how to
know the
gilled
mushrooms

The **Pictured Key Nature Series** has been published since 1944 by the Wm. C. Brown Company. The series was initiated in 1937 by the late Dr. H. E. Jaques, Professor Emeritus of Biology at Iowa Wesleyan University. Dr. Jaques' dedication to the interest of nature lovers in every walk of life has resulted in the prominent place this series fills for all who wonder **"How to Know."**

John F. Bamrick and Edward T. Cawley
Consulting Editors

The Pictured Key Nature Series

How to Know the

AQUATIC INSECTS, Lehmkuhl
AQUATIC PLANTS, Prescott
BEETLES, Arnett-Downie-Jaques, Second Edition
BUTTERFLIES, Ehrlich
ECONOMIC PLANTS, Jaques, Second Edition
FALL FLOWERS, Cuthbert
FERNS AND FERN ALLIES, Mickel
FRESHWATER ALGAE, Prescott, Third Edition
FRESHWATER FISHES, Eddy-Underhill, Third Edition
GILLED MUSHROOMS, Smith-Smith-Weber
GRASSES, Pohl, Third Edition
IMMATURE INSECTS, Chu
INSECTS, Bland-Jaques, Third Edition
LAND BIRDS, Jaques
LICHENS, Hale, Second Edition
LIVING THINGS, Jaques, Second Edition
MAMMALS, Booth, Third Edition
MARINE ISOPOD CRUSTACEANS, Schultz
MITES AND TICKS, McDaniel
MOSSES AND LIVERWORTS, Conard-Redfearn, Third Edition
NON-GILLED FLESHY FUNGI, Smith-Smith
PLANT FAMILIES, Jaques
POLLEN AND SPORES, Kapp
PROTOZOA, Jahn, Bovee, Jahn, Third Edition
SEAWEEDS, Abbott-Dawson, Second Edition
SEED PLANTS, Cronquist

SPIDERS, Kaston, Third Edition
SPRING FLOWERS, Cuthbert, Second Edition
TREMATODES, Schell
TREES, Miller-Jaques, Third Edition
TRUE BUGS, Slater-Baranowski
WATER BIRDS, Jaques-Ollivier
WEEDS, Wilkinson-Jaques, Third Edition
WESTERN TREES, Baerg, Second Edition

how to
know the
gilled
mushrooms

Alexander H. Smith, *Professor Emeritus*
Helen V. Smith
Nancy S. Weber
University of Michigan

The Pictured Key Nature Series
Wm. C. Brown Company Publishers
Dubuque, Iowa

Copyright © 1979 by Wm. C. Brown Company Publishers

Library of Congress Catalog Card Number: 78—69782

ISBN 0—697—04772—5 (Cloth)
ISBN 0—697—04773—3 (Paper)

Printed in the United States of America

Contents

Preface

Both gilled and non-gilled fleshy fungi have been objects of interest throughout much of history, but our progress in building up a fund of knowledge about them has been slow. This volume and the companion volume "How to Know the Non-Gilled Fleshy Fungi" represent an introduction to the study of fleshy fungi from the taxonomic or "what is it" approach.

The study of gilled mushrooms is a study of diversity within a clearly delimited group of organisms. The basic techniques of collecting, studying, and preserving fleshy fungi are discussed in the companion volume and are not repeated here in detail. An effort has been made to make this work useable to those without a microscope, but both macroscopic and microscopic features are needed in the final identification process. Identifications based solely on macroscopic characters are tentative to a greater or lesser extent depending on the genus involved. In short, in the recognition of species among the gilled mushrooms we need to use all features that appear to be reasonably constant and are inherited from one generation of mycelium to the next. The specialists are still finding new characters and re-evaluating those previously used.

Only a small fraction of the gilled mushrooms known from North America are included here; the selections have been made to a great extent to include those which can be reliably recognized at sight. However, one will still find more species in the field than will key out in this—or any other—volume yet written. The mushroom flora of North America is anything but completely known.

Introduction

All fleshy fungi, including the gilled mushrooms, are the spore-bearing phase of the fungous plant much as apples are the seed-bearing phase of the apple plant. In order to see how the familiar mushroom relates to the mushroom plant, a representative life cycle is shown in Fig. 1. The mushroom itself is a fleshy structure typically consisting of a *stalk*, or *stipe*, and a *cap*, or *pileus*, with plates of tissue called *gills*, or *lamellae*, on the under side. The surface of the gills is covered with a palisade-like layer of cells including the *basidia* (*basidium*, singular). All the cells of the mushroom initially contain two nuclei; in the basidia the two nuclei fuse and then divide to form four daughter nuclei. Each daughter nucleus migrates into a spore. When the spores are mature, they are forcibly discharged from the basidium. If the spores land in a suitable place, they germinate and each gives rise to a mass of thread-like structures called *hyphae* (*hypha*, singular) which have one nucleus per cell. This mass of hyphae is called the *mycelium* (*mycelia*, plural) or spawn. If two compatible mycelia come into contact, two cells fuse and the nucleus from one migrates into a cell of the other mycelium producing a cell with two nuclei (binucleate). The cells formed from this binucleate cell will also be binucleate or a multiple of two nuclei will be present. This mycelium with binucleate cells is the principal vegetative or food-gathering phase of the organism that extracts nutrients from the substrate much as the apple tree is the vegetative phase of the apple plant. When adequate food reserves are built up and suitable environmental conditions occur, small knots of threads are formed by the mycelium. These in time become recognizable as button (young) mushrooms. They will grow and expand into mature fruiting bodies if conditions are appropriate. Since the mushroom is the structure analagous to the fruit of flowering plants it is also called a *fruiting body*. The fruiting body is generally the only phase one sees since the hyphae of the mycelium are hidden in the substrate and are too fine to be seen individually without a microscope. The fruiting body is specialized to insure and maximize the production of spores and many of the variations of the basic mushroom type aid in effecting these goals. The gills collectively are known as the *hymenophore*. The presence of a gilled or lamellate hymenophore is the uniting feature of the fleshy fungi discussed in this book. Fleshy fruiting bodies with some other type of hymenophore, such as a smooth surface, spines, or pores; or whose spores are not formed on basidia, are treated in the companion volume "How to Know the Non-Gilled Fleshy Fungi."

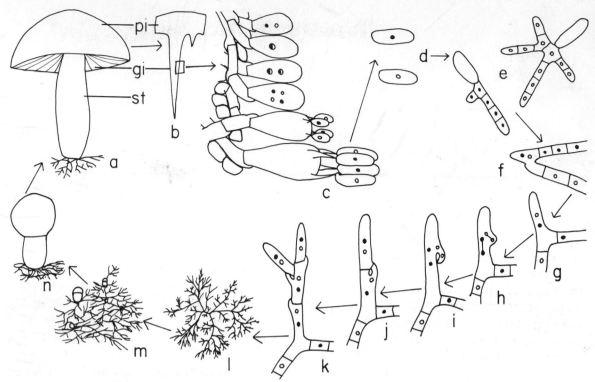

Figure 1 Life cycle of a mushroom. a) Mature fruiting body showing pileus (pi), gills (gi), and stipe (st). b) Tangential section of pileus showing pileus (pi) and a gill (gi). c) A portion of the hymenium showing basidia in various stages of maturity: uppermost young with 2 nuclei, next the nuclei fuse, then the fusion nucleus undergoes a 2-step division resulting in 4 nuclei, each nucleus migrates into a young spore, finally the spores mature. d) 2 discharged mature spores. e) Germinating spores. f) Hyphae from different spores meet and fuse, a nucleus from one hypha migrates into the other. g) The first 2-nucleate cell of the new mycelium. h-j) Stages in the formation of a clamp connection showing how the two nuclei may divide and the cell divides so that each new cell has the same kinds of nuclei as the original cell. k) A hypha consisting of 2-nucleate cells. l) Mycelium or spawn. m) Mycelium with the beginnings of fruiting bodies. n) A young fruiting body.

The Parts of a Mushroom

Whether you are trying to identify a mushroom yourself or to describe it to another person, careful observation and detailed note taking are first required. Toward this goal a number of the descriptive terms used to describe some of the more important features are discussed below.

MACROSCOPIC FEATURES

Cap (also called the *pileus*). The cap is the first part of a mushroom most people see. It bears the gills and also offers them some protection while developing. Among the features of mushroom caps which are routinely important in making identifications are: 1) *Size*. The size is usually recorded in millimeters (mm) or centimeters (cm) and includes the diameter of the cap and its height if the cap is taller than it is wide. 2) *Shape*. The shape and how it changes from youth to age is frequently important. Some of the frequently used terms to describe shape are illustrated in Figs. 2, and 3. Frequently the cap, as seen in section, will not be a smooth curve, but the region over the stipe, usually the center of the cap (Fig. 4) may have a *cusp, papilla,* or *umbo*. Many times a cap will be inter-

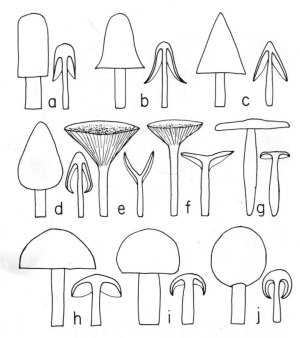

Figure 2   Pileus shapes. a) Cylindric. b) Campanulate or bell-shaped. c) Conic. d) Ovate. e) Funnel-shaped or infundibuliform. f) Depressed. g) Plane. h) Convex. i) Hemispheric or pulvinate. j) Subglobose.

mediate between two of the shapes, i.e., plano-convex or depressed-umbonate. The curvature of the cap margin may also be important (Fig. 5). 3) *Color*. This is frequently the most striking feature of a mushroom. A good

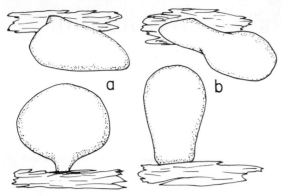

Figure 3   Fruiting body shapes. a) Conchate. b) Spathulate.

Figure 4   Modifications of the pileus disc. a) Cuspidate. b) Papillate. c) Obtuse. d) Umbonate. e) Umbillicate.

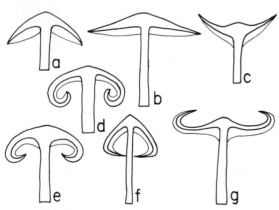

Figure 5   Curvature of the pileus margin. a) Deflexed. b) Straight or flaring. c) Uplifted. d) Inrolled. e) Incurved. f) Connivent. g) Recurved.

color guide is a great asset in recording colors so they can be accurately recalled at will. Color may change from youth to age; if the color fades as moisture is lost, the cap is said to be *hygrophanous*. Often the color is unevenly distributed, i.e., the cap may be *zonate* or spotted (*scrobiculate*) with regions of darker color. The *disc* (center portion of the cap) may be darker or lighter than the marginal area, or the color may be in radiating streaks (*virgate*). In some species the surface layer (*cuticle*) may change color when bruised. Be as specific as reasonably possible when describing the color of the pileus and any changes it may undergo. 4) *Surface appearance*. So far it has been assumed that the surface of the cap is smooth, but this is not always true. For example, the cuticle may crack in the pattern of a drying mud flat and is then termed *areolate*. A bald (*glabrous*) cap is one that lacks any type of hairiness or fuzziness, i.e., lacks *fibrils* and *scales*. However, many mushrooms have some type of fibrils (fine hairlike hyphae) on the cap. Sometimes the fibrils are flat on the cap and do not project at all; this condition is termed *appressed fibrillose*. Depending on the coarseness, density, and distribution of the fibrils, a variety of conditions may be distinguished. In some species the cuticle appears wrinkled or *rugose* (*rugulose* if the wrinkles are small). 5) *Surface feel*. The "feel" of the cuticle when touched is often a useful character in identifying mushrooms. Some caps feel velvety and dry, others are dry but not velvety, still others are moist, sticky, or slimy. A continuous spectrum of degrees of sliminess (or *viscidity*) can be found from instances in which the slime is not discernable by the touch test but is visible under the microscope, to cases where the slime is so thick it literally drips off the fruiting body. Many species that are viscid to some degree when young may appear shiny and glazed at maturity and feel dry, especially during dry weather. 6) *Cap margin*. The margin of the cap may be similar to the rest of the cap in color, appearance, and feel, or it may be distinctive in one or more features. Often the cap is quite thin toward the margin and the radiating ridges formed by the gills are apparent as ridges or lines (*striations*); at times the ridges are so prominent that the margin appears pleated (*plicate*) or *plicate-striate*. In many genera fibrils are present only on the outer one-third to one-fourth of the cap making the margin pubescent, hirsute, or strigose. In some species the margin is quite thick and soft and composed of a roll of tissue described as cottony as in *Lactarius deceptivus*. 7) *Context*. The context or flesh is the bulky portion of most mushroom caps. Its color, texture, and thickness may provide useful information. At times, the context will change color on exposure to air. Sometimes a liquid (also called a *latex*) is released when some part of the fruiting body is broken or cut. The latex may be clear, opaque, or have small flecks of material in a clear matrix (whey-like); furthermore, the latex may be colored or colorless. The color of the freshly exposed latex may be different than that of drops of latex which have been in contact with intact or injured surfaces of the fruiting body and a record of such changes should be made. 8) *Odor and taste*. Many mushrooms have distinctive odors and/or tastes. The odors are often more pronounced when the flesh of the mushroom is crushed or in freshly unwrapped collections. Taste is determined by chewing a piece of the raw pileus (including gills and context) for a few seconds (all most people want of an acrid species) to a minute or so if the taste is mild or slow to develop. Do not swallow the chewed material since the mushroom may be poisonous. Specialists in certain groups will taste each region of the fruiting body separately, but here we give only "whole pileus" taste unless otherwise noted. Many odors and tastes are described in terms of more or less familiar items such as the odor of fresh corn husks (odor of green corn), the odor or taste of radishes (raphanoid), the odor of hyacinths, bed bugs, or freshly ground meal (farinaceous). A strong

burning taste is termed acrid and is possibly best described as intensely peppery to those who have not experienced it.

Gills (or *lamellae*, Fig. 1). The gills resemble the pages of a book when the book is held upside down by its spine. A number of features of gills may be useful in the identification of species: 1) *Attachment*. Attachment (or insertion) refers to the manner in which the gills and the stalk are related as shown in Fig. 6. In some species the gills are

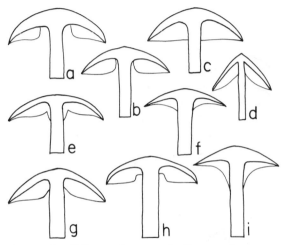

Figure 6   Gill attachment. a) Free and remote. b) Free and approximate. c) Adnate and horizontal. d) Adnate and ascending. e) Uncinate. f) Arcuate. g) Sinuate. h) Adnexed. i) Decurrent.

attached to the stalk at first and become free by maturity (*seceding*). 2) *Breadth*. This is the distance from the pileus to the free edge of the gill. Whether the gills are broad or narrow is a relative character. 3) *Thickness*. Thickness, i.e., thin or thick, is seldom mentioned unless an extreme condition is present. 4) *Spacing*. Like the previous two characters, this is a somewhat subjective one. Generally (Fig. 7) *crowded* denotes a condition where it is hard to distinguish one gill from another whereas *distant* is the opposite extreme; there does not seem to be a term for the "average"

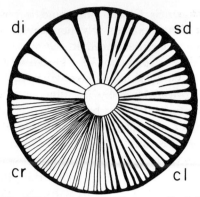

Figure 7 Gill spacing. di) Distant. sd) Subdistant. cl) Close. cr) Crowded.

condition unless it is *close*. 5) *Color*. Gill color may change from youth to maturity as the spores mature as in *Agaricus* and *Cortinarius* where the sequence of changes is important. Color changes which follow injury or contact with the latex should also be noted. 6) *Margin*. The margin is the free edge of the gill and is typically the same color as the sides (also called the *faces*). If the margin differs in color from the faces, the gill is *marginate*. Typically the margin appears to be a smooth curve; however, it may be ragged or eroded depending on the species (Fig. 8). 7) *Behavior*. In some species, the gills change in texture with age as in *Coprinus* where they undergo a process of self-digestion (*deliquescent*); however, in most species no major changes occur.

Stipe (also called the *stalk*, Fig. 1). Most species of gilled mushrooms possess a distinct stipe, but some characteristically lack a stipe or have only a poorly developed one. If a

stipe is absent, the fruiting body is said to be *sessile* on the substrate (Fig. 9). In species with a stipe it elevates the cap above the substrate and provides mechanical support as well as conducting water and nutrients from the mycelium to the cap. When a stipe is present, the following characters deserve attention: 1) *Location*. The stipe may be attached to the cap at its margin (*lateral*), off center (*eccentric*), or in the middle (*central*). Unless the stipe is not basically central, no comment on its position is made in the descriptions. 2) *Size*. The size includes the length from the base to the apex and the diameter measured at the apex. 3) *Shape*. A variety of shapes

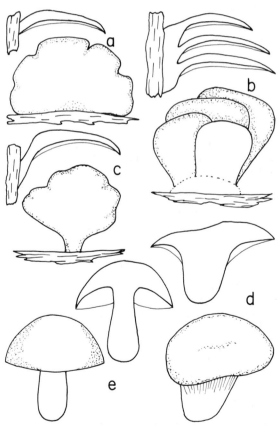

Figure 9 Stipe options. a) Absent (sessile). b) Absent but a tubercle present. c) Lateral. d) Eccentric. e) Central.

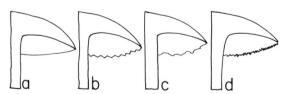

Figure 8   Gill margins. a) Entire. b) Serrate. c) Eroded. d) Fimbriate.

(Fig. 10) may occur. Frequently the shape changes with age. Special attention should be given to the stipe base as it may be enlarged into a bulb of some type (Fig. 11). 4) *Color and color changes.* The same guidelines mentioned in the discussion of the cap also apply

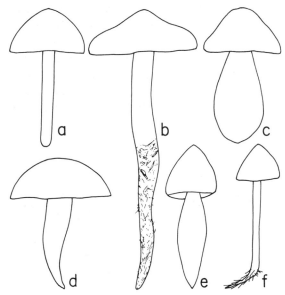

Figure 10 Stipe shape. a) Equal. b) Pseudorhiza present. c) Clavate. d) Tapering toward the base. e) Ventricose (enlarged in the middle). f) Radicating.

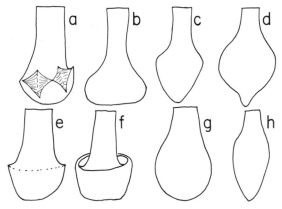

Figure 11 Types of bulbs. a) Cleft. b) Abrupt. c) Oblique. d) Napiform or turnip-shaped. e) Marginate. f) Marginate-depressed. g) Clavate. h) Fusiform.

to the stipe. 5) *Feel.* Again the same considerations discussed for the cap apply to the stipe. 6) *Consistency.* This character varies considerably, being fragile, pliable, cartilage-like, soft, or hard. 7) *Nature of the pith.* In many mushrooms the stipe has a relatively firm outer zone or *cortex* and a distinct inner region or *pith.* Depending on the species, the stipe may be hollow, solid (texture the same throughout), or appear stuffed with cotton.

Veils. In many mushrooms, one or two layers of tissue, known as veils may be present on young fruiting bodies: the *partial veil* (Fig. 12) which extends from the stipe to the margin of the cap, and the *universal veil* (Fig. 12) which envelops the entire fruiting body in the button stage. In many cases it is easy to determine which type of veil is present, but in others it may be hard to make an accurate determination without detailed anatomical and developmental studies. We refer only to the "veil" in the latter situation.

Partial Veil. The partial veil encloses the developing gills in a chamber during the early stages of development. Some of the potentially important characters of partial veils include: 1) *Texture.* The veil may vary from *membranous* (forming a solid sheet of tissue over the gill cavity) to *cortinate* (cortina-like, i.e., resembling a cobweb). A membranous veil may be single or double. In many species of *Agaricus* a cog-wheel-like effect is evident on the outer (lower) surface of the intact partial veil or the free edge of the veil may appear to have two layers (double, Fig. 96). 2) *Color.* The color of both surfaces of the veil and any color changes they undergo should be noted. 3) *Fate.* The fate of the partial veil varies considerably depending on the species involved. The partial veil typically breaks at the cap margin leaving a persistent ring of tissue (the *annulus*, Fig. 12) on the stipe; however, it may break away from the stipe leaving patches of tissue on the edge of the cap

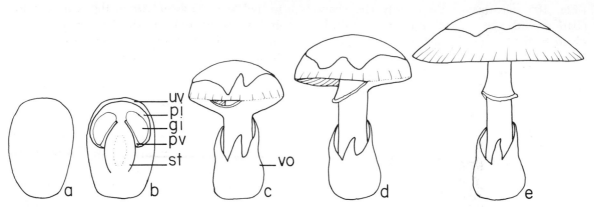

Figure 12 Veil maturation. a) Button with universal veil intact. b) Same button cut longitudinally to expose the universal veil (uv), pileus (pi), gills (gi), partial veil (pv), and stipe (st). c) Older button with universal veil broken, remains at base form the volva (vo), other remains on pileus, partial veil starting to break. d) Older fruiting body with partial veil nearly broken away from pileus margin. e) Mature fruiting body.

causing the cap margin to be *appendiculate.* 4) *Position of the annulus.* The position of the annulus, when one is formed, may be important. The annulus may be attached above the middle of the stipe (*superior*), at or near the middle of the stipe (*median*), or below the middle of the stipe (*inferior*). In some species it is free and moveable as in *Lepiota procera.*

Universal Veil. As it's name implies, the universal veil encloses the entire button during the early part of its development. Expansion of the cap and elongation of the stipe eventually result in the rupture of the universal veil (Fig. 12). The texture, color, and color changes should be noted, but perhaps equally, if not more important, is determining the fate of this veil. The classical example shows the universal veil rupturing and leaving no tissue on the cap, but leaving a persistent cuplike structure (*volva*) around the base of the stipe (Fig. 12). However, many variations exist. For example, patches of universal veil material may persist, at least for a time, on the cap and a distinct volva may be present near the stipe base (Fig. 13a); at times only

a residue of powdery material on the cap and around the base of the stipe remain as evidence of the universal veil (Fig. 13c). In some species the universal veil leaves scales on both the stipe and cap, and the stipe appears to have a stocking over its lower part (Fig. 13e); in others it leaves patches of tissue on the cap and some fragments on the stipe with only a slight suggestion of a cup (Fig. 13d). In some genera, the stipe may be covered with soft fibrils up to the annulus and the cap may be similarly ornamented; in such situations, the partial and universal veils are difficult to distinguish and may actually be grown together. As a final example, the universal veil may be totally gelatinous or viscid, enveloping the button in a coating of slime and leaving the lower portion of the stipe and the cap slimy at maturity. In such cases, field observations may have to be supplemented with anatomical studies to determine if the stipe and cap are intrinsically slimy or if the slime represents a slimy universal veil.

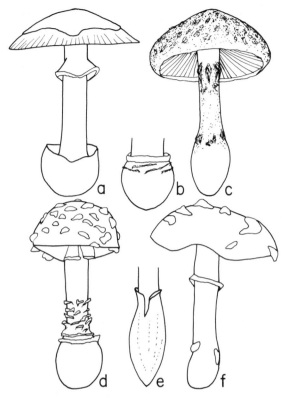

Figure 13 Variations on veils. a) Universal veil present as volva and patch of tissue on pileus, partial veil evident as annulus. b) Collar-like volva of universal veil material. c) Universal veil powdery on both pileus and stipe; partial veil as a few evanescent fibrils. d) Universal veil present as scales and ruffles around stipe base (the volva) and as patches of material on pileus, partial veil just breaking to form annulus. e) Sheathing volva on fusiform stipe base. f) Universal veil easily broken away, most of volva left in soil, a few patches of universal veil on pileus, partial veil represented by annulus.

MICROSCOPIC FEATURES

The hyphae which compose the mushroom fruiting body may be variously arranged in different parts of the fruiting body. Furthermore the hyphal cells may vary in such characters as size, color, shape, and wall thickness. These variations, especially those of hyphal end cells, are frequently important in mushroom identification.

Hymenophore. This is the region of the fruiting body which bears the hymenium, i.e., the gills of the fleshy fungi described in this book. The principal elements of the hymenium are the *basidia* which produce the spores, the *basidioles* (young basidia), and the *cystidia* which are sterile cells.

Basidia (basidium, singular, Fig. 14). As already stated, in the life cycle of a mushroom (Fig. 1), 2 nuclei fuse in each basidium and the resulting nucleus divides to form four nuclei. Typically each daughter nucleus mi-

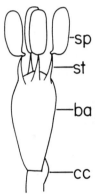

Figure 14 Basidium showing spores (sp), sterigmata (st), body of the basidium (ba), and basal clamp connection (cc).

grates to a different spore. Consequently basidia are extremely important cells. They are usually club-shaped and in the range of 10-70 μm in length (Fig. 14). Each basidium typically has four *sterigmata* (*sterigma*, singular) each of which bears a single spore. Some species may have 2-spored basidia or a hymenium showing a mixture of 2- and 4-spored basidia. Typically spores from 2-spored basidia are larger than those from 4-spored basidia. Except for the Hygrophoraceae in which the basidia are unusually long and narrow, basidial shape is seldom important in mushroom taxonomy. Basidia of species of *Lyophyllum*, some Rhodophyllaceae, and certain other fungi contain siderophilous granules (formerly known as carminophilous granules). These granules can be demonstrated by taking a piece of gill, heating it in a drop of acetocarmine, transferring the fragment to a fresh drop of stain 2-3 times, teasing the fragment apart with iron needles, squashing it, and examining the basidia. The granules, if present, will stain blackish purple to violet-black.

Basidioles. These are club-shaped to rounded cells which resemble immature basidia and in most mushrooms are just that. In the Coprinaceae, however, basidioles become rather large and apparently never function as basidia. They are termed *brachybasidioles* since they evolved, presumably, from basidioles (see *Psathyrella* for examples).

Spores. Mushroom spores are typically unicellular and microscopic, varying from only 2-3 μm long to 15-150 μm depending on the species. The spores serve to disperse the mushroom organism. Important spore characters frequently used in mushroom identification include: 1) *Color.* Color is best and most easily determined by obtaining a spore deposit on white paper (see p. 15). The color of the spores in mass is one of the principal characters used to group mushrooms into genera and families. 2) *Size.* Mature spores such as those from spore deposits are used to establish the size range of the spores. Spore length and width are measured, and in spores which are not round in cross section (*compressed*), three measurements should be made. 3) *Shape.* Shape is described as accurately as possible giving both the *face* and *profile* views. These views are defined by the manner in which spores are borne on the basidia (Fig. 14) and can be surmised on spores which are no longer attached to the basidia. Figure 16 illustrates a number of frequently encountered shapes. 4) *Apex.* The spore apex may be undifferentiated, truncate, or have a discontinuity in the spore wall, forming a *germ pore* of greater or lesser visibility (Fig. 15). In

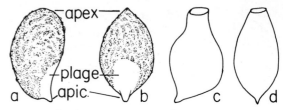

Figure 15   Some variations of spore morphology. a) Spore in profile view showing apex, plage, and apiculus. b) Spore in face view showing apex, plage, and apiculus. c) Spore with snout-like apex ending in a germ pore. d) Spore with a germ pore.

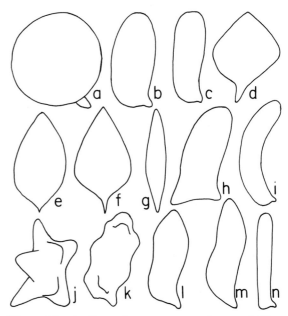

Figure 16   Outlines of common spore shapes. a) Globose. b) Ellipsoid. c) Oblong. d) Quadrate. e) Ovoid. f) Rhomboid. g) Fusiform. h) Bullet-shaped. i) Allantoid or sausage-shaped. j) Nodulose. k) Angular. l) Inequilateral. m) Boletoid. n) Cylindric.

other instances, the apex may be conspicuously elongated to form a *snout* (Fig. 15). 5) *Ornamentation.* Spore ornamentation may be visible as markings on or in the spore wall and may take a variety of forms (Fig. 17). Frequently the ornamentation is unevenly distributed over the spore surface. For example, the ventral surface above the apiculus (Fig. 15) may have consistently lower ornamenta-

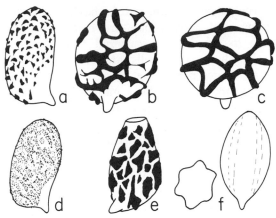

Figure 17 Selected types of spore ornamentation. a) Warty. b) Partial or broken reticulum. c) Reticulate. d) Wrinkled. e) With patches of material over the surface. f) Striate or grooved, left in cross-section, right in face view.

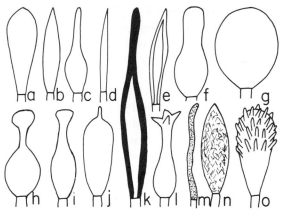

Figure 18 Selected types of cystidia and a seta. a) Clavate. b) Fusoid. c) Fusoid-ventricose. d) Aciculate. e) Lamprocystidium (thick-walled). f) Utriform. g) Saccate or vesiculose. h) Lecythiform. i) Ninepin-shaped. j) Mucronate. k) Seta. l) Horned cystidium. m) Pseudocystidium. n) Macrocystidium. o) Cystidium with projections.

tion or none at all and is then termed a *plage* (Fig. 15). Many types of ornamentation will not stain selectively in commonly available reagents, but others will. The ornamentation of spores in the Russulaceae will turn deep blue to nearly black in iodine-containing reagents such as Melzer's reagent (**p. 15**) and is termed *amyloid*.

Cystidia. Cystidia (cystidium, singular) are specialized hyphal end-cells which do not produce spores. They are not restricted to the hymenium. Both the location of a cystidium and its characters may provide taxonomically useful information. The principal areas where cystidia occur are on the cap or pileus (*pileocystidia*), the stipe or stalk (*caulocystidia*), the faces of the gills (*pleurocystidia*), and the edges of the gills (*cheilocystidia*). No matter where a cystidium occurs the following information should be noted: 1) *Size*. This includes the length from the basal cross wall to the apex and the width in the widest part. 2) *Shape*. Some imagination is useful in interpreting cystidial shapes; a selection of common shapes is shown in Fig. 18. The nature of the apex should also be included when describing the shape, i.e., acute, obtuse, capi-

tate, or rounded. Some cystidia branch like a tree, a bottle brush, or are repeatedly forked in a regular manner (Fig. 18). 3) *Wall thickness*. Cystidia with thin walls are *leptocystidia;* this category includes the majority of cystidia routinely encountered. *Lamprocystidia* have thickened walls; the pattern of thickening may vary as shown in Fig. 18. Wall thickness is seldom mentioned unless the walls are significantly thicker in the cystidium than the walls of other hyphal cells. 4) *Incrustations*. Many cystidia will have incrustations at some stage, especially over the apex. In some cases the incrustations are crystalline, in others, they lack distinctive form. Incrustations may be soluble in certain mounting media or visible only at certain stages of development. 5) *Content*. Many cystidia do not have an obviously specialized content; however, others may appear refractive, oily, or colored. Such cystidia with oily or refractive content are broadly termed *gloeocystidia*. If, as in many members of the Russulaceae, a pleuro- or cheilocystidium of this type is filamentous and appears somewhat irregular in outline, it is a *pseudocystidium* (Fig. 18); if a gloeocystidium is relatively large and appears to have relatively rigid walls and a consistent, regular form, it is a *macrocystidium* (Fig. 18); intermediates between these types may also be encountered. If the content of a cystidium either fresh or as revived in KOH is yellowish, as in many members of the Strophariaceae, the term *chrysocystidium* is employed. In this type the coagulated content as seen in material revived in KOH is a sharply defined amorphous mass or a globule.

Gill Trama. The trama or context of the gill usually forms the bulk of the gill. Several distinctive patterns of hyphal arrangements in the gill trama are used in mushroom identification. These patterns are based on the study of sections of gills (Fig. 19). The four principal types are: 1) *Interwoven* (also known as intermixed or irregular). In this type the hyphae appear randomly interwoven. 2) *Parallel* (also known as regular). As might be expected, the hyphae are oriented in a parallel fashion from the cap to the edge of the gill. 3) *Divergent* (also known as bilateral). In this case there is a central strand of parallel to interwoven hyphae with hyphae diverging from it in a down and out pattern to the hymenium. 4) *Convergent* (also known as inverse). In this type, the elements of the trama appear to converge toward the edge of the gill. Generally gills at early maturity should be used when determining the tramal types. *Lactifers,* part of the latex-producing system, or oleiferous hyphae, may also be present in the gill trama where they are visible as irregular wormlike hyphae lacking divisions into cells but having a distinctive content.

Cap Context or Trama. The bulky portion of most caps is composed of hyphae which vary from interwoven to distinctly radially arranged and vary in diameter from extremely narrow to quite large (often referred to as "inflated cells" in the case of hyphae of large diameter). The Russulaceae are unique in the gilled mushrooms in having nests of columns of cells which are essentially globose to subglobose scattered through their flesh. These large cells are called *sphaerocysts;* tissues possessing sphaerocysts are *heteromerous,* i.e., they have more than one type of hypha. In addition, lactifers may be present.

Cap Cuticle. The cap cuticle is the outermost differentiated layer or aggregation of layers on the cap. At times it is quite simple, sometimes quite complex with several recognizable zones. The structure of the cuticle is usually described from tangential sections of the cap and reflects different arrangements and types of hyphae (Fig. 20). Some of the

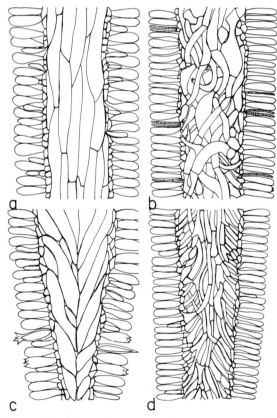

Figure 19 Selected types of gill trama. a) Parallel or regular. b) Interwoven or irregular. c) Convergent or inverse. d) Divergent or bilateral.

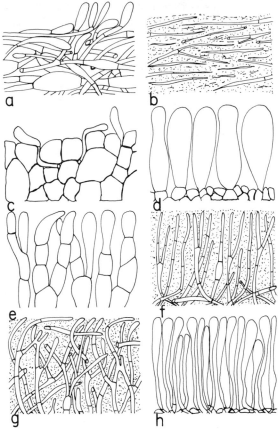

Figure 20 Selected types of cuticle. a) Cutis. b) Ixocutis. c) Cellular. d) Hymeniform. e) Trichoderm. f) Ixotrichoderm. g) Ixolattice. h) Turf.

major cuticle types include: 1) *Cutis*. In a cutis the hyphae typically are interwoven to radially oriented and the hyphal cells are usually relatively long and narrow. The hyphae may be compact, producing a glabrous surface, or, if the tips are free, the surface may be fibrillose to scaly. If the walls of the hyphae gelatinize or if a layer of slime is present, the cuticle is an *ixocutis*. 2) *Trichodermium*. In this type, the hyphae are oriented perpendicular to the pileus surface and the upright portion is several cells long; if slime or gelatinization is present, the later is called an *ixotrichodermium*. A trichodermium may result

in a velvety pileus, whereas an ixotrichodermium is usually tacky to slimy to the touch. 3) *Ixolattice*. An ixolattice is intermediate between the first two types and consists of ascending, branching, and anastomosing hyphae in a layer of slime. 4) *Hymeniform cuticle*. A hymeniform cuticle consists of a single layer of cells arranged in a palisade much as the elements of the hymenium form a palisade. 5) *Turf*. A turf is formed by a palisade of greatly elongated often clavate to cylindric cells (pileocystidia). 6) *Cellular cuticle*. A cellular cuticle appears to be composed of "cells," i.e., hyphae of considerably larger diameter than the hyphae of the context and which are compactly arranged with a minimum of intercellular spaces. The hymeniform cuticle is one extreme of this type; commonly a cellular cuticle will be several cells thick. Various types of pileocystidia may be present if the cap is not viscid.

Stipe Context. The hyphae of the outer portion (*cortex*) of the stipe are predominantly vertical in orientation, but may vary to interwoven, especially toward the center. Members of the Russulaceae typically have vertically oriented columns of sphaerocysts in the stipe. Evidence of the lactiferous system may also be present in the stipe.

Stipe Cuticle. The stipe cuticle seldom is very thick, but it may vary in form along the same lines as the cap cuticle. In species with large smooth spots (scrobiculi) on the stipe, the cuticle is often different over the spots from that of the rest of the stipe.

Clamp Connections. Clamp connections are specialized branches which occur at the cross walls of hyphae (Fig. 1). They are most easily observed on narrow hyphae such as those of the cap cuticle and stipe cortex. They are not present on all mushrooms or all parts of every mushroom. In fact, the Russulaceae as a family almost totally lack them. Frequently, clamp connections are difficult to demonstrate.

In conclusion, the basic aim of examining a mushroom is to describe it accurately and completely so you, or some one else, can make an accurate identification. Not all characters will be present in all species, so no standard check list of items to note will be universally applicable. Use your own talents and follow a consistent pattern, such as the one outlined above, in describing mushrooms and you will soon develop the knack of careful observation and note taking.

Collecting
and Identifying Mushrooms

Mushrooms are collected for a variety of purposes that vary from collector to collector. Whatever the purpose, everyone seemingly wants to know a name for the mushroom(s) they find. Collectors will need either to identify their collections themselves or get help from some one else. Before collections can be identified they first must reach home undamaged. The basic guidelines for collecting mushrooms are quite simple. Collect the entire fruiting body. A knife or small trowel is necessary when digging up the base of terrestrial species or cutting fruiting bodies from woody substrates. Collect both young and mature fruiting bodies of each species. Keep each collection separate in your container. This may be done by wrapping each one separately in pieces of wax paper and placing the packages in an open basket—with the heavy collections at the bottom so that the fragile ones will not be crushed beyond recognition. Plastic wraps tend to hold in too much moisture, and, especially in warm weather, the bacteria and yeasts become active—rapidly making even the best specimens of edible species inedible in a short time. Keep the collections cool. Finally, note what kinds of plants, especially trees, are in the area.

Identifying mushrooms is a matter of paying attention to detail. The first step is to set up one or two caps from each collection for spore prints. To do this, lay the cap gills down on a piece of white paper, removing the stipe if necessary, and either wrap the set-up in wax paper or place a bowl or glass over the cap to restrict air movement. Leave this set-up alone for 2-4 hours or overnight if need be. If the spores are mature, they will be deposited on the paper. If the spores are deeply colored, they will show distinctly. If they are white you may need to tilt the paper to see if spores have fallen, but be sure spores are present. A small piece of dark colored paper placed under the cap alongside the white paper makes it easier to observe if a deposit has been made in the case of light-spored species. Use *only* deposits on white paper for determining spore color.

Before one can use the key effectively, he/she should become familiar with the parts of the mushroom and how to describe them as discussed in the previous chapter. At some point, the need for ascertaining various characters with the aid of a microscope may arise. To study the spores, scrape up a few from a spore print with the edge of a razor blade or a scalpel and mount these in 2.5% KOH (potassium hydroxide). Also mount some in Melzer's reagent (22 gm water, 20 gm chloral hydrate, 0.5 gm iodine, 1.5 gm potassium iodide).

15

Place a number 1 cover slip over each mount. The shape, size, and ornamentation of the spores can then be determined as can whether any part of the spore is amyloid (bluish to black in Melzer's reagent). To determine the type of gill trama, cut a wedge out of the cap with gills attached and make thin tangential sections of it. These will be longitudinal sections of the gills. For sectioning, we use a hollow ground straight edged razor such as an old fashioned shaving razor which can be sharpened repeatedly. Single edged safety razor blades may also be used. The material to be sectioned is held between the thumb and first finger of the left hand (for right handed people) if the wedge is firm and relatively thick. For thinner or softer tissues, the wedge may be held between pieces of elder pith (available from some biological supply houses) or between pieces of a carrot split longitudinally. Slice across the material with smooth strokes saving the thinnest sections for study and discarding pieces of pith or carrot. Mount the sections in a drop of water or 2.5% KOH, tease them apart, add a cover slip, and examine. Thicker sections may be needed when studying the pileus cuticle than are needed for the gill trama. The thinnest sections are used to study the hymenium. To check for the presence of cheilocystidia, pick off a gill, mount it flat on a slide in a drop of mounting medium, add a cover slip and press or tap lightly on the cover slip (do not use your fingers since they will leave grease marks on the cover slip). The gill margin can then be studied easily and the cystidia, if present, should be visible. Cross sections of the stipe cortex can provide information on the cuticle and its caulocystidia. Caulocystidia can also be studied by stripping off a piece of cuticle and mounting it for study.

The next step is to turn to the key. Keys are devices to help one work through the maze of alternatives and correctly match the collection with a name. The keys have sets of choices in pairs (couplets) called leads. Read the first pair of choices and decide which best fits the collection in hand, scan to the right of that choice to the name or number given there. If a number is given, proceed to that pair of choices, read both, decide which is best and continue in this manner until a name is reached. When in doubt as to which lead to choose, try first one then the other and see which way produces the most reasonable answer. Many of the leads may read "not as above" or similar wording. In such cases unless the mushroom in hand corresponds in *all* particulars with the information given in the first lead, accept the "not as above" choice as the correct one. Eventually you will arrive at a name accompanied by a description. If the choices have been made correctly, and if the mushroom is included in this book, that name should be the correct one for that collection. Check the description against the features of the specimens to see if they agree. If there is some difference not likely attributable to size or growing conditions, then several alternatives exist: It is the correct species but not a typical specimen; it is a species related to the one in the book but not treated here; or, if there is very little correspondence in characters between the mushroom and the description, you do not have an identification and more technical works will be needed before an identification can be made.

Scientific rather than common names are used in the keys because every species we discuss has a scientific name, but not every species has a common name. Furthermore, some species have several common names which may vary in different areas. Each species name consists of two words, the name of the genus (the first word, the first letter of which is capitalized) and the specific epithet. Scientific names are Greek, Latin or words which have been latinized. The names frequently tell something about the organism such as color (*albus, luteus*), size (*magnus, minimus*), place where collected (*tahquame-nonensis*), or collector (*truebloodii*).

If you are interested in keeping specimens for further study, to document your identification, or establish a distribution pattern, it will be necessary to preserve the specimens. The first job is to write an accurate description of the collection, being sure to include those features which are not easily or accurately discernable from dried material. Follow a pattern in the descriptions such as the one used in the discussion of the macroscopic and microscopic features. In addition to the description, also record the place, habitat, date, collector, and collector's number. We keep a log in which each field trip is mentioned with a list of all collections saved from that trip and the number assigned to each collection. On a smaller piece of paper (the field label) record place, habitat, date, collector, and collector's number as well as any tentative identification. Drying is the preferred method for preserving most fleshy fungi. A home-made or commercial dryer (some food dryers will work) can be used (see the companion volume). Place the collections, along with the field label, on the dryer so the air flows freely around them.

When the specimens are completely dry, they may be stored in boxes, always keeping the field label with the proper collection. The drying apparatus should not be inside a home or office as many people develop various types of allergies and irritations from drying mushrooms. A garage or porch may be preferable. Insects like dried mushrooms so for long term storage, steps must be taken to prevent their depredations. Some type of fumigation of new collections should be done before they are stored in insect-proof cabinets. Large institutions may have regular fumigating equipment, but for home use, insecticide-impregnated strips of material may be used. The specimens to be fumigated are placed in a sealed container (a room down to a garbage can) along with the insecticide and then allowed to sit for several days. The specimens are then aired to release excess fumes and flake naphthalene (not hard moth balls which may break up the specimens) is added to each box to repel insects. The method outlined here is only for drying and preserving material for study, not for eating. The fumigant and the naphthalene render the material unfit for consumption.

Mycophagy and Mycotoxins

Mycophagy is the name applied to the eating of fungi by man, beast, or worm. Our discussion concerns mushrooms and man. We are frequently asked by someone with a basket of mushrooms "Can I eat them?" There is always a strong temptation to reply "Of course you *can,* but I will not predict what will happen to you." Eating wild mushrooms without learning something about them is frequently and aptly likened to playing Russian roulette. Most of the time, nothing bad will happen, but occasionally serious illness or even death may result. It can not be emphasized too strongly that there are no quick tests which distinguish edible from poisonous species. Learning to identify accurately the species you wish to eat as well as those to avoid is the best safeguard there is. In this book we have tried to point out not only the species which are easily identified and generally safe and good to eat, but also to indicate most of the frequently collected poisonous species.

There is a saying that there are bold mycophagists and old mycophagists, but no *old bold* mycophagists. There are several steps involved in becoming an "old" mycophagist. First be careful and thorough when collecting the mushrooms initially as discussed in the previous section. Keep each kind separate! When collecting for the table, only fresh, worm

free specimens should be saved and they should be kept as clean as reasonably possible. Young and old specimens may be needed in the identification process as well. Second, know your mushroom. Once you have identified a species, study it. Become familiar with the characters of that species and learn the combination which makes that particular species unique. It may take some time and many collections to become familiar with the variations of each species. Once the identity of a collection is established to your satisfaction, check the edibility rating. If the species is rated "poisonous" most people will be poisoned if they eat it. If it is listed as "edible" it means that cooked specimens have been eaten safely in moderate quantities by people in good health. However, most species will not carry a rating as either edible or poisonous because there is insufficient, or no, information about them. Finally, some species are safe but have a bad taste or are essentially tasteless. The decision of which species to try is yours.

Testing the edibility is the third step in successful mycophagy. Choose only firm, fresh specimens without worm holes (usually visible when the specimen is cut in half longitudinally). Begin by cooking a small quantity and eat only about 1-2 tablespoonsful. Do not drink alcoholic beverages at the same meal because alcohol-mushroom interactions are known for some species (see discussion of coprine p. 20). If no ill effects are felt 12-24 hours later, you probably can eat that species safely and may wish to try it again in a larger quantity. Test species new to you no closer than one day apart so that possible delayed reactions will not be attributed to the wrong fungus. Each person must try each species for himself or herself as there is a considerable variation from individual to individual (even in a family) in reactions to mushrooms. By keeping a record of your opinion of each species and its effects, if any, a list of safe locally available species which can be eaten with pleasure and safety will gradually be built up.

Once the safety of a species is established and its characters are firmly in mind, one can modify the collecting process. By checking the characters in the field and trimming away dirty or wormy parts of the fruiting bodies, one can collect much cleaner specimens. However, when in doubt collect the entire specimen and check it carefully against the description. It is always best to bring some intact fruiting bodies back and hold them in reserve should they be needed for identification in case of poisonings.

Assuming you are still interested in eating mushrooms and wish to preserve them for future use, any of several methods may be tried. Always use fresh specimens free of worms and process each species separately. Following instructions in a reputable cookbook, mushrooms may be partially cooked, cooled, packaged (friends of ours package meal size portions) and frozen for later use. Drying is also effective if you have the facilities to do it. Stringing mushrooms up in the attic or leaving them out in the sun is likely to result in an inferior, bug-infested, or somewhat dusty product, at least in the more humid parts of the country. We use a standard mushroom dryer (see the companion volume).

Home food dryers are also available commercially. Slice the specimens fairly thinly if they are fleshy, and dry them until they are crisp, i.e., until the flesh breaks rather than bends and does not feel moist in the center when broken open. Store the dried mushrooms in tightly closed plastic bags or in screw top jars in a cool dry place. Canning mushrooms can be risky if done incorrectly. Be sure to can only one kind at a time and use a pressure canner according to directions to insure that the organisms which cause botulism are killed.

Broadly speaking, mycotoxins are toxins produced by fungi. However, we will only consider those toxins present in fleshy fungi. Somewhat the reverse of eating mushrooms safely is knowing how to recognize the symptoms of mushroom poisoning so that appropriate treatment may be administered if necessary. A few observations apply to mushroom poisoning in general. First, be sure it is mushroom poisoning—not food poisoning or the flu. Our family tried a mushroom once and the following day one of us had a stomach upset which was attributed to the mushroom; the next day another one became ill with the same symptoms, and a few days later the third one got sick and was taken to a doctor who diagnosed all three cases as flu! If in doubt see a physician first. Second, when experimenting with mushrooms always keep some intact specimens on hand; they may be useful if a case of poisoning does occur and will aid in identification so that the correct treatment may be given. Third, do not gorge yourself on mushrooms. Many people find them hard to digest in the best of times. Fourth, never force mushrooms on unwilling or unwell people—they may literally become sick from fright. People in poor health, the very young, and the very old are more likely to have problems with mushrooms than healthy adults. Fifth, eat only cooked mushrooms; some species are more likely to cause problems when consumed raw than when cooked, and some toxins are inactivated by proper cooking.

The principal types of mushroom poisoning known to occur in North America may be divided into seven main groups. No universal antidote exists for mushroom poisoning; each type of poisoning requires different treatment and this is best left to qualified physicians working in conjunction with poison control centers. In general for a healthy person, the sooner symptoms appear the greater the likelihood of complete recovery. The major types of mushroom poisoning are discussed in terms of rapidity of onset and type of symptoms.

Coprine Poisoning. There is very little that is even potentially amusing about mushroom poisoning except possibly for the disulfiram-like type of poisoning caused by coprine. The principal species involved is *Coprinus atramentarius*. The only people likely to be affected are those who consume alcoholic beverages shortly before or up to about 48 hours (occasionally even 4-5 days) after eating the mushrooms. The onset of symptoms is fairly rapid, i.e., twenty minutes to at most an hour or two. Symptoms include a pronounced feeling of apprehension, flushing of the face and neck, tingling in the arms and legs, rapid heart beat, a metallic taste in the mouth, and finally nausea and vomiting. The effects vary in severity depending on the person and relative amounts of fungus and alcohol involved. Some people experience very little discomfort, others become quite emotionally upset. The symptoms usually pass off spontaneously. It has been reported in the literature and confirmed by friends of ours that *Clitocybe clavipes* may also cause this type of reaction.

Gastrointestinal Problems and Individual Idiosyncracies. These are probably the most common types of problems. Certain mushrooms produce gastric distress in most people who consume them. The onset of symptoms varies from about 30 minutes to 2-3 hours from time of consumption, and often include

nausea, vomiting, diarrhea, and abdominal cramps. Usually the symptoms are more severe when raw mushrooms are consumed. The toxins causing such reactions are not fully known, but for a healthy person, recovery is usually rapid, and treatment of the symptoms and rest are usually all that is needed. Some species of *Agaricus, Lactarius, Amanita* (but see below), *Entoloma,* and *Hebeloma,* to name just a few, fall in this category. *Chlorophyllum molybdites* is a frequent cause of this type of poisoning. Some people can eat this species with no difficulty, but others are not so fortunate. The green tinge of the *Chlorophyllum* spore deposit is distinctive so by checking the spore deposit, trouble can usually be avoided. However, we encountered a case where the people had set up caps for a deposit, left them over night, and found the paper was still white the next morning. Believing they did not have *Chlorophyllum* they ate the specimens and became ill, one person even required hospitalization. We later examined the specimens and discovered that they were sterile, i.e., no spores were formed. The paper was white because nothing had fallen on it!

Individual idiosyncracies and allergies may also be involved in apparent mushroom "poisonings," and such reactions may be species-specific. At least two cases have come to our attention where a couple ate the same meal including a course of wild mushrooms and one member became ill while the spouse had no reaction. One member of our family can not eat *Boletus edulis*, a non-gilled fleshy fungus, without having her eyes swell shut, but the swelling is reversed when she takes an antihistamine. Finally, many people are bothered in some way by drying mushrooms.

Muscarine Poisoning. Muscarine was isolated from *Amanita muscaria* and once thought to be the causative agent in all types of mushroom poisoning. More recent research has shown that the muscarine level in *A. muscaria* is relatively low; it is not even the principal toxin in that species. Furthermore, muscarine is only one of several poisonous compounds which may occur in mushrooms. However, muscarine has been detected in species of *Omphalotus, Inocybe,* and *Clitocybe,* particularly in the common lawn mushroom *C. dealbata,* in quantities sufficient to cause illness. It is suspected in poisonings by a number of other mushrooms. The onset of symptoms is usually from 15 minutes to 2 hours after ingestion. The symptoms are characterized by profuse sweating, salivation, and tear formation (lacrimation) accompanied by muscle spasms, constriction of the pupils, blurred vision, slowed heart beat, reduced blood pressure, headache, nausea, vomiting, and diarrhea. The mortality rate from muscarine poisoning has been estimated by various authors to be as high as 5-12% with children being the principal victims. If the combination of profuse sweating, salivation, and lacrimation is present, muscarine poisoning is the likely cause, and atropine can be administered by a physician as an antidote. Species of *Omphalotus* cause a type of poisoning which resembles muscarine poisoning in many respects but typically fails to produce the profuse sweating characteristic of that type.

Ibotenic Acid-Muscimol Poisoning. These compounds and their derivatives are the principal toxins in a number of Amanitas including *A. cothurnata, A. gemmata, A. muscaria,* and *A. pantherina.* Delirium and hallucinations accompanied by deep sleep with visions or a coma are typical symptoms of this type of poisoning. The symptoms appear within two hours of ingestion and affect the central nervous system primarily. Most victims recover rapidly and spontaneously from this type of poisoning; however, side effects may cause problems. For example, if the victims are in a deep sleep or coma, they may choke on their own secretions if not attended. Atropine is worse than useless in this type of poisoning as it acts synergistically with the toxins.

Much lore has evolved around the use of *Amanita muscaria* in deliberately inducing visions and hallucinations. However, it is difficult to predict reactions to this species as the amount of toxin varies within the species from area to area. Furthermore, how it affects the user depends in part on the attitude and surroundings of the user and the user's susceptibility to the toxins.

Psilocybin and Psilocin Poisoning. This group encompasses a second class of compounds which induce delirium and hallucinations within a short time after ingestion, but not, typically, accompanied by "deep sleep" or coma. The principal genera involved include *Psilocybe, Panaeolus, Conocybe,* and *Gymnopilus,* especially species in all these genera that develop blue or green stains in age or where bruised. In addition to the hallucinations, bad headaches may also be present. These are dangerous fungi no matter how glamorized they may be in legend and can be especially dangerous when administered to children who may experience convulsions rather than hallucinations. Many of the species containing these compounds are actively sought for use in inducing hallucinations, particularly in the southern United States south into Mexico and along the Pacific Coast, especially in the Pacific Northwest. There are state laws and some federal statutes which pertain to the collecting, transporting, and possession of hallucinogenic fungi.

Accidental poisonings by members of this group do occur. We know of a case in which a hallucinogenic *Gymnopilus* was confused with the honey mushroom (*Armillariella mellea*). The victims did not enjoy the sensations they experienced and were briefly hospitalized for observation. A check of the spore deposit (reddish brown for the *Gymnopilus,* white or nearly so for the *Armillariella*) would have saved these people some bad moments.

Monomethylhydrazine Poisoning. We

come now to the first of the types of poisoning in which the onset of symptoms is delayed several hours or even days after ingestion. Gyromitrin releases monomethylhydrazine as a decomposition product. Gyromitrin occurs in several species of *Gyromitra*, a genus of non-gilled fleshy fungi sometimes sought for food. Symptoms typically occur 6-8 (2-12) hours after ingestion and may include a feeling of fullness in the stomach, nausea, vomiting, abdominal cramps, and watery diarrhea which may be followed by evidence of liver damage, jaundice, convulsions, and possibly death. No specific antidote is known for this type of poisoning. However, the toxin content of the fungi may be lowered or even removed by repeated (2-3) parboilings. Evidentally the toxin is very slowly degraded in the body so even if only small quantities of the mushroom are eaten over a period of several days, the concentration of the poison can reach dangerous levels. Finally, there is some evidence that indicates that hydrazines may be carcinogenic.

Cyclopeptide Poisoning. It has been estimated that as much as 95% of all the fatal mushroom poisonings are due to this group of toxins. They occur in some members of the genus *Amanita*, especially *A. phalloides*, *A. virosa*, and *A. bisporigera*, as well as in the genus *Galerina*, particularly in the *G. autumnalis* group. The amatoxins are the principal toxins involved. Usually at least six hours, and more likely 10-14 hours, elapse between ingestion and the onset of symptoms. The first stage of poisoning is characterized by severe vomiting and diarrhea (often bloody), and abdominal pain. This is followed by an apparent remission which may last about a day. The third stage is marked by the appearance of cumulative liver and kidney damage which commenced early in the poisoning but only now may be apparent if liver function has not been monitored. Secondary involvement of the heart and central nervous system may occur with death coming 2-4 days after ingestion. As little as one cap of *Amanita phalloides* may contain enough toxin to kill an adult. No specific antidote is generally accepted as the preferred treatment for this type of poisoning, but many people do survive if proper supportive medical care is administered in time.

Cortinarius Poisoning. To date, few cases of this type of poisoning have been reported from North America and relatively few are known from Europe. This is the extreme in delayed onset of symptoms with symptoms first occurring three or more days after ingestion. Thirst and profuse urination are followed by signs of kidney failure. The causal agent(s) is (are) unknown at the present time.

In conclusion, the chemical composition of most mushroom species is unknown and reports on edibility are not available for many. Potentially toxic compounds have been isolated from various species of mushrooms and are present in minute quantities even in apparently harmless mushrooms. For example, *Flammulina velutipes* contains small quantities of a protein that is toxic to heart muscle but which loses its toxicity when heated. This species is safely consumed in large quantity on this continent and in the orient. Furthermore, minute quantities of amanitins have been found in several good edible species. Much remains to be learned about poisonous mushrooms and their constituent poisons. The best defense against poisoning is a combination of careful collecting, accurate identification, and moderate eating. Neither the authors nor the publisher accept responsibility for identifications made by users of this work nor do we accept responsibility for possible effects which may arise from eating mushrooms, either edible or poisonous fungi. Conservatives in this field may outlive adventurers.

General Considerations

The use of a key is discussed in the chapter on collecting and identifying mushrooms.

Responsibility for Identifications. Neither the authors nor the publisher accept responsibility for identifications made by users of this work nor do we accept responsibility for possible effects which may arise from eating mushrooms, especially in regard to edible and/or poisonous species. No book has been written that covers all the species of mushrooms which occur in North America. While data regarding the edibility of many species has been amassed over the years, many others have not been tested. It is the responsibility of the user to decide which species he/she wishes to experiment with. We have tried to point out which species are edible for most people and which poisonous, but we can not predict individual reactions to individual species.

Distribution. The mushroom flora of many parts of North America is poorly documented, so the distribution data is necessarily general. Since many mushrooms are associated with particular higher plants, especially trees, habitat is emphasized.

Illustrations. The drawings are generally less than life size for obvious reasons. The divisions on the scale accompanying each drawing indicate centimeters.

Abbreviations and Symbols
± more or less, or about
mm millimeter
cm centimeter
μm micron, micrometer
10 mm equal 1 cm
2.5 cm equal 1 inch
1 μm equals 0.001 mm

General References

There is no manual for identification of all North American mushrooms. Any one wishing to go beyond the beginner's level of handbooks and field guides must refer to various technical monographs and/or scattered journal articles. Many good handbooks are available; we cite only some of the more advanced, and often less well-known works here. For a more complete list of sources, see Shaffer (1968); he cites references for all the genera. Miller and Farr (1975) also have a useful bibliography.

Gilliam, M. S. 1976. The genus *Marasmius* in the northeastern United States and adjacent Canada. Mycotaxon 4:1-144.

Hesler, L. R. 1969. North American species of *Gymnopilus*. Mycologia Memoir 3, Hafner Publishing Co., New York. 117 pp.

Hesler, L. R., and A. H. Smith. 1963. North American species of *Hygrophorus*. The University of Tennessee Press, Knoxville. 416 pp.

———. 1965. North American species of *Crepidotus*. Hafner Publishing Co., New York. 168 pp.

———. 1979. North American species of *Lactarius*. The University of Michigan Press, Ann Arbor. 814 pp.

Jenkins, D. T. 1977. A taxonomic and nomenclatural study of the genus *Amanita* section *Amanita* for North America. Bibliotheca Mycologica Bd. 57. J. Cramer, Vaduz. 126 pp.

Kauffman, C. H. 1919. The Agaricaceae of Michigan. Michigan Geological and Biological Survey Publication 26. Republished as "The Gilled Mushbooks (Agaricaceae) of Michigan and the Great Lakes Region" by Dover Publications, Inc., New York, New York in 1971.

Kühner, R., and H. Romagnesi. 1974. Flore Analytique des champignons superieurs. Masson et Cie., Paris. 556 pp.

Largent, D. A. 1977. The genus *Leptonia* on the Pacific Coast of the United States. J. Cramer, Vaduz. 286 pp.

Largent, D. L. 1977. How to identify mushrooms to genus I: Macroscopic features. Mad River Press, Inc., Eureka CA. 86 pp.

Largent, D., D. Johnson, R. Watling. 1977. How to identify mushrooms to genus III: Microscopic features. Mad River Press, Inc., Eureka, CA. 148 pp.

Largent, D. L., and H. D. Thiers. 1977. How to identify mushrooms to genus II: Field identification of genera. Mad River Press, Inc., Eureka, CA. 32 pp.

Lincoff, G., and D. H. Mitchel. 1977. Toxic and hallucinogenic mushroom poisoning. Van Nostrand Reinhold Company, New York. 267 pp.

MacIlvaine, C., and R. K. Macadam. 1973. One thousand American fungi. Dover Publications, Inc., New York, New York. 729 pp. An unabridged republication of the 1902 edition with a list of nomenclatural changes by R. L. Shaffer.

Miller, O. K., Jr., and D. F. Farr. 1975. An index of the common fungi of North America (Synonymy and common names). Bibliotheca Mycologica Bd. 44. J. Cramer, Vaduz. 206 pp.

Moser, M. 1978. Die Röhrlinge und Blätterpilze Bd. II b/2 of 'Kleine Kryptogamenflora' by H. Gams. Gustav Fischer, Stuttgart. 532 pp.

Rumack, B. H., and E. Salzman, eds. 1978. Mushroom poisoning: Diagnosis and Treatment. CRC Press, West Palm Beach, Florida, 263 pp.

Shaffer, R. L. 1968. Keys to Genera of Higher Fungi. Ed. 2. University Herbarium and Biological Station, The University of Michigan, Ann Arbor. 131 pp.

Singer, R. 1975. The Agaricales in modern taxonomy. J. Cramer, Vaduz. 912 pp.

Smith, A. H. 1947. North American species of *Mycena*. The University of Michigan Press, Ann Arbor. 521 pp.

————. 1972. The North American species of *Psathyrella*. Memoirs of the New York Botanical Garden 24:1-633.

Smith, A. H., and L. R. Hesler. 1968. The North American species of *Pholiota*. Hafner Publishing Co., New York. 402 pp.

Smith, A. H., and R. Singer. 1964. A monograph on the genus *Galerina* Earle. Hafner Publishing Co., New York. 384 pp.

Smith, H. V., and A. H. Smith, 1973. How to Know the Non-Gilled Fleshy Fungi. Wm. C. Brown Co. Publishers, Dubuque, Iowa. 402 pp. (To be revised as "How to Know the Non-Gilled Mushrooms." To appear in 1980.)

Stuntz, D. E. with D. L. Largent and R. Watling. 1977. How to identify mushrooms to Genus IV: Keys to families and genera. Mad River Press, Inc., Eureka, CA. 94 pp.

Many journals carry articles on mushroom taxonomy; some of the more important ones published in North America include the following:

Brittonia
Bulletin of the Torrey Botanical Club
The Canadian Journal of Botany
Journal of the Elisha Mitchel Scientific Society
Lloydia
The Michigan Botanist
Mycotaxon
Mycologia
The Papers of the Michigan Academy of Science, Arts, and Letters

Key to Families

1a   Parasitic on fruiting bodies of other mushrooms (chiefly Russulaceae); hyphae of pileus context soon breaking up into thick-walled spores; hymenium not well-developed and basidiospores not or sparsely produced ....
.... (p. 78) *Asterophora*

1b   Not as above: if parasitic, gills well-developed 2

2a   Gills present as veins or narrow gills with obtuse edges at least when young, gills often intervenose to almost poroid ....
.... *Cantharellales* (see "How to Know the Non-gilled Fleshy Fungi")

2b   Not as above 3

3a   Spore deposit white to yellow or tinted with pink, lilac-gray, buff, or olive 4

3b   Spore deposit distinctly pink to vinaceous or some shade of brown, black, or gray
.... 8

4a   Gills free from the stipe; stipe and pileus often separating cleanly (like a ball and socket joint) 5

4b   Gills attached to stipe (attachment sometimes so slight that gills are practically free), or stipe absent and gills radiating from base of pileus; stipe and pileus not separating cleanly 6

5a   Spore deposit white or nearly so; often both a partial veil and a universal veil present; gills trama bilateral at maturity
.... (p. 155) *Amanitaceae*

5b   Spore deposit white or nearly so to greenish or olive; universal veil as a volva absent in most species; gill trama regular to interwoven .... (p. 172) *Lepiotaceae*

6a   Gills appearing waxy (clean and ±[1] shining), often thick (if pinkish to purple see *Laccaria*, p. 102 also); basidia often long in relation to width (4-6 times longer than broad) ....(p. 53) *Hygrophoraceae*

1. This symbol (±) will stand for "more or less" throughout the key.

26

6b Not as above 7

7a Fruiting bodies typically coarse and fragile (brittle); neither partial nor universal veil present; tissue of pileus and stipe with groups of inflated cells in a matrix of filamentose hyphae; spores with amyloid ornamentation .... (p. 28) *Russulaceae*

7b Not as above .... (p. 71) *Tricholomataceae*

8a Spore deposit with distinct pink to red tones to reddish cinnamon or brownish-pink (see *Coprinaceae* also; if pileus fan-shaped see *Crepidotus*) 9

8b Spore deposit typically not as above 10

9a Gills free; stipe and pileus often cleanly separating; spores typically smooth; gill trama convergent .... (p. 184) *Pluteaceae*

9b Gills attached; stipe and pileus not cleanly separating; spores typically angular or grooved; gill trama more or less regular .... (p. 304) *Rhodophyllaceae*

10a Spore deposit ochraceous, yellowish clay-color, tawny, orange-brown, dark rusty brown, or earth-brown 11

10b Spore deposit dark bluish fuscous, black, deep olive-brown, purple-brown or various shades of cocoa- or chocolate-brown 14

11a Gill layer usually readily separable from pileus; veils absent .... (p. 309) *Paxillaceae*

11b Not as above 12

12a Partial veil usually present as a cortina on young specimens (membranous only in *Rozites*, absent in some species of *Galerina* and other genera); stipe central and present except in *Crepidotus*; spores mostly roughened and lacking an apical germ pore; pileus cuticle of appressed hyphae or a lax trichodermium (if lignicolous and spores smooth see *Pholiota*) .... (p. 263) *Cortinariaceae*

12b Not as above 13

13a Spore deposit bright to dull rusty brown; pileus cuticle cellular or hymeniform .... (p. 226) *Bolbitiaceae*

13b Spore deposit bluish fuscous to dark vinaceous brown, rusty brown, or clay-color; pileus cuticle of appressed, often gelatinous, narrow hyphae (occasionally with ascending tips) .... (p. 237) *Strophariaceae*

14a Pileus and stipe cleanly separable; annulus typically present; gills typically pallid to pink or vinaceous red when young, free; spores lacking an obvious germ pore; pileus cuticle of appressed to fascicled hyphae (or of globose cells in *Melanophyllum*) .... (p. 194) *Agaricaceae*

14b Not as above 15

15a Gills relatively thick, decurrent; spore deposit grayish to olive-brown; spores long and narrow (10 μm or more long) 16

15b Not as above 17

16a Pileus dry, suede-like; cuticle different in color than the context; pileus cuticle a trichodermium ...... (p. 310) *Phylloporus*

16b Pileus viscid, or if dry and fibrillose, ochraceous with the cuticle and context the same color .... (p. 311) *Gomphidiaceae*

17a Spore deposit black to dark brown, cocoa-brown, to (rarely) dull vinaceous; pileus cuticle cellular or hymeniform; spores with an apical pore; fruiting bodies typically fragile and usually ± cinnamon brown when moist, deliquescent in some .... (p. 207) *Coprinaceae*

17b Spore deposit tinged violet-gray to violet-brown, vinaceous brown to purple-brown, yellow-brown, or duller; pileus cuticle of appressed hyphae, their tips ascending or not; fruiting bodies typically not fragile and not deliquescent .... (p. 237) *Strophariaceae*

RUSSULACEAE Roze

Pileus and stipe confluent; annulus and volva lacking; tissue of stipe and pileus consisting at least in part of groups of inflated cells (rosettes) surrounded by matrical hyphae; spores large and mostly broadly ellipsoid to globose, ornamented variously but the ornamentation always amyloid in some degree.

This family accounts in a large measure for our "summer" mushroom flora. The fruiting bodies are small to large and mostly fragile. They are a popular group with the mycophagists; none of our species are known to be deadly poisonous, though this is not true for the family in the Orient.

KEY TO GENERA

1a Latex present: milk-white, orange, brown or water-like, often changing color on exposure to air .... (p. 28) *Lactarius*

1b Latex absent though gills may be at times beaded with droplets of a clear liquid .... (p. 47) *Russula*

Lactarius (D. C. ex) S. F. Gray

Pileus fleshy, firm, often fragile; where cut or broken exuding a latex; latex clear and watery to opaque and white to variously colored. Gills attached. Stipe central, fragile to hard. Spore ornamentation amyloid; color in deposit white to orange-yellow. Context heteromerous (of groups of inflated cells or these in columns) surrounded by filamentous hyphae. Pileus and stipe confluent. Veils absent in North American species.

Of the roughly 300 species of "Milk Mushrooms" reported from North America, about 60 are treated here. The genus contains a number of edible species, a lot that are unpalatable, and a number which are mildly poisonous.

KEY TO SPECIES

1a Latex when first exposed blue, red, orange or dull brownish yellow to orange-brown **2**

1a Latex at first opaque and white to creamy or clear and colorless **10**

2a Entire fruiting body and latex blue; staining green on injury or in age ....
.... *L. indigo* **(Schw.) Fr.**

Pileus (3) 5-15 cm, convex-depressed, grayish to silvery when faded, thinly slimy; taste mild to faintly acrid. Gills often tinged yellowish from maturing spores. Stipe 2-8 x 1-2.5 cm, hard, thinly slimy, soon dry. Spores 7-9 x 5.5-7.5 μm, ± reticulate. Pileus cuticle an ixocutis.

Scattered to gregarious under both conifers and hardwoods, summer and fall, abundant in the Southeast, rare in the Great Lakes area. Edible and readily identified by beginners.

2b Fruiting body and latex differently colored than in "2a" **3**

3a Pileus dry, chalky to subvelvety, white at first; latex salmon color ....
.... *L. salmoneus* Peck var. *salmoneus*

Pileus (1.5) 2.5-6 cm, convex to depressed, azonate; taste mild. Latex not staining injured tissues. Gills narrow, close, bright salmon color when young. Stipe 1-2.5 cm x 3-6 (10) mm, whitish. Spores 8-9 x 5-6 μm, ± reticulate. Pileus cuticle of dry, interwoven to ascending hyphae.

On soil (often bare of vegetation) which has been flooded; especially under pine or in mixed woods, summer, southeastern United States. In var. *curtisii* (Coker) Hes. & Sm. the taste is slightly acrid and injured areas stain green. Edibility not reported?

3b Pileus moist to lubricous or slimy at first; pileus and latex with a different combination of colors **4**

4a Pileus whitish to pale pinkish brown, often flushed green to olive; latex deep red (port-wine-red) when first exposed ....
.... *L. barrowsii* **Hesler & Smith**

Pileus 3-10 cm, convex-depressed, thinly slimy at first, azonate or faintly zoned; taste mild. Latex scanty, staining flesh greenish. Gills close, narrow, ochraceous to pinkish orange. Stipe 2-4 cm x 1-2.5 cm, dry, yellowish beneath a white bloom. Spores 8-10.5 x 6-7.5 μm, ± reticulate. Cuticle of pileus an ixocutis.

Under pine, New Mexico, September. Edible according to its discoverer.

4b Not as above **5**

5a Pileus at first wine red; latex wine red; usually found near hemlock ....
.... *L. subpurpureus* **Peck**

Pileus 3-10 cm, convex-depressed, zonate, in age silvery to dingy ochraceous to the purplish margin; taste mild to bitterish. Latex slowly staining injured places green. Gills wine red at first. Stipe 3-8 cm x 6-15 mm, often spotted. Spores 8-11 x 6.5-8 μm, ± reticulate. Pileus cuticle an ixocutis.

Solitary to gregarious under conifers, especially eastern hemlock and pine, also in mixed woods, summer and fall; eastern North America. Edible.

5b Not as above **6**

6a Pileus with a silvery, dull blue to grayish green or dingy blue coloration at first **7**

6b Pileus some shade of orange when young and fresh **8**

7a Latex dark reddish brown ....
.... *L. paradoxus* **Beards. & Burl.**

Pileus 5-8 cm, convex-depressed, zonate, viscid at first; taste mild to ± peppery. Latex slowly staining injured tissues green. Gills close, narrow at first, near putty color. Stipe 2.5-3 x 1-1.5 cm, colored like the pileus or bluer. Spores 7-9 x 5.5-6.5 μm, ± reticulate. Pileus cuticle an ixocutis.

Scattered to solitary, often under pine, live oak, and cabbage palmetto, fairly abundant in the Southeast but less frequent to rare northward, late summer and fall in the north, fall and winter in the south. Edible?

7b **Latex dull yellow to yellow-brown (color of grasshopper juice, Peck)** .... *L. chelidonium* **Pk.** var. *chelidonioides* **(Sm.) Hes. & Sm.**

Pileus 3-8 cm, plano-depressed, thinly slimy at first, soon dry, azonate to weakly zonate, at first azure blue with brown zones; taste ± peppery; context slowly staining greenish. Gills narrow, crowded, yellowish to yellowish brown or olive-buff. Stipe 3-8 x 1-2.5 cm, concolorous with pileus or paler. Spores 7-9 x 5-6.5 (7) μm, not appreciably reticulate. Pileus cuticle an ixocutis.

Scattered to gregarious under conifers, especially pine, fall, eastern north America, infrequent. In var. *chelidonium* the flesh is initially the color of the latex, then becomes blue and finally green. In var. *chelidonioides* the flesh is initially blue near the cuticle and yellowish near the gills.

8a **Latex dark red to orange-red when first exposed** .... *L. rubrilactis* **Hesler & Smith**

Pileus 6-12 cm, depressed to broadly funnel-shaped, slimy, zonate with carrot-color zones on a paler ground color; latex scanty; all parts staining green where injured. Gills close to crowded, narrow light pinkish cinnamon to dark dull purplish red. Stipe 2-6 x 1-3 cm, often duller and paler than pileus. Spores 7.5-9 x 6-7.5 μm, ± reticulate. Pileus cuticle an ixocutis.

Gregarious to scattered, especially under pine, summer and fall, from the Rocky Mountains westward. Edible.

8b **Latex orange when first exposed** **9**

9a **Both pileus and stipe viscid at first; fruiting bodies not staining green in age or when injured. Fig. 21** .... *L. thyinos* **Smith**

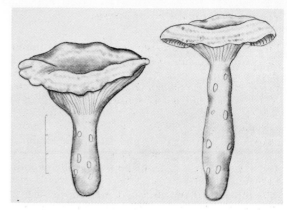

Figure 21

Figure 21 *Lactarius thyinos*

Pileus 3-9 cm, convex-depressed, thickly to thinly slimy, zonate with shades of bright orange and pale yellow-orange; taste mild. Latex cadmium orange; injured areas slowly wine red. Gills close at first, subdistant in age, bright orange. Stipe 4-8 cm x 8-35 mm, soon dry. Spores 9-12 x 7.5-9 μm, ± reticulate. Pileus cuticle an ixocutis.

Solitary to gregarious in cool white cedar (*Thuja*) bogs and swamps, late summer and fall, common, Great Lakes area to the maritime provinces of Canada. Edible.

9b **Pileus and stipe moist to dry at first; fruiting bodies staining green within several hours of injury or in age. Fig. 22** .... *L. deliciosus* **ss. lato**

Figure 22

Figure 22 *Lactarius deliciosus*

Pileus 5-14 cm, broadly convex to depressed, slimy viscid at first, soon dry; taste mild to bitterish. Gills crowded, narrow, pale orange-yellow to ocher-orange. Stipe 3-7 x 1-2.5 cm, pruinose, in some variants slowly staining red at the base where injured. Spores 7-9 x 6-7 μm (or in 2 varieties 8-11 x 7-8 μm). Pileus cuticle an ixocutis.

Solitary to gregarious under conifers, especially pine in late summer and fall. Several varieties may be distinguished as follows: In var. *areolatus* Smith pleurocystidia are absent, the pileus is soon dry and areolate, and the spores 8-11 x 7-8 μm. In var. *deterrimus* (Gröger) Hes. & Sm. pleurocystidia are absent, but the pileus does not become areolate. In var. *piceus* Smotlacha pleurocystidia are present and 40-70 x 3-5 μm and cut surfaces change to wine red before becoming green as is also the case in var. *deterrimus*. All the variants are edible but some are superior to others in flavor. Truely, it is a variable species.

10a **Pileus dry and white to light tan over the disc; (generally occurring east of the Rocky Mountains)** **11**

10b **Not as above** **16**

11a **Bruised or cut gills or cut base of stipe staining deep rosy salmon** .... *L. subplinthogalus* **Coker**

Pileus 3-8 (10.5) cm, plano-depressed, unpolished to minutely pruinose, whitish to yellowish often tinged gray in age or on drying; odor pleasant; taste acrid. Latex white, staining injured areas deep rosy salmon. Gills very distant, broad, near cinnamon-buff at maturity. Stipe 3-8 cm x 7-15 mm, dry, concolorous with pileus or paler. Spores 7.5-9.5 x 7-8 μm, not reticulate (elements of ornamentation not connected .up sufficiently). Cuticle of pileus ± of a trichodermium to an hymeniform layer (some of the elements septate).

Solitary to scattered, usually in deciduous woods, summer and fall, southeastern United States. *L. subvernalis* may also be whitish and with reddish stains but it has close, narrow gills.

11b **Not as above** **12**

12a **Latex copious, soon staining injured tissue brown; taste mild** .... *L. luteolus* **Peck**

Pileus 2.5-6 (8) cm, convex to plane, white to pale buff or brownish in age, dry, velvety, azonate; odor mild to strong and foetid. Gills white becoming yellowish, close, narrow to moderately broad. Stipe 2.5-6 cm x 5-12 mm, white to buff, dry, velvety. Spores 7-9 x 5.5-7 μm, ornamentation mostly of isolated warts. Cuticle of pileus a zone of inflated cells with an epicutis of a turf of pileocystidia ± capitate at apex and 37-70 x 3-5 μm.

Scattered to gregarious under hardwoods and in mixed woods, eastern North America, summer to fall. Edible.

12b **Not as above `(see *L. controversus* also) 13**

13a **Stipe surface at least in part velvety (use a handlens)** **14**

13b **Stipe surface glabrous** **15**

14a **Pileus velvety; margin thin, not cottony when young; taste very acrid. Fig. 23** .... *L. subvellereus* **Pk. var. *subdistans* Hes & Sm.**

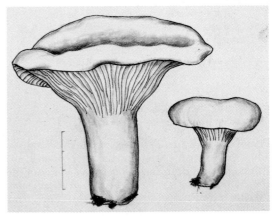

Figure 23

Figure 23 *Lactarius subvellereus* var. *subdistans*

Pileus 5-15 cm, convex then depressed, white to ± tinged yellowish to grayish, dry; odor mild; latex white, slowly dull yellowish, close to subdistant but finally distant, ± narrow. Stipe 2-5 x 1.2-3.5 cm, white, hard. Spores 7.5-9 x 5-7 μm, ornamentation low, mostly of isolated warts. Cuticle of pileus a turf of essentially cylindric, thick-walled pileocystidia 150-200 x 3-5 μm.

Scattered to gregarious on soil in deciduous and mixed woods, summer to early fall, eastern North America. In var. *subvellereus* the gills are crowded. *L. vellereus* (Fr.) Fr. is much less common in North America. Its spores are 7.5-9 x 6.5-8 μm. *L. subvellereus* var. *subdistans* is the one on which most reports of *L. vellereus* in the American literature are based. Not edible.

14b Pileus glabrous or at length areolate to scaly over the disc; margin at first cottony. Fig. 24 .... *L. deceptivus* Peck

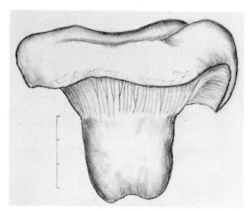

Figure 24

Figure 24 *Lactarius deceptivus*

Pileus (5) 8-24 cm, convex to convex-depressed, white to whitish becoming tan to brownish over all in age, dry, dull, surface ± fibrillose; odor mild at first becoming strong and pungent in age; taste (slowly) strongly acrid; latex white, slowly staining injured tissue brownish. Gills whitish becoming ochraceous, becoming subdistant, rather broad. Stipe 4-9 x (1) 2-4 cm, white with brownish stains in age, velvety to pubescent. Spores 9-12

(13) x 7.5-9 μm; ornamentation of isolated warts. Cuticle of pileus not well differentiated, of dry interwoven hyphae with ascending fascicles of hyphae at the surface.

Solitary to gregarious under conifers, especially hemlock, also in mixed woods and oak woods with an understory of *Vaccinum*, eastern North America, summer and fall. Edibility: Not recommended.

**15a Gills extremely crowded, narrow; spores (4.5) 5-7 × 5-5.5 μm; taste very quickly and sharply acrid. Fig. 25 ....
.... *L. piperatus* sensu lato**

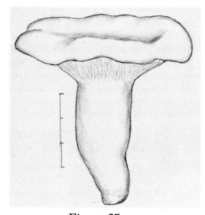

Figure 25

Figure 25 *Lactarius piperatus*

Pileus 4-15 cm, convex to plane or depressed, white, at times with cream-color to pale tan stains, dry, glabrous; latex white drying yellowish, at times staining tissues greenish. Gills white to cream color, often forked 1-3 times. Stipe 2-8 x 1-2.5 cm, white, dry, unpolished. Spores (4.5) 5-7 x 5-5.5 μm, ornamented with very inconspicuous lines and warts. Cuticle of pileus a zone of inflated cells with scattered hypha-like pileocystidia projecting (see young specimens).

Scattered to gregarious in deciduous woods, eastern North America, summer, common. In var. *glaucescens* (Crossl.) Hes. & Sm. the dried latex droplets are a dingy pale green. Neither variety is recommended for the table: var. *glaucescens* is reportedly poisonous here in North America.

15b Gills close, moderately broad; spores 7.5-9.5
× 6.5-8.5 μm ....
.... *L. neuhoffii* Hes. & Sm. var. *neuhoffii*

Pileus 6-12 cm, convex-depressed, dry, glabrous,
white; odor mild, taste very acrid. Latex white
at first, soon dull yellow, staining injured gills
dingy ochraceous. Gills white at first, pale pinkish
buff at maturity. Stipe 2.5-3.5 x 1.5-3 cm, white,
dry, unpolished. Spores ornamented with low
warts and ridges forming a broken reticulum. Cuticle of pileus a mixture of inflated cells and narrow hyphae.

Gregarious to scattered under oak, Great
Lakes area south and eastward, probably wide-
spread east of the Great Plains, summer, sporadic.
Not recommended.

16a Pileus dry and appearing somewhat velvety
.... **17**

16b Pileus not velvety: it may be moist, slimy,
glabrous or fibrillose **23**

17a Pileus gray, brown or black **18**

17b Pileus yellow, light yellow-brown or reddish
brown **22**

18a Gills at maturity distant, subdecurrent; spore
deposit white; spores 8-10 × 7.5-9 μm, ornamented with a low reticulum (prominences
0.5-0.8 μm) ....
.... *L. gerardii* Pk. var. *gerardii*

Pileus (3) 5-10 (13) cm, convex-umbonate to
plane or depressed, with an acute umbo, dark
yellowish brown, dry, velvety, often finely
wrinkled; taste mild to ± acrid; latex white, unchanging. Gills white, finally cream color. Stipe
3.5-8 cm x 8-15 (20) mm, concolor with pileus.
Cuticle of pileus with a turf of pileocystidia.

Scattered to gregarious in deciduous and
conifer forests, summer to fall Great Lakes area
east and southward; not common. In var. *subru-
bescens* (Sm. & Hes.) Hes. & Sm. the latex stains
injured tissue pinkish vinaceous.

18b Not as above **19**

19a Pileus smoky tan to smoky brown; gills
crowded and narrow; cut surfaces slowly
reddish .... *L. fumosus* Pk. var. *fumosus*

Pileus 3-10 cm, convex to plane or shallowly depressed, dry, dull to velvety or unpolished, smoky-
pallid to dingy tan or grayish-alutaceous, color
often uneven; taste peppery; latex white staining
cut surfaces reddish. Gills crowded, narrow, whitish becoming yellowish in age. Stipe 4-11 cm x
6-15 mm, dry, about concolor with pileus. Spores
6-8 x 6-7.5 μm, ornamented with a broken reticulum. Pileus cuticle ± of a lax palisade (hymeniform type).

Scattered to gregarious in deciduous, mixed
or conifer woods, summer and fall in the area
east of the Great Plains, not rare. In var. *fumo-
soides* (Sm. & Hes.) Hes. & Sm. the taste is consistently mild.

19b Pileus deep brown to blackish brown **20**

20a Associated with hardwoods. Fig. 26 ....
.... *L. fuliginellus* Sm. & Hes.

Figure 26

Figure 26 *Lactarius fuliginellus*

Pileus 4-12 cm, convex to plano-depressed or infundibuliform, dark olive-brown to sepia, unpolished to pruinose, often wrinkled in age; taste
not distinctive; latex white, staining cut surfaces
dingy salmon. Gills whitish when young, tan in
age. Stipe 3-10 cm x 9-20 mm, about concolor
with pileus. Spores 6-7.5 μm, ± reticulate, the

ornamentation ± 1-1.5 (2) μm high. Cuticle of pileus a staggered palisade of clavate to ± cylindric or fusoid-ventricose cells.

Scattered to gregarious on wet soil with *Vaccinium* bushes as an understory, summer and fall, sporadic but often abundant when it fruits, Great Lakes area. Edibility not tested.

20b Associated with conifers **21**

21a Gills close to crowded at maturity, narrow. Fig. 27 .... *L. fallax* Sm. & Hes. var *fallax*

Figure 27

Figure 27   *Lactarius fallax* var. *fallax*

Pileus 3-9 (10) cm, convex to plane and umbonate becoming plane to depressed, umbo persistent or not, velvety, dark sooty brown to blackish; taste mild to faintly peppery; latex white, slowly staining injured areas pale purplish red to vinaceous. Gills narrow, crowded, white becoming creamy buff, marginate. Stipe 2.5-6 cm x 8-15 mm, often ± paler than pileus, unpolished to velvety. Spores 7.5-10 μm in diameter, ± globose, ± reticulate, prominences of ornamentation 0.8-2 μm high. Cuticle of pileus a staggered pallisade (actually a compacted trichodermium with the basal cells enlarged).

Under conifers, scattered to gregarious, late summer and fall, Pacific Northwest; it has often been identified as "*L. lignyotus.*" Var. *concolor* Sm. & Hes. has non-marginate gills.

21b Gills subdistant at maturity, relatively broad. Fig. 28 .... *L. lignyotus* Fr. var. *lignyotus*

Figure 28

Figure 28   *Lactarius lignyotus* var. *lignyotus*

Pileus 2-7 (10) cm, convex-umbonate to nearly plane or depressed-umbonate, dull, velvety; taste mild to bitterish; latex white, slowly staining cut flesh rosy red to reddish cinnamon. Gills white becoming pale ochraceous. Stipe 5-12 cm x 4-10 (20) mm, dry, dull, concolorous with pileus, base often paler. Spores 7-9 μm, ± globose, ± reticulate, prominences 1.8-2.4 μm high. Cuticle of pileus a staggered trichodermium, the lower cells greatly inflated.

Gregarious to scattered, often in *Sphagnum* or in damp conifer forests generally, eastern North America. It is a variable species. In var. *nigroviolascens* (Burl.) Hes. & Sm. the latex stains violet. In var. *canadensis* Sm. & Hes. the gills are usually more or less marginate. The latter is the common variant in the *Sphagnum* bogs of the Lake Superior area.

22a Pileus yellowish to orange-tawny, typically not wrinkled; spores 7.5-10 × 7.5-9 μm. Fig. 29 ...... *L. volemus* (Fr.) Fr. var. *volemus*

Figure 29

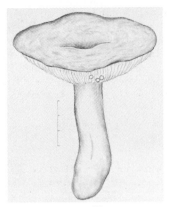

Figure 30

Figure 30   *Lactarius corrugis*

Figure 29   *Lactarius volemus* var. *volemus*

Pileus 5-10 (13) cm, convex to expanded and then ± depressed at times, at times umbonate, dry, pruinose, dull rusty tawny to rusty orange or tawny; odor ± fishy, strong; taste mild. Latex white to cream color, copious, sticky, changing to brown and staining injured tissue brown. Gills whitish to pale tan, close, ± broad. Stipe 5-10 cm x 8-12 (20) mm, concolorous with pileus or paler, dry, unpolished to ± velvety. Spores ornamented with a well developed reticulum. Pileus cuticle cellular with a turf of versiform pileocystidia (16) 50-112 x (1.5) 4-6 μm.

Predominantly in deciduous woods, east of the Great Plains, summer, during hot showery weather common and abundant. Edible. In var. *flavus* Hes. & Sm. the pileus is light yellow to buff-yellow. This species is recommended for use in casserole dishes.

22b Pileus dark reddish brown, typically wrinkled conspicuously at maturity; spores 9-12 × 9-11 (12) μm, ornamented with a distinct reticulum. Fig. 30 .... *L. corrugis* Peck

Pileus 5-12 (2) cm, convex then depressed, a dark reddish brown to orange cinnamon or about rust color, dry, velvety; odor slight; taste mild. Latex copious, white, sticky, staining tissues brown and droplets sometimes brown in a few minutes after exposure. Gills pale yellow to buff, close, moderately broad. Stipe 5-11 x 1-3 cm, usually paler than pileus.

Solitary to scattered in deciduous and mixed woods, east of the Great Plains but most abundant in the Southeast, summer and early fall. Edible (but see *L. volemus*).

23a Latex drying or staining injured areas purple to dull magenta 24

23b Latex not drying or staining as in above choice 29

24a Pileus margin fibrillose at least when young 25

24b Pileus margin glabrous 26

25a Pileus pale golden yellow, ± zonate to azonate; associated with conifers. Fig. 31 .... *L. repraesentaneus* Britz.

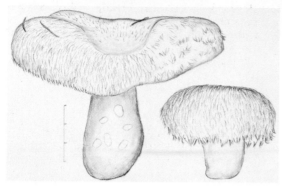

Figure 31

Figure 31 *Lactarius repraesentaneus*

Pileus (4) 6-15 (20) cm, convex-depressed to plane or broadly funnel-shaped, viscid, fibrillose over marginal area; fibrils yellowish to dull clay color; taste slowly bitterish to acrid; latex white to cream color, copious. Gills close to crowded, broad in age, finally pale ochraceous. Stipe 5-12 x 1-3 (4.5) cm, hard, scrobiculate (the spots viscid at first), whitish to concolorous with pileus. Spores (8) 9-11 (12) x 6.5-8 (9) μm, ornamentation of warts and ridges not forming a reticulum.

In spruce-fir forests, Canada and northern United States, late summer and fall, often abundant. Poisonous?

25b Pileus dull buff, distinctly zonate; associated with hardwoods ...... L. speciosus Burlingham

Pileus 5-10 cm, convex-depressed, thinly viscid, soon dry, zones alternating buff and pale dingy tan, thinly fibrillose at first becoming matted in age; margin bearded; taste mild to weakly bitterish-acrid; latex white. Gills close, ± broad, pale buff. Stipe 3-5 x 1-2.5 cm, buff with yellower spots which are slightly viscid. Spores 9-12 (13.5) x 8-11 μm, ornamented with a broken reticulum. Cuticle of pileus a thin ixocutis with fascicles of radiating hyphae.

A typical member of our Southeastern mushroom flora. Reports of it from the Great Lakes area need verification. It is frequently encountered in the Great Smoky Mountains during good seasons.

26a Pileus pale yellow, azonate ....
.... L. aspideoides Burlingham

Pileus 3-8 cm, convex to convex-depressed, glabrous, slimy-viscid; taste bitterish to slightly acrid; latex white staining injured areas lilac. Gills crowded, narrow, pale yellow. Stipe 3-6 x 1-1.5 cm, slimy-viscid when fresh, concolor with pileus. Spores 7-9 (10) x 7-8 μm, ornamented with branching ridges but these not forming a reticulum. Pileus cuticle an ixolattice of narrow (2-3 μm) hyphae.

Gregarious under hardwoods and conifers, Great Lakes region east and southward, rare in the Pacific Northwest. *L. aspideus* (Fr.) Fr. has a dry to only slightly tacky stipe when fresh. Its occurrence here in North America is not firmly established in spite of reports in the literature to date.

26b Not as above 27

27a Pileus milk-white at first, becoming pale grayish vinaceous in age; pileus and stipe very slimy; stipe not spotted. Fig. 32 ....
.... L. pallescens Hes. & Sm.

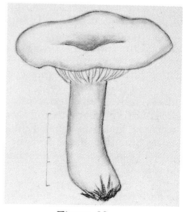

Figure 32

Figure 32 *Lactarius pallescens*

Pileus 4-10 cm, plano-convex to plano-depressed, slimy viscid becoming shiny when dry, glabrous, typically azonate, at times with ochraceous to rusty stains; odor slight; taste slowly but distinctly slightly acrid; latex copious, white, staining injured areas lilaceous. Gills close to subdistant, moderately broad, milk-white. Stipe 3-8 cm x 7-17 mm, slimy viscid fresh, shiny when dry, whitish. Spores 9-11 x 7-9 μm, ornamentation a broken reticulum. Cuticle of pileus an ixotrichodermium to ixolattice.

Under conifers, scattered, Pacific Northwest and adjacent areas, late summer and fall, often abundant. Edibility: not tested.

27b Not as above **28**

28a Pileus 10-20 cm broad, dingy drab gray to dingy yellow-brown, often spotted; stipe 1.5-2.5 cm thick; KOH not staining pileus cuticle olive-green. Fig. 33 ....
.... *L. subpalustris* **Hes. & Sm.**

Figure 33

Figure 33 *Lactarius subpalustris*

Pileus plano-convex, viscid when fresh, glabrous, azonate to obscurely zoned; latex copious, pale dingy cream color staining tissues purplish to lilac; taste mild. Gills broad, close to subdistant, cream-buff at first, finally pale tan, broad. Stipe 5-10 cm long, thinly viscid, spotted, hard, colored like pileus. Spores 8-11 x 7-8 (9) μm, ornamentation with prominences 0.8-2 μm high, of ridges and warts not forming a reticulum. Pileus cuticle an ixocutis.

Gregarious to scattered in low hardwood forests, summer and early fall, Michigan, Tennessee, and Texas. It has been confused with *L. maculatus* Pk. which is similar but is prominently zonate and has an acrid taste.

28b Pileus 3-10 (13) cm broad, whitish where protected, otherwise lilac-drab or pale lavender-brown, seldom spotted; stipe 1-2 (2.5) cm thick; KOH on pileus cuticle staining it olive-green. Fig. 34 ....
.... *L. uvidus* **(Fr.) Fr. var.** *uvidus*

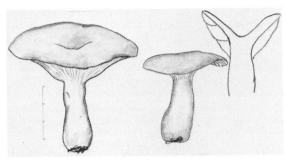

Figure 34

Figure 34 *Lactarius uvidus* var. *uvidus*

Pileus convex-umbonate to plane or depressed, glabrous, viscid to slimy, typically azonate; odor slight; taste slowly bitter to slightly acrid; latex white to cream color, staining tissues dull lilac to pinkish tan. Gills white, moderately broad, close. Stipe 3-7 x 1-2 (2.5) cm thick, slimy at first, off-white but developing ochraceous stains. Spores (7.5) 9-11 x (6.5) 7-8.5 μm, ornamented with ridges and warts not forming a reticulum. Cuticle of pileus an ixolattice.

Scattered in mixed and conifer woods, late summer and fall, frequent in eastern North America. In the Rocky Mountains and westward var. *montanus* Hes. & Sm. occurs. It has practically no viscidity on either pileus or stipe, stouter fruiting bodies, and, often slightly larger spores. Poisonous, at least so reported in the North American literature.

29a Pileus white to whitish, slimy at first; gills narrow, ± crowded, distinctly vinaceous-pink at maturity; latex unchanging. Fig. 35 ....
.... *L. controversus* **(Fr.) Fr.**

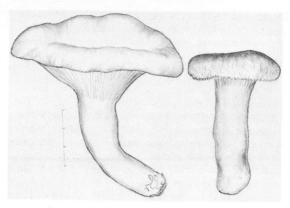

Figure 35

Figure 36

Figure 35   *Lactarius controversus*

Pileus (4) 7-16 (22) cm, convex becoming depressed, white to whitish at times with lavender to dull pink stains, margin short-tomentose at first; taste slowly but strougly acrid; latex white, not staining. Stipe 2.5-5 (8) x 1.5-3 (5) cm, white, tacky but soon dry. Spores 6-7.5 x 4.5-5 μm, ornamented with a partial reticulum. Cuticle of pileus an ixocutis.

Under willows (*Salix*), aspen or cottonwood (*Populus*), widely distributed but predominantly northern or montane, summer and fall, found almost every season. Not recommended.

29b Not as above 30

30a Pileus margin and/or surface, fibrillose to wooly at some stage of development, fibrils at times in a layer of slime (see *L. griseus*, p. 42 if gray-brown) 31

30b Pileus margin not bearded and surface not distinctly fibrillose 36

31a Pileus white to whitish at first, flushed yellowish in age. Fig. 36 ....
.... *L. resimus* (**Fr.**) **Fr.** var. *resimus*

Figure 36   *Lactarius resimus* var. *resimus*

Pileus 6-15 cm, depressed, viscid, white at first, in age often with pale ochraceous zones especially near the margin, disc glabrous to tomentose at first; marginal area with agglutinated fibrils; latex white quickly turning pale greenish yellow on injured surfaces. Gills narrow, crowded, pale dull yellow at maturity. Stipe 6-9 x 1-2.5 cm, white to pale dull yellow, dry. Spores 6-8 x 5-6 μm, ornamented with a partial reticulum. Cuticle of pileus an ixocutis.

Scattered in deciduous and coniferous woods, late summer and fall, widely distributed but predominantly northern or mantane. In var. *regalis* (Pk.) Hes. & Sm. the spores are 7.5-9 (10.5) x 6-7.5 (8) μm.

31b Pileus more highly colored than in above when young 32

32a Pileus margin pruinose to ± pubescent at first, yellow stains very slow to develop ....
.... *L. alnicola* **Smith**

Pileus 8-15 (2) cm, convex-depressed, viscid to slimy, yellow-ochre, typically somewhat zonate, matted fibrillose near the margin, taste quickly strongly acrid; latex scanty, white unchanging or very slowly yellowing. Gills crowded, narrow, whitish becoming pale ochraceous buff. Stipe 3-6 x 2-3 cm, whitish to ochraceous tan, spotted. Spores 7.5-10 x 6-7.5 (8.5) μm, ornamented with a partial reticulum. Pileus cuticle an ixocutis.

Gregarious under alder and conifers, western

North America, summer and early fall, common at times. *L. scrobiculatus* has a bearded pileus margin and wounds stain yellow fairly rapidly.

32b At least some fibrils or woolly tissue present on pileus margin of young specimens (margin ± bearded) **33**

33a Fibrils of pileus margin grayish to fuscous in age; latex slowly staining wounded areas dull yellow; gills close to subdistant ....
.... ***L. payettensis* Smith**

Pileus 8-16 cm, plano-depressed, dull buff with an olive tinge to dark straw color or dingy dark ochraceous, viscid to slimy, glabrous or nearly so over disc, agglutinated-fibrillose toward margin, fibrils grayish in age; margin coarsely bearded; taste strongly acrid; latex staining gills ochraceous. Stipe 2-5 x 2-4 cm, white with ochraceous spots. Spores 8-10 (11) x 7-8 μm, ornamentation not forming a distinct reticulum. Cuticle of pileus an ixocutis.

In spruce-fir forests, summer and fall, central Rocky Mountains. Untested?

33b Fibrils near margin of pileus not becoming gray to fuscous **34**

34a Pileus viscid at first, ochre-yellow; stipe conspicuously scrobiculate. Fig. 37 ....
.... ***L. scrobiculatus* (Fr.) Fr. var. *scrobiculatus***

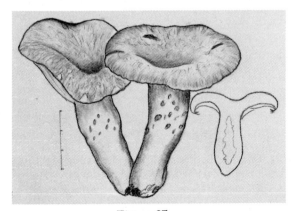

Figure 37

Figure 37 *Lactarius scrobiculatus* var. *scrobiculatus*

Pileus 4-12 cm, convex to plano-depressed, viscid, pale olive buff at times, margin bearded to coarsely pubescent when young; taste very acrid to nearly mild; latex white quickly becoming yellow on injured tissues. Gills crowded, finally broad, whitish becoming pale dull yellow. Stipe 3-11 x 1-3 cm, spotted with honey colored spots, whitish otherwise, at least at first. Spores 7-9 x 5.5-7 μm, ornamented with ridges and warts but not reticulate. Pileus cuticle an ixocutis.

Solitary to gregarious under conifers and especially in montane forests or open areas with scattered trees, common, abundant, and widely distributed. Not recommended. Var. *scrobiculatus* is reported in recent European literature to have a bright ochre spore deposit, whereas var. *canadensis* in North America has a white to cream colored deposit. However, specimens which Smith collected in Switzerland had a faintly colored spore deposit. For this reason the character is not emphasized in the present work.

34b Pileus toned pink to vinaceous or salmon at least on disc **35**

35a Spores 7.5-10 × 6-7.5 μ. Fig. 38 ....
.... ***L. torminosus* (Fr.) S. F. Gray**

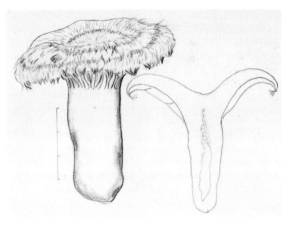

Figure 38

Figure 38 *Lactarius torminosus*

Pileus 5-12 cm, convex to plano-depressed, soon dry, glabrous over disc, fibrillose toward the margin, zonate, with shades of orange-pink and pink, often fading to nearly white in age; margin bearded when young; taste burning acrid; latex white, not staining injured tissues. Gills close to crowded, narrow, whitish becoming more or less cream color in age. Stipe 3-7 cm x 6-15 (2) mm, dry, glabrous, usually not scrobiculate. Spores ornamented with a partial reticulum. Cuticle of pileus an ixocutis over disc becoming an ixolattice near margin. Edibility: Not recommended here in North America because of the numerous variants that have been found. Their edibility has not been tested. In the U.S.S.R. it is very popular, but, apparently, only after special preparation.

Usually found near birch during late summer and fall. It is common and widely distributed. In var. *nordmanensis* (Sm.) Hes. & Sm., the latex stains injured tissues yellow. This is the common variety in northern Idaho. Also, *L. pubescens* and its variants are difficult to distinguish from *L. torminosus* without the aid of a microscope.

35b Spores 6-8 × 5-6.5 μm
.... *L. pubescens* **Fr.** var. *pubescens*

Pileus 2.5-9 cm, convex-depressed, disc viscid at first, white to cream-color, ochraceous to nearly pale salmon at times; fibrillose toward the margin; margin at first with coarse soft fibrils (bearded); taste acrid; latex white unchanging. Gills crowded, narrow, yellowish to pale flesh color. Spores ornamented with a partial reticulum. Pileus cuticle an ixocutis over the disc to a fibrillose dry cutis over marginal area.

Associated primarily with birch and to be expected wherever birch occurs in North America, late summer and fall. In var. *betulae* (Sm.) Hes. & Sm. the latex stains injured areas yellow. Not recommended. *L. pubescens* has only recently been recognized as occurring in North America, and we have no accurate data on the edibility of it and its variants. See *L. torminosus* also.

36a KOH (2.5%) or ammonia on fresh pileus cuticle coloring it magenta **37**

36b KOH not reacting as above **38**

37a Pileus dull to dark green, often spotted ....
.... *L. atroviridis* **Peck.**

Pileus 6-15 cm, convex to plano-depressed, light to dark olive-green, often with fuscous spots, tacky but very soon dry, ± glabrous but rough, margin naked; taste acrid; latex white slowly staining tissues dull olivaceous to greenish gray. Gills close, narrow, becoming broad in age, whitish to pinkish buff. Stipe 2-8 x 1-3 cm, colored like the pileus, scrobiculate, dry. Spores 7-9 x 5.5-6.5 μm, ornamented with a partial reticulum. Cuticle of pileus (button stages) a thin ixocutis.

In hardwoods, especially under oak, east of the Great Plains, summer and fall, often abundant during warm wet weather. Not recommended.

37b Pileus dull honey brown on margin to dingy brown or ± olive brown over the disc ....
.... *L. sordidus* **Pk.**

Pileus 5-10 (15) cm, convex-depressed, pale brownish yellow ± olive-brownish, viscid but soon dry; margin somewhat cottony at first; odor slight, taste slowly acrid. Latex white, slowly staining injured tissues dingy gray-brown to sepia. Gills whitish to yellowish. Stipe 4-12 x 1-2.5 cm, pale near the apex but about concolor with pileus lower down to dingy olive-brown, scrobiculate. Spores 5.5-7.5 x 5-6 μm, ornamentation ± in form of a reticulum. Cuticle of pileus an ixocutis or in old specimens as a lattice.

Typically in damp conifer woods, late summer and fall, often near edge of bogs, Great Lakes area eastward and the Pacific Northwest. Not recommended for table use.

38a Latex colorless (water-like) in young specimens **39**

38b Latex ± opaque, white to cream color as exuded **40**

39a Fruiting bodies with a strong odor of burnt sugar; stipe 3-15 × 1-2 cm, very fragile. Fig. 39 .... *L. aquifluus* **Peck**

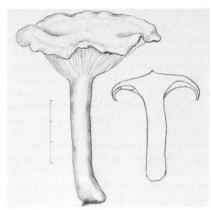

Figure 39

Figure 39 *Lactarius aquifluus*

Pileus (3) 4-15 cm, convex then plane or depressed, at times umbonate, dull brownish rose to fawn color, dry, typically azonate, glabrous becoming ± areolate to squamulose in age; taste mild; latex not staining injured areas. Gills white becoming light pinkish cinnamon, close, finally broad. Stipe 4-8 cm long, slightly paler than pileus, dry. Spores 6.5-8 x 5.5-6 (6.5) μm, ornamented with an irregular reticulum. Cuticle of pileus a cutis of loose fibrils.

Often gregarious in conifer forests but especially in bogs or low wet areas, Great Lakes area eastward and southward, common late summer and fall. Not recommended. Most reports of *L. helvus* in North America are based on this species. *L. helvus* should have a white latex and an acrid taste.

39b Lacking a pronounced odor; stipe 3-7 mm thick, firm; in upland, well-drained hardwood forests .... *L. subserifluus* **Longyear**

Pileus 2-7 cm, plano-umbonate, glabrous, smooth, dull rusty orange to rufous becoming paler in age; odor slight; taste mild to slowly slightly peppery; latex sometimes staining injured gills dull cinnamon. Gills narrow to broad, subdistant. Stipe 5-12 cm long, hard, orange-cinnamon or darker below, base with orange-cinnamon hairs. Spores 6-7.5 x 6-7 μm, ornamentation a nearly complete reticulum. Cuticle a zone of inflated cells 3-5 cells deep.

Common during hot wet summer weather, probably widely distributed east of the Great Plains.

40a Pileus when young violaceous-fuscous fading to cinnamon or tan in age; both pileus and stipe slimy-viscid; associated with conifers in the Pacific Northwest ....
.... *L. trivialis* **(Fr.) Fr.**

Pileus 5-18 cm, convex to plano-convex or depressed, azonate; taste mild to slowly acrid; latex white, drops drying olive-buff on gills or gills staining olive-brown where injured. Gills pale tan at maturity, close becoming subdistant, broad. Stipe 5-15 x 1-2.5 cm, concolor with gills. Spores 7.5-9 (10) x 6-7.5 (8) μm, ornamentation scarcely or not all reticulate. Cuticle of pileus an ixotrichodermium collapsing to an ixolattice.

Solitary to gregarious under conifers, fall, not uncommon. This name has been frequently misapplied in the North American literature.

40b Not as above **41**

41a Pileus pale to dark gray or grayish brown (nearly white where shielded from light) ......
.... **42**

41b Pileus some shade of tan, pink, red or orange **48**

42a Fruiting body with a pronounced odor of coconut (check when first unwrapping specimens). Fig. 40 ....
.... *L. glyciosmus* **(Fr.) Fr.**

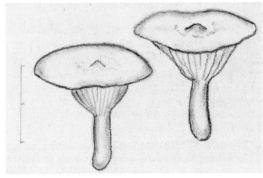

Figure 40

Figure 40 *Lactarius glyciosmus*

Pileus 1.5-6 (9) cm, convex to plane or slightly depressed, dull purplish gray to pinkish gray, dry, appressed fibrillose, azonate; tardily slightly acrid. Latex white, not staining tissues of the fruit body. Gills pinkish buff, close to crowded, narrow. Stipe 2-5 (10) cm x 1.5-5 (9) mm, dry, concolorous with or slightly paler than pileus, pruinose. Spores 6-8 x 5-6 (7-9 x 5.5-7) μm, ornamented with ridges and a few isolated warts. Pileus cuticle a cutis.

Scattered to gregarious, usually under birch and alder, late summer and fall, Canada and the northern United States; not common. *L. hibbardae* Peck may also have a fragrant odor, but the pileus is darker (violaceous drab) and the fruiting bodies are stouter.

42b Not as above **43**

43a Pileus 1.5-5 cm, squamulose to scaly at maturity; on or close to decaying wood ....
.... *L. griseus* **Peck**

Pileus depressed to funnel-shaped with a papilla, violaceous-fuscous becoming gray and then ochraceous tones developing, dry, odor slight, taste of young fruiting bodies slowly slightly acrid; latex white, drying in yellowish droplets. Gills yellowish, close becoming subdistant, ± broad. Stipe 2-6.5 cm x (2) 3-6 (10) mm, pallid to grayish, dry. Spores 7-8 (10) x 6-7 (8) μm; ornamentation not forming a reticulum. Cuticle of pileus dry, of hyphae aggregated into fascicles to form scales.

Gregarious to scattered on or adjacent to very decayed logs, and on rich humus; eastern North America, summer to fall, common during most seasons.

43b Not as above **44**

44a Pileus 4-15 (18) cm; gills discoloring in age or where injured to grayish brown to brown; spores not at all reticulate; cuticle of pileus an ixolattice .... *L. argillaceifolius* **Hes. & Sm. var.** *argillaceifolius*

Pileus convex-depressed, cinnamon-drab to drab gray to buff or cinnamon buff, azonate, viscid, glabrous; taste acrid in young material; latex dull cream color staining injured tissue grayish brown to tan or olivaceous. Gills broad at maturity, close, cream color then brown to tan or dingy clay-color in age. Stipe 6-9 x 1.5-3.5 cm, dry or at most thinly slimy at first, buff to tan. Spores (7) 8-10 (11) x 7-8 μm; Cuticle of pileus an ixolattice.

Scattered to gregarious in deciduous woods, especially with oak. It is one of our very common early summer mushrooms east of the Great Plains. A western variety, var. *megacarpus* Hes. & Sm. from California may have caps to 27 cm broad and slightly more reticulate spores. *L. argillaceifolius*, previously in North America, has been reported under the name *L. trivialis*.

44b Not as above **45**

45a Pileus slightly tacky when wet; stipe dry; latex staining injured gills olive-gray to gray-brown .... *L. vietus* **(Fr.) Fr.**

Pileus (1) 3-8 cm, convex-depressed, glabrous, dark vinaceous-brown to violaceous-gray or vinaceous fawn to whitish; odor slight; taste acrid; latex white, the droplets drying olive-gray, staining gills olive-gray to grayish brown. Gills close, moderately broad at maturity, dingy pinkish buff. Stipe 3-6 cm x 8-18 mm, dry paler than the pileus. Spores 7.5-9 x 6-7.5 μm, ornamentation not forming a reticulum. Cuticle of pileus an ixocutis, hyphae often with brown incrustations.

Scattered to gregarious or cespitose in woods containing birch, Canada and northern United States, common when it fruits, late summer and fall.

45b Pileus and stipe slimy to the touch when fresh and moist; gills seldom brownish where injured **46**

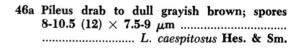

46a Pileus drab to dull grayish brown; spores 8-10.5 (12) × 7.5-9 μm ....
.... *L. caespitosus* **Hes. & Sm.**

Pileus 4-10 cm, convex to shallowly depressed, glabrous, azonate, viscid, drab to dull grayish brown; taste slowly acrid; latex scanty, white, staining injured areas slowly yellowish or brownish. Gills close, narrow, whitish becoming pinkish buff. Stipe 3-4 (8) x 1-2.5 cm, viscid but soon dry, whitish to pale brown. Spores ornamented with a well defined reticulum. Cuticle of pileus an ixotrichodermium.

Gregarious to caespitose or scattered, under conifers, summer, Rocky Mountains. Edibility untested.

46b Pileus blackish brown to dark reddish brown; spores smaller than in above choice 47

47a Margin of pileus typically much lighter than rest of pileus. Fig. 41 ....
.... L. mucidus Burl. var. mucidus

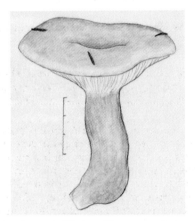

Figure 41

Figure 41 *Lactarius mucidus* var. *mucidus*

Pileus 3-9 cm, convex-expanded, depressed, at times with a low umbo, azonate, slimy-viscid, dingy purplish brown to sepia, glabrous; taste acrid; latex white drying in glaucous green droplets on the gills. Gills white becoming cream color. Stipe 4-8 cm x 7-10 mm, viscid, paler than pileus. Spores 7.5-10 x 6-7 (8) μm, ornamented with a distinct reticulum. Cuticle of pileus an ixotrichodermium.

Solitary to scattered in moist coniferous woods, eastern North America south into North Carolina, rare in the western States where *L. pseudomucidus* Hes. & Sm. with a darker stipe and pileus is more common. Varieties in *L. mucidus* are distinguished on color of the spore deposit and features of the latex.

47b Margin of pileus not markedly lighter than the disc and stipe tan at maturity ....
.... L. kauffmanii Hes. & Sm. var. kauffmanii

Pileus 5-15 (20) cm, convex-depressed, glabrous, azonate, slimy-viscid, blackish brown to fuscous gray over all; taste slowly acrid; latex white, staining injured areas olivaceous to grayish brown. Gills close, broad at maturity, whitish to pale pinkish tan. Stipe 5-10 cm long, slimy at first, glabrous. Spores 7-10 x 6.5-8 μm, ornamented with a distinct reticulum. Cuticle of pileus an ixotrichodermium.

Scattered to gregarious under conifers, summer and fall, rare in the Great Lakes region, common in the Pacific Northwest. Not recommended for the table.

48a Latex white at first, quickly yellow; pileus 4-12 cm broad, moist to viscid, pallid to pale pinkish cinnamon, becoming dark wine-red in age. Stipe also dark wine-red in age; taste slowly acrid. Fig. 42 ....
.... L. vinaceorufescens Smith

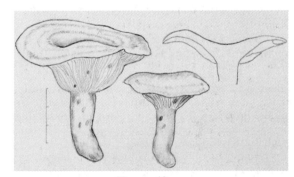

Figure 42

Figure 42 *Lactarius vinaceorufescens*

Pileus 4-12 cm, broadly convex to shallowly depressed, buff to pinkish cinnamon, pink, vinaceous-rose to finally dark vinaceous-red in age or when water-soaked; glabrous, faintly zoned; odor slight. Gills close, narrow, pale pinkish tan becoming darker in age. Stipe 4-7 x 1-2.5 cm, pale pinkish buff at first, glabrous, dry. Spores 6.5-8 (9) x 6-7 μm, ornamented with ridges and warts but not forming a reticulum. Cuticle of pileus a thin ixocutis.

Scattered to gregarious often under pine, eastern North America, more frequent in the northern area. Not recommended for the table.

48b Not as above **49**

49a Pileus slimy, zonate, various shades of orange; taste acrid; latex unchanging; stipe dry, associated with conifers. Fig. 43 ....
.... *L. olympianus* **Hes. & Sm.**

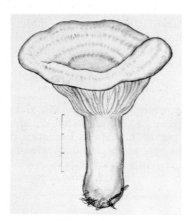

Figure 43

Figure 43 *Lactarius olympianus*

Pileus 6-12 cm, convex-depressed, glabrous; taste acrid; latex white, staining injured gills orange to orange-brown. Gills narrow, close to subdistant, dingy yellow at maturity. Stipe 4-6 x 1.5-3 cm, whitish, dry. Spores (7) 8-11 (13) x 7.5-9 (11) μm, somewhat reticulate. Cuticle of pileus an ixocutis.

Scattered to gregarious under conifers, summer and fall in the Pacific Northwest, common. Not recommended for the table.

49b Not as above **50**

50a Pileus whitish to cream color or yellow to orange; latex white at first, quickly becoming bright yellow **51**

50b Not with above combination of features **53**

51a Stipe slimy at first, spotted; pileus slimy, whitish, with cream color to yellowish spots .... *L. maculatipes* **Burlingham**

Pileus 5-10 cm, convex-depressed to shallowly funnel-shaped, glabrous, nearly white at first, becoming tinted honey yellow to pale pinkish buff, zonate; taste acrid. Gills crowded to close, narrow. Stipe 3-8 x 1-2.3 cm, concolorous with pileus or paler. Spores 6-8 x 6-7.5 μm, not reticulate. Pileus cuticle an ixocutis.

Scattered, usually under oak, Great Lakes area south to Florida, late summer to fall in the north, winter in the south. Not recommended.

51b Not as above **52**

52a Pileus saffron yellow to cadmium orange; spores 7.5-10 $\times$ 5.5-7.5 μm ....
.... *L. croceus* **Burlingham**

Pileus 5-10 cm, convex-depressed, bright orange-yellow, viscid at first, azonate to zonate; taste bitterish becoming acrid; latex white staining injured tissues cadmium yellow. Gills close to subdistant, ± broad, dull yellowish at maturity. Stipe 3-6 x 1-2 cm, glabrous, at times spotted, concolorous with pileus or paler. Spores at times somewhat reticulate. Pileus cuticle an ixocutis.

Solitary to scattered in deciduous woods, summer, Massachusetts south to North Carolina and west to Ohio, probably more widely distributed; infrequent. Not recommended for the table.

52b Pileus pale dull yellowish tan to pinkish buff; spores 6-8 (9) $\times$ 5.5-6.5 μm. Fig. 44
.... *L. chrysorheus* **Fries**

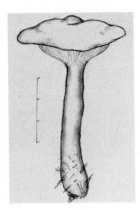

Figure 44

Figure 44   *Lactarius chrysorheus*

Pileus 3-7 (9) cm, convex-depressed, glabrous, moist to lubricous or subviscid but soon dry, azonate or with "watery" spots arranged in zones, pale yellowish to pale yellowish cinnamon at first, often fading to nearly white; odor slight; taste slowly acrid; latex staining injured surfaces bright yellow. Gills close, off-white to pale orange-buff. Stipe 3-4 (8) x 1-2 cm, concolorous with or paler than pileus, never vinaceous red. Spores not reticulate. Cuticle of pileus a thin ixocutis.

Typically in deciduous or mixed woods with oak, summer and fall, widely distributed but often confused with *L. vinaceorufescens*.

53a Pileus 6-15 (20) cm, nearly white where protected, soon pinkish tan to brick red where exposed to light; stipe 2-4 (7) × 1-3 cm, hollow, hard, white at first, soon colored like the pileus .... *L. allardii* **Coker**

Pileus convex-depressed, often irregular in outline, dry, glabrous, becoming cracked over the disc in age, azonate; odor mild to unpleasant in age; taste acrid and unpleasant. Latex copious, viscous, white, slowly drying greenish to olive or finally brownish on injured surfaces. Gills close to subdistant when young, often distant in age, light buff at maturity. Stipe dry. Spores (7.5) 8-10 (10.5) x 5.5-8 μm, ornamented with very low ridges and warts. Cuticle of pileus of loosely interwoven hyphae with rather erect fascicles of pileocystidia.

In well drained deciduous and mixed woods,

late summer and fall east of the Great Plains, often abundant during a good year. Not recommended for table use.

53b Not as above **54**

54a Both pileus and stipe slimy when fresh and moist, often shining when dry .... *L. affinis* **Peck var.** *affinis*

Pileus 6-15 (18) cm broad, convex-depressed, pale cinnamon buff to pale ochraceous, azonate; taste acrid; latex white, unchanging. Gills rather broad, whitish tinged with yellow, close to subdistant. Stipe 4-12 x 1-3 cm, about concolorous with pileus. Spores 9-10.5 x 7-8 μm, ornamentation of separate elements to a partial reticulum. Pileus cuticle an ixolattice or ixocutis at maturity.

Scattered to gregarious in mixed woods, and pastures, Great Lakes area to New England and adjacent Canada, late summer and fall. In var. *viridilactis* (Kauff.) Hes. & Sm. the latex dries as glaucous green droplets on the gills.

54b Neither pileus nor stipe slimy **55**

55a Fruiting bodies decidedly fragrant in mass; pileus dark red-brown. Fig. 45 .... *L. camphoratus* **(Fr.) Fr.**

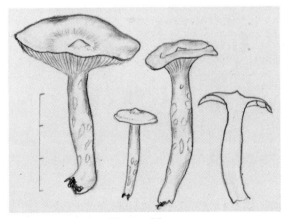

Figure 45

Figure 45 *Lactarius camphoratus*

Pileus 2-4.5 cm, convex to convex-depressed, often with a papilla, glabrous, moist, soon dry, dull dark red-brown fading to dingy vinaceous pink; taste somewhat unpleasant to bitter; latex not staining cut surfaces. Gills close to crowded, narrow at first finally ± broad, pale pinkish cinnamon becoming darker. Stipe 1.5-6 cm x 3-11 (13) mm, moist to dry, about concolorous with pileus. Spores 7-8.5 x 6-7.5 μm, not reticulate. Cuticle of pileus a zone of inflated cells several cells deep.

In coniferous and mixed woods, often with pine or hemlock, late summer and fall, eastern North America. In the southeast and Pacific coast, *L. fragilis* Burl. May be mistaken for *L. camphoratus* because of the similar odor, but its spores are distinctly reticulate.

55b Not with the odor and colors of *L. camphoratus* **56**

56a Pileus 1-3.5 cm broad, tacky at first, dull rosy pink over all but darker over disc; typically fruiting in bogs where *Sphagnum* is present. Fig. 46 .... *L. oculatus* **(Pk.) Burl.**

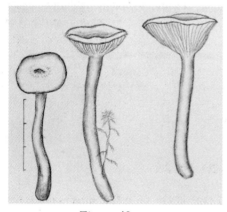

Figure 46

Figure 46 *Lactarius oculatus*

Pileus plano-depressed with a low papilla, soon dry and shining, glabrous, deep brownish rose to reddish cinnamon over the disc, dingy rose to vinaceous buff over margin; taste slowly faintly peppery, odor slight; latex scanty, whey-like to white, staining white paper yellow (use young pilei). Gills close becoming subdistant, broad, dull pinkish cinnamon at maturity. Stipe 2-3 cm x 2-4 (6) mm, dull pinkish cinnamon, moist. Spores 7.5-9.5 x 6-7 μm, not reticulate. Cuticle of pileus with some ascending hyphal tips, otherwise more or less an ixocutis of interwoven hyphae.

Late summer to early fall, eastern North America.

56b Not as above **57**

57a Pileus dry to moist, often becoming cracked to minutely fibrillose at maturity in dry weather, deep brick red; taste (slowly) exceedingly acrid; spores 8.5-10.5 (12) × 7.5-8.5 μm; latex white and not staining. Fig. 47 .... *L. rufus* **(Fr.) Fr. var.** *rufus*

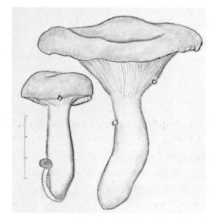

Figure 47

Figure 47 *Lactarius rufus* var. *rufus*

Pileus 4-12 cm, convex to plane or shallowly depressed, dry to moist or rarely tacky; odor slight. Gills crowded, narrow, in age pinkish tan. Stipe 5-11 cm x 9-17 mm, dry, about concolorous with pileus or lighter basally. Spore ornamentation forming a partial reticulum. Pileus cuticle a thin cutis or of rather appressed radially arranged hyphae.

Scattered to gregarious under conifers, particularly pine, late summer and fall, widely distributed and common in the cooler parts of North America. Not recommended for North Americans even though it is popular in some European countries. The common variant which is usually found in *Sphagnum* bogs under spruce is known to be edible.

57b Not as above **58**

58a Typically associated with birch; pileus ferrugineus to orange-cinnamon; latex staining white paper yellow; spore ornamentation of isolated warts; pileus cuticle several cells deep .... *L. thejogalus* (Fr.) S. F. Gray

Pileus 2-7 (9) cm, convex, often with a low umbo, fading to orange-buff, moist, glabrous; taste slowly slightly acrid; latex white, staining injured tissues yellowish (use young specimens). Gills close to crowded, narrow, pale pinkish buff to ± orange-cinnamon. Stipe 4-6 x 1-1.5 cm, moist, ± concolor with pileus. Spores 7-9 x 6-7.5 μm. Pileus cuticle a zone of inflated cells several deep, with occasional projecting filamentous hyphae but these not forming a turf.

Scattered to gregarious on wet soil such as edges of bogs summer and fall, common and often abundant, eastern North America and Alaska, to be expected in areas where *Betula* species occur.

58b Associated with alder (*Alnus*); latex staining white paper yellow; pileus ± olive-brown to bister young, becoming tawny to vinaceous cinnamon; pileus cuticle a staggered palisade of clavate to vesiculose cells .... *L. occidentalis* Smith

Pileus 1-3.5 cm, convex or with a papilla, expanding to plane or the margin uplifted, surface often rugulose; taste mild; latex white to whey-like, slowly changing to yellow on exposure to air at times. Gills close, narrow, slowly staining incarnate tan when broken. Stipe 3-6 cm x 4-6 mm, slowly reddish brown where wounded, glabrous, moist. Spore deposit white. Spores 8-10 x 6.5-8 μm, ornamentation of warts and ridges partially connected to form ± a broken reticulum.

Gregarious, summer and fall, under Alder in the Pacific Northwest, very abundant at times late in the season.

Russula Pers. ex S. G. Gray

Pileus and stipe confluent; all parts fragile and brittle except the stipe which may be quite hard in larger fruiting bodies; context of pileus and stipe heteromerous (with nests or columns of sphaerocysts bounded by narrow filamentose connective hyphae); spores globose to broadly ellipsoid, with amyloid ornamentation in the form of warts, short to long ridges, or these connected to form a partial to complete reticulum; clamp connections absent; aspect of fruiting body short and stocky (rather characteristic); forming mycorrhiza with woody plants.

The genus is large, probably ± 200 species in North America. They are very difficult to identify. Consequently only a few of the common and more easily identified species are included here. The genus is popular, however, among those collecting mushrooms for food, most of whom, literally, do not know what they are eating—but they survive because so few of the species are poisonous. The apparently dangerous group consists of those with white caps at first which blacken in age, so a number of these are included here even though they are the most unattractive in the genus. However, to our knowledge they have caused no fatalities in North America.

KEY TO SPECIES

1a Pileus white to pallid when young, blackening and soon dark over all; consistency relatively hard and firm **2**

1b Pileus not both white and blackening where injured **4**

2a Cut surface of stipe near apex staining reddish then black **3**

2b Cut or bruised surfaces staining gray to black
directly; pileus often very large. Fig. 48 ....
.... *R. albonigra* (Krombh.) Fr.

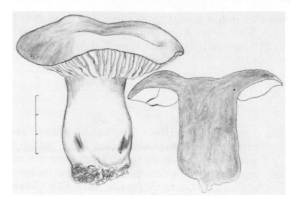

Figure 49

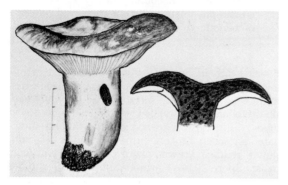

Figure 48

Figure 48   *Russula albonigra*

Pileus 5-15 (20) cm, convex to plano-depressed,
surface soon dry and dull; taste mild to ± acrid.
Gills finally broad, close to crowded. Stipe 2.5-10
x 2-8 cm, white at first, dry, gradually darkening.
Spores 7-10 x 6-7 μm, ornamentation of warts
usually connected by fine lines into ± a broken
reticulum. Pleurocystidia conspicuous (50-106 x
4-15 μm). Cuticle of pileus a cutis, or rarely an
ixocutis in very young caps.

Solitary to gregarious in conifer and hardwood forests, widely distributed, common in the
Pacific Northwest, summer and fall. Not recommended.

3a Gills distant to subdistant; spores 6.3-8 ×
5.2-6.8 μm; spore deposit white. Fig. 49 ......
.... *R. nigricans* Fries

Figure 49   *Russula nigricans*

Pileus 7-20 cm, convex becoming broadly funnel-
shaped, surface dull and ± felted, at times rimose-
areolate, margin entire; taste slightly acrid to
mild. Gills thick, yellowish, finally blackish like
the pileus. Stipe 2-7 x 1-4 cm, rigid, staining like
the pileus, dry and unpolished. Spore ornamentation of prominences 0.1-0.3 μm high, of warts
and fine lines forming ± of a reticulum. Pileus
cuticle in very young specimens ± of an ixocutis.

Solitary to gregarious, mostly under conifers, Pacific Northwest where it is common. Its
occurrence in other areas of North America, apparently, is open to question, but it is widely reported in the literature.

3b Gills close to crowded; spores (7) **7.5-10.2**
(11) × 6-8 (8.6) μm ....
.... *R. densifolia* (Secr.) Gillet

Pileus 4-15 cm, convex-depressed, finally ± funnel-shaped, viscid but soon dry, white slowly becoming dingy brown and finally black; taste
slightly to burning acrid. Gills narrow, yellowish
at first, darkening in age. Stipe 2-9 x 1-3.5 cm,
surface dry and glabrous or minutely furfuraceous.
Spore deposit white; spore ornamentation with
prominences 0.5-0.7 μm high, of lines ± connected to make a reticulum. Pileus cuticle duplex,
the upper layer an ixolattice (check young pilei).

Solitary to gregarious under hardwoods and
conifers, widely distributed, summer and early
fall, rather common; not recommended.

4a Pileus soon rust to reddish brown over most of surface; staining ochraceous to brown where injured; odor of old specimens disagreeable and becoming more so when dried. Fig. 50 .... *R. compacta* **Frost in Peck**

Figure 50

Figure 50 *Russula compacta*

Pileus 6-12 (18) cm, pulvinate, expanding to plano-depressed, viscid at first, glabrous, often areolate, white to pale buff at first, soon tan to tawny on disc; taste slight to bitter. Gills finally moderately broad, close to subdistant, discoloring like the pileus. Stipe 3-9 (12) x 1-3.5 (4.5) cm, white then discoloring, hard when young. Spore deposit white; spores 7.6-9.9 x 6.3-8.6 µm, ornamentation of warts up to 1.2 µm high connected by fine lines. Pileus cuticle a thick cutis.

Solitary, scattered, or gregarious in northern conifer forests, Great Lakes area and eastward, fairly common.

4b Not as above **5**

5a Cuticle of pileus thick and rubbery; pileus white to pale yellow, cut flesh slowly staining brownish; context slightly acrid-bitter ....
.................................*R. crassotunicata* **Singer**

Pileus 3-8 cm, pulvinate at first then convex-depressed, viscid, soon dry, becoming rimose over disc, white to yellowish white or pale yellow, staining brownish to olive-brown; odor of an old *Lycoperdon*. Gills narrow, subdistant to distant, yellow when young, slowly brownish where bruised. Stipe 3.5-5 x 1-2 cm, pallid, dry. Spore deposit white; spores 8.5-11 x 7-9.3 µm, ornamentation of isolated warts up to 1.2 µm high.

Solitary to gregarious, usually under conifers, summer and fall, frequent in the Pacific Northwest, often in habitats with devil's club, rare in the Great Lakes area. Not recommended.

5b Not with a thick rubbery pileus cuticle **6**

6a Pileus white **7**

6b Pileus typically colored red, purple, green, etc. **8**

7a Upper stipe area and gills often tinged blue-green; pileus 6-20 cm broad; spores 8-10.7 × 6.7-8.6 (9.6) µm; taste slowly but strongly acrid. Fig. 51 ....
.... *R. brevipes* **var.** *acrior* **R. L. Shaffer**

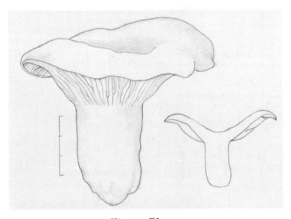

Figure 51

Figure 51 *Russula brevipes* var. *acrior*

Pileus convex-depressed, margin inrolled, dry and unpolished, white to pale buff, discoloring finally to ± clay-color; taste typically slowly but strongly acrid. Gills narrow to moderately broad, close, often stained brownish. Stipe 2.5-8 x 1.5-5.5 cm, white, unpolished, slowly discolored around damaged areas. Spore deposit white to pale buff. Spore ornamentation with prominences

0.7-1.7 μm high, the elements forming a broken to complete reticulum.

Solitary to gregarious in conifer forests, summer and fall, widely distributed in North America. Edible, popular in some areas of the Pacific Northwest. In the Great Lakes region var. *brevipes* Peck usually is more abundant. It is the *Russula* that has generally been identified as *R. delica* Fr. here in North America. Var. *acrior* is often found developing under the duff (hypogeously), and many of these fruiting bodies mature and rot without ever becoming visible.

7b **Fruiting body lacking blue or greenish tinges on gills or apex of stipe; pileus 4-9 cm broad; spores 6.7-8.2 × 4.8-6.7 μm; taste intensely acrid. Fig. 52** .... *R. cascadensis* **R. L. Shaffer**

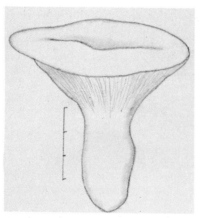

Figure 52

Figure 52 *Russula cascadensis*

Pileus convex to shallowly depressed, dry and unpolished, white gradually flushed pale tan. Gills narrow, becoming subdecurrent, close to crowded, staining dingy ochraceous on injured areas. Stipe 3-4 cm x 2-2.5 cm, white, unpolished, firm. Spore ornamentation 0.2-0.7 μm high, of lines and isolated warts with some spores ± reticulate. Pileus cuticle two-layered, the upper a lattice (loosely interwoven hyphae).

Under conifers in the Pacific Northwest, fall, not uncommon. Not recommended for table use. From time to time reports of gastrointestinal upsets from eating (supposedly) this species reach us, but have not been verifiable. Without question, many people have eaten it thinking it was "*Russula delica*."

8a **Many of the gills forked once or twice (some distance from the stipe); pileus dull olive to brownish vinaceous or colors mixed to present a confusing picture. Fig. 53** .... *R. variata* **Banning**

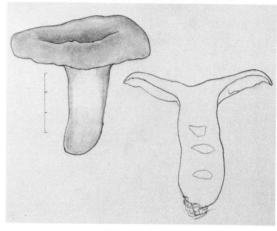

Figure 53

Figure 53 *Russula variata*

Pileus 5-15 cm, convex to plano-depressed, slightly viscid, margin short-striate only in age; context unchanging, odor and taste mild. Gills narrow, close, sometimes stained brownish. Stipe 3-9 x 1-3 cm, dry, dull, whitish or at base stained brownish. Spore deposit white; spores 7.5-10 (11.4) x 5.7-8.5 (9.5) μm, ornamentation as warts 0.3-0.9 μm high (no reticulum formed).

Common, scattered to gregarious under hardwoods, summer and early fall, east of the Great Plains. It is exceptionally abundant during wet summer weather in barren oak-aspen stands in the Great Lakes area where it is one of the first "summer mushrooms" to fruit in quantity. Edible.

8b **Gills not forked or if so forking not conspicuous and mostly near the attachment to the stipe** **9**

9a **Pileus with flat areolate patches on a more or less green to gray-green background; taste mild; fruiting under hardwoods, especially oak and beech. Fig. 54** .... *R. virescens* **Fries**

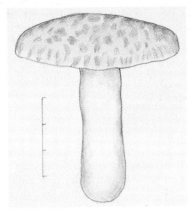

Figure 54

Figure 54 *Russula virescens*

Pileus 5-10 (15) cm, convex to ± plane, dry; context fragile, odor and taste not distinctive. Gills white, close, narrowed toward the stipe. Stipe 3-7 x 1-2 cm, white, brittle. Spore deposit white; spores (5.5) 6.2-8.5 (10) x 5-6.5 (7) μm, ornamentation variable (from isolated warts to reticulate). Cuticle of pileus a modified trichodermium.

Scattered to gregarious in deciduous and mixed woods, summer east of the Great Plains, common. Edible: the best in the genus (in Europe) according to some.

9b **Pileus lacking areolate patches of tissue 10**

10a **Under conifers; pileus orange-red to yellow and red mixed; context becoming ash-color in age or on injury; taste mild** .... *R. decolorans* **Fries**

Pileus 5-12 cm, subglobose becoming plano-depressed, subviscid, margin striate in age; odor and taste mild. Gills close to subdistant, moderately broad, becoming pale ochraceous and in age stained gray. Stipe 5-12 x 1-2.5 cm, firm then fragile, staining gray. Spore deposit pale ochraceous; spores (8.5) 9-12 (13) x (6.5) 7-9

(10) μm, ornamentation of isolated spines up to 1.5 μm high.

Solitary to scattered in conifer forests, especially pines, late summer and fall, Great Lakes area east and southward, common. Edible—and rather easy to recognize.

10b **Not as above** **11**

11a **Context slowly becoming (or staining) ash-color; taste mild; pileus evenly dull yellow** .... *R. claroflava* **Grove**

Pileus (3) 4-12 cm, subglobose then convex-depressed, soon dry, golden yellow to duller, margin becoming short-striate; context white at first, odor and taste mild. Gills close, often forked near the stipe, becoming creamy-ochraceous, spotting gray to darker. Stipe 3-8.5 x 1-2 cm, white to pale yellow. Spore deposit ochraceous; spores 8.5-10 x 7.5-8 μm; ornamented with conic warts about 1 μm high and these connected by lines to form ± a reticulum.

Solitary to scattered in conifer or mixed forests, summer and fall, common and widely distributed. Edible. *R. flava* is another name that has been used for this species.

11b **Not changing to or staining gray to blackish** **12**

12a **Pileus glabrous, viscid, dull green and color more or less persistent; spore deposit creamy white; taste mild** .... *R. aeruginea* **Lindblad**

Pileus 5-18 cm, pulvinate becoming ± plane to shallowly depressed, olive tinged with gray or yellow or both, slightly viscid, soon dry, margin striate; cuticle separable as a thin skin; taste mild. Gills close, broad, yellowish pallid often with brownish stains. Stipe 4-8 x 1-2 cm, dry, yellowish pallid and often with brown stains near base. Spore deposit cream color; spores 6-8.5 x 5-6.5 (7) μm, ornamentation mostly of isolated short-cylindric warts and occasional ridges, prominences up to ± 0.8 μm high.

Scattered to gregarious in deciduous and mixed stands, most abundant in stands of aspen, Great Lakes area and northern Rocky Mountains.

12b **Not as above** **13**

13a Pileus 15-35 cm, olive becoming deep red, often entirely red in age; stipe usually flushed red; spore deposit yellow; taste mild ....
.... *R. olivacea* (Secr.) Fries

Pileus subglobose becoming broadly convex to slightly depressed, dry, pruinose, margin even; context thick, firm, white to yellowish pallid, taste mild. Gills finally ± distant, becoming pale ochraceous. Stipe 6-12 x 2-6 cm, dry, dull, consistency hard. Spores 8-11 x 7-9 (10) μm, ornamentation as warts 0.5-1 μm high. Pileus cuticle a lax trichodermium arising from a subgelatinous subcutis.

Solitary to scattered under conifers, fall, frequent in the Olympic National Park and in the Priest Lake district of Idaho. Edible. It favors a habitat of old-growth Douglas fir and hemlock.

13b Fruiting body less robust than in above choice, and color pattern not the same **14**

14a Pileus dingy ochraceous brown; gills often beaded with hyaline drops; odor and taste offensive. Fig. 55 ....
.... *R. laurocerasi* **Melzer**

Figure 55

Figure 55 *Russula laurocerasi*

Pileus 3.5-13 cm, pulvinate becoming plano-convex or disc depressed, slimy, shining when dry, glabrous, margin tuberculate-striate; context with odor of benzaldehyde varying to foetid, taste strongly nauseating-acrid. Gills moderately broad, becoming subdistant, pale to distinctly ochraceous,

spotted brownish. Stipe 2.5-11 x 1-3 cm, dry, often with brownish stains. Spore deposit orange-ochraceous; spores 7-10.7 x 7-9 μm, ornamented with spines and ridges sometimes forming a coarse partial or complete reticulum.

Solitary, scattered, or gregarious in deciduous or mixed woods, late summer and fall, widely distributed. This species has been identified as "*R. foetens*" in the Pacific Northwest. The fungus commonly identified as *R. foetens* in the United States is more properly identified as *R. fragrantissima* Romag. None in this group is edible.

14b Not as above **15**

15a Stipe staining dingy ochraceous brown where handled; odor in age or in drying disagreeable; pileus color variable; taste mild. Fig. 56 .... *R. xerampelina* (Secr.) Fries

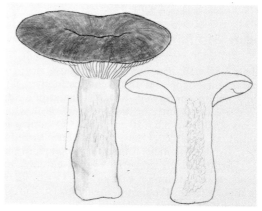

Figure 56

Figure 56 *Russula xerampelina*

Pileus 6-15 cm, convex becoming plano-depressed, purple black to olive-purplish, at times dark red and sometimes brownish olive, soon dry; taste mild. Gills close then subdistant, broad, cream color becoming pale ochraceous. Stipe 4-10 x 1-3 cm, rose-red or only tinged rose color, dry. Spore deposit ochraceous; spores (7.5) 8-10 (11.5) x 7-8.5 μm, ornamentation of mostly unconnected warts with the longest about 0.8 μm high.

Scattered to gregarious in conifer and mixed forests, often with hemlock, summer and fall, widely distributed and variable; in the Pacific

Northwest it is considered one of the best for table use. Generally it is not highly recommended.

15b Stipe not staining when handled **16**

16a Pileus 5-10 cm, bright red, fragile; taste very sharply acrid; spore deposit white to dull white. Fig. 57 .... *R. emetica* **Fries**

Figure 57

Figure 57   *Russula emetica*

Pileus 3-10 cm, convex to convex-depressed, viscid, pellicle separable, scarlet red, paler in age, at times rose-red when young; margin tubercu-late-striate; pileus cuticle readily separable from the context; context white. Gills broad, close, white, scarcely changing. Stipe 4.5-10.5 x 7-24 mm, white, dry, very fragile. Spores 8-11.5 x 6.5-9 μm; spore ornamentation of warts and spines up to 0.7 μm high, these connected by low ridges to form a partial or complete reticulum.

Scattered to gregarious, usually in *Sphagnum* bogs but also on very rotten wood or rich humus in conifer forests, summer and fall, common, widely distributed and not recommended for table use. Almost every red *Russula*, at one time or another, has been identified as this species!

16b Pileus 9-15 cm, dull red and not especially fragile; stipe thick and firm; taste mild to faintly acrid; spore deposit yellowish .... *R. paludosa* **Britzelmayr**

Pileus convex becoming expanded, often depressed in age, bright red to blood red, at times slightly purplish tinted, fading slowly to orange tones especially over the margin; taste mild. Gills close but finally subdistant, broad, creamy-white becoming pale ochraceous. Stipe 5-12 x 2-4 cm, white or tinted rose-color. Spores 8-10 (11.5) x 6.5-8 μm, ornamented with warts and ridges. forming at most a partial reticulum.

Solitary to scattered in *Sphagnum* bogs, and wet mossy areas in conifer forests generally, Great Lakes area eastward, seldom in large numbers but certainly not rare either.

HYGROPHORACEAE Roze

Fruiting body appearing clean and somewhat shiny; stipe central, continuous with the pileus; gills waxy in appearance and in consistency, at first attached to the stipe, sometimes seceding. Basidia typically about 5-7 times as long as the spores; spore deposit white; spores typically smooth and thin-walled, usually ellipsoid but varying to oblong or to globose; pleuro- and cheilocystidia present in a few species, thin-walled and hyaline, fusoid-ventricose to cylindric or clavate; gill trama bilateral (*Hygrophorus*), of interwoven hyphae (*Camarophyllus*), or ± parallel hyphae (*Hygrocybe*); clamp connections present or absent; cuticle of pileus diverse, gelatinizing in some species.

Since a microscope is necessary to make the decisions as to the correct genus, all the species included in this family here are arranged in a single key. In the following key cystidia are mentioned only if present; odor and taste are not stated unless they are distinctive, a mild taste, for instance is significant in some comparisons but not in others.

The spores are assumed to be ± ellipsoid unless otherwise mentioned.

KEY TO SPECIES

1a Pileus viscid at least when young 2

1b Pileus not viscid at any stage 3

2a Pileus viscid; stipe dry (check immature specimens) 14

2b Pileus and stipe both viscid to slimy 36

3a Pileus white, whitish, grayish, or olive-brown 4

3b Pileus differently colored than in above choice 7

4a Pileus white to creamy white. Fig. 58 .... *Camarophyllus borealis* (**Pk.**) **Murr.**

Figure 58

Figure 58 *Camarophyllus borealis*

Pileus 1-4.5 cm, when moist translucent-striate, becoming chalky white when faded; context thin, unchanging. Gills white, decurrent, ± distant. Stipe 2-9 cm x 2-5 (8) mm, glabrous, dull white. Spores 7-9 (12) x 4.5-6.5 μm, non-amyloid. Gill

trama interwoven. Cuticle of pileus a thin poorly defined cutis.

Solitary to gregarious on humus in mixed and conifer woods, common in northern United States and southern Canada, late summer and fall or early winter, weather permitting.

4b Pileus grayish to brownish gray 5

5a Gills adnate, whitish, pinkish when bruised, usually blackening in age or when dried .... *Hygrocybe ovina* (**Fr.**) **Kühner**

Pileus 2-5 cm, grayish brown becoming paler on aging and more grayish in fading; context brittle, odor faintly fruity, taste slightly alkaline. Stipe 4-7 cm x 5-10 mm, pallid or concolor with pileus, pinkish brown when handled, finally blackish. Spores 7-9 x 4.5-6 μm, non-amyloid. Gill trama subparallel. Cuticle of pileus a cutis.

Gregarious on soil in deciduous, conifer or mixed woods, Southeast and in California, summer and fall, apparently rare in North America.

5b Stipe not staining when injured and not blackening in age 6

6a Pileus 1-2.5 cm; stipe 3-6 mm thick, whitish to pale olive-brown; no veil present; spores 7-9 × 4-5 μm .... *Camarophyllus recurvatus* (**Pk.**) **Murr.**

Pileus dark to pale olive-brown, subviscid when wet, cuticle often cracking and at times lacerate. Gills grayish white, decurrent, broad, ± distant. Stipe 2-4 cm x 3-6 mm, glabrous, dry. Spores non-amyloid. Gill trama of interwoven hyphae. Cuticle of pileus a clearly defined ixocutis over a brownish hypodermium. Clamp connections present.

Gregarious under conifers and in pastures, northern United States especially the Pacific Northwest, October into January, often abundant.

6b Pileus 3-6 cm, a dry fibrillose veil present on young specimens causing stipe to be streaked with dark fibrils; spores 9-14 × 6-8 μm .... *Hygrophorus inocybiformis* **Smith**

Pileus dark gray over all or with dark gray fibrils over a pallid ground color. Gills pallid to grayish, broad, subdistant to ± decurrent. Stipe 3-6 cm x 5-12 mm, ± equal, solid. Spores non-amyloid. Gill trama of divergent hyphae. Cuticle of pileus a cutis. Clamp connections present.

Gregarious to scattered under spruce and fir, northern Rocky Mountains, July to October, frequent at times.

7a Pileus glabrous when faded (see *Hygrophorus kauffmanii* also) 8

7b Pileus furfuraceous to fibrillose, sometimes innately fibrillose when faded 10

8a Pileus essentially red; gills red to orange; stipe equal, fragile and hollow. Fig. 59 .... *Hygrocybe coccinea* **(Fr.) Kummer**

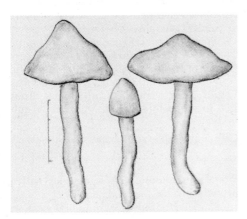

Figure 59

Figure 59 *Hygrocybe coccinea*

Pileus 2-5 cm, surface moist to sublubricous or subviscid, lacking a well defined gelatinous pellicle. Gills broad, thickish, intervenose, adnate to adnexed. Stipe 3-7 cm x 3-8 mm, red to orange-red, yellowish below. Spores 7-10.5 x 4-5 μm, non-amyloid. Gill trama of subparallel hyphae. Cuticle of pileus a simple cutis and not sharply differentiated. Clamp connections present.

Gregarious on soil or humus in hardwoods and conifer woods alike, chiefly east of the Great Plains, summer and fall, not common.

8b Pileus not red (see *Hygrocybe marginata* also) 9

9a Pileus yellow to orange; gills whitish to pale yellow; stipe 2-3 mm thick, naked. Fig. 60 .... *Hygrocybe parvula* **(Pk.) Murrill**

Figure 60

Figure 60 *Hygrocybe parvula*

Pileus 1-3 cm, translucent-striate moist and at times lubricous, thin. Gills decurrent, subdistant, broad. Stipe 3-6 cm long, yellow, becoming red over lower half. Spores 5-7 (8) x 3.5-5 μm, non-amyloid. Gill trama of subparallel hyphae. Cuticle of pileus a poorly differentiated cutis. Clamp connections present.

Solitary to caespitose in open places or grassy areas, in thickets or dense forests; common throughout the United States and Southern Canada, May to December depending on the weather.

9b Pileus rufous to orange fading to pallid buff; gills paler than the moist pileus; stipe 5-20 mm thick, whitish to tinged like the pileus, glabrous. Fig. 61 .... *Camarophyllus pratensis* **(Fr.) Kummer**

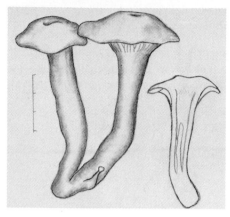

Figure 61

Figure 61 *Camarophyllus pratensis*

Pileus 2-7 cm, often irregularly cracked around the disc. Stipe 3-8 cm long, equal, stuffed whitish. Spores 5.5-8 x 3.5-5 μm, non-amyloid. Gill trama of interwoven hyphae. Cuticle of pileus not clearly differentiated. Clamp connections present.

Solitary to gregarious in open places or grassy areas in thickets or dense forests; common throughout the United States and southern Canada, summer and fall.

10a Pileus cream-buff to honey-yellow; squamulose when fresh; stipe becoming dingy olive-brownish below ....
.... *Hygrocybe caespitosa* (**Murr.**) **Murr.**

Pileus 1-6 cm, scales somewhat recurved and old-gold to dull brown, the tips often blackish. Gills white, becoming yellowish, broad, thick, subdistant to distant. Stipe 2-5 cm x 3-7 mm, concolor with cap above. Spores 6.5-9 (10) x 4-6 (7) μm. Hyphae of gill trama subparallel to ± interwoven. Cuticle of pileus a rudimentary trichodermium. Clamp connections present but rare.

10b Pileus yellow-orange, orange or scarlet when fresh **11**

11a Gills remaining deep yellow to reddish orange after pileus has faded. Fig. 62 ....
.... *Hygrocybe marginata* (**Pk.**) **Murr.**

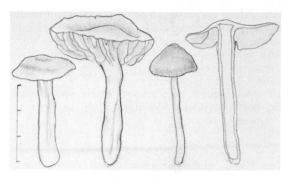

Figure 62

Figure 62 *Hygrocybe marginata*

Pileus 1-5 cm, yellow-orange to orange with a tinge of olive when moist, at times lubricous; context concolor with surface, Stipe 4-10 cm x 3-6 mm, pale orange-yellow, naked and moist, fragile. Spores 7-10 x 4-6 μm, non-amyloid. Gill trama of subparallel to interwoven hyphae, lactifers scattered in the layer. Pileus of ± a cutis to a lattice. Clamp connections absent.

Solitary to gregarious on soil and humus in mixed woods, widely distributed, summer and fall, common in the Great Lakes region and eastward but not in great quantity. One variety has yellow gills paler than the fresh pileus. Another has olive to green tones on the disc of the pileus.

11b Gills not as above **12**

12a Pileus squamulose with squamules with dull brown tips ....
.... *Hygrocybe turunda* (**Fr.**) **Karsten**

Pileus 1-3 cm, the ground color variable, scarlet to orange or yellow, brightest when young and becoming dingy in age; context orange. Gills pale dingy yellow to pallid, broad, distant to subdistant. Stipe 3-6 cm x 2-3.5 mm, orange in midportion, pale above and below. Spores 9-14 x 5-8 μm, non-amyloid. Pleuro- and cheilocystidia similar, 40-60 x 12-20 μm, clavate to subcapitate. Gill trama of ± interwoven hyphae. Cuticle of pileus a trichodermium. Clamp connections present.

Scattered to gregarious on moist soil and wet moss, often on *Sphagnum*, northern, abundant at times in the Cascade Mountains.

12b Pileus lacking fuscous brown squamules .. 13

13a Stipe long and slender (4-9 cm × 1.5-4 mm); gills distant and decurrent; pileus squamulose when faded. Fig. 63 .... *Hygrocybe cantharellus* (Schw.) Lange

Figure 64

Figure 64 *Hygrocybe miniata*

Figure 63

Figure 63 *Hygrocybe cantharellus*

Pileus 1-3.5 cm, glabrous when moist, flame scarlet fading to ochraceous buff. Gills orange to yellow (usually paler than the pileus), not staining, broad. Stipe concolor with pileus or paler, base whitish, naked, moist. Spores 7-12 x 4-6 μm or 8-13 x 5-8 μm in 2-spored forms, non-amyloid. Hyphae of gill trama becoming ± interwoven. Cuticle of pileus ± of a trichodermium. Clamp connections present.

Solitary to gregarious or caespitose on rich humus or very rotten wood, late spring on into the fall, very common in the Great Lakes area and eastward, but seldom in quantity.

13b Stipe shorter than in above; gills adnate and close. Fig. 64 .... *Hygrocybe miniata* (Fr.) Kummer

Pileus 2-4 cm, glabrous and scarlet when moist, fading to orange-yellow and then squamulose; context concolor with surface or paler. Gills almost concolor with pileus and soon fading, broad, not spotting. Stipe 3-5 cm x 3-4 (5) mm, concolor with pileus and fading more slowly. Spores 6-8 x 4-5 μm. Gill trama of subparallel hyphae. Cuticle of pileus of erect to repent septate elements with clavate end-cells. Clamp connections present.

Gregarious on humus and among mosses or on very rotten logs in mixed woods, summer and fall, common and widely distributed.

14a Pileus conic or conic-umbonate 15

14b Pileus obtuse to convex or disc slightly depressed 20

15a Fruiting body blackening in some part when bruised or in age. Fig. 65 .... *Hygrocybe conica* (Fr.) Kummer

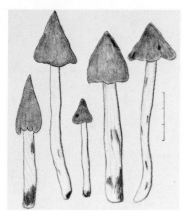

Figure 65

Figure 65 *Hygrocybe conica*

Pileus 2-7 (9) cm, usually reddish or scarlet-orange around and on the umbo, paler orange toward the margin, olive-gray to black when bruised or in age, slightly viscid when moist, soon dry. Gills nearly white at first, then olive-grayish to olive-yellow, or bright yellow, close, broad, narrowly attached. Stipe 6-11 cm x 5-11 mm, equal, base whitish, remainder red, orange or yellow, becoming dingy to blackish on aging. Spores 9-12 x 5.5-6.5 µm, non-amyloid. Gill trama of parallel hyphae and with broad lactifers variously disposed. Cuticle of pileus a thin ixocutis to an ixolattice. Clamp connections present.

Solitary to scattered or sparingly gregarious, summer and fall, widely distributed but seldom in quantity. It can be collected almost every season, but not in large numbers.

15b Fruiting body not blackening **16**

16a Pileus dull pinkish red to bright pink; pleurocystidia 50-105 × 4-25 µm ....
.... *Hygrocybe calyptraeformis* (**Berk. & Br.**) **Fayod**

Pileus 2.5-6 cm, occasionally tinged with lavender, the disc sometimes whitish, slightly viscid if moist. Gills bright pale pink, narrow to ± ventricose, close to ± subdistant. Stipe 5-16 cm x 4-8 mm, whitish, tinged with flesh color, very fragile, splitting readily. Spores 6.3-8 x 4.5-5 µm, non-amyloid. Pleurocystidia clavate to fusoid-ventricose. Cheilocystidia similar but smaller (62-79 x 10-15 µm). Gill trama of parallel to subparallel hyphae. Cu-

ticle of pileus a narrow gelatinous zone, some hyphae slender and with long cells, others constricted at the septa; terminal cells cystidioid. Clamp connections present.

Scattered to gregarious on humus under mixed hardwoods and conifers, Southeast north to the Great Lakes area, also in California, sporadic, summer and fall.

16b Pileus not as above **17**

17a Pileus olive to citrine-drab, or showing olive at least on the disc ....
.... *Hygrocybe spadicea* (**Fr.**) **Karsten**

Pileus 3-4 cm, olive-brown at first, margin becoming yellowish, context pale greenish yellow. Gills chartreuse yellow, close, broad and ventricose, edges eroded. Stipe 4-5 cm x 6-8 mm, concolor with gills or paler, overlaid with a thin layer of olive-brown fibrils. Spores 8-11 x 4-5.5 µm, non-amyloid. Gill trama of parallel hyphae. Cuticle of pileus an ixocutis, the hyphae fuscous. Clamp connections present.

Scattered under sumac on dry soil after heavy rains; Great Lakes area, July, apparently rarely collected. One form has a sharp odor and a glabrous stipe.

17b Pileus not as above **18**

18a Pileus disc grayish brown to ± bister; odor of fresh green corn; context staining pink. Fig. 66 .... *Hygrocybe acutoides* (**Sm. & Hes.**) **A. H. Smith comb. nov***

Figure 66

Hygrophorus acutoides Sm. & Hes. Sydowia 8: 325. 1954.

Figure 66 *Hygrocybe acutoides*

Pileus 3-5 cm, soon dry, context watery pallid. Gills whitish to pallid, subdistant, broad, adnate to adnexed. Stipe 6-8 cm x 4-6 mm, ± equal, white in age, staining salmon color where bruised. Spores 7-8 x 5-6 μm, non-amyloid. Gill trama of subparallel hyphae. Cuticle of pileus a thin ixocutis. Clamp connections present.

Gregarious to scattered on humus; Great Lakes area, summer and fall, sporadic and not common. One variety has a pallid pileus and a more poorly developed ixocutis on the pileus.

18b Pileus bright yellow, orange or red 19

19a Pileus deep red fresh and moist ....
.... *Hygrocybe cuspidata* (Pk.) Murr.

Pileus 2-7 cm, pellicle separable, fading to bright orange. Gills orange to yellow, free or just reaching apex of stipe, close to crowded, becoming broad. Stipe ± 5-9 cm x ± 10 mm, yellow to orange, the base whitish. Spores 8-12 (14) x 4-6.5 (9) μm, non-amyloid. Pleurocystidia present at times. Cheilocystidia somewhat fusoid, 52-68 x 4-5 μm. Gill trama parallel, lactifers yellowish. Cuticle of pileus an ixocutis, hyphae mostly colorless. Clamp connections present.

Gregarious on humus in mixed woods, widely distributed, spring and fall, abundant during some wet years.

19b Pileus orange to yellow when moist; spores
9-15 × 5-9 μm. Fig. 67 ....
.... *Hygrocybe acutoconica* (Clements) Singer

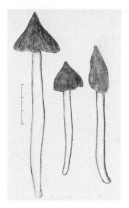

Figure 67

Figure 67 *Hygrocybe acutoconica*

Pileus 2-10 cm, sharply conic, thin, margin ± striatulate when moist, glabrous, readily splitting radially. Gills yellow, free to narrowly adnexed, close to subdistant, moderately broad. Stipe 6-12 x 3-6 (12) mm, concolor with pileus inside and out, paler or white as the base, lubricous at times. Spores non-amyloid. Cuticle of pileus a narrow ixocutis, hyphae mostly colorless. Clamp connections present.

Solitary to scattered on soil and humus, in deciduous and conifer forests, widely distributed in the United States and Canada, summer and fall, often collected but not in quantity. A variety with small spores (7-10 x 5-6 μm) is sometimes encountered.

20a Pileus white to pallid at first or on disc tinged
buff to brownish 21

20b Pileus more distinctly colored when young
.. 24

21a Gills pale apricot to pinkish tan ....
.... *Hygrophorus saxatilis* Sm. & Hes.

Pileus 3-8 (10) cm, whitish to very pale buff with a cinnamon tinge developing, occasionally watery-spotted or zoned, ± viscid; context soft, odor faint of dried peaches. Gills short-decurrent, pale pinkish cinnamon at first, narrow to moderately broad. Stipe 6-8 (15) cm x 10-15 mm, concolor with pileus, thinly appressed fibrillose, pruinose at apex. Spores 7-9.5 x 5-6 μm, non-amyloid. Gill trama of divergent hyphae. Cuticle of pileus a weakly differentiated ixocutis (the hyphae ± the same diameter as those beneath it). Clamp connections present.

Under conifers, Pacific Northwest; late fall.

21b Gills white at least at first 22

22a Growing under hardwoods. Fig. 68 ....
.... *Hygrophorus sordidus* **Pk.**

Figure 68

Figure 68   *Hygrophorus sordidus*

Pileus 8-20 cm, pure white or tinged yellowish on disc, viscid, smooth; context firm thick, unchanging. Gills yellowish in age, ± subdistant, broad, acuminate at the extremities, not spotting. Stipe 6-10 cm x 5-30 mm, tapered to a point below or nearly equal, solid, firm, surface glabrous. Spores 6-8 x (3.5) 4-5.5 μm, non-amyloid. Gill trama of divergent hyphae. Cuticle of pileus an ixocutis, 2-layered, the upper layer of brownish hyphae as revived in KOH. Clamp connections present.

Gregarious in open oak-hickory woods, eastern and central United States, late summer and fall. Common and abundant. Edible.

22b Growing under conifers 23

23a Fruiting body short and squatty; with a white fibrillose veil. Fig. 69 ....
.... *Hygrophorus subalpinus* **Smith**

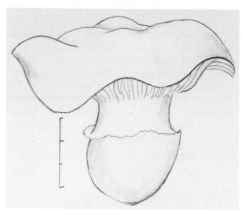

Figure 69

Figure 69   *Hygrophorus subalpinus*

Pileus 4-12 cm, snow-white and with a luster, subviscid, patches of the broken veil often adhering along the margin; context thick, white, unchanging. Gills white to whitish, close, decurrent, narrow, not staining. Stipe 3-9 cm x 1-3 cm, base often bulbous when young, often with a flaring but evanescent annulus at the apex of the bulb, white throughout. Spores 8-10 x 4.5-5 μm, non-amyloid. Gill trama of divergent hyphae. Cuticle of pileus an ixocutis. Clamp connections present.

Gregarious under conifers, Pacific Northwest and Rocky Mountains, spring and summer. It is one of the species comprising the "snow bank mushroom flora" of both regions. Deer feed on it to the extent that at times it is difficult to get undamaged specimens. It is edible (for humans) but has, according to reports, very little flavor.

23b Fruiting body with a slender stipe and lacking a veil. Fig. 70 ....
.... *Hygrophorus piceae* **Kühner & Romagnesi**

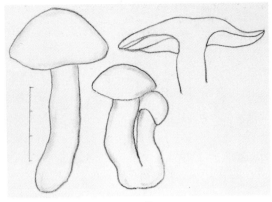

Figure 70

Figure 70 *Hygrophorus piceae*

Pileus 2.5-8 cm, snow white, viscid, glabrous; context soft and white. Gills becoming pale pinkish buff, subdistant to distant, adnate to decurrent, edges even, not staining. Stipe 3-8 cm x 3-5 (12) mm, upper half with a white cottony fibrillose coating, dry, not staining. Spores 6-8 (10) x 4-5 (6) μm, non-amyloid. Gill trama of divergent hyphae. Cuticle of pileus an ixolattice. Clamp connections rare.

In woods of spruce and fir in wet areas, northern and western United States, late summer and fall, often late in the season. It is frequently abundant in the Cascade Mountains.

24a Stipe thick and at the apex having points and/or scurf which becomes orange-yellow in KOH and which dry reddish brown. Fig. 71 .... *Hygrophorus pudorinus* (Fr.) Fr.

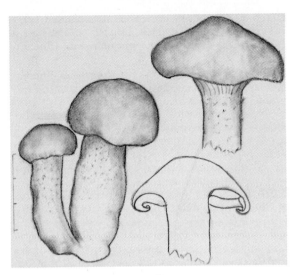

Figure 71

Figure 71 *Hygrophorus pudorinus*

Pileus 5-15 (20) cm, pale tan to pale flesh-color, margin at first inrolled and minutely downy. Gills white to pallid but flushed pinkish (but not staining reddish), $\pm$ decurrent, narrow, subdistant. Stipe 4-12 cm x 10-25 mm, $\pm$ equal, solid, white to tinged vinaceous, dry. Spores 6.5-9.5 x 4-5.5 μm, non-amyloid. Gill trama of divergent hyphae. Cuticle of pileus an ixotrichoderm, the hyphae 2-3 μm wide. Clamp connections present.

Scattered to gregarious under spruce and fir, northern United States and adjacent Canada, abundant at times, late summer and fall. Edible. Var. *fragrans* (Murr.) Hes. & Sm. is bright ochraceous at the base of the stipe, has a strong tendency to stain yellow where injured, and is found in the Pacific Northwest. Var. *subcinereus* Sm. & Hes. is tinged grayish on the pileus and is found in the Great Lakes region.

24b KOH reaction on apex of stipe not as above 25

25a Gills soon spotted vinaceous or becoming vinaceous red over all or this color from the beginning 26

25b Gills not spotting or colored as above 30

26a A fibrillose veil present in unexpanded specimens (see *H. amarus* also) .... *Hygrophorus purpurascens* (**Fr.**) **Fr.**

Pileus (3) 6-12 (20) cm, fibrillose layer mineral red to darker, margin paler (pinkish), the exposed context whitish, often streaked with purplish red, subviscid; context bitter to (rarely) mild. Gills soon spotted pinkish to purplish red, becoming decurrent, narrow, close to subdistant. Stipe 8-15 cm long, 10-25 mm at apex, ± narrowed downward, colored ± as in pileus, at first with a faint fibrillose zone from the veil. Spores 5.5-7 (8) x 3-4.5 μm, non-amyloid. Gill trama of divergent hyphae. Cuticle of pileus an ixocutis. Clamp connections present.

Gregarious to scattered on soil under conifers, spruce in particular, northern United States and adjacent Canada, fall, not rare. Edible but the bitter specimens are the ones usually found. It is abundant in the northern Rocky Mountains. Not recommended.

26b A fibrillose veil lacking or very rudimentary 27

27a Taste bitter; pileus where exposed to light fading to yellow; gills pale yellow at first .... *Hygrophorus amarus* **Sm. & Hes.**

Pileus 3-8 cm, obtuse to ± expanded-umbonate, ± vinaceous at first. Gills soon ± decurrent, close to subdistant, spotted vinaceous broad. Stipe 3-7 cm x 10-15 mm, narrowed downward, solid, surface ± white-fibrillose, at times with a very slight cortina. Spores 7-9 x 4.5-6 μm, non-amyloid. Gill trama of divergent hyphae. Cuticle of pileus an ixotrichoderm to an ixolattice. Clamp connections present.

Scattered under spruce, Rocky Mountains, summer, not rare. The bitter taste is persistent: not recommended.

27b Not as above 28

28a Gills close to crowded; mostly under oak; with the aspect of a *Russula*. **Fig. 72** .... *Hygrophorus russula* (**Fr.**) **Quél.**

Figure 72

Figure 72 *Hygrophorus russula*

Pileus 5-12 cm, color variable (shrimp pink, coral pink, vinaceous to purplish red), margin often whitish, streaked with red fibrils, at times staining yellow where bruised; context thick, whitish, taste mild. Gills white at first, soon flushed pinkish, finally spotted vinaceous red. Stipe 3-10 cm x 15-35 mm, white becoming stained; veil lacking. Spores 6-8 x 3-4.5 (5) μm, non-amyloid. Gill trama of slightly divergent hyphae. Cuticle of pileus an ixocutis to an ixolattice. Clamp connections present.

28b Gills distant to subdistant, rarely close 29

29a At maturity the pileus, gills, and stipe evenly dark vinaceous red .... *Hygrophorus capreolaris* (**Kalchbr.**) **Sacc.**

Pileus 3-7 cm, delicately streaked with purplish fibrils, appressed-scaly on the disc in age; the margin thick and white silky; context thick, whitish then ± concolor with surface, taste mild. Gills at first pallid, soon decurrent, ± distant, thickish. Stipe 4-10 cm x 6-10 mm, at first white with a reddish tinge, floccose-punctate at apex; veil lacking. Spores 6.5-8 x 4.5-5 μm, non-amyloid. Gill trama of divergent hyphae. Cuticle of pileus an ixolattice. Clamp connections present.

Scattered under spruce and in *Sphagnum* bogs, northern United States, fall and early winter.

29b Gills paler than pileus at maturity. Fig. 73. .... *Hygrophorus erubescens* (**Fr.**) **Fr.**

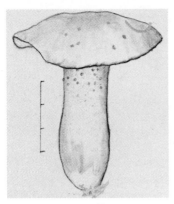

Figure 73

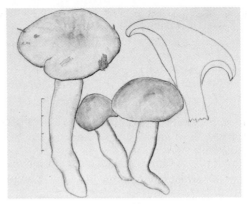

Figure 74

Figure 73 *Hygrophorus erubescens*

Pileus vinaceous red or margin paler, fading, a pink tinge often pervading the entire cap; margin incurved and minutely tomentose, often beaded with drops of moisture, surface streaked with fibrils, finally with spotlike scales on disc; context white, often staining yellowish where bruised; taste mild. Gills pinkish, soon spotted or stained red, adnate then decurrent, close becoming subdistant. Stipe 4-7 cm x 6-12 mm, at first beaded with drops of moisture, appressed-fibrillose to scurfy below, apex white, otherwise pale brownish vinaceous and at times yellowish where bruised. Spores 7-10 (11.5) x 5-6 μm, non-amyloid. Gill trama divergent. Cuticle of pileus an ixolattice. Clamp connections present.

Gregarious under conifers, especially pine and spruce, northern United States and adjacent Canada, fall, not infrequent.

30a Pileus pink, yellow, brown or rusty to vinaceous brown **31**

30b Pileus gray to black, blackish brown or dark violaceous to brownish violaceous (see *C. recurvatus* also) **33**

31a Gills creamy white; stipe apex beaded with drops when fresh. Fig. 74 ....
.... *Hygrophorus bakerensis* **Sm. & Hes.**

Figure 74 *Hygrophorus bakerensis*

Pileus 4-15 cm, slimy viscid, dark to pale clay-color, margin pallid at first; odor heavy, somewhat of almonds. Gills decurrent, becoming subdistant, moderately broad in age. Stipe (4) 7-14 cm x 8-25 mm, narrowed downward, solid lower part dry, cottony-pruinose above, not staining, white to pale pinkish buff. Spores 7-9 (10) x 4.5-6 μm, non-amyloid. Gill trama of divergent hyphae. Cuticle of pileus an ixocutis to an ixolattice. Clamp connections present.

Scattered to gregarious, very common under conifers at elevations of 1000-4000 ft., Pacific Northwest, fall and early winter, common. Edible but not highly rated.

31b Gills distinctly colored when young **32**

32a Gills pinkish gray (avellaneous) at first, paler in age. Fig. 75 .... *Camarophyllus colemannianus* **(Blox. in Berk.) Ricken**

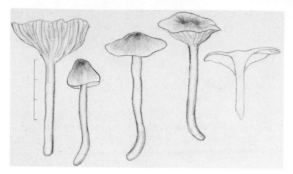

Figure 75

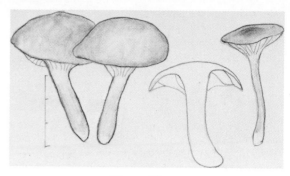

Figure 76

Figure 75 *Camarophyllus colemannianus*

Pileus 1-4.5 cm, dull deep vinaceous brown fading to pinkish gray or buff, pellicle thin and separable, margin translucent-striate when moist. Gills close then subdistant, ± broad, decurrent. Stipe 3-6 (8) cm x 4-7 mm, dry, glabrous and white. Spores 6-8 x 4.5-6 μm, non-amyloid. Gill trama of interwoven hyphae. Cuticle of pileus an ixocutis over a hypodermium of conspicuous parallel brownish hyphae. Clamp connections present.

Gregarious on humus in oak and beech woods as well as in mixed woods; in Great Lakes region and Pacific Northwest, fall, not uncommon but not in quantity.

32b Gills vinaceous brown when young, darker in age .... *Hygrophorus kauffmanii* Sm. & Hes.

Pileus 2-11 cm, canescent, with minute spotlike scales, hazel to chestnut color when moist, fading to apricot buff; context pale pinkish cinnamon, odor and taste mild. Gills subdistant, broad, finally ± decurrent. Stipe 3-8 cm x 4-12 mm or more, narrowed downward, dry; veil lacking, soon concolor with pileus. Spores 6-8 x 4.5—6 μm, non-amyloid. Gill trama of divergent hyphae. Cuticle of pileus a thin ixolattice. Clamp connections present.

Gregarious to scattered in open hardwoods, Michigan and Tennessee, late fall in the north, winter in the south, not common.

33a With a distinct almond-like odor; stipe typically whitish at first. Fig. 76 .... *Hygrophorus agathosmus* (Fr.) Fries

Figure 76 *Hygrophorus agathosmus*

Pileus (3) 4-8 (11) cm, evenly light drab or dull ashy gray, viscid, margin faintly tomentose. Gills whitish then pale cinereous, close in one variant, usually subdistant to distant, adnate then ± decurrent. Stipe 48 (16) cm x 6-14 mm, equal or narrowed downward, dry, at first fibrillose-pruinose. Spores (7) 8-10.5 x 4.5-5.5 μm, non-amyloid. Gill trama of divergent hyphae. Cuticle of pileus an ixolattice, uppermost hyphae fuscous. Clamp connections present.

Scattered under spruce and pine, northern United States and adjacent Canada, late summer and fall, fairly common.

33b Not as above 34

34a Gills violaceous .... *Camarophyllus subviolaceus* (Pk.) Singer

Pileus 2.5-6 cm, dark violet to brownish violaceous, hygrophanous, subviscid and pellicle separable, margin translucent-striate when wet; odor slight, taste at first mild then bitter to subnauseous, at times leaving a burning sensation in the throat. Gills whitish at first, decurrent, ± distant, broad. Stipe 3-7 cm x 4-11 mm, soon tinted like the pileus, dry, appressed fibrillose. Spores 6-7 (8) x 4-5 (6) μm, non-amyloid. Gill trama of interwoven hyphae. Pileus cuticle an ixolattice or ± of an ixotrichodermium. Clamp connections present.

Gregarious on soil in swamps and deep humus in deciduous and conifer forests in northern United States and adjacent Canada.

34b Gills not as above 35

35a Gills white to creamy at first but soon flushed a delicate pink ....
.... *Hygrophorus calophyllus* **Karsten**

Pileus 5-11 cm, slimy-viscid, raw umber to olive-brown or slightly paler near the margin; context whitish, odor faintly fragrant, taste mild. Gills narrow, decurrent, ± distant. Stipe 6-10 (12) x 10-15 mm, brown to a paler zone near gills. Spores 5.5-8 x 4-5 μm, non-amyloid. Gill trama of divergent hyphae. Cuticle of pileus an ixolattice. Clamp connections present.

Solitary to scattered under fir and pine, western United States, late summer and fall, not common.

35b Gills grayish to pallid or white; pileus merely subviscid to viscid. Fig. 77 ....
Hygrophorus camarophyllus **(Fr.) Dumée, Grandjean et Maire**

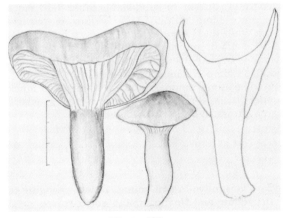

Figure 77

Figure 77 *Hygrophorus camarophyllus*

Pileus 4-7 (13) cm, turbinate or with a slight umbo, fuscous over all, often streaked, margin pubescent to pruinose. Gills adnate to decurrent, ± distant at maturity, broad, thin. Stipe 3-8 (13) cm x 10-20 mm, pallid to fuscous, pruinose above; context cinereous. Spores 7-9 x 4-5 μm, non-amyloid. Gill trama of divergent hyphae. Cuticle of pileus poorly defined to merely a weak ixocutis. Clamp connections present.

Scattered to gregarious under conifers,

abundant in the Pacific Northwest, not common in the Great Lakes area, usually late in the fall or earlier during cool seasons. Edible.

36a Stipe with a slime veil, the apex dry and pruinose to scabrous 37

36b Stipe slimy or viscid to apex from a gelatinous cuticle 49

37a Pileus white to whitish 38

37b Pileus more distinctly colored 40

38a Stipe typically short and thick (15-33 mm) .... *Hygrophorus ponderatus* **Britzelmayr**

Pileus 5-14 cm, white, slimy-viscid, margin floccose; context white, unchanging, taste mild. Gills becoming decurrent, subdistant, broad, white. Stipe 2.3-6 (9) cm long, silky fibrillose beneath the slime; partial veil cortinate. Spores 6.5-9 (10) x 4-5.5 μm, non-amyloid. Gill trama of divergent hyphae. Cuticle of pileus an ixolattice. Clamp connections present.

Under mixed hardwoods and pines, southern, November to January. Not common.

38b Stipe typically only 5-10 mm thick 39

39a Gills white becoming brownish in age ....
.... *Hygrophorus chrysapsis* **Métrod**

Pileus 2-7 (10) cm, matted fibrillose beneath the slime, white becoming pale pinkish buff to tawny, usually drying darker, odor often faintly fragrant. Gills dark brown as dried, white at first, often staining yellow where bruised. Stipe 4-6 (15) cm x 2-8 mm, dull white becoming pale pinkish buff to yellow where bruised, apex often beaded with pale yellow drops. Spores 7-8 (9) x 3.5-4.5 μm. Gill trama of divergent hyphae. Cuticle of pileus an ixolattice.

On humus under hardwoods, especially beech, Great Lakes area and both south and eastward, summer and fall.

**39b Gills white, drying yellowish to pale buff.
Fig. 78 .... *Hygrophorus eburneus* (Fr.) Fr.**

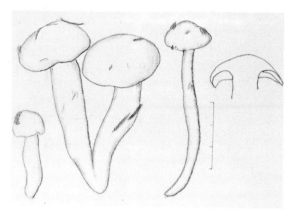

Figure 78

Figure 78 *Hygrophorus eburneus*

Pileus 2-7 (10) cm, pure white overall and slimy, drying whitish or yellowish, glabrous or with a silky lustre, margin floccose-pubescent, odor and taste mild. Gills subdistant, soon decurrent, broad, Stipe 4.5-15 x 2-8 (15) mm, usually narrowed downward, slimy, near apex fibrillose-punctate to ± squamulose, white, unchanging where injured. Spores 6-8 (9) x 3.5-5 μm, non-amyloid. Gill trama of divergent hyphae. Cuticle of pileus an ixolattice. Clamp connections present.

Gregarious under either conifers or hardwoods or grassy areas near trees, east of the Great Plains, summer and fall, uncommon.

40a Pileus bright or pale-colored (buff to tan or yellowish) or if dark at first becoming yellow to red in age 41

40b Pileus in gray to black or fuscous range 44

**41a Pileus bright red fading soon to orange, growing under larch. Fig. 79 ....
.... *Hygrophorus speciosus* Peck**

Figure 79

Figure 79 *Hygrophorus speciosus*

Pileus 2-5 cm broad, very slimy when fresh; context white to yellowish, odor and taste mild. Gills white to yellowish, edges yellowish, ± narrow, decurrent, distant to subdistant. Stipe 4-10 cm x 4-8 mm, slime staining stipe yellow or orange; apex white and pruinose above the veil line. Spores 8-10 x 4.5-6 μm, non-amyloid. Gill trama of divergent hyphae. Cuticle of pileus an ixotrichodermium. Clamp connections present.

Scattered to gregarious on humus and muck under larch, throughout North America where larch grows, fall, often abundant.

41b Not as above 42

**42a Pileus olive-brown young, slowly changing to yellow and finally orange going to red ....
.... *Hygrophorus hypothejus* (Fr.) Fr.**

Pileus 2-8 cm, bone brown to olive-brown on disc, yellow ochre to greenish elsewhere, slimy, agglutinated-fibrillose toward the margin. Gills white becoming pale yellow, decurrent, ± subdistant. Stipe 6-16 cm x (3) 6-12 mm, partial veil floccose and leaving a subapical fibrillose evanescent annular zone, apical region silky and yellowish, lower down the colors various (olive-brown, olivaceous yellow, bright yellow, orange or scarlet). Spores 7-9 x 4-5 μm, non-amyloid. Gill trama of divergent hyphae. Cuticle of pileus an ixolattice to an ixocutis. Clamp connections present.

Gregarious under pine throughout most of the United States and Canada where pine grows, late summer and fall, common.

42b Not as above **43**

43a Pileus yellowish to pale cream-color, not changing much in aging. Fig. 80 .... *Hygrophorus gliocyclus* **Fr.**

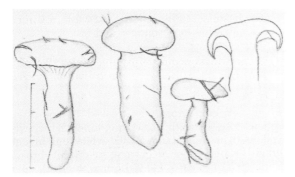

Figure 80

Figure 80 *Hygrophorus gliocyclus*

Pileus (2) 4-9 cm, broadly umbonate, slimy, margin involute at first; context thick, soft, taste mild. Gills ivory-yellow to darker becoming decurrent, broad toward the stipe. Stipe (2) 3-6 cm x 8-12 (20) mm, whitish, sheathed by a hyaline slime veil which terminates in a narrow slime-annulus; the apical region at first white floccose and then silky-fibriloose. Spores 8-10 (11) x 4.5-6 μm, non-amyloid. Gill trama of divergent hyphae. Cuticle of pileus an ixotrichoderm arising from an ixo-subcuticle. Clamp connections present.

Gregarious to caespitose under pine rarely spruce, southeastern and western United States, fall and winter. Edible and choice but wipe off the slime.

43b Pileus ± clay-color, the slime becoming smoky brownish in age and gills and apex of stipe tending to stain olivaceous; spores 8-11 × 5-7 μm .... *Hygrophorus paludosus* **Pk.**

Pileus 4-10 cm, dull yellowish in buttons, often zoned near the margin in age; taste mild. Gills soon decurrent, white, subdistant. Stipe 5-12 cm x 10-20 mm, slimy over lower 2/3rds, the slime discoloring; cortina thin, white, and fibrillose; near apex punctate. Gill trama of divergent hyphae. Cuticle of pileus an ixotrichoderm collapsing into an ixolattice. Clamp connections present.

Scattered to gregarious on humus in deciduous woods, Great Lakes area south and eastward, late fall.

44a Stipe with a layer of dark colored fibrils beneath the slime veil. Fig. 81 .... *Hygrophorus olivaceoalbus* **(Fr.) Fr.**

Figure 81

Figure 81 *Hygrophorus olivaceoalbus*

Pileus 3-8 cm, conspicuously streaked beneath the pellicle from smoke-gray to black fibrils, disc umber to black, margin paler; context soft, white, taste mild. Gills pure white to somewhat ashy, becoming subdistant, thickish. Stipe 8-12 (15) cm x (5) 10-20 mm, with a double sheath to near apex (outer layer slimy), in age the sheath breaking into zones or patches; white and pruinose above the veil line. Spores 9-12 x 5-6 μm, non-amyloid. Gill trama of divergent hyphae. Pileus cuticle an ixocutis of fuscous hyphae. Clamp connections present.

Caespitose to scattered under conifers including redwood, the western United States and Canada, late summer and fall. Var. *intermedius* Sm. & Hes. has a thin inner veil. Var. *gracilis* Maire has spores 10-14 x 5.5-7.5 μm and the hyphae of the cuticle contain dark granules in Melzer's medium.

44b Not as above **45**

45a Slime veil very thin and soon evanescent; fibrils on stipe staining ashy gray. Fig. 82 .... *Hygrophorus tephroleucus* (Fr.) Fr.

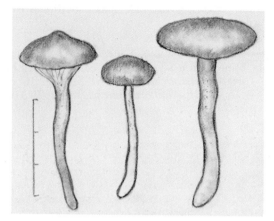

Figure 82

Figure 82 *Hygrophorus tephroleucus*

Pileus 1-3 cm, dark ashy gray on disc, pale gray over all in age, appressed fibrillose under the slime, in age squamulose. Gills white becoming creamy, broad, subdistant. Stipe 4-6 cm x 2-3 (4) mm, white over all at first, ± fibrillose below, base in young specimens coated with a thin layer of slime, soon dry. Spores (7) 8-10 x 4-5 μm, non-amyloid. Gill trama of divergent hyphae. Pileus cuticle an ixolattice of fuscous hyphae. Clamp connections present.

Gregarious under conifers and in *Sphagnum* bogs, Great Lakes area south and eastward, also in Canada, fall and winter, common during wet seasons.

45b Slime veil copious; fibrils on stipe not staining gray **46**

46a Spores 10-13 (15) μm long **47**

46b Spores 7-10 μm long **48**

47a Pileus fuscous to cinereous; spores 9-13 × 5-7 μm .... *Hygrophorus fuscoalbus* (Lasch) Fr.

Pileus 2-5 cm, margin pale and incurved, white-tomentose; context grayish white; taste mild. Gills white with a pale pinkish buff reflection, close, broad, soon decurrent. Stipe 3-6 cm x 8-15 mm, with a layer of white floccose fibrils beneath the slime, white floccose at apex. Spores non-amyloid. Gill trama of divergent hyphae. Cuticle of pileus an ixolattice. Clamp connections present.

On soil, eastern, central, and western United States, sporadic, late summer and fall.

47b Pileus dark sepia at first; spores 10-17 × 6-9 μm .... *Hygrophorus limacinus* Fries

Pileus 3-7 cm, appearing streaked to appressed squamulose beneath the slime, in KOH slowly yellow then dull orange. Gills white but in age grayish-watery, soon decurrent, ± distant, broad. Stipe (2.5) 6-8 cm x (4) 8-12 mm, ± equal, apex white, slightly grayish from fibrils below, at times naked, with KOH apex lemon yellow changing to orange; no inner veil evident. Spores non-amyloid. Gill trama of divergent hyphae. Cuticle of pileus an ixolattice of fuscous hyphae. Clamp connections present.

On soil, under hardwoods and conifers, Michigan and California, October and December. Apparently rare.

48a Pileus with pallid margin; stipe 3-10 (15) mm thick at apex .... *Hygrophorus occidentalis* Sm. & Hes.

Pileus 2-8 (10) cm, color variable (hair brown to fuscous), at times yellowish to smoky, the taste mild. Gills soon decurrent, subdistant, finally moderately broad, white to tinged cream color. Stipe 2-7 cm long, pallid or concolor with pileus, with appressed white fibrils beneath the slime. Spores 6-9 x 3.5-5 μm, non-amyloid. Gill trama of divergent hyphae. Cuticle of pileus an ixotrichodermium. Clamp connections present.

Gregarious to scattered on soil in mixed oak-pine and in deciduous woods; east of the Great Plains, fall, abundant at times.

48b Pileus blackish overall; stipe 20-25 mm thick .... *Hygrophorus fuligineus* Frost in Peck

Pileus 4-12 cm, ± virgate after slime dries; odor and taste not distinctive. Gills rather thin, whitish to creamy white, fairly broad at maturity, becoming ± decurrent. Stipe 4-10 (12) cm long, whitish fresh, lower part covered by hyaline slime, naked near apex or in some ± scabrous. Spores 7-9 x 4.5-5.5 μm, non-amyloid. Gill trama of divergent hyphae. Cuticle of pileus an ixotrichodermium, over a hypodermium of brownish hyphae. Clamp connections present.

On humus and muck under conifers, eastern United States and Great Lakes area, also in northern Idaho. To be expected in Canada; late summer and fall.

49a Taste of pellicle bitter; pileus red when young .... *Hygrocybe reai* (Maire) Lange

Pileus 1-3 cm, in age fading to deep orange, glabrous, faintly translucent-striate toward the margin; context whitish but becoming yellow. Gills bluntly adnate, seceding, soon yellow, subdistant, broad. Stipe 3-5 cm x 1.5-3.5 mm, concolor with pileus or paler, often translucent. Spores 6.5-8 x 4-4.5 μm, non-amyloid. Gill trama of subparallel hyphae. Cuticle of pileus an ixocutis. Clamp connections present.

Gregarious under conifers, northern United States, summer and fall, abundant at times.

49b Not as above **50**

50a Stipe very slimy-viscid **51**

50b Stipe merely viscid to subviscid at first, soon dry **54**

51a Pileus parrot green young, soon changing to yellow or pinkish to reddish tan. Fig. 83 .... *Hygrocybe psittacina* (**Fr.**) **Karsten**

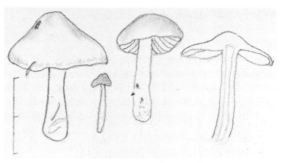

Figure 83

Figure 83 *Hygrocybe psittacina*

Pileus 1-3 cm, obtuse, striate when fresh. Gills ± distant, green at first and fading like pileus, broad. Stipe 3-7 cm x 2-3 mm, green above or overall when young, becoming yellow to orange then pinkish. Spores 6.5-8 (10) x 4-5 (6) μm, non-amyloid. Hyphae of gill trama ± interwoven. Cuticle of pileus an ixotrichodermium. Clamp connections present.

Gregarious to scattered in conifer and deciduous woods, in pastures and along roadsides, widely distributed but seldom in large numbers, spring, summer and fall. A variety from California, has blue colors at first.

51b Not as above **52**

52a Gills yellow and long-decurrent; cap fading to whitish. Fig. 84 .... *Hygrocybe nitida* (**Berk. & Curt.**) **Murr.**

Figure 84

Figure 84 *Hygrocybe nitida*

Pileus 1-4 cm, yellow at first, striatulate when moist. Gills very fragile. Stipe 3-8 cm x 2-5 mm, concolor with pileus and fading like it, glistening when dry. Spores 6.5-8 (9) x (3.5) 4-5 μm, non-amyloid. Hyphae of gill trama subparallel. Cuticle of pileus an ixotrichodermium. Clamp connections present.

Gregarious to scattered on humus and wet soil and in bogs, widely distributed, summer and fall.

52b Not as above **53**

53a Gills pale vinaceous; faded cap some shade of vinaceous. Fig. 85 ....
.... *Hygrocybe laeta* (**Fr.**) **Karsten**

Figure 85

Figure 85 *Hygrocybe laeta*

Pileus 1-4 cm glabrous, slimy-viscid, translucent-striate, pale violet gray, orange, orange red or tawny olive when young (color variable); odor often fishy, taste mild. Gills at first variously colored (like the cap), subdistant, broad, adnate then ± decurrent. Stipe 3-12 cm x 2-4 (6) mm, ± concolor with pileus, glabrous, slimy-viscid. Spores 5-7 (8) x 3-4 (5) μm. Cheilocystidia 25-52 x 1.5-2.5 μm, at times branched. Hyphae of gill trama subparallel, subhymenium gelatinizing. Cuticle of pileus an ixotrichodermium. Clamp connections present.

Scattered to gregarious on damp soil in woods and bogs, widely distributed and common, summer and fall. Forma *pallida* (Sm.) Bon has a whitish pileus when young.

53b Gills white to grayish; pileus blackish to dark or pale gray. Fig. 86 ....
.... *Hygrocybe unguinosa* (**Fr.**) **Karsten**

Figure 86

Figure 86 *Hygrocybe unguinosa*

Pileus 2-5 cm, glabrous, slimy when fresh, shining when dry, becoming pallid along the margin in age, translucent-striate. Gills broad, thick, adnate to adnexed. Stipe 3-9 cm x 2-5 mm, concolor with or paler than pileus, glabrous, slimy, appearing varnished when dry. Spores (6) 7-10 x 4-5 (6) μm, non-amyloid. Hyphae of gill trama subparallel to ± interwoven, lactifers numerous. Cuticle of cap an ixotrichodermium. Clamp connections present.

Gregarious to scattered on humus and soil, in conifer and hardwoods, in swamps, etc., widely distributed, summer and fall. Seldom found in quantity. One variety has a faint but disagreeable-aromatic odor and clamp connections are very hard to find.

54a Pileus 0.5-1.5 cm, scarlet when young ....
.... *Hygrocybe minutula* (**Pk.**) **Murr.**

Pileus fading to yellow, glabrous, silky on drying, margin striatulate when fresh. Gills orange to orange buff, adnate to adnexed, broad, becoming subdistant. Stipe 1.5-5 cm x 1-3 mm, at first red near apex, yellowish or whitish near base, fading to yellow overall in age, fragile. Spores 7-10.3 x 4-5 (6) μm, non-amyloid. Hyphae of gill trama subparallel. Cuticle of pileus an ixocutis. Clamp connections present.

Gregarious to scattered on grassy soil, waste land, etc., summer and fall, widely distributed in North America but not common.

54b Pileus 1-4 cm, yellow when young. Fig. 87. .... *Hygrocybe ceracea* **(Fr.) Karsten**

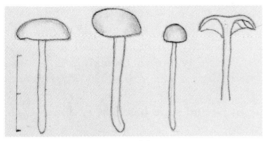

Figure 87

Figure 87 *Hygrocybe ceracea*

Pileus fading to straw yellow, glabrous, slightly viscid, hygrophanous, translucent-striate when moist. Gills pale yellow to nearly white, decurrent. Stipe 2-5 cm x 1-3 (4) mm, concolor with pileus, glabrous, slightly viscid but soon dry. Spores 5.5-8 x 4-5 μm, non-amyloid. Gill trama of subparallel to slightly interwoven hyphae. Cuticle of pileus an ixocutis, no hypodermium differentiated. Clamp connections rare.

Scattered to gregarious on moss and soil, widely distributed in North America, summer and fall or winter in the south.

TRICHOLOMATACEAE Roze

Of all the families of the gilled mushrooms, this is the most difficult one to define, especially if emphasis is to be placed on macroscopic characters. At the same time it is the most interesting family from the standpoint of the evolution of the features we use in the taxonomy of the Agaricales. It contains the hyaline-spored (under the microscope) agarics with the pileus and stipe confluent as well as closely related species with pale-colored spore deposits.

KEY TO GENERA

1a Habit pleurotoid (fruiting body sessile or stipe typically eccentric to lateral) .... **Key A**

1b Stipe centrally attached (specimens with eccentric stipe occur rarely) .... **Key B**

Key A

1a Spores amyloid, gills with serrate edges .... **(p. 104)** *Lentinellus*

1b Not with both the above features 2

2a Spore deposit pink (see *Clitocybe martiorum* also) 3

2b Spore deposit yellowish to white or lilac-gray 4

3a Pileus sessile; gills bright orange ....
.... (p. 134) *Phyllotopsis*

3b Pileus mostly with eccentric stipe; pileus
± reticulate and watermelon pink ....
.... (p. 136) *Rhodotus*

4a Pileus trama at least in part gelatinous
(pileus feels rubbery) 5

4b Pileus trama tough to fleshy-soft (lacking gelatinized layer or layers) 6

5a Spores amyloid .... (p. 131) *Panellus*

5b Spores not amyloid ....
.... (p. 101) *Hohenbuehelia*

6a Fruiting body tough, reviving ....
.... (p. 133) *Panus*

6b Fruiting body fleshy, decaying readily ....
.... (p. 134) *Pleurotus*

Key B

1a Gills dichotomously forked, yellow to
orange; crowded; spores dextrinoid; pileus soft to the touch ....
.... (p. 102) *Hygrophoropsis*

1b Not as above 2

2a Inhabiting cones of magnolias and conifers; fruiting bodies ± pliant; spores non-
amyloid .... (p. 137) *Strobilurus*

2b Not as above 3

3a Stipe 1-3.5 mm thick near apex, or if
thicker having a distinct cartilaginous
cortex or very tough in consistency 4

3b Stipe typically more than 4 mm thick at
apex and fleshy (at times rather firm and
fibrous) 17

4a Spores amyloid 5

4b Spores not amyloid 9

5a Stipe rusty brown below and base strigose
with rusty brown tomentum ....
.... (p. 152) *Xeromphalina*

5b Stipe and stipe base not as above 6

6a Pileus ± granulose from a ± powdery
veil which also often sheaths the stipe at
first .... (p. 96) *Cystoderma*

6b Veil (if present) not as in above choice
.... 7

7a Pileus margin straight at first or only
bent inward slightly .... (p. 120) *Mycena*

7b Pileus margin distinctly incurved to inrolled at first 8

8a Gills adnexed to adnate or short-decurrent .... (p. 89) *Collybia*
and (p. 88) *Clitocybula*

8b Gills decurrent ....
.... (p. 79) *Cantharellula*

9a Spore deposit pale brown; spores echinulate .... (p. 136) *Ripartites*

9b Spore deposit white to buff; spores smooth or ornamented 10

10a Gills flesh color, thick, waxy; spores ornamented (very weakly so on large ellipsoid spores), globose and 8-15 mm diam. .... (p. 102) *Laccaria*

10b Not as above 11

11a Pileus cuticle of differentiated cells (clavate and in a palisade or with various types of projections—often giving a "brush-like" effect); fruit body tough and reviving when moistened (if dextrinoid hairs occur on pileus; see *Crinipellis* p. 95) .... (p. 112) *Marasmius* and (p. 96) *Cyptotrama*

11b Not as in any of the above 3 genera 12

12a Stipe with a prominent pseudorhiza (dig out specimen carefully), and spores 5-8 μm or more broad .... (p. 130) *Oudemansiella*

12b Stipe and spores not as above 13

13a Pileus rubbery in consistency; on wood; stipe soon pubescent and pubescence becoming dark brown .... (p. 100) *Flammulina*

13b Not as above 14

14a Gills decurrent and fruit body ± fleshy to membranous and fragile (see *Mycena* and *Clitocybe* also) .. (p. 127) *Omphalina*

14b Not as above 15

15a Veil present and ± granulose .... (p. 96) *Cystoderma*

15b Not as above 16

16a Fruiting body in some part staining gray to black finally ...... (p. 110) *Lyophyllum*

16b Not staining as above; gills usually adnexed to sinuate or nearly free (if gills are broadly adnate to decurrent see *Clitocybe* and also *Lyophyllum*—the nonstaining species) .... (p. 89) *Collybia*

17a Consistency of fruit body tough and gills serrate at maturity ...... (p. 106) *Lentinus*

17b Fruiting body fleshy to brittle 18

18a Stipe annulate or with an annular zone where veil breaks; veil often in zones or scales beneath the terminal zone or ring 19

18b Stipe not annulate; veil absent to rudimentary 22

19a Annulus double; stipe massive (± 3 cm or more at apex), pointed at base usually .... (p. 80) *Catathelasma*

19b Not as above 20

20a Veil ± granulose as evidenced by the granulose dry pileus and remnants of veil on stipe .... (p. 96) *Cystoderma*

20b Veil fibrillose to cottony; pileus appressed-fibrillose to scaly 21

21a Terrestrial; seldom clustered; spores amyloid (or if veil is double the spores may be non-amyloid) .... (p. 75) *Armillaria*

21b In large clusters, on dead wood (often buried), or parasitic on living tree roots; annulus cottony; mycelium producing black rhizomorphs ....
.... (p. 77) *Armillariella*

22a Spores amyloid (note: large fruit bodies of some narrow-stiped species will key out here) 23

22b Spores non-amyloid 24

23a Pileus glabrous and moist; gills crowded and ± horizontal; stipe strict; cheilocystidia usually sharp-pointed ....
.... (p. 117) *Melanoleuca*

23b Pileus dry and fibrillose to silky or kidglove like; gills usually arcuate; stipe fleshy and not strict; cheilocystidia seldom sharp-pointed ....
.... (p. 107) *Leucopaxillus*

24a Gills flesh-color to violet, thick, waxy; spores globose and echinulate or ellipsoid and weakly ornamented; stipe fibroustough .... (p. 102) *Laccaria*

24b Not as above 25

25a Pileus ± rubbery; stipe at maturity covered over lower area by dark brown pubescence; on wood especially aspen and elm .... (p. 100) *Flammulina*

25b Not as above 26

26a Clearly terrestrial—in arcs, gregarious, or in troops 27

26b On wood or coming from buried wood such as dead roots 30

27a Gills sinuate to adnexed (if adnexed see *Collybia* and *Clitocybe* also) clamps mostly absent .... (p. 137) *Tricholoma*

27b Not as above 28

28a Gills adnate to decurrent, staining black (finally) where injured, or scarcely changing; spores ± globose and with fruit bodies in large clusters ....
.... (p. 110) *Lyophyllum*

28b Not as above 29

29a Gills ± distinctly decurrent ....
.... (p. 81) *Clitocybe*

29b Gills ± adnate to adnexed ....
.... (p. 89) *Collybia*

30a Fruit body yellow to orange; gills crowded, decurrent, phosphorescent when fresh (glowing in the dark); typically in large clusters from buried wood ....
.... (p. 129) *Omphalotus*

30b Not as above 31

31a Stipe with a distinct pseudorhiza arising from buried wood; spores 5-8 μm or more broad .... (p. 130) *Oudemansiella*

31b Not as above 32

32a Yellow colors commonly present but mixed with red, gray etc.; cheilocystidia typically large; pileus cuticle of fibrils the end-cells of which are often clavate to cystidium-like; mostly on wood of conifers .... (p. 147) *Tricholomopsis*

32b Not as above: see some species of *Omphalina*, *Clitocybe* and *Collybia* which are aberrant in some of the features emphasized here.

Armillaria (Fr.) Kummer

Pileus and stipe confluent; veil single or double; gills attached to the stipe but in some species seceding; stipe fleshy; volva absent; spore deposit white or practically so; spores amyloid or if the veil is double the spores may be inamyloid; if an outer veil is present and ± granulose in texture see *Cystoderma*. In *Armillaria* the general aspect of the fruit bodies is that of *Tricholoma*. *Armillaria* contains several very popular edible fungi, the matsutake of the Orient and *A. ponderosa*, the pine mushroom or white matsutake of North America. In Colorado *A. straminea* var. *americana* is popular. The genus contains less than 25 species for North America as currently defined.

KEY TO SPECIES

1a Spores amyloid 2

1b Spores non-amyloid 7

2a Pileus conspicuously scaly with rusty brown scales; on wood of hardwoods ....
.... *A. decorosa* (Pk.) Sm. & Walters

Pileus 3-6 cm, broadly convex to ± plane, margin incurved. Gills close, ± broad, adnexed, white. Stipe 3-7 cm x 6-11 mm, sheathed up to an annular zone, the fibrils of the sheath concolorous with those on the cap. Spores ± 6 x 4 μm, ellipsoid.
Great Lakes area and eastward, not often collected; late summer and fall. Edible (?).

2b Not growing directly from wood 3

3a Fruit bodies white when young. ....
.... see *A. albolanaripes* and *A. straminea*

3b Fruit bodies distinctly colored 4

4a Pileus with conspicuous bright yellow scales; gill trama regular. Fig. 88 ....
.... *A. straminea* (Krombh.) Kummer var. *americana* Mitchel & Smith

Figure 88

Figure 88 *Armillaria straminea*

Pileus 4-18 cm, obtuse then umbonate to convex, appressed fibrillose when young, pigment fading rapidly in sunlight; taste mild. Gills sinuate, close, broad, pallid becoming lemon yellow. Stipe 5-12 x 1.5-2.5 cm, ± equal, smooth and white above annular zone, soon scaly (like pileus) below. Spore deposit white; spores 6-8 x 4-5 μm. Clamp connections present.

Under aspen, Rocky Mountains, often abundant in Colorado, summer. Edible. An albino variant is sometimes found also.

4b   Pileus not scaly as in above choice 5

5a   Pileus when fresh fuscous to gray, no yellow tints present .... A. *fusca* Mitchell & Smith

Pileus 4-7 cm, obtuse to plane, ± glabrous but streaked with wood brown to fuscous fibrils; margin appendiculate, finally the surface appressed-squamulose; taste mild. Gills close, adnexed, white to grayish. Stipe 6-7 cm x 10-15 mm, equal, floccose below the annular zone, veil remnants finally grayish buff. Spores 6-8 x 4-5 μm, strongly amyloid.

Solitary to scattered under spruce, Colorado, not rare but not appearing in quantity. Edibility not known.

5b   Pileus, gills, or stipe showing at least weak yellow tints 6

6a   Pileus margin bright yellow, disc gradually dingy yellow-brown. Fig. 89 .... A. *albolanaripes* Atkinson

Figure 89

Figure 89   *Armillaria albolanaripes*

Pileus 4-12 cm, obtuse to convex-umbonate, subviscid, soon dry, appressed fibrillose (squamulose only in age); taste mild. Gills close, adnexed, broad, white. Stipe 2-8 cm x 9-25 mm, equal, sheathed below annular zone with veil remains, squamules white but with ochraceous to brownish tips. Spores 6-8 x 4-5 μm, weakly amyloid.

Scattered to gregarious under conifers, Pacific Northwest and the Rocky Mountains, summer and fall, not rare (one can find it almost every season). Edible.

6b   Pileus margin ivory yellow to pale olive-buff, disc grayer (near avellaneous in age) .... A. *pitkinensis* Mitchel & Smith

Pileus 4-10 cm, obtuse to convex or plane, slightly viscid, margin appendiculate. Gills white then dingy yellowish, close, adnexed, not staining. Stipe 3-7 x 0.5-2.5 cm, ± equal, with grayish-yellow veil material below the veil line, basal mycelium white. Spores 6-8 x 4-5 μm, weakly amyloid.

Scattered under spruce and fir, after summer rains, Colorado.

7a   Pileus with patches of dark rusty brown to chestnut innate veil material and this continued on the stipe below the annulus. Fig. 90 .... A. *caligata* Viv.

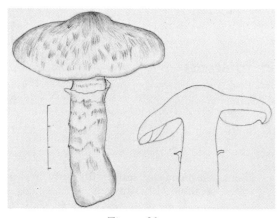

Figure 90

Figure 90   *Armillaria caligata*

Pileus 6-10 cm, broadly convex, rarely with bluish stains near margin, odor fragrant, pungent or lacking. Gills pallid, close, ± adnate. Stipe 4-9 x 1-2 cm, pallid above the annulus or annular zone. Spores 6-8 x 4.5-5.5 μm.

Under hardwoods in the Great Lakes area and eastward, under conifers (but rare) in our western states; sporadic in appearance. Edible. It is closely related to the matsutake of the Orient.

7b Not as above **8**

8a Pileus, gills, and stipe white at first, slowly staining cinnamon; annulus membranous. Fig. 91 .... *A. ponderosa* **Peck**

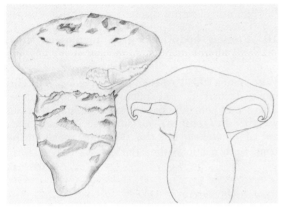

Figure 91

Figure 91 *Armillaria ponderosa*

Pileus 6-15 (20) cm, convex with incurled margin, glabrous to appressed fibrillose; odor not strong but distinctly fragrant. Gills crowded, narrow, adnexed. Stipe 4-10 x 1-3 cm, very hard, firm, unpolished above the annulus, appressed fibrillose with more or less ingrown veil material below. Spores 5-7 x 4.5-5.5 μm, non-amyloid.

Scattered to gregarious under pines and occasionally other conifers, northern United States and in Canada, late summer and fall, often abundant. Edible and choice. In our western states it is known among the orientals as the white matsutake.

8b Pileus viscid at first, color orange, brown, olive and yellow mixed. Fig. 92 ....
.... *A. zelleri* **Stuntz & Smith**

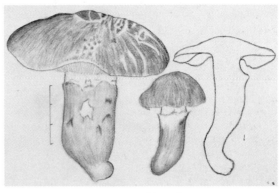

Figure 92

Figure 92 *Armillaria zelleri*

Pileus 5-15 cm, obtuse to expanded-umbonate, appressed fibrillose beneath the slime; context slowly staining orange-brown where cut, taste $\pm$ farinaceous. Gills soon showing rusty brown stains. Stipe 4-13 x 1-3 cm, $\pm$ tapered to a point below, sheathed to the ragged annulus with fibrils like those of the pileus in color. Spores 4-4.5 x 3.5 μm, non-amyloid.

Scattered to gregarious under pine, northern United States and in Canada, abundant in the Pacific Northwest. Not recommended.

Armillariella Karsten

Pileus and stipe confluent, pileus when young fibrillose to squamulose, often somewhat viscid (under the fibrils). Gills close to subdistant, adnate to decurrent. Stipe fibrous to fleshy in age, typically with black rhizomorphs at the base. Spore deposit white to light cream, spores non-amyloid; clamp connections absent. Often fruiting in dense clusters.

While slightly over 20 species have been reported, only two are well known in North America, both are popular, edible mushrooms. *Armillariella* is an example of a genus ambiguous to delimit but distinct nevertheless.

KEY TO SPECIES

1a **Fruiting body with a veil usually leaving a superior annulus on the stipe. Fig. 93** .... *A. mellea* (**Fr.**) **Karsten**

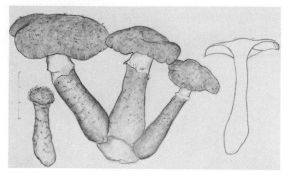

Figure 93

Figure 93 *Armillariella mellea*

Pileus 3-15 cm, obtuse, usually with fibrillose squamules at first, color variable (dark to pale yellow, or honey color to medium brown). Gills adnate to decurrent, staining brown by old age. Stipe 5-15 cm x 6-35 mm, often connate below. Spores 8-10 x 5-6.5 μm.

Common, causing root rot of conifers and hardwoods alike, summer and fall, widely (unfortunately) distributed. Edible but do not eat it raw. It is commonly known as the honey mushroom.

1b **Fruiting body lacking an annulus on stipe; veil absent** .... *A. tabescens* (**Fr.**) **Singer**

With much the "aspect" of *A. mellea* but gills more decurrent, and pileus never squamulose. There has been discussion in the literature as to whether *A. tabescens* was simply a southern variant of *A. mellea*, but this does not appear to be true. Both occur in the South.

Asterophora Ditmar ex S. F. Gray

Agarics parasitic on other mushrooms (especially the Russulaceae) and producing mushroom-like fruiting bodies characteristically with aborted hymenium which produces few if any (in most cases) basidiospores. The hyphae of the fruiting body round off into spores (chlamydospores) characteristic of the species (smooth in one, spiny in the other). We have two species in North America.

On rotted fruiting bodies of species of *Russula* and *Lactarius,* widely distributed; very sporadic in appearance but to be expected in the area east of the Great Plains.

1b **Pileus 1-1.5 (2.5-3) cm, white, soon lilac-gray to pale brownish and appressed silky, with a slight veil. Gills pallid, thick, decurrent, breaking up into chlamydospores 12-15 × 8-10 μm which are smooth; stipe 1-4 cm × 2-3 mm; basidiospores 5-6 × 3-3.5 μm. Fig. 94** .... *A. parasitica* (**Fr.**) **Singer**

KEY TO SPECIES

1a **Pileus 1-2 cm, ± hemispheric, whitish and floccose, soon brown and pulverulent as hyphae form the brown, globose, spiny chlamydospores which are 12-18 μm in diam; stipe 2.5 cm × 3-8 mm; basidiospores seldom formed** .... *A. lycoperdoides* **Ditmar ex S. F. Gray**

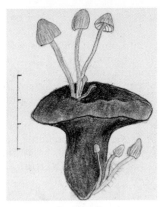

Figure 94

Figure 94 *Asterophora parasitica*

This species is rare in North America. We have one record of it from the Cape Lookout area of Oregon.

Cantharellula Singer

Aspect of fruiting body that of a thin *Cantharellus* or a medium small *Clitocybe;* many of the gills forked; staining reddish in age; spores amyloid; pileus cuticle a cutis; clamp connections present; pileus and stipe confluent. This is a small genus with only a few species.

We treat only 1 species. Fig. 95 ....
.... *C. umbonata* (Fr.) Singer

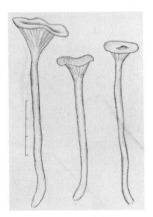

Figure 95

Figure 95 *Cantharellula umbonata*

Pileus 2-4 cm, funnel-shaped at maturity, with a slight central umbo, brownish gray to violaceous gray, dry, pruinose to flocculose, margin often wavy; context staining reddish where cut. Gills decurrent, thickish, narrow, crowded. Stipe 3-8 cm x 4-7 mm, ± equal, pallid to grayish, silky. Spores 9-11 x 3-4.5 μm, subfusoid in profile, deposit white.

Gregarious on beds of hair-capped moss (*Polytrichum*), common and widely distributed, late summer and fall. We have not seen it in "swampy woods" as reported by Kauffman for Michigan. Reported as edible but too small to be of interest.

Catathelasma Lovejoy

Pileus and stipe confluent, firm, fleshy; spore deposit white; spores amyloid, distinctly elongate; veil "double" leaving two rings on the stipe—one below the pileus margin where it touched the stipe and the other just above it; stipe typically narrowed downward; gills decurrent; gill trama at maturity interwoven or weakly bilateral.

Only two species are well known; both are edible but not choice.

KEY TO SPECIES

1a Pileus 15-40 cm broad, viscid at first, dingy brown; spores 11-14 × 4-5.3 μm. Fig. 96. .... *C. imperiale* (Fr.) Singer

Figure 96

Figure 96 *Catathelasma imperiale*

Pileus 12-15 cm in button stages, at times becoming areolate, blackish brown when young; context thick, hard, white, taste sharply farinaceous. Gills narrow becoming broad in age, close, yellowish gradually becoming pale grayish olivaceous. Stipe 12-18 x 6-8 cm, narrowed downward; with a sheath which is membranous and dingy yellow-brown; lower ring gelatinous, upper membranous and striate on its upper surface.

Solitary in old growth conifer stands in the Pacific Northwest, usually one fruiting body is all a collector wants to carry. It fruits in the fall after heavy rains.

1b Pileus 8-20 cm broad, not viscid when young, dull white at first becoming grayish in places in age; spores 9-12 (13) × 4-5 μm. Fig. 97. .... *C. ventricosum* (Pk.) Singer

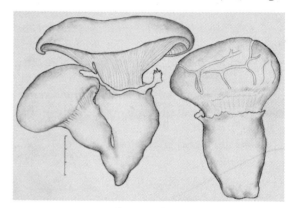

Figure 97

Figure 97 *Catathelasma ventricosum*

Pileus usually areolate in age; context very thick and hard; taste mildly disagreeable. Gills narrow becoming broad, close, whitish. Stipe 6-15 x 3-7 cm, narrowed downward, sunken in the soil; annulus double (as in above), whitish.

Scattered to gregarious under conifers, especially spruce, northern United States and Canada. It is the most frequently collected species in the genus.

Clitocybe (Fr.) Kummer

Spore deposit white to cream color, pinkish buff or truly pink (if the latter, the spores smooth and not angular); pileus and stipe confluent, the gills broadly adnate to decurrent; stipe typically central, fleshy and lacking evidence of a veil; margin of pileus incurved to incurled at first; gill trama of hyphae parallel to interwoven in the fully developed hymenophore.

KEY TO SPECIES

1a Spore deposit white (taken on white paper) 2

1b Spore deposit at least slightly colored (on white paper) 11

2a Growing from the remains of the fruiting body of another fungus (presumably a *Helvella*), the latter reduced to a fleshy mass of tissue at times .... *C. sclerotoidea* (Morse) Bigelow

Pileus 1-4 (4) cm, convex to plane or broadly umbonate, the margin elevated in age at times, canescent, dingy buff to clay-color, often with watery sordid buff spots; context pallid, soft, taste mild. Gills adnate to short decurrent, subdistant, broad, pallid buff darkening to gray or olive-brown. Stipe 2-4 (8) cm x 3-11 (15) mm, central to eccentric, fleshy, matted with white tomentum and watery buff beneath it; fleshy base up to 6 x 4 cm. Spores 8-11 x 3-4 μm, non-amyloid. Pleurocystidia absent.

   Late fall along the Pacific Coast, rather frequent in some areas.

2b Not as above 3

3a Pileus white or whitish at first 4

3b Pileus colored 6

4a Stipe clavate, 1-3 cm at apex; pileus 10-20 cm broad (see *C. irina* also) 10

4b Stipe (3) 5-12 (25) mm thick 5

5a Pileus finely areolate-cracked in age; on lawns, grassy areas, old fields, etc. .... *C. dealbata* (Fr.) Kummer

Pileus 1-4 cm, convex to plane or shallowly depressed, lubricous when wet, discolored to pale alutaceous at times in age; context thin, pallid, taste ± unpleasant. Gills adnate to decurrent, close, ± broad, whitish. Stipe 1.5-4 cm x (1) 3-9 mm, often slightly wider at apex, pliant, sordid at base. Spores 4-5 x 2-3.5 μm, non-amyloid. Pleurocystidia none.

   Gregarious, summer and fall, frequent, very widely distributed. Poisonous, often causing acute perspiration. It is often found growing in with rings of the fairy ring mushroom, and at times is accidentally included in a gathering of the latter.

5b Pileus surface continuous, cap typically with an irregular wavy margin; taste sour and disagreeable; often in dense masses along country roads. Fig. 98 .... *C. dilatata* Pers. ex Karst.

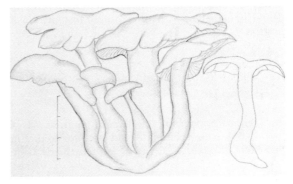

Figure 98

Figure 98   *Clitocybe dilatata*

Pileus 5-15 cm, soon plane or margin uplifted, dry, shining white to dull white, often zoned near the margin. Gills close, narrow, broadly adnate to decurrent, white to buff colored. Stipe 4-12 x 3-10 (25) mm, ± equal, whitish. Spores 4.5-6.5 x 3-3.5 μm. Pleurocystidia none.

Abundant, Pacific Northwest in the fall. Not recommended.

6a   Pileus pinkish tan to vinaceous cinnamon **7**

6b   Pileus olive-brown to fuscous or drab 9

7a   Pileus (4) 7-30 cm broad, pinkish tan at first, finally funnel-shaped .... *C. gibba* var. *maxima* (**Fr.**) **Bigelow**

Pileus ± plane then depressed and finally broadly funnel-shaped, margin often lobed, surface soon dry and unpolished and ± fibrillose, often scaly around the disc; taste mild. Gills narrow, close, decurrent, pale buff. Stipe 3-15 x 1-2.5 (3) cm, clavate or equal, solid, glabrous becoming fibrillose-striate, whitish to pale buff. Spores 6.5-8.5 (10) x 4.5-6 μm, non-amyloid. Pleurocystidia none.

Solitary to gregarious, under hardwoods, summer and fall, infrequent. Edible. The best fruiting seen to date was below Lake Mills on the Elwha River, Olympic Mountains of Washington.

7a   Pileus 3-8 cm broad **8**

8a   Pileus vinaceous cinnamon; spores 4-5 × 3.5-4 μm, echinulate and non-amyloid. Fig. 99 .... *C. inversa* (**Fr.**) **Gillet**

Figure 99

Figure 99   *Clitocybe inversa*

Pileus plano-depressed, then funnel-shaped, often with watery spots in the depression; context thin, taste mild. Gills close, narrow, decurrent, pale pinkish cinnamon. Stipe 3-5 cm x 5-9 mm, slightly clavate or equal, cortex tough, whitish becoming orange-rufous in age. Pleurocystidia none.

Gregarious in conifer and mixed forests, widely distributed in northern areas and especially in the Pacific Northwest.

8b   Pileus pinkish cinnamon to pinkish tan; spores 6-8 (10) × 4-5 (6) μm, smooth, non-amyloid .... *C. gibba* (**Fr.**) **Kummer var.** *gibba*

Pileus soon funnel-shaped, glabrous, becoming diffracted scaly; context whitish, taste mild. Gills long-decurrent, thin, crowded, narrow, readily separable from pileus. Stipe 3-7 cm x 4-12 mm, equal to ± clavate, base with copious tomentum, glabrous, appressed innately fibrillose (under a lens), whitish to pale flesh-color. Pleurocystidia none.

Common, usually under hardwoods, July to October, Great Lakes region eastward and southward, not so common in the Northwest. Edible.

9a   Stipe 2-6 cm long and about as thick; becoming brownish where bruised .... *C. crassa* **Bigelow**

Pileus 4-15 cm, convex to ± plane, surface dry and heavily fibrillose, gray-brown; context thick, tough, taste mild. Gills short-decurrent, broad (to

13 mm), yellowish then finally pale tan. Stipe bulbous at base, whitish at first, heavily fibrillose (but veil absent). Spores 5.5-7 x 4-5 μm, non-amyloid. Pleurocystidia none.

June and July, under spruce, Salmon River region of central Idaho, apparently rare.

9b **Stipe 4-10 (12) mm thick at apex, clavate; not staining brown where injured. Fig. 100.**
.... *C. clavipes* **(Fr.) Kummer**

Figure 100

Figure 100 *Clitocybe clavipes*

Pileus 2-10 cm, plane with a slight umbo, margin soon elevated, glabrous, often mottled with watery spots, olive-brown to gray-brown, often pallid at margin; context watery and flaccid, odor fragrant at times, taste mild. Gills decurrent, close to sub-distant, narrow (finally fairly broad), white becoming weakly yellowish. Stipe 1-3.5 cm broad at base, fibrillose-streaked above, typically paler than pileus. Spores 6-8.5 x 3.5-5 μm.

Common under conifers, especially in plantations of white pine, fall, widely distributed. Edible but some people experience the *Coprinus atramentarius* type of intoxication if an alcoholic beverage is consumed shortly before or after the meal.

10a **Pileus long remaining white. Fig. 101** ....
.... *C. candida* **Bresadola**

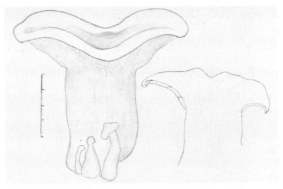

Figure 101

Figure 101 *Clitocybe candida*

Pileus 8-20 cm, flat at first, the margin inrolled, finally shallowly and broadly funnel-shaped, sulcate-grooved at edge at times, dry, surface matted-fibrillose; disc ± sordid in age; context thin, odor ± farinaceous. Gills crowded, decurrent to short-decurrent, becoming yellowish, separable from pileus. Stipe 4-9 x 1.5-3.5 cm ± equal to clavate, surface matted fibrillose, white, finally pale buff. Spores 6-8.5 x 3-4.5 μm, weakly amyloid, smooth. Pleurocystidia none.

Gregarious in northern hardwood forests, often abundant during wet seasons. It is more frequent than reports indicate.

10b **Pileus whitish at first but soon dingy buff to brownish, finally colored overall; 10-45 cm broad, margin often grooved. Fig. 102** ....
.... *C. gigantea* **(Fr.) Quélet**

Figure 102

Figure 102 *Clitocybe gigantea*

Pileus glabrous, in age often rimulose to squamulose over the disc; context whitish, soon flaccid, taste mild to disagreeable. Gills ± decurrent, crowded, thin, narrow but 5-13 mm broad, some of them forked, soon pale buff and finally alutaceous. Stipe 4-10 x 2-5 cm, ± equal, tomentose at base, surface fibrillose-striate, fibrils becoming dull brown on the paler ground color. Spores 6-8 x 3-4.5 μm, weakly amyloid, smooth. Pleurocystidia none.

Gregarious to scattered or in fairy rings, open woods and waste areas (habitat rather generalized), widely distributed but not commonly collected. The cap is so thin in relation to its width that it usually becomes badly broken when collected.

11a Pileus white to whitish at first 12

11b Pileus colored 13

12a In dense clusters in hardwood forests; stipe ± equal. Fig. 103 ...... C. subconnexa Murrill

Figure 103

Figure 103 *Clitocybe subconnexa*

Pileus 3-9 cm, convex then ± plane with margin undulating, at first shining white and satiny, slowly discoloring; context brittle, white, taste pleasant in fresh young caps, astringent to metallic (unpleasant) in old ones. Gills adnate then short-decurrent; crowded, narrow, separable from pileus, white but soon discolored dingy buff. Stipe 3-10 cm x 5-10 (20) mm, ± equal, dry, whitish silky, discolored in age. Spore deposit pale vinaceous buff. Spores 4.5-6 x 3-3.5 μm, non-amyloid, minutely roughened. Pleurocystidia none.

Common in the hardwood forests of the Great Lakes area eastward and southward, late summer and fall. Edible, but use fresh young fruiting bodies and eat them the day you collect them. If kept overnight either cooked or raw the taste becomes ± disagreeable.

12b Not as above 13

13a In open grasslands, often in fairy rings, Great Plains and Rocky Mountains below timberline .... C. praemagna (Murr.) Bigl. & Sm.

Pileus 10-30 cm, convex, dry, dull, glabrous, becoming areolate-rimose, becoming light brown in age; context thick, white, taste mild. Gills close to subdistant, broad (up to 1.2 cm), whitish. Stipe 3-7 cm x 1.5-5 cm, ± equal, at times with a marginate bulb, white or spotted brown, fibrillose (but veil lacking). Spores 6-8 x 4-5 μm, non-amyloid, roughened. Pleurocystidia none.

Apparently a species of our western grass lands and adjacent habitats such as sage brush areas; June to September. Edible; look for it after periods of heavy thunderstorms.

13b Habitat not as above 14

14a Gills white and scarcely changing (yellowish finally); spore deposit pale yellow. Fig. 104. .... C. robusta Peck

Figure 104

Figure 104 *Clitocybe robusta*

Pileus 5-17 cm, convex then broadly convex, surface with a satin-like lustre, tacky to touch when wet, pale dingy buff in age; context thick in disc, white, taste ± rancid-disagreeable. Gills adnate then short-decurrent, close to crowded, narrow at first (finally broad), white then cream color. Stipe 4-10 x 1-3.5 cm, bulbous to clavate or finally ± equal, whitish, ± fibrillose-striate. Spores 6-8 x 3-4 (5) μm, non-amyloid.

    Common during wet fall seasons in the Great Lakes area and eastward as well as southward; less abundant in the conifer forests of our western states. Not edible because of the flavor.

14b Gills soon grayish buff to vinaceous gray (dingy); spore deposit pale vinaceous buff to whitish .... *C. irina* (Fr.) Bigl. & Sm.

Pileus 4-13 cm, obtuse then expanded-umbonate, subviscid but soon dry, at times watery-spotted, soon dingy vinaceous buff; flesh thick, soft, odor usually fragrant, taste mild. Gills broadly adnate to ± decurrent, narrow to ± broad (finally), close. Stipe 4-8 x 1-2.5 cm, clavate to (finally) ± equal, rough in age, somewhat fibrillose with innate fibrils (no veil), becoming dingy like the gills. Spores 7-9 (10) x 4-5 μm, non-amyloid, faintly roughened. Pleurocystidia none.

    Gregarious or in fairy rings, on soil rich in lignicolous debris, late summer and fall, widely distributed, common. Edible but apparently a few people are allergic to it.

15a Spore deposit bright pink; gills very crowded and narrow; pileus dingy vinaceous brown. Fig. 105 .... *C. martiorum* Favre

Figure 105

Figure 105 *Clitocybe martiorum*

Pileus 3-6 cm, broadly convex, hoary at first, soon naked, dull cinnamon to vinaceous brown, often rivulose, subzonate; context dingy vinaceous buff, taste ± disagreeable. Gills short-decurrent, not readily separable from cap, dingy vinaceous cinnamon. Stipe 3-8 cm x 8-12 mm, ± equal, solid, ± concolor with pileus; no veil present. Spores 4.5-5 x 2-3 μm, non-amyloid. Pleurocystidia none.

    Gregarious on rich humus, hardwood and conifer forests alike, abundant at times in pine plantations; fall, widely distributed but seldom reported.

15b Not as above 16

16a Spore deposit pale vinaceous buff; pileus deep vinaceous brown; gills grayish brown .... *C. subalpina* Bigelow & Smith

Pileus 4-12 cm, soon plane or depressed, faintly hoary at first, soon naked, becoming minutely appressed-squamulose, the context colored like the pileus, taste usually disagreeable. Gills crowded, adnate to decurrent, close, fairly broad. Stipe 3-14 x 1-2.5 cm, ± narrowed downward, base with rhizomorphs, ± wood brown (gray brown). Spores 4.5-5.5 x 2.8-4 μm, non-amyloid, roughened slightly. Pleurocystidia none.

Caespitose in soil by the side of a road, conifers nearby, late summer and fall, Pacific Northwest. Edibility not tested. Apparently rare.

16b Not as above **17**

17a Spores amyloid; cap minutely scaly and brownish ochraceous; on wood of conifers. Fig. 106 .... *C. ectypoides* (Pk.) Sacc.

Figure 106

Figure 106 *Clitocybe ectypoides*

Pileus 2-7 (10) cm, soon with disc depressed and margin spreading to uplifted; finely virgate with dark appressed fibrils; context thin, odor and taste mild. Gills decurrent, subdistant to distant, narrow (± 4 mm), some forked, yellowish. Stipe 2-6.5 cm x 2-9 mm, eccentric at times, ± honey-yellow, staining brown to olivaceous on handling. Spores 6.5-8 (9) x 3.5-5 (6) μm, smooth. Pleurocystidia rare and filamentose, 2-5 μm wide.

Common but seldom in quantity, Pacific Northwest, Great Lakes area and both eastward and southward following the distribution of hemlock, late summer and fall. Probably common in Canada.

17b Spores not amyloid **18**

18a Odor strong of anise; pileus with olive to greenish gray tints to pea-green at least when young. Fig. 107 .... *C. odora* (Fr.) Kummer

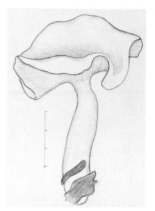

Figure 107

Figure 107 *Clitocybe odora*

Pileus 2-8 (10) cm, convex to plane, margin becoming elevated and undulating, surface finely matted fibrillose; context thin, pliant, whitish, taste of anise or mild. Gills adnate at first, close to crowded, 2-4 mm broad, pallid. Stipe 2-6 (9) x 4-10 (16) mm, ± equal or either (or both) ends enlarged, buff colored, darker if wet. Spores (5) 6-9 x 3.5-5 μm, non-amyloid, smooth. Pleurocystidia absent.

18b Lacking an anise-like odor **19**

19a Spore deposit distinctly pale yellow **20**

19b Spore deposit pinkish buff to vinaceous **21**

20a Pileus gray; stipe 2.5-4 cm thick. Fig. 108. .... *C. nebularis* (Fr.) Kummer

Figure 108

Figure 108 *Clitocybe nebularis*

Pileus 6-15 cm, convex-umbonate to broadly expanded, disc depressed at times, ± virgate; context white, odor and taste disagreeable. Gills short-decurrent, close, broad, white then yellowish. Stipe 8-10 cm. long, ± enlarged downward, fleshy-fibrous, fibrils olive-brown on a pallid ground color, dingy from handling. Spores 5.5-8 x 3.5-4.5 μm, non-amyloid. Pleurocystidia none.

Gregarious on humus in conifer and mixed forests, August to December, common in the Pacific Northwest, less frequent east of the Great Plains. Edible but not palatable.

**20b Pileus ferruginous to reddish cinnamon; stipe 5-9 mm thick. Fig. 109 ....
.... C. sinopica (Fr.) Kummer**

Figure 109

Figure 109 *Clitocybe sinopica*

Pileus 2-7 cm, convex-depressed, soon nearly plane and finally broadly funnel-shaped, often with minute squamules over the disc, margin appressed-fibrillose; context with a strong farinaceous taste. Gills short-decurrent, ± equal or apex enlarged, eccentric at times; concolor with cap. Spores 7-9 (10.5) x 4.5-6 μm, non-amyloid Pleurocystidia none.

Solitary to scattered on naked soil, along fire lines, lanes, paths, etc. May to October, widely distributed.

21a Stipe 2-8 cm × (1.5) 3-8 mm; gills subdistant .... C. tarda Peck

Pileus 2-7 cm, soon broadly funnel-shaped; margin translucent-striate when moist, color various shades of violaceous to violaceous brown or vinaceous brown progressively as it ages; context thin, odor and taste mild. Gills moderately broad, ± vinaceous drab. Stipe ± equal, at first with a thin coating of whitish fibrils, ± vinaceous drab over all in age (color dingy and variable). Spores 6-8 (10) x 3.5-5 (5.5) μm, roughened slightly, non-amyloid. Pleurocystidia absent.

Clustered to gregarious on lawns, piles of organic debris such as old haystacks and sawdust piles, summer and fall, widely distributed.

21b Stipe 1-3 cm thick; gills crowded 22

**22a Pileus 6-15 cm, pallid with faint lilac to vinaceous tints and the gills pallid violaceous ......
.... C. glaucocana (Fr.) Bigl. & Sm.**

Pileus broadly convex, then plane, at times with a slight umbo; context white tinged vinaceous, odor and taste pleasant. Gills narrow, becoming pallid grayish vinaceous. Stipe 5-9 cm long, enlarged downward; surface floccose-scabrous, pallid (about concolor with gills). Spores 5.5-7.5 x 3-4.5 μm, roughened, non-amyloid. Pleurocystidia none.

Gregarious to cespitose in cold cedar swamps or along roads where organic material was used as a fill, Michigan and Washington. Probably common but seldom recognized. Edible.

22b Pileus 4-15 cm, distinctly violet at first, then violet gray and finally vinaceous brown; gills concolor with cap at first. Fig. 110 .... *C. nuda* (**Fr.**) **Bigl. & Sm.**

Figure 110

Figure 110   *Clitocybe nuda*

Pileus 4-12 cm, convex with margin inrolled, becoming plane with the margin still inrolled, glabrous, smooth, often lubricous when young and fresh; context violaceous at first, fading to pallid, odor pleasant, taste mild. Gills adnexed to sinuate, narrow. Stipe 3-6 (10) cm long, concolorous with pileus or paler, clavate to bulbous becoming ± equal; surface ± fibrillose to scurfy; veil absent. Spores 5.5-8 x 3.5-5 μm, non-amyloid, roughened slightly. Pleurocystidia absent.

Common and widely distributed and collected for food. It grows on organic matter in the soil but especially on compost piles and the like; late summer and fall, often in quantity. Edible. Commonly known as blewits.

Clitocybula (Singer) Métrod

Pileus and stipe confluent; spore deposit white; spores amyloid; stipe slender and fragile; pileus surface streaked from dark radial fibrils to somewhat furfuraceous; cheilocystidia usually numerous; veils absent.

About a half dozen species occur in the North Temperate zone. The genus seems hardly distinct from *Mycena*. Its recognition here is tentative.

We treat only 1 species. Fig. 111 .... *C. familia* (**Peck**) **Singer**

Figure 111

Figure 111   *Clitocybula familia*

Pileus 2-4 cm, convex to nearly plane, glabrous, moist, fuligineous (gray); margin incurved then spreading and in age lacerated; taste slightly disagreeable. Gills crowded, narrow, adnate then seceding, cinereous (ash gray) to pallid. Stipe 4-8 cm x 2-3.5 mm, fragile, gray, finely pubescent, base white-mycelioid. Spores 3.5-4.5 μm, ± globose, amyloid. Pleurocystidia and cheilocystidia none. Pileus cuticle a cutis from which clavate pileocystidia arise. Clamp connections present.

In large clusters, mostly on conifer logs, late summer and fall, often in great abundance, widely distributed. Listed as edible.

Collybia (Fr.) Kummer

Pileus centrally stipitate, thin-fleshed and pliant, often reviving somewhat when moistened, margin usually incurved or inrolled at first; stipe cartilaginous, often pubescent, typically thin and fairly pliant; lamellae broadly adnate to nearly free, often crowded and narrow; spore deposit white to creamy yellow or pinkish buff; cuticle of pileus typically of appressed filamentous hyphae often with clamp connections; spores non-amyloid or rarely amyloid, smooth; gill trama regular.

Certain species with a cellular cuticle are included here for historical reasons. Their fruit bodies are not marasmioid. As far as systematists are concerned, *Collybia* as a genus is in a state of flux and name changing is to be expected in the near future. We have elected to use names that are found in the general literature. Our treatment here in no way reflects our opinions on the phylogeny of the group as a whole. In the following key amyloidity of the spores is mentioned only for those species in which the spores are amyloid.

KEY TO SPECIES

1a Stipe with a distinct pseudorhiza 2

1b Stipe not deeply rooting by a pseudorhiza 4

2a Stipe 10-16 mm thick; odor rather heavy and aromatic; spores 5-5.5-4.5-5 μm. Fig. 112 .... *C. subsulcatipes* Smith

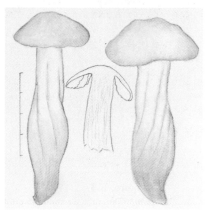

Figure 112

Figure 112 *Collybia subsulcatipes*

Pileus 5-8 cm, obtuse with an inrolled margin, becoming umbonate with a spreading margin, moist, glabrous, when moist slightly translucent-striate, dull vinaceous brown to vinaceous-pink, in age pale vinaceous buff over margin and opaque; context thin, concolorous with pileus surface, taste mild. Gills close, becoming subdistant, broad (± 1 cm) and somewhat ventricose, narrowly adnate, pale grayish pink, thick, edges even. Stipe 6-10 cm long, tapered down to the pseudorhiza, solid and fibrous, colored like pileus above, becoming dark vinaceous brown from base upward, unpolished, longitudinally grooved.

Solitary to gregarious on humus under conifers, Pacific Northwest, fall, infrequent. Edibility not known.

2b Stipe typically 2-6 (10) mm thick; odor lacking 3

3a Under coastal redwoods, California, fall and winter. Fig. 113 .... *C. umbonata* Peck

Figure 113

Figure 113 *Collybia umbonata*

Pileus (2) 5-10 (17) cm, obtuse to convex becoming plane and with a conspicuous conic umbo, surface glabrous, moist, hygrophanous, chestnut brown to russet or tawny, fading in streaks to pale tan or clay-color. Gills broad, close, deeply adnexed, pale tan to vinaceous-buff, rarely with brownish spots. Stipe 5-15 cm x (3) 6-12 (20) mm, with a pseudorhiza up to 30 cm long, cartilaginous, surface unpolished, pale buff to alutaceous, often twisted striate. Spores 5-6 x 3 μm. Pleurocystidia 57-86 x 9-15 μm, very abundant.

Solitary to scattered, common in the range of the coastal redwood. Edible?

3b   Under hardwoods in Great Lakes and eastern North American areas; fruiting during May to early July .... *C. hygrophoroides* Peck

Pileus 2-5 cm, conic becoming campanulate, glabrous, moist, hygrophanous, dark reddish to reddish brown becoming a reddish tan and fading to isabelline or pale dingy clay-color, margin straight at first; odor not distinctive. Gills close, almost free, fairly broad, becoming ventricose, white at first, flushed dingy vinaceous pink in age, edges becoming eroded. Stipe 5-12 cm x 2-6 mm, deeply rooting, often twisted-striate, pruinose and reddish pallid above, white tomentose at ground line. Spores 5.5-7 x 3-3.5 μm. Pleurocystidia 50-70 x 4-7 μm, ± aciculate to narrowly fusoid.

Scattered to gregarious in low hardwoods, infrequent, late spring. Edible?

4a   Gills narrow, crowded and persistently lilac to violaceous; spores 4-5 $\times$ 2.5-3 μm, amyloid .... *C. myriadophylla* Peck

Pileus 2-5 cm, plano-convex, with inrolled margin, becoming plane or finally with uplifted margin, glabrous, moist, dull violaceous brown becoming dull cinnamon, when faded dingy pale buff, opaque at all stages; context thin, pliant, odor and taste ± mild. Gills adnate, very crowded. Stipe 1-5 cm long, 1-3 mm thick, equal, ± silky-pruinose, pliant, concolorous with gills above.

On rotting wood of hardwoods and conifers, spring and summer. Widely distributed but common in the Great Lakes region, infrequent in Colorado.

4b   Not with lilac gills and amyloid spores 5

5a   Gills dark fuscous brown, staining olive with KOH; pileus about 1-4 cm broad .... *C. alcalivirens* Singer

Pileus broadly convex with margin incurved, plane or margin recurved, glabrous, blackish brown to burnt umber (reddish fuscous) fading to dingy vinaceous brown, opaque at all times, margin wavy in age. Context thin, pliant, concolorous with surface, taste very bitter, odor none, dark olive in both KOH and in $FeSO_4$. Gills close, narrow, adnate, concolorous with pileus. Stipe 5-6 cm x 2-3 mm, often flattened above, unpolished, bases covered with dark burnt-umber, mycelium. Spores 6-7 x 3-3.5 μm, white in deposit.

Solitary to gregarious on very rotten wood of conifers, late spring to fall, not rare in the Great Lakes area but seldom collected. Not edible.

5b   Gills white, yellowish, vinaceous or (in *C. racemosa*) gray 6

6a   Pileus 3-12 mm broad; fruit body on blackened remains of a dead decomposed mushroom fruiting body 7

6b   Pileus regularly 1 cm or more broad; on wood or humus 8

7a Stipe with several horizontally projecting short branches. Fig. 114 ....
.... *C. racemosa* **(Fr.) Quélet**

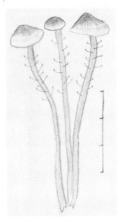

Figure 114

Figure 114 *Collybia racemosa*

Pileus 3-10 mm, conic to convex, becoming plano-umbonate or broadly convex, surface dry, opaque, innately silky, dark drab (or with a paler margin); odor and taste slight. Gills ± broad, deeply adnexed, close, brownish gray. Stipe 4-6 mm thick, watery gray inside; horizontal branches bearing asexual spores (conidia). Basidiospores 4-5 x 2 μm.

On decayed remains of mushroom fruiting bodies, particularly in the Pacific Northwest. It differs from *C. tuberosa* and similar species in color and in having branches on the stipe.

7b Stipe lacking lateral branches; growing from a sclerotium. Fig. 115 ....
.... *C. tuberosa* **(Fr.) Quélet**

Figure 115

Figure 115 *Collybia tuberosa*

Pileus (3) 5-10 mm, convex becoming broadly convex to plane, rarely ± umbonate, glabrous but unpolished, whitish or only very weakly tinted or discolored buff. Gills pallid, close, narrow, adnate. Stipe 1-3 cm x ± 1 mm, whitish, equal, often flexuous, unpolished, attached to an apple-seed-like sclerotium (red-brown to black). Spores 4-5.5 μ 2-3 μm.

On remains of old mushroom fruiting bodies in which the sclerotia are imbedded. Hence the fruiting bodies are found in a very restricted small area. If no sclerotia can be found, one most likely has *Collybia cirrhata* (Pers.) Quélet. If sclerotia are present and are ± globular and ochraceous to tan in color one has *C. cookei* (Bres.) J. D. Arnold. All three species have very wide distribution at least over the Northern Hemisphere.

8a Fruiting bodies in dense clusters (as in a bundle) on old conifer logs, etc.; pileus deep red-brown to vinaceous brown fading to pallid; spores 5-6.5 × 2-2.5 μm. Fig. 116 ....
.... *C. acervata* **(Fr.) Kummer**

Figure 116

Figure 116 *Collybia acervata*

Pileus (0.5) 1-4 cm, convex to obtuse, becoming broadly convex, margin long remaining inrolled, glabrous, moist, ± hygrophanous, lubricous at first, dark vinaceous brown gradually paler and when faded ± vinaceous buff or paler; context thin, pliant, taste bitter when cooked. Gills crowded, narrow, rounded at stipe, whitish to dingy pale vinaceous, edges even. Stipe 8-12 (2) cm x 3-5 mm, equal, hollow, glabrous but fibrillose over lower area, concolorous with or darker than pileus. Spore deposit white.

Common in conifer country in North America, summer and fall. Edible but not palatable.

8b Fruiting bodies if clustered not in compact bundles **9**

9a Fruiting body soon developing reddish stains **10**

9b Not developing reddish stains **11**

10a Pileus white at first, odor slight. Fig. 117 .... *C. maculata* **(Fr.) Quél. var.** *maculata*

Figure 117

Figure 117 *Collybia maculata* var. *maculata*

Pileus 4-10 cm, obtuse then convex to nearly plane or umbonate, canescent then naked and whitish becoming pale tan and at times ± scrobiculate, soon stained dingy reddish; context white, firm, taste bitter. Gills crowded, narrow to ± broad (finally), adnate, pale pinkish buff to whitish, soon reddish stained. Spores 4.5-5.5 (6) x 3.5-4 (5) μm, typically subglobose.

Solitary to clustered on conifer wood, common, northern United States and southern Can-

ada, late summer and fall. Var. *moschata* Lovejoy has a strong odor of musk; var. *occidentalis* Smith has spores 5-7 x 3.5-4.5 μm; and var. *scorzonerea* (Fr.) Gillet has yellow gills and is by some workers regarded as a distinct species. Not palatable.

10b Pileus deep vinaceous brown at first; odor resembling that of benzaldehyde. Fig. 118. .... *C. oregonensis* **Smith**

Figure 118

Figure 118 *Collybia oregonensis*

Pileus 5-10 cm, very broadly convex becoming plane, subviscid, finally pale pinkish buff (pallid); taste bitterish. Gills close to crowded, narrow, ivory-yellow, pallid in age and then often stained reddish brown, edges eroded. Stipe 6-12 cm x 10-16 mm, equal to subventricose, ± pointed below and with attached rhizomorphs, white, dingy in age, staining reddish, stuffed becoming hollow. Spores 6-8 x 3.5-4 μm.

Solitary to scattered on conifer logs and debris, Pacific Northwest, fall, infrequent. Edible?

11a Pileus dark bay-red at first, fading through ferruginous to pinkish buff over margin; spores 3-5 μm, globose. Fig. 119 .... *C. badiialba* **Murrill**

Figure 119

Figure 119 *Collybia badiialba*

Pileus 2-7 cm, obtuse to expanded-umbonate, lubricous, color slowly becoming rusty chocolate brown before fading; odor none, taste mild to bitterish. Gills narrow to moderately broad (finally), crowded, adnexed, edges serrulate, faces shining white. Stipe 5-11 cm x 5-9 mm, ± equal, abruptly narrowed at base and rhizomorphs present, toward the apex longitudinally striate, color pale pinkish buff or more dingy, surface unpolished.

Solitary to scattered on conifer wood, rarely on hardwood, Pacific Northwest, fall, not rare.

11b Not as above **12**

12a Pileus whitish at first; gills staining yellowish; stipe short (1-4 cm); spores 4-5 × 3-4 μm; on conifer logs and debris .... *C. bakerensis* **Smith**

Pileus 2-4 cm, broadly convex, in age ± plane or with a low umbo, glabrous, moist, appearing appressed fibrillose under a lens when faded, with a flush of vinaceous at times; context 3-4 mm thick, watery white; odor and taste mild. Gills very narrow and crowded, short-decurrent, white to flushed vinaceous. Stipe (2) 3-5 mm thick, equal, hollow, pliant, white above, dingy vinaceous below, thinly white-fibrillose at first.

Solitary to scattered on rotting conifer logs, Pacific Northwest, fall, not common.

12b Not as above **13**

13a Stipe with short white pubescence over lower two-thirds **14**

13b Stipe glabrous to unpolished except for near the base **16**

14a Odor and taste of crushed flesh ± like garlic or more disagreeable; pileus 2-7 cm broad .... *C. polyphylla* **(Pk.) Singer**

Pileus convex, soon plane or with margin uplifted, glabrous, dry to moist, disc dull cinnamon to vinaceous brown, margin soon whitish and edge lacerated in age; context pliant, white. Gills very crowded, free or barely attached, narrow, white, edges even. Stipe 3-7 cm x (1) 2-5 (6) mm, ± equal, pliant, evenly covered by white short tomentum, with a mass of white mycelium at base, pinkish brown color showing through the tomentum near base. Spores 5-6 x 3 μm.

Gregarious to clustered on hardwood debris and leaf mats, Great Lakes area and eastern North America, common at times, summer and fall. Edible?

14b Not with a garlic-like odor and/or taste **15**

15a Gills close to subdistant and moderately broad; spores 1.5-2.5 μm wide (very narrow) .... *C. cylindrospora* **Kauffman**

Pileus 4-7 cm, obtuse to broadly convex when expanded, ± plane or with a low umbo, in age wavy or lobed at the margin, striatulate when moist, pale yellow to pale buff becoming dingy yellow-brown, fading to pale ochraceous, odor and taste not distinctive. Gills adnate, pallid, rarely with rusty brown stains, pliant, edges even. Stipe 5-10 (12) cm long, 4-8 mm thick, twisted-striate to furrowed, hollow, pliant, clay-color below, paler above, base strigose and with numerous rhizomorphs. Spores 5-6 μm long.

Clustered to gregarious on debris of alder and cottonwood and in conifer forests, Pacific Northwest, fall, not common.

15b Gills very crowded and narrow; spores 3-3.5 μm wide. Fig. 120 .... *C. confluens* **(Fr.) Kummer**

Figure 120

Figure 120   *Collybia confluens*

Pileus 2-6 cm, convex with margin incurved, soon nearly plane with margin undulating, flaccid, glabrous, faintly striatulate before fading, dull reddish brown to ± crust-brown when moist, pale buff to pallid when faded, surface becoming rather uneven; context thin and tough; odor and taste mild. Gills scarcely reaching the stipe, pallid, edges even. Stipe 5-10 cm x 2-6 mm, ± equal, often compressed, tough, reddish beneath a dense whitish pubescence, sometimes grooved, base with floccose mycelium. Spores 6-8 μm long.

In clusters or gregarious on mats of fallen hardwood leaves, common both in the United States and Canada, summer and fall after heavy rains. Reported as edible, but the consistency is tough.

16a Spore deposit yellowish. Fig. 121 ....
.... *C. butyracea* (**Fr.**) **Quélet**

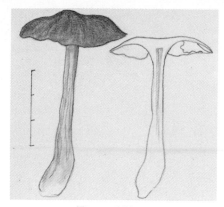

Figure 121

Figure 121   *Collybia butyracea*

Pileus 3-7 cm, obtuse to convex to broadly umbonate, glabrous, lubricous, dark reddish brown, gradually paler to pale reddish tan, consistency rather soft; context watery fresh, odor and taste not distinctive. Gills ± adnexed, close to crowded, becoming only moderately broad, pallid, edges crenulate. Stipe 3-8 cm x 4-8 mm, ± equal to a slightly enlarged base, longitudinally striate, ± glabrous to mycelioid at base, pale tan to honeycolor. Spores 6-7 x 3-3.5 μm.

Scattered to gregarious under conifers, common in pine plantations, fall, northern United States and adjacent Canada. A dark gray variant (f. *asema* (Fr.) Sing.) occurs in the Pacific Northwest in addition to the type form. Both are edible and fairly popular.

16b Spore deposit white **17**

17a Pileus rusty to tawny brown when fresh. Fig. 122 .... *C. dryophila* (**Fr.**) **Kummer**

Figure 122

Figure 122 *Collybia dryophila*

Pileus 2.4-5 (7) cm, broadly convex, margin inrolled, surface smooth, glabrous, moist, rusty brown to tawny or finally ± ochraceous; odor and taste not distinctive. Gills crowded, ± adnexed, white to pallid, edges even and not stain-

ing. Stipe 4-7 cm x 3-7 mm, hollow, cartilaginous, glabrous, unpolished; paler than pileus, base with numerous rhizomorphs. Spores 5-6 x 3 μm.

Scattered to clustered on wood and lignicolous debris such as sawdust piles, spring, summer and fall, common in North America. An early spring variant has bright yellow gills. The typical variety is a popular edible mushroom.

17b Pileus pale dingy yellow or disc with a tinge of cinnamon; stipe attached to leaves by a mycelial pad .... *C. strictipes* **Peck**

Pileus 3-7 cm, broadly convex to plane with incurved margin, merely ± plane in age, glabrous, moist, hygrophanous, margin slightly striate before fading; odor and taste mild. Gills crowded, ± adnexed, narrow to only moderately broad, white to pallid, not spotting. Stipe 2-6 cm x 3-6 mm, equal, strict, hollow, at times twisted-striate, pruinose, usually a dull translucent white. Spores 6-7.5 (8) x 3-3.5 μm.

Gregarious on fallen hardwood leaves, late summer and fall, Great Lakes area eastward and southward, abundant at times. Reported as edible.

Crinipellis Patouillard

This genus is aptly characterized as containing species resembling *Marasmius* species but differs in having pseudoamyloid hairs over the surface of the cap. The fruiting bodies are small, often inserted directly on the substrate, revive when moistened, and have non-amyloid spores. In the past the species have been placed in *Collybia* or *Marasmius*. This is a small genus of less than two dozen species.

We treat only 1 species Fig. 123 .... *C. campanella* (**Pk.**) **Singer**

Figure 123

Figure 123 *Crinipellis campanella*

Pileus 1-2 cm, campanulate, chestnut brown to ferruginous, densely fibrillose with long hairs, margin ± fimbriate, dry, pliant. Gills narrow, close, white, free. Stipe 1-3 cm x 1-1.5 mm, ferruginous like the pileus, densely pubescent over all. Spores 8-9 x 4-4.5 μm.

On twigs of conifers (the lower branches but well off the ground) during long periods of high humidity, summer and fall, not rare but seldom collected, northern United States and Canada.

Cyptotrama Singer

Pileus dry and unpolished, pubescent under a lens, confluent with stipe; gills ± distant, adnate; spore deposit white; spores non-amyloid; gill trama bilateral; habit collybioid; clamp connections present. Less than a dozen species are known in this genus, and most of them are tropical or subtropical.

We treat only 1 species Fig. 124 .... *C. chrysopeplum* (**Berk. & Curt.**) **Singer**

Figure 124

Figure 124 *Cyptotrama chrysopeplum*

Pileus 5-20 mm, convex to plane, margin sulcate; color lemon yellow to golden yellow over all but the gills. Gills broad, subdistant, thickish, adnate to decurrent, white to yellow. Stipe 1-5 cm x 2-3 mm, firm, tough, lemon yellow or paler. Spores 9-12 x 6-7.5 μm. Pleurocystidia: (1) narrowly fusoid and 50-60 x 4-5 μm, and (2) 80-110 x 12-12 μm and fusoid-ventricose. Cheilocystidia similar to pleurocystidia. Gill trama at maturity of interwoven hyaline ± gelatinous hyphae. Pileus cuticle a lax palisade of golden yellow cells some having thick walls, ± 40-50 x 9-12 μm along with some projecting filaments.

Scattered on hardwood sticks, etc., Great Lakes area east and especially southward; spring, summer, and fall; common but never abundant. It was formerly known under the name *Collybia lacunosa* and later as *Xerulina chrsopepla*.

Cystoderma Fayod

Pileus and stipe confluent, the surface of both usually granular to powdery; gills attached to the stipe, seceding at times; annulus present and flaring or merely a poorly formed mealy zone; spore deposit white, spores smooth, thin-walled; pleuro- and cheilocystidia present in some species; gill trama typically regular or nearly so; cuticle of the pileus usually formed of chains of globose to variously shaped inflated cells, but in some the cells cylindric to ellipsoid; the wall olivaceous, yellowish or reddish brown in KOH depending on the species, clavate-pedicellate cells present at times. Habitat terrestrial or lignicolous. Clamp connections present as noted.

About 20 species are known; none are recommended for the table.

KEY TO SPECIES

1a Pileus surface appearing innately appressed fibrillose to slightly squamulose, lacking a covering of globose cells at maturity but these present on the stipe surface 2

1b Pileus surface powdery, finely granular, or with granular patches 3

2a Stipe 1-3.5 mm thick; spores globose, amyloid, 4-5 μm ....
.... *C. contortipes* **Smith & Stuntz**

Pileus 5-15 mm, dull purplish on disc, paler lilac-gray toward the margin, the disc at times having tiny recurved scales; context grayish. Gills distant, broad, arcuate-adnate, thickish, pale dull purplish. Stipe 1-3.5 cm long, fibrillose downward, minutely scurfy at apex, grayish with a buff to brownish mass of fleshy tissue at the base. Cuticle of pileus of large cells with free hyphal ends projecting.

Solitary to caespitose on logs or in moss under Douglas Fir; Pacific Northwest, fall, rare.

2b Stipe 3-6 mm thick; spores ellipsoid, 9-10 × 4-5 μm, non-amyloid ....
.... *C. paradoxum* **Smith & Singer**

Pileus 1-3 cm, pallid lilac to dark violaceous drab, button stages covered by a brownish granulose veil which soon vanishes and the surface appears fibrillose, lilaceous. Gills broad, adnexed, subdistant, pale lilac. Stipe 4-8 cm long, pale lilac and longitudinally striate as well as lacerate scaly above, lower 2/3 sheathed by a granulose, buff veil which breaks into concentric rings or scales. Cells on surface of buttons globose to short ellipsoid, on mature caps the surface cells filamentose to mostly ellipsoid and repent.

Solitary or in small clusters from a fleshy basal mass of tissue; on humus and among mosses; Pacific Northwest, fall, rare.

3a Spores amyloid 4

3b Spores not amyloid 11

4a Terrestrial species 5

4b Lignicolous species 8

5a Annulus usually poorly formed and soon disappearing; pileus ochraceous brown to yellowish 6

5b Annulus well developed, usually persistent 7

6a Pileus with conspicuous radial ridges; odor typically of freshly husked green corn. Fig. 125. .... *C. amianthinum* (Fr.) Fayod var. *rugosoreticulatum* (Lorinser) **Smith & Singer**

Figure 125

Figure 125 *Cystoderma amianthinum* var. *rugosoreticulatum*

Pileus 3-5.5 cm, tawny to ochraceous tawny or paler and near ochraceous buff, the margin fringed at first. Stipe 4-8 cm x 3-8 mm, granulose, concolorous with cap to the evanescent annulus or the veil broken into zones or patches; smooth above the annulus; annulus superior, two-layered, the outer like the pileus surface in color and texture, the inner smooth and pale buff. Spores 5-6 x 3 μm. Cuticle of pileus of globose to inflated saccate cells in chains.

Scattered to gregarious on soil, mats of conifer needles, or beds of moss; widely distributed; late summer and fall (during the winter rainy season in California).

6b Pileus smooth to only slightly wrinkled (not radially grooved); odor mild. Fig. 126 ....
C. amianthinum (Fr.) Fay. var. *amianthinum*

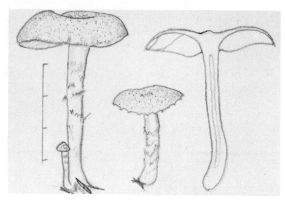

Figure 126

Figure 126   *Cystoderma amianthinum* var. *amianthinum*

Pileus 2-3.5 cm, the margin at first fringed, surface even to only somewhat wrinkled, ochraceous brown on disc, yellow toward the margin, with KOH fulvous to ferruginous. Gills usually pale orange-yellow at maturity. Stipe 2.5-6 cm long, with a granular sheath concolor with pileus on lower side and buff above, annulus evanescent. Spores 4.5-6.5 x 2.8-3.5 μm. Cuticle of pileus of chains of globose to ellipsoid cells which are rusty cinnamon in KOH.

Solitary to densely gregarious on beds of moss (*Polytrichum*), on fallen leaves, in mixed woods or on needle carpets under conifers, widely distributed, late summer and fall, common. Edible (?)

7a   Pileus pinkish, lilaceous or white ....
.... *C. carcharias* (Secr.) Fayod

Pileus 2.5-4 cm, dry and finely to coarsely granulose. Margin often appendiculate, KOH on fresh pileus olive-yellow to dull yellow, odor and taste disagreeable. Stipe 3-6 cm x 4-8 mm, granulose and concolorous with pileus below; annulus well developed, flaring at first, then collapsing and sometimes evanescent. Spores 4.5-5.5 x 3-4 μm. Cuticle of pileus readily separable, the globose cells hyaline in KOH. Clamp connections present.

Scattered to gregarious under conifers, among mosses or on needle beds; northern United States, late summer and fall, rare.

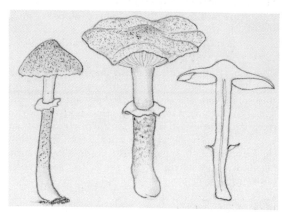

Figure 127

Figure 127   *Cystoderma fallax*

Pileus 2-5 cm, surface at first covered with erect granulose scales, becoming evenly granulose or powdery finally, blackish where KOH is applied. Gills adnate to adnexed, close, whitish to tinged yellowish. Stipe 3-6 (7) cm x 3-7 mm, annulus flaring, ± ferruginous on under side, buff above. Spores 3.5-5.5 x 2.8-3.6 μm. Cells from cuticle of pileus very dark brown in KOH.

Scattered, gregarious or subcaespitose on humus, moss, needle beds or on very rotten conifer logs; Pacific Northwest and Great Lakes area, fall, common in the Northwest.

8a   Pileus bright orange; annulus flaring and persistent; stipe 8-15 mm thick ....
.... *C. granosum* (Morg.) Sm. & Sing.

Pileus 4-9 cm, surface with small granulose warts or finely powdery, sometimes wrinkled. Stipe 5-10 cm x 8-15 mm, sheathed below with a granulose covering, the sheath similar to cap surface and often broken into several annular zones; annulus rather large, flaring, persistent. Spores 4-5 x 3 μm. Cells of the pileus cuticle with reddish brown walls in KOH. Lactifers present in the pileus trama.

Gregarious to caespitose on rotten wood of deciduous trees, central and eastern United States, summer and fall, not infrequent in hardwood slashings.

8b Stipe less than 5 mm thick at apex 9

9a Pileus at first covered with numerous powdery pyramidal warts; spores 9-11.5 × 5-6 μm .... *C. gruberianum* **Smith**

Pileus 1-3 cm, broad, the ground color between the warts clay-color, margin ragged. Gills becoming ventricose, yellowish, thickish, close, becoming ± decurrent. Stipe 3-4.5 cm x 1-2.5 mm, sheathed with a granulose sheath which may break up into scales or tufts; annulus merely a fibrillose zone. Cuticle of pileus of globose cells dark rusty cinnamon in KOH.

Scattered or in small groups on decaying conifer logs, Pacific Northwest, fall, apparently rare.

9b Pileus merely granulose; spores less than 6 μm long 10

10a Pileus whitish to pallid or tawny .... *C. pulveraceum* (**Pk.**) **Sm. & Sing.**

Pileus 1-2.5 cm, finely powdery or minutely granulose and at first squamulose. Stipe 2.5-5 cm x 3.5-4 mm, like the pileus in color and surface features; annulus poorly formed. Spores 4-4.5 x 2-2.5 μm. Cuticular cells of pileus often with a flexuous projection from the apex, the walls hyaline or faintly yellowish in KOH.

Solitary to scattered on old conifer logs, central and northeastern United States, August and September, rare.

10b Pileus dark vinaceous brown; cells of cuticle of pileus as revived in KOH olivaceous .... *C. subvinaceum* **Smith**

Pileus 1-2.5 cm, granular to warty, pale vinaceous in age. Gills close to subdistant, broadest near stipe, pallid tinged buff. Stipe 3-5 cm x 3-5 mm, sheathed with veil material to the superior evanescent annulus or sheath broken into zones. Spores 3.5-4.2 x 2-3.5 μm.

Scattered on mossy rotten logs, Great Lakes area, rather rare, late summer and fall.

11a Pileus white over all at first, cuticular cells not distinctly colored in KOH .... *C. ambrosii* (**Bres.**) **Sm. & Sing.**

Pileus 4-6 cm, at first with small conic scales; becoming cottony-fibrillose to glabrescent, in age flushed dingy tan. Gills broad, adnexed, close, white to cream-color. Stipe 5-9 cm x 8-12 mm, white, fibrillose to lacerate-scaly below the thin fibrillose annulus, glabrescent. Spores 4-5 x 2.5-3 μm. Cuticle of pileus of globose to sausage-shaped cells with intermingled filaments.

In mossy places under larch or alder, on road banks, etc., Pacific Northwest, fall, rare.

11b Pileus colored; cuticular cells tawny to deep rusty brown or reddish when revived in KOH 12

12a Growing on decaying logs; southern in distribution .... *C. australe* **Sm. & Sing.**

Pileus about 1.5 cm, covered with wartlike persistent scales, evenly dark rusty brown. Stipe about 2 cm x 2 mm, fibrillose-scaly, tinged with color of cap in lower part; annular zone median or lower (annulus not distinct). Spores 4-5.4 x 2.5-3.5 μm. Pleurocystidia similar to cheilocystidia which are 16-22 x 4-6 μm. Cuticle of pileus of ovoid ellipsoid or elongated cells and irregular in shape, the walls rusty brown as revived in KOH.

Solitary to scattered, fall, southeastern United States, rare.

12b Not as above 13

13a Pileus 3-12 cm broad 14

13b Pileus 1-4 cm broad 15

14a Pileus yellowish brown; cheilocystidia lacking .... *C. ponderosum* **Sm. & Sing.**

Pileus squarrose-scaly or toward the margin appressed scaly with pallid ground color showing, the scales quite persistent. Gills broadly adnate or with a decurrent tooth, close, narrow, pale buff. Stipe 6-8 cm x 8-15 mm, base white-mycelioid, the sheath thin and soon broken into scales concolorous with those of pileus; annulus poorly formed, evanescent. Spores 3-3.5 x 2.5-3 μm. Cuticle of pileus chiefly of interwoven branched hyphae and a few enlarged irregular cells also in the scales; the hyphae with encrusting brown pigment.

On mossy soil or among rocks, southeastern United States, summer, rare.

14b Pileus cinnabar-red to orange-brown or orange; sharp-pointed cheilocystidia present ....
.... *C. cinnabarinum* **(Secr.) Fayod**

Pileus 3-8 cm, with granulose pyramidal scales. Gills adnate-seceding, close to crowded, narrow, white to pallid. Stipe 3-8 cm x 8-15 mm, sheathed up to the evanescent annulus with a granulose sheath similar in color and texture to the pileus surface. Spores 3.5-5 x 2-3 μm. Pleurocystidia and cheilocystidia similar, 32-46 x 4-9 μm, fusoid-pointed. Cuticle of pileus of globose and elongated cells, the wall bright reddish brown as revived in KOH.

Scattered to gregarious on decayed conifer wood, on needle beds, on humus, or among mosses under hardwoods, widely distributed and fairly common. Edibility questionable.

15a Pileus 1-4 (6) cm, color dark vinaceous brown, brick red, tawny, or whitish where bleached by sunlight ....
.... *C. granulosum* **(Fr.) Fayod**

Pileus convex to nearly plane, surface granular or at first with conic granulose warts. Gills close, broad, rounded to adnexed at the stipe, white to pallid. Stipe 2-6 cm x 2-6 mm, sheathed up to the evanescent annulus with a granulose sheath similar in color and texture to the pileus surface. Spores 3.5-5 x 2-3 μm. Cuticle of pileus of chains of globose to ellipsoid cells having the walls brown when revived in KOH.

Scattered to gregarious, on waste ground, on moss and soil under hardwoods and conifers alike, and in barren places, widely distributed, late summer and fall, rather common.

15b Not as above **16**

16a Cap grayish with a purplish cast; spores ovoid, 4-4.5 × 2.5-3 μm ....
.... *C. subpurpureum* **Sm. & Sing.**

Pileus 4-8 mm, convex, powdery at first, becoming pale ashy pink or merely ashy gray in age at times. Gills pale hematite color. Stipe 1-2.5 cm long, 1 mm or less thick, concolorous with pileus, powdery; annulus fibrillose, soon evanescent. Spores smooth. Cuticle of pileus of globose to short-ellipsoid cells, their walls dark violaceous drab at first when revived in KOH, slowly becoming dull olivaceous.

Scattered on soil where a brush pile had been burned, Pacific Northwest, fall, apparently rare.

16b Pileus ochraceous to pale yellow; spores subrhomboid 5-6 × 3.8-4.5 μm ....
.... *C. rhombosporum* **(Atk.) Sm. & Sing.**

Pileus 8-15 mm, surface granulose to squamulose-granulose. Stipe 3-4 cm x 1-3 mm, squamulose to granulose at first. Gills clay-color, sinuate, ventricose. Pleurocystidia and cheilocystidia similar, 26-38 x 5-7 μm. Cuticle of pileus of globose to ellipsoid cells in chains, their walls tawny as revived in KOH.

Solitary to gregarious on leaf mold at the edge of mixed woods, northeastern United States; late summer, rare.

Flammulina Karsten

Pileus and stipe confluent, pileus viscid, glabrous; gills yellowish, adnate to adnexed or sinuate, trama weakly bilateral; stipe distinctly strigose at the base and often somewhat extended below into a rhizomorph, usually velvety from numerous caulocystidia; veils absent in North American species.

We treat only one species. Fig. 128 ....
.... *F. velutipes* **(Curt. ex Fr.) Sing.**

Figure 128

Figure 128 *Flammulina velutipes*

Pileus 2-5 (7) cm, ± convex with an inrolled margin, in age broadly convex to nearly plane, disc orange-red to pinkish cinnamon or paler and tawny to clay-color, margin paler orange-buff to ochraceous; taste mild. Gills often flesh-tinged in age. Stipe 2-7 (10) cm x 3-7 (10) mm, ± equal, pliant, velvety over lower portion, pallid at first, then yellow to tawny above and dark rusty brown below. Spores 6.5-8 x 2.5-3 μm. Pleurocystidia 32-48 x 10-18 μm, fusoid-ventricose, apex obtuse; cheilocystidia similar. Pileus cuticle an ixotrichodermium, non-gelatinous pileocystidia also present.

More or less clustered on wood of hardwoods, especially elm; common and widely distributed, late fall, winter, and early spring. It is abundant on aspen in the Rocky Mountains. Edible when cooked; known as the winter mushroom.

Hohenbuehelia Schulzer in Schulz., Kanitz & Knapp

Pleurotoid agarics with a gelatinized layer in the pileus or on it, lamprocystidia in the hymenium, white spore print and non-amyloid spores. A stipe is usually lacking.

They are saprophytes on lignicolous debris. About 25 species are recognized on a world wide basis.

tidia like the pleurocystidia but some thin-walled fusoid-ventricose to clavate cells also present.

On hardwood logs and detritus, not common, summer and fall after heavy rains; widely distributed.

1b Pileus pale pinkish buff; taste mild; spores 3-4 μm, globose. Fig. 129 .... *H. angustatus* (**Berk.**) Sing.

KEY TO SPECIES

1a Pileus mouse-gray to drab, pallid when faded; taste nauseous to subfarinaceous; spores 7-9 $\times$ 5-6 μm .... *H. mastrucatus* (**Fr.**) Sing.

Pileus 2-7 cm, resupinate becoming fan-shaped, covered by gelatinous ridges and spines connected to form a reticulum; context a thick gelatinous upper layer and a floccose lower layer; odor strongly fungoid. Gills broad, ± subdistant, white becoming grayish. Spores 7-9 x 5-6 μm. Pleurocystidia 50-90 x 10-18 μm, apices or apical region in some more or less incrusted. Cheilocys-

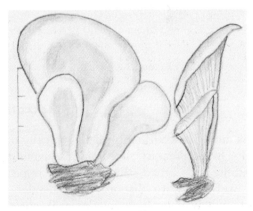

Figure 129

Figure 129 *Hohenbuehelia angustatus*

Pileus 2-5 (7) cm, spathulate to fan-shaped, often narrowed to a stipe-like base, surface lubricous and with a rubbery feel, hoary-pruinose at first. Gills crowded narrow, whitish, finally alutaceous. Stipe a narrowed pileus base, numerous white rhizomorphs present in substrate around the base.

Pleurocystidia 40-60 x 10-15 μm, apex often incrusted. Cheilocystidia like the pleurocystidia but also some thin-walled clavate cells present.

On hardwood detritus, often abundant on debris around sawdust piles, abundant during some seasons, summer and early fall, east of the Great Plains.

Hygrophoropsis (Schröt. in Cohn) R. Maire in Martin-Sans

Pileus and stipe confluent; gills decurrent, dicotomously forked repeatedly; veil absent; spores dextrinoid, walls cyanophyllic (blue in cresyl blue); pileus surface soft to touch but not viscid. A small genus with only one species in our area. Fig. 130 ....
H. aurantiaca (Fr.) R. Maire in Martin-Sans

Figure 130 *Hygrophoropsis aurantiaca*

Pileus 2-6 cm, convex to plane, finally shallowly depressed, yellow orange, brownish orange or shaded fuscous over disc; taste mild. Gills crowded and narrow. Stipe 3-6 cm x (1) 2-7 mm, unpolished, yellowish to brownish orange. Spore deposit white. Cystidia none.

Scattered to caespitose on humus and rotten wood, often on charred wood, late summer and fall, common in northern United States in either conifer or hardwood forests. Kauffman lists it as edible. It has also been reported as poisonous.

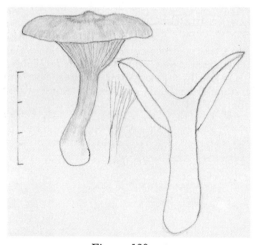

Figure 130

Laccaria Berk. & Br.

Pileus and stipe confluent; pileus typically distinctly hygrophanous, becoming squamulose in fading; gills broad, thick, waxy in appearance, subdistant to distant; stipe slender to thick and fibrous, not fragile; veil absent; spores white in deposit or pale violaceous,

either (1) large and typically globose to subglobose and echinulate, or (2) ellipsoid, large, and very weakly ornamented, both types nonamyloid; clamp connections present.

Terrestrial and very widely distributed over the Northern Hemisphere. About 18 species are known. All reportedly non-poisonous, but of low quality.

KEY TO SPECIES

1a Growing in sand dunes or sand generally; gills violaceous at first; spores 16-22 × 6-9 μm. Fig. 131. .... *L. trullisata* (Ellis) Peck

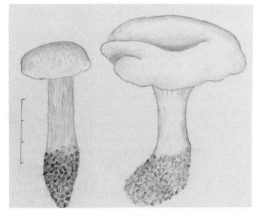

Figure 131

Figure 131 *Laccaria trullisata*

Pileus 3-10 cm, convex then ± plane, moist, virgate, reddish flesh-color fading to pale dusky pink and then furfuraceous, in age often scaly. Gills distant, soon reddish flesh color. Stipe 3-10 cm x (3) 10-20 mm, ± clavate from adhering sand, innately fibrillose. Spore deposit white; spores appearing smooth under "high dry" lens. Basidia 4-spored, 54-67 x 12-15 μm. Cheilocystidia not differentiated.

Solitary to scattered; Great Lakes area eastward; not common or perhaps not commonly collected.

1b Habitat and spores not as above 2

2a Stipe 1-3 cm thick near apex, Fig. 132 .... *L. ochropurpurea* (Berk.) Peck

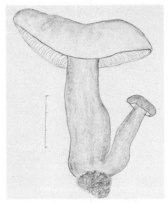

Figure 132

Figure 132 *Laccaria ochropurpurea*

Pileus 4-15 (30) cm, convex to plane, the margin often decurved, purplish to purplish brown to purplish flesh-color, fading through grayish to finally nearly white, in age lacerated squamulose; taste unpleasant. Gills distant, broad, thick, purple. Stipe 6-30 x 1-3 cm, equal to subfusoid, solid, hard, ± concolor with cap. Spore deposit white to faintly lilac; spores globose, 6-8 μm, echinulations ± 2 μm high. Basidia 4-spored, 40-50 x 10-11 μm. Cheilocystidia 18-26 x 4-6 μm, irregular in shape.

Grassy open oak woods, but under other deciduous trees as well, common late summer and early fall east of the Great Plains; noted as a "dry weather" species; edible but mediocre.

2b Stipe 2-10 mm thick 3

3a Pileus, gills, and stipe violet, the gills persistently so, Fig. 133 .... *L. amethystina* (Hooker) Murr.

Figure 133

Figure 133 *Laccaria amethystina*

Pileus 1-5 cm, convex then convex-depressed, or finally shallowly funnel-shaped, fading to light purplish lilac and then furfuraceous from breaking up of cuticle, ± striate when moist. Gills broad, distant, decurrent. Stipe 3-8 (10) cm x 4-10 mm, fibrous, dingy when faded, basal mycelium white. Spore deposit pale violaceous to whitish; spores echinate, 7-9 μm, globose. Cheilocystidia not differentiated.

Gregarious in wet areas under hardwoods, especially in dried up pools, east of the Great Plains, common, summer and fall.

3b　Fruiting body dull pink to dull orange pink (about flesh color) over all, Fig. 134 ....
.... *L. laccata* (**Fr.**) **Berk. & Br.**

Figure 134

Figure 134 *Laccaria laccata*

Pileus (1) 1.5-4 (5) cm, convex then plane or with uplifted margin, dull pinkish fading in age and then scurfy from breaking up of cuticle. Gills broad, distant, adnate to short decurrent. Stipe 2-6 (8) cm x 2-6 (10) mm, fibrous. Spores deposit white; spores 7.5-10 x 7-8.5 μm, globose to broadly ellipsoid, echinulate. Basidia 34-40 x 9-11 μm, 4-spored. Cheilocystidia not well differentiated.

Scattered to gregarious, summer and fall, widely distributed. Over a half dozen species will key out here in addition to numerous "variants" which may not deserve recognition at the rank of species. Critical taxonomic work on the North America variants is needed.

Lentinellus Karsten

Pileus and stipe confluent (when a stipe is present); consistency tough; not readily decaying; taste of raw context often acrid or bitter; gills typically decurrent, margins serrate; spore deposit white to buff, spores minutely echinulate with strongly amyloid ornamentation; growing from decaying wood of deciduous and coniferous trees.

Less than a dozen species are known from North America; none are reported to be choice edibles.

KEY TO SPECIES

1a　Fruiting bodies with sulcate stipes which are often fused into clusters; pilei often very irregular from crowding; taste of raw flesh mild .... *L. cochleatus* (**Fr.**) **Karsten**

Pileus 2-7 cm, plano-depressed, dark reddish brown to clay color, glabrous to scrupose, the margin inrolled, often quite irregular; odor ± of anise. Gills crowded, long-decurrent, pallid becoming pale cinnamon, easily breaking transversely, edges soon serrate. Stipe 3-10 cm x 3-10 mm, central to lateral, often scrupose, conspicuously sulcate, base dark reddish brown in age. Spores 4-5 x 3.5-4.5 μm. Pleurocystidia ± basidiole-like. Cheilocystidia as short filaments.

Caespitose at base of hardwood stubs and stumps (often appearing terrestrial), summer and fall, not uncommon; Great Lakes area eastward and southward. Kauffman lists it as edible.

1b **Fruiting bodies sessile or nearly so; pilei not irregular from crowding; taste acrid** 2

2a **Gills distant; spores 4.5-6.5 μm long** .... *L. montanus* **O. K. Miller**

Pileus 4-11 cm, fan-shaped, sessile, moist, only the central area hirsute and dark vinaceous brown, paler (to pale cinnamon) toward the margin, deep vinaceous brown overall in age; taste sharply acrid. Gills broad, serrate, soon pallid buff, drying gray. Spores 4.5-6.5 x 4-5 μm. Pleuro- and cheilocystidia rare, versiform, 26-39 x 4.5-8.5 μm.

On conifer wood, often near snowbanks on wood partly buried in the snow, spring and summer in the mountains of the western United States and in Canada. The fruiting period is of short duration, but the species is common.

2b **Gills close; spores 3-5 μm long** 3

3a **Pileus soon developing dark brown pubescence from base toward the margin; pleurocystidia fusoid-ventricose to clavate. Fig. 135** .... *L. ursinus* **(Fr.) Kühner**

Figure 135

Figure 135 *Lentinellus ursinus*

Pileus 3-11 cm wide, 2-5 cm from back to front, ± fan-shaped, yellowish brown to reddish brown, surface at maturity scrupose and ribbed; taste slowly strongly acrid. Gills crowded, broad, light dingy pink becoming light reddish brown. Spores 2.5-3.5 x 1.2 μm. Pleurocystidia 16-30 (45) 3.5-5 (7.5) μm, some fusoid-ventricose, some clavate; cheilocystidia similar.

Solitary to gregarious, on wood of conifers (western North America) or on hardwoods (Great Lakes and eastward), summer and fall to early winter depending on the weather, widely distributed.

3b **Pileus rough and radially ribbed, somewhat pubescent, the pubescence white to whitish; pleurocystidia pointed. Fig. 136** .... *L. vulpinus* **(Fr.) Kühner & Maire**

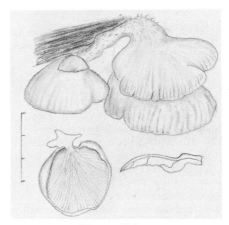

Figure 136

Figure 136 *Lentinellus vulpinus*

Pileus 3-10 (25) cm, fan-shaped, often in dense imbricate masses, white to pale pinkish cinnamon. Gills broad, crowded, white becoming dingy flesh-color, short decurrent, breaking transversely by maturity. Spores 3-4.5 x 2.5-3.5 μm. Pleuro- and cheilocystidia similar, 25-35 x 5-8 μm, absent to rare.

Common on hardwoods, Great Lake area eastward and southward, summer and fall.

Lentinus Fries

Pileus and stipe confluent; stipe central to eccentric; consistency hard and tough; spore deposit white, yellowish, or orange-buff; spores non-amyloid; gill edges typically serrate to toothed but in some species this is evident only in old specimens; no truly gelatinous layers present in the fruiting bodies, thick-walled hyphae often present in gill and/or pileus trama; clamp connections present but rare in some species. Less than two dozen species are placed in the genus, all lignicolous. *L. edodes,* the shiitake is a highly prized edible mushroom in the Orient.

KEY TO SPECIES

1a On Sitka spruce (along the Pacific Coast); veil absent; stipe 5-12 mm thick; spores 5-6 × 2-2.5 μm ....
.... *L. kauffmanii* Smith

Pileus 3-8 cm, convex to broadly convex and finally ± plane or margin wavy and lobed, hoary at first, soon dingy pinkish-alutaceous to pale tan. Gills crowded, adnate with decurrent lines, moderately broad, whitish to ± pinkish buff. Stipe 3-6 cm long, central to eccentric, concolor with cap. Pleurocystidia 60-125 x 5-9 μm, subequal, apex in some enlarged.

  Scattered on logs, stumps, etc.; fall, often frequent in dry seasons but within the fog belt.

1b Not as above 2

2a Pileus 1-5 cm broad; on wood of hardwoods 3

2b Pileus 10-50 cm broad; on wood of conifers 4

3a On ± water-soaked wood; pileus at maturity with dark brown to blackish squamules on a whitish ground .... *L. tigrinus* (Fr.) Fr.

Pileus 1.5-5 cm, convex to convex-depressed, dry, fibrillose to squamulose, the squamules dark brown to blackish. Gills crowded, narrow, becoming ± short decurrent, white to pallid. Stipe central to eccentric, 2-6 cm x 4-10 mm, narrowed downward; veil leaving a superior zone, whitish above it, darkening below. Spores 6-7 x 3 μm, oblong. Cheilocystidia 20-30 x 4-5.5 μm, filamentose to contorted.

  Gregarious to clustered on hardwood logs often partly sunken in mud, widely distributed but more abundant southward. An "abortive stage" often occurs with normal fruiting bodies or by itself. In it the gills remain covered by the veil, and very few spores can be discharged from the basidia. This stage was once recognized as a species, "*Lentodium squamosum*" and was regarded as a Gasteromycete since the basidiospores presumably were not discharged from the basidium. It is now known, however, that both are sexually compatible with each other, indicating they represent a single species.

3b Fruiting on dry habitats such as decorticated dry wood in rail fences or debarked fallen trees; pileus pecan-brown to orange-cinnamon .... *L. sulcatus* Berkeley

Pileus 1-4 cm, convex to plano-depressed, margin conspicuously ribbed, dry and fibrillose, becoming appressed-squamulose. Gills whitish then dingy tan, close, broad. Stipe 1-3 cm x 3-6 mm, solid, fibrillose, scaly near base from lacerated cuticle and pinkish tan, pallid near apex. Spore deposit orange-buff. Spores 11-16 (20) x 5-7 μm, bean-shaped in profile. Pleurocystidia and cheilocystidia 60-90 (110) x 7-9 μm, subcylindric.

  Summer and fall, widely distributed, especially on avalanche debris of aspen in the Rocky Mountains.

4a Veil lacking (check young fruiting bodies). Fig. 137 .... *L. ponderosus* O. K. Miller

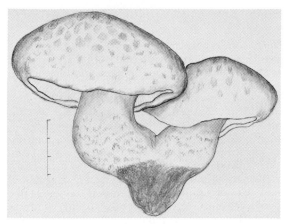

Figure 137

4b Stipe annulate or veil remnants obvious somewhere on young specimens. Fig. 138 ....
.... *L. lepideus* Fries

Figure 138

Figure 137 *Lentinus ponderosus*

Pileus 10-30 (50) cm, convex becoming plano-depressed, at first with a continuous avellaneous cuticle, this breaking up into broad scales, margin cottony, ground color white then yellowing to orange; odor fragrant (as in *Armillaria ponderosa*). Gills decurrent, narrow but broad in age (± 2 cm), gradually yellowish to orange and finally rusty brown. Stipe central to eccentric, 5-15 x 1-5 cm, narrowed to a pseudorhiza, surface furfuraceous with avellaneous patches but not with a distinct veil, near base finally vinaceous brown. Spores 8-11 (12) x 4.5-5.5 μm. Pleurocystidia 40-50 x 7-9 μm, fusoid-ventricose. Cheilocystidia present as projecting filaments of tramal hyphae.

Solitary on conifer wood, late summer and fall, in the western United States. It is one of our largest mushrooms but not recommended for the table unless fresh young fruiting bodies are found.

Figure 138 *Lentinus lepideus*

Pileus 5-20 cm, convex, then ± plane or broadly umbonate, often beaded with drops on margin when young, cuticle breaking into broad appressed spotlike scales; context slowly lutescent, odor pungent or disagreeable. Gills decurrent, subdistant, broad, pallid becoming dingy yellowish in aging. Stipe 4-15 x 1-3 cm, tapered to a point (±) at the base in some, solid, tough, scaly to fibrillose to submembranous annulus, base staining vinaceous, remainder yellowing in age. Spore deposit yellowish. Spores 10-14 x 4-5.5 μm, subcylindric. Pleurocystidia 28-55 x 7-10 μm, cylindric to fusoid-ventricose. Cheilocystidia about 60 x 5 μm, crooked and with slightly thickened walls in some.

Common on decaying conifer wood; solitary to scattered; widely distributed in the Northern Hemisphere; spring, summer, and fall.

Leucopaxillus Bousier

Pileus and stipe confluent; stipe fleshy, dry and unpolished; pileus dry, fibrillose to unpolished; gills in some species readily separable from pileus, adnate to decurrent, often arcuate; spore deposit white, spores with strongly amyloid ornamentation; cheilocystidia ± unspecialized (not fusoid-pointed as in *Melanoleuca*); mycelium in area surrounding the fruiting bodies white, copious and conspicuous; clamp connections present; veils absent at least in our species. Less than two dozen species known.

KEY TO SPECIES

1a Taste mild to farinaceous 2

1b Taste distinctly bitter-disagreeable 4

2a Pileus, gills, and stipe yellow ....
.... *L. subzonalis* (Pk.) Bigl.

Pileus 4-10 cm, convex then shallowly depressed, hygrophanous but also unpolished; context yellowish. Gills close, narrow very few anastomosing. Stipe 2-5 cm long, 1-2 cm thick, solid, yellow within, basal mycelium white. Spores 4-5 x 3.5-4.5 μm, echinulate. Pleuro- and cheilocystidia none.

Gregarious under beech and other hardwoods, eastern North America to the western Great Lakes area, fall not common.

2b Fruiting body not yellow as in above choice
.... 3

3a Pileus 9-30 cm, pinkish buff at first; gills faintly yellowish; stipe 1-4 cm thick at apex. Fig. 139 ....
.... *L. tricolor* (Pk.) Kühner

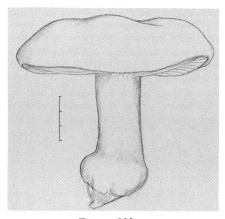

Figure 139

Figure 139 *Leucopaxilius tricolor*

Pileus convex to plane, margin long inrolled, surface dry and unpolished, pinkish buff gradually becoming alutaceous, in drying often becoming vinaceous red; context thick, firm, white, odor pungent, taste mild to ± unpleasant. Gills finally broad, crowded, adnate at first. Stipe 4-10 cm long, often abruptly bulbous, whitish, dry and unpolished, with conspicuous white mycelium in the duff. Spore deposit white; spores 6-8 x 4-5.5 μm, ornamentation of isolated warts. Pleuro- and cheilocystidia rare.

Usually solitary to scattered under hardwoods, eastern North America to the western Great Lakes area, summer and fall after heavy rains, uncommon. Listed as edible by some authors.

3b Pileus 5-10 cm, white at first; gills white; stipe white-pubescent to near apex in age
.... *L. paradoxus* (Cost. & Duf.) Bours.

Pileus 5-10 cm, convex to broadly convex, dull and unpolished, white, in age with pinkish buff areas as epicutis is worn away, margin cottony and ribbed; odor fungoid, taste disagreeable to mild (not bitter). Gills narrow, decurrent finally, ± crowded, yellowish in age (staining yellow slightly at times). Stipe (3) 6-12 cm x 6-25 mm, white, unpolished at first. Spores 5-7.5 x 3.5-5 μm. Cheilocystidia none.

Solitary to scattered under hardwoods, Great Lakes area and the western United States, sporadic, late summer and fall; not common. Edible?

4a Pileus dark vinaceous brown, walnut-brown or pecan brown, margin finally paler. Fig. 140 .... *L. gentianeus* (Quél.) Kotlaba

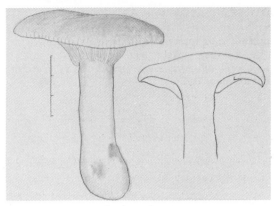

Figure 140

Figure 141

Figure 140   *Leucopaxilius gentianeus*

Pileus 5-12 (15) cm, convex, margin inrolled, finally ± plane, at times with an obtuse umbo, dry and subtomentose to unpolished, becoming areolate at times; context dry, thick, firm, odor ± pungent, taste very bitter. Gills separable from pileus, white then creamy, rarely ferruginous spotted, close, long remaining narrow. Stipe 5-10 cm x 8-45 mm, equal to bulbous at base, white but in age base brownish where bruised. Spores 4.5-6 x 4-5.5 μm, subglobose; ornamentation of low warts. Cheilocystidia abundant, 25-38 x 2-6.5 μm, versiform.

Common under conifers in the western area of North America. A number of varieties and forms have been described. In North America it has been known under the name *Leucopaxillus amarus*. We have used the current European name here pending further studies.

4b   **Pileus white to pale tan or dingy clay-color** **5**

5a   **Pileus pallid except for a flesh-tinge (dull pinkish) over the disc; spores 3.5-5.5 × 3.5-4.7 μm. Fig. 141** .... *L. laterarius* (Pk.) Sing. & Sm.

Figure 141   *Leucopaxillus laterarius*

Pileus (4) 7-15 (20) cm, obtuse to convex becoming plane or with a low umbo, margin inrolled at first, surface dry and unpolished to minutely scurfy, the margin often grooved; odor farinaceous, taste very bitter. Gills white to cream color, crowded, adnate and decurrent by lines. Stipe 4-10 x 1-2 cm, solid, firm, ± clavate, dry, unpolished, white, with copious mycelium at base. Spore deposit white; spores ornamented with amyloid warts. Cheilocystidia 2-5.5 μm thick, ± filamentose.

Solitary to scattered under hardwoods, one of the first large terrestrial mushrooms to fruit when the spring *Mycena* flora is past. It is seldom abundant, but appears almost every year in the Great Lakes area. Entirely white fruiting bodies can be recognized by the small spores. Not edible because of the bitter taste.

5b   **Pileus white with buff to pale crust brown disc; spores 5-8 × 3.5-5 μm. Fig. 142** .... ***L. albissimus* var. *piceinus* (Pk.) Sing. & Sm.**

Figure 142

Figure 142 *Leucopaxillus albissimus* var. *piceinus*

Pileus 5-12 (25) cm, convex, white to cream color or pale crust over disc, surface unpolished to scurfy, margin often ribbed; context thick, white, dry; odor pungent and unpleasant. Gills close to subdistant, short decurrent or extending down the stipe by anastomosing lines. Stipe 3-8 cm x 8-30 mm, often eccentric, tapered near base, equal, or clavate. Spores 5-8 x 4.5-5 μm. Cheilocystidia 20-32 x 3 μm, scattered, filamentose.

Scattered to gregarious on humus in conifer forests east of the Great Plains, late summer and fall, not common. Not edible.

Another variety, Fig. 143 .... *L. albissimus* var. *paradoxus* f. *albiformis* (Murr.) Sing. & Sm.

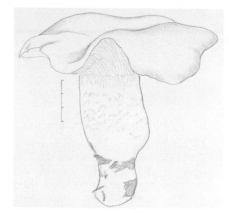

Figure 143

Figure 143 *Leucopaxillus albissimus* var. *paradoxus* f. *albiformis*

Is found solitary to scattered or clustered on old conifer stumps, logs, and rich humus in the Pacific Northwest during fall and early winter.

Lyophyllum Karsten

Pileus and stipe confluent; gills adnate to decurrent; stipe mostly central; spores white to whitish in deposits on white paper and non-amyloid; pileus color white to black but chiefly in the gray to gray-brown color range; injured places in many species staining finally to black or dark gray; basidia with siderophilous (aceto-carmine positive) granules; clamp connections usually present; veil typically lacking.

The siderophilous granules of the basidia are not an automatic indication that the specimen being tested is a *Lyophyllum* but a positive test is the principal character of the genus, though one not readily available to beginners.

For the latter, specimens which stain gray to black, and which resemble those of *Tricholoma, Clitocybe, Collybia* or *Mycena* in stature, belong in *Lyophyllum*. As for the non-staining species, if pleurocystidia and cheilocystidia are absent to poorly differentiated, and the pileus is glabrous, hygrophanous, and whitish to gray or darker, *Lyophyllum* is probably indicated. The genus is relatively large but as yet there is no critical treatment for the North American species. A few of the species, however, are edible and choice, and well-known to many collectors.

KEY TO SPECIES

1a Fruiting bodies in large clusters; spores globose 2

1b Fruiting bodies scattered to gregarious, or if in clusters then the spores elongate (oblong to ellipsoid, etc.) 3

2a Pileus blackish at first; spores 6-7 μm. Fig. 144. .... *L. loricatum* (Fr.) Küh.

Figure 144

Figure 144 *Lyophyllum loricatum*

Pileus 3-10 cm, broadly convex to plane, margin at first incurved, surface hoary at first, slowly fading to brownish, margin paler; taste ± farinaceous. Gills crowded, narrow, adnate, grayish becoming paler. Stipe 8-15 cm x 10-20 mm, often compound (or fused at the base), grayish becoming pallid to whitish. Spores smooth.

Occurring in massive clusters on grassy, waste ground, around sawdust piles, hedges, etc., frequent during wet fall seasons. It is widely distributed in North America, but seldom treated in our popular books on edible mushrooms. It is edible, but not as highly regarded as the following species.

2b Pileus pallid to grayish brown at first; spores (3.5) 4-5.5 × 4-5 μm. Fig. 145 ....
.... *L. decastes* (Fr.) Sing.

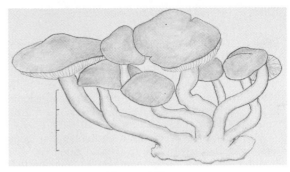

Figure 145

Figure 145 *Lyophyllum decastes*

Pileus 3-12 cm, convex to ± plane, margin finally uplifted, surface lubricous; odor and taste slightly pungent. Gills crowded, narrow, whitish, brownish in age. Stipes connate at base in many clusters, 4-10 x 1-2 cm, pallid, in age with pale tan discolorations. Spores smooth.

In large clusters on waste ground and especially in weeds around old sawdust piles, late summer and fall, widely distributed and very popular as an edible species. It is often referred to as the fried chicken mushroom.

3a Staining dark gray to blackish eventually where injured; gills gray at first. Fig. 146 ....
.... *L. semitale* (Fr.) Küh.

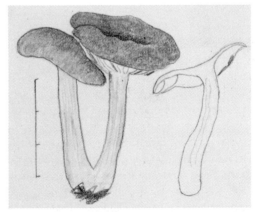

Figure 146

Figure 146 *Lyophyllum semitale*

Pileus (3) 4-10 cm, convex to expanded-umbonate, glabrous, opaque when moist; odor and taste farinaceous. Gills adnate to subdecurrent, close, staining yellowish then bluish and finally black. Stipe 6-10 cm x 9-15 mm, pale gray, long-striate and/or fibrillose. Spores 7-9 x 4-4.5 μm, smooth. Clamp connections present.

Gregarious or in small clusters under conifers, widely distributed in North America, late summer and fall. It is common in our western mountains and during warm wet seasons in the Great Lakes area.

3b   Not staining dark gray to black 4

4a   **Pileus pallid to ochraceous at first; gills white to yellowish, staining ochraceous slowly. Fig. 147** .... *L. multiforme* (**Pk.**) **Bigelow**

Figure 147

Figure 147 *Lyophyllum multiforme*

Pileus 3-8 (10) cm, convex to plane and margin undulating in age, lubricous, dingy cinereous when faded; taste mild. Gills narrow, crowded, broadly adnate, slowly staining dingy ochraceous. Stipe 4-7 cm x 5-10 mm, often eccentric, hollow, fibrous-striate in age. Spores 5-6 x 3-3.5 μm, smooth. Clamp connections present.

Densely gregarious to caespitose on soil around accumulations of lignicolous debris, fall, common east of the Great Plains generally. Edible.

4b   **Pileus lead-color beneath a hoary coating when young; not staining where injured .... *L. montanum* Smith**

Pileus 2-6.5 cm, convex with an incurved margin, at times finally with a low umbo, slowly becoming clay-color in aging, lubricous when fresh; context umber soon fading to pallid, taste mild. Gills drab becoming cinereous, close, broad, nearly free. Stipe 3-7 cm x 10-16 mm, ± equal, canescent, ground color umber at first. Spores 6.5-8 x 3.5-4 μm, white in deposit. Clamp connections present.

Gregarious-subcaespitose under spruce and fir in close proximity to melting snow banks, spring and early summer in the Rocky Mountains.

Marasmius Fries

Fruiting body with a white to pale cream-colored spore deposit and typically non-amyloid spores; the pileus and stipe are confluent and the latter typically central to rarely eccentric; stipe typically thin and pliant or resembling a coarse horsehair, glabrous and shining or dull and pubescent; cuticle of pileus highly differentiated: consisting of cells in a hymeniform layer or the cells in the layer staggered somewhat, or the cells variously branched or with irregular protrusions (the so-called "broom cells").

It has always been difficult to distinguish between *Collybia* and *Marasmius* because of intergrading species. The cuticle in *Collybia* as now defined by some authors is a true cutis of repent hyphae. However, in the following key a few of the truly marasmioid *Collybia* species are treated here because they revive readily and are more "marasmioid" than "collybioid" in appearance. This is done because there are problems in studying the cuticle in *Marasmius* that tax the patience of even a professional mycologist. The genus is a large one numbering over 200 species. *M. oreades,* the fairy ring mushroom, is the one common good edible species in North America.

KEY TO SPECIES

1a Stipe under a handlens minutely pubescent to tomentose at ± the midportion 2

1b Stipe glabrous and polished over most of its length **6**

2a **Pileus and gills violet at first; odor "strong"** .... *M. iocephalus* (**Berk. & Curt.**) **Penn.**

Pileus 1.5-4 cm, striate to plicate. Gills adnate, distant, narrow, paler than pileus. Stipe 4-6 cm x 2-4 mm, attenuated upward, white to yellowish. Spores 7-8 x 3-3.5 μm.
    Gregarious to ± clustered on wet leaves in low woods and swamps, typically southern but reported as far north as New York.

2b **Not with above combination of features** 3

3a **Growing in lawns and grassy places, often in "fairy rings"; pileus ± fleshy. Fig. 148** .... *M. oreades* (**Fr.**) **Fries**

Figure 148

Figure 148 *Marasmius oreades*

Pileus 2-5 cm, obtuse, then campanulate to broadly convex or finally plane with or without an umbo, margin often crenate in age, surface glabrous, color dull red to orange-cinnamon or pale dingy tan to cream-color (gradually becoming paler the longer it is exposed to light); context thickish, pallid to buff; odor faint. Gills broad, subdistant, rounded at the stipe, often intervenose, pallid, edges even. Stipe 4-8 cm x 3-7 mm, equal, base ± striogose, tough, pallid above, ± colored toward the base. Spores 7-9 x 4-5.5 μm. Pleurocystidia none.
    Widely distributed in the Northern Hemisphere, spring, summer or fall if moisture and temperature are favorable. Edible and choice.

3b **Habitat and pileus not as above** **4**

4a **On matted leaves under deciduous trees; taste very distinctly acrid. Fig. 149** .... *M. urens* (**Fr.**) **Fr.**

Figure 149

Figure 149 *Marasmius urens*

Pileus 1-5 cm, convex-expanded, soon plane with margin wavy at times, plicate-striate in age, dry, dull dark reddish brown, gradually paler and a dull orange-cinnamon, in age ± scurfy at times; context thin, pliant; odor none. Gills adnexed, soon free, subdistant, narrow, pallid becoming dingy buff and in age reddish stained at times, edges even. Stipe 3-6 cm x 2-4 mm, soon darker than pileus in basal region, solid, surface densely pubescent. Spores 8-11 x 3-4 μm. Pleurocystidia absent.

4b   Not as above (taste slight) 5

5a   Stipe 3-7 cm × 2-4 mm; pileus 2-4 cm, not staining red in age; on humus in wet areas .... *M. umbilicatus* Kauffman

Pileus 2-4 cm, with an abruptly depressed disc, in age the margin uplifted, disc at times tinged pinkish gray but white over most of surface; odor and taste slight. Gills close then subdistant, narrow, ± decurrent, whitish. Stipe subequal, longitudinally sulcate at times, pinkish brown to dark smoky brown over lower part, pallid near apex, base with brownish tomentum. Spores 9-12 x 3-4.5 μm. subcylindric. Pleurocystidia 50-72 x 5-7 μm, subfusoid.

Scattered to gregarious, Pacific Northwest; frequent but rarely in abundance; fall, often in wet areas under Devil's Club.

5b   Stipe 1-2.5 cm × 1-2 mm; pileus and gills white but staining red finally; on berry canes, dead small branches, often covering the substrate .... *M. magnisporus* Murrill

Pileus (5) 10-30 (40) mm, broadly convex, disc soon depressed, margin often spreading in age and sulcate to undulating, white, thin, dry, pliant, shining at first; odor and taste mild. Gills distant, often strongly intervenose, white but discoloring brownish red, narrow, adnate. Stipe short, often eccentric, white, blackening slowly upward, unpolished. Spores 10-13 x 5-6 μm, drop-shaped. Pleurocystidia 60-150 x 7-9 μm, cylindric. Setae on pileus 150-200 μm long.

Common in the fall in the Pacific Northwest, apparently rare in the Great Lakes area and eastward.

6a   Base of stipe anchored to substrate by a dense mat of mycelium and substrate (but see also *M. plicatulus*); thick-walled pleurocystidia present 7

6b   Not as above 9

7a   Pileus in late button stages pale ochraceous but by maturity entirely white. Fig. 150 .... *M. delectans* Morgan

Figure 150

Figure 150 *Marasmius delectans*

Pileus 1-4 cm, obtuse to broadly convex to finally plano-umbonate or with margin uplifted; disc at times depressed, dry, dull, in age quite rugulose at times, yellowish pallid then white, ± sulcate-striate in age; context with a ± disagreeable odor, taste mild. Gills soon broad, adnexed to appearing free finally, subdistant to distant, white. Stipe 2-8 cm x 1-3 mm, enlarged near base, glabrous above the mycelioid base, lower portion soon dark brown, upper area ± shining white. Spores 6-8 (10) x 3-5 μm. Pleurocystidia 15-70 x 4-12 μm, of many shapes but generally ± fusoid.

On fallen leaves of hardwoods, summer and fall, common in the central and eastern United States generally.

7b   Pileus definitely colored at maturity 8

8a   Pleurocystidia with brown walls. Fig. 151 ....
.... M. cohaerans (Fr.) Cke. & Quél.

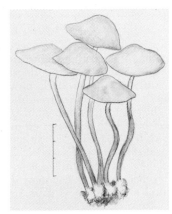

Figure 151

Figure 151   *Marasmius coherans*

Pileus 1-4.5 cm, conic to campanulate or convex, glabrous, dry, unpolished, smooth to rugulose, dull yellow-brown to dark reddish brown; context brownish fading to pallid, odor lacking to ± pungent, taste mild or tardily bitterish. Gills broad, subdistant to distant (in one variant ± narrow and crowded), pallid at first, becoming ± brown from the cystidia. Stipe 2-8 cm x 1-3 mm, dry, shining, naked to near base, becoming dark brown below, with a basal pad of ± colored mycelium. Spores (6) 7-10 (11) x 3-5.5 μm.

On decaying debris of hardwoods, Great Lakes area east and southward, also in Canada, common during late spring and summer.

8b   Pleurocystidia with hyaline to weakly yellowish walls. Fig. 152 ....
.... M. cystidiosus (Sm. & Hes.) Gilliam

Figure 152

Figure 152   *Marasmius cystidiosus*

Pileus 2-4 (6) cm, obtuse to obtusely campanulate, finally broadly expanded; glabrous, striate when moist; taste slight. Gills crowded, adnate-seceding, pale buff. Stipe 6-12 cm x (2) 3-6 (8) mm, with white basal mycelium, cartilaginous, often twisted-striate, pallid above, ± fulvous below. Spores 7-9 (10.5) x 2.5-3.5 μm. Pleurocystidia 36-67 x 3-8 (12) μm, subfusoid, apex often nipple-like.

Clustered on very decayed wood of hardwoods, spring and summer, Great Lakes area eastward and southward, not common. The variant described here, in the older literature was known as *Marasmius fasciatus* Pennington.

9a   Taste of onions or garlic; spores 8-9 × 4-5 μm .... M. scorodonius (Fr.) Fr.

Pileus 1-2 cm, convex to ± expanded, reddish becoming pallid, faded, radially wrinkled. Gills pallid, adnate at first, crowded, narrow, often connected by veins. Stipe 2-5 cm x 1-2 mm, smooth, shining, brittle, base naked. Pleurocystidia none.

Scattered to gregarious on bits of organic debris: grass stems, twigs, conifer needles, etc., northern United States and in Canada. It is more common in these regions than collections in herbaria indicate.

9b   Taste and/or odor not of onions or garlic ....
.. 10

10a On needle beds under conifers **11**

10b On mats of fallen leaves under hardwoods or near or on decaying hardwood **12**

11a Pileus 2-14 mm, dark reddish brown young but whitish (pallid) by maturity; stipe horse-hair-like .... *M. pallidocephalus* **Gilliam**

Pileus convex becoming plano-convex or disc slightly depressed, typically dry (if wet slightly tacky), opaque, smooth to faintly rugulose; odor and taste mild. Gills narrow, subdistant, attached to stipe, edges usually entire, faces pallid to buff. Stipe 12-43 x 0.2-0.8 mm, usually central, shining, blackish brown below, paler reddish brown upward, inserted on fallen needles. Spores 6-10 x 2.5-4 μm. Pleurocystidia lacking.

Gregarious in troops on spruce and fir needle carpets, June to October, Maine to Washington, common.

11b Pileus 1-3.5 cm, wine-red to dark rusty brown; stipe 6-12 cm × 1.5-3.5 mm; spores 11-15 × 5-6.5 μm ....
.... *M. plicatulus* **Peck**

Pileus obtusely conic to campanulate or convex, finally often broadly convex, dry and velvety, becoming plicate-striate nearly to disc, pliant; odor and taste slight. Gills broad, ± distant, rounded-adnate, pallid or tinged pink, more rarely buff. Stipe equal, pink to purplish down to a reddish black base (in a brown variant the apex is pallid to clay-colored and the base dark chestnut), brittle, polished, attached by a dense mat of mycelium at times. Pleurocystidia none.

Densely gregarious under second-growth Sitka spruce along the Pacific Coast, common, fall; less abundant in other habitats.

12a Gills broad, distant, attached to a collar around the stipe **13**

12b Gills attached directly to the stipe **14**

13a Densely gregarious on leaf mats; pileus ± grayish brown but paler to whitish in the depression. Fig. 153 ....
.... *M. capillaris* **Morgan**

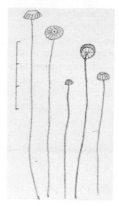

Figure 153

Figure 153 *Marasmius capillaris*

Pileus 3-15 mm, obtuse with an abrupt central depression, plicate, whitish in the depression, remainder of surface pale to dark brownish, becoming paler in age, margin straight; odor and taste slight. Gills distant, broad, whitish. Stipe 3-6 cm x 1 mm ± horsehair-like, inserted on leaf mat, polished, black to (at apex) slightly paler. Spores 8-9 x 4-4.5 μm. Pleurocystidia none.

Densely gregarious on fallen leaves, summer and fall after heavy rains, common during wet seasons, central and eastern United States.

13b Clustered on decaying hardwood and debris; pileus soon whitish except for a dark central spot. Fig. 154 .... *M. rotula* **(Fr.) Fr.**

Figure 154

Figure 154 *Marasmius rotula*

Pileus 10-15 (20) mm broad, convex-depressed, the disc usually flat at first but soon depressed, surface dry, soon plicate-striate, brownish on disc, the margin pallid, soon predominantly white but with a dark spot in the depression; context thin and pliant, odor slight, taste mild to bitterish. Gills broad, distant, white. Stipe 1.5-8 (10) cm x 1-2 mm, base ± bulbous, surface shining and appearing wiry, pallid but soon black except for the whitish apex. Spores 6.5-9 (10) x 3-4.5 μm. Pleurocystidia none.

Typically in dense clusters on or near decaying hardwood, very common and widely distributed, late spring, summer, and fall.

14a Gills close; pileus bright rusty red .... *M. sullivantii* Montagne

Pileus 6-25 mm, convex becoming plane, margin only faintly striate, dull and unpolished; context pallid, taste faintly bitter, odor none. Gills free but reaching the stipe ±, narrow but slightly ventricose, edges faintly pinkish then concolorous with faces. Stipe 5-25 x 1-1.5 mm, hornlike and rigid, with a faint bloom at first, reddish brown to blackish below, attached by a strigose enlarged base, Spores 7-9 x 3-3.5 μm, smooth. Pleurocystidia 16-38 x 3-7 μm, versiform and smooth or with short projections, scarcely projecting beyond the basidia.

Solitary to scattered or gregarious, under hardwoods on debris on the forest floor, the Southeast north to Massachusetts, Michigan, and Minnesota, not common.

14b Gills distant, pileus rusty orange to rusty brown .... *M. siccus* (Schw.) Fr.

Pileus 1-3 cm, convex to campanulate or disc depressed, soon rugulose to deeply plicate, rusty orange to rusty brown or paler tawny; odor and taste slight. Gills distant, broad, pallid to buff, edges even. Stipe 2-7 cm x 1-2 mm, ± equal, becoming dark brown from base upward, attached by a patch of white mycelium. Spores (13) 16-21 (23) x 2.8-4.5 (5) μm, narrowly clavate. Pleurocystidia fusoid-ventricose, 25-70 x 3-14 μm.

Scattered to gregarious on fallen leaves mostly under hardwoods July to October, east of the Great Plains in North America, very common.

Melanoleuca Patouillard

Pileus and stipe confluent; pileus usually hygrophanous; stipe strict and narrow compared to width of the cap; gills adnate to sinuate, usually ± horizontal at maturity and ± crowded; spore deposit cream color to white, rarely buff; spores with amyloid ornamentation and a distinct plage; cheilocystidia when present usually with incrustations near apex and apex pointed; clamp connections absent; growing on humus and on waste ground but probably mycorrhiza-formers with woody plants for the most part. The genus here in North America contains about 30 species of which none are known to be poisonous, though most have not been tested.

KEY TO SPECIES

1a Pileus white becoming lemon-yellow; surface viscid .... *M. lewisii* Sm. & P. M. Rea

Pileus 4-8 cm, convex to plane, appearing varnished when dry; odor and taste mild. Gills white, broad, rounded at the stipe, crowded. Stipe 3-6 cm x ± 10 mm, flared somewhat at apex, white. Spores 6-8.5 x 4-5 μm. Pleuro- and cheilocystidia 46-64 x 9-14 μm, fusoid-ventricose, pointed apex incrusted. Pileus with a thick ixocutis.

Gregarious to subcaespitose under Monterey Pine, near sea level, southern California.

1b Not with both the above features 2

2a Stipe eccentric .... *M. eccentrica* Smith

Pileus 4-7 cm, plano-umbonate, glabrous, moist, pale yellow, margin pallid yellowish, ± pale tan over all in age; context pallid; taste and odor *Inocybe*-like (nauseous and disagreeable). Gills crowded, narrow, adnexed, pallid. Stipe 4-5 cm x 9-10 mm, equal, pinkish gray and fibrillose striate. Spores 7-8 x 4-5 μm. Cystidia none. Cuticle of pileus a thin cutis of narrow (3-6 μm hyphae).

Under conifers, Olympic Mountains, Washington, October, scattered, apparently rarely collected.

2b Stipe central, pileus not pale yellow at first 3

3a Pileus creamy but tinged gray; gills whitish .... M. *reai* **Singer**

Pileus 2-6.5 cm, convex to plane, odor and taste mild. Gills broad, sinuate, close. Stipe 4-5 cm x 4-7 mm, thick, usually central, fibrillose-striate, basal tomentum white. Spores cream color in deposit, 8-9 x 6-7 μm, broadly ovoid, warts strongly amyloid. Cheilocystidia rare, 28-42 x 5-6 μm, apex slightly incrusted.

On a lawn, southern California, September to November, rarely collected.

3b Not as above 4

4a Gills at maturity pinkish cinnamon to tan. Fig. 155 .... M. *cognata* (Fr.) Kon. & Maüb.

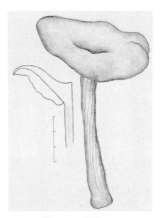

Figure 155

Figure 155 *Melanoleuca cognata*

Pileus 9-13 cm, plane, becoming depressed, glabrous, viscid, color bister to snuff brown fading to pale tan; odor and taste peculiar but hard to define. Gills crowded, finally broad, sinuate, whitish when young, thin. Stipe 6-11 cm x 10-16 mm, longitudinally striate from parallel ridges, or twisted-striate, brownish above, soon bister over basal area. Spores cream-color in deposit, 7-8 x 4-5.5 μm, warts strongly amyloid. Pleuro- and cheilocystidia abundant, 52-80 x 8-15 μm, fusoid-ventricose, pointed, apex incrusted. Cuticle an ixocutis, hyphae 4-7 μm wide.

On wet soil in dense conifer forests and on wet ground under weeds at edge of forest, summer and fall, widely distributed but not common. It has been found regularly, however, in the spruce-fir zone in the mountains of Colorado.

4b Gills white to grayish 5

5a Gill edges staining brownish where bruised 6

5b Gill edges not staining where bruised 7

6a Gills gray at first, becoming white; cheilocystidia absent .... M. *angelesiana* Smith

Pileus 5-7 cm, expanded-umbonate, glabrous, subviscid, olive brown to drab; taste mild. Gills crowded, broad, adnate. Stipe 5-6 cm x 10-12 mm, fibrous-striate, dingy gray within. Spores 7-9 x 4.5-6 μm, with strongly amyloid warts. Pleuro- and cheilocystidia none. Cuticular hyphae of pileus with dark brown content.

Scattered under conifers, Pacific Northwest, June, rarely collected.

6b Gills white at first; cheilocystidia abundant .... M. *humilis* (Fr.) **Pat.**

Pileus 2-4.5 cm, convex to plane, glabrous, fuscous to dark drab, fading to drab gray, odor and taste faintly like that of *Lepiota cristata*. Gills crowded, white. Stipe 4-6 cm x 3-4 mm, equal, pallid throughout, in age surface pale cinereous, fibrillose-striate to pruinose near apex. Spores white in deposits, 7-9 x 4-5 μm, with strongly amyloid warts. Pleuro- and cheilocystidia 46-62 x 9-12 μm, versiform: clavate to fusoid-pointed and incrusted, also the wall somewhat thickened.

Scattered on moss, Pacific Northwest, rarely collected, September.

7a Pleurocystidia absent; stipe with dark fibrils or dark ± overall. Fig. 156 ....
.... M. melaleuca (Fr.) Murr.

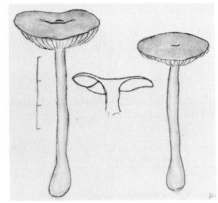

Figure 156

Figure 156 *Melanoleuca melaleuca*

Pileus 3-8 cm, thin, plano-convex, often with a low umbo, glabrous, hygrophanous, dark smoky brown to blackish moist, dingy ochraceous tan faded; context pallid; odor and taste slight. Gills adnexed, narrow, close, pure white, dingy in age. Stipe 3-8 cm x 3-6 mm, equal, strict, cartilaginous, streaked with dark fibrils or almost as dark as the pileus overall. Spores 7-8 x 4-5.5 μm. Pleurocystidia none. Cheilocystidia rare and ± imbedded in the gill edge, 18-26 x 5-9 μm, clavate to fusoid-ventricose.

Solitary to gregarious on waste land, under conifers and hardwoods, widely distributed, summer and fall. In Europe it is regarded as a good edible species. In North America it is likely to be confused with other species.

7b Pleurocystidia present; stipe white to pallid
.. 8

8a Pileus dark to pale honey-color fading to yellowish pallid; stipe 7-15 cm × (5) 8-12 mm. Fig. 157 ...... M. alboflavida (Pk.) Murr.

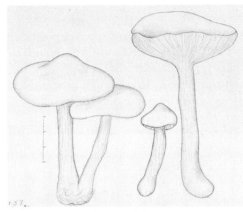

Figure 157

Figure 157 *Melanoleuca alboflavida*

Pileus 5-12 cm, obtuse becoming expanded-umbonate to plane, at times ± depressed around the umbo, surface tacky when moist, soon dry; context pallid, odor and taste mild. Gills very crowded, horizontal, broad, adnexed, whitish or finally buffy-pallid in age. Stipe strict, ± equal, base weakly bulbous, fibrous, cartilaginous, longitudinally striate, dingy pallid, ± fibrillose-lacerate at times. Spore deposit white; spores 7-9 x 4-5.5 μm. Pleuro- and cheilocystidia similar, 50-65 x 9-16 μm.

Scattered to gregarious on soil in hardwood forests, under brush, on waste land, along country roads, etc.; common, summer and fall east of the Great Plains. Edible according to Kauffman.

8b Pileus 2-4 (7) cm, black to dark gray ....
.... M. brevipes (Fr.) Patouillard

Pileus convex to plane, dull and unpolished, slowly fading to buffy brown or paler; context white, odor and taste mild. Gills crowded, narrow, white then cream-color. Stipe 1-3 cm x 3-6 mm, clavate at first, white to pale buff, fibrous-pruinose near apex. Spores white in deposit, 6.5-8 x 5-6 μm, ornamentation of warts and fine lines. Cheilocystidia 30-42 x 6-9 μm, cylindric with obtuse tips and somewhat thickened walls.

Scattered to gregarious in grassy areas or on waste land, sometimes near compost piles, summer and fall, widely distributed, probably more common than records indicate.

Mycena (Fr.) S. F. Gray

Pileus and stipe confluent; spore deposit white; stipe thin and fragile (mostly 1-3 mm thick at apex); pileus margin typically appressed against the stipe at first or merely approaching it; pileus typically conic or with a conic umbo; cuticular region of pileus in most species consisting of a cutis or ixocutis and subcuticular zone in which the hyphae have greatly inflated cells and typically contain a dissolved pigment in the cell sap; spores amyloid or not, smooth.

Over 200 species occur in North America. None are recommended for table use.

KEY TO SPECIES

1a Stipe when sectioned near base with a sharp instrument exuding a drop of dull red latex. Fig. 158 .... *M. haematopus* (Fr.) Kummer

Figure 158

Figure 158 *Mycena haematopus*

Pileus 1-3.5 cm, conic to campanulate, with a sterile band at edge which becomes crenate, surface pruinose at first, ± dull red to reddish brown or pinkish brown; taste mild to bitterish. Gills with or without reddish margins, close to subdistant, often stained dull reddish brown. Stipe 3-8 (14) cm x 1-3 mm, pruinose ± dull red-brown. Spores 8-11 x 5-7 μm, amyloid.

Solitary to clustered, on wood of hardwoods, common and widely distributed, spring, summer, or fall.

1b Lacking a latex when tested as in above choice 2

2a Gill edges marginate (a different color than the faces) 3

2b Gill edges not differently colored than the faces (or merely paler) 7

3a Growing in troops (densely gregarious) to scattered on needle beds under conifers 4

3b Habitat on wood or humus generally 5

4a Pileus pinkish to grayish pink; gill edges dull reddish (at times rather pale) ....
.... *M. rosella* (Fr.) Kummer

Pileus 5-20 (30) mm, conic to campanulate to broadly convex, lubricous, striate, flesh-color to pink, tinted ochraceous in age or toned with gray; context pliant, pinkish-pallid. Gills ± horizontal, subdistant, broadly adnate to arcuate. Stipe 2.5-7 cm x 1-1.5 (2) mm, pliant, white-strigose at base, pale rose to grayish, lubricous but not viscid. Spores 7-9 x 4-5 μm, amyloid. Pleurocystidia 60-80 x 10-14 μm, with reddish content, fusoid-ventricose. Cheilocystidia subfusoid, 21-36 x 9-15 μm, enlarged part with short obtuse projections, cell content dull pink to red.

Gregarious and common in the conifer areas of North America, late summer and fall after heavy rains.

4b Pileus bright scarlet; gill edges flame scarlet. Fig. 159 .... *M. strobilinoides* **Peck**

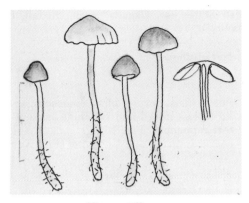

Figure 159

Figure 159 *Mycena strobilinoides*

Pileus 1-2.5 cm, conic to campanulate, striate, fading to cadmium yellow; taste mild. Gills ascending, subdistant, yellow to pinkish orange. Stipe 3-6 cm x 1-2.5 mm, strigose at base with orange fibrils, surface covered with orange pruina at first, ground color orange-chrome. Spores 7-9 x 4-5 μm, amyloid. Cheilocystidia and pleurocystidia similar, clavate and covered by rod-like projections, content bright to pale orange.

Common in the mountains of the Pacific Northwest, sporadic in the Great Lakes area, late summer and fall.

5a Under hardwoods on humus or on very rotten remains of hardwoods; stipe 3-10 mm thick; taste of context radish-like; gill edges dingy reddish purple .... *M. rutilantiformis* **Murrill**

Pileus 2-7 cm, convex to ± plane, often split on margin, glabrous, striatulate; dark vinaceous brown to vinaceous buff and soon developing yellowish tinges over margin; odor raphanoid. Gills sinuate to adnexed, broad (± 1 cm), close to subdistant. Stipe 3-8 cm long, equal, hollow, fragile, longitudinally striate, with scattered purplish fibrils near apex and ground color in apical region yellowish. Spores 8-10 x 3.5-5 μm, amyloid. Pleuro- and cheilocystidia similar, 40-80 x 9-15 μm, content dark red-brown.

Solitary to gregarious on rotting wood and rich humus, Great Lakes area eastward, and in the Pacific Northwest. *M. pelianthina* (Fr.) Quélet is a similar species with smaller spores but lacks yellow tints in the apex of the stipe. It is often confused with Murrill's species.

5b Obviously lignicolous; taste not radish-like **6**

6a On wood of hardwoods; fruiting body bright orange to yellow; stipe with orange scurf at first. Fig. 160 .... *M. leaiana* **(Berk.) Sacc.**

Figure 160

Figure 160 *Mycena leaiana*

Pileus 1-4 cm, obtuse then campanulate to convex, viscid, shining, striate on margin. Gills close, broad, light ochraceous salmon with brilliant orange-red edges. Stipes clustered, 2-10 x 2-4 mm, orange-strigose at base. Spores 7-10 x 5-6 μm, amyloid. Pleuro- and cheilocystidia similar, 32-46 x 8-13 μm, content orange, fusoid-ventricose to clavate or with 1-several protuberances.

Caespitose, east of the Great Plains, spring, summer and fall, common. The southern *M. euspeirea* (Berk. & Curt.) Sacc. and *M. texensis* Smith are closely related but differ in having gray to pallid colors.

6b On conifer logs, pileus dark purple-umber to purplish vinaceous .... *M. purpureofusca* **(Pk.) Sacc.**

Pileus 5-25 mm, obtusely conic to campanulate, hoary at first, soon naked. Gills narrow, equal, close, grayish to pallid, edges dark grayish purple. Stipe 3-10 cm x 1-2.5 mm, equal, base white-strigose. Spores 8-10 x 6-7 μm (10-14 x 6.5-8.5 μm from 2-spored basidia). Cheilocystidia 30-50 (65) x 7-15 μm, fusoid-ventricose, filled with a dull purple sap.

Solitary to gregarious on conifer logs and stumps, northern United States and in Canada, abundant at times in the Pacific Northwest, and in the mountains of the Southwest. *M. elegantula* Peck is easily confused with *M. purpureofusca* but the gills edges are reddish and paler.

7a   Pileus and/or stipe ± brightly colored (blue, red, lilac, or yellow) 8

7b   Pileus and/or stipe white to gray to reddish brown brown or black 13

8a   Pileus coral red fading to white. Fig. 161 ....
.... *M. amabilissima* (Pk.) Sacc.

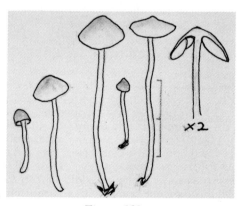

Figure 161

Figure 161   *Mycena amabilissima*

Pileus 3-20 mm, conic then conic-campanulate, in age expanded-umbonate, glabrous and moist, evenly colored, striate when moist. Gills adnate, narrow, subdistant, tinged coral red but soon white, edges pallid. Stipe 3-5 cm x 1-2 mm, equal, watery, tinged coral red, often white at maturity. Spores 7-9 x 3-4 μm, non-amyloid. Pleuro- and

cheilocystidia similar, fusoid-ventricose, 40-65 x 8-15 μm, apex acute.

Scattered to gregarious on moss in bogs and on needle carpets, widely distributed in northern United States and Canada, spring to fall, fairly common.

8b   Not as above 9

9a   Pileus lilac, purple, blue, vinaceous, or pallid (colors mixed and variable); taste of context raphanoid. Fig. 162 ....
.... *M. pura* (Fr.) Kummer

Figure 162

Figure 162   *Mycena pura*

Pileus 2-4 (6.5) cm, obtuse to convex, becoming broadly umbonate, odor raphanoid. Gills broad, subdistant, adnate to adnexed, color variable as for the pileus, edges pallid. Stipe 3-7 (10) cm x 2-6 mm, fragile, equal, somewhat scabrous at times, more often glabrous, pallid or colored as the pileus. Spores 6-9 (10) x 3-3.5 μm, amyloid. Pleuro- and cheilocystidia ± similar, 40-70 (100) x 10-20 (25) μm, ventricose, the apex obtuse, or fusoid-ventricose, or ± ellipsoid (rarely), some with a few protuberances on the upper part.

Scattered to widely gregarious in hardwood and conifer forests alike, common, summer and fall, widely distributed. We suspect it of being poisonous.

9b   Not as above 10

10a Stipe showing blue somewhere (especially at base or on the hairs attached to it); stipe not viscid .... *M. subcaerulea* (Pk.) **Sacc.**

Pileus (3) 5-25 mm, ovoid to broadly conic or convex, often in age broadly convex, glabrous, pellicle completely separable from cap, color at very first a bright blue but soon gray to brownish with only a tint of blue, often yellowish in age. Gills close, ± broad finally, white to grayish. Stipe 3-8 cm x 1-2.5 mm, elastic, densely pruinose to pubescent. Spores 6-8 x 6-7 (8) μm, ± globose, amyloid. Cheilocystidia 32-60 x 5-8 μm, ± cylindric.

Solitary to scattered in debris of hardwoods, on bits of wood, stumps, rotting logs, etc.; common east of the Great Plains but seldom in large numbers, spring, summer and fall. On conifer debris the very similar *M. amicta* (Fr.) Quélet occurs but its spores are ellipsoid.

10b Stipe viscid, not blue **11**

11a Pileus lilac but very soon yellow; gills usually remaining lilac to maturity. Fig. 163 ......
.... *M. lilacifolia* (Pk.) **Sm.**

Figure 163

Figure 163 *Mycena lilacifolia*

Pileus 8-25 mm, convex and disc ± flattened, becoming plano-depressed, viscid, striate. Gills subdistant, unequally decurrent. Stipe 1-3 (4.5) cm x 1-2 mm, equal, concolorous with gills but soon yellow, basal mycelium remaining lilac.

Spores 6-7 x 3-3.5 μm, non-amyloid. Cheilo- and pleurocystidia none.

Solitary or scattered in small numbers on rotting conifer logs, northern United States and Canada; spring, summer, and fall.

11b Lilac colors not present on the fruiting body **12**

12a Taste of raw flesh rancid farinaceous. Fig. 164 .... *M. viscosa* (Secr.) **Maire**

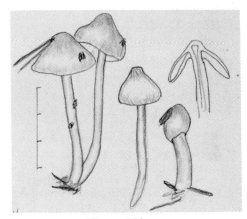

Figure 164

Figure 164 *Mycena viscosa*

Pileus 5-30 mm, ovoid then convex to broadly campanulate, viscid, in age sulcate-striate, yellowish to greenish gray, dingy brown in age, margin a sterile band at first appressed to stipe; context staining reddish; odor strong of fresh cucumber. Gills subdistant, often spotted reddish. Stipe 3-10 cm x 1-3 mm, tenacious, lemon yellow, slimy, reddish variously in age. Spores 9-11 x 6.5-8 μm from 4-spored basidia. Cheilocystidia 40-60 x 6-9 μm, pedicels gelatinous, apex clavate and with numerous crooked projections.

Gregarious under pine, late in the fall, common after prolonged cold soaking rains, widely distributed.

12b Taste mild. Fig. 165 ....
.... *M. epipterygia* (Fr.) **S. F. Gray**

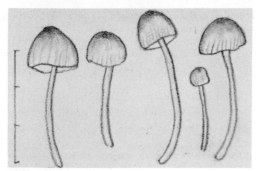

Figure 165

Figure 166

Figure 165 *Mycena epipterygia*

Pileus 8-20 mm, ovoid then campanulate, viscid, pellicle separable, in age plicate-striate, color old-gold to mustard yellow fading to pallid or white but drying pale gray. Gills subdistant, yellowish, fairly broad. Stipe 6-8 cm x 1-2 mm, slimy-viscid, lemon yellow fading to white, yellow as dried. Spores 8-11 x 5-6 μm, amyloid. Cheilocystidia clavate with apex roughened with rodlike projections, gelatinizing and difficult to measure.

Common under conifers and widely distributed but sporadic; late fall after heavy rains. A variety occurs on rotting conifer logs (var. *lignicola* Smith), which is common in the Great Lakes area, summer and fall, but never in large numbers.

13a Minute species (stipe thread-like up to ± 1 mm thick) 14

13b Stipe 1-3 mm thick or more 16

14a Stipe with a flat circular disc at base. Fig. 166 .... *M. stylobates* (**Fr.**) **Kummer**

Figure 166 *Mycena stylobates*

Pileus 3-15 mm, conic to convex, then campanulate to plane, smooth or spinulose on disc, translucent-striate, pale gray, fading to nearly white. Gills close becoming distant, finally ventricose, often seceding and adhering to each other forming a collar around the stipe, gray becoming white. Stipe 10-60 x 0.5-1 mm, basal disc striate; surface above disc covered with fine white fibrils, when fresh bluish gray, in age pallid. Spores 6-8 x 3.5-4.5 μm (in 2-spored variants the spores 8-10 μm long). Cheilocystidia ± clavate and with 2-5 obtuse projections, 26-38 x 8-13 μm.

Scattered on bits of debris, fallen oak leaves, conifer needles, small pieces of bark, etc., widely distributed in North America, spring, summer, and fall.

14b Stipe not as above 15

15a Stipe 5-15 mm long; gills broad. Fig. 167 .... *M. tenerrima* (**Berk.**) **Quél.**

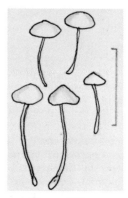

Figure 167

Figure 167 *Mycena tenerrima*

Pileus 2.5-3.5 mm, obtuse to obtusely campanulate then convex, margin straight, surface granulose, soon white overall, sulcate to disc, membranous. Gills ± free, broad, distant, white. Stipe 5-15 mm long, filiform, setose under a lens. Spores 8-10 x 5-6.5 (7) μm, amyloid. Pleurocystidia when present similar to cheilocystidia and both 28-44 x 8-12 μm, fusoid-ventricose or with 2-3 needle-like projections from near the apex, enlarged area verrucose. Cells on pileus also verrucose.

    Scattered on twigs and debris, mostly on alder and conifer twigs, spring and fall, Washington to California.

15b Stipe 2-3 cm long; gills narrow. Fig. 168 ....
.... *M. osmundicola* **Lange**

Figure 168

Figure 168 *Mycena osmundicola*

Pileus (2) 3-6 mm, conic to convex, dry and powdery, grayish to chalk-white, membranous, at times sulcate; taste mild. Gills ± distant, narrow, nearly free, white. Stipe densely white-villous from verrucose cells and hyphae. Spores 7-9 (10) x 4-5 μm, weakly amyloid. Cheilocystidia clavate, verrucose, 18-28 x 9-15 μm.

    Scattered to gregarious on debris in the forest: on conifer needles, debris of ferns, old leaves of deciduous trees, etc., spring, summer, and fall, not uncommon, widely distributed.

16a Stipe distinctly pubescent under a handlens; spores 5-6.5 μm, verrucose, not amyloid ......
.... *M. cooliana* **Oort**

Pileus 10-30 mm, conic, then campanulate, hoary at first, fuscous brown, margin paler; taste mild. Gills close, broad in age, grayish at first, margin pruinose (under a lens). Stipe 4-12 cm x 1-2.5 mm, gray above, darker below. Pleurocystidia and cheilocystidia similar, 40-90 x 8-12 μm, fusoid-ventricose, neck and apex smooth to incrusted.

    Scattered under redwood, California, sporadic, fall and winter.

16b Stipe at most pubescent near the base; spores smooth, amyloid, usually larger than in preceding choice 17

17a Growing scattered to gregarious on humus and needle carpets; pileus and stipe gray (tin-color) .... *M. murina* Murrill

Pileus 1-3 (4) cm, obtusely conic, then campanulate, striate, dull gray or paler; taste mild. Gills subdistant, pale to dark gray (like the pileus), edges pallid. Stipe 3-8 cm x 1-4 mm, fragile, dark to pale gray. Spores 8-11 x 5-6 (7) μm, amyloid. Pleuro- and cheilocystidia fusoid-ventricose or with one or more obtuse protuberances from the apical region.

    Scattered to gregarious, common and widely distributed in North America, summer and late fall.

17b Not as in above choice 18

18a Stipe with a well-developed pseudorhiza; spores 12-17 × 6-9 μm. Fig. 169 ....
.... *M. megaspora* **Kauffman**

Figure 169

Figure 170

Figure 169 *Mycena megaspora*

Pileus 2-5 (7) cm, obtuse to convex, finally plano-umbonate, often campanulate, glabrous, ± wrinkled, lubricous, blackish over all and fading through gray to ± pinkish gray or dingy yellowish brown; odor and taste mild. Gills broad, subdistant, ± adnate, ventricose in age, finally stained reddish brown. Stipe 5-15 cm long with an additional 3-10 cm of pseudorhiza, 1-4 (5) mm thick, naked, cartilaginous. Spores amyloid. Basidia 2-, 3-, and 4-spored. Cheilocystidia 38-46 x 14-22 μm, clavate, apex studded with rod-like projections.

Scattered to solitary, rarely in small clusters, on wet humus and in bogs or swamps, apparently from dead wood. We have seen it regularly in dried up bogs near bushes of *Vaccinium*. Not rare in the Great Lakes area and to be expected eastward.

18b Not as above **19**

19a Stipe innately white-fibrillose; odor often nitrous; on debris of hardwoods; solitary to scattered; pleurocystidia 50-90 × 8-15 μm. Fig. 170 .... *M. niveipes* **Murrill**

Figure 170 *Mycena niveipes*

Pileus 2-7 cm, ellipsoid at first, becoming campanulate to broadly conic, striate, olive-brown to gray, paler on margin, nearly white in age; taste acidulous to ± farinaceous, odor nitrous (or in some collections lacking). Gills broad, subdistant, ascending-adnate, grayish becoming white. Stipe 4-10 cm x 2.5-7 mm, fragile, surface grayish but usually white by maturity. Spores 8-10 x 5-6 μm, amyloid. Cheilocystidia similar to pleurocystidia, apex obtuse to acute.

Spring and early summer, east of the Great Plains and also in the Rocky Mountains.

19b Not as above: obviously and consistently on wood of conifers **20**

20a Odor sharp (nitrous to alkaline); pleurocystidia prominent and projecting distinctly beyond the hymenium .... *M. alcalina* **(Fr.) Kummer**

Pileus 1-4 cm, conic becoming broadly conic to campanulate, blackish to bluish gray or in age yellowish gray or brownish. Gills close to subdistant, ascending-adnate, at times spotted reddish brown in age. Stipe 4-9 (11) cm x 1.5-3 (4) mm, grayish to pallid, lubricous. Spores 8-11 x 5-7 μm, amyloid. Pleurocystidia (35) 40-60 x 8-15 (20) μm; cheilocystidia similar to pleurocystidia or smaller.

Solitary to caespitose on conifer wood, abundant in the spring and fall, widely distributed in northern regions.

20b Odor slight; pleurocystidia not projecting from hymenium **21**

21a Gills at maturity with reddish brown stains; fruiting in the fall. Fig. 171 .... *M. maculata* **Karsten**

Figure 171

Figure 171 *Mycena maculata*

Pileus 2-5 cm, conic to convex, soon campanulate to broadly convex, finally plano-umbonate, lubricous, striate if moist, blackish brown; context gray staining reddish when cut, taste farinaceous. Gills ± subdistant, broad, gray at first. Stipe 4-8 cm x 2-5 mm, somewhat rooting at times, white-strigose over lower part. Spores 7-9 (10) x 4-5 (6) μm, amyloid. Cheilocystidia clavate, apex with short rodlike projections. Pleurocystidia rare and resembling cheilocystidia, inconspicuous.

Caespitose on wood of conifers, fall, common and widely distributed in northern regions.

It is the most abundant *Mycena* on conifer wood in the Pacific Northwest.

21b Gills staining gray when bruised; fruiting in the early spring to midsummer. Fig. 172 .... *M. overholtsii* **Smith & Solheim**

Figure 172

Figure 172 *Mycena overholtsii*

Pileus 2-5 cm, obtuse to convex becoming ± plane or obtusely umbonate, at times remaining campanulate, glabrous, lubricous, striate, dark to pale watery gray or bluish gray. Gills ± subdistant, broadly adnate to ± decurrent, broad. Stipe 4-10 cm x 2-5 mm, pallid to gray above, downward becoming reddish brown slowly. Spores 6-8 x 3.4-4 μm, amyloid. Cheilocystidia smooth, 26-32 x 5-8 μm.

Caespitose on conifer logs partly covered by snow, early spring to midsummer, common in the higher mountains of the western area. In this area it has come to be recognized as a member of the "snowbank mushroom flora."

Omphalina Quélet

Pileus 5-25 (45) mm, convex to plane, becoming depressed to funnel-shaped, margin incurved at first, ± hygrophanous, glabrous to fibrillose or squamulose, typically brightly colored; gills clearly decurrent, often appearing waxy, white to brightly colored (yellow to orange); stipe usually 1-3 (6) mm thick, fragile; spores non-amyloid, white to yellowish in deposits, rarely tinged salmon; hyphal pigment dissolved in the cell sap; habitat on mosses, lichens, wood or soil.

A total of 14 species and varieties are currently recognized from North America.

KEY TO SPECIES

1a **On moss in wet springy areas; pileus pinkish ferruginous to orange-red fading to orange-yellow** .... *O. postii* **(Fr.) Singer**

Pileus 1-3 cm, soon plano-depressed, striatulate when moist, glabrous; context thin, flaccid, dull orange. Gills distinctly decurrent, intervenose, white then yellowish to pinkish, appearing waxy (clean). Stipe 2.5-8 (10) cm x 1-3 (5) mm, pale orange to yellow, pruinose, soon naked, fragile, hollow. Spores white in deposit, 6.5-11 x 4.5-6 (6.5) μm. Clamp connections absent.

    Scattered to gregarious, spring, summer or fall, Great Lakes area and eastward as well as in the Pacific Northwest. In its favorite habitat it fruits almost every season.

1b **On wood, especially that of conifers; if habitat otherwise then pileus not red to orange** **2**

2a **Pileus salmon-orange or pinker, fading to yellow (rarely whitish in age). Fig. 173** .... *O. luteicolor* **Murrill**

Figure 173

Figure 173 *Omphalina luteicolor*

Pileus 1-3 cm, convex to plane and finally shallowly depressed, striate when moist; context pinkish to orange buff; taste and odor mild. Gills adnate to short-decurrent, ± distant, narrow, arched, orange to salmon buff. Stipe 1-2 (3) cm, 1.5-2.5

cm thick, pale orange becoming pallid finally, glabrous, base strigose at times. Spores (6.5) x 7-9 (11.5) x 4-5 (5.5) μm, elliptic to obovate. Clamp connections absent.

    Densely gregarious on rotting, wet, conifer logs and stumps, fall, common in the Pacific Northwest.

2b **Pileus brown to brownish to olive-ochraceous** **3**

3a **Pileus with an olive tone and gradually brighter greenish yellow. Fig. 174** .... *O. wynniae* **(Berk. & Br.) Ito**

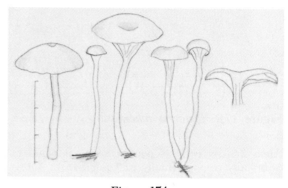

Figure 174

Figure 174 *Omphalina wynniae*

Pileus 1-2.5 cm, convex to ± plane and finally with uplifted margin, glabrous, moist, hygrophanous, striate when moist, disc ± olive-brown to brownish olive; margin ± greenish yellow, paler overall in age. Gills distinctly decurrent, ± broad, olive-yellow, brighter and paler in age. Stipe 1-3 cm x 1-4 mm, equal, ± naked, pallid to yellow. Spores 7-9 (10.5) x 4-5 (6) μm, elliptic. Clamp connections present.

    On wet rotting conifer wood, solitary or in small clusters, fall, Pacific Northwest.

3b **Pileus vinaceous brown to various shades of brownish ochraceous to buff (but not olive); on wood, among lichens or on soil covered with "algae" (a green scum, actually the vegetative phase of a lichen). Fig. 175** .... *O. ericetorum* **(Fr.) M. Lange**

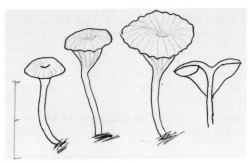

Figure 175

Figure 175 *Omphalina ericetorum*

Pileus 5-35 mm, plane with margin inrolled; finally broadly funnel-shaped, various shades from dark vinaceous brown through clay-color to ochraceous or even pallid ochraceous, glabrous, moist, conspicuously striate. Gills decurrent, broad, distant, yellowish. Stipe 1-3 cm x 1-3 mm, finely pubescent to naked, brownish slowly becoming yellowish to pallid. Spores 7-9 (10) x 4-6 μm (up to 12 x 8 μm on 1-spored basidia). Basidia 1-, 2-, 3-, and 4-spored.

Scattered on the lichen *Botrydina vulgaris* Breb which often covers wet wood, mosses and soil as a green scum. This mushroom is regarded as one of the most common mushrooms in the arctic and extends southward across Canada to the cooler places in the United States. In the Pacific Northwest we have one variant with a white spore deposit and one with a yellow one.

Omphalotus Fayod

Fruiting bodies in large clusters associated with decaying hardwood logs, stumps, trees, and roots; gills phosphorescent in fresh material, narrow, decurrent, close; stipe often fused at base to form the clusters, central to eccentric; stipe and pileus confluent; spore deposit white to yellow, spores non-amyloid; veils absent; clamp connections present.

Four species are known from North America, all should be regarded as poisonous.

KEY TO SPECIES

1a Pileus dull orange to brownish orange becoming olivaceous in age; gills olive mottled with honey yellow when young; spores 7-8 $\times$ 6-6.5 (7.5) μm. Fig. 176 ....
.... *O. olivascens* Bigl., Mill. & Thiers

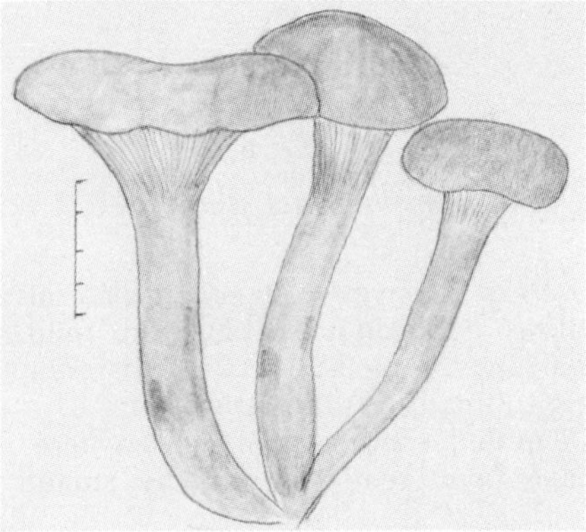

Figure 176

Figure 176 *Omphalotus olivascens*

Pileus 4-10 (24) cm, broadly convex to $\pm$ plane with a decurved margin, glabrous; context olivaceous to dull orange, odor not distinctive, taste mild. Gills close to subdistant, short decurrent. Stipe 4-22 x 0.7-8 cm, tapering toward the base, olive to olive-yellow or dull sulphur-yellow, glabrous to $\pm$ longitudinally fibrillose, sometimes fused at the base.

Known from northcentral California where, around the Bay Region, it is fairly abundant from late fall into winter.

1b Pileus orange to orange-yellow, duller in age but lacking olive tones; gills orange, often beaded with orange droplets; spores usually smaller **2**

2a Spores globose to drop shaped, 3.5-5 μm in diam. Fig. 177 .... *O. illudens* (Schw.) **Bigl.**

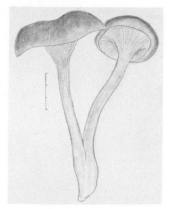

Figure 177

Figure 177 *Omphalotus illudens*

Pileus 5-18 cm, convex to ± plane, glabrous; context yellow, odor disagreeable, taste mild. Gills close, narrow. Stipe 9-20 x 2-4 cm, orange-yellow, longitudinally fibrous-striate.

Common, especially in cities where shade trees have been removed and the stumps covered with dirt, late summer and fall. Although heavy spore deposits are yellowish, white deposits have been reported for this species, but here one may be dealing with thin deposits. This species is to be expected east of the Great Plains, and often fruits during relatively dry seasons.

2b Spores ellipsoid, or globose and larger **3**

3a Spores 5-7 × 4.5-6.5 (8 × 7) μm .... *O. olearius* (Fr.) **Fayod**

This species, apparently relatively common in southern Europe, has been considered to be the same as our *O. illudens* by some, who then of course, report *O. olearius* as occurring in North America.

3b Spores 4.5-6 × 3-3.5 μm .... *Monadelphus subilludens* **Murr.**

Monadelphus is a later name for *Omphalotus;* we have not found this species transferred to *Omphalotus*. This species differs from *O. illudens* chiefly in shape of the spores. Its center of distribution appears to be the Gulf Coast area, but both species are found there. Those who reduce all these species to synonymy under *O. olearius* put greatest emphasis on the fact that all, to some degree, are interfertile. Those who recognize four species recognize that since they are sympatric to a degree, they hybridize—a feature well established for many groups of plants.

Oudemansiella Speg.

Pileus and stipe confluent; gills adnate to adnexed, broad; stipe with a well-developed pseudorhiza; veil absent; spore deposit white, spores broad (usually over 6 μm), non-amyloid; basidia and cystidia very large; clamp connections typically present.

In a sense this genus is the counter part of *Phaeocollybia* in the Cortinariaceae, at least on the aspect of the fresh fruiting bodies, particularly the well-developed pseudorhiza. Probably less than a dozen species occur in North America.

KEY TO SPECIES

1a Pileus thinly viscid when fresh and moist; spores 12-18 × 9-12 μm. Fig. 178 .... *O. radicata* (Fr.) **Singer**

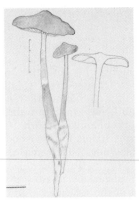

Figure 178

Figure 178 *Oudemansiella radicata*

Pileus (3) 4-10 (12) cm, campanulate to ± plano-umbonate, glabrous, often rugose, dark brown to yellowish brown, gray, or nearly white; margin incurved; taste mild. Gills broad, ± subdistant; thickish. Stipe 6-20 cm x 4-8 (15) mm above the pseudorhiza, rigid, erect, unpolished to furfuraceous, often twisted-striate, pallid above, smoky brown lower down. Spores subellipsoid, smooth. Pleurocystidia (80) 100-150 x 16-36 (45) μm, utriform; cheilocystidia versiform. Pileus cuticle ± gelatinous, a hymeniform layer of clavate to cystidioid elements.

Solitary to scattered on and around hardwood stumps and trees (presumably from dead roots), widely distributed, summer and fall. Edible according to Kauffman. A white small variant is not uncommon and a dark, almost black variant with a furfuraceous stipe (var. *furfuracea* Peck) is also common as are several other color variants which may deserve species rank.

1b Pileus moist to dry and unpolished; spores 8-11 × 6-8 μm ....
.... *O. longipes* (St. Amans) Moser

Pileus 3-7 cm, campanulate, dark watery gray to pale gray, scarcely hygrophanous. Gills broad, subdistant, pallid often with a reflection of pink in age. Stipe 6-10 cm x 4-8 mm above the pseudorhiza, dark watery gray, some with rusty stains in age. Pleurocystidia and cheilocystidia ± similar, 60-100 x 12-20 μm, utriform. Pileus cuticle hymeniform but layer studded with narrow, thick-walled, hyaline setae.

Solitary to gregarious around dead aspens, fallen trunks, etc., Rocky Mountains, summer, not uncommon during rainy periods. *"Collybia longipes"* has been confused in North America with *Oudemansiella radicata* var. *furfuracea* because of the initially dry pileus of the latter. Edible according to some European authors.

Panellus Karsten

Pileus sessile on the substrate or stipe, if present, eccentric or lateral and confluent with pileus; pileus surface viscid to dry or moist, glabrous or pubescent to woolly; spores amyloid, hyaline and thin-walled as seen under the microscope; hyphae of the gill trama thick-walled at least in part. Clamp connections present.

About 15 species of these wood-rotting fungi are currently recognized; none are generally recommended for eating.

KEY TO SPECIES

1a Pileus up to 10 cm or more broad; violaceous, green, or yellow, or these colors mixed; gills when young bright ochraceous to yellow, often with violet margins. Fig. 179 ....
.... *P. serotinus* (Fr.) Kühner

Figure 179

Figure 179 *Panellus serotinus*

Pileus 3-10 cm broad, sessile, fan-shaped to reniform, viscid in age, color finally yellowish olive. Gills crowded, narrow. Spores 4-6 x 1.5 μm, in some collections non-amyloid when fresh, generally amyloid after storage in an herbarium.

Scattered to imbricate, late in the fall on wood of hardwoods and conifers, widely distributed. We consider its appearance an indication that the end of the mushroom season is near at hand. It is a variable species, and, at least in North America, deserves further study. Edible but not choice.

1b Pileus small (1-3 cm) and colors not as above **2**

2a Fruiting body stipitate; pileus 5-25 mm, dry and unpolished, pale buff to tan; taste $\pm$ acrid-astringent. Fig. 180 .... *P. stipticus* (**Fr.**) **Karst.**

Figure 180

Figure 180 *Panellus stipticus*

Pileus spathulate to reniform, usually depressed over point of attachment to stipe, furfuraceous to pubescent, tough, the margin arched. Gills crowded, narrow, $\pm$ decurrent finally, cinnamon buff. Stipe 5-10 x 3-8 mm, flattened at times, tough, pallid buff, base matted-pubescent. Spores 3-4 x 2 μm, $\pm$ oblong, smooth. Cheilocystidia 30-40 x 4-5 μm, filamentose to contorted, some with apical branching. Gill trama of thick-walled hyphae.

Densely gregarious to caespitose; common, most abundant in the fall but found during spring and summer also, widely distributed, on wood of hardwoods in relatively dry situations. Not edible.

2b Not as above; taste mild **3**

3a Pileus purplish-vinaceous to purple-drab; gills grayish pink; spores (4) 5-7 $\times$ 1.2-2 μm .... *P. ringens* (**Fr.**) **Romag.**

Pileus 5-20 (30) mm, sessile, cupulate to fan-shaped, with a rather dense pallid pubescence over the area of attachment. Gills radiating from a point, close, moderately broad. Spores allantoid in profile view. Gill trama of thick-walled hyphae.

Densely gregarious on hardwood debris, especially alder, willow, and birch, northern United States and in Canada; abundant but sporadic in its fruiting pattern.

3b Pileus avellaneous (pinkish gray) to whitish; spores 3.5-6 $\times$ 1-1.5 μm .... *P. mitis* (**Fr.**) **Sing.**

Pileus 5-15 mm, fan-shaped to spathulate or conchate, moist under fine felt-like fibrils, appearing glabrous when water-soaked, vinaceous-buff moist, pallid faded, with a separable gelatinous cuticle; margin incurved. Gills crowded, arising from a single point, pallid to pale avellaneous. Stipe lacking or represented by a tubercle. Spores allantoid in profile view. Gill trama of thin-walled hyphae.

Scattered on conifer debris (small branches, etc.), widely distributed, late summer and fall.

Panus Fries

Pileus and stipe (if the latter is present) confluent; in aspect the fruiting bodies are *Pleurotus*-like, but tough and not readily decaying; spore deposit white to yellowish; spores non-amyloid; clamp connections present; gill trama of mostly thick-walled hyphae.

Possibly a dozen species occur in North America; all fruit on rotting wood.

KEY TO SPECIES

1a   Stipe 8-15 × 1-4 cm, conspicuously hairy-strigose toward the base ....
.... *P. strigosus* **Berk. & Curt.**

Pileus 10-20 (40) cm, broadly convex to ± plane or fan-shaped if stipe is not central, dry and strigose-roughened over all, white slowly becoming yellowish; context thick, white then yellowish, taste mild. Gills broad, close to subdistant, decurrent, white, yellowing somewhat in age. Stipe eccentric to lateral, solid. Spore deposit white; spores 11-13 x 3.5-4.5 μm, smooth. Cheilocystidia merely the ends of tramal hyphae.

Solitary or 2-3 in a cluster from wounds in hardwood trees; maple, yellow birch, and others; August through September, Great Lakes area east and southward.

1b   **Stipe absent to weakly developed** 2

2a   **Pileus surface ± glabrous. Fig. 181** ....
.... *P. conchatus* **(Fr.) Fr.**

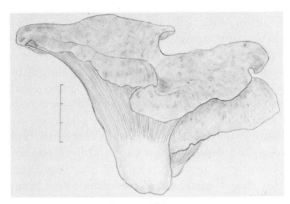

Figure 181

Figure 181   *Panus conchatus*

Pileus 5-10 (15) cm, plano-depressed, the margin inrolled, becoming broadly vase-shaped, in age often wavy and lobed (quite irregular), surface moist; cuticle often broken into small patches, when young violet toned with red, going to dark vinaceous brown, paler in age. Stipe 2-5 x 1-3 cm, widest at apex, central to lateral, solid. Spores 5-6 x 2.5-3 μm, smooth. Pleurocystidia 35-45 x 8-11 μm, ventricose-capitate. Cheilocystidia clavate to fusoid-ventricose, 30-40 x 8-12 μm.

Scattered to caespitose on hardwood slash, stumps, logs, etc., common and widely distributed, summer and fall. The fruiting bodies are very long-lived and consequently a collector will almost always find old specimens that have lost their original colors. Reported to be edible.

2b   **Pileus hispid to strigose** ....
.... *P. rudis* **Fries**

Pileus 2-7 (10) cm, spathulate to fan-shaped or reniform, margin long inrolled, dry, ± violaceous to vinaceous young, later reddish brown to alutaceous; taste bitter. Gills decurrent, crowded, narrow, violaceous but soon pallid, finally ± alutaceous. Stipe when present lateral to eccentric, 1-2 cm x 4-10 mm, densely hairy like pileus. Spores 5-6 x 2.5-3 μm. Pleurocystidia 40-55 x 9-14 μm, clavate to subcylindric, apex obtuse; cheilocystidia similar.

Gregarious to caespitose on hardwood slash, summer and fall, common and widely distributed.

Phyllotopsis (Gilbert & Donk in Pilát) Singer

Fruiting bodies pleurotoid; pileus 2-8 cm, fan-shaped and sessile, the surface densely tomentose, orange-yellow; gills bright orange-yellow or paler; spore deposit pink slowly fading to white in time in the herbarium; spores non-amyloid, smooth, allantoid in profile view; gill trama interwoven; context fleshy-pliant; growing on wood of both coniferous and hardwood trees, but especially on aspen. Only 1 species generally recognized. Fig. 182 ....
.... *P. nidulans* (Fr.) Sing.

Figure 182 *Phyllotopsis nidulans*

This species is widely distributed and common, but in North America has found little favor for table use. Various American and European authors have reported different spore sizes for it. Because there are variants of this species worth further taxonomic study, we do not recommend North American collections for table use.

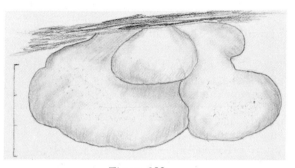

Figure 182

Pleurotus (Fr.) Quélet

Stipe eccentric, lateral or lacking; spores thin-walled, non-amyloid, hyaline under the microscope, in deposit white to cream buff or pale lilac-gray; context of pileus firm-fleshy; pileus typically not viscid, lacking gelatinous layers; clamp connections present; habitat primarily on decaying wood. It is a small genus in the modern sense, with probably less than 25 species in North America north of Mexico.

Pileus 4-12 cm, broadly convex, appressed fibrillose from gray fibrils of the veil, margin fringed for a time, ground color paler to pallid beneath the fibrils; context firm; taste mild; odor ± pungent. Gills close, narrow, decurrent, anastomosing on the stipe, white. Stipe 4-10 x 1-3.5 cm, annulate from remains of membranous veil, sheath on stipe soon ruptured, white beneath the veil. Spores 9-12 x 3.5-4 μm.

    Solitary or in small groups, on alder, Pacific Northwest, fall, not common. Edible.

1b   Stipe present or absent but lacking a veil 2

KEY TO SPECIES

1a   Stipe typically eccentric; a veil present with the remains usually present on pileus and/or stipe .... *P. dryinus* (Fr.) Kummer

2a   Stipe eccentric to almost central; fruiting body usually solitary from knotholes in hardwood trees .... *P. ulmarius* of American authors

Pileus 5-15 cm, convex, compact and firm, moist but not viscid, glabrous, white or over disc creamy tan to pale crust brown, surface often areolate; context thick, firm, white, odor fungoid, taste mild. Gills broad, adnexed to sinuate, close to subdistant, pallid to white. Stipe 4-12 x 1-3 cm, enlarged toward base, fibrous and firm, solid. Spores 5-7 μm, globose, deposit white.

Late fall or early winter, mostly on old-growth hardwood, often collected, but a ladder is often needed to reach most of the fruiting bodies. This is the species known as *Hypsizigus tessulatus* in Singer's system. *P. ulmarius* of Europe is now placed in *Lyophyllum*. Edible.

2b   Not as above 3

3a   Pileus ± drab to brownish gray; spore deposit when air-dried a dull lilac-gray; spores 7-9 × 3-3.5 μm. Fig. 183 .... *P. ostreatus* (Fr.) Kummer

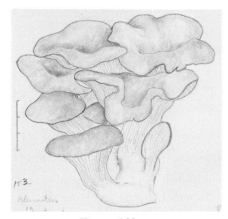

Figure 183

Figure 183   *Pleurotus ostreatus*

Pileus 4-10 (15) cm, spathulate to fan-shaped or conchate, at times the stipe lateral, glabrous, moist and then slightly lubricous; taste mild. Gills close, broad, anastomosing where they are decurrent on the stipe-like base, edges staining brown where bruised at times. Stipe eccentric, lateral or absent. Spores smooth, ± oblong in face view. Pileus trama of thin-walled hyphae.

On decaying hardwood logs especially elm, imbricate to caespitose, late fall and spring. Ed-

ible and choice, but some variants have a somewhat disagreeable taste. The species is a "collective" one, or one might say very variable, but the different variations are often constant in their characters in a given region. The "oyster" as it is often called, is easy to grow in culture.

3b   Not as above 4

4a   Pileus bluish umber to greenish gray .... *P. columbinus* Quélet

Pileus 4-9 cm, fan-shaped, glabrous, hygrophanous, fading to pinkish gray (avellaneous); taste mild. Gills close, narrow at first, pallid. Stipe lacking or present as the narrowed base of the pileus. Spores 9-2 x 3.5-4 μm, oblong in face view, smooth. Cheilocystidia inconspicuous, 30-35 x 6-8 μm, subcylindric to subventricose.

Imbricate on conifer logs, central Idaho, June, apparently rare in North America.

4b   Not as above 5

5a   Pileus white; on conifer wood; spores 6-7 × 5-6 μm; gills yellowish white in age. Fig. 184 .... *P. porrigens* (Fr.) Kummer

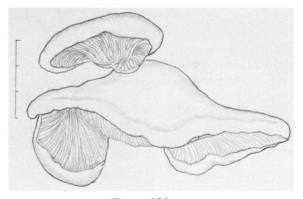

Figure 184

Figure 184   *Pleurotus porrigens*

Pileus 4-8 cm in widest dimension, 2-5 cm in short dimension, obovate, ear-shaped, etc., glabrous to the mycelioid point of attachment, glistening, milk-white in age, not striate; taste mild. Gills attached to the basal tubercle (point of attachment of fruiting body to the substratum), narrow, close then subdistant, white becoming yellowish. Stipe none (just a tubercle). Spore deposit white.

Scattered to closely gregarious on decaying conifer wood, northern United States and in Canada, abundant in the Pacific Northwest, and both edible and highly regarded. A common name is angel's wings.

5b On hardwood especially beech and aspen. White variants of *P. ostreatus*

These occur especially in the spring and summer. The spore deposits are usually lilac-gray after air drying. There is much intergradation of color of the pileus with that of the type variety. Studies are currently in progress in several laboratories to resolve the taxonomic problems in this group. These mushrooms, however, are among our most popular spring and summer edibles.

Rhodotus Maire

Pileus broadly convex, 3-8 cm, margin inrolled, surface reticulate, watermelon-pink when fresh, fading and becoming orange toned with yellow; consistency rubbery because of the gelatinous context. Gills adnate, broad, close, intervenose, salmon color at maturity. Stipe usually eccentric, 2-5 cm x 3-6 mm, fibrillose, tough. Spore deposit pink; spores non-amyloid, 6-8 μm, globose, weakly ornamented. Clamp connections present. Veil absent. Only one species known. Fig. 185 ....
.... *R. palmatus* (Fr.) R. Maire

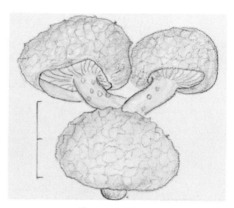

Figure 185

Figure 185 *Rhodotus palmatus*

On wood of hardwoods, summer and early fall, widely distributed but rare; during some seasons frequently found in the hardwood slashings of the upper Great Lakes area.

Ripartites Karsten

Pileus and stipe confluent; lamellae adnate to decurrent; spore deposit dull brown; spores pale brown under microscope, ± echinulate and globose, ornamentation non-amyloid, apex lacking a germ pore; stipe typically central and veil present but thin and evanescent; clamp connections present.

The genus is a small one, containing about a half dozen species, but the only species commonly collected in North America is the one treated here ....
.... *R. tricholoma* (Fr.) Karsten

Pileus 2-4 cm, convex, margin incurved, becoming plane, snow-white, soft and subviscid to touch, appressed silky but not scaly, marginal hairs present or absent; context pallid, very soft. Gills close, broad, squarely adnate, white becoming dull pinkish cinnamon, seceding, very soft. Stipe 2-4 (6) cm x 3-3.5 mm, equal, hollow, fragile, whitish becoming dingy ochraceous, faintly hoary to ± furfuraceous a first. Spores 4-5 x 3.5-4 μm, warty.

Late summer and fall in forest situations, widely distributed but usually only a few fruiting bodies found at a time, on humus or very decayed wood.

Strobilurus Singer

Pileus and stipe confluent; stipe 0.5-2 mm thick, pliant, often strigose over a rooting basal area (if arising from a buried cone); pileus convex to broadly convex, olive-brown to gray or finally white; spores hyaline, non-amyloid; cuticle of pileus hymeniform; habitat on cones of magnolia and of various conifers.

A small group about which questions are still being raised. The type species of the genus, S. coniginoides (Ellis) Singer, inhabits magnolia cones, and is very abundant in the range of that genus. Singer places S. albipilata in Marasmius. We include it here as an example of the genus, Fig. 186 ....
.... S. albipilata (Pk.) Wells & Kempton

Figure 186 *Strobilurus albipilata*

Pileus 1-2 cm, convex, margin inrolled, dark olive brown, fading to gray and in age bleached to whitish, densely pruinose when moist; context pliant and tough, taste mild. Gills close, broad, sinuate to adnate, grayish then white, pruinose from cystidia. Stipe 2-4 cm x 1-2 mm, with a strigose base (if coming from a buried cone), surface above pubescent (under a lens) from caulocystidia. Spores 5-6 x 3-3.5 μm, non-amyloid. Pleuro- and cheilocystidia similar and abundant, (40) 50-70 x 8-12 μm, elongate fusoid-ventricose, apex obtuse to pointed.

Solitary or in groups from buried cones or those lying on the forest floor, fall, Pacific Northwest, probably more common than the records indicate.

Figure 186

Tricholoma (Fr.) Quélet

Pileus fleshy, confluent with stipe; gills sinuate to adnexed or at times ± adnate; stipe typically central, fleshy to fibrous; veils present in some species and cortinate to membranous, when breaking leaving a fibrillose zone or a ± membranous annulus; spore deposit white to pale cream-color; spores smooth, non-amyloid; pleuro- and cheilocystidia usually absent. Usually terrestrial and occurring in association with woody plants with which they presumably form mycorrhiza.

About 35 species are either treated or mentioned here. This is about a third of the number found so far in the genus for North

America. Several are edible and good, but some are poisonous, and many are merely unpalatable. Be sure you *know* the species you plan to eat.

KEY TO SPECIES

1a Veil present and forming a membranous annulus, or a ± persistent fibrillose zone, or a distinct line marking the termination of a sheath **2**

1b Veil absent, or thin and fibrillose or cortinate, all traces soon vanishing **4**

2a Pileus dry and fibrillose, pale drab to brownish gray, usually found under willow .... *T. cingulatum* (Fr.) Jacobsh.

Pileus 2-4 (6) cm, obtuse then expanded-umbonate, at times with appressed scales, often with a bluish gray cast, in age dark avellaneous; margin cottony at first; odor and taste farinaceous. Gills close, narrow, adnate, equal, grayish becoming pallid, in age at times staining greenish yellow. Stipe 4-6 cm x 3-6 mm, ± equal, pallid to bluish gray, silky above the annulus; annulus submembranous or a fibrillose zone. Spores 4-5 x 2-3 μm, non-amyloid.

Scattered to gregarious; fall; Pacific Northwest; not common. To be expected in the Great Lakes area and eastward. Edible.

2b Pileus viscid at least when young **3**

3a Veil membranous; stipe narrowed downward; scattered to gregarious under pine .... *T. zelleri* (Stuntz & Smith) Ovrebo & Tylutki

Pileus 5-12 (20) cm, obtuse to broadly umbonate or nearly plane, when young (and cuticle is continuous) thinly slimy-viscid when wet but soon dry, becoming scaly from rupture of the cuticle; color variable (orange, greenish, ochraceous, orange-brown, or mixtures of these); context with a farinaceous odor and taste, slowly orange-brown where bruised. Gills close to crowded, finally broad, adnate to ± decurrent;

pallid then rusty stained. Stipe 4-13 x 1-3 cm, below the annulus with zones and scales colored like the pileus cuticle; annulus ragged and submembranous, upper surface pallid. Spores 4-5.5 x 3.5 μm.

Common in the Pacific Northwest, less so in the Rocky Mountains and infrequent in the Great Lakes area and eastward. Edible (?), the taste does not encourage experimentation. Previously known as *Armillaria Zelleri*.

3b Veil present as a colored sheath on stipe which terminates in a line but no actual veil tissue present to form an annulus, only a line visable. Fig. 187 .... *T. aurantium* (Fr.) Ricken

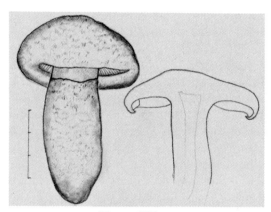

Figure 187

Figure 187 *Tricholoma aurantium*

Pileus 5-7 cm, convex then expanded and ± plane to obtusely umbonate, viscid and glabrous at first, ochraceous-fulvous, tawny orange-red or at times splashed with green; cuticle soon breaking into small appressed scales; odor and taste farinaceous-rancid. Gills close, ± adnexed, rather narrow, pallid and soon spotted rusty brown. Stipe 4-7 cm x 8-15 mm, equal or narrowed downward, pallid above the veil-line, ± squamulose below. Spores 4-5 x 3-5 μm.

Scattered to gregarious in mixed woods, possibly associated with aspen as well as conifers, summer in the Rocky Mountains, fall in the Great Lakes area and eastward, abundant during some seasons. Unpalatable.

4a Pileus viscid at first (cuticle an ixocutis), often soon dry 5

4b Pileus moist and glabrous, or dry and fibrillose, or squamulose 13

5a Pileus, stipe and gills white. Fig. 188 .... *T. resplendens* (Fr.) Quél.

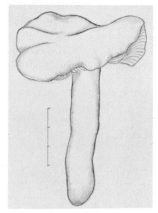

Figure 188

Figure 188 *Tricholoma resplendens*

Pileus 4-10 cm, convex then plane or margin uplifted, glabrous, shining when dry, odor and taste mild. Gills close, medium broad, adnexed. Stipe 4-8 cm x 7-20 mm, ± equal, dry, glabrous, solid. Spores 6-7.5 x 4 μm.

Scattered to gregarious in deciduous and mixed woods, late summer and fall, not uncommon, Great Lakes area eastward and southward. Edible, but some white species are poisonous!

5b Pileus colored at least on the disc 6

6a Pileus ± lead-color; gills pallid with a lemon color reflection in places; under pines. Fig. 189 .... *T. portentosum* (Fr.) Quélet

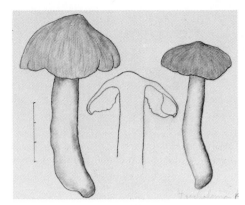

Figure 189

Figure 189 *Tricholoma portentosum*

Pileus 6-12 cm, obtuse to expanded-umbonate or broadly convex, ground color tinged violet in some, in others lemon-yellow, virgate from dark fibrils; odor and taste ± farinaceous, cut flesh slowly yellowish. Gills broad, close to subdistant, ± adnexed, often tinged grayish and yellowish. Stipe 6-10 x 1-2 cm, ± equal, whitish or with a yellow flush, innately fibrillose-striate. Spores 6-7 x 3-4 μm.

Scattered to gregarious on sandy soil as a rule, common late in the fall in both the Pacific Northwest and Great Lakes area and eastward. Edible.

6b Pileus not lead-color 7

7a Gills, stipe and pileus all showing some yellow tints 8

7b Yellow lacking or more restricted than in above choice 9

8a Pileus conic-umbonate, disc blackish to brown and ± virgate with the colored fibrils. Fig. 190 .... *T. sejunctum* (Fr.) Quélet

Figure 190

Figure 190 *Tricholoma sejunctum*

Pileus 4-8 cm, convex-umbonate to expanded-umbonate, only slightly viscid; innately fibrillose but not squamulose except in age; taste ± bitterish to nauseous. Gills subdistant to close, white, soon yellow near the cap margin, broad. Stipe 5-8 (12) x 1-2 cm, ± equal, pallid but soon with yellowish discolorations, ± glabrous. Spores 6-7 x 4-5.5 μm.

Scattered to gregarious in hardwood and conifer forests alike, late summer and fall, common; Pacific Northwest, Great Lakes area, and both east and southward.

8b   Stipe and gills bright yellow, pileus yellow at least on the margin; disc of pileus lacking radiating dark fibrils. Fig. 191 ....
.... *T. flavovirens* (Fr.) Lundell

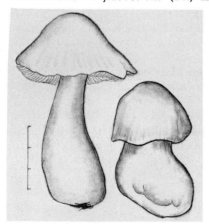

Figure 191

Figure 191 *Tricholoma flavovirens*

Pileus 4-12 cm, obtuse to convex, then plane or with a low umbo, fibrillose-streaked beneath the ixocutis, soon dry and slightly squamulose; odor and taste farinaceous. Gills adnexed, close, broad, not staining. Stipe 3-10 x 1-2.5 cm, ± equal, pale yellow varying to whitish, unpolished; veil absent. Spores 6-7.5 x 4-5 μm.

Scattered to gregarious under pine, less frequently under aspen, Pacific Northwest, Great Lakes area and east and southward, fall; widely distributed. Edible and popular, be sure to get rid of all the sand.

9a   Stipe colored like pileus to a clearly defined line: see *T. aurantium*

9b   Stipe not as above 10

10a Gills very pale yellowish at first; pileus a dingy rusty brown ....
.... *T. flavobrunneum* (Fr.) Kummer

Pileus 3-8 cm, convex to plane or with a low umbo, only slightly viscid and somewhat fibrillose-squamulose in age; dark yellow-brown to reddish brown; odor farinaceous. Gills pale yellow, soon spotted or stained reddish brown. Stipe 4-8 x 1-1.5 cm, ± equal, pallid but soon concolor with cap over lower part, ± fibrillose. Veil absent. Spores 5-6.5 x 3-4.5 μm, non-amyloid.

Scattered to gregarious, under hardwoods, especially late summer and fall, not common, Great Lakes area and eastward.

10b Gills white to pallid at first 11

11a Fruit bodies densely caespitose-gregarious on soil near cottonwood trees. Fig. 192 ....
.... *T. populinum* Lange

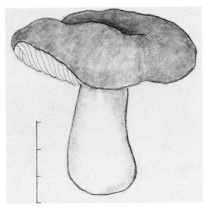

Figure 192

Figure 192 *Tricholoma populinum*

Pileus 6-16 cm, convex to plane, margin inrolled; surface virgate, at times with watery spots, dull cinnamon to dull vinaceous brown, margin pallid; context thick, white, firm, odor and taste strongly farinaceous. KOH on cuticle dingy lilaceous. Gills close, narrow, adnexed, white becoming pallid vinaceous buff, staining vinaceous brown especially on the edges. Stipe 3-6 x 1.5-3 cm, solid, equal or ± clavate; surface white, unpolished, staining dingy reddish brown where handled, ± innately fibrillose. Spores 5-6 x 3.5-4 μm.

Common around cottonwood, late in the fall in the Pacific Northwest, but its distribution in North America is not adequately known as yet. It is to be expected throughout the range of the cottonwoods. Edible (but be sure you collect it near cottonwoods).

11b Fruiting bodies scattered to gregarious under various species of tree but especially under conifers **12**

12a Gills, white, staining dingy reddish brown. Fig. 193. ....*T. albobrunneum* **(Fr.) Kummer**

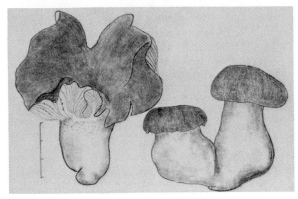

Figure 193

Figure 193 *Tricholoma albobrunneum*

Pileus 4-8 (10) cm, convex to plane or with a broad low umbo, dingy reddish brown over disc, pinkish brown to the pallid margin, streaked with innate fibrills; odor and taste farinaceous. Gills close to crowded, finally broad, adnexed, white at first. Stipe 3-6 (8) x 1-2 cm, equal, dry, silky-fibrillose (or in age squamulose below), white but soon stained reddish brown. Spores 5-6 x 3-3.5 (4) μm.

Gregarious under conifers especially pine, late in the fall, northern United States and southern Canada. Indicated by some authors as *poisonous*.

12b Gills white and not staining ....
.... *T. leucophyllum* **Ovrebo & Tylutki**

Pileus 4-10 cm, convex to plano-umbonate, brownish over disc, pale yellow over remainder, ± glabrous, only slightly viscid, soon dry; odor and taste farinaceous. Gills close, ± sinuate, broad, edges becoming eroded. Stipe 3-9 x 1-2.5 cm, white over all or slightly yellowish near base, glabrous to silky fibrillose. Spores 5.5-7 x 4-4.5 μm.

Solitary to gregarious under conifers and hardwoods (especially aspen), fall, northern United States and adjacent Canada. It has the stature of *T. flavovirens* and is probably edible: it has often been mistaken for the latter.

13a Fruiting body white except for disc of pileus which may be ± vinaceous buff to avellaneous **14**

13b Pileus more highly colored than in above choice **16**

14a Readily staining yellow where bruised. Fig. 194 .... *T. sulphurescens* **Bres.**

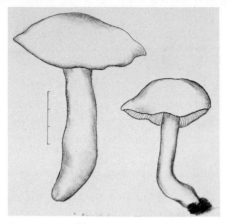

Figure 194

Figure 194 *Tricholoma sulphurescens*

Pileus 5-10 cm, convex to ± umbonate or plane, dry, glabrous, white becoming creamy and with disc brownish; odor pungent, taste not distinctive. Gills close to crowded, rounded-adnate, white. Stipe 3-8 x 1-2 cm, white, dry, unpolished; clavate at first, becoming equal, ± appressed-fibrillose. Spores 4-5.5 x 3-3.5 μm.

    Scattered to clustered in deciduous woods, especially under oak, common, Great Lakes area eastward and infrequent under conifers in the Northwest. Late summer and fall.

14b Not as above **15**

15a Odor and taste of "coal tar" (pungent and disagreeable); spores 10-12 × 6.5-8 μm. Fig. 195 .... *T. platyphyllum* **(Murr.) Murr.**

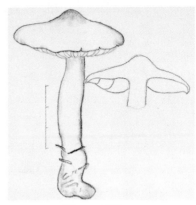

Figure 195

Figure 195 *Tricholoma platyphyllum*

Pileus 3-5 cm, convex to slightly depressed, sub-glabrous, white, to creamy white. Gills white, very broad, subdistant, not staining. Stipe 4-9 cm x 4-9 mm, ± equal or enlarged downward to a swollen base, glabrous, dry, whitish. Spores non-amyloid.

    Solitary to scattered under conifers, Pacific Northwest, fall, not uncommon. *T. inamoenum* (Fr.) Quélet is the most closely related species; in fact *T. platyphyllum* may be only a variety of it.

15b Taste bitter to disagreeable, odor slight; spores 6-7 × 4-5 μm.....................................
.... *T. venenatum* **Atkinson**

Pileus 4-9 (11) cm, obtuse to convex becoming convex-expanded, umbonate or plane, dry, appressed fibrillose to minutely fibrillose-squamulose, squamules pale yellowish brown, ground color becoming pale buff; odor and taste mild to weakly farinaceous; injured areas developing a pale buff tinge. Gills adnexed to broadly sinuate, moderately broad, subdistant, whitish staining dull clay-color. Stipe 6-10 x 1.2-1.5 cm, clavate to subbulbous, white with dull clay-color stains, innately fibrillose; veil none. Spores 5-7 (8.5) x 3.5-5 μm, non-amyloid. Pleurocystidia none. Cheilocystidia scattered to rare 25-36 x 7-10 μm.

    Scattered to gregarious in deciduous woods, summer and fall; fairly frequent and to be expected from the Great Lakes area eastward during wet seasons. *Poisonous.*

16a Pileus appressed-fibrillose to squamulose .. 17

16b Pileus glabrous and moist to dry but not fibrillose or scaly 28

17a Pileus orange-brown to reddish or bay-brown 18

17b Pileus gray to drab, or dingy brown 19

18a Margin of pileus cottony; pileus conic at first and coarsely fibrillose to squamulose. Fig. 196 ...., *T. vaccinum* (Fr.) Kummer

Figure 196

Figure 196 *Tricholoma vaccinum*

Pileus 4-7 cm, soon campanulate to expanded-umbonate, dry, cinnamon-rufous to dark reddish brown, ± rimose at times, fibrillose-squamulose; odor and taste ± disagreeable to farinaceous; context slowly reddening in age or at times when bruised. Gills adnate then sinuate, moderately broad, close, whitish becoming toned reddish in age or slowly where bruised. Stipe 5-7 x 1-1.5 cm, subequal, fibrillose to lacerate-fibrillose, the fibrils brown. Spores 4-5 x 4-5 μm, non-amyloid.

Gregarious to clustered in association with conifers, late summer and fall, widely distributed in the northern areas of the United States and adjacent Canada. Apparently not very poisonous: it is rated suspected to not recommended. There are several color variants in the species.

18b Margin of pileus more or less naked; pileus more or less glabrous when young, at times scaly in age, broadly convex at first. Fig. 197 .... *T. imbricatum* (Fr.) Kummer

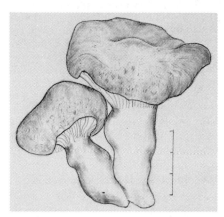

Figure 197

Figure 197 *Tricholoma imbricatum*

Pileus 5-10 cm, convex to obtuse becoming broadly convex to obtusely umbonate in age, dry, dull reddish brown, at times dull cinnamon brown, innately fibrillose, rarely scaly; odor and taste mild to slightly farinaceous; cut flesh slowly reddish. Gills close, broad, sinuate to adnexed; pallid becoming grayish vinaceous or with dingy reddish spots; edges even to slightly eroded. Stipe 4-8 (11) x 1-2 cm, clavate becoming equal, whitish but soon brownish to reddish brown from the base upward, unpolished. Spores 5.5-7 x 4-4.5 μm.

Scattered to gregarious under conifers, fall, especially late fall, widely distributed in northern North America. Edible. This species is distinct from *T. vaccinum* by the broadly convex, dull, brown, typically less fibrillose pileus, but the two are closely related.

19a Injured parts staining reddish to pinkish orange or gills beaded with reddish droplets in age 20

19b Not staining as above 23

20a Odor somewhat like coal tar; taste very disagreeable; stipe coated with gray fibrils or squamules .... *T. michiganense* **Smith**

Pileus 5-9 cm, convex to obtuse becoming plane or plano-umbonate, dry, minutely squarrose scaly over the margin, matted fibrillose over the disc, fibrils fuscous (gray) to grayish brown or drab gray in age. Gills crowded, narrow, rounded-adnexed, pale drab to whitish, in age stained pale salmon color; edges even. Stipe 3-8 x 1-1.2 cm, with a narrowly clavate base. Spores 6-7 x 3-3.5 μm.

On soil and humus around oak stumps in particular, fall, Great Lakes region. Edibility: not known.

20b Odor and taste merely farinaceous **21**

21a Gill edges beaded with red droplets ....
.... *T. huronense* **Smith**

Pileus 6-9 (12) cm, obtusely conic at first becoming convex to plane or with a low obtuse umbo, dry, pale to moderately deep gray, fibrillose, soon fibrillose-scaly with the flesh exposed; margin slightly fringed to somewhat cottony, often beaded with clear pink droplets or streaked pinkish; injured areas unchanging. Gills close to crowded, adnexed, rather narrow, dull white; edges slightly eroded. Stipe 4-8 x 1-2 cm (or up to 4 cm at base in some), whitish, lower part appressed-fibrillose scaly like the pileus, often beaded with pinkish droplets. Spores 7-9 x 5-6 μm, non-amyloid. Pleurocystidia none. Cheilocystidia 28-39 x 6-12 μm.

Gregarious to caespitose in oak woods, Great Lakes region; late summer and fall. Edibility not reported but probably poisonous.

21b Not beaded with droplets as in above choice **22**

22a Pileus conic, yellow with dingy to pale fuscous disc; under conifers; with the aspect of *T. sejunctum* ....
.... *T. cheilolamnium* **Ovrebo & Tylutki**

Pileus 3-11 cm, broadly conic to convex becoming plano-convex, obtusely umbonate, dark brown over the disc, yellowish to buff with a tinge of

pink toward the margin, dry, tomentose over the disc to innately fibrillose to fibrillose-scaly toward the margin; odor and taste farinaceous. Gills sinuate, uncinate, subdistant, whitish then light buff or pinkish, yellowish near pileus margin in age; edges even. Stipe 5-15 cm x 7-30 mm, equal to ventricose or clavate, whitish to yellowish, pink at the base, dry, silky fibrillose. Spores 6-7.5 x 3.8-4.5 μm. Pleurocystidia and cheilocystidia 26-40 x 12-22 μm.

Gregarious to solitary under conifers, fall, Pacific Northwest frequent. Edibility: apparently not tested. Pleurocystidia are found near the gill edges in some collections and resemble the cheilocystidia.

22b Pileus broadly expanded, some shade of drab; growing under hardwoods ....
.... *T. orirubens* **Quélet**

Pileus 3-10 cm, convex to plane, dry, dark violaceous gray over the disc, pale gray to nearly white to the margin, in age often tinged light salmon-orange; appressed fibrillose to minutely squamulose; odor and taste strongly farinaceous, cut or bruised areas becoming light salmon-orange. Gills close, broad, adnexed, whitish flushed light salmon-orange in age. Stipe 4-7 cm x 10-18 mm, white but in age flushed light salmon-orange, at first faintly silky. Spores 4.5-5.5 x 4-4.5 μm, non-amyloid.

Scattered to widely gregarious under hardwoods, especially oak, late fall, Great Lakes region; found mostly during rainy seasons.

23a Readily staining yellow where bruised ....
.... *T. luteomaculosum* **Smith**

Pileus 4-10 cm, obtuse, becoming broadly convex to nearly plane, dry, innately appressed fibrillose over disc and minutely scaly near the margin at times, dark to light bluish gray; odor and taste farinaceous; injured areas (or cap in age) tinged yellow-green. Gills close, broad, adnexed, whitish to pale gray; edges eroded, and sometimes stained blackish. Stipe 4-8 x 1-2 cm, about equal, white or tinged pale gray, innately fibrillose. Spores 5.5-7 x 4-5 μm, non-amyloid. Pleurocystidia rare to abundant, 36-40 x 10-15 μm, ± clavate. Cheilocystidia 36-52 x 12-18 μm.

Gregarious in oak woods, fall, Great Lakes region. Edibility not tested.

23b Not staining yellow where bruised **24**

24a Pileus blackish-fuscous, squamulose; gill edges soon stained fuscous; stipe 1-3 cm thick. Fig. 198 .... *T. atroviolaceum* Smith

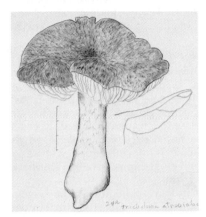

Figure 198

Figure 198   *Tricholoma atroviolaceum*

Pileus 5-12 (14) cm, obtuse becoming expanded-umbonate to plane, dry, densely fibrillose squamulose with minute recurved blackish violet to violaceous brown scales; margin often splitting radially in age; odor and taste farinaceous; injured flesh unchanging. Gills close, sinuate to adnexed, broad, dull light cinnamon with a gray tint; edges becoming uneven to eroded, typically staining blackish. Stipe 6-14 cm long, equal or at times with a bulbous base, soon dark brown (violaceous brown) or darker, appressed-fibrillose. Spores 7-9 x 4.5-6 μm.

Gregarious under conifers, fall, Pacific Northwest. Edibility apparently untested.

24b Not as above **25**

25a Pileus 4-16 cm; margin becoming pallid; gill edges not darkening in age or if bruised; stipe 1-2 (4) cm thick. Fig. 199 ....
.... *T. pardinum* Quélet

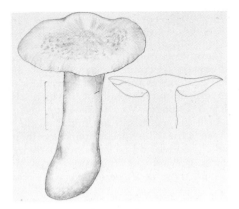

Figure 199

Figure 199   *Tricholoma pardinum*

Pileus convex becoming plane or at times with a low umbo, dry, fibrillose, the fibrils very pale to ± dark gray, soon ± squamulose, darkest on disc, whitish near margin; taste farinaceous. Gills sinuate to deeply broadly adnexed, moderately broad, close, creamy to white or at times flushed pinkish; edges finally eroded. Stipe 8-15 cm long, clavate becoming ± equal, whitish or at times tinged ashy or with rusty basal stains, glabrous but appressed fibrillose. Spores 6-9 (10) x 5-6 μm, non-amyloid.

Gregarious to scattered under conifers or in mixed hardwoods, fall, widely distributed in the cooler parts of North America. Poisonous. With us, its appearance has been very sporadic: abundant one year and then not appearing for several years in a row.

25b Not as above **26**

26a Cortina present at first; pileus fuscous tinged violaceous .... *T. myomyces* Lange

Pileus 3-7 cm, fibrillose to fibrillose-squamulose, margin ± fibrillose-fringed at times; context often grayish near the cuticle, odor and taste slight. Gills grayish at first, white to pallid in age, close, adnexed, narrow to moderately broad, edges tending to stain brownish where bruised. Stipe 5-7 cm x 10-12 mm, equal to narrowly clavate, dull white, at most only faintly fibrillose. Spores 5-6 x 3.5-4 μm, non-amyloid. Pleurocystidia resembling the cheilocystidia, the latter 26-38 x 6-11 μm, clavate to saccate.

Caespitose-gregarious in troops of hundreds of individuals in conifer plantations of pine or spruce, Great Lakes region, fall. Variations of this species are found throughout northern United States and Canada. Var. *triste* Lange is one of these. In it grayish fibrils are found on the lower part of the stipe. The variant found locally in S.E. Michigan is edible and collected regularly by some collectors. Beware of confusing large fruiting bodies with those of *T. pardinum!*

26b Cortina lacking (check unexpanded buttons)
.... **27**

27a Pileus gray and ± sharply conic to conic-umbonate. Fig. 200 ....
.... *T. virgatum* **(Fr.) Kummer**

Figure 200

Figure 200   *Tricholoma virgatum*

Pileus 4-8 (10) cm, surface dry and fibrillose, the fibrils at times forming squamules, often streaked, disc dark grayish toned with violaceous to violaceous black, pale gray toward the margin; odor earthy, cut flesh soon grayish. Gills broad, close, deeply adnexed, whitish becoming grayish or spotted grayish; edges uneven to eroded. Stipe 8-15 x 1-2 cm, whitish, unpolished to innately fibrillose. Spores 6-7.5 x 5-6 μm. Pleurocystidia absent. Cheilocystidia basidiole-like but 9-12 μm broad.

Solitary to scattered in conifer and mixed forests, not uncommon, Pacific Northwest and Great Lakes area eastward and southward. Edibility: not recommended. It fruits during cool wet weather.

27b Pileus olive to grayish olive, broadly convex with an inrolled margin ....
.... *T. palustre* **Smith**

Pileus 4-8 (9) cm, finally plane, moist to dry, matted fibrillose, grayish olive to brownish gray over disc to pale yellowish olive elsewhere, margin at times pale yellow; odor none; taste slowly sharply acrid; bruised flesh unchanging. Gills broad, close to crowded, adnexed, ± concolor with the olive tinted part of the pileus; edges eroded. Stipe 5-6 x 1-1.8 cm, equal, whitish or faintly tinged olive, glabrous to silky fibrillose. Spores 5-6 x 4-5 μm.

Scattered on humus at the edges of bogs, fall, southern Michigan. Its distribution has not been established.

28a Gills yellowish, distant, broad; odor of coal tar (strongly unpleasant). Fig. 201 ....
.... *T. sulphureum* **(Fr.) Kummer**

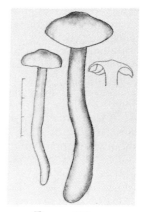
Figure 201

Figure 201   *Tricholoma sulphureum*

Pileus 2-8 cm, convex-expanded, typically umbonate, glabrous or nearly so, moist to dry, dingy brown over the disc, otherwise sulphur-yellow to olivaceous yellow; taste disagreeable. Gills adnexed with a tooth, subdistant, moderately broad, thick, at first yellow. Stipe 4-8 cm x 5-10 mm, ± equal, innately fibrillose, yellow to olivaceous. Spores 8-10 x 5-6 μm, non-amyloid.

Gregarious in deciduous woods, summer to early fall in the Great Lakes area, but widely distributed. The entire fruiting body is yellow in the early stages. The odor and taste discourage eating it.

28b Gills pallid at first, close; odor not as above 29

29a Stipe becoming orange-pink especially in the base; on well-drained soil; pileus olive to gray or yellowish-olive. Fig. 202 ....
.... *T. saponaceum* (Fr.) Kummer

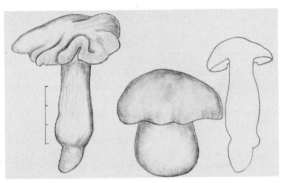

Figure 202

Figure 202 *Tricholoma saponaceum*

Pileus 4-8 cm, convex-expanded, glabrous to finely areolate-scaly, dry to moist; odor and taste strong, unpleasant, soapy or slightly farinaceous, or nearly mild; injured areas often staining pinkish orange. Stipe 5-8 x 1.5-2 cm, wider in the midportion and

tapering toward the base or almost radicating, white or flushed with color of pileus, glabrous to minutely squamulose (but no veil). Spores 5-6 x 3.5-4 μm.

Solitary to gregarious in deciduous woods, fall, also in mixed and in conifer forests generally, widely distributed in the northern areas. It is a variable species in color, odor, and taste as well as in the staining reaction. It is not one that the beginner can recognize with sufficient accuracy to justify testing it as to its edibility.

29b Stipe not staining; growing in bogs. Fig. 203 .... *T. fumosiluteum* Peck

Figure 203

Figure 203 *Tricholoma fumosiluteum*

Pileus 3-8 (1) cm, obtuse to expanded-plane or umbonate, moist, subhygrophanous, often with watery spots, smoky yellow at first, becoming brighter yellow in age; context whitish; odor and taste farinaceous. Gills broad, close, adnexed, pallid to yellowish, edges becoming eroded. Stipe 5-12 x 1-2 cm, ± equal, dull white, in age yellowish to smoky yellowish, often fibrous-striate. Spores 6-7 x 4.5-5 μm.

Common in *Sphagnum* bogs in the Great Lakes area and eastward, late summer and fall.

Tricholomopsis Singer

Stipe and pileus confluent; veil typically absent, if present, rudimentary; gills attached to stipe variously, rarely seceding in age; stipe fleshy to ± cartilaginous; spore deposit white or nearly so; spores thin-walled, pseudoamy-loid; cheilocystidia regularly present and typically voluminous though variable in size between species; gill trama typically ± parallel, of hyaline thin-walled hyphae; cuticle of pileus of innate fibrils usually radially arranged and with cystidium-like end-cells; clamp connections present. Habitat typically lignicolous (apparently never forming mycorrhizae).

About 15-20 species are known; none are highly rated as edible.

KEY TO SPECIES

1a Pileus blackish to grayish or pallid, virgate to squamulose 2

1b Pileus not colored as in above choice (if pileus has dark fibrils, the over all color is yellow) 5

2a Stipe distinctly radicating (with a pseudorhiza) .... *T. radicata* (Pk.) Sing.

Pileus 5-7 cm, silky fibrillose, pale grayish brown, the center often darker brown with a reddish tinge. Gills thin, close, adnate to adnexed and with a decurrent tooth, white. Stipe 4-10 cm x 6-10 mm, firm, hollow, white. Spores 6-7 x 3.5-5 μm, Cheilocystidia 22-35 x 5-9 μm, clavate to fusoid-ventricose. End-cells of pileus cuticle hyphae 30-160 x 11-35 μm, cylindric, clavate, or fusoid-ventricose. Pleurocystidia absent (?).

Scattered under conifers, northeastern United States, September; apparently rare.

2b Stipe not radicating 3

3a Pileus tomentose, evenly livid; gills and stipe also livid .... *T. totilivida* (Murr.) Sing.

Pileus 6-8 cm, tomentose, convex to plane, dry; context white, taste mild. Gills broad, ± crowded. Stipe 5 x 1.5 cm, yellow within. Spores 5.5-7 x 3.5 μm. Pleurocystidia numerous, 45-66 x 12-20 μm, fusoid-ventricose, content of some dark-colored. Cheilocystidia same as for pleurocystidia. Pileocystidia with brown content and rounded apices, abundant.

Florida, fall. Edibility not reported (?).

3b Not as above 4

4a Stipe whitish tinged gray; gills white to grayish. Fig. 204 .... *T. platyphylla* (Fr.) Sing.

Figure 204

Figure 204 *Tricholomopsis platyphylla*

Pileus 5-12 cm, margin often frayed in age, at times whitish except for a grayish disc. Gills white to grayish, broad, subdistant. Stipe 6-12 x 1-3 cm, ± equal, base with white rhizomorphs, ± glabrous. Spores 7-9 x 4-5 μm. Pleurocystidia absent or resembling cheilocystidia, the latter 26-37 x 8-15 μm.

Scattered or in small groups on and around hardwood debris, less often on conifer wood, common and widely distributed, spring and early summer, uncommon in the fall. Edible.

4b Stipe and gills yellowish to some degree .... *T. fallax* Smith

Pileus 4-7 cm, dry and virgate with dark gray fibrils; context white; margin lobed and lacerate. Gills pallid at first, broad and subdistaant. Stipe 8-10 x 1-2 cm, surface varying to whitish, ± with appressed fibrils or naked. Spores 6-8.5 x 5-6 μm. Pleurocystidia absent. Cheilocystidia 28-35 x 9-12 μm.

Scattered to gregarious on conifer wood and debris, Northern Rocky Mountains, spring and early summer, not rare. Edibility not tested (?).

5a Pileus and/or stipe with purple, red, vinaceous or vinaceous brown fibrils over surface 6

5b Pileus and/or stipe yellow and if fibrillose the fibrils ochraceous, brown to rusty brown (rarely fuscous) 9

6a Odor and/or taste strong (disagreeable); usually on hardwoods 7

6b Odor and/or taste not distinctive, usually on conifer wood 8

7a Taste bitter, odor slight; gill edges entire; spores 7-9 × 6-7 μm .... *T. squamosa* **Thiers**

Pileus 3.5-4.5 cm, surface dry, densely fibrillose- to squarrose-scaly, dark red young, paler and browner later; context thin. Gills lavender-gray at first, yellowish in aging. Stipe 2-3.5 cm x 5-8 mm, orange-brown, paler in age, appressed fibrillose. Spores non-amyloid. Pleurocystidia and cheilocystidia similar, 30-46 x 12-18 μm.
  On hardwood stumps, etc., Texas, June. Edibility not tested (?).

7b Taste and odor both disagreeable; gill edges fringed; spores 6-7 × 4-5 μm .... *T. formosa* (**Murr.**) **Sing.**

Pileus 5-8 cm, with conspicuous lateritious elongate recurved scales; context firm. Gills crowded, white to yellowish. Stipe 6-8 x 1-2 cm, fibrillose-scaly like the pileus. Pleurocystidia absent. Cheilocystidia 30-76 x 7-18 μm. Scales of pileus of slender brown hyphae.
  November, Florida, on pine sawdust. Edibility not tested (?).

8a Stipe glabrous, sulphur yellow .... *T. flammula* **Métrod**

Pileus 1.6-2.2 cm, squamulose, ground color yellow, squamules, reddish violaceous; context yellow. Gills golden yellow, edges white-fimbriate. Stipe 3-4 cm x 2-3 mm. Spores 6.5-8 x 3.5-4.5 μm. Pleurocystidia 40-50 x 8-12 μm. Cheilocystidia 35-60 x 15-25 μm. Squamules on pileus of hyphae with clavate terminal cells.
  Summer and fall, on conifer wood, Pacific Northwest and Great Lakes area. Most of the

North American collections identified as this species might well be considered a small variant of *T. rutilans*.

8b Stipe ± coated with purplish red fibrils; on conifer wood. Fig. 205 ....+.... .... *T. rutilans* (**Fr.**) **Sing.**

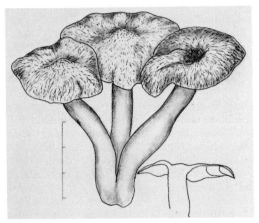

Figure 205

Figure 205 *Tricholomopsis rutilans*

Pileus 4-10 cm, dry and squamulose, the fibrils and squamules bright purplish red, margin often ribbed, often yellowish where bruised; context pale yellow, odor ± fragrant and pungent. Gills yellow. Stipe 5-10 x 0.5-2 cm, yellowish within, staining yellow where handled, ± fibrillose. Spores 5-7 x 3.5-4 μm, non-amyloid. Pleurocystidia 36-52 x 6-9 μm. Cheilocystidia 50-80 x 12-20 μm or larger. End-cells of cuticular hyphae cystidium-like.
  Solitary to ± caespitose on conifer wood, summer and fall, not uncommon; widely distributed in northern regions. Edible but of poor quality.

9a Context pallid to grayish .... *T. glaucipes* **Smith**

Pileus 3-7 cm, surface unpolished from a dark innate pruinose covering, cream color to yellowish brown with a grayish cast from the pruina, more or less streaked; flesh watery. Gills intervenose, yellow. Stipe 6-8 cm x 9-12 mm, surface pallid with a reflection of yellow, becoming dingy brown.

Spores 5-6.5 x 4.5-5 μm. Pleurocystidia lacking. Cheilocystidia 35-46 x 7-11 μm. Cuticle of cap a tangled turf of clavate to subfusoid pileocystidia 30-70 x 8-16 μm.

Solitary on old logs of conifers, Pacific Northwest, summer, apparently rare. Edibility not reported (?).

9b Context of pileus yellow 10

10a Pileus glabrous; veil absent ....
.... T. *thompsoniana* (**Murr.**) **Sm.**

Pileus 2-6 cm, surface moist and hygrophanous, when moist yellow variegated with pallid areas, when faded merely pale yellow; context staining yellow where injured; odor and taste mild. Gills yellowish, edges pallid, staining darker yellow where bruised. Stipe 4-7 cm x 4-11 mm, ± equal, pallid staining ochraceous. Spores 6.5-8 x 5.5-6.5 μm. Pleurocystidia 30-42 x 6-8 μm, clavate. Cheilocystidia 50-85 x 12-22 μm, often fusoid-ventricose. End cells of cuticular hyphae not significantly differentiated from the other cells of the hypha.

On decaying wood of pine, Great Lakes region eastward (It was described from New York as *Agaricus flavescens*).

10b Pileus fibrillose at least over the disc 11

11a Pileus with blackish fibrils or scales in the center at least. Fig. 206 ....
.... T. *decora* (**Fr.**) **Sing.**

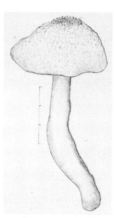

Figure 206

Figure 206 *Tricholomopsis decora*

Pileus 4-6 cm, surface appearing moist beneath a coating of fibrillose scales, firm, yellow under the fibrils. Gills often readily seceding, bright yellow or tinged with orange. Stipe 4-6 cm x 5-10 mm, yellow within, surface paler, glabrous to slightly fibrillose. Spores 6-7.5 x 4.5-5 μm. Pleurocystidia rare, 34-42 x 5-8 μm, scarcely projecting beyond the hymenium. Cheilocystidia 36-62 x 9-20 μm, abundant.

Solitary, scattered to gregarious; on conifer logs etc., common but seldom in quantity, northern United States and in Canada, late summer and fall. Edible?

11b Fibrils over disc of pileus not blackish to fuscous 12

12a Pileus margin fringed; spores globose 7-9 μm. Fig. 207 .... T. *flavissima* (**Sm.**) **Sing.**

Figure 207

Figure 207 *Tricholomopsis flavissima*

Pileus 3-5 cm, dry and innately fibrillose, at times becoming ± scaly around the disc; marginal fibrils at times in fascicles; surface evenly yellow over all or the disc darker; context dull yellow, odor faintly fragrant, taste slightly peppery. Gills bright yellow, edges a brighter color and appearing gelatinous under a lens. Stipe 2-5 cm x 3-6 mm, equal, pallid at first from a thin yellowish partial veil, concolorous with pileus in age and then appressed-fibrillose. Pleurocystidia absent. Cheilocystidia 40-200 x 3-5 μm, filamentose and septate, subgelatinous. Pilear cuticle of greatly elongated hyphae with the end-cells rounded.

Scattered to subcespitose on conifer wood, fall, Pacific Northwest, not uncommon. Edibility not tested.

12b Pileus margin and spores not as above 13

13a Stipe rusty brown when handled. Fig. 208 ....
.... *T. fulvescens* Smith

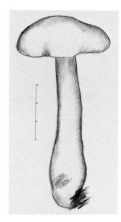

Figure 208

Figure 208   *Tricholomopsis fulvescens*

Pileus 3-5 cm broad, yellow, ochraceous tawny to tawny, dry and appressed fibrillose, the fibrils in obscure fascicles especially near the margin, ground color yellow, the fascicles becoming tawny. Gills pale yellow. Stipe 6-9 x ± 1 cm, dull watery ochraceous within and darkening where cut, appressed fibrillose, the fibrils becoming rusty brown where handled, basal mycelium yellow. Spores 8-10 x 6-7 μm. Pleurocystidia 50-80 x 6-9 μm. Cheilocystidia 28-40 x 6-9 μm. Cuticle of pileus a layer of tangled hyphae with thickened ochraceous walls.

Solitary on very rotten conifer wood; Pacific Northwest, fall, not common. Edibility not tested.

13b Stipe unchanging when handled 14

14a A veil evident on button stages of fruiting body; cheilocystidia 33-50 × 7-13 μm. Fig. 209 .... *T. sulfureoides* (Pk.) Sing.

Figure 209

Figure 209   *Tricholomopsis sulfureoides*

Pileus 3-7 cm, pale yellow variegated with paler areas at times, usually sparsely innately fibrillose over the disc, becoming finely squamulose, the squamules darkening to brownish in age; context pale yellow, unchanging when cut or bruised. Gills almost concolorous with pileus, edges fimbriate and beaded with hyaline drops at first, not staining when bruised. Stipe 3-6 cm x 3-7 mm, yellow, fibrillose below. Spores 5.5-6.5 x 4.5-5 μm. Pleurocystidia 35-47 x 6-9 μm. Cheilocystidia 46-75 x 12-18 μm. Cuticle of pileus of radial hyphae, the end-cells merely cylindric.

Solitary to gregarious on conifer logs, often on hemlock, Great Lakes area eastward and southward, late summer and fall. Var. *megaspora* Smith occurs in the Pacific Northwest and has spores 7-9 x 5-6 μm and cheilocystidia 60-120 x 16-33 μm.

14b Veil absent; some cheilocystidia 56-70 × 12-20 μm .... *T. bella* Smith

Pileus 5-7 cm, depressed around the low umbo, coarsely fibrillose, becoming slightly squamulose over disc, dull yellow; context dull yellow, thin; odor and taste mild. Gills close, dull yellow, the edges staining dull rusty brown when bruised. Stipe about 2 x 1 cm, concolorous with pileus, dull yellow, fibrils slowly staining brown where handled. Spores 6-7 x 4.5-5 μm. Pleurocystidia present but hardly projecting beyond the basidia. Cheilocystidia variable in size and shape: clavate to filamentose and often with apical projections.

Solitary, on conifer logs, etc., Great Lakes and northern Rocky Mountain region, late summer and fall, apparently rare.

Xeromphalina Kühner and Maire

Pileus thin and pliant, confluent with the pliant-cartilaginous stipe; margin of pileus usually incurved; gills broadly adnate to decurrent; stipe tawny-pubescent at the base, the fulvous mycelium often very conspicuous; spores white in deposit, amyloid, thin-walled; hyphae of pileus and gill-trama with slightly to distinctly thickened walls which are often highly refractive when revived in KOH, and are often incrusted, the pigments intercellular; clamp connections present. Fewer than a dozen species are known.

KEY TO SPECIES

1a Pileus dark vinaceous brown; known only from redwood logs and stumps. Fig. 210 .... *X. orickiana* (Smith) Singer

Figure 210

Figure 210 *Xeromphalina orickiana*

Pileus 1-2.5 cm, surface moist to dry, faintly innately fibrillose under a lens; context concolor with the surface, pliant and cartilaginous. Gills pale grayish, becoming brownish. Stipe 1-3 cm

long concolorous with pileus or darker. Spores 4.5-6 x 2-2.5 μm, Pleurocystidia scattered, 30-40 x 8-14 μm. Cheilocystidia similar but more variable. Pileus trama dark vinaceous brown when revived in KOH, vinaceous red in KOH when fresh. Cuticle of pileus having slender irregular pileocystidia 20-50 x 6-12 μm variously disposed.

Caespitose to gregarious, fall and winter, northern California.

1b Habitat and pileus color not as above 2

2a Stipe swollen at apex and gills attached to swelling by their margins. Fig. 211 .... *X. picta* (Fr.) Smith

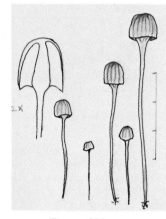

Figure 211

Figure 211 *Xeromphalina picta*

Pileus 2-10 mm broad, cylindric or with a slightly flaring margin but not expanding, the disc and striations brown, remainder yellowish. Gills yellow, subdistant to distant, broad. Stipe 2-6 cm long, thread-like but very rigid, concolorous with pileus. Spores 8-10 x 4-5 μm. Pleurocystidia absent (?). Cheilocystidia 15-20 x 10-14 μm, clavate, echinulate. Gill trama dingy brown in KOH, pale orange-brown in Melzer's solution. Pileus trama with a zone of large cells which stain rusty red in Melzer's.

Gregarious to somewhat caespitose, at times solitary, on rich humus in dense forests or thickets, summer and fall, rare, known in North America from Quebec, Ontario, Michigan, Tennessee and the Pacific Northwest.

2b   Not as above **3**

3a   Pileus 2.5-7 cm broad; growing on hardwood logs, stumps, etc. Fig. 212 ....
.... *X. tenuipes* (Schw.) **Smith**

Figure 212

Figure 212   *Xeromphalina tenuipes*

Pileus dry and velvety, becoming ± granulose or wrinkled, orange-brown with an olive-brown sheen when fresh, the margin usually opaque; context pliant, watery brown. Gills white, becoming pale yellow. Stipe 5-8 cm long, 3-8 mm thick, at times with a pseudorhiza, concolorous with pileus, surface velvety to tomentose. Spores 7-9 x 4.5-5 μm. Pleurocystidia embedded in the hymenium, 23-30 x 5-8 μm. Cheilocystidia similar. Cuticle of pileus a tangled turf of thick-walled hyphal tips or pileocystidia singly or in groups.

Solitary to subcaespitose, east of the Great Plains, spring and summer. This is the largest species in the genus. Edible (?).

3b   Pileus smaller than in above, habitat various
.... **4**

4a   Densely caespitose on hardwood (especially oak) in groups of 50-100 or more fruiting bodies. Fig. 213 .... *X. kauffmanii* **Smith**

Figure 213

Figure 213   *Xeromphalina kauffmanii*

Pileus 5-25 mm, glabrous, ferruginous when young, the margin soon yellowish and ± striate, fading to dingy yellowish. Gills pale yellow, strongly interveined, soon subdistant, narrow, decurrent. Stipe 1-4 cm x 1-2 mm, ferruginous and becoming glabrous above, darker red-brown below, with rusty brown mycelium at base. Spores 5-6 x 3.3 μm. Pleurocystidia and cheilocystidia similar, 40-70 x 8-12 μm. Cuticle of pileus a cutis.

Central and eastern United States, spring and summer, fairly common and usually mistaken for *X. campanella*.

4b   Not as above **5**

5a   On hardwood debris (especially ash) in low hardwood swamps; pileus bister going to pale tawny .... *X. fraxinophila* **Smith**

Pileus 1-3 cm, moist and hygrophanous, buttons faintly hoary, bister at first, then ochraceous tawny or brown, margin closely and faintly striate when moist, often concentrically zoned in age; context concolorous with surface. Gills honey-yellow. Stipe 5-7 x 2-3 mm, evenly brownish pubescent, the base with matted yellow tomentum. Spores 4.5-5.5 x 2.5-3.3 μm. Cystidia lacking. Gill trama bright pinkish red in KOH, fading to orange-brown.

Gregarious to subcaespitose on very old debris of ash, or on humus under ash, Great Lakes area, apparently rare, fall.

5b **On conifer wood, on debris in bogs or on conifer debris on the forest floor** **6**

6a **Taste bitter; aspect of fruit body collybioid (gills adnate). Fig. 214** ....
.... *X. fulvipes* **(Murr.) Smith**

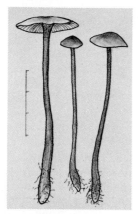

Figure 214

Figure 214 *Xeromphalina fulvipes*

Pileus 1-2.5 cm, bright yellow-brown on disc, ochraceous tawny on the margin, slowly fading, when moist faintly striate, glabrous; context concolorous with surface, pliant and tough, reviving when moistened. Gills yellowish to brownish, close. Stipe 2-8 cm x 1-2.5 mm, ferruginous to blackish brown and covered with an orange tomentum, base strigose and often sunken in the substrate. Spores 4.5-6 x 1.5-2 μm. Pleurocystidia rare to abundant, 20-32 x 3-9 μm, soon elongating greatly and with flexuous hairlike prolongations. Cheilocystidia similar. Gill trama subgelatinous, pallid to brown in KOH.

Solitary to scattered on debris of conifers, more rarely on alder; Pacific Northwest, spring and fall, uncommon, not found in quantity.

6b **Taste mild; gills ± decurrent at maturity** **7**

7a **Typically densely gregarious to caespitose on conifer wood; stipe usually 1-4 cm long. Fig. 215** .... *X. campanella* **(Fr.) Küh. & Maire**

Figure 215

Figure 215 *Xeromphalina campanella*

Pileus 1-2.5 cm, glabrous, moist opaque, then striate before fading, dull orange-yellow to tawny, darker in age; context pliant, yellow. Gills thickish, subdistant, narrow, deeply decurrent in age. Stipe yellow ochre at first, with a yellowish pruina, becoming glabrous near apex and strigose at base, horny-cartilaginous at maturity, darkening to date brown from base upward. Spores 6-7.5 x 3-3.5 μm. Pleurocystidia 26-40 x 5-14 μm. Cheilocystidia similar. Gill trama of interwoven brownwalled hyphae.

Gregarious to cespitose on decaying conifer wood. Throughout the conifer areas of North America, spring to winter, common.

7b **Scattered on debris; stipe 4-8 cm long and ± bulbous at the base. Fig. 216** ....
.... *X. cauticinalis* **(Fr.) Küh. & Maire**

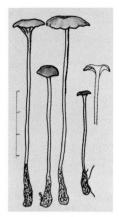

Figure 216

Figure 216 *Xeromphalina cauticinalis*

Pileus 1-2.5 cm, margin becoming irregular to lacerate in age, russet to tawny or ochraceous tawny, fading to yellow, at times staining ferruginous in age, buttons a rich rusty brown; context concolorous with pileus surface. Gills pale to dingy yellow, many of them forked near the margin of the cap, strongly intervenose. Stipe 3.5-8 cm long, basal bulb coated with tawny mycelium which binds the debris. Spores 5.5-7 x 3-4 μm. Pleurocystidia lacking. Cheilocystidia rare to scattered, 26-30 x 4-7 μm.

Gregarious to scattered under conifers, in bogs, and on very decayed conifer debris, summer and fall, Great Lakes area eastward and in the Pacific Northwest, common at times in the northern Rocky Mountains.

AMANITACEAE Roze

Pileus and stipe easily and cleanly separated, gills typically free from the stipe or nearly so, spore deposit white to slightly tinted, gill trama bilateral (Fig. 19d).

KEY TO GENERA

1a Stipe with a volva (remains of an outer veil) in the form of a cup at the base of the stipe, or as particles of tissue or powder, patches or warts of the tissue of this veil around the base of the stipe or on the pileus or on both .... (p. 155) *Amanita*

1b Remains of the outer veil (for all practical purposes) lacking ....
.... (p. 171) *Limacella*

Amanita Pers. ex Hooker

The volva is the most important macroscopic structure in the identification of species of *Amanita*. For this reason it is important to dig up carefully, any fruiting body suspected of being in this genus. The outer veil encloses the entire young fruiting body and is left at the base of the stipe when the fruit body expands. The volva may appear as a cup enclosing the base of the stipe, as somewhat ingrown rolls or ridges of tissue low down on the stipe, or its remains may simply be powdery and the powder may adhere to the soil around the base of the stipe when the specimen is collected. Some of the remains often appear as warts or particles on the pileus. The principal microscopic characters are the smooth, thin-walled, globose to ellipsoid or more elongate spores and bilateral gill trama.

Many amanitas are edible and some are said to be very tasty, however, since some of the most deadly poisonous mushrooms are found in this genus we recommend that no amanitas be eaten unless the mycophagist has become an expert in the identification of the species. The genus is large and world-wide in distribution. As yet we have no critical inventory of the North American species, but we have over 100 known at present. Most are terrestrial, form mycorrhiza with woody plants, and fruit most abundantly during hot wet weather. The center of distribution for North America, based on the number of species occurring there, is our southeastern area combined with the Gulf Coast region.

KEY TO SPECIES

1a Volva distinct, cuplike or sacklike at the base of the stipe (Fig. 12a, e); pileus glabrous or with only a patch or two of volval material on it at times 2

1b Volva intergrown almost completely with the base of the stipe, or very fragile and soon breaking into small pieces (or merely powdery) (Fig. 12b, c, d, f); pileus surface usually having warts or small patches of material on it 8

2a Stipe lacking a membranous annulus (a faint fibrillose zone may be present) 3

2b Stipe with a membranous annulus formed by the breaking of the partial veil from the margin of the pileus (in a few species the annulus may be ragged or fragmentary so examine several fruiting bodies to avoid being mislead by accidents at the time the specimen expanded) 10

3a Pileus 6-18 cm, blackish brown, often with a flat piece of the volva on the surface; gill edges umber brown. Fig. 217 ....
.... A. pachycholea Stuntz

Figure 217

Figure 217 *Amanita pachycholea*

Pileus ovoid to obtuse then umbonate or plane, viscid, margin coarsely plicate-striate and often splitting at maturity, becoming date-brown from margin inward; context white, thin, odor mild. Gills broad, thickish, free, white to pallid. Stipe 10-20 x 1-2.5 cm, slightly enlarged downwards, becoming hollow, surface colored like the pileus but paler, base set in a thick, rigid volva which is white but finally stained rusty brown, 2-3 lobed. Spores ± globose 10-13 µm, non-amyloid.

Solitary to scattered under conifers, Pacific Northwest, fall, not common.

3b Not as above 4

4a Pileus smoke-gray to drab and gill edges white-floccose. Fig. 218 ....
.... A. *vaginata* (Fr.) Vitt.

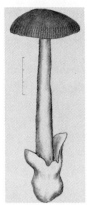

Figure 218

Figure 218 *Amanita vaginata*

Pileus 3-8 cm, oval then convex and finally ± plane, glabrous, viscid, soon dry, margin plicate-striate. Gills free but approximate, broad in front, close, white. Stipe 8-12 x 0.5-1.2 cm, ± equal, unpolished, at times with pallid to ash-colored appressed zones of fibrils; volva white, 2-3 lobed. Spores 10-13 μm, ± globose, non-amyloid.

Solitary to scattered, summer and fall, widely distributed in conifer and hardwood forests.

4b   Not with the above combination of features 5

5a   Pileus orange-buff and nearly always with a patch of volva remains on it; odor strong and pungent. Fig. 219 .... A. *velosa* (Pk.) Lloyd

Figure 219

Figure 219 *Amanita velosa*

Pileus 4-9.5 cm, convex to nearly plane, viscid but soon dry, margin sulcate-striate, pale buff; context white, unchanging. Gills close, white to pale cream-color, in age often tinged pink, decurrent on stipe by lines. Stipe 8-15 x 0.6-1 cm, evenly enlarged downward, only an obscure veil-line present as an annulus. Volva white, 2-layered. Spores 8.4-11 (12.6) x 6-11 μm, non-amyloid.

Solitary to scattered under oak, Oregon and California, spring and summer, abundant at times. Old caps are easily mistaken for *Volvariella* species.

5b   Not as above 6

6a   Pileus tan to rusty brown, margin distinctly sulcate-striate; volva becoming stained or flushed tan to reddish tan. Fig. 220 .... A. *fulva* Persoon

Figure 220

Figure 220 *Amanita fulva*

Pileus 5-10 cm, ovoid to obtuse, then convex and finally expanded-umbonate or plane, usually glabrous. Gills free, close, broad, white to cream-color, not marginate. Stipe 8-16 x 0.4-1.3 cm, ± equal, lacking a distinct bulb, surface ± appressed fibrillose. Volva ± fragile, soft, white at first, lobed. Spores 8-10 μm, globose, non-amyloid.

Solitary to scattered, ubiquitous in wooded areas and especially in drying-up bogs, summer and early fall, common and often abundant.

Amanitaceae   157

6b Not as above 7

7a Odor strong and distinctive 8

7b Odor none or slight 9

8a Odor strong of garlic ....
.... *A. alliacea* (**Murr.**) **Murrill**

Pileus ± 8 cm, margin appendiculate and not sulcate, white, dry or subviscid, with scattered volval patches 4-12 mm wide. Gills crowded, attached to stipe, narrow, white. Stipe 10 x 2 cm, tapered upward from a fusoid ± rooting bulb 4 x 2.5 cm, solid, white; annulus soon obliterated; volva collapsing against the stipe, soft. Spores 12-14.5 x 4-4.5 μm, amyloid.

Under *Quercus* (oak) in mixed woods, Florida, summer, not well known.

8b Odor strong and peculiar but not of garlic
.... *A. roanokensis* **Coker**

Pileus 8-12 cm, convex to plane, at times with a slight umbo, margin appendiculate, white overall or disc cream-color, sparsely decorated with volval patches 4-12 mm wide. Gills crowded to ± distant, attached to stipe, finally ± broad, white to pallid. Stipe 9-14 x 1-2 cm, tapered upward from a ± fusoid-rooting base 4-5 x 2-3 cm, solid, white, no annulus or only with a faint annular zone; volva with a free but torn upper edge (limb), the free margin collapsing on the stipe. Spores 12-15 x 3.5-5 μm, amyloid, some with small amyloid warts.

In dry mixed forests, eastern and southern United States, summer and fall, rare (?).

9a Fruiting body staining reddish where bruised; spores 8-11 × 5.5-6.5 μm, amyloid ....
.... *A. agglutinata* (**Berk. & Curt.**) **Lloyd**

Pileus 4-8 cm, ovoid, then convex to plane, subviscid, ± coated first with outer veil fibrils, margin striate at maturity, whitish but soon dingy brown over disc. Gills white, broad, close, remote from stipe. Stipe 9-11 x 1-2.5 cm, enlarged downward, whitish to reddish brown (in age); annulus seldom well-formed; volva tough, thick, membranous, white but reddish where bruised.

Solitary to scattered under hardwood, summer, southeastern United States north to Great Lakes area and eastward, not rare.

9b Fruiting body not reddish where bruised. Fig. 221 .... *A. peckiana* **Kauff. in Peck**

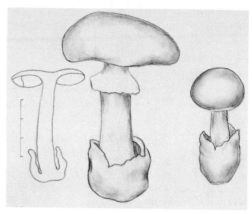

Figure 221

Figure 221 *Amanita peckiana*

Pileus 4-9 cm, ovoid becoming convex to ± plane, glabrous or with a patch or two of volval tissue, soon dry and minutely squamulose, at first the margin fringed but not striate, whitish to cream-buff, or pinkish buff to pinkish gray; context thick, soft, white. Gills free or attached by a line, broad in front, whitish, close. Stipe 3-8 x 1-2 cm, white, floccose from inner veil (annulus soon obliterated); volva thick, fleshy, 2-3 lobed, double (inner layer often inconspicuous), pinkish tan in stipe base on aging. Spores 13-16 x 4.5-6 μm, amyloid.

Scattered to gregarious on sandy soil under aspen and oak, summer, Great Lakes area southward, abundant at times.

10a Pileus obviously colored 11

10b Pileus white at least when young; disc may be tinted slightly in age 14

11a Pileus red to orange-red to rich yellow-orange; spores non-amyloid. Fig. 222 ....
.... *A. caesarea* (**Fr.**) **Pers. ex Schw.**

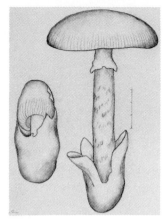

Figure 222

Figure 222 *Amanita caesarea*

Pileus 5-12 (15) cm, convex becoming nearly plane, glabrous, viscid, margin plicate-striate. Gills close, broad, free but not remote, light yellow. Stipe 8-15 x 1-2 cm, ± equal, base scarcely bulbous, yellow; annulus yellow, pendant, superior; volva white, thick, tough. Spores 8-11 x 6-7.5 μm.

Solitary to gregarious in open stands of conifers, Gulf Coast to southeastern states and north to the Gulf of St. Lawrence, not common but occasionally found in abundance. Edible and choice according to those who have eaten it.

11b Not as above **12**

12a Pileus olive-yellowish, olive to olive gray or yellowish gray to yellowish brown. Fig. 223 .... *A. phalloides* **(Fr.) Secr.**

Figure 223

Figure 223 *Amanita phalloides*

Pileus 5-12 cm, obtuse to convex, finally nearly plane, glabrous, viscid, margin scarcely striate; context whitish, odor nauseous. Gills close, moderately broad, free, white to pallid, not staining where injured. Stipe 5-10 x 1-2 cm above a distinct bulb 2-3.5 cm broad; surface below the annulus zoned with the color of the pileus; annulus subapical, pendent, white to olive yellowish; volva pallid to tinged olive-yellow. Spores 8-11 x 5.5-7 μm, amyloid.

Scattered to gregarious under hardwoods, summer and fall, sporadic, Pacific coast area and eastern United States. POISONOUS.

12b Not as above **13**

13a Volva thick, rigid and very prominent. Fig. 224 .... *A. calyptroderma* **Atk. & Ballen**

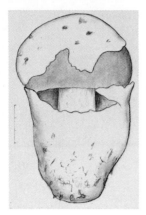

Figure 224

Figure 225

Figure 224 *Amanita calyptoderma*

Pileus 10-22 cm, convex, then broadly convex to plane, viscid, with a large piece of the volva usually somewhere on or near the disc, dark date brown over disc and more ochraceous over the margin, becoming yellower as it ages, margin soon becoming tuberculate-striate. Gills broad, crowded, adnate by a line at first, soon free, white to yellow. Stipe 10-20 x 2-3 cm, appearing bulbous; annulus ± superior, membranous, yellowish; volva with a double margin. Spores 9-11 x 5-6 μm, non-amyloid.

Scattered to gregarious, mixed woods, Pacific Northwest, not common, spring and fall. Edible and choice but BE SURE of your identification.

13b Volva very small and inconspicuous; pileus pale to dark gray or brownish gray, rarely almost white. Fig. 225 .... A. *spreta* Peck

Figure 225 *Amanita spreta*

Pileus 5-12 cm, ovoid to obtuse, soon conic to convex and finally plane or with an umbo, viscid, margin sulcate-striate, surface glabrous, rarely with adhering veil material; context soft fragile, no color change on injury. Gills close to subdistant, ± broad in front, attached by a line, white to creamy. Stipe 6-12 x 1-2 cm, ± equal, floccose-pruinose above the annulus, ± lacerate-fibrillose below, white to pallid throughout, base inserted in a small inconspicuous, white, lobed volva (easily lost in collecting); annulus superior, white above, gray beneath. Spores 10-12 x 6-7.5 μm, non-amyloid

Solitary to gregarious on sandy soil under oak, summer and early fall, Great Lakes area eastward and southward, common during warm wet seasons. Probably poisonous: the question deserves further study. The one fatality attributed to it in Michigan could have been caused by another species.

14a Spores ± globose 15

14b Spores ± ellipsoid 16

15a Basidia 2-spored. Fig. 226 ....
.... A. *bisporigera* Atkinson

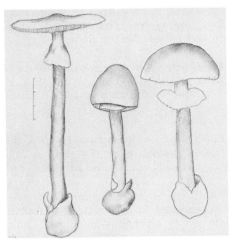

Figure 226

Figure 226 *Amanita bisporigera*

Pileus 3-7 (10) cm, ovoid to cylindric, expanding to campanulate, convex or broadly expanded, viscid, glabrous, white, disc finally ± creamy, margin even; context white, thin, odor nauseous, KOH on cuticle yellow. Gills free or at first attached by a line, ± broad in front, close to crowded, white. Stipe 6-12 x 0.8-2 cm, nearly equal to a basal bulb, white; volva 2-3 lobed, membranous, white. Spores 7-10 μm, globose, amyloid.

Solitary to scattered under hardwoods, east of the Mississippi River, summer and fall. POISONOUS.

15b Basidia 4-spored. Fig. 227 .... A. *virosa* (Fr.) Bertillon

Figure 227

Figure 227 *Amanita virosa*

Pileus 6-15 cm, obtuse becoming broadly convex to plane or expanded-umbonate, shining white, glabrous. Gills close, broad, free or attached by a line, white and unchanging. Stipe 8-15 (20) x 1-2.5 cm, ± equal down to a large bulb, white; KOH yellow on upper surface and on cuticle of pileus; surface usually ± scaly below the subapical annulus; annulus ample, membranous, white; volva forming a cup with a free, lobed margin, fleshy-tough. Spores 8.5-11 or 9-11 x 7-9 μm, globose to subglobose, amyloid.

Scattered to gregarious especially under birch and aspen, late summer and fall; eastern United States (east of the Great Plains), and in Canada. Very rare in the western United States. Common and POISONOUS.

16a Pileus white to cream-color and soon orange-buff over the disc; usually with a patch or two of volval tissue around the disc; southwestern in distribution .... A. *ocreata* Peck

Pileus 5-7 cm, convex to plane, viscid, margin even or slightly striate. Gills free but approximate, narrow, crowded, not staining where injured. Stipe 8-15 x 1.5-1.8 cm, nearly equal above a bulbous base, white throughout, floccose; annulus superior, white to yellowish; bulb 2-3.5 cm thick and elongate-ovate, pointed below; volva white, thin, with a free limb flaring and then collapsing on stipe. Spores 9-11 x 7-8.5 μm, amyloid.

Scattered on ground under oak, central and southern California and apparently widely distributed in the Southwest, spring. POISONOUS.

16b Pileus white to maturity, glabrous; distribution east of the Great Plains 17

17a Bulb of stipe tending to stain brownish, disc of pileus often appearing wet; spores 10-13 × 6.5-8 μm .... A. *hygroscopica* Coker

Pileus 4-10 cm, convex to plane, viscid, disc with a wet appearance, glabrous, margin scarcely striate, dull white, in age dull yellowish and drying this color. Gills broad, close, rounded at stipe, white becoming tinged vinaceous. Stipe 5-8 cm x 5-7 mm, with a distinct rounded bulb, white, at times stained brownish below; annulus white, median to superior, often ragged; volva as in *A. virosa*.

Scattered under hardwoods, southern United States but northward to the Great Lakes area, summer and fall.

17b Bulb not staining; pileus lacking a "wet" disc under normal conditions; spores 9-12 × 6.5-8 μm .... A. verna sensu American authors

Pileus 3-10 cm, convex to ± plane, subviscid, glabrous, white, in age the disc yellowish; odor slight; KOH on cuticle no reaction. Gills crowded, ± reaching the stipe, unchanging if injured, a faint pinkish flush present in age. Stipe 8-12 x 1-2 cm, bulb 3-4 cm; white overall; annulus spreading then pendent.

Scattered in rich beech maple woods, east of the Great Plains, not uncommon during warm wet seasons: POISONOUS. It seems likely that *A. hygroscopica* is merely a slight variant of *A. verna*, but the time to make this comparison will be when a type collection has been designated for *A. verna*.

18a Stipe lacking a membranous annulus but an annular zone may be present (partial veil rudimentary) 19

18b A membranous annulus present at the time the veil breaks (in some species it is thin and soon broken) 24

19a Pileus scarlet to yellow at first 20

19b Pileus white to gray or lead-color 21

20a Pileus rich scarlet to bright orange .... A. parcivolvata (Pk.) Gilbert

Pileus 4-9 cm, convex to broadly convex or plane, viscid, with scattered warts of veil material over surface, margin plicate-striate; context yellow. Gills pale cream, close, narrow to ± broad, edges floccose from yellow veil particles. Stipe 5-10 x 0.3-1.2 cm, ± equal, stuffed, base hardly bulbous, surface dusted yellow; volva white to yellow, friable and leaving particles adhering to soil. Spores 9-12 x 6-8 μm, non-amyloid.

Scattered to gregarious on lawns and cultivated soil, spring, less common in the fall, southeastern and eastern United States.

20b Pileus pale yellow to egg-yellow when young, paler in age .... see page 166 A. russuloides

21a Pileus dingy white; spores 10-15 × 5-6 μm (see A. silvicola page 170 also) .... A. baccata (Fr.) Gillet

Pileus 4-12 cm, pulvinate to broadly convex, the disc ± depressed in age, margin at first appendiculate, white to slightly discolored, subviscid, coated at first with white volval remains which break into patches or warts. Gills crowded, free or nearly so, broad, white to cream-color, not staining. Stipe 5-15 x 0.5-2 cm, ± equal above an elongate rooting bulb, solid, white fibrillose to floccose; annulus present or absent, usually not evident, rim of bulb decorated with floccose material at first. Spores amyloid.

Scattered to gregarious on sandy soil under scrub oak, Great Lakes area, common locally after heavy July rains.

21b Pileus cinereous, drab or lead-color 22

22a Pileus with fairly persistent warts over disc; spores 10-14 μm in diam., ± globose, non-amyloid. Fig. 228 .... A. inaurata Secretan

Figure 228

Figure 228 *Amanita inaurata*

Pileus 4-8 (12) cm, ovoid to convex then broadly convex or obtusely umbonate, viscid, at first with grayish warts and patches of volval tissue, color lead-gray to blackish brown; context thin, fragile, soft, odor and taste mild. Gills close, broad, free but approximate, whitish. Stipe 6-8 x 1-2 cm, ± equal or evenly enlarged downward, hollow, ± coated below with ashy gray fibrils, apex pallid; annulus merely a zone of fibrils soon evanescent; volva gray to pallid, with rusty stains in some, very fragile.

Scattered in mixed woods, late summer and fall, seldom in quantity but widely distributed in North America.

22b Pileus and spores not as above **23**

23a Odor of chloride of lime or "old ham;" spores 8.5-11 × 5-6 μm, amyloid. Fig. 229 ....
.... *A. cinereiconia* **Atkinson**

Figure 229

Figure 229 *Amanita cinereiconia*

Pileus 3-7 cm, convex to ± plane, finally depressed around disc, margin appendiculate, whitish to gray, covered by pale yellowish gray to brownish, pulverulent, soft warts of volval tissue. Gills close, soon free, broad, white to cream-color, floccose on edge. Stipe 5-10 x 0.4-1 cm, ± equal above a napiform to fusoid, rooting bulb 6-18 mm thick; surface of stipe more pulverulent downward; annulus imperfect to evanescent, pulverulent-floc-

cose; volva friable, remains often on margin of bulb.

The name of this species used here is in the sense of Bas (Atkinson's type). The species is southeastern in distribution, and fruits in the summer. Apparently it is not rare.

23b Odor not distinctive; spores 7-9 × 5-6 μm, amyloid. Fig. 230 .... *A. farinosa* **Schw.**

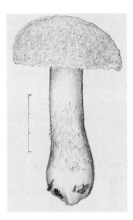

Figure 230

Figure 230 *Amanita farinosa*

Pileus 3-7 cm, obtuse to convex, finally plane to ± depressed, surface dry, pale gray and at first covered by remains of a powdery veil; margin appendiculate at first and surface coarsely tuberculate-striate beneath veil remnants. Gills close, narrowly attached, ± broad, white to pale gray; edges white fimbriate. Stipe 6-8 x 1-1.5 cm, clavate, hollow, finally equal, with a short pseudorhiza, granulose from the veil.

Solitary to scattered often under spruce, along the Pacific Coast, late fall. It was described from the Southeast where it is abundant. Not rare, but apparently rarely collected.

24a Pileus distinctly pinkish, or injured places staining red to vinaceous **25**

24b Pileus and staining reactions not as above **27**

25a Pileus pink to vinaceous at first; spores amyloid, 11-13.5 × 8-10 μm......................................
.... *A. salmonea* **Thiers**

Pileus 4-8 cm, obtuse to convex or plano-umbonate, margin appendiculate, surface smooth, volval material breaking up to form warts and these vinaceous to subferruginous. Gills crowded to subdistant, free or narrowly attached, white, ventricose. Stipe 6-9 x 0.8-1.6 cm, equal or base ± enlarged, white; annulus submembranous, edge thick, often poorly formed.

Scattered in lawns, pastures and open areas generally, Texas, apparently abundant at times after heavy rains in late August or September.

25b Injured tissues staining red to vinaceous, often slowly, pileus never pink **26**

26a Pileus yellow to yellow brownish; volva yellow and friable. Fig. 231 ....
.... *A. flavorubescens* **Atkinson**

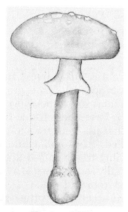

Figure 231

Figure 231 *Amanita flavorubescens*

Pileus 5-14 cm, obtuse to convex, finally broadly convex to plane, at first dotted with yellow warts of volval material, viscid, fading to pinkish buff, margin finally ± striate. Gills close, white, broad, remote from stipe. Stipe 6-12 (15) x 1-2 cm, equal to a bulbous base, squamulose below annulus; annulus with yellow patches on margin; volva friable, particles often left adhering to the soil. Spores 8-10 x 5-6 μm, amyloid.

Gregarious to scattered in oak woods, early summer, Great Lakes area and southward, not uncommon.

26b Pileus whitish to dark brown or tinged olive to near date-brown; volval remnants pallid, all tissues staining reddish and slowly becoming brown. Fig. 232 ....
.... *A. rubescens* **(Fr.) S. F. Gray**

Figure 232

Figure 232 *Amanita rubescens*

Pileus 5-12 cm, ovoid to campanulate, finally expanded-umbonate or broadly convex, viscid, with scattered warts of broken volva, glabrescent. Gills ± broad, approximate, close, white to dingy. Stipe 8-15 x 0.8-2.5 cm, equal above a distinct bulb; pallid; annulus superior, often flushed vinaceous; volva friable, the pieces often adhering to soil around bulb. Spores 8-10 x 5-6 μm, amyloid.

Scattered to gregarious under hardwoods or in mixed forests, common east of the Great Plains, summer and fall. It is one of our most abundant edible species (but we do not recommend any *Amanita*).

27a Taste oily-bitter; on lawns in Texas ....
.... *A. thiersii* **Bas**

Pileus 3-10 cm, obtuse to convex or with a low umbo, margin appendiculate, white, at first with soft subpulverulent floccose woolly white volval remnants, ± glabrescent, odor not distinctive. Gills close, free, narrow (finally broad), white. Stipe 8-20 x 1-2 cm, hollow, ± equal to a slightly enlarged subfusoid base, white; annulus apical, thin, white, finally disappearing. Spores 7.5-9.5 x 7-9 μm, amyloid.

Late summer, rare (?), probably Gulf Coast area in distribution.

27b Not as above **28**

28a Pileus disc red to orange to yellow **29**

28b Pileus not colored as in above choice **34**

29a Spores amyloid **30**

29b Spores non-amyloid **31**

30a Pileus greenish yellow fading to olive-buff. Fig. 233 .... *A. citrina* **S. F. Gray**

Figure 233

Figure 233 *Amanita citrina*

Pileus 5-12 cm, obtuse to convex, finally plane, viscid, with thin patches of volval material grayish in color variously distributed, odor faintly of chloride of lime. Gills white, finally often yellowish, crowded, broad, free but approximate. Stipe 6-12

x 1-1.5 cm, equal above an abrupt bulb often showing one to three longitudinal clefts or splits (as in *A. brunnescens*); annulus olive yellowish to pallid; volva fibrillose-floccose, remains often on rim of bulb. Spores 7-9 μm, amyloid.

Solitary to scattered under hardwoods, Great lakes area and both east and southward to Gulf Coast, summer and fall, common.

30b Pileus bright orange to yellow. Fig. 234 .... *A. flavoconia* **Atkinson**

Figure 234

Figure 234 *Amanita flavoconia*

Pileus 3-10 cm, convex to broadly convex with a decurved margin, viscid, at first with soft yellow warts of volval tissue, margin even to slightly striate. Gills free, ± approximate, close, broad, white to pale yellow. Stipe 6-10 x 0.5-1 cm, equal above a bulbous base, yellow-pulverulent above annulus, unpolished and yellow below it; bulb and lower part of stipe typically with patches of volval material adhering to the surface or to the surrounding soil. Spores 7-9 x 5-6.5 μm.

Solitary to scattered in hardwood and mixed forests. Great Lakes area east and southward; summer and fall common.

31a Pileus dull yellow, with flat patches of volval material over surface at first (these readily washed off) ....
A. junquillea **Quélet, sensu American authors**

Pileus 4-10 cm, convex to convex-depressed finally, margin tuberculate-striate at maturity, volval patches white to pallid tan. Context thin and white. Gills close, ± broad in front finally, attached by a line, whitish to cream color. Stipe 6-12 x 1-2 cm, evenly enlarged downward; annulus superior, persistent, often with volval patches adhering to edge; volva evident as a collar-like roll of tissue at apex of bulb. Spores 8-11 x 6-8 μm.

Solitary to scattered in mixed forests, Pacific Northwest, fall, frequently collected.

31b Not as above 32

32a Pileus deep red, orange-red, orange-yellow to whitish (in different variants); volval remains on pileus in form of warts and patches; volval remains on bulb and lower part of stipe present as scales and zones. Fig. 235 .... *A. muscaria* **(Fr.) S. F. Gray**

Figure 235

Figure 235 *Amanita muscaria*

Pileus 7-15 (2) cm, convex to plano-depressed at maturity, viscid, warts on cap white to yellow, margin even. Gills free, approximate to stipe, broad, close, white to yellowish, edges floccose, Stipe 8-15 x 1-3 cm, bulbous, fibrillose; annulus median to superior, ample, margin often with yellow patches; bulb rounded below. Spores 9-11 x 7-8 μm.

Scattered to densely gregarious under conifers and also aspen and birch, rarely oak, spring

and fall, common and widely distributed. POISONOUS.

32b Not as above 33

33a Pileus persistently pale yellow, margin coarsely tuberculate-striate. Fig. 236 .... *A. russuloides* **Peck**

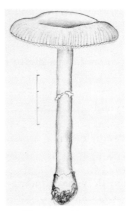

Figure 236

Figure 236 *Amanita russuloides*

Pileus 4-10 (12) cm, at maturity broadly convex to plane or shallowly depressed on the disc. Gills free, ± crowded, broad in front, white to yellowish, edges floccose. Stipe 6-12 x 1-2 cm, clavate to bulbous, white to yellowish, annulus nearly basal to median and ± collar-like, often absent; volva intergrown with the bulb, its upper edge collar-like around base of stipe. Spores 9-11 x 7-8.5 μm.

Scattered to densely gregarious under second growth oak on sandy soil, summer, common from the Great Lakes southward and in the east.

33b Pileus white or only the disc yellowish to raw umber; slimy at first; volva a tight fitting collar at apex of bulb in most fruiting bodies. Fig. 237 .... *A. cothurnata* **Atkinson**

Figure 237

Figure 238

Figure 238 *Amanita pantherina*

Figure 237 *Amanita cothurnata*

Pileus 5-10 cm, obtuse to convex becoming plane to expanded-umbonate; odor ± pungent. Gills white, broad in front, close, remote. Stipe 6-15 x 1-1.5 cm, equal above a bulb with a pointed base; surface silky above the annulus, below it often scaly, white; annulus median, white or tinged avellaneous. Spores 8-11 x 6-8 μm.

Solitary to scattered under scrub oak on sandy soil, Great Lakes area southward and eastward, common in some areas during late summer and fall. It occurs in 3 variants: white, white with pale yellow disc, and white with a brownish gray disc. All are to be regarded as POISONOUS.

34a Spores non-amyloid; volva a collar-like roll of tissue at apex of bulb (see *A. cothurnata* also). Fig. 238 ....
.... *A. pantherina* (**Fr.**) **Krombhz.**

Pileus 5-10 (12) cm, at maturity broadly convex to plane, viscid, with warts of volval material over surface at first, color variable but dull: grayish brown, deep yellowish brown, dull amber brown to amber yellow or at times ± pinkish gray over margin. Gills close, crowded, broad in front, attached by a line, remote in age. Stipe 6-10 x 1-2 cm, clavate (2-3 cm at base); fibrillose below annulus with 2-4 zones of volval tissue near bulb at times; annulus median to superior, yellowish to pinkish gray or pallid. Spores 9-11 x 6.5-8 μm.

Scattered under conifers or rarely under hardwood, spring and fall, Pacific Northwest, the Great Lakes area, and the Southeast (generally east of the Great Plains), but most abundant in the Rocky Mountains and the Pacific Northwest.

34b Spores amyloid; volva friable and not leaving a collar around stipe 35

35a Spores globose, 8-10 μm, amyloid; bulb of stipe usually split lengthwise in 1-3 places; under hardwoods. Fig. 239. .... *A. brunnescens* **Atkinson**

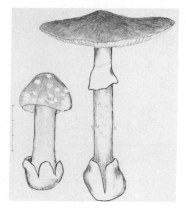

Figure 239

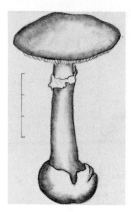

Figure 240

Figure 239 *Amanita brunnescens*

Pileus 4-10 cm, obtuse to convex, then broadly expanded or with a low umbo, viscid, soon glabrous, with volval patches at first, virgate, olive-brown to drab or brownish gray to pallid or white. Gills close, broad in front, attached by a line, stained brown in age at times. Stipe 6-12 x 1-2 cm, equal above the bulb, white to pallid; volva leaving patches over pileus and along apex of bulb or adhering to the soil.

Gregarious and often abundant under hardwoods, mixed woods, and often in stands of pole-sized saplings, midsummer to fall, Great Lakes area southward and eastward, very common.

35b Not as above 36

36a Under conifers; annulus, stipe and pileus drab or darker; bulb of stipe often split as in *A. brunnescens.* **Fig. 240** .... *A. porphyria* **(Fr.) Secr.**

Figure 240 *Amanita porphyria*

Pileus 4-10 (12) cm, convex to nearly flat, sub-viscid, volval remnants on cap ash-colored, margin even. Gills ± broad in front, close, narrowly attached, whitish to cinereous. Stipe 5-10 x 1-1.5 cm, equal above the abrupt bulb; annulus median, ample; volva floccose-pulverulent. Spores 7-10 μm, globose, amyloid.

Solitary in rich humus especially under hemlock, late summer and fall, to be expected where hemlock grows in North America; not rare but seldom abundant.

36b Not as above 37

37a Spores 7-9 $\times$ 5-6 μm; warts on cap dark gray; volva friable as in *A. rubescens.* **Fig. 241** .... *A. spissa* **(Fr.) Kummer**

Figure 241

Figure 241 *Amanita spissa*

Pileus 3-10 (12) cm, obtuse to convex, finally plane or slightly umbonate, viscid, dark grayish brown at least over the disc, margin paler to pallid, at first decorated by block-like to pyramidal warts of gray veil tissue, margin even; odor slight, of chlorine? Gills close, broad, soon remote, not staining. Stipe 8-12 x 0.8-1.5 cm, enlarged down to an oval bulb 3-4 cm thick; annulus soon ragged and with gray patches on underside; volva gray. Spores amyloid.

Solitary to gregarious in mixed woods, Southeast, Gulf Coast, and north to the Great Lakes area and New England, not common, summer and fall.

37b Not as above; fruit body predominantly white but veil gray in two species 38

38a Stipe with an abrupt broad bulb flattened below; odor not dinstinctive; spores 9-11 × 6.5-9 μm .... *A. abrupta* **Peck**

Pileus 4-10 cm, convex then broadly convex, subviscid, white or disc slowly ± yellowish, with numerous conic warts often in concentric rows, margin at times finally slightly striate. Gills white, close, broad in front, approximate. Stipe 6-12 x 0.5-1.2 cm above a bulb 4-5 cm wide, white; annulus superior, white, delicate; volva present around stipe base as particles or the veil remnants adhering to soil. Spores amyloid.

Scattered under hardwoods, southeastern and Gulf Coast states north to the Great Lakes area (where it is rare); summer and early fall.

38b Not as above (bulb not broad and flattened) 39

39a Volval material white at first but at times discoloring to buff or brown (or remaining white) 41

39b Volval material gray to grayish brown when young and fresh 40

40a Annulus often stained clay color to more ochraceous; cut cortex of stipe staining yellow; odor pungent and unpleasant .... *A. atkinsoniana* **Coker**

Pileus 7-15 cm, broadly convex to plane, ground-color whitish, surface at first with ± pyramidal warts scattered over disc at least. Gills close, ± broad finally, reaching the stipe, white to creamy, at times staining ochraceous where injured. Stipe 7-20 x 1-2.5 cm, evenly enlarged to a fusoid-pointed bulb up to 4 cm thick, whitish to pallid and variously decorated with remains of the veils; annulus when well-formed striate above and floccose below, apical, fragile. Spores 9-12 x 5-6 μm, amyloid.

Scattered on low ground under hardwoods, apparently throughout eastern and central United States, but more numerous southward, late summer and fall.

40b Annulus gray, cut surfaces not staining yellow; odor fragrant .... *A. cinereopannosa* **Bas**

Pileus 8-16 cm, convex to plane or depressed over disc, margin slightly appendiculate, pallid to cinereous, subviscid, covered at first with low, gray, patches or warts of volval material. Gills crowded, free, finally broad (6-12 mm), pure white. Stipe 10-16 x 1-1.5 cm, equal above a broadly fusiform bulb up to 6 x 4 cm and slightly rooting; white above, brownish gray below and lacerate-fibrillose; annulus apical; volva grayish, friable, bulb at times ± scaly. Spores 9-12.5 x 5-6 μm, amyloid.

Solitary under pine, southeastern United States, summer, rare (?)

41a Spores 7-9 (10) × 5-5.5 μm, amyloid; pileus and bulb of stipe typically with imbricate scales; odor not pungent .... *A. ravenelii* **(Berk. & Curt.) Sacc.**

Pileus 6-15 cm, globose, convex or (finally) broadly expanded, surface dry, the scales soon brownish; odor ± fragrant. Gills close, ± remote from stipe, dark cream color. Stipe 10-20 x 1-2.5 cm above the bulb, bulb up to 11 x 6 cm, lower part of stipe with ± pinkish-gray scales on a white ground color; annulus superior, double (with patches on under side).

Solitary to gregarious under oak and pine, Southeast, summer, not common. Previously this species has been known in the region as *Amanita strobiliformis*.

41b Spores larger and base of stipe not scaly as in above 42

42a Odor strong and pungent; spores 8-10.5 × 5-6 μm; outer veil ± powdery .... *A. chlorinosma* Peck

Pileus 8-25 cm, subglobose to convex, finally nearly plane, margin at first decorated with powdery veil remnants and these extending over cap as very fragile warts, white over all or cream-buff on disc. Gills approximate to stipe (± attached at first), broad in front, white becoming cream-color. Stipe 6-12 (18) x 1-3 cm, ± equal down to a napiform bulb 3-5 cm thick, usually conspicuously rooting, cortex hard. Annulus superior, torn and ragged in many specimens; volva of powdery material.

Solitary to caespitose, mixed woods, roadsides, waste land, etc., most frequent in the Gulf Coast and Southeast areas but extending northward to the Great Lakes and eastward. A similar species but with spores 10-13 x 6-8 μm is *A. polypyramis* (Berk. & Curt.) Saccardo.

42b Not as above 43

43a Pileus floccose from veil material; annulus floccose and often obliterated. Fig. 242 .... *A. silvicola* Kauffman

Figure 242

Figure 242 *Amanita silvicola*

Pileus 5-12 cm, convex to plano-convex, margin appendiculate, white, subviscid, coated by a soft ± continuous floccose layer of veil material breaking up to form poorly defined patches which soon become reduced to a powder. Odor slight, ± soapy. Gills barely attached to stipe, crowded, broad, edges floccose. Stipe 6-12 x 1.5-2.5 cm, ± equal to a ± marginate bulb 3-4 cm thick; white thoughout, covered by floccose veil remnants. Spores 9-12 x 5-6 μm, amyloid.

Solitary to scattered in conifer forests, fall, Pacific Northwest, not infrequent.

43b Not as above 44

44a Pyramidal warts on pileus well formed and persistent; annulus well formed and persistent .... *A. cokeri* (E. Gilb. & Küh.) E. Gilb.

Pileus 8-15 cm, pulvinate to plano-convex, margin appendiculate, white to ivory-color, viscid, surface with scattered large (to 4 mm wide) white to brownish pyramidal warts over disc; odor and taste mild. Gills crowded, free, narrowly adnate, broad, white, developing a yellowish to pinkish tint. Stipe 12-20 x 1.2-2 cm, tapered upward from a ventricose rooting bulb; often with warts in zones on the bulb and just above it; annulus double and fibrillose-lacerate. Spores 11-13.5 x 7-9 μm, amyloid.

Solitary to gregarious, southern, not infrequent during warm wet seasons in hardwood stands or mixed forests. It has passed under the name *A. solitaria* Fr. previously.

44b Warts on disc of pileus poorly defined; annulus fragile and ragged .... *A. smithiana* Bas

Pileus 6-11 cm, convex becoming plane, margin conspicuously appendiculate, subviscid, white to whitish, surface with patches of veil tissue up to 3 mm broad and white to brownish; odor faintly fragrant. Gills crowded, nearly free, 6-10 mm broad, whitish. Stipe 10-18 x 1-3 cm, evenly enlarged down to a fusiform bulb ± 4.5 cm thick; surface above the bulb up to the annulus conspicuously ragged with zones and patches of veil material; annulus apical; volva as floccose-zones and squamules mostly near or on apex of bulb. Spores 10.5-13.5 x 7-8 μm, amyloid.

Solitary to scattered under conifers, fall, Pacific Northwest, rare (or rarely collected ?).

Limacella Earle

Pileus subviscid to slimy, glabrous, sometimes appearing fibrillose-streaked beneath the slime; stipe dry or slimy to merely viscid below the annulus; annulus usually present; volva lacking; gills free from the stipe or practically so, gill trama bilateral; spores white to whitish in deposit, typically small and non-amyloid; clamp connections present.

This is a small genus of a little over a dozen species. Some species are reputedly edible but they are usually not abundant and have no economic importance. They fruit either on the ground or on very decayed wood.

KEY TO SPECIES

1a Stipe dry 2

1b Stipe viscid or slimy 3

2a Annulus membranous, flaring and usually persistent; pileus pale pinkish cream color ....
.... *L. lenticularis* (Lasch) Earle

Pileus 6-15 cm, often streaked, often splitting radially, the disc in age sometimes marked with roundish watery spots. Gills crowded, sometimes staining olive-gray in age. Stipe 10-15 cm x 1-2.5 cm; annulus thin, pallid. Spores 4-5 x 3.5-4 μm. Pileus cuticle of ± upright, subgelatinous, rather short, attenuated hyphal end cells.

Gregarious to scattered under elm (*Ulmus*) or ash (*Fraxinus*) on swampy ground, Great Lakes

region. Var. *fischeri* (Kauff.) H. V. Smith has a smaller pileus (4-9 cm), the gills do not stain, and the odor is strong when the fruiting bodies are drying. It is the variety commonly collected in the Great Lakes area.

2b Annulus lacking or merely a fibrillose zone; pileus dark reddish to orange-brown or chestnut brown. Fig. 243 ....
.... *L. glioderma* (Fr.) Earle

Figure 243

Figure 243 *Limacella glioderma*

Pileus 3-8 cm, fading to pale pinkish brown, in age the surface breaking up into crustlike patches with the white to pale vinaceous flesh showing; context very soft and fragile, odor and taste strongly farinaceous. Gills close, broad, ± touching the stipe, pallid. Stipe 5-9 cm x 5-10 mm, ± annulate with zones and patches of veil material below the annulus. Spores globose, 3-4 μm. Pileus cuticle of ± erect hyphal ends 2-15 μm wide, ± 30 μm long, gelatinized, the ends tapered to a point.

Solitary, scattered, or gregarious on rich humus in forests, rarely in winter in greenhouses; widely distributed.

3a **Slime on the pileus and stipe bright reddish brown (burnt sienna). Fig. 244** .... *L. glishera* **(Morg.) Murr.**

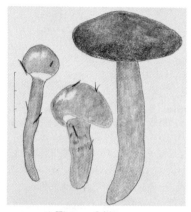

Figure 244

Figure 244 *Limacella glishera*

Pileus 2-4 cm, pale beneath the copious slime. Gills close, broad, white. Stipe 6-8 cm x 9-12 mm; annulus evanescent. Spores 4.5-5.5 x 5-6.3 μm, appearing finely stippled under an oil immersion lens. Pileus cuticle of long interwoven hyphae mostly 4-5 μm in diameter.

Solitary on rich soil in woods; widely distributed but seldom found in quantity.

3b **Slime on the pileus and stipe hyaline (colorless). Fig. 245.** .... *L. illinita* **(Fr.) Earle**

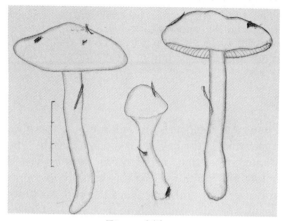

Figure 245

Figure 245 *Limacella illinita*

Pileus 2-7 cm, slime copious, often dripping from the margin in wet weather, surface pure white to creamy white. Gills close, broad, ± reaching the stipe at first. Stipe 5-9 cm x 3-8 mm, white or whitish. Spores 4.5-5.5 x 5-6.3 μm, globose to broadly ellipsoid. Pileus cuticle of gelatinized hyphae 3-4 μm wide and the cells ± 120 μm long.

Solitary, scattered, or gregarious on soil in woods, cedar swamps, fields and on sand dunes; widely distributed and relatively common. In var. *rubescens* H. V. Smith the slime at the base of the stipe stains red. In var. *argillacea* (Fr.) H. V. Smith the pileus is grayish brown to clay color on the disc when fresh.

LEPIOTACEAE Roze

Pileus and stipe usually cleanly separable; gills free from stipe or scarcely touching it; spore deposit white to buff, or in *Chlorophyllum*, olive to green; gill trama regular, parallel to interwoven; veil typically leaving an annulus or annular zone on stipe; habitat terrestrial,

rarely lignicolous; fruiting during summer and fall or in greenhouses during winter.

The family is fairly large; it contains about 200 species in North America. Both dangerously poisonous and excellent edible species occur here. Singer (1975) has proposed a very elaborate taxonomic arrangement for these fungi, and places them in the family Agaricaceae. In his system the species we have included in the following key are placed in the genera *Lepiota, Cystolepiota, Macrolepiota, Leucocoprinus, Leucoagaricus,* and *Chlorophyllum.* Our treatment is conservative, and emphasizes the "*Lepiota* aspect" of the included species.

KEY TO GENERA

1a Spore deposit green to olive ....
.... *Chlorophyllum*

1b Spore deposit white to light buff ....
.... *Lepiota*

Chlorophyllum Massee

For the generic description see that of the family and key to genera. It is a small genus of possibly only two species, both widely distributed and most abundant in warmer climates. The single species we have treated here is included in the key to *Lepiota.*

Lepiota S. F. Gray

For the generic description see that of the family and key to genera.

The species of this genus are widely distributed and erratic in their fruiting patterns. They are much more frequently encountered in the Southeast, Gulf Coast, and California than in northern areas here in North America. As to distribution, one may expect that eventually any species described from the Northern Hemisphere will be found in North America.

KEY TO SPECIES

1a Annulus membranous and ± persistent (sometimes absent in age, and moveable in some species 2

1b Annulus poorly formed (cortinate, powdery, fibrillose, floccose, or submembranous) 18

2a Stipe typically 8 mm or more thick in well developed specimens (see *L. rubrotincta* also) 3

2b Stipe usually less than 7 mm thick at apex 9

3a Pileus surface usually smooth and appressed fibrillose, dull white to (rarely) cinereous. Fig. 246 .... *L. naucina* (Fr.) Kummer

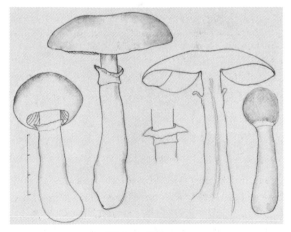

Figure 246

Figure 246   *Lepiota naucina*

Pileus 4-8 (12) cm, subglobose to ovoid, then broadly convex, at times finely squamulose near the margin, at times slowly staining yellowish where injured; context thick, firm. Gills white becoming grayish vinaceous to finally dingy vinaceous brown as dried. Stipe 7-12 cm x 6-12 mm, equal or base slightly enlarged, white, glabrous, sometimes staining yellow then slowly discoloring to pale brown; annulus double-edged, white, persistent. Spores 7-9 x 5-6 μm, $\pm$ ovoid. Cheilocystidia 28-39 x 7-12 μm, fusoid-ventricose to clavate or saccate. Clamp connections absent. Cuticle of pileus not sharply differentiated.

Scattered to gregarious in grassy areas; summer and fall after heavy rains; widely distributed and common. Edible, but some people cannot tolerate it and experience severe gastrointestinal upsets from eating it.

3b   Pileus not as above, disc and scales colored **4**

4a   Fruiting body when injured showing a distinct color change within $\pm$ 60 minutes **5**

4b   Not staining as above **7**

5a   Stipe staining brown where handled; scales on pileus large, thick, brown; fruiting bodies rarely clustered. Fig. 247 .... **L.** *rachodes* **(Vitt.) Quél.**

Figure 247

Figure 247   *Lepiota rachodes*

Pileus 6-20 cm, convex, becoming nearly plane, cuticle continuous at first, rupturing into coarse concentrically arranged scales, margin appendiculate; context white, staining slightly reddish but soon going to brown. Gills white, finally brownish when bruised. Stipe 6-20 x 1-3 cm, bulbous at base, glabrous to $\pm$ innately fibrillose, annulus thick, appearing double. Spores 8-10.5 x 5-6.5 μm, ovoid. Cheilocystidia 18-47 x 10-25 μm, mostly clavate. Clamp connections present, often rare. Cuticle of pileus a hymeniform layer of $\pm$ clavate cells.

Solitary, gregarious, or rarely caespitose on soil in open areas or under trees, often forming fairy rings. Fall, widely distributed. Edible and choice, but not recommended because of the danger of confusing it with the poisonous *Chlorophyllum molybdites*.

5b   Not as above, usually staining yellow at first when young and fresh **6**

6a   Pileus cuticle smooth and continuous at first, rupturing into vinaceous to reddish brown flat scales or fibrillose scales; fruiting body dull vinaceous red when dried. Fig. 248 .... **L.** *americana* **Peck**

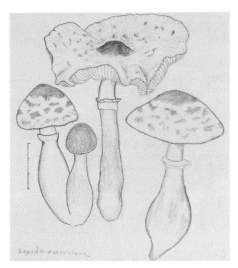

Figure 248

Figure 248   *Lepiota americana*

Pileus 3-15 cm, soon convex to plane, smooth but soon the cuticle rupturing into flat scales or toward the margin the scales fibrillose, disc and scales pinkish buff to reddish or reddish brown, surface staining as in the stipe. Gills white at first, often staining like the stipe. Stipe 7-14 cm x 8-22 mm, equal, ventricose-fusiform or clavate, or ± clavate; annulus large, firm, double. Spores 8.5-14 x 6.5-10 μm, ± ellipsoid. Cheilocystidia clavate with or without a neck. Cuticle of erect hyphal tips. Clamp connections rare to absent.

Usually in large clusters on or around stumps, sawdust piles, etc., summer and fall, widely distributed. Edible. Easily recognized when dried by the dull vinaceous red color of the entire fruiting body.

6b   Pileus cuticle white with numerous small pointed pale chestnut scales .... *L. tinctoria* Murrill

Pileus 5-10 cm, convex to expanded or umbonate, white with numerous small pointed pale chestnut scales; context thin, immediately yellow when cut then darkening. Stipe 6-7 x 0.5-1.5 cm, slightly fibrillose, white becoming yellow when bruised then ± chestnut brown; annulus persistent, becoming pale chestnut. Spores 7.5-9 x 6-6.5 μm, ovoid. Cheilocystidia 18-120 x 10-30 μm, clavate to fusoid-ventricose. Pleurocystidia none. Scales of pileus of tufts of pileocystidia 70-130 x 13-18 μm. Clamp connections absent.

Caespitose on lawns, Florida, September. It stains the fingers yellow from handling it, and when dried the gills are dark gray and the remainder pale chestnut.

7a   Stipe glabrous or nearly so 8

7b   Stipe furfuraceous or finely squamulose. Fig. 249 .... *L. procera* (Fr.) S. F. Gray

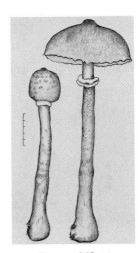

Figure 249

Figure 249   *Lepiota procera*

Pileus 7-20 cm, ovate then ± plane or umbonate; cuticle ± reddish brown and continuous but soon broken into scales and patches except on the disc, exposed context between scales floccose; context white, soft, finally ± reddish. Gills white becoming pinkish to avellaneous then brownish, broad. Stipe 15-40 cm x 8-10 mm, paler than pileus; annulus moveable, margin thick. Spores 12.5-15 x 7.5-10 cm, broadly ellipsoid. Cheilocystidia 20-38 x 5-12 μm, clavate to subcylindric. Pleurocystidia none. Cuticle of disc and scales a turf of brown cells 30-70 μm long; fibrillose scales of septate easily separated hyphae, clamp connections rare.

Solitary to widely scattered or gregarious, on the ground in woods of either conifers or hardwoods, late summer and fall. Edible and choice. Widely distributed in North America, but apparently very abundant at times in New England. This is often called the parasol mushroom.

8a Spore deposit grayish olive; cuticle of pileus rupturing into flattened or uplifted scales; gills white to yellowish, then olive. Fig. 250 .... *Chlorophyllum molybdites* (Fr.) Sacc.

Figure 250

Figure 250 *Chlorophyllum molybdites*

Pileus 10-30 cm, hemispheric to broadly convex, cuticle pale pinkish buff at first but darkening, white context showing between; context thick, white, finally discolored to dingy reddish where cut or bruised. Gills broad, close, with dark margins at times. Stipe 5-25 cm x 8-25 mm, equal to clavate, whitish, slowly dingy clay-color; annulus double, large, becoming moveable. Spores (8) 10-12 x 6.5-9 µm, subovoid. Cheilocystidia 22-68 x 10-26 µm, clavate to fusoid-ventricose. Pleurocystidia absent. Clamp connections present.

Usually forming fairy rings in lawns, meadows, pastures, etc., summer and early fall, widely distributed, but very common in the Gulf Coast area. Poisonous.

8b Spore deposit white; pileus gray to brownish gray and fibrillose .... *L. barsii* Zeller

Pileus 7-15 cm, subglobose becoming convex to expanded, at times umbonate, evenly fibrillose or finely fibrillose-squamulose; context thick in the disc, whitish. Gills white, on injury becoming straw-color to brownish. Stipe 6-13 cm x 8-25 mm,

equal or enlarged below but pointed at base, glabrous or nearly so, becoming brown at base where handled; annulus white, the margin grayish brown. Spores 6-11 x 4.5-5 µm, ovoid to short-ellipsoid. Cheilocystidia 20-56 x 8-15 µm, clavate to broadly ventricose, saccate or cylindric. Pileus cuticle over disc a tangled turf of tubular hyphae. Clamp connections absent.

Gregarious to caespitose in pastures, plowed fields, stubble of wheat fields, around straw stacks or manure piles, fall, western Oregon. Edible and choice.

9a Pileus context thin, margin often becoming striate to rimose-striate; spores with a thick wall and an apical germ pore 10

9b Not as above 11

10a Fruiting body bright yellow .... *L. lutea* (Fr.) Loq.

Pileus 3-6 cm, campanulate becoming broadly conic to expanded to umbonate, finely fibrillose to powdery; gills attached to a ring, pale yellowish white, edges sometimes yellow. Stipe 2.5-8 cm x 1.5-5 mm, covered with lemon yellow powder; annulus cottony-fibrillose, bright yellow, evanescent. Spores 8-12.7 x 5.5-8 µm. Cheilocystidia 24-84 x 9-21 µm, clavate to fusoid-ventricose, apex obtuse, mucronate or having neck elongated. Clamp connections absent. Pileus cuticle mostly cellular, cells irregular to regular in shape, readily disarticulating.

Widely distributed in the southern part of the United States and fruiting during the summer, not uncommon in greenhouses in the north in winter. Not edible, may cause gastro-intestinal problems in some people. This is known as *Leucocoprinus birnbaumii* (Corda) Singer in the modern classification.

10b Fruiting body white to dingy white at first, slowly becoming brownish to purple-drab on aging. Fig. 251 .... *L. cepaestipes* (Sow. ex Fr.) Kummer

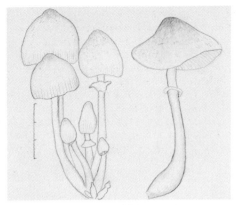

Figure 251

Figure 251 *Lepiota cepaestipes*

Pileus 2-8 cm, ovate with a truncate apex, becoming campanulate, or finally expanded-umbonate, surface at first with mealy warts, becoming fibrillose-scaly, fibrils and scales finally brownish to purplish drab, when bruised context may become straw yellow. Gills remote, crowded. Stipe 4-14 cm x 3-6 mm, glabrous to faintly pruinose or fibrillose, white to tinged brownish, often yellow where handled; annulus persistent. Spores 7-10 (12) x 6-7.5 (8) μm, broadly ellipsoid. Cheilocystidia 32-45 (79) x 10-32 μm, fusoid ventricose, mucronate, or ± rostrate. Cuticle of pileus of pileocystidia 45-90 x 3-11 μm. Clamp connections absent.

On rich soil, compost, etc.; summer and fall; in greenhouses in winter; widely distributed. Edible for some but may cause gastric distress for others.

11a Fruiting body having a distinct color change on injury or on drying **12**

11b Not showing a characteristic color change as above **14**

12a Pileus white with brownish disc and scales; fruiting body turning caerulean blue on drying, eventually fading ..*L. caerulescens* **Peck**

Pileus 1-2 cm, convex to plane or umbonate, disc and scales brown, ground color white. Gills distant, moderately crowded, white, edges even.

Stipe 3-5 cm x 1.5-2 mm, while, glabrous; annulus small, white, persistent. Spores 7-9 x 4-3.5 μm, in profile often slightly inequilateral but varying to ovate or elliptic, in face view ovate to elliptic. Cheilocystidia 35-44 x 9-12 μm, clavate to at times irregular in outline. Cuticle of disc and scales of narrowly elongate-clavate pileocystidia 30-110 x 8-12 μ, many variously incrusted with bands or patches of a dextrinoid incrustation. Clamp connections not found.

Scattered to gregarious in rich humus, late summer, eastern United States to Great Lakes area, rare. It is easily identified by the blue color the entire fruiting body assumes when freshly dried. The color disappears after a time in the herbarium.

12b Not as above **13**

13a Pileus pinkish red, quickly staining bright orange then becoming blackish ....
.... *L. roseotincta* **A. H. Smith**

Pileus 2.5-4 cm, convex or disc flattened, appressed fibrillose, slightly squamulose near margin, the disc and fibrils along with the squamules pinkish red; context white, unchanging. Gills close to crowded, white or flushed pink near cap margin. Stipe 3-5 cm x 3-5 mm, ± clavate and tapered to a point below at times; surface staining like the pileus; annulus with scattered pink fibrils on lower surface. Spores 7-10 x 4-5 μm, narrowly subovoid. Cheilocystidia 36-48 x 9-14 μm, fusoid-ventricose. Cuticle a layer of irregularly arranged hyphae 8-15 μ diam. Clamp connections absent.

Gregarious on vegetable debris such as compost piles or very rich humus, early fall, Michigan, rare.

13b Pileus and stipe with brown fibrils which turn flame scarlet when injured and then dark brown; spores 6-8.5 $\times$ 4-4.8 μm, ellipsoid. Fig. 252 .... *L. flammeotincta* **Kauff.**

Figure 252

Figure 253

Figure 252 *Lepiota flammeotincta*

Pileus 1-4.5 cm, convex then plane or ± umbo-nate, appressed fibrillose becoming squamulose; context thin away from disc, white changing to red and then fading. Gills crowded, edges some-times brownish. Stipe 3-9.5 cm x 1.5-6 mm, ap-pressed fibrillose below the annulus, the fibrils staining like those on pileus; annulus flaring at first then appressed, with brown fibrils on lower side. Cheilocystidia 22-70 x 6-18 μm, clavate to cylindric or irregular. Cuticle of interwoven hy-phae, with numerous upright hyphal tips. Clamp connections lacking.

Solitary to scattered under conifers along the Pacific Coast of Washington to California. When dried the fruiting bodies are blackish ± tinged red; the gills being a little paler.

14a Pileus pink to red or purple 15

14b Pileus not colored as above 16

15a Pileus purple. Fig. 253 ....
.... *L. roseilivida* **Murr.**

Figure 253 *Lepiota roseilivida*

Pileus 1-4 cm, convex then plane to umbonate, glabrous to finely tomentose on disc, evenly fi-brillose to furfuraceous toward the margin, ground color white. Gills approximate, white and mostly unchanging. Stipe 3-7.5 cm x 2-6 mm, glabrous and white above the annulus, innately fibrillose with purple fibrils below, dingy after handling; annulus membranous, collar-like with a flaring margin, white, tinged purplish to vinaceous on lower surface. Spores 6.3-9 x 4-5 μm, ovoid to short ellipsoid. Cheilocystidia 14-38 x 4-15 μm, clavate to cylindric to fusoid-ventricose. Cuticle a lax trichoderm, the terminal cells up to 240 μm long and 10-15 μm wide. Clamp connections ab-sent.

Solitary, scattered or gregarious in stands of conifers, Pacific Coast area, fall, not common.

15b Pileus with pinkish to red tones dominant. Fig. 254 ....*L. rubrotincta* **Peck**

Figure 254

Figure 254 *Lepiota rubrotincta*

Pileus 3-8 cm, ovoid with flattened apex, expanding to conic to convex and finally plane or margin uplifted, in age tending to be radiately rimose, cuticle continuous and smooth over all at first, finally minutely fibrillose-squamulose, in age the margin paler than the disc. Gills white, unchanging. Stipe 4-16 cm x 4-10 mm, narrowly clavate to subbulbous, glabrous to finely fibrillose, white, where handled pale buff; annulus membranous, persistent, margin thickened somewhat. Spores 6.3-10 x 4-5.5 μ, ovoid-ellipsoid. Cheilocystidia (18) 30-37 x 11-16 μm, clavate to ventricose. Cuticle on disc of pileus of upright hyphae and pileocystidia; scales of pileus of fascicles of radially arranged hyphae. Clamp connections absent.

Solitary to scattered in humus and compost as well as in hardwood forests, widely distributed late summer and fall, fairly common, eastern United States and Pacific Coast. Considerable color variation is encountered in the Pacific Northwest.

16a Pileus white or whitish pale avellaneous over all in age; taste strongly acidulous ....
.... *L. pulcherrima* Graf sensu Kauff.

Pileus 1.5-4 cm, campanulate becoming broadly convex to nearly plane or umbonate, disc remaining smooth, cuticle elsewhere appressed fibrillose becoming almost powdery to finely squamulose, toward the margin the squamules recurved; context thin and fragile. Gills crowded. Stipe 3-9 cm

x 1.5-4 mm, enlarging downward, glabrous, white or slowly discoloring to brownish; annulus superior, small. Spores 5.5-7 x 3.8-4 μm, ovoid to ellipsoid. Cheilocystidia 20-40 x 4-8 μm clavate to cylindric. Pileus cuticle of radial hyphae with fascicles turned up at the ends to form squamules, hyphal cells often narrowed at the septa, the cells usually having numerous globules which stain rusty in Melzer's. Clamp connections lacking.

Solitary or in clusters in alder flats along rivers in gravel, Pacific Northwest, and in the eastern United States. The strong acid taste persists for several years after the specimens have been placed in the herbarium.

16b Pileus with brown, gray or blackish fibrils or scales; taste not as in above choice 18

17a Pileus gray to blackish ...... *L. atrodisca* Zeller

Pileus 1-5 cm broad, convex becoming broadly expanded to plane, the margin uplifted at times, at times umbonate, surface tomentose to densely appressed fibrillose to squamulose, the cuticle gray to black, ground color white; context white, unchanging. Gills close, white. Stipe 2-6 cm x (1) 2-7 mm, enlarged toward the base, glabrous, to innately fibrillose, white, unchanging or flushed pale clay-color near the base from handling; annulus thin and delicate, not moveable, easily obliterated, margin gray. Spores 6-8 x 3-5 μm, subellipsoid to ellipsoid. Cheilocystidia 21-65 x 6-16 μm, elongate-clavate to cylindric or somewhat inflated. Cuticle of septate filamentous hyphae 8-15 μ wide, the cells often short and $\pm$ rounded at the septa and containing grayish cytoplasmic granules. Clamp connections lacking.

Solitary to scattered on dead wood of conifers already quite well rotted, fall, Pacific Coast area, not common.

17b Pileus with $\pm$ crust brown disc and scales. Fig. 255 .... *L. cristata* (Fr.) Kummer

Figure 255

Figure 255 *Lepiota cristata*

Pileus 1-7 cm, convex becoming expanded-umbonate, cuticle at first continuous, soon ruptured into concentric zones of small scales, continuous over the disc; context white thin, fragile, odor pungent, spicy, to lacking. Gills approximate, white, fragile. Stipe 1.5-8 cm x 2-6 mm, equal to subbulbous, surface glabrous and shining, usually somewhat silky fibrillose, white to pale pinkish buff to (near base) brownish; annulus small, white, persistent for a time. Spores 6-7 (8) x 3-4.5 μm, wedge-shaped, spurred. Cheilocystidia 22-45 x 10-14 μm, clavate to globose with a long narrow base. Cuticle of pileus a layer of pear-shaped to clavate cells 37-74 x 9-16 μm. Clamp connections present.

Scattered to gregarious on humus in woods, along roads, on waste land, etc., habitat terrestrial but no definite association with higher plants observed, common, encountered almost every season, widely distributed.

18a Pileus and stipe cinnamon brown to orange buff; stipe and sometimes gills and pileus becoming rusty orange after injury; spores 8.7-11 $\times$ 4-5 μm, bullet-shaped, Fig. 256 ....
.... *L. castanea* **Quélet**

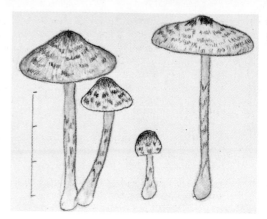

Figure 256

Figure 256 *Lepiota castanea*

Pileus 1-3 cm, obtusely conic becoming convex, densely fibrillose and scales brown to tawny to orange buff, ground color white to buff and finally changing to brownish, in age often stained rusty orange. Gills white to buff, edges at times stained rusty brown. Stipe 2.8-6.5 cm x 1-3 mm, appressed fibrillose to scaly, fibrils brown to tawny and ground color white becoming orange to rusty after handling; annulus an evanescent zone of fibrils often in patches. Cheilocystidia 19-37 x 5-8 μm, narrowly clavate to cylindric, hyaline. Pileus cuticle a turf of upright hyphae and pileocystidia. Clamp connections absent.

Solitary to scattered on humus under conifers, Western United States and Great Lakes region, fall, not common.

18b **Not as above** **19**

19a **Pileus surface powdery, mealy or granular**
.... **20**

19b **Pileus not as above** **23**

20a **Pileus yellow or grayish lavender** **21**

20b **Pileus white to flushed pale pink at times or buff on disc** **22**

21a **Pileus yellow** .... *L. flavescens* **Morgan**

Pileus 2.5-4 cm, cylindric to ovate becoming ± plane. Gills pale yellow. Stipe 3-4.5 (8) cm x 2 mm, pale sulfur yellow, finely floccose, annulus pale yellow, evanescent. Spores 4.8-6.6 (7.2) x (3.5) 4.8-5.5 μm, broadly ellipsoid to subglobose or globose. Cheilocystidia 28-43 x 8-15 μm, clavate, subcylindric-capitate. Cuticle a palisade of elongate pear-shaped to globose thin-walled cells.

On humus in greenhouses, the distribution remains to be established.

**21b Pileus pale dull lavender to lilac, odor strong; annulus seldom formed. Fig. 257 ....
.... L. bucknallii (Berk. & Br.) Sacc.**

Figure 257

Figure 257 *Lepiota bucknallii*

Pileus 2.5-4.5 cm, campanulate becoming broadly convex, margin at first appendiculate. Gills approximate, pale yellow. Stipe 4-10 cm x 2-4 mm, lavender becoming dark violaceous within at base. Spores 6-7.5 (8.4) x (2) 2.8-3 μm, ± bullet-shaped. Pleuro- and cheilocystidia none. Cuticle of pileus of globose cells with filamentose narrow hyphae bearing clamp connections interwoven among them.

On humus in mixed conifer and hardwood forests, widely distributed; the best fruitings we have seen were along the Pacific Coast and in northern Idaho.

22a Pileus 1-2.5 (5) cm, often flushed pale pink, slightly powdery; pleurocystidia absent. Fig. 258 .... L. seminuda (Lasch) Kummer

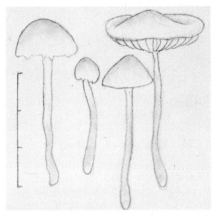

Figure 258

Figure 258 *Lepiota seminuda*

Pileus convex to plane, at times campanulate, powdery, white at first, ± micaceous by old age; context very thin and fragile. Gills white, at times becoming flushed pale pink. Stipe 2-4 cm x 1.5-3 (4) mm, powdery at first, glabrescent and at times pale dingy pinkish, usually pallid. Spores 4-5 x 2.5-3 μm, ellipsoid. Pleuro- and cheilocystidia lacking. Clamp connections present. Cuticle of pileus of globose cells.

Scattered to gregarious, under conifers and/or hardwoods, summer and fall, fairly common. In North America it is to be expected east of the Great Plains but it also occurs in the Pacific Northwest.

**22b Pileus 3-9 cm, copiously powdery, dull white slowly becoming pale buff to pale clay-color, pleurocystidia present. Fig. 259 ....
.... L. cystidiosa A. H. Smith**

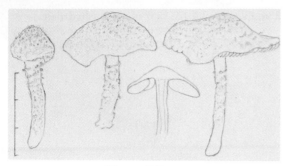

Figure 259

Figure 259 *Lepiota cystidiosa*

Pileus conic to convex then broadly convex, nearly glabrous in age; context slowly sordid where cut or bruised. Gills white becoming discolored in age. Stipe 4-8 cm x 3-7 mm, densely powdery over lower portion. Spores 4-4.5 x 2.5 μm, ellipsoid or the base slightly truncate. Pleurocystidia 25-42 x 7-12 μm, fusoid, ventricose-subcapitate or saccate, 20-30 x 8-12 μm. Cheilocystidia similar to pleurocystidia. Cuticle of pileus of globose cells.

Gregarious on rich humus, compost, piles of organic debris generally, summer and fall, Great Lakes area (but probably widely distributed in North America). It is very similar to *L. petasiformis* Murr. which lacks pleurocystidia.

23a Pileus with warts ± persistent at least over disc (or if warts deciduous the surface layer ± thinly fibrillose or floccose) 24

23b Not as above, pileus fibrillose to lacerate scaly 26

24a Pileus dull yellow .... *L. scabrivelata* Murr.

Pileus 2-3 cm, convex to expanded, densely warty. Gills white. Stipe 4-5 cm x 4-5 mm, equal, covered at least below with yellow scales and warts which are evanescent; veil ample, cobwebby, not forming a distinct annulus, thickly beset with dull yellow warts. Spores 3-3.5 (4) x 2-2.5 μm, elliptic. Warts pyramidal and ochraceous brown as revived, of globose cells 8-22 μm diam, some irregular in shape, and chains of short, cylindric

cells mostly 22-26 x 7-12 μm, the terminal cell pointed. Clamp connections present.

Gregarious on the ground, Gulf Coast area, September.

24b Pileus brown 25

25a Spores 3-5.5 × 2-2.5 (3) μm; pileus with numerous small warts; context thin and brittle .... *L. eriophora* Peck

Pileus (1.5) 2-7 cm, convex becoming plane with a low umbo, often splitting or breaking, rather evenly fibrillose to floccose-fibrillose or scaly toward the margin and densely covered with small pointed dark brown warts. Gills white, soon pallid to buff or pinkish, thin and brittle, not forking, edge even. Stipe 2-10 cm x 2-7 (10) mm, equal or slightly thicker at the base, cottony fibrillose and warty below, the small warts often evanescent, glabrous and white to pallid above; annulus a dense fibrillose zone. Spores oblong. Cheilocystidia 12-33 x 6-12 μm, clavate to fusoid ventricose. Clamp connections present.

Solitary, gregarious or caespitose, often in rich humus in woods, late summer and fall, widely distributed.

25b Spores 6.5-9 × 2-3 μm; context thick and ± firm; warts relatively large and soon deciduous. Fig. 260 .... *L. acutaesquamosa* (Weinm.) Kummer

Figure 260

Figure 260 *Lepiota acutaesquamosa*

Pileus (1.5) 3-11 cm, convex to ± plane, appressed fibrillose over all and with pyramidal wars soon deciduous. Gills very crowded, thin, white to pale cream-color, edge even to ± eroded or serrate. Stipe 6-11 cm x 3-12 mm, clavate to bulbous, fibrillose below annulus; annulus cortinate to fibrillose-floccose, if membranous soon collapsing, when membranous with brown warts along outer edge. Spores subfusoid. Cheilocystidia 14-27 x 9-15 μm, subcylindric to clavate, or globose with a pedicel. Cuticle of pileus of interwoven brown-walled hyphae with frequent cross walls; warts composed of chains of globose, ovoid, or inflated short-cylindric, readily separating cells with some binding hyphae present. Clamp connections present.

Solitary to scattered in humus, often around rotting wood, widely distributed.

26a Pileus cuticle entire, becoming rugulose; gills bright yellow. Fig. 261 ....
.... *L. luteophylla* **Sundberg**

Figure 261

Figure 261 *Lepiota luteophylla*

Pileus 0.8-4 cm, conic becoming plano-convex, smooth at first, light to dark brown, in age the margin pale brown to cream-color. Gills unchanging. Stipe 1.5-4.5 cm x 2.5-7 mm, pale to dark yellow above, brown below; annulus thin, appressed, evanescent. Spore deposit white, spores 4.5-5.1 x 2.6-3.2 μm. Cuticle nearly hymeniform,

composed of inflated, clavate, to almost globose cells 11-38 μm wide with short pedicels. Pleuro- and cheilocystidia lacking. Clamp connections present.

Scattered, gregarious or cespitose in humus; under Monterey cypress in California in winter, and under hardwoods in summer in Michigan.

26b Pileus cuticle fibrillose, scaly, or floccose; gills not yellow **27**

27a Veil cortinate, soon evanescent; spores 7.5-10 × 3-4 μm, truncate ....*L. cortinarius* **Lange**

Pileus 3-10 cm, convex becoming nearly plane with the margin irregularly elevated, cuticle except on the disc ruptured into ± concentric rings of small scales with the white context showing, disc, fibrils and scales tawny to near burnt umber; context thick, fragile. Gills remote from stipe, crowded, white, sometimes stained yellowish in age. Stipe 3-9 cm x 7-20 mm, bulbous, glabrous at apex, ± fibrillose-squamulose downward, colored like the pileus; annulus a fibrillose zone. Spores truncate at base. Cheilocystidia 18-26 x 8-12 μm, clavate. Pleurocystidia 28-40 x 3-4 μm, rare. Clamp connections present. Cuticle of pileus of pileocystidia 120-360 x 10-20 μm, with thick brown walls.

On needle carpets under conifers or in mixed woods in the Great Lakes area and rarely in the Pacific Northwest, fall, fairly common.

27b Not as above **28**

28a Stipe shaggy at first from floccose to fibrillose scales and patches; disc and scales yellowish brown to orange-tawny; spores 14.3-19 × 3.5-4.7 μm, fusiform. Fig. 262 ....
.... *L. clypeolaria* **(Fr.) Kummer**

Figure 262

Figure 262 *Lepiota clypeolaria*

Pileus 2-7 cm, campanulate to expanded-umbonate, with margin appendiculate with veil remnants at first, surface becoming diffracted squamulose as well as floccose-fibrillose, cuticle ± continuous over disc; context white, or yellowish in the disc. Gills approximate, white becoming cream color. Stipe 3.5-15 cm x 4-10 mm, appressed silky fibrillose above, shaggy below, ground color ± tawny but often ochraceous orange after handling; annulus a poorly defined ring or zone of veil material, soon evanescent. Cheilocystidia 19-37 x 8-14 μm, Cuticle of pileocystidia 52-304 x 9-15 μm. Clamp connections present.

Solitary, scattered or gregarious under conifers, hardwoods, or mixed woods, late summer and fall. Variable and perhaps including a number of variants. Mildly poisonous.

28b **Stipe with zones and patches of veil remnants but not shaggy, disc of pileus and**

scales burnt umber; spores 6-8.5 × 3.7-5.6 μm, ellipsoid. Fig. 263 ....
.... *L. clypeolarioides* **Rea**

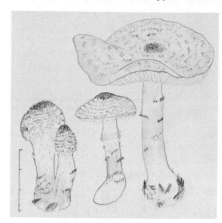

Figure 263

Figure 263 *Lepiota clypeolarioides*

Pileus 2.5-5 cm, cylindric becoming conic to convex to nearly plane; cuticle except for the disc ruptured into ± concentric rings of squamules with white ground color showing between, disc and scales becoming paler on fading. Gills white, usually unchanging. Stipe 4-9 cm x 6-9 mm, equal or nearly so, lower portion with a white fibrillose to floccose sheath with bands or patches of brown scales, becoming dingy reddish brown in age; annulus variable, a few fibrils to a distinct band of white tissue bearing rows of dark brown scales. Cheilocystidia 23-30 x 7-14 μm, clavate with an elongate base. Cuticle of disc and scales composed of pileocystidia 75-150 x 10-15 μm. Clamp connections present.

Scattered to gregarious under conifers, Pacific Northwest, fall, not uncommon.

PLUTEACEAE Kotl. and Pouz.

Pileus and stipe cleanly and readily separable; gills free from the stipe, gill trama of elongate convergent cells originating near the subhymenium and extending downward toward the gill edge and slanted toward the hymenial layer opposite their point of origin; spore deposit dull pink, rose, or brownish pink; spores smooth and non-amyloid; fruiting body generally soft and fleshy to almost deliquescent.

The family may contain as many as 100 species in North America, with species of *Pluteus* being the most numerous. *Pluteus cervi-*

nus and related species here in North America are highly rated for table use, as is *Volvariella bombycina*. A variant of *Volvariella volvacea*, under the name paddy straw mushroom, is grown commercially in the Orient. *V. speciosa* and *V. gliocephala* have been listed as poisonous here in North America.

KEY TO GENERA

1a **Volva present, annulus absent** .... (p. 191) *Volvariella*

1b **Volva and annulus lacking** .... (p. 185) *Pluteus*

Pluteus Fries

For a characterization of the genus see family description and key to genera. The species are mostly wood-inhabiting or terrestrial on soil containing much lignicolous debris. The common larger species around *P. cervinus* are edible—they have frequently been confused with *P. cervinus*. There are approximately 100 species in the genus, but as yet it is not clear how many occur in North America.

KEY TO SPECIES

1a **Fruit body showing greenish to blue stains, especially around the base of the stipe** **2**

1b **Lacking blue to green or olive stains where bruised** **3**

2a **Pileus striatulate when moist, rugulose around disc; pleurocystidia lacking apical horns** .... *P. cyanopus* Quélet

Pileus 2-4 cm, convex to plano-umbonate, ± rugose-reticulate, cinnamon brown; context white, odor and taste mild. Gills broad, subdistant, white then pink. Stipe 2-5 cm x 2-8 mm, fragile, longitudinally striate, watery gray to grayish olive near base, staining greenish gray to bluish where handled. Spores 6-7.5 x 5-6 μm. Pleurocystidia 59-83 x 12-17 μm, fusoid-ventricose, apex obtuse. Cheilocystidia 30-77 x 8.5-21 μm, obtusely fusoid-ventricose.

Solitary to scattered on hardwood chips, etc., widely distributed (California, Wyoming, Michigan) summer and fall, rare?

2b **Pileus margin opaque, surface not striate; pleurocystidia with apical horns. Fig. 264 ....** .... *P. salicinus* (Fr.) Kummer, var. *salicinus*

Figure 264

Figure 264 *Pluteus salicinus* var. *salicinus*

Pileus 3-5 cm, plane to shallowly depressed or margin at times uplifted, ± umbonate at times, often minutely squamulose near margin, dark gray brown, in age more bluish-gray, not hygrophanous; odor disagreeable, taste unpleasant. Gills crowded, ± broad, remote finally, whitish at first, gray on edges where bruised. Stipe 4-7 cm x 2.5-4 (6) mm, whitish, stained bluish around base, glabrous. Spores 7-9 x 5-6 μm. Pleurocystidia 50-70 x 11-18 μm, crowned with 3-5 horns, walls not appreciably thickened. Cheilocystidia like the pleurocystidia or clavate to vesiculose. Clamp connections present. Note: If cystidia are horned and pileus margin is striate when moist, the collection most likely is *P. salicinus* var. *achloes* Singer.

Solitary to scattered on hardwood logs and stumps, summer and fall, east of the Great Plains, not common.

3a   Gill edges brown and pleurocystidia with ± thick walls and with horns at apex **4**

3b   If gill edges brown, then the pleurocystidia not horned **6**

4a   Odor of fresh crushed flesh pungent and strong; stipe blackish brown .... *P. bartelliae* **Smith**

Pileus 4-10 cm, convex to umbonate, appressed-fibrillose, rimose near margin, scurfy over disc, blackish brown overall; context pallid, odor reminding one of crushed inner bark of elderberry. Gills ± remote, broad, grayish to dingy pallid at first, the edges blackish brown. Stipe 6-10 x 1-2 cm, solid, equal, surface blackish brown, dull and unpolished to scurfy. Spores 7-8 x 5-5.5 μm, or globose and 6-7 μm, Pleurocystidia 50-80 x 10-20 μm, thick-walled in some part, with poorly developed horns at apex. Cheilocystidia 40-70 x 12-20 μm, clavate to fusoid-ventricose, apex rounded, content brown in KOH. Clamp connections present.

On debris such as sawdust piles and wood piles, Great Lakes area, fall. It is not clear whether the species prefers conifer or hardwood.

4b   Lacking a pungent distinctive odor **5**

5a   Northern; on wood of conifers; pleurocystidia with horns only at the apex. Fig. 265 .... *P. atromarginatus* (Kon.) **Küh.**

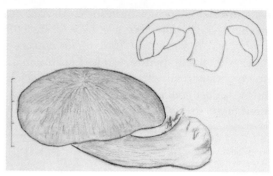

Figure 265

Figure 265   *Pluteus atromarginatus*

Pileus 3-10 cm, obtuse to convex, finally plane or with a low umbo, blackish brown, streaked from appressed black fibrils, at times squamulose; context white, cottony and soft, taste not distinctive. Gills close, broad, fairly remote, white at first, edges dark brown. Stipe 5-10 cm x 5-12 mm, ± equal, surface coated with dark fibrils but paler than pileus. Spores 6.5-8 x 4.5-5 μm. Pleurocystidia thick-walled, 50-90 x 10-20 μm. Cheilocystidia 30-60 x 10-22 μm, clavate, content dark brown. Clamp connections present.

Solitary to scattered on conifer logs and debris, late summer and fall, widely distributed, fairly frequent during some seasons.

5b   Southern (described from British Honduras); horns and spines on the pleurocystidia present on apex, neck and ventricose portion .... *P. spinulosus* **Murrill**

Pileus 4-5 cm, convex, glabrous, subviscid, avellaneous (pinkish gray) on margin, disc darker, margin even. Gills crowded, narrow, white at first, edges brown. Stipe 4-5 cm x 3-4 mm, solid, glabrous, concolorous with pileus. Spores 6-8 x 5.5-7.5 μm. Pleurocystidia (50) 60-90 x 10-20 μm, fusoid, thick-walled, pointed at apex. Cheilocystidia similar to pleurocystidia but smaller and content brown. Clamp connections present.

One would expect to find this species in the Gulf Coast area.

6a Pileus gray-brown to dull cinnamon, surface subviscid; taste ± raphanoid; pleurocystidia horned. Fig. 266 .... *P. cervinus* (Fr.) **Kummer**

Figure 266

Figure 266 *Pluteus cervinus*

Pileus 3-12 cm, obtuse then expanded-umbonate to convex or plane, ± radially streaked, around the disc minutely squamulose at times, pale to dark dull brown, taste ± raphanoid. Gills close, free, broad, pallid. Stipe 5-12 cm x (3) 5-15 mm, pallid but with appressed grayish to brownish fibrils variously disposed. Spores 5.5-7 x 4.5-5 μm. Pleurocystidia 54-90 x 10-20 μm, fusoid-ventricose with 2-5 horns around apex, walls in neck at least slightly thickened Cheilocystidia smaller but ± similar otherwise to the pleurocystidia, some clavate cells also present. Clamp connections present.

Widely distributed on wood of hardwoods in North America, common, spring, summer and fall. Edible and considered good. Like *P. petasatus*, it often occurs in quantity on old sawdust piles.

6b Not as above **7**

7a Pleurocystidia with horns at or near apex; pileus white or streaked with brown fibrils on a pallid ground color **8**

7b Pleurocystidia lacking horns; pileus white or colored **9**

8a Pileus glabrous, dull white .... *P. pellitus* (Fr.) **Kummer**

Pileus 4-8 cm, obtuse then ± plane to convex, glabrous, moist, taste mild. Gills white at first, close, remote, broad. Stipe 7-10 cm x 5-10 mm, ± equal, white, ± squamulose around base, naked above. Spores 7-8 x 5-6 μm. Pleurocystidia 60-90 x 10-20 μm, fusoid-ventricose, walls thickened, apex with 2 or more horns. Cheilocystidia ± similar to pleurocystidia and some clavate cells also present. Clamp connections absent to rare.

Solitary to scattered on wood of hardwoods, not common in North America but widely distributed, summer and fall. Edible.

8b Pileus soon streaked with brownish fibrils, and scales around the disc soon dingy yellow-brown .... *P. petasatus* (Fr.) **Gillet**

Pileus 4-10 cm, obtuse then umbonate to expanded plane, moist, streaked with brownish fibrils on a pallid ground color. Gills broad, close, remote finally, pallid then pinkish. Stipe 4-10 cm x 7-15 mm, equal, firm, whitish, finally dingy yellow-brown below, naked or slightly streaked from fibrils. Spores 6-7.5 x 4.5-5 μm. Pleurocystidia 40-90 x 8-17 μm, fusoid-ventricose, wall thickened, apex with a variable number of horns. Clamp connections absent.

Caespitose especially on sawdust piles, widely distributed in North America and common; often misidentified as *P. cervinus*. Edible.

9a Pileus (under a handlens) ± velvety from projecting pileocystidia **10**

9b Pileus ± glabrous or merely micaceous under a hand lens **13**

10a Fruit body entirely white before gills become pink; pileus floccose-tomentose .... *P. tomentosulus* **Peck**

Pileus 3-10 cm broad, soon expanded-umbonate, white over all, dry, margin even. Gills ± remote, broad, crowded, white then pink. Stipe 5-10 cm x 4-10 mm, equal, fibrillose-striate, unpolished often with a slight ± tomentose bulb. Spores 5-7 x 4.5-6 μm. Pleurocystidia 60-95 x 10-20 (25) μm, fusoid-ventricose. Cheilocystidia clavate to fusoid ventricose (± like pleurocystidia).

Solitary to scattered on wood or conifers and hardwoods, summer and early fall, Great Lakes area eastward and southward, frequently collected but not in quantity.

10b Not as above **11**

11a Pileus fissured-striate, soft and soon collapsing; evenly gray. Fig. 267 ....
.... *P. longistriatus* **Peck**

Figure 267

Figure 267 *Pluteus longistriatus*

Pileus 1-3 (5) cm, oval to convex, expanding to nearly plane or depressed on disc, at times squamulose around disc; context very soft and readily collapsing, pallid. Gills remote in age, ± narrow (finally broad), pallid, soon very soft. Stipe 2-5 (8) cm x 1.5-3 mm, longitudinally fibrillose-striate, not darkening from base upward. Spores 6-7.5 x 5-5.5 μm. Pleurocystidia 50-70 x 18-30 μm, clavate to utriform and 40-60 x 9-14 μm, fusoid-ventricose with acute apex. Cheilocystidia mostly clavate, 40-60 x 12-30 μm.

On hardwood debris, spring to fall after heavy rains, Great Lakes area and both east and southward, often solitary and never in any quantity.

11b Not as above **12**

12a Pileus soon yellow with a darker disc; stipe not plush-like. Fig. 268 ....
.... *P. flavofuligineus* **Atkinson**

Figure 268

Figure 268 *Pluteus flavofuligineus*

Pileus 2-7 (9) cm, obtuse to convex, finally ± plane and umbonate or broadly convex, appearing granulose to furfuraceous, margin hardly striate, nearly blackish brown young, soon yellow on margin and progressively toward the disc, finally ± yellow ochre overall; taste mild. Gills approximate to stipe, broad, close, nearly white at first. Stipe 4-10 cm x 4-8 mm, ± equal, surface pinkish, gradually becoming dull yellow. Spores 6-7 x 4.5-5.5 μm. Pleurocystidia abundant, 50-90 x 12-25 μm, fusoid-ventricose with obtuse to acute apices. Cheilocystidia 23-50 x 5-18 μm, clavate to utriform or fusoid-ventricose.

Solitary to scattered on hardwood debris, late spring to fall, Great Lakes area east and southward, rare in the Northwest.

12b Pileus and stipe plush-covered; colors dark brown with only a slight yellowish tint ....
.... *P. granularis* **Peck**

Pileus 2-5 (10) cm, convex to ± plane, surface granulose to the naked eye, taste slightly disagreeable. Gills free, crowded, broad, ventricose, pallid at first. Stipe 3-8 cm x 2-5 (10) mm, equal, velvety to plushlike, this material in patches toward the base. Spores 5-6.5 x 4-5 μm, broadly ellipsoid in profile. Pleurocystidia 50-70 x 12-20 μm, obtusely fusoid-ventricose. Cheilocystidia similar to pleurocystidia but smaller. Clamp connections absent.

Scattered to solitary on rotting wood of either conifers or hardwoods; Great Lakes area east and southward, summer and fall, not rare. If one finds a collection with yellow gill margins, it is more than likely var. *umbrosellus* Atkinson in Kauffman.

13a Pileus pinkish gray; taste disagreeable .... *P. pallidus* **Homola**

Pileus 2.5-4 cm, broadly convex to plane or slightly depressed, glabrous, striatulate moist, fading to whitish. Gills broad, close, white at first. Stipe 2-4 cm x 1.3-4 mm, fragile, silvery streaked, watery brownish at base. Spores 5-7 x 4.5-6 μm. Pleurocystidia (40) 50-60 x (9) 15-17 μm. Cheilocystidia 30-37 x 9-18 μm, obtusely fusoid-ventricose to clavate. Clamp connections present.

Scattered on rotting logs of hardwoods, Great Lakes region, summer, infrequent.

13b Not as above **14**

14a Pileus with yellow, orange or red colors **15**

14b Pileus with somber colors (grays, browns etc.) **17**

15a Pileus brilliant red when young and fresh .... *P. aurantiorugosus* (**Trog**) **Sacc.**

Pileus (1.5) 2-5.5 cm, obtuse to convex then nearly plane, or expanded-umbonate, brilliant red to orange-red, fading to bright yellow (cadmium yellow); odor and taste not distinctive. Gills whitish at first, broad, close, becoming remote from stipe. Stipe 3-6 cm x 3-8 mm, equal, fibrillose, whitish to yellowish, becoming reddish near base but basal mycelium yellowish to white. Spores 6-7 x 4.5-5 μm. Pleurocystidia 44-76 x 18-31 μm, saccate to clavate to fusoid-ventricose. Cheilocystidia smaller than pleurocystidia but as variable in size. Clamp connections absent.

Solitary to gregarious or in small clusters on rotting hardwood debris, Great Lakes area to Colorado, summer and fall, rare, but one of our most striking species because of the color.

15b Pileus in yellow range of tints when young and fresh **16**

16a Pileus greenish yellow .... *P. rugosodisca* **Murrill**

Pileus 1-3 cm, campanulate, then nearly plane, umbo when present flattened, translucent striate when moist, tinged smoky to olive-green at times; context yellow to olivaceous, odor slightly fragrant, taste mild. Gills ± broad, approximate, subdistant in age, yellowish olive at first. Stipe 2-5 cm x 2-3 mm, ± equal, glabrous, basal mycelium white, stipe itself pale yellow and glabrous. Spores 6-8 x 4.5-6 μm. Pleurocystidia 40-60 (80) x 9-15 (20) μm, fusoid-ventricose, apex frequently incrusted (revived in KOH). Cheilocystidia 30-46 x 10-23 μm, clavate to fusoid-ventricose to a rounded apex. Clamp connections none.

Solitary to gregarious on wood of deciduous trees or on debris, Great Lakes eastward, summer and fall, also in Washington and Oregon, not common.

16b Pileus lemon-yellow to ochre yellow .... *P. admirabilis* **Peck**

Pileus 1-3 cm, obtuse then expanded-umbonate to ± plane, glabrous and moist, brilliant yellow young, duller in age, context pallid becoming yellow, taste mild. Gills broad, close, approximate, pallid but soon yellow. Stipe (2) 3-6 cm x 1-2.5 mm, equal, fragile, glabrous, lemon yellow, not darkening below, basal mycelium white. Spores 6-7 x 4.5-5.8 μm. Pleurocystidia 40-60 x 12-18 μm, obtusely fusoid-ventricose, apex frequently incrusted (as revived in KOH). Cheilocystidia 30-46 x 10-23 μm, clavate to broadly fusoid-ventricose. Clamp connections absent.

Usually densely gregarious on rotting hardwood logs and debris, summer and fall, Great Lakes area eastward and southward, common and conspicuous, but too small to be considered for table use.

17a Stipe yellow; pileus ± olive-brown .... *P. lutescens* (**Fr.**) **Bres.**

Pileus 1-5 cm, convex to plane or umbonate, rarely depressed, finely striate on edge, olive-brown to yellowish-olive; context pallid to yellow, taste mild. Gills subdistant, ventricose, broad, white, soon pale yellow. Stipe 2-4 cm x 1.3-3 mm, equal, ± fibrillose, fragile, yellow, brighter near base. Spores 5.8-7 x 5-6 μm. Pleurocystidia 48-74 x 14-49 μm, clavate to oval-pedicellate, some utriform. Cheilocystidia 31-60 x 9-26 μm, generally similar to the pleurocystidia. Clamp connections absent.

Gregarious to scattered on debris of hardwoods and on soil rich in lignin, summer and fall, Great Lakes region to Colorada, also eastward and southward; infrequent but widely distributed.

17b Not as above **18**

18a Pileus greenish gray; spores 7-8.5 (10) × 5.5-6.6 μm .... *P. californicus* McClatchie

Pileus 2-4 cm, convex to plane, greenish gray becoming cinnamon gray, margin thin, short-striate. Gills broad, crowded, pale gray to pinkish gray. Stipe 2-6 cm x 2-3 mm, shining, pale yellowish gray, hollow, fibrous. Spores 7-9 (10) x 5.5-6.6 μm. Pleurocystidia 45-60 x 10-18 μm, ± utriform. Cheilocystidia 35-47 x 9-16 μm, clavate to elliptic. Clamp connections absent.

On the ground among decayed leaves and branches, southern California.

18b Pileus blackish brown to rusty brown 19

19a Pleurocystidia 50-80 × 10-20 μm; pileus dull cinnamon brown. Fig. 269 ....
.... ***P. chrysophaeus* (Fr.) Quél.**

Figure 269 *Pluteus chrysophaeus*

Pileus 1-3 cm, obtuse to convex, finally ± plane, distinctly rugulose around disc, dull cinnamon brown; context pallid to brownish, taste ± farinaceous. Gills ± remote, pallid at first, broad, close. Stipe pallid near apex, becoming yellowish brown from base upward, 2-4 cm x 2-5 mm, fragile, streaked grayish to silvery. Spores 5-7 x 5-6 μm, subglobose. Pleurocystidia 50-80 x 10-20 μm, fusoid-ventricose, apex obtuse. Cheilocystidia 32-65 x 10-20 μm, clavate, mucronate or fusoid-ventricose with the apex obtuse.

Scattered on hardwood debris, stumps, etc., summer and fall, fairly common in Great Lakes area east and southward.

19b Pleurocystidia 36-63 × 8-10 μm; pileus blackish brown and reticulate-veined around disc .... *P. thompsonii* (Berk. & Br.) Dennis

Pileus 1-3.5 cm, obtuse to convex, then expanded-umbonate, paler and dull brownish faded. Gills broad, free, close, becoming subdistant, white to gray before colored by spores. Stipe 2-4.5 cm x 1.5-6 mm, equal, densely pruinose, in age silky and silvery streaked. Spores 6-8 x 5.5-6 μm. Pleurocystidia 36-63 x 8-10 μm fusoid-ventricose, apex obtuse. Cheilocystidia 39-61 x 8-18 μm, clavate to utriform or with projections originating near or on the apex.

Scattered on debris and wood of hardwoods, Great Lakes area eastward and southward, summer and fall, not rare but seldom collected.

Figure 269

Volvariella Speg.

Pileus small to large; gills white at first becoming pink to brownish pink as the spores mature, the gill edges often whitish and finely fringed; pleurocystidia and cheilocystidia generally present and prominent; hyphae of the pileus cuticle mostly radially arranged, sometimes gelatinized; clamp connections generally lacking.

One authority estimated the world's flora for this genus at 100 species.

KEY TO SPECIES

1a Growing on other mushrooms, usually on *Clitocybe nebularis*. **Fig. 270** .... *V. surrecta* (**Knapp**) **Sing.**

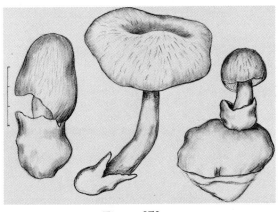

Figure 270

Figure 270 *Volvariella surrecta*

Pileus 2.5-8 cm broad, silky fibrillose, the margin even, white to light gray, the disc becoming yellowish or brownish at times. Gills close, broad, white then pink, ± free from stipe. Stipe 4-9 cm x 4-12 mm, appressed fibrillose, pruinose near apex, white to light gray; volva up to 2.5 cm high, white, lobed. Spores 5.5-7.5 x 3.5-7 μm. Pleurocystidia 21-57 x 8-29 μm. Cheilocystidia 25-50 x 6-20 μm. Pileus cuticle not gelatinized.

Solitary to gregarious on species of *Clitocybe*, northeastern United States to Minnesota and Idaho, fall.

1b Not growing on other mushrooms 2

2a Typically growing on wood 3

2b Typically terrestrial, on compost, etc. 4

3a Pileus margin striate .... *V. peckii* (**Atk. in Pk.**) **Shaffer**

Pileus ± 7.5 cm, thin, viscid, whitish, glabrous, marginal striations fine. Stipe 7-8 cm x 3-6 mm, glabrous, whitish; volva membranous. Spores 7.7-10.7 x 5-6.5 μm. Pleurocystidia 41-69 x 10-25 μm. Cheilocystidia 30-83 x 10-19 μm. Pileus cuticle apparently non-gelatinized.

Solitary, northeastern United States, fall, rare.

3b Pileus margin appressed-fibrillose but not striate. **Fig. 271** ...... *V. bombycina* (**Fr.**) **Sing.**

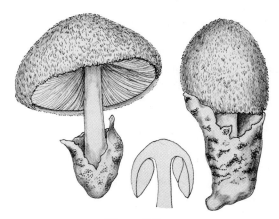

Figure 271

Figure 271 *Volvariella bombycina*

Pileus 5-20 cm, silky fibrillose, becoming ± squamulose, margin somewhat fringed, white or in age yellowish, or dingy on the disc, bright yellow over all in var. *flaviceps*. Gills crowded, broad and ventricose, remote from stipe. Stipe 6-20 x 1-2 cm, glabrous, white; volva ample, areolate, whitish, becoming dingy yellowish in age or darker than the scales. Spores 6.5-10.5 x 4.5-6.5 μm. Pleurocystidia 26-122 x 8-57 μm. Cheilocystidia 26-144 x 8-46 μm. Pileus cuticle not gelatinized.

Solitary to gregarious on hardwoods, widely distributed but the yellow variety is known only from Florida; summer and early fall. Edible and choice.

4a   Pileus truly viscid (if less than 3 cm broad see *V. pusilla*)**. Fig. 272** ....
.... *V. speciosa* **(Fr. ex Fr.) Sing.**

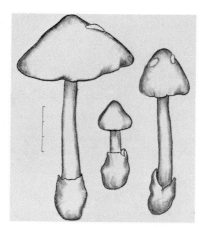

Figure 272

Figure 272   *Volvariella speciosa*

Pileus 5-15 cm, glabrous, at times with patches of the outer veil variously scattered, dull white to cream-color, or light brownish gray; odor and taste unpleasant. Gills broad, crowded, free. Stipe 9-20 x 1-2 cm, white to cream-color; volva white to light gray. Spores 11.5-21 x 7-12.5 μm. Pleurocystidia 30-118 x 10-69 μm. Cheilocystidia 23-108 x 8-24 μm. Pileus cuticle of gelatinized hyphae.

Solitary to gregarious on dung or rich soil in lawns, gardens, greenhouses, fields, and woods. Throughout the country and the growing season, but not found every year.

4b   Pileus typically dry and fibrillose **5**

5a   Volva covered with long mycelioid hairs. Fig. 273 .... *V. villosavolva* **(Lloyd) Singer**

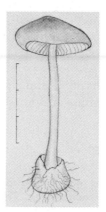

Figure 273

Figure 273   *Volvariella villosavolva*

Pileus 2.5-3.5 cm, innately fibrillose and ± rimose, drab-gray except for the smoky disc. Gills free, broad, ventricose, pinkish cinnamon. Stipe 5-6 cm x 2-4 mm, white; volva 7-10 mm high, white. Spores 5.5-7.3 x 3.5-4.5 μm. Pleurocystidia 34-51 x 9-22 μm. Cheilocystidia 25-91 x 9-23 μm. Pileus cuticle not gelatinized.

Solitary, attached to dead leaves; eastern United Statee and Great Lakes area, summer, sporadic.

5b   Outer surface of volva merely appressed-fibrillose **6**

6a   Pileus colored over all **7**

6b   Pileus white or only the disc faintly colored **8**

7a   Pileus 5-10 cm, fuligineous to blackish brown. Fig. 274 .... *V. volvacea* **(Fr.) Sing.**

Figure 274

Figure 275

Figure 274 *Volvariella volvacea*

Pileus often radially rimose, not striate, smoky gray to blackish brown; taste mild. Gills close broad, free, edges fimbriate. Stipe 4.5-14 cm x 3-20 mm, off-white to dull brown; volva large, floccose, brownish. Spores 7-10.5 x 4.5-7 μm. Pleurocystidia 35-113 x 8-36 μm. Cheilocystidia 23-107 x 4-29 μm. Pileus cuticle not gelatinized.

Solitary to gregarious on soil or compost; also in hothouses and cellars, eastern United States south to Florida, spring and summer.

7b   Pileus 2-6 cm, pale gray to avellaneous .... *V. taylori* (Berk. & Br.) Sing.

Pileus prominently fibrillose, the margin often lacerate; context thin. Gills only moderately broad, close to subdistant free, edges fimbriate. Stipe 3.5-6.5 cm 3-7 mm, glabrous, white; volva up to 1 cm high, 3-5 lobed, brown or grayish over exterior, inner surface white. Spores 5.5-8.7 x 4-6 μm. Pleurocystidia 23-76 x 7-30 μm. Cheilocystidia 23-79 x 8-31 μm. Pileus cuticle not gelatinized.

Solitary to gregarious, eastern seaboard west to Minnesota and Kansas, summer.

8a   Stipe glabrous. Fig. 275 .... *V. pusilla* (Fr.) Sing.

Figure 275 *Volvariella pusilla*

Pileus up to 3.5 cm broad, slightly viscid at first, soon dry and appressed fibrillose, white or on the disc tinged gray, the margin becoming striate. Gills becoming subdistant, broad, free, edges entire, white becoming pink. Stipe 1-5 cm x 1-3 (5) mm, white to grayish; volva white becoming grayish, 2-5 lobed. Spores 5.5-8 x 4-5.7 μm. Pleurocystidia 24-76 x 7-24 μm. Cheilocystidia 21-61 x 7-23 μm. Pileus cuticle sometimes gelatinized.

Solitary to gregarious in lawns, gardens, greenhouses and occasionally in woods, east of the Great Plains generally, summer, seldom found in quantity.

8b   Stipe pubescent 9

9a   Volva ochraceous to brownish; spores 3-4 μm wide .... *V. smithii* Shaffer

Pileus 3.2 cm, dry, glabrous and unpolished over disc, appressed fibrillose and rimose along the margin, dull white except for the pinkish buff disc. Stipe 4 cm long, 5 mm thick, densely pubescent, white, volva matted fibrillose on exterior. Gills close, broad, free. Spores 4.7-7 x 3-4 μm. Pleurocystidia 33-79 x 6-18 μm. Cheilocystidia 17-67 x 8-29 μm. Pileus cuticle not gelatinized.

Solitary to scattered on soil and humus in mixed woods, Pacific Northwest, fall, rare.

9b   Volva white; spores 4-6 μm wide. Fig. 276 .... *V. hypopithys* (Fr.) Shaffer

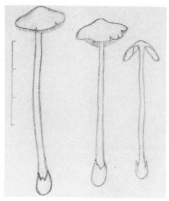

Figure 276

Figure 276   *Volvariella hypopithys*

Pileus 2-5 cm broad, innately fibrillose and silky, becoming squamulose, the margin finely fringed, not or only slightly striate, white, the disc at times yellowish. Gills close, narrow, free, edges white fimbriate. Stipe 2-8 cm x 2-4 mm, densely pubescent to long-hairy, becoming glabrous near base. Spores 6-8.5 x 4-6 μm. Pleurocystidia 14-70 x 7-33 μm. Cheilocystidia 22-90 x 7-36 μm. Pileus cuticle not gelatinized.

Solitary to scattered on humus in woods, Great Lakes area eastward and west to California, summer and early fall, in the winter in California. Edible.

AGARICACEAE Fries

Pileus and stipe typically cleanly separable from each other; stipe typically fleshy and furnished with an annulus; volva absent; gills free (or almost free) from the stipe, often pink before being colored by spores; spore deposit purple-brown, blackish brown, or dark cocoa-brown, rarely with olive tints in moist deposits; pileus typically dry and glabrous varying to appressed fibrillose to scaly, rarely powdery.

KEY TO GENERA

1a   **Pileus powdery from outer veil material; spore deposit when fresh with a tinge of olive to blue-green** .... **(p. 206)** *Melanophyllum*

1b   **Pileus glabrous to fibrillose or fibrillose-scaly; spore deposits never with bluish or greenish tints** .... **(p. 194)** *Agaricus*

Agaricus Fries

With the characters of the family but emphasizing the glabrous to fibrillose to fibrillose-squamulose pileus; the gills may be white when very young but nearly always become some degree of pink before darkening by the maturation of the spores. The stipe is 5-30 mm thick and furnished with a membranous annulus, which, however, is fragile and at times becomes broken or obliterated.

Although a number of species are well known and popular as edible mushrooms, and one is the "backbone" of the American mush-room industry, caution is the word if one is thinking of eating one of the more unusual species. A number are "mildly" poisonous—at least to *some* people. The species are very difficult to recognize and as yet we have no comprehensive systematic work on the species occurring in North America. The genus is large, we estimate over 100 species for North America.

KEY TO SPECIES

1a Pileus white when young and usually long remaining so or only faintly tinted tan to yellow over the disc in age; lacking colored fibrils when young 2

1b Pileus distinctly colored or with colored fibrils over a white to whitish ground color when young 14

2a Pileus cuticle and flesh breaking up to form large conspicuous scales; spores 8-11 × 5.5-7 μm. Fig. 277 .... *A. crocodilinus* Murrill

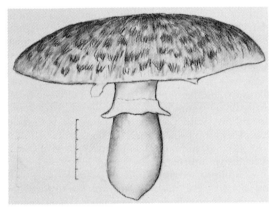

Figure 277

Figure 277 *Agaricus crocodilinus*

Pileus 10-35 cm, convex, appressed fibrillose, often areolate over disc, scales and fibrils becoming pale crust-brown. Gills pale vinaceous at first, finally chocolate brown. Stipe (7) 10-15 cm x 2-4 (7) cm, becoming dark reddish brown in age; annulus 2-layered, the lower layer present as pale cinnamon buff patches. Pleurocystidia none. Cheilocystidia abundant, 42-50 x 8-13 μm.

In pastures and meadows, bottom lands along the Pacific coast, fall; edible and choice, frequently collected.

2b Not as above (spores much smaller than in above) 3

3a Cut or bruised surfaces of fresh young pilei promptly staining blood red 4

3b Not as above 5

4a Stipe 10-16 cm long; annulus large and 2-layered; spores 5-6.5 × 4-4.5 μm. Fig. 278 .... *A. benesii* Pilat

Figure 278

Figure 278 *Agaricus benesii*

Pileus 6-15 cm, subglobose then plane and somewhat squamulose. Gills russet-vinaceous becoming purple-brown. Stipe 13-16 cm x ± 1 cm, base sometimes slightly bulbous, silky above the annulus, slightly floccose below the annulus but finally glabrescent; annulus large, with patches of tissue on the underside (double). Pleurocystidia none; cheilocystidia 7-14 x 10-18 μ, clustered, abundant, clavate to saccate.

Solitary to scattered in woods; Washington to California, not common. Not recommended.

4b Stipe 2.5-5 cm × 1.5-2.5 cm; annulus delicate, "slight"; spores 6-7 (8) × 5-6 μm .... *A. halophilus* Peck

Pileus 5-20 cm, subglobose becoming nearly plane, becoming dingy brown in age, glabrous or slightly squamulose with appressed scales. Gills narrow, close, pinkish at first, purplish brown in age. Stipe stout, base sometimes slightly bulbous. Pleurocystidia none; cheilocystidia 40-50 x 6-12 μm, abundant, clavate.

On sandy soil near salt water, Massachusetts and Washington. Edible—highly regarded by its discoverer who ate it for 14 years. It is said to have an odor of the seashore, and a slightly disagreeable taste raw. The latter apparently disappears as the specimens are cooked.

5a Annulus flaring and later pendant, margin thick and floccose or with patches of tissue on the lower surface 6

5b Annulus not as above 10

6a Spores 7-9 × 4.5-6 μm; gills white to grayish (never a bright pink) Fig. 279 ....
.... A. *arvensis* Fries

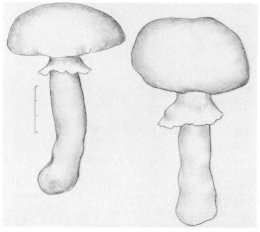

Figure 279

Figure 279 *Agaricus arvensis*

Pileus 7-15 cm, ovoid becoming convex, white to creamy or on the disc yellowish, fibrillose, sometimes becoming fibrillose-scaly, margin frequently with adhering veil remnants. Gills broad, finally blackish brown. Stipe 6-12 x 1-2 cm, equal with a slightly clavate base, glabrous above and below the annulus; annulus with cottony patches on the under side, white to yellowish in age; bruised areas yellowish, especially on pileus cuticle; odor and taste mild to slightly almond-like. Pleurocystidia none; cheilocystidia (11) 14-25 (33) x 8-11 μm, abundant, saccate to clavate.

Scattered to gregarious in meadows, grassy waste ground and on manured soil, summer and fall, widely distributed. Edible and popular. Occasional cases of "mild" poisonings are reported as caused by closely related species.

6b Spores shorter and/or narrower than in above choice; gills pinkish before becoming purple-brown 7

7a Pileus readily staining amber yellow where bruised, entirely yellow as dried; spores (5) 6-7 (8) × 3.5-4.5 μm; gills grayish pink at first .... A. *albolutescens* Zeller

Pileus 10-18 cm broad, convex to nearly plane, glabrous to slightly fibrillose when young, somewhat fibrous to floccose in age; context staining yellowish; odor like that of anise or almonds; taste pleasant. Gills close, broad, grayish pink at first, finally fuligineous to ± black. Stipe 5-9 (14) x 2-2.5 cm, base bulbous (up to 4.5 cm); surface silky-fibrillose above the annulus, with scattered fibrils below; annulus thin, ample whitish becoming yellow, with patches or scales on the under side. Pleurocystidia none; cheilocystidia 16-24 x 7-11 μm, abundant, clavate to fusoid-ventricose with obtuse apices.

Solitary to gregarious under oaks and conifers on the Pacific seaboard of California and Oregon, November to February. Not recommended: it causes rather severe gastrointestinal upsets in some people. Also, it is very similar to A. *xanthodermis* Genevier. The latter stains yellow, has a disagreeable, phenol-like odor and is also poisonous. Its occurrence in North America is not well established.

7b Not as above 8

8a Pileus soon becoming appressed squamulose with small pale crust-brown squamules, disc soon dingy pinkish gray ....
.... A. *magniceps* Peck

Pileus 5-15 cm, convex becoming plane; gills close, white becoming grayish vinaceous then dull reddish brown; context unchanging, odor and taste anise-like. Gills broad, close, free, lacking a pink stage. Stipe 7-10 x 1-2.3 cm, with a clavate to bulbous base, silky above annulus, ± cottony fibrillose below; annulus with white cottony patches on under surface. Spores (5) 6-7.5 x 3-3.5 μm. Pleurocystidia none; cheilocystidia 14-20 x 8-11 μm.

In thin woods, eastern United States, August. Edible, when young the entire fruiting body is good, later only the caps are good.

8b **Pileus not as above** 9

9a **Spores 5-6.5 × 4-4.5 μm, fruiting body readily staining lemon yellow where bruised. Fig. 280** .... *A. sylvicola* (Vitt.) **Fr.**

Figure 280

Figure 280 *Agaricus sylvicola*

Pileus 5-15 (20) cm, convex to nearly plane, silky fibrillose to obscurely fibrillose-scaly, white over all, becoming yellowish over disc; context unchanging or yellowish where bruised; odor not pronounced; taste somewhat almond-like. Gills narrow to ± broad, crowded, at first whitish then pinkish, finally pale chocolate brown. Stipe 8-15 cm x (8) 10-20 (25) mm, slightly enlarged toward base, with or without a flattened, bulbous base, silky above annulus, ± appressed fibrillose below and glabrescent; annulus membranous, lower surface with white the yellowish floccose patches. Pleurocystidia none; cheilocystidia 15-28 x 8-15 μm, abundant, clavate to fusoid-ventricose.

Scattered to gregarious in forested areas across North America, summer and fall, usually appearing every season. This is a collective species with many variations recorded; reports on edibility vary, possibly, with the variants, or possibly from person to person of those trying it. We do not recommend it.

9b **Spores 4-5 (5.5) × 3-3.5 (4) μm; yellow staining reaction weak and erratic** .... *A. cretacellus* **Atkinson**

Pileus 4-7.5 cm, ovoid to convex, margin often appendiculate, surface white over all, appressed fibrillose to appressed-scaly; odor faintly pungent; taste mild to almond-like. Gills narrow, crowded, white at first, finally deep brown. Stipe 8-10 cm x 6-10 mm, clavate, glabrous above the annulus, with powdery patches or scales below; annulus with the under surface ornamented like lower part of stipe. Pleurocystidia none; cheilocystidia 15-24 x 6-10 μ, rare, saccate to clavate.

On humus in woods, east of the Great Plains, late summer to fall. Edibility not well established.

10a **Annulus collar-like or terminating volva-like sheath** 11

10b **Not as above** 12

11a **Annulus collar-like, with a free upper and lower limb; stipe 1-3 cm thick, short; spores 5-6 × 4-5 μm. Fig. 281** .... *A. bitorquis* **Quélet**

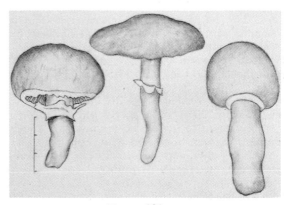

Figure 281

Figure 281 *Agaricus bitorquis*

Pileus 5-15 cm, at first broadly convex, nearly plane to broadly depressed at maturity; innately appressed fibrillose, at times areolate to rimose, in age sordid yellowish or dirt brown; context unchanging; odor and taste mild to fungoid. Gills narrow, at first grayish pink, finally deep brown. Stipe 2-5 (7) cm long, base ± pointed at first glabrous above the annulus, glabrous below it; annulus ± median. Pleurocystidia 28-36 x 9-14 μm, scattered, clavate to saccate; cheilocystidia 10-18 x 6-12 μm, saccate.

Scattered to caespitose on packed earth such as school yards, roadsides, tennis courts, etc., widely distributed, common, fruiting both in the spring and fall. Edible and choice.

11b Annulus terminating a volva-like sheath; stipe 10-12 mm thick; spores 8-9 (10) × 6-7.5 (8) μm .... *A. chlamydopus* **Peck**

Pileus 5-7.5 cm broad, convex, glabrous or minutely pulverulent on the margin, chalky white; context apparently not changing when injured; odor and taste not recorded. Gills close, chocolate color becoming black. Stipe 3-5 cm long, nearly equal, with numerous rhizomorphs at base. Neither pleurocystidia nor cheilocystidia present.

Solitary to scattered along roadsides, Colorado, spring. Edibility not reported.

12a Spores 7-9 (10) × 5-6 (7) μm; stipe solid, 6-10 mm thick; annulus single, often obliterated .... *A. solidipes* **Peck**

Pileus 2-7 (9) cm, convex to plane, white slowly becoming purplish brown, appressed fibrillose to areolate or squammulose in age; context unchanging, taste pleasant. Gills close, dull pink to dull sepia becoming brownish black. Stipe 2-4 cm long, ± equal, glabrous; veil remnants often left on pileus margin. Pleurocystidia none; cheilocystidia basidium-like (18-20 x 7-8.5 μm or smaller).

Scattered to gregarious in grassy areas and prairies pastures, Colorado, early summer, also Texas, California, and Oregon. Edible, easily confused with *A. campestris*.

12b Not as above **13**

13a Spores 6.5-7.5 (8) × 4-5 μm; stipe 8-12 mm thick; context not yellowish where injured. Fig. 282 .... *A. campestris* **Fries**

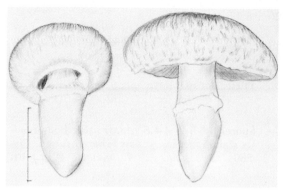

Figure 282

Figure 282 *Agaricus campestris*

Pileus (2) 3-7 (10) cm, convex, remaining white or the fibrils becoming cinnamon to reddish brown, fibrillose to ± squamulose; context white slowly vinaceous brown in aging; odor not distinctive, taste pleasant. Gills crowded, broad, pale to bright pink, then chocolate color to blackish. Stipe 2-4 (6) cm long, often tapered downward, glabrous above the annulus, ± fibrillose below it; annulus thin, single, often obliterated. Pleurocystidia none; cheilocystidia absent to inconspicuous and basidium-like, 20-24 x 7-8 μm, rarely up to 20 μm broad.

Scattered to gregarious in meadows, lawns, etc., temperate North America, spring summer and fall, depending on the area but mostly in the fall. Edible and good, often called pink bottom or meadow mushroom and highly prized wherever found.

13b Spores 4.5-5 (6) × 3-3.5 μm; context readily changing to yellow; stipe 3-6 mm thick. Fig. 283 .... *A. comptulus* **Fries**

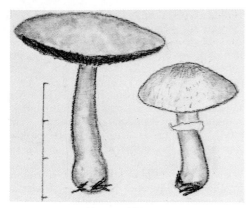

Figure 283

Figure 284

Figure 283   *Agaricus comptulus*

Figure 284   *Agaricus haemorrhoidarius*

Pileus 2-5 cm broad, convex becoming broadly convex to slightly umbonate, soon tinted lilac gray to brownish or rosy on the disc, often yellowish in age; odor and taste not distinctive. Gills crowded, whitish at first, finally dirty purple brown. Stipe 3-6 cm long, slender, tapered upwards, soon staining yellowish, glabrous to appressed silky; annulus thin, single, at times evanescent. Pleurocystidia absent; cheilocystidia 12-18 (25) x 6-8 (10) μm, inconspicuous, saccate to clavate.

Solitary to scattered, in pastures and grassland generally, its distribution in North America remains to be established. It was reported from Oregon.

14a Stipe typically 1 cm or more thick near apex
.... 15

14b Stipe typically less than 1 cm thick near apex
.... 31

15a Injured areas of fruiting body quickly changing to red; spores 5-6.5 $\times$ 3.5-4 μm. Fig. 284 .... *A. haemorrhoidarius* Schulzer in Kalchbrenner

Pileus (3) 4-8 (10) cm broad, disc flattened, convex to plane at maturity, fibrils dark purplish brown and breaking up into fibrillose squamules; odor and taste mild. Gills close, moderately broad, whitish at first, then pinkish, finally dull chocolate color. Stipe 6-12 cm x 10-20 mm, equal with an abrupt flattened bulb, white and silky above the annulus, becoming dull pinkish gray in age, with deep pinkish gray fibrillose patches below the annulus; annulus often not persistent. Pleurocystidia none; cheilocystidia 28-32 x 8-10 μm, fusoid-ventricose, saccate or clavate.

Gregarious in woods, especially damp areas, central and eastern United States summer and early fall. Edibility: not recommended.

15b Not with the above features 16

16a Stipe with an abruptly bulbous flattened base
.... 17

16b Stipe base not flattened (a small rounded bulb may be present), often sunken deep in the humus 00

17a Unbroken partial veil with brown droplets of liquid on the under side (or brown spots in dry weather). Fig. 285 ....
.... *A. placomyces* Peck

Figure 285

Figure 285 *Agaricus placomyces*

Pileus 4-10 (15) cm, obtuse to flattened-convex to ± plane; cuticle of radial fibrils cinereous to pale drab, in age rimose or fibrils aggregated into fascicles but not squamules; context pallid, in age brownish; odor unpleasant but slight; taste mild to slightly disagreeable. Gills soon pale grayish pink, finally chocolate brown, crowded, narrow. Stipe (3) 7-15 cm x 9-15 mm, with numerous basal rhizomorphs; annulus flabby, white at first, soon pinkish gray, underside with floccose patches. Spores 5-6 x 3.5-5 μm. Pleurocystidia none; cheilocystidia 15-24 x 8-16 μm, saccate to clavate.

Scattered to gregarious in woods, on old sawdust piles and rich humus generally, under hardwoods, eastern North America to Great Lakes area summer and fall. Edible, but not recommended. The species which is poisonous and which has passed under the name A. *placomyces* is A. *melagris*.

17b Not as above (annulus lacking brown water-spots on under side) **18**

18a Pileus with dark to blackish brown squamules; odor strong of phenol; gills very soon bright pink .... *A. meleagris* **J. Shaffer**

Pileus 4-15 cm, obtuse to convex but with disc ± flattened, surface dry and fibrillose; cuticle of ± radial blackish brown fibrils soon separating and tips recurved to form squamules; context white, soon pink when water-soaked; taste ± dis-

agreeable. Gills close, broad. Stipe 7-15 x 1-1.5 cm, equal to a flanged base, white, finally discolored brownish; annulus superior to median, double. Spores 5.5-6.5 x 3.5-4 μ, Pleurocystidia none; cheilocystidia 12-20 x 9-15 μm, saccate to clavate, abundant.

Gregarious on lawns near hedge rows, in cemetaries and grassy areas generally but often also under hardwoods on rich humus, summer and fall, Great Lakes area east and southward. A. *placomyces* has brown droplets on the under side of the annulus and the pileus cuticle does not become squamulose though it is rimose at times and typically very pale gray. A. *meleagris* is poisonous, and has frequently been reported under the name A. *placomyces* (see above).

18b Not as above **19**

19a Pileus with ochraceous-tawny fibrils or squamules; spores 8-10 (12) × 5-5 (6) μm. Fig. 286 .... *A. perrarus* **Schulzer**

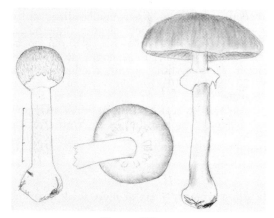

Figure 286

Figure 286 *Agaricus perrarus*

Pileus 8-15 cm, convex to obtuse to nearly plane, at first innately fibrillose, the fibrils aggregated into fascicles or squamules by maturity; tending to stain yellowish where bruised; odor ± pungent; taste distinctly of almonds. Gills crowded, whitish, slowly becoming chocolate brown. Stipe 8-15 cm x 10-15 mm, equal above the abruptly bulbous base; annulus with floccose patches on the under side colored like fibrils on pileus; below annulus

± fibrillose, silky above. Pleurocystidia none; cheilocystidia 8-12 μ broad, balloon-shaped.

Scattered to gregarious fall and winter along our Pacific Coast especially in groves of Sitka spruce. Edible.

19b Not as above (spores distinctly smaller, habitat not under Sitka spruce) **20**

20a Pileus evenly rosy avellaneous (Murrill) at first; annulus single, (lacking patches on underside); spores ellipsoid ....
.... *A. praemagniceps* **Murrill**

Pileus ± 15 cm, flattened-convex to finally depressed, disc minutely fibrillose. Gills white at first, almost black in age. Stipe 6-10 cm x 1-1.5 cm, glabrous; annulus persistent. Spores 5-6.5 x 3.5-4 μm. Pleurocystidia none; cheilocystidia basidium-like (12-15 x 5-6 μm).

Under evergreen oaks, Florida, late summer and fall. Murrill reported the flavor as good but the fruiting bodies were tough and stringy.

20b Pileus color not as above; annulus single or double **21**

21a Spores 4.5-5.5 × 4-5 μm; pileus dingy yellow-brown; annulus only slightly floccose on under side .... *A. kauffmanii* **Smith**

Pileus 5-7 cm, ovoid becoming convex-flattened, dry, appressed fibrillose, dingy to dark clay-color; context white, unchanging; odor and taste not distinctive. Gills white then pink, finally chocolate brown, crowded, narrow, free. Stipe 5-8 (10) cm, equal to a small rounded evanescent bulb; glabrous; annulus superior, very slightly floccose on under side. Spores 4.5-5.5 x 4.5 μm.

Gregarious, on soil, southeastern United States, summer, apparently rarely collected. Edibility: not tested.

21b Annulus with patches on under surface or a very thick edge **22**

22a Pileus innately fibrillose, the fibrils soon aggregated into ± appressed fascicles and ± dingy pinkish brown to merely dark brown. Fig. 287 .... *A. sylvaticus* **Fries**

Figure 287

Figure 287 *Agaricus sylvaticus*

Pileus 4-12 (15) cm, with a flattened disc, subovate at first. Gills crowded, narrow to moderately broad, at first pale purplish gray then dull pink, cut context slowly reddish brown, finally dark reddish brown. Stipe 6-11 x 1-2 cm, base subbulbous; appressed silky above and below the annulus; annulus with vinaceous tinged floccose scales or patches on under side or merely white fibrillose below. Spores 5-6 x 3-3.4 (4) μm. Pleurocystidia none; cheilocystidia 12-18 x 7-10 μm, saccate to clavate, abundant to scattered.

In wooded areas across the continent but most abundant along the west coast, fall. Edible but easily confused with *A. hondensis* which is poisonous to some people; caution is advised.

22b Not as above **23**

23a Pileus glabrous and pale grayish pink, not squamulose in age; spores 4.5-5.5 (6) × 3-3.5 μm .... *A. hondensis* **Murrill**

Pileus 8-15 cm broad, with a flattened disc, hemispheric to convex at first, rarely with appressed squamules. Gills close to crowded, narrow, pale grayish vinaceous at first, finally dark purplish brown. Stipe 8-14 x 1-2 cm, darkening like pileus in age; annulus with vinaceous fibrillose patches on under side near margin or occasionally only white fibrillose. Pleurocystidia none; cheilocystidia inconspicuous, basidium-like (16-22 x 5-6 μm or slightly broader).

Scattered to gregarious in woods, British Columbia south into California, fall, abundant at times. It is a variable species and in some collections the context stains yellowish then pinkish gray and has an odor of phenol. This species reportedly causes nausea when eaten raw and is poorly flavored when cooked: not recommended.

23b Not as above **24**

24a Fruiting bodies stout in appearance (length of stipe typically less than width of pileus when latter is expanded) **25**

24b Fruiting bodies with stipe as long or longer than the width of the expanded pileus **28**

25a Pileus with pale pink fibrils; surface where bruised staining tawny, becoming purplish umber in age; spores 5-6 × 4-4.5 μm .... *A. lilaceps* **Zeller**

Pileus (4) 7-13 cm, hemispheric to convex. Gills whitish to pale flesh color then "lilacy" and finally fuscous, close. Stipe 5-9.5 cm x 1.5-3 cm, slightly bulbous, white to tinted as the pileus and smooth to minutely floccose above the annulus, below with light brown fibrils and yellow-ochre basal stains; annulus white, narrow, drooping and adhering to stipe, finally evanescent. Pleurocystidia none; cheilocystidia basidium-like or shorter and broader, 12-18 x 6-9 μm.

Gregarious to caespitose under Monterey pine, California, December to March. Edibility not reported. The taste raw is slightly of almonds.

25b Not as above **26**

26a Annulus membranous and double. Fig. 288 .... *A. pattersonae* **Peck**

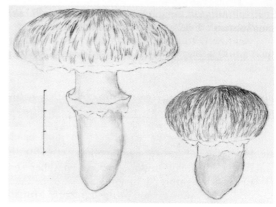

Figure 288

Figure 288 *Agaricus pattersonae*

Pileus 6-14 cm, convex to nearly plane, appressed-fibrillose, breaking up into reddish brown squamules; context not staining significantly; taste fungoid. Gills close, pink when young, blackish brown at maturity. Stipe 7-12 cm x 2-3 cm, equal or slightly tapering upward, base slightly bulbous. Spores 6-8 x 4.5-5.5 μm. Pleurocystidia none; cheilocystidia up to 20 x 10 μm, saccate.

Caespitose to gregarious in packed soil, California and Michigan, summer to fall. The thick, firm flesh and mild taste make this a popular species for eating. It is apparently most frequently found in suburban and urban areas in lawns, along streets, etc. Edible and choice.

26b Annulus simple, membranous to cottony .. **27**

27a Annulus membranous and skirt-like; spores 5-6 × 4-5 μm; pileus with small brownish scales .... *A. subfloridanus* **Murrill**

Pileus 10-12 cm, convex; odor pleasant; taste "pronounced." Gills free, broad, crowded, pallid at first, at length dark brown. Stipe about 6 cm x 1-1.5 cm (near base 2-3 cm), somewhat bulbous, glabrous. Pleurocystidia none; cheilocystidia basidium-like, 12-16 x 7-8 μm.

Scattered to gregarious in an open field on sterile soil, Florida, March. Edibility not reported, but Murrill suggested that this handsome species should be cultivated.

27b Annulus cottony to felt-like; spores 7-7.5 (8) × 4.5-6 μm; dull white at first but very soon brownish. Fig. 289 .... A. *brunnescens* **Peck**

Figure 289

Figure 289 *Agaricus brunnescens*

Pileus 5-10 (15) cm, broadly convex at first, expanding to plane or the margin uplifted, appressed fibrillose to squamulose or areolate over disc, in age sordid dark reddish brown; margin often appendiculate. Gills crowded to close, broad, grayish at first then dull grayish pink, finally deep rusty brown. Stipe 2-7 (9) x 1-2.5 cm, equal to somewhat clavate, silky; annulus usually persistent. Pleurocystidia none; cheilocystidia 14-22 x 7-11 μm, saccate, abundant.

Gregarious to scattered on manured soil or fertile soil in open areas, Massachusetts to Michigan. Edible and choice. It fruits sporadically (spring or fall) and has been found on piles of muck dug from bogs.

28a Spores 8-10 (11) × 5-6 μm; stipe narrowed downward and sunken deeply in the substrate. Fig. 290 .... A. *augustus* **Fries**

Figure 290

Figure 290 *Agaricus augustus*

Pileus 10-18 (28) cm, when young subcylindric with a flattened disc, convex with a flattened disc in age; fibrillose to fibrillose squamulose, the squamules dull yellowish brown to grayer brown, surface staining yellowish where bruised; taste of bitter almonds, often quite pronounced. Gills whitish at first then pinkish and finally dull vinaceous brown, close, broad at maturity. Stipe 8-12 x 2-3.5 cm, enlarged downward then tapered somewhat, appressed silky above the annulus, densely fibrillose squamulose below but soon glabrescent; annulus ample, with patches of brownish fibrils on the lower side. Pleurocystidia none; cheilocystidia 8-12 x 7-10 μm.

Solitary to scattered, rarely subcaespitose, along roads, in grassy areas, school yards, etc., late summer and fall, Michigan and the Pacific Northwest where it is sufficiently abundant to be sought for by the "gourmet set." In that area it is known as "The Prince."

28b Spores 5-7.5 μm long; stipe base often flattened or flanged 29

29a Stipe with white fibrillose veil remnants below the annulus as a sheath which becomes broken up; pileus streaked with dark vinaceous-brown fibrils. Fig. 291 .... A. *subrutilescens* (**Kauff.**) **Hot. & Stuntz**

Figure 291

Figure 291   *Agaricus subrutilescens*

Pileus (4) 6-12 (15) cm, with a flattened disc, nearly plane in age, fibrils often aggregated into fascicles or scales in age; context often tinged vinaceous in age; odor and taste not distinctive or taste slightly unpleasant. Gills narrow, crowded, white at first, then pinkish, finally deep purplish brown. Stipe 8-15 x (0.6) 1-2 cm, (at base up to 3 cm), glabrous above the annulus; annulus ample, thin, with vinaceous patches of fibrils on lower side or on the thickened margin. Spores 5-6 x 3-3.5 μm. Pleurocystidia none; cheilocystidia 10-20 x 8-15 μm.

Solitary to gregarious in woods (Sitka spruce usually present) along the Pacific coast from California northward, rather frequent, late summer and fall. Not recommended. It has caused considerable discomfort to a number of people—but it is one of the best flavored species in the genus.

29b Not as above **30**

30a Pileus with fuscous brown fibrils becoming arranged in squamules; annulus collar-like .... *A. cervinifolius* **Zeller**

Pileus 10-25 cm, fibrillose scales bruising yellowish; context of pileus yellowish where bruised. Gills moderately broad, crowded pale pinkish gray at first, becoming dark purplish brown. Stipe 8-16 x 2-3.4 (4) cm, with a slightly bulbous base, staining reddish brown where handled.

Spores 5-6 x 3.5-4.2 μm. Pleurocystidia and cheilocystidia 10-18 x 6-8 μm, saccate to clavate.

Gregarious to caespitose on rich humus at edges of conifer forests and along roads, especially where horses have been pastured, November, Washington and Oregon. Edibility: not tested.

30b Pileus with tawny fibrils or squamules; annulus ample and skirt-like. Fig. 292 ....
.... *A. subrufescens* **Peck**

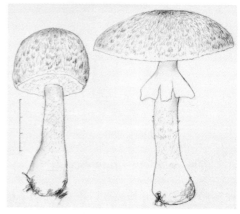

Figure 292

Figure 292   *Agaricus subrufescens*

Pileus (6) 8-18 (20) cm, with a flattened disc, finally nearly plane. Gills whitish at first, slowly dull pinkish brown, finally dark vinaceous brown to blackish, crowded, narrow. Stipe 7-15 x 1-2 cm, (at base up to 4 cm), base rarely flattened and generally sunken into the substrate, white and silky above the annulus, floccose-fibrillose or with patches or zones of fibrils below the annulus; annulus thin, lower surface with white to tawny patches of fibrils. Spores 6-7.5 x 4-5 μm. Pleurocystidia none; cheilocystidia 10-15 x 4 x 5 μm, abundant, somewhat inflated.

Solitary to subcaespitose on rich humus, compost heaps, etc., east of the Great Plains, summer and fall, not rare. Edible and choice. The raw flesh has a taste and odor of almonds but it is often weak and hardly distinctive. There are reports that this species was cultivated some 80 years ago in the eastern United States.

31a Stipe furnished with a distinct pseudorhiza .... *A. ciscoensis* **Smith**

Pileus 2-3.5 (4) cm, convex becoming plane, dull brown, silky-fibrillose; context dingy reddish brown in age. Gills close, moderately broad, pink when young, finally dark chocolate brown. Stipe 3-5 cm x 3-6 mm, with a somewhat bulbous base at ground line; annulus single, narrow, whitish, sometimes evanescent. Spores 7-8 x 4.5-5.5 μm. Pleurocystidia none; cheilocystidia basidium-like.

Scattered on soil under live oaks, Texas, September.

31b Lacking a distinct pseudorhiza 32

32a Surface of cap or the flesh readily staining red to pink 33

32b Not staining as in above choice 34

33a Pileus chamois to dingy yellow or clay-color, shaggy fibrillose near margin; spores 4-5 × 3.5-5 μm .... *A. flavitingens* **Murrill**

Pileus 4-10 cm broadly convex or with a flattened disc or nearly plane; taste slightly nutty. Gills pinkish at first, finally sordid purplish brown, close, narrow. Stipe 4-7 cm x 8-12 mm, with a somewhat enlarged to clavate base (± 2 cm thick), glabrous and silky above the annulus, densely white fibrillose or with fibrillose zones or patches below the annulus, becoming glabrous; annulus thin, often appearing single with white or yellowish fibrils on the lower surface. Pleurocystidia none; cheilocystidia 18-30 x 9-15 μm abundant, clavate to saccate.

Gregarious on soil under brush, fall, Washington. Apparently rare.

33b Pileus whitish but very soon rusty to reddish brown, bay as dried; surface appressed fibrillose; spores 5.5-7 (8) × 4-4.5 μm .... *A. rutilescens* **Peck**

Pileus 2.5-6 cm, convex becoming plane, surface even to rimose and minutely fibrillose. Gills close, narrow, reddish becoming blackish brown. Stipe 5-10 cm x 6-10 mm, equal or nearly so, often abruptly bulbous at the base; annulus distinctly double as in *A. bitorquis* but evanescent at times, or often adhering partly to the pileus margin.

Pleurocystidia none; cheilocystidia 18-26 x 6-7.5 μm, clavate to saccate, inconspicuous.

On manured ground in pastures, Colorado. Not much is known about this species.

34a Odor and taste strongly of almonds; pileus cadmium yellow on disc, margin white to whitish but with cadmium yellow squamules .... *A. auricolor* **Krieger**

Pileus 3-6 cm, obtuse when young expanding to plane; context staining yellow when bruised. Gills moderately close, whitish at first, deep sooty brown at maturity. Stipe 4-5 cm x 5-7 mm, with the base slightly bulbous and usually deeply sunken into the soil, glabrous above the annulus, with yellow floccose patches below the annulus; annulus thin, delicate, with yellowish floccose patches on the under side. Spores 4.5-5.5 x 3.5-5 μm. Pleurocystidia none; cheilocystidia inconspicuous, basidium-like 16-19 x 5-7 μm, clavate.

Single to gregarious on cultivated ground, along woods borders and in open places, southeastern United States, summer and fall. Edible and good. It is reported to fruit later than *A. campestris*.

34b Not as yellow as in above choice 35

35a Stipe 6-10 mm thick. Fig. 293 .... *A. micromegathus* **Peck**

Figure 293

Figure 293   *Agaricus micromegathus*   Figure 294   *Agaricus diminutivus*

Pileus 2-7 cm, convex or with a flattened to slightly depressed disc at first, more or less plane in age, innately fibrillose, the fibrils sordid yellowish brown gradually discoloring to brown or grayish brown, staining yellowish to ferruginous when bruised. Gills white to grayish at first, then pinkish and finally dark vinaceous brown, close, narrow. Stipe 2-5 cm long, equal or slightly tapering upward, silky above the annulus, scantily white fibrillose below it; annulus thin, single, with appressed fibrils on the lower side, soon evanescent. Spores 4.5-5.5 (6) x 3.5-4 μm. Pleurocystidia none; cheilocystidia basidium-like (12-14 x 5-6 μm).

Scattered to gregarious on rich ground, pastures and meadows, widely distributed east of the Great Plains.

Pileus 1-4 (6) cm, ovoid then convex to expanded-umbonate, dry, faintly appressed fibrillose, fibrils rosy brown to purplish gray, paler near margin, finally purplish gray overall. Gills close, broad, dull pink at first, finally dark dull vinaceous brown. Stipe 3-7 cm long, equal or with a slightly flattened basal bulb, white and silky above the annulus, with white floccose zones below at first, becoming yellowish brown from base upward; annulus single, white. Spores 4.5-5.5 x (3) 3.5-5 μm. Pleurocystidia none; cheilocystidia differentiated as sterile basidia.

Solitary to scattered on humus in woods, fall, in the eastern half of North America. Its occurrence in the Pacific Northwest needs critical study. There is a "swarm" of variants around this species in this region.

35b Stipe 2-5 mm thick. Fig. 294 ....
.... *A. diminutivus* **Peck**

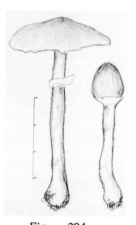

Figure 294

Melanophyllum Velenovsky

Only one species known in our area. Fig. 295
.... *M. echinatum* (Fr.) **Singer**

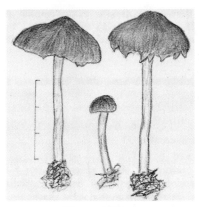

Figure 295

Figure 295 *Melanophyllum echinatum*

Pileus powdery from remains of outer veil, 1.5-3.5 cm, conic to nearly plane, dark dull grayish brown, at first covered with conic scales soon breaking down to a powder, with the margin at first appendiculate. Gills bright brick- to hematite-red when young, brownish drab in age. Stipe 3-7 cm x 1-3 mm, upper part colored as the young gills, powdery but soon glabrous; annular zone very soon obliterated. Spores subcylindric to subellipsoid.

Solitary to scattered on humus and leaf litter, widely distributed in the Northern Hemisphere but seldom abundant; summer and fall. Edibility unknown (?), the most closely related species are reportedly poisonous.

COPRINACEAE Roze

Cuticle of pileus various; a hymeniform layer of ± upright clavate cells, a layer of inflated ± isodiametric cells 1-3 cells deep, or a combination of both types; more rarely of greatly inflated hyphal cells ± radial in arrangement and with the cells ± elongated (in sections tangential to the pileus the cuticle appears as the cellular type mentioned above); spore deposit black to various shades of chocolate brown, gray-brown, reddish or coffee-brown; spores with pigment in the wall, and an apical to ± eccentric (in some species of *Coprinus*) germ pore often broad enough to cause the apex of the spore to appear flattened (truncate); fruiting body typically fragile; living mostly on dead organic matter such as the dung of herbivores, wood, fallen leaves, dead grass, etc., rarely parasitic on other fungi.

It is a large family of over 600 species. Fruiting occurs during spring, summer and fall, and substrate brought into the laboratory can be induced to produce fruiting bodies during winter months. This is true especially for dung inhabiting species.

KEY TO GENERA

1a Gills turning into a black inklike fluid .... (p. 208) *Coprinus*

1b Not liquifying as above 2

2a Pileus plicate-striate and hymenium regularly showing brachybasidioles .... (p. 226) *Pseudocoprinus*

2b Not with both the above features 3

3a Gills when just reaching maturity mottled obscurely with light and dark areas; spores black in deposit .... (p. 211) *Panaeolus*

3b Gills not mottled (rarely so in a few species); spores seldom truly black in deposit .... (p. 215) *Psathyrella*

Coprinus (Fr.) S. F. Gray (The Inky Caps)

Spore deposit black to dark brown, rarely tinged reddish; spores typically with an apical pore; gills undergoing autodigestion as the spores are shed (gills deliquescing into a black liquid); brachybasidioles support the sporulating basidia in the hymenium; occurring on dung of herbivores or on organic debris such as wood, straw, old bales of hay, compost heaps, soil, etc. A number of species are edible and popular; only a few are poisonous.

The genus is medium-sized and world wide in distribution, and has an estimated 200 species. Most of them culture readily and make good subjects for laboratory studies in elementary courses in mycology.

KEY TO SPECIES

1a Pileus large ± columnar (5-12 cm high), often with an apical smooth "skull cap," the remaining surface soon torn into fibrils or scales exposing the white flesh; annulus present, inferior; gills and flesh often becoming red at the stage just before the spores mature; terrestrial. Fig. 296 ....*C. comatus* (Fr.) S. F. Gray

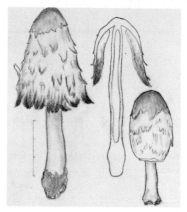

Figure 296

Figure 296 *Coprinus comatus*

Pileus 2-6 cm across the base just prior to sporulation, dominant color white with brownish disc. Stipe ± rooting, white, unpolished. Spores (12) 13-17 (18) x 7-9 μm, germ pore apical to ± eccentric.

Very common and widely distributed in North America. A number of variants are known. It fruits sparingly in the spring and abundantly in the fall on hard-packed soil along roads, in lawns and on waste ground; edible and popular. The most widely used common name is shaggy mane.

1b Not as above; veil if present granulose or of radially arranged fibrils, or felt-like to submembranous 2

2a Pileus with a submembranous patch of veil over disc and segmented into starlike rays; spores 14-20 × 10-12 μm ....*C. asterophorus* Long & Miller

Pileus 3-6 cm broad, becoming plane, marginal area soon fissured-striate, central area (disc) beneath the veil smooth, up to 12 mm wide, the gills are attached to it. Gills white becoming black, close, remote from stipe, narrow. Stipe 5-11 cm x 3-5 mm, base bulbous, fairly tough. Volva apparently viscid. Spores with a slightly eccentric pore.

Solitary to clustered on dry sandy soil, southwestern United States, after rains. This species is treated here as a mushroom but it is closely related to *Montagnites* which is classed as a Gasteromycete. The latter, however, is very closely related to *Coprinus*.

2b   Outer veil not as in above choice; spores very rarely up to 10 μm wide 3

3a   Outer veil of ± radially arranged superficial fibrils often becoming arranged in fascicles and soon removed by weathering (the pileus is then glabrous) 4

3b   Outer veil absent or if present mostly of interwoven hyphae, or granulose in texture at least in part 6

4a   Spores ornamented; pileus soon glabrous (outer veil very thin); on rotting wood especially of sugar maple. Fig. 297 ....
.... *C. insignis* **Peck**

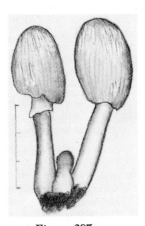

Figure 297

Figure 297   *Coprinus insignis*

Pileus 1.5-3 cm across the base, 2-4.5 cm high, sulcate to rimose-striate to disc, disc dingy brown,

marginal area pallid at first. Gills blackening directly, narrow to moderately broad. Stipe (5) 10-14 cm x 6-12 mm, scarcely any veil remnants evident on it. Spores 10-12.5 x 7-8.5 μm, with a snout-like apex. Pleurocystidia very soon collapsing.

Occurring east of the Great Plains, summer and fall, solitary or in small clusters. It is most likely to be confused with *C. atramentarius* especially if the veil has been obliterated. Poisonous.

4b   Not as above **5**

5a   Spores 10-12 × 6-7 μm ....
.... *C. lagopus* **Fries**

Pileus 8-15 mm wide at base, up to 15 mm high before expanding, veil well developed but remnants soon obliterated, surface becoming fissured-striate as expansion takes place. Gills narrow, close, free, soon black (no red zone present). Stipe 6-10 cm x 2-3.5 mm, white, very fragile. Pleurocystidia voluminous.

Solitary to scattered on lignicolous debris such as compost piles, rotting fallen branches in the woods or on humus rich in lignicolous material; common during some wet seasons, widely distributed.

5b   Spores 7-8.5 (9) × 5.5-7.3 μm ....
.... *C. lagopides* **Karsten**

Pileus 1.5-3 cm high, 1.5-2 cm across the base before expanding, ellipsoid when young, veil remnants soon vanishing, margin finely striate. Gills crowded, broad, attached to apex of stipe, changing from white to brown to black. Stipe densely fibrillose to pubescent at first, white, in age ± glabrous. Pleurocystidia voluminous (80-150 x 30-60 μm), thin-walled, ellipsoid to subcylindric.

Scattered to gregarious on lignicolous debris, Great Lakes area, fall, abundant at times, in the field easily confused with *C. lagopus*.

6a   Outer veil felt-like (mostly of interwoven hyphae) and breaking up into patches and/or warts over surface of pileus; occurring in large clusters on hardwood debris. Fig. 298 .... *C. quadrifidus* **Peck**

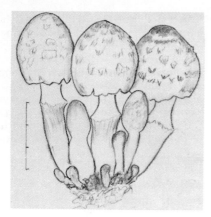

Figure 298

Figure 298 *Coprinus quadrifidus*

Pileus 2-5 cm broad at base, 2-4 cm high, veil remnants whitish at first but soon dingy buff or darker at least on surface where exposed to light; surface of cap pallid beneath the veil, darkening as spores mature, not distinctly striate. Gills white then purplish and then black, crowded, reaching the stipe. Stipe 4-12 cm x 5-8 mm, whitish, the basal fibrillose zone usually evident, base connected to brownish rhizomorphs. Spores 7.5-10 x 4-5 (5.5) μm.

Common on hardwood, especially of ash and elm, late spring and early summer, Great Lakes area and eastward, edible but not popular because of the flavor.

6b Not as above 7

7a Pileus surface glabrous or silky at first, or innately appressed-squamulose around disc. Fig. 299 .... *C. atramentarius* (**Fr.**) **Fr.**

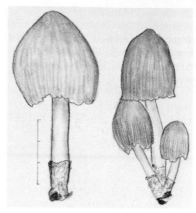

Figure 299

Figure 299 *Coprinus atramentarius*

Pileus 4-6 cm across the base, up to 6 cm high or more, margin connected at first to a thin fibrillose veil sheathing the stipe base; pileus color gray as spores mature, the disc usually dingy brown. Gills white becoming brownish then black. Stipe 8-15 cm x 8-12 mm, white except for the veil remnants at the base. Spores 7-9 x 3.5-4 x 4-5 μm, slightly compressed. Pleurocystidia ± 150 x 30 μm.

Clustered on or near stumps and buried wood generally, very common and widely distributed; spring and fall.

It is edible but one should not partake of alcoholic beverages for a number of hours before or after eating it since some people (not all) get a peculiar type of poisoning from the combination.

7b Outer veil granulose (check buttons) or a mixture of globose cells and hyphal filaments (fibrillose and granulose mixed) 8

8a Veil remnants granulose (often absent by maturity), never in patches or squamules; spores slightly compressed; habitat on rotting wood. Fig. 300 ...... *C. micaceus* (**Fr.**) **Fr.**

Figure 300

Figure 300 *Coprinus micaceus*

Pileus 1.5-5 cm across the base, 2.5-4 cm high, broadly conic, at first granular from remains of veil, soon glabrous, color ± tawny to crust brown or pale tan, striate to near disc, the striate ± plicate. Gills ± broad, close, pale buff to brownish and then black. Stipe 4-8 (12) cm x 3-5 mm, white, slightly pruinose, in some fibrillose at base. Spores 8-11 x 5-6 x 5.5-6.5 μm. Pleurocystidia 40-70 x 20-40 μm.

Caespitose, spring and fall, very common and widely distributed. It is edible and popular. The most used common name is mica cap.

8b **Not as above** **9**

9a **Growing on wood; pileus tawny to crust-brown** .... *C. radians* **Desmaziers**

Pileus 1.5-3 cm high, 2-2.5 cm wide at base, conic to cylindric, surface at first covered with fine mealy particles and hyphae, together these forming patches which soon wear away, surface finely wrinkled-striate to disc; clay-color to pale tawny, darkening to lead-color as spores mature. Gills broad, crowded, attached to stipe apex; white changing to brown then black. Stipe 4-8 cm x 3-6 mm, tomentose, no evidence of volva or annulus, usually a coarse brown mycelium (an ozonium) around the area containing the fruit body. Spores 8-10 x 4.5-6 μm, in profile slightly bean-shaped. Pleurocystidia scattered, 60-150 x 15-50 μm, soon collapsing.

Scattered, usually a few in an area, widely distributed. It often occurs on wet wood in dwellings, such as around sinks, bathtubs, etc.

9b **Pileus white; growing on dung** .... *C. niveus* **(Fr.) Fr.**

Pileus 1.5-4 cm high, 2.5-5 cm wide, snow-white to creamy white, surface at first with a conspicuous powdery covering of veil material which is soon evanescent. Gills broad, white at first. Stipe 4-9 cm x 2.5-5 mm, surface at first powdery from veil. Spores 13-17 x 7.5-9 x 10-13 μm, appreciably compressed.

Solitary or only 2-3 together, widely distributed, spring and summer or fall.

Panaeolus (Fr.) Quélet

Pileus conic, campanulate or convex; cuticle cellular; basidia maturing in patches hence gills mottled by groups of darker and paler spores; brachybasidioles not clearly differentiated from basidioles; spores black in deposits, with an apical pore; stipe thin in comparison to diameter of the pileus; growing on dung, soil, moss, or wood but apparently are not mycorrhiza formers.

This genus is close to *Psathyrella*. It is a small genus of about 25 species or less in North America. A number have been reported as poisonous and at least some of these contain psilocybin and psilocin. In the following key cystidia are mentioned only if they are significant.

KEY TO SPECIES

1a **Common on lawns and other grassy habitats during late spring and early summer; veil lacking** .... **see page 222** *Psathyrella foenisecii*

1b Not as above **2**

2a Annulus typically present; fruiting on horse dung mainly. Fig. 301 .... *P. semiovatus* (Fr.) Lundell & Nanfeldt

Figure 301

Figure 301   *Panaeolus semiovatus*

Pileus (3) 5-9 cm, ovoid becoming obtusely conic to broadly conic; surface glabrous, viscid, pale tan fading to pallid; context very soft, pallid, becoming dingy. Gills pallid becoming mottled with black. Stipe 8-15 cm x 6-12 mm, equal down to an enlarged base; surface whitish to buff; annulus median, evanescent. Spores 15-20 x 8-11 μm. Pleurocystidia present as chrysocystidia.

Solitary or 2-3 at a location, widely distributed, spring and summer. Specimens in which the annulus has disappeared are likely to be confused with the following species.

2b Annulus absent (check young fruiting bodies) **3**

3a Pileus 4-10 cm; stipe 3-15 mm thick; chrysocystidia present in hymenium. Fig. 302 .... *P. solidipes* (Pk.) Sacc.

Figure 302

Figure 302   *Panaeolus solidipes*

Pileus convex, glabrous, white, in age yellowish. Gills broad and ventricose, close, white at first. Stipe (4) 9-20 cm x 3-15 mm, solid, apex beaded with drops at first and also striate, white. Spores 14-19 x 9-12 μm.

Gregarious on heavily manured soil, manure piles containing much straw, and rarely on rotting straw stacks; spring, occurrence erratic. Singer considers it to be a synonym of *Anellaria sepulchralis* (Berk.) Sing.

3b Fruiting body less robust than in 3a and chrysocystidia absent **4**

4a Pileus dark reddish brown and when faded long retaining a dark moist marginal band; stipe reddish brown beneath a pruinose-fibrous outer covering; on dung or manured soil; spores 11-14 × 7-9 μm. Fig. 303 .... *P. subbalteatus* (Berk. & Br.) Sacc.

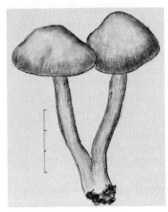

Figure 303

Figure 303 *Panaeolus subbalteatus*

Pileus 3-5 cm, obtusely conic to expanded umbonate, fading to dingy ochraceous buff, surface
often pitted to rugulose, margin not appendiculate. Gills broad, close, dull reddish brown then
mottled black. Stipe 4-8 (11) cm x 3-6 mm, longitudinally striate.

   Scattered to gregarious, spring and early
summer, sporadic but widely distributed. Poisonous.

**4b   Pileus in white to gray or darker range, or
   if red-brown not on dung or manured soil
   .... 5**

**5a   Pileus margin at first crenate with sterile
   flaps of veil tissue; pileus olive-brown to
   paler (if faded); spores 13-16 × 8-11 μm.
   Fig. 304 .... *P. campanulatus* (Fr.) Quél.**

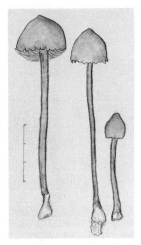

Figure 304

Figure 304 *Panaeolus campanulatus*

Pileus (1) 2-5 (6) cm, obtusely conic then campanulate, when faded ± pale olive buff. Gills
subdistant, broad (to 1 cm), seceding, pallid at
first, edges white. Stipe 6-14 cm x 1.5-5 mm,
equal, tubular, concolorous with fresh cap, densely
pruinose. Pleurocystidia none.

   Clustered to solitary on dung of horses and
cows; spring, summer and fall after heavy rains,
widely distributed.

5b   Pileus margin not crenate at first 6

**6a   Scattered on soil; pileus 1-2 cm, dark choco-
   late brown; stipe 8-12 cm × 1.5-2 mm, very
   brittle. Fig. 305 ....
   .... *P. acuminatus* (Sec.) Quél.**

Figure 305

Figure 305 *Panaeolus acuminatus*

Pileus hygrophanous, often conic-umbonate, cinereous when faded, glabrous; context fragile, odor and taste mild. Gills ± close, grayish at first, seceding, broad. Stipe dark brown over all, grayish from a dense pruinose coating. Spores (11) 12-15 x 8-10 μm. Cheilocystidia 25-35 x 7-9 μm, narrowly fusoid-ventricose.

Spring and summer, Pacific Northwest, apparently widely distributed.

6b Habitat on wood, moss beds, or on dung
.... 7

7a Growing on wood of hardwoods (especially ash) .... *P. fraxinophilus* **Smith**

Pileus 8-15 mm surface hoary, blackish, drab when faded. Gills close, ± broad, adnate, drab then mottled black, edge whitish. Stipe 1-2 cm x 2 mm, dark grayish brown, pruinose, beaded with droplets above, hollow. Spores 9-11 x 5.5-7 μm.

Eastern United States, apparently rare, early fall. The habitat is most unusual for the genus. Because of the habitat and the small spores this species might well be regarded as primitive in the genus.

7b Habitat on moss beds or on dung 8

8a Scattered on beds of species of *Mnium* (a moss) in swamps; spores 7-9 × 4-5 μm
.... *P. fontinalis* **Smith**

Pileus 1-2 cm, conic, olive-buff to olive-brown, margin paler, fading to grayish olive-buff. Gills olive-buff at first, broad, close, edges ± floccose. Stipe 5-10 cm x 1-2 mm, very fragile, pruinose, pallid, beaded with droplets if fresh. Spores 7-9 x 4-5 μm.

Scattered, late spring and early summer, apparently rarely collected, Great Lakes area.

8b On dung or heavily manured soil 9

9a Pileus and/or stipe when bruised changing to blue at least slightly; thick-walled pleurocystidia present in hymenium ....
.... *P. cyanescens* **(Berk. & Br.) Sacc.**

Pileus 2.5-4 cm wide, 1.5-2 cm high, convex to campanulate, dark brown, margin translucent striate if moist. Gills adnate, ventricose, grayish black. Stipe 6.5-11.5 cm x 2.5-3 mm, with a slight bulb, longitudinally striate, grayish pallid, brownish flesh-color near base, pruinose. Spores 12-14 x 8.5-11 μm.

On dung, Gulf Coast region, widely distributed in southern portions of North America. Poisonous.

9b Not staining blue and lacking thick-walled pleurocystidia but with pileus margin appendiculate at first .... *P. retirugis* **Fries**

Pileus 3-6 cm high and wide, glabrous, surface often pitted and/or wrinkled, pale tan but often whitish in age; taste slightly nauseous. Gills close, broad, vinaceous gray at first. Stipe 9-15 cm x 3-7 mm, hollow, densely pruinose, beaded with droplets if fresh; some with a slight subapical evanescent annular zone. Spores (11) 12-16 (18) x 8-11 μm. Cheilocystidia mostly ± capitate.

Widely distributed but sporadic, spring and early summer.

Psathyrella (Fr.) Quelet

Pileus typically fragile, thin, partial and outer veils absent to present and well-developed. Stipe fragile. Gills attached to stipe at least at first. Spore print typically cocoa-color to chocolate black, dull brick red, or pinkish gray. Spores typically with a germ pore and if well developed the apex truncate, smooth or ornamented. Fruiting bodies not undergoing autodigestion and if brachybasidioles are present the pileus is not plicate-striate.

About 400 species occur in North America of which 35 common and/or conspicuous species are included in this book. The species of this genus occur on wood and other plant debris, beside drying up woodland pools, and on burned areas especially in late summer and fall. The edibility of many species has not been established.

KEY TO SPECIES

1a Stipe 6-15 (20) mm thick near apex p. 215
.... **Key A**

1b Stipe 1-5 (6) mm thick near apex p. 221
.... **Key B**

Key A

1a Pileus innately fibrillose, the fibrils white to variously colored and often arranged radially in fascicles 2

1b Pileus fibrillose from remains of a superficial veil but all traces of it soon vanishing, or pileus glabrous 9

2a Fruiting body growing from a fruiting body of the shaggy mane (*Coprinus comatus*) ......
.... *P. epimyces* (Pk.) Sm.

Pileus 2-6 cm, finally convex to ± plane, dry, silky fibrillose, white but dingy in age; margin at first appendiculate. Gills pallid at first, close, narrowly adnate. Stipe 2-7 cm x 5-15 mm, equal, at times with a white annulus or appearing volvate, surface floccose-mealy. Spores 7-9 (10) x 4-5 μm, ovate to elliptic in face view, in profile ± inequilateral. Pleurocystidia 40-64 (70) x 9-15 μm, fusoid-ventricose, apex obtuse to rounded.

Late summer and fall, northern United States and in Canada, not common.

2b On wood, debris, humus, etc. (but not parasitic on mushrooms) 3

3a Fibrils on pileus white; gills soon toned reddish (see *P. lacrymabunda* (Fr.) Moser also)
.... *P. insignis* Smith

Pileus 3-7 cm, obtuse then expanded-umbonate to convex, at first coated with white veil fibrils, these soon aggregated into fascicles, glabrescent, ground color white becoming vinaceous fawn, at first with an appendiculate margin; context brittle, pallid, not staining. Gills pale grayish vinaceous then vinaceous brown, depressed-adnate, close to crowded, finally broad. Stipe 6-10 cm x 8-12 mm, white, fibrillose from veil remnants. Spore deposit vinaceous-brown. Spores 6.5-7.5 x 3.2-3.8 μm, oblong to elliptic in face view, in profile ± bean-shaped, smooth. Pleurocystidia 32-45 x 10-15 μm, apex rounded to obtuse.

Clustered around beech and locust stumps, late summer and fall, Michigan; not rare during wet seasons.

3b Fibrils on pileus colored or soon becoming so
.... 4

4a Pileus with blackish brown patches of veil fibrils especially near or on the disc; spores 5-6 × 3-3.5 μm. Fig. 306 ....
.... *P. maculata* (Parker) Moser

Figure 306

Figure 306 *Psathyrella maculata*

Pileus 2-6 cm, obtuse then campanulate, finally plane or umbonate; margin typically appendiculate; context soft, whitish. Gills crowded, narrow, depressed-adnate, pallid becoming cinnamon-drab. Stipe 6-12 cm x 6-14 mm, slightly narrowed downward, pinkish in base when cut, fibrillose, at times ± annulate. Spores in face view elliptic to oblong, in profile ± bean-shaped. Pleurocystidia abundant, 32-46 x 9-15 μm, obovate-mucronate or with an apical finger-like projection.

Caespitose ot gregarious on alder stumps and logs; summer and fall; Pacific Northwest; abundant when it fruits.

4b Not as above; central and eastern United States **5**

5a Pileus with dark brown to blackish radially arranged fibrils or fascicles of fibrils .... *P. echiniceps* **(Atk.) Sm.**

Pileus 3-10 cm, soon ± plano-umbonate; context thickish, brittle, buff-colored, olivaceous with FeSO$_4$; odor and taste slightly disagreeable. Gills broad, close, adnate-seceding, deep reddish brown at maturity. Stipe 8-12 cm x 10-15 mm, pale alutaceous, lower two-thirds coated with dark fibrils from veil. Spores ovate to elliptic in face view, ± inequilateral in profile, minutely ornamented, 7-9 x 4-5 μm. Pleurocystidia 40-70 x 9-18 μm, often in groups, ± cylindric, apex rounded to obtuse.

Appearing terrestrial but growing from buried wood, late summer and fall, Great Lakes area, rare in the Northwest.

5b Veil remnants on pileus pallid to buff, grayish or brownish (distinctly paler than in above choice) **6**

6a Pileus ± rusty brown; pleurocystidia ± in bunches; spores 9-12 × 6-7 μm, minutely roughened. Fig. 307 .... *P. velutina* **(Fr.) Singer**

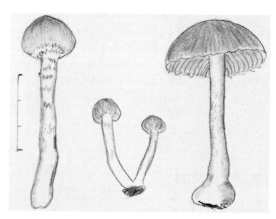

Figure 307

Figure 307 *Psathyrella velutina*

Pileus (3) 5-12 cm, obtuse to convex then plane or obtusely umbonate, surface often rugulose beneath the fibrils, ground color ochraceous to dull tawny; context watery brown to dingy buff, with KOH dark rusty brown, with FeSO$_4$ slowly olive-gray. Gills weakly ochraceous, finally deep rusty brown and ± mottled, edges often beaded with drops of moisture. Stipe 5-15 cm x 4-20 mm, floccose-squamulose to tawny annular zone. Spores blackish brown in deposit; germ pore prominant (apex snout-like). Pleurocystidia 48-62 x 9-14 μm, clavate to utriform, often in groups of 3-4.

Scattered to clustered on accumulations of organic debris such as compost heaps; summer and fall, widely distributed and abundant at times. Edible.

6b Pileus whitish to grayish brown in color; spores ± under 9 μm long 7

7a Basal mycelium pale yellow; spores 6-7.5 × 3.2-4 μm .... *P. lacrymabunda* (Fr.) Moser var. *lacrymabunda*

Pileus 4-10 cm, convex to campanulate or plane, fibrillose-squamulose, the fibrils gray-brown, ground color whitish to yellowish. Gills crowded, narrow, adnate-seceding, white becoming dark gray-brown. Stipe 6-12 cm x 6-15 mm, ± equal, white, with colored patches of veil material over lower part, at times stained yellow. Spores bean-shaped in profile. Pleurocystidia 32-46 x 10-16 μm, utriform, some with ± colored content.

Caespitose around dead trees and stumps of hardwoods, late summer and fall, Great Lakes area south and eastward.

7b Basal mycelium if present not yellow 8

8a Spores 7.5-9 × 4-4.5 μm; basal mycelium white but base of stipe often stained orange-pink; on hardwood .... *P. alboalutacea* Smith

Pileus 2-6 cm, obtuse to convex, soon plane or nearly so, dry and fibrillose, fibrils soon forming patches and discoloring to grayish brown, disc often alutaceous, discolored over all in age; margin fibrillose to cottony-appendiculate. Gills adnate-seceding, close, finally ± broad, white becoming drab gray. Stipe 3-5 x 10-12 μm, hard, with dingy fibrils or patches over lower half. Spores smooth, lacking an evident pore, in profile bean-shaped to ± inequilateral. Pleurocystidia: 1) clavate to subvesiculose, 25-40 x 10-14 μm, and 2) fusoid, 40-53 x 9-14 μm, apex obtuse to subacute or mucronate.

Clustered on dead wood of alder; Pacific Northwest; abundant when it fruits.

8b Spores 6-6.5 × 3-3.5 μm; base of stipe not stained orange pink; growing on soil under spruce .... *P. duchesnayensis* Smith

Pileus 3-6 cm, convex, appressed fibrillose near margin, pale pinkish buff, disc glabrous, margin for a time decorated with patches of dingy veil tissue. Gills whitish then vinaceous, finally pinkish gray, close, narrow, adnate. Stipe 3-6 cm x 9-12 mm, lower 3/4 coated with dingy buff to gray veil remnants terminating as an annular zone. Spores in profile bean-shaped, in face view oblong. Pleurocystidia 33-52 x 10-15 μm, broadly utriform.

Caespitose on soil under spruce and fir; fall; Province of Quebec, Canada.

9a Spores 9-11 × 6-7.5 μm; pileus 6-10 cm, radiately rugulose; gills mottled from maturing spores .... *P. rugocephala* (Atk.) Smith

Pileus convex to plane or broadly umbonate, glabrous, watery brown to tawny fading to dull pale clay-color; context yellowish. Gills adnate, seceding, ± broad, close, brownish becoming purplish fuscous and obscurely mottled. Stipe 8-12 cm x 6-10 mm, ± equal, hollow, brownish below, paler above; annular zone of veil remnants colored dark from an accumulation of spores. Spores ± inequilateral in profile, in face view ± ovate but with a snout-like apex with the germ pore lens-shaped. Pleurocystidia scattered, 45-63 x 9-12 μm, apex broadly rounded to obtuse.

Gregarious on humus and around stumps, summer and fall; Great Lakes area eastward, occasional.

9b Not as above 10

10a Annulus membranous 11

10b Annulus absent or present only as a fibrillose zone 16

11a Pileus whitish at first; odor aromatic; habitat on burned ground .... *P. gruberi* Smith

Pileus 3-6 cm, obtuse, becoming campanulate and finally expanded-umbonate, covered with a dense coating of white squamules; surface whitish, darkening to grayish brown or the disc a grayish clay-color; at first with a heavily appendiculate margin. Gills whitish becoming violaceous brown, adnate, close, ± broad. Stipe 5-8 cm x 8-10 mm, ± equal, usually with a thick superior cottony annulus, below annulus white and fibrillose-scaly, discoloring on handling or in age. Pleurocystidia 40-60 x 10-20 μm, apex obtuse to broadly rounded, some with 1-3 subapical protrusions.

Caespitose, late fall, Oregon, apparently rare.

11b Not as above **12**

12a Spores 9-12 × 4.5-6 μm; odor aromatic ......
.... *P. caputmedusae* (Fr.) Kon. & Maubl.

Pileus 4-5 cm, obtusely conic becoming campanulate, at first with superficial deciduous fibrillose squamules, the tips of which usually darken; cuticle ± medium date brown before fading. Gills close, broad, adnate, pinkish gray becoming grayish brown. Stipe 8-10 cm x 7-8 mm, ± equal, whitish, fibrillose scaly below the membranous annulus. Spores obscurely inequilateral in profile, ovate to ± elliptic in face view. Pleurocystidia 36-54 x 12-22 μm, apex obtuse to rounded.

Clustered on or beside conifer wood and debris, Pacific Northwest, fall, apparently rare.

12b Not as above **13**

13a On conifer duff; spores 11-14 (15) × 6-7.5 μm (but see *P. longistriata* also, it has small spores) .... *P. annulata* Smith

Pileus 3-5 cm, obtuse then ± campanulate to expanded-umbonate, at first with minute squamules from the veil, honey-brown beneath the scales. Gills close, broad, adnate-seceding, pale dull cinnamon becoming dark cinnamon. Stipe 9-13 cm x 5-9 mm, equal, hollow, fragile; annulus membranous, superior, striate on upper side, squamulose underneath. Pleurocystidia 46-77 x 13-20 μm, apex broadly rounded.

Scattered, fall, northern Idaho, apparently rare, but easily mistaken for a large specimen of *P. longistriata* in the field.

13b Spores smaller than in above choice; fruiting bodies on remains of hardwood trees or on humus under them **14**

14a Pleurocystidia absent ....
.... **see page 224** *P. candolleana*

14b Pleurocystidia present **15**

15a Pleurocystidia broadly rounded. Fig. 308 ....
.... *P. kauffmanii* Smith

Figure 308

Figure 308 *Psathyrella kauffmanii*

Pileus 3-9 cm, campanulate to plane, glabrous, moist, hygrophanous, honey-brown at first, finally grayish brown, grayish clay-color faded; taste slightly bitter. Gills adnate, seceding, ± narrow, close to crowded, pallid becoming dusky gray. Stipe 6-12 cm x 3-10 mm at base, white, hollow, fragile; annulus membranous, distant from stipe apex but not median, striate on upper surface. Spores 7-9 x 4.5-5 μm, smooth. Pleurocystidia (34) 40-60 x 10-18 μm, ± utriform, some with 1-3 subapical protuberances.

Gregarious to scattered under hardwoods, spring and early summer, Great Lakes area south and eastward, also in aspen areas of the Rocky Mountains.

15b Pleurocystidia ± acute at apex. Fig. 309 ....
.... *P. longistriata* (Murr.) Smith

Figure 309

Figure 309   *Psathyrella longistriata*

Pileus 3-10 cm, conic to convex, becoming plane or umbonate-expanded, at first thinly coated with veil fibrils, glabrescent, smooth to rugulose, ± translucent-striate when moist, color variable but in honey brown to vinaceous-brown or brownish gray ranges. Gills close, adnate-seceding, ± broad, pale buff when young. Stipe 4-10 cm x 4-10 mm, equal, fragile, pallid to white, veil remnants scattered from annulus downward; annulus membranous, striate on upper side. Spores 7-9 x 4-5 μm. Pleurocystidia 40-72 x 10-17 μm, apex typically acute.

Scattered on humus and duff in conifer and mixed forests, Pacific Northwest, fall, common.

16a   Pleurocystidia absent **17**

16b   Pleurocystidia present **19**

17a   Pileus reddish brown; stipe staining yellow .... *P. waltersii* **Smith**

Pileus 3-9 cm, subovoid, becoming campanulate, finally broadly conic to expanded-umbonate, canescent from a thin coating of whitish fibrils, glabrescent, dark reddish brown fading finally to whitish, margin often splitting radially. Gills ± crowded, adnate-seceding, ± broad, white, slowly becoming dark violaceous brown. Stipe 5-12 cm x 8-10 mm, hollow, fibrous, scurfy above. Spores 9-12.5 x 5-6 μm, in face view ovate to elliptic, in profile obscurely inequilateral.

Clustered on hardwood stumps and debris, Great Lakes area, summer and fall, not uncommon during warm wet seasons.

17b   Pileus white to grayish at first **18**

18a   Pileus white, becoming grayish as spores mature; habitat lignicolous (on hardwoods) .... *P. huronensis* **Smith**

Pileus 4-8 cm, conic to campanulate, glabrous; margin appendiculate, white becoming grayish as spores mature. Gills white, finally cocoa- to chocolate-brown, crowded, narrow, ascending. Stipe 9-14 cm x 6-10 mm, fragile, white. Spores 8-11 x 5-6 μm, ovate to elliptic in face view, in profile obscurely inequilateral.

Clustered on wood of maple, including scars on living trees, fall, Great Lakes area (the Huron Peninsula of Michigan).

18b   Pileus pallid to gray at first; habitat on humus under aspens in Rocky Mountains. Fig. 310 .... *P. uliginicola* McKnight & Smith

Figure 310

Figure 310   *Psathyrella uliginicola*

Pileus 5-10 cm, obtuse to globose, becoming hemispheric to broadly convex, pallid to grayish, darker as spores mature, faintly silky at first, context pallid becoming grayish. Gills 5-6 mm broad (wider in old caps), close, thin, pallid then dark vinaceous brown to purple-brown at maturity. Stipe 8-12 cm x 12-15 mm, equal, hollow, rigid and brittle, white, decorated with scattered veil fibrils, basal area discoloring from handling. Spores 10-12 x 5-6 μm, in face view oblong to elliptic or ovate, in profile ± bean-shaped.

Solitary to scattered on wet soil under aspen, especially around beaver ponds, spring and summer; a characteristic species of the aspen stands of the Rocky Mountains.

19a Pileus pale to dark gray or brownish gray before spores mature .... *P. subagraria* (Atk.) Sm.

Pileus (2) 3-7 (10) cm, convex to broadly convex, surface first thinly coated with veil fibrils, soon glabrous, color not changing much from youth to age. Gills narrow, ± subdistant to close, pallid to grayish, finally dull purplish brown. Stipe 6-12 cm x 3-12 mm, ± equal, white, rather fragile. Spores 8-10 x 4.5-5.5 μm (10-12 x 4.5-5.5 μm from 2-spored basidia), in face view oblong to elliptic, in profile obscurely inequilateral to ± bean-shaped.

Scattered to gregarious on wet soil (as in elm swamps), summer and fall; Great Lakes region and on the Oregon coast; not uncommon in the Lakes area.

19b Pileus dark rusty brown to a redder brown when young 20

20a Veil present (check unexpanded pilei) 21

20b Veil absent 24

21a Pleurocystidia with a finger-like apical prolongation or the cell ninepin-shaped 22

21b Pleurocystidia fusoid-ventricose to utriform 23

22a On wood of hardwoods; stipe whitish at maturity and not distinctly discoloring .... *P. delineata* (Pk.) Sm.

Pileus 3-10 cm, obtuse to convex or ± plane, at first with a thin coating of superficial fibrils, dark rusty brown to dark bay brown, slowly fading to tan, surface often rugulose; margin at first appendiculate, glabrescent. Gills close, ± broad, adnate, soon concolorous with pileus. Stipe 6-10 cm x 5-15 mm, hollow, whitish, fibrillose below. Spores 6.5-9 x 4.5-5.5 μm, ovate in face view, in profile obscurely bean-shaped. Pleurocystidia 34-68 x 10-22 μm.

Scattered to gregarious on debris of hardwoods, mostly east of the Great Plains, rare on the Pacific Coast; summer and fall.

22b On wood of conifers; stipe pale brown at maturity and ± glabrous .... *P. tsugae* Smith

Pileus 4-10 cm, obtuse then expanded-umbonate or broadly convex, glabrous, rugulose, dark cinnamon brown, with the margin appendiculate with veil remnants at first. Gill close, broad, adnate, dark rusty brown when young. Stipe 5-10 x 1-1.5 cm, ± equal, brownish when mature. Spores 7-9 x 3.7-4.5 μm, ± wedge-shaped in face view, somewhat bean-shaped in profile. Pleurocystidia 34-78 (90) x 9-13 μm, ninepin-shaped.

Clustered on logs and stumps of hemlock, late summer, northern Michigan.

23a Veil pale tan; fruiting on conifer debris .... *P. turnagainensis* **Wells & Kempton in Smith**

Pileus 3-9 cm, convex becoming broadly convex or at times with a low umbo, dark rich chestnut brown; margin at first appendiculate with veil remnants. Gills adnexed, narrow, close, pale tan then chocolate brown. Stipe 5-14 cm x 8-18 mm, equal, ivory-white, with a median zone where the veil breaks and patches of the veil present below it. Spores 7.5-9.5 x 4.2-5.3 μm. Pleurocystidia capitate or the apex divided into 2-3 lobes, 35-65 x 9-13 μ.

Gregarious to clustered, Alaska, summer and fall.

23b Veil white (see young pilei); on hardwood debris and humus in low wet woods. Fig. 311 .... *P. larga* (Kauffman) Smith

Figure 311

Figure 312

Figure 311 *Psathyrella larga*

Pileus 4-14 cm, ovoid to campanulate then expanded to plane to broadly umbonate, at first dotted with white deciduous veil particles, bay brown fading to pale tan. Gills broad, close, adnate, white at first then fuscous. Stipe 5-10 cm x 5-15 mm, ± equal, shining, white, ± longitudinally striate. Spore 7-9.5 x 4-4.5 μm. Pleurocystidia 64-80 x 12-20 μm, apex broadly rounded.

Solitary or in small clusters, spring and early summer, Great Lakes region.

24a Spore deposit with a strong red tone (to dull brick red) .... *P. sublateritia* **Smith**

Pileus 3-10 cm, obtuse to convex or with a low umbo, moist, glabrous, vinaceous-brown, paler vinaceous faded; margin often uplifted in age. Gills ± close to subdistant, broad, adnate, brownish pallid, in age dull brick red. Stipe 6-10 cm x 8-20 mm, white to dingy, ± equal. Spores 7.5-9 (10) x 4.5-5.5 μm, in profile ± bean-shaped. Pleurocystidia 40-60 x 10-20 μm, broadly fusoid, wall thickened to 2-3 μm in some, apex often incrusted at first.

Clustered on and around hardwood stumps, logs, etc., often on *Populus.* (cottonwood and aspen), widely distributed in the United States and Canada, summer and fall.

24b Spore deposit gray-brown with hardly a tinge of vinaceous and as air dried fuscous gray. Fig. 312 .... *P. spadicea* **(Fr.) Sing.**

Figure 312 *Psathyrella spadicea*

Pileus 3-6 (10) cm, obtuse to convex or nearly plane, glabrous, moist, hygrophanous, pale date brown to pale or dark chocolate brown or pale dingy clay-color faded. Gills ± adnate, narrow at first then broad, close, pallid becoming dark purple-brown. Stipe 4-8 (12) cm x 4-10 (12) mm, ± equal, pruinose above. Spores 7-9 (10) x 4-5.5 μm, in profile obscurely inequilateral. Pleurocystidia 36-58 (67) x 9-15 (18) μm, broadly fusoid, wall 2-3 μm thick in neck in some, apex acute.

Clustered on stumps and dead trees of cottonwood and aspen, spring and fall, widely distributed and fairly common.

Key B

1a **On grassy ground; spring and summer; veil absent; spores ornamented with plate-like patches of outer wall material. Fig. 313** .... *P. foenisecii* **(Fr.) Sm.**

Figure 313

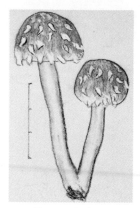

Figure 314

Figure 313 *Psathyrella foenisecii*

Pileus 1-3 (4) cm, obtusely conic to convex, fin-ally nearly plane, glabrous, moist, hygrophanous, dark reddish to grayish or violaceous brown, pale to pallid faded; context fragile, taste acidulous. Gills adnate, seceding, close to subdistant, broad and ventricose, chocolate brown to violaceous brown at maturity. Stipe 4-8 cm x 1.5-3.5 mm, equal, fragile, dingy brownish to pallid, ± naked. Spore deposit dark vinaceous brown. Spores 12-15 x 6.5-9 μm (ornamentation visible under an oil-immersion lens). Pleurocystidia present as scat-tered pseudocystidia.

The haymaker's mushroom is widely dis-tributed, common, fruits in the spring and sum-mer on grassy areas, and is poisonous if eaten in quantity.

1b Not as above 2

2a Growing on burned areas. Fig. 314 ....
.... *P. carbonicola* **Smith**

Figure 314 *Psathyrella carbonicola*

Pileus (1.5) 3-6 cm, obtusely conic to convex, at first with a heavy coating of outer veil fibrils but these superficial and soon weathered away, color chocolate brown to dark yellow-brown or finally paler grayish brown and then striatulate, finally fading. Gills narrow, close to crowded, adnate, pallid brown then dark yellow-brown to finally chocolate brown. Stipe 3-7 cm x 2-5 (6) mm, equal, white, fibrillose (from veil) up to the an-nular zone (rarely with a membranous annulus). Spores (6) 6.5-7.5 (8) x 3-4.2 μm. Pleurocys-tidia 34-58 x 9-14 μm, apex sharply pointed.

Gregarious to clustered on burned areas within a year or two after the fire; western United States and adjacent Canada, also in the Great Lakes region, common after rains.

2b On wood, duff, humus, sandy areas, etc 3

3a On sand dunes along with dune grasses ....
.... *P. arenulina* (Pk.) **Sm.**

Pileus 1-3 cm, convex becoming plane or mar-gin uplifted, rarely umbonate, dark brown young, grayer as spores mature, pallid when faded. Gills close, adnate, broad, cinnamon brown becoming fuscous brown. Stipe 3-5 cm x 1.5-3.5 mm, pal-lid, originating deep in the sand and this portion greatly enlarged by bound sand. Spores 9-12 (15) x 5-6 μm. Pleurocystidia none or very rare.

Scattered in proximity of dune grass, caps often hardly projecting above the sand; summer and fall; Great Lakes region. A closely related species, *P. ammophila* (Dur. & Lév.) Orton, is more widely distributed but favors the same habitat.

3b   Not associated with sand-dune plants 4

4a   Universal veil pale yellow ....
.. P. luteovelata Smith

Pileus 2-4 cm, obtusely conic becoming broadly campanulate, surface covered by delicate pale yellow veil fibrils which soon disappear, dull cinnamon to rusty brown, grayer as spores mature, margin at first appendiculate. Gills adnate, seceding, close, broad, brownish then brownish gray from spores. Stipe 4-5 cm x 2.5-3.5 mm, fragile, whitish, with yellow fibrils from veil at first. Spores 7-9 x 3.5-4 μm. Pleurocystidia 38-56 x 10-15 μm, apex obtuse to $\pm$ acute.

Solitary to gregarious under hardwoods, spring and fall, Pacific Northwest, apparently rare.

4b   Outer veil (if present) white to pallid 5

5a   Brown-walled setae scattered on (projecting from) the cuticle of the pileus 6

5b   Lacking brown-walled setae in cuticle of pileus 7

6a   Solitary to gregarious; no ozonium around base of stipe. Fig. 315 ....
.... P. conopilea (Fr.) Pears. & Dennis

Figure 315

Figure 315   *Psathyrella conopilea*

Pileus (1.5) 2-4 cm, conic and 2-3 cm high, glabrous, moist, smooth, bright fulvous, duller as spores mature. Gills close, narrow, adnate, pale dingy tan then finally blackish brown. Stipe 6-15 cm x 2-3.5 mm, equal, strict, fragile, hollow, dull white; veil rudimentary to absent. Spores 14-17 x 7-8.5 μm. Pleurocystidia none. Setae of pileus 100-250 x 4-8 μm, with thick brown walls.

Solitary to gregarious on sticks and debris, rich humus or well manured soil; widely distributed; spring and fall.

6b   Growing in dense clusters; stipe bases showing tanwy mycelium but not always in abundance (an ozonium) ....
.... P. circellatipes Benoist

Pileus 1-4.5 cm, ovate, expanding to conic or convex, glabrous, moist, striatulate before fading, fulvous becoming grayer as spores mature; margin straight at first. Gills close, moderately broad, adnate-seceding, pallid to brownish, finally $\pm$ fuscous as spores mature. Stipe 4-7 cm x 1-5 mm, equal, fragile, white to pallid with brownish flecks of tomentum around base or a tawny mycelium present. Spores (10) 11-14 x 6-8 μm. Pleurocystidia none. Setae on pileus cuticle scattered, with thick brown walls, up to 250 x 11 μm.

In extensive clusters or densely gregarious on or near wood of aspen and cottonwood; western North America. It is characteristic of the aspen areas of the Rocky Mountains.

7a Pleurocystidia absent 8

7b Pleurocystidia present 10

8a Pileus rusty tan before fading or the spores
    have matured. Fig. 316 ....
    .... *P. hymenocephala* (**Pk.**) **Sm.**

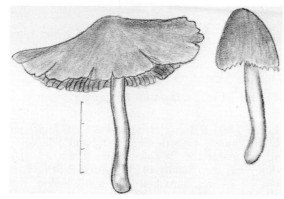

Figure 316

Figure 316 *Psathyrella hymenocephala*

Pileus 2-4 (7) cm, obtusely conic, then convex
to plane or expanded-umbonate, at first thinly
coated with pale buff veil fibrils, glabrescent,
fading to dingy buff; margin at first appendiculate. Gills close, narrow, adnate-seceding, pallid
when young, slowly changing to purplish brown.
Stipe 3-6 (10) cm x 1.5-5 (10) mm, white, hollow, at first with scattered veil fibrils. Spores
6-8 (9) x (3.5) 4-4.5 (5) μm.
     Scattered to gregarious under hardwoods,
summer and early fall, widely distributed and
common in North America.

8b Pileus pallid to pale yellow or honey-color
    9

9a Pileus ± honey-color when moist; spores 7-9
    (10) × 4-5 μm. Fig. 317 ....
    .... *P. candolleana* (**Fr.**) **Maire**

Figure 317

Figure 317 *Psathyrella candolleana*

Pileus 3-7 (11) cm, obtusely conic, remaining so
or finally convex to expanded-umbonate, ± pale
to medium buff when faded, surface soon glabrous; margin appendiculate at first. Gills ±
crowded, narrow, adnate, pallid becoming grayish brown or violaceous toned. Stipe 4-10 (13)
x 3-8 (10) mm, whitish, fibrillose from veil at
first (rarely with a membranous annulus). Spores
7-10 x 4-5 μm.
     Gregarious to caespitose on or near hard-
wood stumps and debris, spring and early summer, common and widely distributed—one of the
very common species in "suburbia." Edible.

9b Pileus pale yellow; spores 6-7.5 × 3.5-4 μm
    .... *P. incerta* (**Pk.**) **Sm.**

This species is often mistaken for *P. candolleana*,
but has the combination of characters given above.
Both are edible and have the same range.

10a Fruiting bodies in a dense cluster arising from
    a cordlike pseudorhiza; veil rudimentary.
    Fig. 318 .... *P. multipedata* (**Pk.**) **Sm.**

Figure 318

Figure 318 *Psathyrella multipedata*

Pileus 1-4.5 cm, ovoid to obtusely conic, finally broadly conic to ± plane, very soon glabrous over all, pale date brown fading to buff. Gills close, narrow, ascending adnate, pallid then purplish brown. Stipe 5-10 cm x 2-4 mm, whitish, only moderately fragile, pruinose above. Spores (6.5) 7-9 x (3) 3.5-4.5 μm. Pleurocystidia scattered, apex acute to subacute.

Clustered on debris (such as sawdust piles) of hardwood origin; Great Lakes area, frequent after wet weather in late August.

10b Lacking a pseudorhiza **11**

11a Fruiting bodies in large clusters on hardwood remains; veil leaving a thin zone of fibrils along the pileus margin; spores (4) 4.5-5.5 (6) × 3-3.5 μm. Fig. 319 ....
.... *P. hydrophila* **(Fr.) Maire**

Figure 319

Figure 319 *Psathyrella hydrophila*

Pileus 2-5 (7) cm, obtusely conic to convex, finally broadly expanded, glabrous, moist, hygrophanous, dark rusty brown becoming more fuscous as spores mature, finally fading to ± pale tan. Gills crowded, ± narrow, buff-colored at first then dark reddish brown, rarely beaded with droplets. Stipe 3-7 (15) cm x 2-6 (8) mm, equal, pallid. Pleurocystidia with obtuse to broadly rounded apices.

Caespitose to gregarious on hardwood debris, common in North America, mostly fruiting fairly late in the fall.

11b Fruiting bodies scattered to gregarious; terrestrial **12**

12a Stipe 6-12 cm × 1-2.5 (3) mm; veil absent, spores (10) 11-14 (15) × 6.5-8 μm ....
.... *P. gracilis* **(Fr.) Quél.**

Pileus 1.5-3.5 (5) cm, conic to conic-campanulate or nearly plane, at times convex, glabrous, striate, clay-color to darker yellowish brown, becoming lead-color as spores mature, when faded often tinged pink along margin. Gills ± broad, close, adnate, pallid becoming ± fuscous, edges at times tinged pink. Stipe equal, strict, pallid, ± pruinose but soon naked. Pleurocystidia 54-75 x 10-16 μm, apex acute to subacute.

Scattered to gregarious on soil and debris, at times in grassy places, widely distributed in North America.

12b Stipe 4-12 cm × 2.5-6 mm; veil present but thin; spores 7-9 (10) × 5-6 μm ....
.... *P. spadiceogrisea* (Fr.) Maire

Pileus 2-8 cm, conic to convex to campanulate or plane to umbonate, with scattered patches of fibrils near the margin, soon glabrous, when moist ± translucent-striate, rusty brown becom-ing grayer as spores mature. Gills close, adnate, ± broad, pallid brown becoming grayer as spores mature. Stipe whitish, hollow. Pleurocystidia 32-48 x 9-15 μm, obtuse to rounded at apex.

Gregarious on wet muck along edges of swamps and pools, spring and early summer, not uncommon, Great Lakes area.

Pseudocoprinus Kühner

Pileus thin, fragile, plicate-striate; hymenium with brachybasidioles as supporting elements for the basidia; spores ± black in deposits, with an apical germ pore; pileus cuticle cellular to hymeniform; autodigestion not destroying the gill tissue following spore discharge (at most occurring along the gill edges under condi-tions of very high humidity).

The genus is distinguished from *Psathy-rella* by having both a plicate-striate pileus and brachybasidioles in the hymenium as the fruiting body reaches maturity. *Psathyrella* may have one or the other or neither of these two features. In *Coprinus* the gills are de-stroyed by autodigestion. Fewer than a dozen species of *Pseudocoprinus* are known.

We treat only one species. Fig. 320 ....
.... *P. disseminatus* (Fr.) Kühner

Figure 320

Figure 320   *Pseudocoprinus disseminatus*

Pileus 5-10 (15) mm broad, conic to convex, plicate ± to disc, pale buff to honey brown, be-coming gray over marginal area as spores mature. Gills subdistant, broad, white then black from spores but paler in age after spores are dispersed. Stipe 2-3 cm x 0.5-1 mm, white, very delicate. Spores 7-9 (10) x 4-4.5 μm, apex truncate from a hyaline pore. Basidia of 3 lengths, 4-spored.

Occurring in troops of hundreds of fruiting bodies on, or from, hardwood debris (often buried in the soil); spring, summer, and fall; common and widely distributed.

BOLBITIACEAE Singer

Spore deposit bright rusty brown to fulvous or earth brown; spores with an apical pore often causing the apex to appear flattened or truncate (cut off); cuticle of pileus in the form of an hymeniform palisade of ± upright clavate cells, or in some the layer interrupted but then no cutis (as in the Strophariaceae) is evident; or the cuticle consisting of a layer 1-3 cells deep of short greatly inflated cells (± globose often times in age) thus resembl-ing the cuticle of many species of *Psathyrella* (see Coprinaceae).

The color of the spore deposit inter-grades with that of the Strophariaceae in some species such as *Agrocybe dura* but here a study of the pileus cuticle in young pilei allows a clear distinction to be made.

KEY TO GENERA

1a Pileus viscid, plicate-striate at maturity; brachybasidioles present in the mature hymenium; fruiting body soft and ± readily collapsing ...... (p. 231) *Bolbitius*

1b Not as above 2

2a Spore deposit a dull brown (coffee-brown, earth-brown, etc. but not orange-rusty to bright tawny or ochraceous); stipe mostly over 4 mm wide at apex .... (p. 227) *Agrocybe*

2b Spore deposit bright ochraceous brown to orange-tawny to bright fulvous; stipe mostly under 4 mm thick at apex (but see *C. intrusus* with a thick stipe) .... (p. 233) *Conocybe*

Agrocybe Fayod

Spore deposit rusty brown to earth brown; spores having an apical pore often broad enough so that the spore appears truncate at the apex; stipe typically fleshy but very narrow in a number of species; pileus cuticle at first a layer of inflated cells or cells clavate and in an hymeniform palisade(but the layer in some species collapsing and then difficult to demonstrate in mature caps); partial veil present or absent.

brous, shining white. Spores 9-11 x 5-6.5 μm, truncate. Pleurocystidia 30-55 x 10-18 μm, clavate-pedicellate to fusoid-ventricose and with broadly rounded apices. Cheilocystidia similar to pleurocystidia.

Gregarious on dung, eastern United States, summer, apparently rare.

2b Taste mild to farinaceous 3

3a On wood of hardwood trees; pileus very dark brown when young and fresh. Fig. 321 .... *A. firma* (Pk.) Sing.

KEY TO SPECIES

1a Veil absent 2

1b Veil present (often as an annulus on the stipe) 6

2a Taste of raw context very bitter .... *A. amara* (Murr.) Sing.

Pileus 3-4 cm, convex to nearly plane, dingy ochraceous to isabelline, margin only slightly incurved; context whitish, odor farinaceous. Gills slightly sinuate, crowded, pallid becoming rusty brown, narrow. Stipe about 5 cm x 5 mm, smooth, gla-

Figure 321

Figure 321 *Agrocybe firma*

Pileus 2-7 (9) cm, ± convex becoming plane or with a broad low umbo, glabrous, blackish brown becoming dark grayish brown and finally paler to clay-color; margin inrolled and opaque when moist. Gills earth brown becoming ± clay-color, close, becoming broad, adnate. Stipe 4-8 cm x 5-10 mm, concolorous with gills, grayish pruinose near apex, interior brownish, with white basal rhizomorphs. Spores 7-9 (10) x 4-5 μm, apex not truncate. Pleurocystidia 30-35 (48) x 12-20 μm, ventricose and with hardly any neck, apex broadly rounded. Cheilocystidia 25-36 x 9-13 μm, fusoid-ventricose with narrow necks and subacute apex.

Caespitose to gregarious on rotting hardwood, North Central and Eastern United States and southward, summer and fall, common during wet seasons, at times in abundance. Edibility not known?

3b On soil humus **4**

4a Stipe 4-8 (10) mm thick. Fig. 322 ....
.... **A. sororia (Pk.) Sing.**

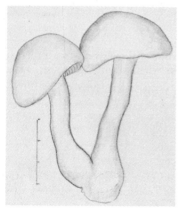

Figure 322

Figure 322 *Agrocybe sororia*

Pileus 5-10 cm, convex to broadly umbonate, sometimes wrinkled and/or pitted, subviscid, tawny, often a darker zone near the margin, fading in age; odor and taste farinaceous. Gills narrow, adnate, pallid, dull brown as spores mature.

Stipe 4-12 mm long, equal, striate at apex, pale tawny within. Spores 8-11 x 6-7 μm, apex truncate. Pleurocystidia 32-48 x 12-20 μm, utriform. Cheilocystidia ± similar to pleurocystidia to smaller and apex merely obtuse.

Solitary to gregarious in open grassy areas, around compost, etc., east of the Great Plains, not common but at times fruiting in great abundance. (Edibility not known?).

4b Stipe 1.5-3 mm thick **5**

5a Gills distant; fruiting body arising from a black sclerotium .... **A. tuberosa (Henn.) Sing.**

Pileus 1-2 cm, campanulate to convex, glabrous, yellow then brown; context tawny, taste mild, odor farinaceous. Gills broad, rather thick, sinuate, cream color then ocher-brownish. Stipe 2-5 x 1-2.5 mm, with an ovoid bulb, with a long pseudorhiza or several rhizomorphs arising from a globose fuscous to black sclerotium having a white homogeneous interior; stipe surface pruinose overall, buff to brownish to a paler area near apex. Spores 8-10 x 4-5 μm, only obscurely truncate. Pleurocystidia abundant, 36-54 x 10-18 μm broadly fusoid-ventricose, apices obtuse to rounded. Cheilocystidia similar to pleurocystidia.

Scattered to gregarious, particularly in garden soil, found so far in Indiana, apparently rare or seldom recognized, widely distributed in the Northern Hemisphere.

5b Gills close; sclerotia absent. Fig. 323 ....
.... **A. pediades (Fr.) Fayod**

Figure 323

Figure 323   *Agrocybe pediades*

Pileus 8-25 mm, hemispheric to broadly convex, glabrous, tacky when young but soon merely moist, rusty brown to clay-color, fading to ochraceous buff, opaque at all times; context thick, whitish, taste farinaceous. Gills close, broad, adnate and seceding, pallid becoming ± rusty brown Stipe 2-5 cm long, 1.5-3 mm thick, equal, at first more or less fibrillose-furfuraceous, glabrescent, pale buff above, yellowish brown near base. Spores 9-13 x 6.6-7.5 x 7.5-9 μm, somewhat compressed, truncate. Pleurocystidia 30-66 x 8-14 μm, fusoid-ventricose with acute to subcapitate tips. Cheilocystidia similar to pleurocystidia.

Scattered to gregarious on grassy areas, waste land, poor pastures; common and widely distributed, summer.

6a   Pileus dark brown from youth to age; gills soon decurrent. Fig. 324 .... *A. erebia* (**Fr.**) **Kühner**

Figure 324

Figure 324   *Agrocybe erebia*

Pileus (1) 2-5 cm, obtuse to convex becoming plane to slightly umbonate, viscid, soon dry, glabrous, dark fuscous brown to dark reddish brown, fading to clay-color; context brownish. Gills adnate to ± decurrent, subdistant, intervenose, broad, brownish then dull rusty brown. Stipe 3-7 cm x 3-10 mm, ± equal, pallid and pruinose near apex, dull brown lower down and fibrillose; an-

nulus pallid, thin but membranous. Spores 11-15.5 x 5-6.5 μm, apex snout-like. Pleurocystidia 50-75 x 9-15 μm, narrowly fusoid-ventricose, apex obtuse. Cheilocystidia 26-35 x 10-16 μm, ventricose and apex broadly rounded, or similar to pleurocystidia.

Scattered to gregarious in hardwoods and conifer woods alike, not uncommon in late summer and fall in northern USA and in Canada. Authors differ on the spore size of this species.

6b   Not as above 7

7a   **Stipe 2-3 mm thick; growing in marshes and bogs; annulus thin and membranous** .... *A. paludosa* (**Lange**) **Küh. & Rom.**

Pileus 1.5-3 cm, convex to broadly convex or nearly plane, glabrous, viscid, olivaceous gray fading to cinnamon buff or along the margin pallid, slightly striate moist; context pallid, soft, odor and taste mild. Gills grayish becoming pale cinnamon-brown, close, broad, adnate at first. Stipe 5-8 cm x 2-3 mm, equal, near base dull brown, pallid to brownish above, glabrous below the superior annulus. Spores 9-11 x 5-6.5 x 4.5-5.5 μm, slightly compressed, apex truncate. Pleurocystidia 36-48 x 15-20 μm, broadly fusoid-ventricose with short necks and obtuse to rounded apices. Cheilocystidia 14-18 x 5-8 μm (small), clavate-pedicellate to fusoid-ventricose.

Scattered in wet meadows, marshes and swamps, on organic debris, northern United States and probably abundant in Canada, summer and early fall, not rare but apparently seldom collected.

7b   **Stipe 4-12 mm thick near apex** 8

8a   **Spores 10-14 × 6.5-8 μm; pileus white at first. Fig. 325** .... *A. dura* (**Fr.**) **Sing.**

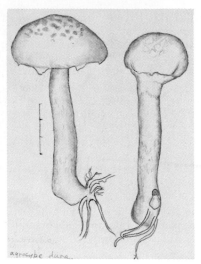

Figure 325

Figure 326

Figure 326   *Agrocybe acericola*

Pileus 3-7 (10) cm, obtuse expanding to plane or with a low umbo, glabrous, moist, hygrophanous, margin even and opaque; odor and taste farinaceous. Gills pallid to buff, becoming grayish brown, crowded, adnate or with a decurrent tooth, broad. Stipe 5-10 cm long, equal, hollow, fibrous, whitish but becoming bister from the base upward, apex pallid and striate; annulus membranous, cream-color. Spores 8-10.5 x 5-6.5 μm, truncate. Pleurocystidia 40-50 x 12-22 μm, clavate-mucronate to $\pm$ utriform or with 1-3 apical projections. Cheilocystidia clavate.

Solitary to scattered on decaying hardwood logs and debris, common and widely distributed in North America, summer and fall. Not recommended for the table.

9b   Pileus $\pm$ cream color at first, clay color in age; veil submembranous and annulus soon broken. Fig. 327 ....
.... *A. praecox* (**Fr.**) **Fayod**

Figure 325   *Agrocybe dura*

Pileus (3) 4-9 (12) cm, convex to plane, at times with a low umbo, glabrous, soft to the touch, smooth becoming areolate, white becoming buff-tinged at least on disc; taste mild to slightly disagreeable. Gills close, broad, adnate to sinuate, white becoming $\pm$ purplish brown. Stipe 4-10 cm x (3) 5-15 mm, equal, solid, white, fibrillose but glabrescent, apex $\pm$ pruinose; veil white, thin, forming a thin superior evanescent annulus or remains of veil appendiculate on pileus margin. Spores truncate. Pleurocystidia 35-48 (56) x 10-18 (24) μm, ventricose-pedicellate and apex broadly rounded.

Gregarious to solitary on lawns, waste grassland, shrub borders, and pastures; summer, common, northern United States and probably southward. It favors hot wet weather for fruiting. Edible.

8b   Spores 8-11 $\times$ 5-7 μm; pileus becoming clay-color **9**

9a   Pileus dark yellow-brown when young; annulus well formed and $\pm$ persistent; on or near hardwood debris. Fig. 326 ....
.... *A. acericola* (**Pk.**) **Sing.**

Figure 327

Figure 327 *Agrocybe praecox*

Pileus (2) 3-9 (11) cm, obtuse to convex, becoming plane or with a low umbo, glabrous, soft to the touch, disc becoming areolate; context white, odor and taste farinaceous. Gills adnate, close, broad, pallid, finally clay color. Stipe 3-10 cm x (3) 4-12 mm, equal, with white rhizomorphs at base, apex pruinose; veil submembranous, often as patches appendiculate on pileus margin. Spores 8-11 x 5-6 μm, truncate. Pleurocystidia 38-50 x 10-18 μm, utriform. Cheilocystidia similar to pleurocystidia.

Scattered to gregarious on humus and chip-dirt, in lawns, fields, and open woods, common, spring and early summer, widely distributed. Edible.

Bolbitius Fries

Spore deposit orange-brown to bright rusty brown, varying to ochraceous or ochraceous brown; pileus viscid and $\pm$ plicate-striate at maturity; brachybasidioles usually present in the hymenium at maturity; consistency of pileus very soft and fruiting body readily collapsing though not deliquescing as in *Coprinus;* gills semi-deliquescing in some species; spores $\pm$ truncate; pileus cuticle hymeniform to cellular. *Pluteolus* is a later name that has been applied to some species in this genus.

Figure 328

KEY TO SPECIES

1a On wood (wet sticks and/or debris on the forest floor) 2

1b On manured soil or manure, or on grassy areas fertilized or not 3

2a Pileus olivaceous fading to rusty red on disc. Fig. 328 .... *P. callistus* Pk.

Figure 328 *Pluteolus callistus*

Pileus 1.5-3.5 cm, obtusely campanulate to expanded-umbonate, glabrous, slimy, at first dull olive to yellowish olive on margin and soon rusty red on disc and orange toward margin, only faintly striatulate at first. Gills free, narrow, close, yellow becoming rusty brown. Stipe 3-5 cm x 1.5-3 mm, densely pruinose, ground-color orange-yellow, olive to bluish-green around the base. Spores 8-10 x 5-6 μm, truncate. Cheilocystidia 28-36 x 7-9 μm, narrowly fusoid-ventricose, with an obtuse apex and often undulating walls.

Scattered on sticks and other lignicolous debris in wet places, usually one or two fruit bodies at a time; rare (or only rarely collected ?); Great Lakes area eastward.

2b Pileus white .... *B. sordidus* C. G. Lloyd

Pileus 2-4 cm, conic becoming campanulate to plane, slimy, glabrous, sulcate-striate on margin in age. Gills narrow, close, free, white, becoming pale ochraceous tawny, soft (but not deliquescing). Stipe 3-8 cm x 4-6 mm, hollow, very fragile, floccose, with snow-white fibrils but no veil evident. Spores 8-10.5 x 5-6 μm. Cheilocystidia 30-40 (50) x 9-14 μm, fusoid-ventricose with obtuse apices.

Solitary on wood of hardwoods, sawdust and shavings, infrequently recognized, Great Lakes area.

3a On grassy areas; lawns, golf courses, etc. Fig. 329 .... *Gasterocybe lateritia* Watling

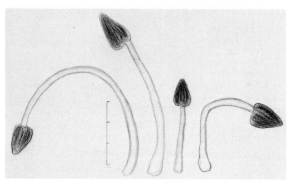

Figure 329

Figure 329 *Gasterocybe lateritia*

Pileus 5-30 mm, ellipsoid to campanulate, not completely expanding, at maturity nodding or bent over and touching the ground (not in an upright position), viscid, striate, chestnut to rusty brown, very soft and mushy. Gills (hymenophore) well formed, rusty brown, interveined and fused (honeycomb-like). Stipe 50-130 x 1-1.5 mm, white, straight at first then bending over. Spore print not obtainable. Spores (9.5) 10-12 (14) x (6) 7-8 μm. Cheilocystidia capitate, head about 4 μm wide, ventricose part ± 7 μm wide, neck flexuous and 1-2 μm thick.

It fruits during hot humid summer weather

in the area east of the Great Plains. This species, often mistaken for a true agaric, is a gasteromycete of the *Secotium*-type (with pileus, "gills," and stipe), and is regarded as representing a mutation from some species of *Bolbitius*.

3b On manure or manured soil 4

**4a Pileus grayish cinnamon ....
.... *P. coprophilus* Pk.**

Pileus 3-7 cm, oval expanding to plane, viscid, glabrous, becoming plicate-striate, grayish cinnamon to dingy brown on disc. Gills close, narrow to ± broad, pale dingy brown, edges pallid. Stipe 6-12 cm x 3-6 mm, white, ± fibrillose to pubescent (veil absent), very fragile. Spores 12-15 x 6-8 μm. Cheilocystidia clavate, 30-40 x 20-28 μm or 28-40 x 9-12 μm.

On horse manure, eastern United States, not common, summer and fall.

**4b Pileus yellow to greenish yellow; stipe yellow or soon becoming so. Fig. 330 ....
.... *B. vitellinus* (Pers.) Fr.**

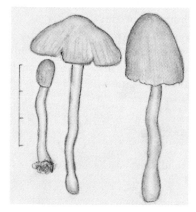

Figure 330

Figure 330 *Bolbitius vitellinus*

Pileus (2.5) 3-7 cm, obtuse to convex becoming plane or disc ± depressed, slimy, tuberculate-striate to plicate, margin often splitting, color ± citron yellow and with disc tinged orange; context watery yellow, soft. Gills attached to stipe, ± close, narrow, pallid to yellow-tinged, finally

± ochraceous tawny. Stipe (4) 6-12 cm x (3) 4-8 mm, very fragile, yellow overall, surface ± scurfy but no veil evident; basal mycelium white. Spores 12-15 x 6-7 μm, apex weakly truncate. Cheilocystidia saccate, about 8-15 μm wide.

Often abundant on manure or manured soil, caespitose-gregarious, summer and fall, Great Lakes area east and southward but widely distributed in addition.

Conocybe Fayod

Spores rusty brown to yellowish brown in deposit, typically with an apical germ pore and apex ± truncate; stipe fleshy to cartilaginous and thin; pileus cuticle hymeniform or of ± greatly inflated cells in a layer one or more cells deep; partial veil annulate, fibrillose, or lacking.

The basidia are 4-spored unless otherwise stated, and clamp connections are present unless the contrary is stated. The genus is a small one, we estimate no more than 50 species for North America. One species contains alpha amanitan, a deadly poison, but the fruiting bodies are so small mushroom hunters pass them by; the danger from poisoning rests mainly from small children picking and eating them raw when, as one doctor put it, they are in the "grazing stage."

KEY TO SPECIES

1a Annulus typically present (veil membranous) 2

1b Annulus absent (if a veil is present it is fibrillose) 9

2a Growing on dung of herbivores 3

2b Habitat other than the above 4

3a Stipe below annulus faintly fibrillose to glabrous; spores 8-10 (11) × 5-6 μm. Fig. 331 .... *C. stercoraria* Watling

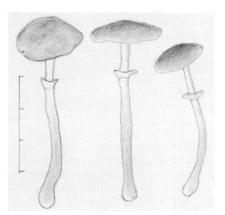

Figure 331

Figure 331 *Conocybe stercoraria*

Pileus 1.5-3.5 cm, obtuse to convex, becoming plane, margin at times with a few veil fragments, otherwise glabrous, yellowish-brown fading to yellowish or pale buff. Gills close, ± broad, depressed-adnate, white at first, soon yellow-brown. Stipe 5-6 cm x 1.5-2 mm, fragile, lower part dark brown, toward apex paler, faintly fibrillose; annulus not striate, its lower surface cottony, very soon evanescent. Spores truncate. Cheilocystidia (28) 30-37 x 7-10 μm, ventricose and apex capitate.

Scattered on horse dung, spring and early summer, Washington, apparently not uncommon along our Pacific Coast.

3b Stipe below annulus fibrillose with buff fibrils; spores 7-9 × 4-4.5 μm........................ .... *C. fimicola* Watling

Pileus 1-2.5 cm and conic, margin straight, becoming broadly conic or margin flaring, glabrous, striatulate, dark rusty brown fading to pale tawny. Gills close, ± broad, adnate, yellow-tawny, edges even. Stipe 3-4 cm x 2-3 mm, ± equal, lower portion yellowish becoming dark brown; annulus ± median, buff-colored, striate on upper surface. Cheilocystidia 24-32 x 7-10 μm, fusoid-ventricose with narrow neck and acute apex.

Gregarious on manure, spring, Washington, apparently rare.

**4a Spores 9-11 × 5-5.5 μm; stipe often flexuous; annulus with a thick cottony margin; growing on debris and detritus from an avalanche in a cold wet mountain habitat ....
.... C. flexipes Watling**

Pileus 5-15 mm, obtusely conic then campanulate, glabrous, hygrophanous, striate when moist, pale tawny fading to pinkish buff. Gills close, broad, adnate but seceding, pale buff becoming pale to medium clay-color. Stipe 5-7 cm x 1-1.5 mm, equal, often flexuous, fragile, tawny near base, pruinose above annulus; annulus pale buff, striate on upper surface, with a thick cottony margin. Spores truncate. Cheilocystidia 26-38 x 6-12 μm, ventricose and narrowed to an obtuse to ± capitate apex but cystidia not lecythiform.

Scattered on avalanche debris, Mt. Rainier National Park, fall, not uncommon in its particular habitat, but not in large numbers.

4b Not as above 5

5a Stipe densely fibrillose below the annulus .... C. pinguis Watling

Pileus 1.5-3.5 cm, convex then plane, glabrous, bright ochraceous brown, margin striate; taste mild. Gills crowded, narrow, depressed-adnate, seceding, pallid then pale tawny. Stipe 7-9 cm x 3-4 mm, equal to slightly enlarged at base, whitish above, dark brown below, fibrillose above the annulus; annulus membranous, striate on upper surface. Spores 7-9 x 4-4.5 μm, apex obscurely truncate. Cheilocystidia 35-45 x 7-10 μm, ventricose-capitate, capitellum 5-7 μm wide.

Gregarious on rotting logs of alder and maple, Washington, spring and early summer, uncommon.

5b Stipe scarcely fibrillose below the annulus 6

6a Veil forming a membranous annulus or more rarely pieces of it adhering to pileus margin; stipe short (1-3 cm); spores 6-8 × 4-5 μm, not truncate .... C. intermedia (Sm.) Küh.

Pileus 1-2 cm, obtusely conic becoming nearly plane, glabrous, hygrophanous, chestnut brown fading to dingy buff, striate when moist, disc often rugose. Gills close, narrow, adnate, ochraceous then tawny brown, edges white-fimbriate. Stipe 2-3 mm thick, dark brown at base paler upward, surface loosely fibrillose above the annulus; annulus median to inferior, its upper surface striate, at times breaking and the pieces adhering to cap margin. Cheilocystidia 18-26 (37) x 6-10 μm, ventricose-capitate.

Scattered on hardwood debris, Great Lakes area, summer and early fall, not common but frequently found.

6b Not as above 7

**7a Annulus seldom well-formed; stipe floccose over all. Fig. 332 ....
.... C. brunnea Lge. & Küh. ex Watl.**

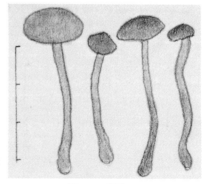

Figure 332

Figure 332 *Conocybe brunnea*

Pileus 5-10 mm, conic to convex, thin, ± plane in age, glabrous except for veil fibrils along margin, bright rusty brown, fading to buff, not striate. Gills close, broad, adnate, pale tawny. Stipe 2.5-3 cm x about 1.5 mm, dark brown near base, clay color toward apex; veil fibrils dingy buff, not forming a true annulus. Spores 8-10 x 4.5-5 μm, not truncate. Cheilocystidia 25-32 x 7-11 x 3-5 μm, capitate.

On rich humus and debris under hardwoods, Washington, spring, apparently rarely collected.

7b Annulus typically well-formed and stipe not floccose overall **8**

8a Spores 9-10.5 × 4-5 μm; pileus rugose-wrinkled. Fig. 333 .... *C. rugosa* (Pk.) Sing.

Figure 333

Figure 333 *Conocybe rugosa*

Pileus (5) 10-25 mm, obtuse then plano-umbonate or remaining campanulate, glabrous, dark rusty brown, fading to clay color, margin striate when moist. Gills adnate to adnexed, crowded, narrow then ± broad, yellowish then tawny, edges white-crenulate. Stipe 2-4 cm x (1.5) 2-3 (4) mm, ± equal, pale ochraceous over all, becoming dark near base, ± glabrous below annulus, pruinose above it; annulus membranous, striate on upper surface, ± cinnamon buff. Spores 9-11 x 4.5-5 μm, truncate. Cheilocystidia 22-30 x 7-12 μm, fusoid-ventricose with obtuse to acute apex.

Gregarious on rich humus and hardwood debris, Great Lakes area, summer and early fall, not common and seldom found in quantity.

8b Spores 7-8.5 (9) × 4-4.5 μm; pileus even (not rugulose) when moist .... *C. arhenii* (Fr.) Kits van Wavern

Pileus 1-3 cm, umbonate to nearly plane, glabrous, cinnamon-brown on disc, margin paler, unicolorous when faded. Gills moderately close, broad, adnate, pale tawny, equal. Stipe 3-5 cm x 2-3.5 mm, lower part dingy tawny and becoming blackish brown, upper area pallid buff and scurfy, fibrillose-striate below the annulus; annulus about median, upper surface striate. Cheilocystidia narrowly fusoid-ventricose the apex obtuse.

On soil, scattered to gregarious, late summer and fall, Great Lakes area, not common. In North America this and several other species together have been identified as *"Pholiota togularis"* previously. For a discussion of *P. togularis* see Kitsvan Wavern, Persoonia 6:119-165 (1970).

9a Stipe greenish to bluish near or at the base; spores 7-9 × 4-4.5 μm .... *C. cyanopus* (Atk.) Kühner

Pileus (3) 5-15 mm, obtusely conic to expanded-umbonate, cinnamon-brown, paler when faded, when fresh translucent-striate, glabrous; context very thin and fragile. Gills close to subdistant, becoming broad, finally cinnamon-tawny. Stipe 1-3 cm x 1-2 mm, with a slight basal bulb, whitish toward the apex. Cheilocystidia (2)0 30-40 x 12-12 μm, fusoid-ventricose, apex ± obtuse.

Scattered on moss and in grass, Great Lakes area and Pacific Northwest, rare (or mostly overlooked ?). *Conocybe smithii* Watling differs from the above chiefly in having subcapitate cheilocystidia.

9a Base of stipe not greenish or bluish **10**

10a Pileus (10) 25-60 mm broad **11**

10b Pileus 5-15 mm broad **13**

11a Stipe 4-15 mm thick, usually abruptly bulbous; pileus 2.5-7 cm broad. Fig. 334 .... *C. intrusa* (Pk.) Singer

Figure 334

Figure 334   *Conocybe intrusa*

Pileus obtuse to convex, becoming nearly plane, glabrous, whitish to dull clay-color or finally ± tawny, viscid; taste slightly of radish. Gills ± adnexed, close, ± broad, whitish then cream-yellow and finally dark brown. Stipe 3-6 cm long, abruptly bulbous, whitish, ± floccose becoming glabrous. Spores 6-8 x 4-5 μm, truncate. Cheilocystidia 20-30 x 7-9 x 4-5 μm, ninepin-shaped, yellow in KOH.

   Scattered to caespitose on compost piles and in greenhouses; probably more common than records indicate. It was placed in *Cortinarius* at the time it was first described.

11b Stipe rarely up to 5 mm thick 12

12a Stipe 4-10 cm × 2-5 mm; gills narrow, crisped and intervenose ....
.... *C. crispa* (Longyr.) Sing.

Pileus 1.5-4 cm, conic-campanulate, glabrous, brownish ochraceous over disc, paler on margin; taste mild. Gills white becoming bright tawny. Stipe white, fragile, slightly enlarged at base. Spores 12-16 x 9-11 μm, truncate. Cheilocystidia 16-19 x 6-9 x 4-5 μm.

   Scattered to gregarious in lawns and other grassy areas, Great Lakes area, not rare, moist warm weather in June and July.

12b Stipe 4-8 (10) cm × 1.5-2 mm, very fragile; gills not crisped or strongly intervenose. Fig. 335 .... *C. lactea* (Lge.) Métrod

Figure 335

Figure 335   *Conocybe lactea*

Pileus 10-25 mm broad, 10-15 mm high, conic, margin often flared, glabrous, creamy white overall or buff on disc; odor and taste not distinctive. Gills very narrow, close, whitish at first, tawny in age. Stipe whitish overall, pruinose, ± equal. Spores 12-16 x 7-9 μm, truncate. Basidia 2-spored. Cheilocystidia 12-16 x 6-10 x 3-4.5 μm, ninepin-shaped.

   Densely gregarious to scattered on lawns and grassy areas generally, northern United States, summer and fall, very common, also common at least at times in the Gulf Coast area.

13a On soil; spores 7-9 × 4-5 μm; stipe darkening in lower part; pileus 6-12 mm; stipe ± 1 mm thick .... *C. filipes* (Atk.) Küh.

Pileus ovoid to conic, glabrous, conspicuously translucent-striate and tawny when fresh. Gills narrow, broad, white then tawny. Stipe pallid above, soon pale tan near base, densely pubescent under a lens. Spores with a small apical pore but not appearing truncate. Cheilocystidia narrowly fusoid, 50-70 x 9-12 μm.

   Scattered on soil, Great Lakes eastward, summer and early fall, not common.

13b On wood 14

14a On rotting conifer wood; spores 8-10 × 4-5 μm .... *C. aberrans* (Kühner) Singer

Pileus 7-16 mm, conic, tawny, striate when moist, at first pruinose. Gills broad, seceding, pale tawny. Stipe 1-2.5 cm x 1-2.5 mm, hollow, fragile, pallid overall, pruinose. Spores with a distinct germ pore. Cheilocystidia 38-55 x 7-10 μm, fusoid with ± acute apex.

Gregarious on rotten conifer logs, Idaho, June, not common.

14b On wood of hardwoods; spores 6-7 × ± 4 μm, apex ± snout-like; taste disagreeable .... C. laricina (Küh.) Küh.

Pileus 5-10 mm, umbonate, with a spreading margin, glabrous, ± cinnamon-brown, striate. Gills dull ochraceous, close, adnate, crenulate. Stipe 2-3 cm x ± 1 mm, dark brown below, minutely pruinose overall. Cheilocystidia 30-40 x 9-16 x 6-8 μm, nine pin-shaped.

Scattered, June, Great Lakes area, apparently rare or at least rarely collected.

STROPHARIACEAE Singer and Smith

Pileus and stipe confluent; stipe typically central in species treated here; spore deposit violaceous brown to fuscous brown or rusty brown; spores with an apical pore usually causing the apex of the spore to appear ± truncate; pileus cuticle a cutis or an ixocutis or an ixotrichodermium, but not hymeniform or cellular.

The family intergrades with the Cortinariaceae through *Galerina*. Most of the species are wood-rotting fungi, but some may be mycorrhiza-formers. The family contains between 400 and 500 species in North America. A number of these are good edible species, and some are conspicuous and common. The family also contains many species having the compounds psilocybin and psilocin. A number

of these are common in some areas such as the Gulf Coast and our Pacific Coast. Species containing these poisons are particularly dangerous to small children if they happen to eat significant amounts.

KEY TO GENERA

1a Spore deposit clay-color (pale tan) to rusty brown .... (p. 237) *Pholiota*

1b Spore deposit ± violaceous brown to cocoa- to chocolate-color ....
.... (p. 249) **see key to**
Stropharia, *Psilocybe*, **and** *Naematoloma*

Pholiota (Fr.) Kummer

Spore deposit rusty brown to earth-brown; spores typically smooth and many with a more or less distinct germ pore; stipe and pileus confluent; Pileus scaly, fibrillose, moist and hygrophanous, viscid or slimy but cuticle neither cellular nor hymeniform; annulus present or absent but fibrillose veil present if no annulus is formed; pleurocystidia present or

absent and if present either as leptocystidia or chrysocystidia or both in a given species; living on dead organic matter, especially on wood.

Pholiota is a large genus of over 200 species in North America some of which are popular with mycophagists. In recent times a number of mildly poisonous species have been discovered, some of which so closely resemble edible ones, that mistakes are very easily made.

KEY TO SPECIES

1a   Occurring on burned ground (following forest fires or where brush has been burned) 2

1b   Habitat on uncharred materials **5**

2a   Veil remnants dull rusty red, scattered over pileus and appendiculate on its margin at first; pileus pale yellow beneath the veil. Fig. 336 .... *P. carbonaria* Smith

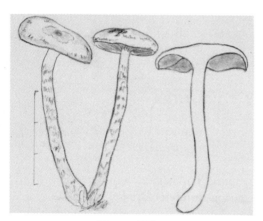

Figure 336

Figure 336   *Pholiota carbonaria*

Pileus 2-4 cm, convex, appendiculate from veil, in age ± cinnamon brown, viscid; odor and taste mild. Gills narrow, crowded, grayish at first. Stipe 3-6 cm x 4-6 mm, ± equal, ground color yellowish. Spores (5) 6-7 (8) x 3.5-4 (4.5) μm. Pleurocystidia 50-88 x 9-14 μm.

   Caespitose to scattered, often abundant in recent burns, Pacific Northwest, summer and fall after rains.

2b   Veil not colored as in above choice 3

3a   Veil remnants orange-brown; pileus tawny on disc and whitish over marginal area. Fig. 337 .... *P. fulvozonata* Smith

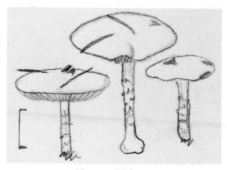

Figure 337

Figure 337   *Pholiota fulvozonata*

Pileus 1-2 cm, conic to campanulate, tawy on disc and margin paler, pellicle tough and separable; odor and taste mild; context quickly green with FeSO$_4$. Gills pallid at first, crowded, adnate. Stipe 1-3 cm x 3-4 mm, pallid beneath the veil remnants. Spores 6-7.5 x 4-4.5 μm. Pleurocystidia 33-46 x 9-16 μm, fusoid-ventricose to utriform. Veil hyphae brown-walled and often with encrusting pigment on the walls as revived in KOH.

   Gregarious, common during some seasons, northern Idaho.

3b   Veil not as above (usually white to yellowish) 4

4a   Stipe (4) 8-10 mm thick, zones of veil on stipe clear yellow; caulocystidia 40-123 × 15-40 μm .... *P. brunnescens* Smith & Hesler

Pileus 2-7 cm, convex to plane, slimy-viscid, ochraceous-brown to dark reddish brown, ± dull orange when faded; taste slightly disagreeable at times (older pilei). Gills whitish at first then ± cinnamon, narrow, crowded. Stipe 4-6 (9) cm long, equal, pallid, staining tawny in age. Spores 6-7 x 4-4.5 μm. Pleurocystidia 48-70 x 9-16 μm, fusoid-ventricose.

   Pacific Northwest, fall, common on recent burns, caespitose to gregarious and on soil as well as charred wood.

4b Stipe (2) 3-6 mm thick; veil remnants on stipe pallid to buff; caulocystidia 45-88 × 7-12 (16) μm .... *P. highlandensis* (Pk.) **Sm. & Hes.**

Pileus 2-4 (6) cm, convex to plano-depressed, viscid, tawny to bright reddish brown, glabrous except for veil remnants along margin at first, fading to pale tan; taste at times ± disagreeable. Gills pallid to yellowish, finally ± cinnamon brown, broad, close. Stipe (1) 2-4 cm long, whitish to yellowish above, lower part soon dark brown; veil remnants pale ochraceous leaving an evanescent fibrillose annular zone. Spores 6-8 x 4-4.5 μm. Pleurocystidia 36-65 (70) x 7-15 μm, fusoid-ventricose.

Common in the United States and Canada; spring summer and fall or winter in the south.

5a Pileus yellow and slimy-viscid, usually scaly; stipe often scaly; usually growing clustered; pleurocystidia lacking a greatly elongated neck (if present mostly as mucronate chrysocystidia) 6

5b Not as above 12

6a Base of stipe surrounded by olive-yellow to tawny pubescence (an ozonium); young lamellae olive-buff .... *P. subvelutipes* **Sm. & Hes.**

Pileus 4-7 cm, convex to plane, margin appendiculate, viscid to slimy, bright pale yellow, olivaceous where bruised, at first decorated with amber brown scales ± 3 mm wide; context white becoming pale yellow. Gills adnate, crowded, fairly broad, finally ± clay-color. Stipe 4-8 x 0.5-1.1 cm, flanged at base, soon yellowish; annular zone of yellow scales; veil pale yellow at first, ± fibrillose. Spores 6.5-8 (9) x 3-4 μm. Pleurocystidia 30-46 x 7-11 μm, content often brown in KOH.

Clustered on hardwood logs, Great Lakes region, late summer and fall, apparently rare.

6b Lacking an ozonium around base of stipe 7

7a Annulus ± persistant, heavy and thick; with tawny patches on under side; on wood of conifers .... *P. filamentosa* (Fr.) **Herpel**

Pileus 4-16 cm, convex, viscid, lemon to ochre yellow, with rusty brown spotlike scales which gelatinize; margin fringed at first; context whitish. yellow-brown around worm holes, with FeSO$_4$ olivaceous. Gills yellow at first, rusty brown in age, broad, close, adnexed. Stipe 4-8 x 1-2 cm, equal, base flanged, yellowish throughout at first but becoming rusty brown below. Spores 6-7.5 (8) x 3.5-4.2 μm. Pleurocystidia 25-40 x 6-13 μm, clavate to mucronate, some with rusty brown content.

Clustered on conifer wood, Pacific Northwest, fall, probably not uncommon in the area.

7b Annulus not well formed (usually absent or merely a zone of fibrils) 8

8a On wood of hardwoods 9

8b On wood of conifers 10

9a Stipe scaly over lower third, less so upward; spores 7-9.5 (11) × 4.5-6 μm. Fig. 338 .... *P. aurivella* (Fr.) **Kummer**

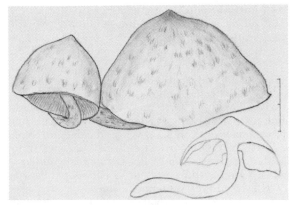

Figure 338

Figure 338 *Pholiota aurivella*

Pileus 4-18 cm, convex to broadly umbonate, ochraceous orange becoming ± tawny, at first with large appressed spot-like scales that gelatinize; context yellow. Gills adnate to sinuate, yellowish becoming rusty brown. Stipe 5-8 x 0.5-1.5 cm, yellowish to pale yellow-brown. Spores in profile view oblong to bean-shaped. Pleurocystidia 30-45 x 4-7 μm, some branched 1-2 times near apex, some with a dark brown content.

On wood of hardwoods, fall and early winter, widely distributed in North America.

9b Stipe ± squamulose up to annular zone; spores 6-7.5 × 4.3-4.8 μm ....
.... *P. squarroso-adiposa* **Lange**

Pileus 3-6 (8) cm, conic to plano-umbonate or broadly convex, slimy-viscid, at first with strap-shaped to triangular recurved scales 3-4 mm long and ± 3 mm wide; dark rusty brown at first but soon bright yellow; context yellow. Gills pale yellow at first, finally rusty brown. Stipe 4-7 x 0.8-1 cm, abruptly flanged at base, pale yellow; inner veil pale yellow, leaving only an evanescent zone. Pleurocystidia 26-35 x 7-11 μm; clavate to oval-pedicellate, content mostly highly refractive.

Clustered to scattered, late summer and fall, especially in the Pacific Northwest, but widely distributed. This is one of the species that has passed under the name of *"Pholiota adiposa"* in the past in North America.

10a Spores 7-9 (10) × 4-5 μm; lamellae with pallid faces and yellow edges at first; scales on pileus wide and gelatinous; stipe also with scattered gelatinous scales ....
.... *P. hiemalis* **Sm. & Hes.**

Pileus 4-11 cm broadly conic to plano-umbonate, very slimy, ochre yellow to lemon yellow; context yellowish, odor ± unpleasant but soon fading, taste mild, with $FeSO_4$ slowly olive. Gills becoming yellow overall, close, broad, adnexed. Stipe 4-9 cm x 6-15 mm, ± enlarged downward to a flaring base, often with an annular fibrillose zone. Pleurocystidia present as chrysocystidia 30-50 x 8-15 μm, clavate-mucronate.

Clustered on wood of *Abies*, late fall and winter, northern Idaho and very likely throughout the Pacific Northwest. POISONOUS.

10b Spores smaller than in above choice **11**

11a Spores 4-5 × 2.5-3 μm. Fig. 339 ....
.... *Pholiota flammans* **(Fr.) Kummer**

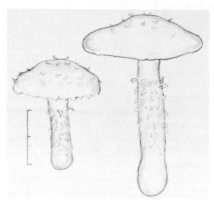

Figure 339

Figure 339 *Pholiota flammans*

Pileus (3) 4-8 (10) cm, broadly umbonate to convex or plane, slightly viscid beneath the coating of recurved fibrillose scales, ± glabrescent, margin fringed at first, brilliant yellow (picric yellow to lemon-chrome); context yellow; odor and taste slight. Gills bright yellow, staining brown on edges where injured, close to crowded. Stipe (3) 5-10 (12) cm x (3) 5-10 mm, ± equal, concolor with pileus, densely recurved-scaly to the veil-line. Pleurocystidia of 2 types: 1) 25-35 x 6-8 μm and clavate to mucronate, content ochraceous; and 2) typical chrysocystidia 26-40 x 6-9 μm (with an amorphous central inclusion.

Solitary to clustered, throughout northern United States south to Tennessee, and the conifer areas of Canada, late summer and fall; not common. Edibility: not recommended.

11b Spores 5.5-7.5 × 3.5-4.5 μm; lamellae pallid brownish at first; scales on pileus not gelatinous .... *P. abietis* **Sm. & Hes.**

Pileus 4-9 (15) cm, broadly convex to plano-umbonate, slimy viscid, margin appendiculate, scales on pileus tawny; context yellow, scales fibrillose and dry; veil leaving an evenescent zone; overall color yellow. Pleurocystidia: 1) 32-46 x 8-12 μm, clavate to mucronate, the content brown; 2) typical chrysocystidia 26-42 x 6-12 μm.

Clustered to gregarious, fall, common in the Pacific Northwest.

12a Pileus powdery to granulose and dry 13

12b Pileus viscid, dry and fibrillose to scaly, or moist and hygrophanous 14

13a Pileus ± orange, 5-15 (30) cm, obtuse to convex then broadly convex to expanded umbonate. Fig. 340 .... *P. aurea* (Fr.) Kummer

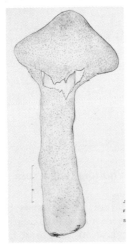

Figure 340

Figure 340 *Pholiota aurea*

Pileus margin often appendiculate; context pallid, odor slight, taste ± astringent. Gills pallid becoming orange-brown, adnate, close, broad in age. Stipe 10-15 (25) x (1.5) 3.5 (6) cm, ± clavate and broader at the base, concolorous with pileus and like it granulose, the granular coating extending up to and including the under side of the membranous annulus. Spores 10.5-13 (14) x 5-6 μm. Pleurocystidia absent to very rare, clavate-mucronate.

Gregarious and clustered on compost piles and rich humus, Pacific Northwest, Canada and Alaska; fall, not common. Edible for some people BUT NOT FOR OTHERS.

13b Pileus dark rusty brown, 1-4 cm broad. Fig. 341 .... *P. erinaceella* (Pk.) Pk.

Figure 341

Figure 341 *Pholiota erinaceella*

Pileus obtuse to convex, then nearly plane, rarely umbonate, the tufted squamules soon broken down to a powder; margin at first appendiculate; context olive-yellowish, with $FeSO_4$ olive, with KOH dark red-brown; taste metallic to bitterish. Gills pallid becoming ochraceous tawny, crowded, broad. Stipe 3-4 (6) x 1.5-4 mm thick, coated with powder and squamules like those on the pileus; annulus soon evanescent. Spores 6-8 (9) x 4-4.5 μm, slightly bean-shaped in profile. Pleurocystidia none. Cheilocystidia (40-) 50-115 x 3.5-6 x (at apex) 9-16 μm, ± cylindric with apex enlarged.

On hardwood debris, solitary to gregarious, summer and fall, northern United States and in Canada.

14a Pileus slimy, blue over all at first .... *P. subcaerulea* Sm. & Hes.

Pileus 2-4 cm, obtuse to convex, becoming expanded-umbonate, surface at first dotted with white flecks of outer veil materials; color fading to pale dingy tan; context thin, bluish, odor and taste mild. Gills brownish becoming cinnamon brown, close, ± broad, adnate. Stipe 3-6 cm x 1.5-4 mm, base with white rhizomorphs, lower half ± covered with floccose patches of the veil, bluish at first, dry; annulus white, evanescent. Spores 7-9 x 4-4.5 μm. Pleurocystidia present as chrysocystidia 24-36 x 9-12 μm.

Solitary or in small clusters on soil and debris, fall, Pacific Northwest, not common.

14b Pileus white to colored, but not blue when young **15**

15a Pileus coarsely innately scaly **16**

15b Pileus not as above (glabrous or with superficial scales) **18**

16a Pileus dark brown; on soil (but from buried wood); spores 4.5-6.5 (7) × 3.5-4.5 μm. Fig. 342 .... *P. terrestris* **Overholts**

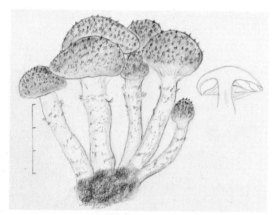

Figure 342

Figure 342 *Pholiota terrestris*

Pileus 2-8 (10) cm, obtuse to expanded-umbonate, at times nearly plane; a gelatinous layer present beneath the scales; margin usually fibrillose-appendiculate; context watery buff to brownish; taste mild. Gills adnate, crowded, pallid to avellaneous (pinkish gray) to dull brown. Stipe 3-8 (10) cm x (2) 5-10 mm, ± equal or narrowed below, staining brownish at base, covered by scales concolorous with those on the pileus. Pleurocystidia as chrysocystidia, 18-34 x (4) 5-10 (12) μm.

Clustered on soil but originating from buried wood, common in the Pacific Northwest, June to January; rare in the Great Lakes area, fall. Edible, but not rated highly.

16b Pileus lighter in color and fruiting bodies clearly lignicolous **17**

17a Gills greenish in age; pileus lacking a gelatinous layer beneath the scales; spores 6-7.5 (8) μm long. Fig. 343 .... *P. squarrosa* (Fr.) **Kummer**

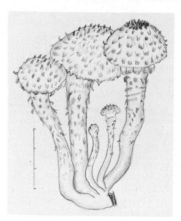

Figure 343

Figure 343 *Pholiota squarrosa*

Pileus 3-10 (12) cm, campanulate to broadly convex, dry; scales recurved to squarrose, veil remnants appendiculate on margin at first; scales yellowish brown; surface yellowish between scales; context pliant, yellowish; odor and taste mild (or taste of garlic in some). Gills crowded, narrow, finally dull rusty brown. Stipe 4-10 (12) x 4-12 (15) mm, ± equal, surface covered with recurved pale tan to tawny dry scales; annulus often poorly formed and evanescent. Pleurocystidia present as chrysocystidia (26) 30-48 x (6) 8-16 μm.

Clustered on wood of conifers and hardwoods, summer and fall, widely distributed, summer in the Rocky Mountains, usually in the fall in other areas. "Mildly" poisonous to some people, but it has been generally rated as an edible species.

17b Gills dull brown in age; spores 4-5.5 (6) × (2.5) 3-3.5 μm; pileus with a gelatinous layer beneath the scales .... *P. squarrosoides* (Pk.) **Sacc.**

Pileus 3-10 cm, convex to umbonate, at times ± plane, whitish except for the crust brown scales, margin fringed, viscid beneath the scales; scales crowded over the disc; context whitish, taste mild. Gills ± crowded, broad in age, whitish when young. Stipe 4-10 (15) cm x 5-12 (15) mm, below veil line covered with scales like those on cap; annulus superior, pallid, more fibrillose than membranous. Pleurocystidia (25) 30-50 (65) x (6) 8-15 (18) μm.

Mostly clustered on hardwood substrates, common in northern United States and southern Canada. Edible: one of the best in the genus. But do not confuse it with *P. squarrosa*.

18a **Pileus viscid, large and dark brown; stipe scaly up to annulus; spores 10-15 (18) × 5.5-7 (8.5) μm; pleurocystidia none** .... *P. albocrenulata* (Pk.) Sacc.

Pileus 2.5-8 (12) cm, broadly conic to convex or broadly umbonate, decorated with superficial brownish fibrillose scales, margin appendiculate; context pallid. Gills broadly adnate, very broad, close, whitish then grayish, at length rusty dark brown, edge crenulate and beaded with droplets when fresh. Stipe 3-10 (15) x 0.5-1.5 cm, ± equal, fibrous, pallid above, dark brown below, with brown scattered scales up to annulus, apex pruinose. Pleurocystidia none. Cheilocystidia 43-75 x 4-9 μm, cylindric-capitate.

Solitary or in groups of 2-3 on hardwood, especially sugar maple trees where it appears to cause a butt-rot, rarely on wood of conifers, appearing nearly every year but not in large numbers; central and eastern United States and in southern Canada. It is rated "nonpoisonous" by some investigators, which means it is not well-flavored.

18a **Not as above** **19**

19a **Pleurocystidia fusoid-ventricose, neck elongated and projecting prominently beyond the hymenium (if a microscope is not available view the gill face with a 10x or 15x hand lens: the cystidia will be seen as minute hairs projecting from the surface)** **20**

19b **Pleurocystidia mucronate to clavate or absent (not prominently projecting beyond the basidia if present)** **35**

20a **Pileus 1.5-2 (3) cm, viscid; stipe 1-3 mm thick, loosely fibrillose; colors over all pallid yellow to pallid cinnamon; spores 7-9 (10) × 4.5-5.5 μm. Fig. 344** .... *P. scamba* (Fr.) Moser

Figure 344

Figure 344 *Pholiota scamba*

Pileus convex to plane, often with a low umbo, appearing siky fibrillose, soon dry, margin appendiculate; context watery yellowish, taste mild. Gills adnate, pale yellow when young, broad, close. Stipe 1.5-3 cm long, apex clear pale yellow, brownish below and woolly tomentose to squamulose, base strigose. Pleurocystidia 28-40 x 8-14 μm, utriform to fusoid-ventricose.

Gregarious on wet conifer wood, June to October, common in the Pacific Northwest, rare in the Great Lakes area.

20b **Not as above** **21**

21a **Scattered on conifer duff and debris; stipe 3-4.5 mm, thick, greenish yellow, decorated with clay-color veil remnants; spores 6.5-8.5 × 5-7 μm, ± angular-ovate in face view; taste usually bitter** .... *P. pulchella* Sm. & Hes.

Pileus obtuse when young, then campanulate to expanded-umbonate, dingy pinkish brown to olive-gray at margin which for a time is appendiculate with veil remnants; surface fibrillose-squamulose at first from delicate yellow squamules; context olivaceous, taste mild at times. Gills adnate, subdistant, pale olivaceous, olive-brown in age, edges fimbriate. Stipe 3-6 cm long, equal, base fibrilose-strigose. Pleurocystidia (38) 50-81 x (8) 12-16 μm, fusoid-ventricose.

Scattered to gregarious, September to November, Pacific Northwest, not common.

21b Not as above **22**

22a Pileus brilliant pinkish orange fresh; lamellae bright yellow; taste bitter. Fig. 345 ....
.... *P. astragalina* **(Fr.) Sing.**

Figure 345

Figure 345   *Pholiota astragalina*

Pileus 2-4 cm, conic to campanulate or convex-umbonate, viscid, glabrous except for scattered veil remnants along margin, in age developing blackish discolorations; context reddish-orange soon yellowish orange. Gills adnexed, broad, discoloring where bruised. Stipe 5-9 cm x 4-7 mm, equal, flexuous or straight, yellow in interior, with yellow veil remnants over surface, base soon sordid brown from handling. Spores 5-7 x 3.8-4.5 μm. Pleurocystidia 35-60 x 8-14 μm, present as both leptocystidia and chrysocystidia, fusoid-ventricose to clavate-mucronate.

In small clusters to scattered, on conifer wood, frequent in the Pacific Northwest, quite rare in the Great Lakes area eastward, late summer and fall.

22b Not with all the above features **23**

23a Pileus color variable: green, olive, purple, drab to purple brown in various combinations; on hardwood slash; lamellae pallid to gray then dark brown; pileus margin typically appendiculate with veil remnants ....
.... *P. polychroa* **(Berk.) Sm. & Brodie**

Pileus (2) 4-10 cm, broadly convex to ± plano-umbonate, viscid, veil remnants creamy to pinkish gray, superficial squamules; context soft, taste mild. Gills close to crowded, ± broad, at first lilaceous to pale cream color, soon grayish brown to purplish brown, edges white fimbriate. Stipe 2-6 (8) cm x 3-5 (8) mm, lower part squamulose from adhering veil remnants; annulus evanescent; apical area blue-green to pallid; near base reddish brown. Spores 6-7.5 x 3.5-4.5 μm. Pleurocystidia 40-60 (70) x 9-15 μm, fusoid-ventricose.

Scattered to clustered on hardwood slash, summer and fall, not uncommon in the Great Lakes area eastward and southward.

23b Not with the above color pattern **24**

24a Stipe 1.5-4 mm thick **25**

24b Stipe 4-10 mm or more thick **28**

25a Pileus ± decorated with veil remnants, often as patches of appressed fibrils over disc **26**

25b Pileus glabrous or only a slight fringe of veil remnants on margin **27**

26a Pileus pale cream color to the tawny disc; on conifer debris (especially mossy stumps) in bogs; hyphae of the pileus cuticle heavily incrusted; spores 7-10 (12) × 4-5 (6) μm; stipe soon rusty brown below ....
.... *P. paludosella* **(Atk.) Sm. & Hes.**

Pileus (2) 3-5 (6) cm, obtuse to convex then broadly convex to plane, at times umbonate, ± viscid at first; veil remnants buff in color, mostly around the disc as appressed patches; margin at first appendiculate. Gills sinuate, close, narrow. Stipe 3-6 (8) cm long, yellowish above, ± floccose-squamulose up to the veil-line. Pleurocystidia 36-52 x 9-12 μm, fusoid-ventricose.

Late summer and fall, Great Lakes region southward; common in its special habitat during dry years, but never in large numbers. Edibility not known.

26b On *Sphagnum* in bogs; hyphae of the pileus cuticle smooth for the most part; spores 7-9 × 4-5 μm; pileus tinged pinkish tan when young ...... *P. sphagnophila* (Pk.) Sm. & Hes.

Pileus 12-25 mm, ± broadly convex, soon dry and appressed fibrillose to slightly squamulose around disc, disc dingy ochraceous to rusty brown at maturity. Gills narrow, crowded, yellowish becoming reddish brown. Stipe 2.5-4.5 cm long, yellowish, coated with grayish veil fibrils to near apex. Pleurocystidia 42-73 x 7-12 μm, neck 5-8 μm thick.

Summer, New England, apparently rare.

27a Pileus reddish tawny at least over disc; stipe reddish tawny near base; veil arachnoid .... *P. totteni* (Murr.) Sm. & Hes.

Pileus 2.5-4 cm, convex to plane, becoming depressed, rarely slightly umbonate, glabrous, shining; context pale buff. Gills broad, ± subdistant, ochraceous then fulvous. Stipe 1.5-4 cm long, apex yellow-pruinose, base decorated with long coarse white hairs. Spores (6) 7-9 (10.5) x 4-5 (6.5) μm. Pleurocystidia 45-65 (75) x 8-16 μm, fusoid-ventricose.

On soil under pine, North Carolina, July and December.

27b Pileus chrome yellow (or darker over disc); stipe ochraceous near base .... *P. tetonensis* Sm. & Hes.

Pileus 10-25 mm, conic to convex or acutely umbonate; context yellowish, odor and taste fungoid. Gills adnate, yellowish, then yellow-brown, ± subdistant, broad. Stipe 1.5-4 cm long, veil yellow and fibrillose. Spores 7-9 x 4-5 μm. Pleurocystidia 40-70 x 10-22 μm, broadly fusoid-ventricose to ellipsoid-pedicellate.

On rotting wood of conifers (?), June, Wyoming, apparently rare.

28a Gills white to pallid at first 29

28b Gills yellow at first 32

29a Stipe with orange to yellow basal mycelium .... *P. crassipedes* Sm. & Hes.

Pileus about 9 cm, convex to plane, reddish tawny on disc, margin yellowish, viscid; context thin, taste mild. Gills adnate, horizontal, narrow, close. Stipe 5-7 x 1-1.3 cm, ± equal, white; veil yellow, membranous at first but soon broken and obliterated. Spores 5.5-7 x 3.5-4.5 μm. Pleurocystidia: both leptocystidia and chrysocystidia (?) present. Leptocystidia 38-73 x 7-21 μm, fusoid-ventricose. Chrysocystidia (?) 12-20 x 4-9 μm, content often not typical for the category.

Solitary to scattered on wood of deciduous trees, Pacific Northwest, apparently rare, fall.

29b Stipe with white to pallid basal mycelium (or none) 30

30a Veil remnants on pileus brown. Fig. 346 .... *P. sublubrica* Sm. & Hes.

Figure 346

Figure 346 *Pholiota sublubrica*

Pileus 4-10 (15) cm, convex-umbonate to ± plane, disc ochraceous tawny to ochraceous orange, margin yellowish, viscid; context white. Gills adnate, close, broad, at times with rusty spots in age. Stipe 4-10 x 1-1.5 cm, equal, whitish, base soon rusty brown; annulus a superior fibrillose zone, below it the surface ragged-fibrillose to squamulose from the pallid veil. Spores 5.5-7 x 3.2-4 μm. Pleurocystidia 45-83 x 9-16 μm.

On or near rotting conifer wood, summer and fall, not infrequent in the Rocky Mountains but rare on the Pacific Coast.

30b Veil remnants whitish (if present) 31

31a Pileus disc dark reddish brown to blackish red. Fig. 347 .... *P. lubrica* (Fr.) Sing.

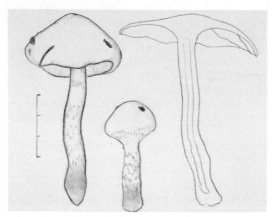

Figure 347

Figure 347 *Pholiota lubrica*

Pileus 4-8.5 cm, convex to plane, glabrous, viscid, marginal area pallid, edge appendiculate at first; context whitish, taste mild, with $FeSO_4$ green. Gills whitish going to dark cinnamon, broad, bluntly adnate, crowded. Stipe 6-8 x 0.9-1.1 cm, equal, pallid, soon bay-brown, scurfy from remains of a veil, apex silky and yellowish pallid. Spores 6-7 x 3 μm. Pleurocystidia 50-65 x 9-16 μm.

On or near conifer wood or on soil rich in organic material in conifer forests, Pacific Northwest; fall. It is more frequent than the literature indicates.

31b Pileus whitish to pinkish buff or pinkish gray. .... *P. lenta* (Fr.) Sing.

Pileus 3-7 (10) cm, convex to plane, slimy, with white squamules from the veil along margin at first, and margin then ± appendiculate, glabrescent. Gills ± adnate, white, finally clay-color, close, ± narrow. Stipe 3-8 (12) x 0.4-1.2 cm, white above, brown at base, fibrillose, apex white-mealy; veil white, copious, cortinate; annulus an evanescent zone. Spores 5.5-7 x 3.5-4.5 μm. Pleurocystidia 42-60 x 8-14 μm, fusoid-ventricose.

On humus and debris of hardwoods, July-December, fairly common on wet years, Great Lakes area eastward and southward.

32a Pileus margin at first with patches of tawny veil remnants; spores 4.5-6 (6.5) × 2.8-3.5 μm; on wood and debris of hardwoods .... *P. innocua* Sm. & Hes.

Pileus 3-7 cm, convex then ± plane, margin at first appressed-fibrillose from remains of the tawny veil, viscid but soon dry, tawny on disc, marginal area bright yellow; context yellowish, with $FeSO_4$ green then black. Gills close, broad, adnate to decurrent. Stipe 4-6 x 0.9-1.2 cm, ± equal, pale yellow, duller toward the rusty brown base, with matted yellowish mycelium. Pleurocystidia 30-46 (60) x 10-15 μm, utriform.

Gregarious on or near hardwood logs, summer and fall, Great Lakes area and in the Adirondack Mountains of New York. Edibility not known.

32b On soil or on wood and debris of conifers 33

33a Pileus becoming spotted green where handled, disc tawny, margin honey-color .... *P. subflavida* (Murr.) Sm. & Hes.

Pileus 3-5 cm, convex-umbonate or remaining conic, glabrous, viscid. Gills sinuate, greenish yellow, subdistant. Stipe 4-7 cm x 5-8 mm, equal, cream-color above, fulvous below, fibrillose; veil greenish yellow, thin (but membranous), annulus soon evanescent. Spores 5.5-7.5 (8.5) x 3.5-4.5 (5) μm. Pleurocystidia abundant, 48-72 x 9-15 μm, fusoid-ventricose.

On conifer debris or near it, fall, Pacific Northwest.

33b Not as above 34

34a Spores 5.5-6.5 (7) × 3.5-4 μm; pileus context white ...... *P. virescentifolia* Sm. & Hes.

Pileus 4-5 cm, conic-campanulate, yellow-brown, viscid; taste slight. Gills white then pale greenish yellow, close, broad, edges fimbriate. Stipe 3.5-4 cm x 8-12 mm, subradicating, apex white, dingy downward, fibrillose; veil copious, yellow, submembranous. Pleurocystidia 45-75 (83) x 10-17 μm, fusoid-ventricose, with a long narrow pedicel.

On soil and humus, under hemlock, September, Tennessee.

34b Spores 6.5-8 (9) × 4-4.5 (5) μm; pileus context greenish yellow .... P. acutoconica Sm. & Hes.

Pileus 3-6 cm, conic-campanulate, finally expanded and with a conic umbo, viscid, virgate, yellow on margin, ± clay-color on disc, with patches of veil tissue along the margin. Gills close, becoming ± decurrent, broad, edges even. Stipe 5-7 cm x 5-8 mm, darkening to dark yellow-brown from base upward. Pleurocystidia 46-70 x 8-16 μm.

Clustered to gregarious on or around conifer wood, October, Oregon.

35a Veil forming a broad membranous persistent annulus; spores 7-9 × 4-4.5 μm .... P. albivelata Murrill

Pileus (2) 4-8 cm, broadly convex to plane, glabrous, viscid, pale to dark pinkish brown; context whitish, soft, pliant. Gills adnate, white then grayish brown, close, ± broad. Stipe 5-10 cm x 4-10 mm, equal, hollow, basal portion becoming discolored, below annulus conspicuously scurfy; with white rhizomorphs at the base; annulus striate above, floccose underneath. Spores 7-9 x 4-5 μm. Pleurocystidia present as chrysocystidia 30-50 (60) x 5-12 μm.

Solitary to scattered on debris in conifer forests, fall, Pacific Northwest; frequently collected. The closely related species, P. sipei Sm. & Hes., has spores 9-12 x 4.5-6 μm, and giant leptocystidia 50-75 x 10-20 μm in addition to chrysocystidia.

35b Veil and spore size not as above 36

36a Stipe 2-5 mm thick, at first covered with recurved fibrillose scales; pileus glabrous .... P. mutabilis (Fr.) Kummer

Pileus 1.5-6 cm, becoming campanulate to convex-umbonate or plane, a few veil fibrils along the margin at first, dull rusty brown and margin striate when moist, fading to ± clay-color; context whitish (pallid). Gills adnate to short-decurrent, close, broad, pallid then cinnamon brown. Stipe 4-10 cm long, soon darkening from base upward; annulus membranous to fibrillose. Spores 5.5-7.5 x 3.7-4.5 μm. Pleurocystidia none.

Clustered on conifer and hardwood logs and stumps, widely distributed in North America but common and abundant in the Pacific Northwest, fall. It is edible but so likely to be confused with Galerina autumnalis that it cannot be recommended.

36b Stipe not covered below veil-line with recurved scales 37

37a Spores 14-17 × 7-9 μm; stipe (6) 10-15 (20) cm × 2-5 (7) mm; gregarious on muck and in bogs; pileus olive-green to olive-bronze .... P. myosotis (Fr.) Sing.

Pileus (10) 15-30 (40) mm, conic to convex, glabrous or at first with fibrils along margin, viscid, opaque, becoming striatulate at times; context olivaceous. Gills broad, adnate, subdistant, olivaceous then brown, edges fimbriate. Stipe with olivaceous patches and zones of veil fibrils, densely pruinose above veil-line. Pleurocystidia present as chrysocystidia 35-50 x 10-15 μm.

Solitary to gregarious, not uncommon in northern United States and very likely abundant in Canada during favorable seasons. The best fruitings we have seen followed hot dry summers.

37b Not as above 38

38a On conifer wood; pileus glabrous and yellow when young. Fig. 348 .... P. subochracea (Sm.) Sm. & Hes.

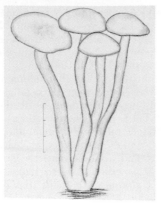

Figure 348

Figure 349

Figure 348 *Pholiota subochracea*

Pileus 2-4 cm, convex to broadly convex, margin inrolled at first, glabrous (or with veil fibrils on margin at first), viscid, pale yellow to the ± tan disc, in age pale clay color over all; context pale yellow. Gills close, ± broad at maturity, adnate, pale yellow then dingy cinnamon. Stipe 5-9 cm x 5-7 mm, ± equal, in age rusty brown near base, apical area yellowish and silky; veil fibrillose and leaving an evanescent zone. Spores 5-6 x 2.5-3 μm. Pleurocystidia present as chrysocystidia, 32-47 x 10-15 μm.

    Clustered to gregarious on decaying conifer wood, Pacific Northwest, fall (often late), rather frequent. Edibility: not recommended.

38b On wood of hardwoods or if on conifer wood the pileus brown at first **39**

39a Gills very narrow and very crowded; spores obscurely truncate; pileus 1-3.5 cm; stipe 1.5-5 mm thick; on wood of either conifers or hardwoods. Fig. 349 ....
........................*P. vernalis* **(Pk.) Sm. & Hes.**

Figure 349 *Pholiota vernalis*

Pileus 10-35 mm, conic-campanulate to nearly plane, glabrous or with veil remnants along margin at first, translucent-striate moist, slightly viscid, honey-color to clay color, fading to a pale tan. Gills adnate, seceding, pale tan then dark cinnamon. Stipe (2) 3-6 cm long, equal, fibrillose; veil remnants pale brownish, leaving an annular zone as well as scattered patches and zones below; interior of stipe darkening to dark brown in lower portion. Spores 5.5-7.5 x 3-4.5 μm. Pleurocystidia none.

    Gregarious to clustered, spring and summer, widely distributed in North America. This is another species easily confused with *Galerina autumnalis* by beginners.

39b Not as above **40**

40a Pileus gills and stipe yellow to orange and staining orange-brown on handling; taste bitter .... *P. multifolia* **(Pk.) Sm. & Hes.**

Pileus 5-8 cm, convex to ± umbonate, dry, brilliant yellow at first, dry and obscurely fibrillose; context thick, yellow. Gills adnexed, narrow, crowded, soon spotted or stained rusty brown, edges crenulate and often with reddish yellow droplets. Stipe (2) 3-7 (10) cm long, 4-10 mm thick, yellow, floccose; annulus a fibrillose evanescent zone. Spores 6.5-9 x 4.5-5.5 μm. Pleurocystidia present as brown basidioles.

    On logs, sawdust pileus, etc., Great Lakes area eastward, summer and fall, not uncommon.

It is closely related to *P. curvipes* (Fr.) Quél. which has a thinner stipe and a mild taste. It is also close to *P. subsulphurea* Sm. & Hes. which is bitter and has a pileus 10-15 mm broad and a stipe 2-3 mm thick. This group of species is likely to be mistaken for the genus *Gymnopilus*. None are recommended for the table.

40b Pileus and color changes not as above 41

41a Stipe 1-3 cm thick at apex, hard; veil copious and at first leaving large patches on pileus; spores 7-9.5 × 4-5.5 μm. Fig. 350 .... *P. destruens* (Brond.) Gillet

Figure 350

Figure 350 *Pholiota destruens*

Pileus (6) 8-16 (20) cm, convex to nearly plane, viscid beneath the veil remnants, creamy white finally going to yellow to dark yellow-brown, con-spicuously decorated at first with whitish to buff patches of soft veil material; margin shaggy from copious veil fragments. Context white; taste ± disagreeable. Gills adnate to sinuate, broad, close, white becoming dull rusty brown. Stipe 5-12 (18) cm long, clavate at first, solid, brownish in base in age, copiously decorated with thick whitish veil remnants; annulus floccose and cottony. Pleurocystidia none.

Solitary to scattered especially on stumps and logs of cottonwood and Lombardy popular late in the season, widely distributed and frequently collected. Edible but not popular in North America. Pileus of cottonwood logs left for a year or two often become infected with this fungus which causes a rapid decay of the soft wood. The fruit bodies usually develop at the cut surfaces of the logs (the ends).

41b Pileus yellow or orange; lubricous to viscid at first; stipe 4-12 mm thick at apex; spores 8.5-11 (12) × 4.5-5.5 μm; gills yellow at first .... *P. malicola* (Kauff.) Sm.

Pileus (3) 6-12 cm, obtusely conic going to conic-campanulate or plano-umbonate, viscid when wet soon dry, decorated at first with patches of brownish fibrils but soon glabrous; context pallid. Gills sinuate, narrow, close, yellow, finally rusty brown. Stipe 4-12 cm long, ± equal, yellowish within, surface yellow like the pileus, becoming rusty brown below; veil remnants yellowish to pallid; annulus thin and soon obliterated. Pleurocystidia none.

Clustered to gregarious on or near either hardwood or that of conifers; not uncommon in northern United States and southern Canada, but it is a variable species belonging to the *P. alnicola* group. Not recommended for the table.

Stropharia (Fr.) Quélet, Naematoloma Karsten, and Psilocybe Kummer

The species of the genera *Stropharia*, *Psilocybe*, and *Naematoloma* have a similar aspect and the genera are maintained on a somewhat arbitrary basis. Annulate species are now placed in *Psilocybe* as well as in *Stropharia*, and the presence or absence of chryso-cystidia in the hymenium, the character now used to distinguish *Psilocybe* from *Naematoloma*, is no longer convincing since we know of species in the family with both types of cystidia in the hymenium of single fruiting bodies. Because of this situation, in our treatment here, the species we include from all three genera are presented in a single key.

KEY TO SPECIES

1a **On dung of various herbivores** **2**

1b **On soil (if it is heavily manured try above choice first), or on organic substrates such as weed and other plant, as well as animal, debris** **12**

2a **Pileus white when young** ....
.... *S. melanosperma* **(Fr.) Quél.**

Pileus (2.5) 3-6 cm, convex then broadly convex, at times disc finally slightly depressed, glabrous, subviscid, gradually becoming cream-color over disc. Gills adnate, broad, close, white then cinereous to violet-fuscous. Stipe 3-5 (8) cm x 4-8 mm, equal or nearly so, finely fibrillose, white; annulus membranous, ± median, easily obliterated. Spores 10-13 x 6.5-8 μm; pleurocystidia present as chrysocystidia.

Scattered to gregarious on manured ground and in pastures, widely distributed but not well known in North America, spring to fall.

2b **Pileus yellow, orange or more deeply colored** **3**

3a **Fruiting body staining blue where injured. Fig. 351** .... *S. cubensis* **Earle**

Figure 351

Figure 351 *Stropharia cubensis*

Pileus 2-8 (9) cm, conic to campanulate or convex to expanded-umbonate, often with an acute papilla, viscid, glabrous or ± decorated with veil remnants, yellow to clay-color to olive-yellow or dingy olive; context pallid; taste farinaceous. Gills gray then violet-gray going to fuscous, close, adnate, broad in age. Stipe 4-15 cm x 4-14 mm, ± enlarged downward, white, dry; annulus membranous, white. Spores 11-17 x 8-12 x 7-9 μm, compressed. Pleurocystidia present as leptocystidia, 18-23 x 10-13 μm, apex obtuse to rounded.

Scattered to gregarious on cow dung, Gulf Coast region, fall, common and collected for its hallucinogenic properties. It is a poisonous species, and against the law in a number of southern states to transport it by automobile without a permit.

3b **Not staining blue when injured** **4**

4a **Pileus yellow to orange when young** **5**

4b **Pileus tan, gray-brown, or dark brown** **7**

5a **Spores 14-17 × 7-8 μm** ....
.... *S. merdaria* **(Fr.) Quél.**

Pileus 1-3 cm, campanulate to broadly convex, glabrous, subviscid, dingy yellowish becoming dull orange brownish. Gills broad, subdistant, yellowish then purple-brown from spores. Stipe 2-4 cm x 1-3 mm, floccose-fibrillose, glabrescent, dry, yellowish; veil leaving a slight zone.

On horse dung, spring, widely distributed but not abundant.

5b **Spores 15-19 × 7.5-10 μm or larger** **6**

6a **Spores 15-19 × 7.5-10 μm, germ pore apical; stipe (2) 3-5 mm thick. Fig. 352** ....
.... *S. semiglobata* ` **(Fr.) Quél.**

Figure 352

Figure 352 *Stropharia semiglobata*

Pileus 1-4 (6) cm, obtuse then convex, glabrous, evenly pale yellow, gradually paler, viscid; taste ± farinaceous. Gills broad, adnate, grayish pallid then purplish fuscous. Stipe 5-8 cm x 2-5 mm, viscid when fresh, ± varnished if dry; annulus soon evanescent. Pleurocystidia present as chrysocystidia.

Common, spring and summer or fall, widely distributed but not found in significant numbers.

6b **Spores 17-23 × 9-12.5 μm; germ pore eccentric; stipe 5-10 mm thick. Otherwise as in** *S. semiglobata* (see above)
.... *S. stercoraria* **(Fr.) Lange**
S. stercoraria **is often considered to be a variety of** *S. semiglobata*.

7a **Annulus and a pseudorhiza both present** ....
.... *S. annellariiformis* **Murrill**

Pileus 1-3 cm, conic then campanulate to expanded-umbonate, glabrous, viscid, faintly striate, bright to dull fulvous, fading to ± olive-brown. Gills close, broad, adnate, seceding, pallid to dull brown, finally purple-brown. Stipe 2-8 cm x 1-4 mm, pale fulvous, pruinose above, at first fibrillose below annulus; pseudorhiza 3-4 cm long; annulus ± superior, flaring, soon evanescent. Spores 9-12 x 6-7.5 μm. Pleurocystidia absent.

On manure, Gulf Coast area but as far north as Michigan and New York, not common.

7b **Lacking the above combination of features**
.... **8**

8a **Pileus grayish brown; stipe 5-10 cm × 1-2 mm** .... *P. panaeoliformis* **Murrill**

Pileus 1-2.5 cm, convex to more or less campanulate, dry, slightly fibrillose to glabrous, dull grayish brown. Gills sinuate to adnexed, broad, ventricose, crowded, finally blackish. Stipe equal, more or less fibrillose, darker than pileus. Spores 9-11.5 x 6-7 μm. Pleurocystidia none.

Solitary to clustered on manured ground, Gulf Coast, not well known. It is possible that the pileus is ± viscid at first.

8b **Pileus tan to rusty brown young; stipe typically less than 5 cm long** **9**

9a **Stipe about 0.5 mm thick; spores 5-6.5 μm wide** .... *P. angustispora* **Smith**

Pileus 2-6 mm broad, 3-5 mm high, conic to campanulate, glabrous, viscid, dark reddish brown, pinkish tan faded, margin at first with white fibrillose flecks (veil remnants). Gills broad, short-decurrent, distant to subdistant, dark purple-brown mature. Stipe 10-20 mm long, delicate, pallid, lower down fibrillose-squamulose, base white-mycelioid. Spores 12-15 x 5-6.5 μm. Pleurocystidia none.

On dung pellets of deer and elk, Olympic National Park, Washington, obviously seldom collected.

9b Not as above **10**

10a Spores 11-14 × 7-8.5 μm. Fig. 353 ....
.... *P. coprophila* (Fr.) Quél.

Figure 353

Figure 353 *Psilocybe coprophila*

Pileus 1-3 cm, convex to broadly convex or plane, with white floccose patches along the margin at first, smooth, dark reddish brown, ± clay-color when faded. Gills broad, adnate, subdistant, pallid to brownish to violaceous-fuscous, when spores are shed the color dull yellow-brown. Stipe 2-4 cm x 2-4 mm, ± equal, fibrillose, pallid, then brownish above and darker toward base. Pleurocystidia none.

Solitary or in small clusters on dung heaps and on manured soil, throughout the growing season, widely distributed, common.

10b Spores smaller than in above choice **11**

11a Gills crowded; stipe shaggy-fibrillose; spores 6.2-7.5 × 4-4.6 μm ....
.... *P. caespitosa* **Murrill**

Pileus 1-2.5 cm, convex to expanded, with a small umbo, smooth, glabrous, striatulate when moist, brownish isabelline. Gills adnate to sinuate, with a smoky purplish tinge. Stipe 1-3 cm x 1-2 mm, ± equal, colored like pileus but base darker. Pleurocystidia none.

Caespitose on or near compost heaps and manure piles; New York Botanical Garden, New York. It was probably introduced.

11b Gills subdistant; stipe merely appressed-fibrillose; spores 7-8 × 4-5 μm ....
.... *P. subviscida* (Pk.) **Kauff.**

Pileus 6-12 mm broad, convex to nearly plane, glabrous, hygrophanous, pale chestnut to reddish tan, subviscid, striatulate when moist, pallid to buff when faded. Gills broad, subdistant, adnate, whitish then chocolate color. Stipe ± 25 x 2 mm, equal, grayish, appressed fibrillose, brown toward base, paler above; veil slight, white, soon vanishing. Pleurocystidia 34-50 x 7-10 μm, ± fusoid-ventricose.

Gregarious on horse manure and manured ground, Great Lakes area eastward, apparently seldom collected. *P. bullacea* (Fr.) Gillet has spores 7-9.5 x 4.5-6 μm. It is very similar to *P. subviscida* otherwise.

12a Stipe typically 4 mm or more thick near apex at maturity **13**

12b Stipe typically 1-3 (4) mm thick near apex at maturity **27**

13a Annulus lacking, or if present at first, soon broken up leaving only a zone of veil material on the stipe **14**

13b Annulus well developed and relatively persistent **21**

14a Pileus blue to greenish blue; gills at maturity and spores dark violaceous brown. Fig. 354 .... *S. aeruginosa* (Fr.) **Quél.**

Figure 354

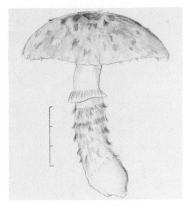

Figure 355

Figure 354 *Stropharia aeruginosa*

Pileus 2-6 (8) cm, campanulate to plano-umbonate or broadly convex, slimy-viscid, yellowish in age, often dotted with white veil particles. Gills more or less adnate, ± close, broad, whitish to grayish and then finally purplish brown. Stipe 3-7 cm x 4-12 mm, ± equal, floccose to squamulose at first and with a white submembranous annulus which soon becomes broken and disappears. Spores 6-8.5 x 4-5 μm. Pleurocystidia present as chrysocystidia.

On debris of hardwoods, Great Lakes area east and southward, and in the Pacific Northwest, not rare. A very similar species with rusty brown spores and cinnamon brown gills also occurs in North America.

14b Pileus some other color 15

15a Pileus dry and conspicuously innately scaly; stipe squamulose also. Fig. 355 ....
.... S. *kauffmanii* Smith

Figure 355 *Stropharia kauffmanii*

Pileus 6-15 cm, convex then broadly convex to plane, margin curved in at first, tawny to grayish brown, ground color yellowish; odor and taste more or less nauseous. Gills depressed-adnate, crowded, very narrow, thin and readily broken transversely, pallid, becoming drab. Stipe 6-10 cm x 1.5-3 cm, ± equal, whitish but ± cream-color below, squamulose above and below the superior veil-line. Spores 6-8 x 4-4.5 μm. Pleurocystidia present as chrysocystidia and leptocystidia both.

On humus rich in organic debris, very decayed piles of brush etc., associated with hardwoods, Pacific Northwest and Rocky Mountains, not common, spring, summer and fall.

15b Pileus smooth or if squamules or scales are present they are appressed or superficial and deciduous 16

16a Pileus pale yellow becoming olivaceous; stipe (3) 4-7 (10) mm thick; associated with aspen. Fig. 356 .... S. *riparia* Smth

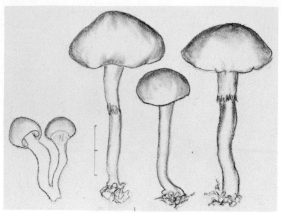

Figure 356

Figure 356 *Stropharia riparia*

Pileus 3-9 cm, obtuse to convex then broadly convex to umbonate, for a time decorated with small
squamules near the margin, margin at first appendiculate, viscid, soon dry, disc tinged orange
at times. Stipe ± equal, brownish below, whitish
above, somewhat fibrillose below annulus; annulus submembranous to lacerated and soon disappearing. Spores 11-14 (15) x 6-8 μm. Pleurocystidia none. Cheilocystidia clavate to flexuous-
filamentose.

    Scattered to gregarious under aspen and
cottonwood, low ground, especially along streams;
Rocky Mountains and Pacific Northwest, common during wet periods in the summer.

16b Not as above **17**

**17a Pileus yellow; stipe 1-2 cm thick; growing on
humus and debris on the forest floor. Fig.
357** .... *S. ambigua* (**Pk.**) **Zeller**

Figure 357

Figure 357 *Stropharia ambigua*

Pileus (3) 5-12 (15) cm, obtuse to convex becoming broadly convex to nearly plane, viscid,
at first with veil remnants along the margin, soon
glabrous. Gills adnate, close, broad, pallid becoming grayish to violaceous brown. Stipe ±
equal, white, fibrillose to the torn floccose evanescent annulus, numerous white rhizomorphs at
base. Spores 11-14 x 6-7.5 μm. Pleurocystidia
present as chrysocystidia.

    Scattered to gregarious in mixed conifer-
hardwood habitats, Devil's club is often present
in the habitat, Pacific Northwest, late summer
and fall common. It is not poisonous but the
flavor is not good.

17b Not as above **18**

**18a Pileus dark reddish brown; stipe 8-18 cm ×
2.5-6 mm; on black muck in swamps** ....
.... **see** *Psilocybe atrobrunnea*

18b Not as above **19**

**19a Pileus ± brick red when young; on hardwood
logs and stumps; stipe often staining yellow
where injured. Fig. 358** ....
.... *N. sublateritium* (**Fr.**) **Karst.**

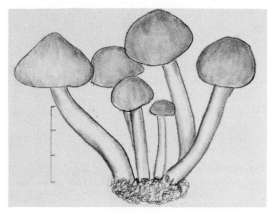

Figure 358

Figure 358 *Naematoloma sublateritium*

Pileus (2) 4-8 (10) cm, convex, margin inrolled, finally broadly convex to plane, surface moist, often canescent; taste mild to bitter. Gills adnate, crowded, pallid then purplish gray from spores. Stipe 5-10 cm long, equal, whitish, at times an annular fibrillose zone present. Spores 6-7 x 4-4.5 μm. Pleurocystidia present as chrysocystidia.

Typically clustered on hardwood logs and stumps, late summer to late fall, common in hardwood area of North America generally. Edible, popularly known as brick-cap.

19b On wood of conifers **20**

20a Pileus cinnamon to rusty cinnamon; gills pallid becoming gray to purple brown. Fig. 359 .... *N. capnoides* **(Fr.) Karst.**

Figure 359

Figure 359 *Nematoloma capnoides*

Pileus 2-7 cm, convex to broadly convex, ± glabrous, odor and taste mild. Gills close, broad, adnate-seceding, pallid then violaceous drab. Stipe 5-7 (10) cm x 3-8 (10) mm, ± equal, pallid becoming rusty brown from base upward. Spores 6-7 x 4-4.5 μm. Pleurocystidia present as chrysocystidia.

Gregarious to caespitose, very common during the fall and early winter, throughout North America where conifers are found. Edible.

20b Pileus yellow to greenish yellow; gills greenish in age. Fig. 360 ....
.... *N. fasciculare* **(Fr.) Karst.**

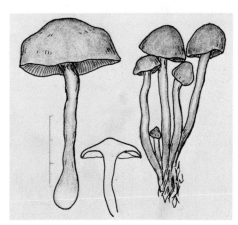

Figure 360

Figure 360 *Nematoloma fasciculare*

Pileus (1) 2-8 cm, obtuse to convex to plano-umbonate, glabrous, moist, bright ochraceous to greenish ochraceous, or the disc amber brown, a green tone pervading entire cap at times; taste very bitter (to mild in some collections). Gills crowded, yellow then flushed green, narrow. Stipe 5-12 cm x (2) 3-10 mm, usually narrowed to base, becoming fulvous from base upward. Spores 6.5-8 x 3.5 μm. Pleurocystidia present as chrysocystidia.

Gregarious to caespitose on conifer wood, very common in conifer country, late summer on into winter. *Naematoloma subviride* (B. & C.) Smith is a second species with greenish gills. It may be found in the Gulf Coast area. Its caps are 1-3 cm broad. Neither species is recommended for the table.

21a Stipe 0.8-2 cm thick, conspicuously white-fibrillose scaly at first; on decaying conifer wood; pileus glabrous and slimy viscid. Fig. 361 .... *S. hornemannii* **(Fr.) Lundell & Nanfeldt**

Figure 361

Figure 361 *Stropharia hornemannii*

Pileus (4) 6-15 cm, campanulate to broadly convex-umbonate, slimy-viscid when wet, with white floccules of veil along margin at first; color dingy purplish brown to smoky reddish brown, a bit paler in age; taste somewhat disagreeable. Gills adnate, broad, close, pallid gray then dull purple-

brown. Stipe 6-12 cm long, ± equal, silky toward apex. Spores 10-14 x 5.5-7 μm. Pleurocystidia: present as both chrysocystidia and leptocystidia.

Solitary to scattered on conifer wood, late summer and fall, to be expected in the northern United States and in Canada.

21b Not as above **22**

22a Annulus thick and splitting into segments especially on the lower surface; growing on bark mulch used around plantings; pileus 5-15 cm broad. Fig. 362 ....
.... *S. rugoso-annulata* **Farlow in Murrill**

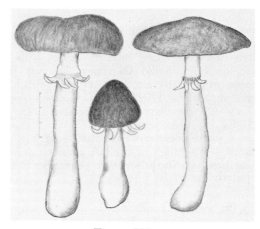

Figure 362

Figure 362 *Stropharia rugoso-annulata*

Pileus pecan-brown to purple-red, finally expanded-umbonate to plane, glabrous, not viscid, sometimes subsquamulose from rupture of cuticle, at times ochraceous tan in age. Gills adnate, broad, crowded, whitish then pale olive, finally deep bluish gray. Stipe 10-18 cm x 1-2 cm, ± equal; annulus superior. Spores 10-13 x 7.5-9 μm. Pleurocystidia present as chrysocystidia.

Scattered to gregarious, often in quantity. Most large findings of this species have been around plantings such as Rhododendrons, its natural habitat appears to be uncertain. It is known in Europe also, and is a popular edible species.

22b Annulus and habitat not as above **23**

23a Pileus and stipe at first conspicuously squamulose from superficial squamules of veil
material; cheilocystidia ± filamentous **24**

23b Not with both the above features **25**

24a Pileus dull yellow to orange-tawny or chestnut brown. Fig. 363 ....
.... *S. squamosa* (Fr.) Quél. var. *squamosa*

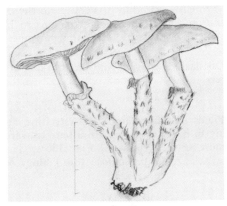

Figure 363

Figure 363 *Stropharia squamosa* var. *squamosa*

Pileus 3-8 cm, conic to obtuse, then campanulate
to expanded-umbonate, viscid, ± olivaceous in
age. Gills adnate, close to subdistant, broad, pallid to bluish gray or darker. Stipe 6-10 (15) x
3-6 (10) mm, equal, dingy brown and squamulose below the annulus, fibrillose-pruinose above;
annulus membranous and ample. Spores 12-14 x
6-7.5 μm. Pleurocystidia none.
    Scatted to gregarious on organic debris in
both conifer and hardwood forests, frequent in
the Pacific Northwest, apparently rare east of the
Great Plains.

24b Pileus orange to brick red ....
.... *S. squamosa* var. *thrausta* (Schulz. in
Kalchb.) Lange

Spores with a slightly eccentric germ pore. For
remainder of details see var. *squamosa*.

25a Pileus white at first ....
........see page 250 *Stropharia melanosperma*

25b Pileus colored **26**

26a Spores 6-7 × 3-4 μm; occurring on ground
in woods of deciduous trees ....
.... *S. hardii* Atkinson

Pileus 4-10 cm, convex to plane, soft to touch,
subviscid, at times with brown spots on the yellow
ground color; taste ± farinaceous. Gills adnate to
sinuate, close, narrow, whitish becoming pale
gray when mature. Stipe (4) 6-12 (14) cm x
6-14 mm, equal or often with a slight abrupt
bulb, pallid to yellowish; annulus thin but membranous, superior; white basal rhizomorphs present. Spores 6-7 x 3.5-4 μm. Pleurocystidia present
as chrysocystidia.
    Summer and fall, southern United States
mostly, not common.

26b Spores 7-9 (8-11) × 4.5-5.5 μm; growing in
lawns and other grassy places. Fig. 364 ....
.... *S. coronilla* (Fr.) Quél.

Figure 364

Figure 364 *Stropharia coronilla*

Pileus 2-4 (6) cm, convex to nearly plane, slightly
viscid, glabrous, pale yellow. Gills adnate, broad,
close, whitish soon violaceous-fuscous. Stipe 2-4
cm x 3-6 (10) mm, ± equal, dry, minutely floccose above the annulus; annulus white, persis-

tent, striate on upper surface. Pleurocystidia present as chrysocystidia.

Scattered to gregarious, summer and fall, widely distributed; common in irrigated areas where lawns are sprinkled regularly.

27a Fruiting body staining blue to greenish blue where injured **28**

27b Fruiting body not staining as above **31**

28a On hardwood slash partly decayed; Great Lakes region; spores 7-10 × 4-5 μm. Fig. 365 .... *P. caerulipes* (Pk.) Sacc.

Figure 365

Figure 365 *Psilocybe caerulipes*

Pileus 1-3 (3.5) cm, obtuse to convex, soon broadly convex to plane, glabrous, viscid when young, closely striatulate when moist, dull watery cinnamon fading to yellowish but dingy tan on aging, taste farinaceous. Gills adnate, narrow, crowded, finally with a decurrent tooth, brownish at first then rusty cinnamon. Stipe 3-6 cm x 2-3 mm, equal, more or less tough, apex pruinose, with a fibrillose zone where veil breaks, whitish downward at first. Pleurocystidia slightly capitate, mostly near the gill edge.

Scattered to gregarious, summer and fall, Great Lakes region east and southward. *Psilocybe quebecensis* O'lah & Heim is a closely related species. Both are hallucinogenic.

28b Habitat and distribution not as above and spores larger **29**

29a On decaying peat moss; cheilocystidia 4-6 μm wide .... *P. baeocystis* Sing. & Sm.

Pileus 1.4-5.4 cm, conic to campanulate or convex, subviscid, glabrous, margin striate, olive-brown to buffy brown, copper-tinged over disc as dried. Gills adnate, more or less close, moderately broad, when mature violet-fuscous. Stipe 5-7 cm x 2-3 mm, more or less equal, with fine white fibrils over surface, yellowish near apex, Spores (8) 10-13 x 6.3-7 μm. Pleurocystidia absent.

Probably introduced; Pacific Northwest. Its distribution and habitat range remains to be determined by critical studies. Hallucinogenic.

29b On slash of conifers and on chip-dirt of conifers **30**

30a Pileus margin straight at first; stipe darkening to bister or darker from base upward and more or less glabrous. Fig. 366 .... *P. pelliculosa* (Sm.) Sing. & Sm.

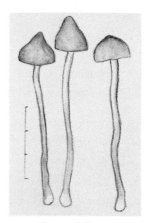
Figure 366

Figure 366 *Psilocybe pelliculosa*

Pileus 8-15 (30) mm, obtusely conic to conic-campanulate, glabrous, viscid, dingy yellow-brown, more olivaceous in age, margin striate when moist, surface pale dull tan when faded. Gills cinnamon brown until darkened by maturing spores, adnate-seceding, close, broad. Stipe 6-8 cm x 1.5-2 mm, ± equal, pallid to grayish, appressed-fibrillose; veil rudimentary. Spores 9.3-11 x 5-5.5 μm. Pleurocystidia absent.

Common slash and debris of conifers, the Pacific Northwest and fruiting during cool weather in the fall on into winter. Hallucinogenic.

30b Pileus margin incurved at first; stipe pallid from a coating of fibrils, staining only slightly where bruised ....
.... *P. strictipes* **Singer & Smith**

Pileus 2-4 cm, convex to plane, glabrous, viscid, pellicle separable, margin striatulate, color dull yellowish brown to olive-brown, fading to cinnamon-buff on disc, finally pallid over all. Gills adnate, close, narrow, pallid becoming chocolate-brown. Stipe 10-13 cm x 2-3 (5) mm, strict, more or less equal, pallid, veil zone indistinct, staining bluish slightly. Spores 9-12.5 x 5-6.5 μm. Pleurocystidia none.

Solitary to scattered or in small clusters on decaying conifer wood, fall, not common, Pacific Northwest. Poisonous (hallucinogenic).

31a Pileus typically sharply conic, olive to olive-gray when young; spores 11-13.5 $\times$ 7-8 μm; in pastures. Fig. 367 ....
.... *P. semilanceata* **(Fr.) Quél.**

Figure 367

Figure 367 *Psilocybe semilanceata*

Pileus 1-2.5 cm high, 8-20 mm across the base, conic to sharply conic, scarcely expanding, glabrous, viscid, dull olivaceous, finally olive-gray before fading to pinkish buff or dingy tan, striate when moist. Gills pale gray, chocolate brown when

mature, adnate, broad, close. Stipe 5-10 cm x 1-2 mm, flexuous, pruinose above, thinly white-fibrillose with the fibrils greenish blue in age. Pleurocystidia absent.

Scattered to gregarious in meadows, late summer and fall, Pacific Northwest in particular but widely distributed. It is collected for its properties as an hallucinogen, as are all the blue-staining species of this family. All, however, are to be regarded as mildly poisonous. There is still a question of whether *P. semilanceata* var. *semilanceata* actually stains from bruising or whether the bluish areas noted on old pilei are the result of aging.

31b Not as above **32**

32a On decaying remains of fireweed (*Epilobium*); pileus with flecks of veil near the margin at first; spores 5-6 $\times$ 4-4.5 μm ....
.... *P. acadiensis* **Smith**

Pileus 1-2.5 cm, obtuse to campanulate becoming expanded-umbonate or plane; viscid, hygrophanous, dark rusty brown fading to clay-color. Gills adnate, narrow, close, pallid then dark violaceous-brown. Stipe 2-4 cm x 2-2.5 mm, equal above an enlarged base, dark brown, densely fibrillose, terminated by a fibrillose zone; base surrounded by a mat of mycelium. Pleurocystidia none. Cheilocystidia 28-40 x 5-6 μm, elongating to 50-70 x 3-4 μm in age.

Probably widely distributed in eastern Canada, but as yet its distribution has not been determined.

32b Not as above **33**

33a Gills flushed green by maturity (not resulting from injury); scattered or in clusters on conifer wood (see page 255) *Naematoloma fasciculare* also). Fig. 368 ....
.... *N. dispersum* **(Fr.) Karst.**

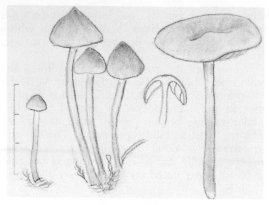

Figure 368

Figure 368 *Naematoloma dispersum*

Pileus 1-4 cm, conic, campanulate or umbonate-expanded, glabrous, moist, orange-tawny to tawny, fading and developing yellow tints. Gills broad, adnate, close, pallid becoming dingy olive, purplish brown finally. Stipe 6-10 cm x 2-5 mm, nearly equal, rather tough, silky fibrillose, or with an annular zone from the veil, dark reddish brown to bister below, yellowish above. Spores 7-9 (10) x 4-5 μm. Chrysocystidia present as pleurocystidia.

Often abundant late in the season, northern United States and in Canada. It is a variable species found in smaller clusters than *N. fasciculare*.

33b Not as above 34

34a Species with specialized habitats as follows: (see p. 261 for 34b)

1. On *Polytrichum* (Hair-Capped Moss) on barren sandy soil. Fig. 369 ....
.... *P. polytrichophila* Peck

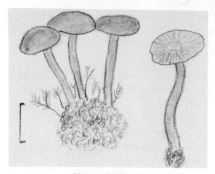

Figure 369

Figure 369 *Psilocybe polytrichophila*

Pileus 4-12 mm, convex to more or less campanulate, glabrous, striatulate when moist, dull rusty brown fading to buff; usually with a faint odor. Gills broad, subdistant, adnate, at times short-decurrent, colored ± like pileus. Stipe 2.5-5 cm x 1-1.5 mm thinly whitish-fibrillose, colored like the pileus. Spores 6-7.5 x 4-5 μm. Pleurocystidia rare and resembling cheilocystidia. Cheilocystidia 16-23 x 5-7 μm, fusoid-ventricose, apex obtuse.

Early spring (April in Michigan). The Michigan variant lacks a distinctive odor.

2. On *Sphagnum* in bogs; with white patches of veil on cap margin; gills grayish brown at first; spores 5.5-6.5 x 4-4.5 μm .... *P. sphagnicola* Smith

Pileus 10-15 mm, conic-campanulate, dark brown fading to yellowish. Gills close to subdistant, broad, adnate, becoming violaceous brown. Stipe 7-9 cm x 1-1.5 mm, equal, surface covered to near apex with clay-colored fibrils, base dark rusty brown beneath the fibrils. Pleurocystidia none.

Scattered, inconspicuous, and hence "rare." Known from Michigan.

3. Caespitose in arcs or rings on grass in lawns, etc.; stipe surrounded by copious mycelium, California; spores 6-7 x 3.5-4 μm .... *P. castanella* Peck

Pileus 1.5-3.5 cm, convex to broadly convex, glabrous or margin silky at first, subviscid, dark reddish brown over disc at first, margin pinkish tan, fading to pale tan overall. Gills broadly adnate, subdistant, fairly broad, pale brown, finally fuscous. Stipe 3-5 cm x 2-3 mm, equal or enlarged near apex, attached to grass by copious mycelium. Pleurocystidia none.

Little is known about the seasonal occurrence and general distribution outside of California, but it is more frequent than the records indicate.

4. Found on relatively undecayed fallen leaves of hardwood trees, with a flat disc of mycelium at base of stipe; spores 5-6.5 x 4-4.6 x 5-6 μm .... *P. phyllogena* Peck

Pileus 4-8 mm, convex to umbonate, reddish brown moist, dingy tan faded. Gills adnate, broad, close, horizontal, brown. Stipe 1.5-2.5 cm x 1-2 mm, fibrillose, brownish, expanding at base into a flat disc which adheres closely to the leaf; veil none. Spores 5-6.5 (7) x 4-4.6 x 5-6 μm. Pleurocystidia none.

Great Lakes area eastward, summer, not rare during warm wet summers, but never in large numbers.

5. On partly decayed wood of conifers; stipe base surrounded by a mat of gray mycelium .... *P. washingtonensis* Smith

Pileus 1-2 cm conic to convex, hygrophanous, dark dull reddish brown fading to more or less clay-color; taste ± bitter. Gills adnate to subdecurrent, close to subdistant, broad, dull vinaceous-brown. Stipe 3-5 cm x 1.5-2 mm, dark brown within, surface with appressed grayish fibrils. Spores 6.3-7.5 (8) x 3.8-4.5 μm. Pleurocystidia abundant, 38-56 (64) x 9-12 μm, fusoid-ventricose, subacute. Cheilocystidia more variable than above.

Pacific Northwest, not uncommon in the fall but rarely collected.

6. On muck in bogs; veil remnants on cap sparse to absent; gills yellowish at first; spores 14-18 x 5-7 μm; Fig. 370 ....
.... *N. udum* (Fr.) Karst.

Figure 370

Figure 370 *Naematoloma udum*

Pileus 1-3 (5) cm, obtusely conic to convex, color orange cinnamon to tawny, slowly becoming yellower and if water-soaked ± olivaceous; taste ± bitter. Gills adnate, more or less close, broad, finally dingy purple-brown. Stipe 4-12 cm x 1.5-4 mm, equal, fragile, ± ferruginous to rusty brown below. Pleurocystidia present as chrysocystidia.

Scattered to gregarious in bogs, especially along rabbit runways, northern United States and Canada, very common during late summer and fall.

34b Species with unspecialized habitats 35

**35a Stipe 6-12 (18) cm × 2-4 (6) mm; spores 9-12.5 × 5-7 μm; pileus viscid and dark reddish brown. Fig. 371 ....
.... *P. atrobrunnea* (Lasch) Gillet**

Figure 371

Figure 371 *Psilocybe atrobrunnea*

Pileus 1.5-4 (5.5) cm, conic-campanulate to convex or plane, glabrous, viscid, dark reddish brown, in age blackish brown, pale tan faded, striate when moist; taste farinaceous. Gills close, broad, adnate, pale cinnamon-buff then dark violaceous brown. Stipe flexuous to strict, cartilaginous, coated with pallid fibrils, in age becoming bister from base up. Pleurocystidia (as leptocystidia) inconspicuous and scattered to rare.

Scattered to gregarious in swamps and bogs generally (low wet ground), late fall, Great Lakes area eastward; probably common in Canada.

35b Not as above **36**

36a Chrysocystidia absent; spores (5) 6-7 (8) x 4-5 μm; cheilocystidia clavate to globose .... *P. rhomboidispora* **Atkinson**

Pileus 1-2.5 cm, becoming convex, umbonate or plane; with veil remnants on margin at first, chestnut brown fading to clay-color; viscid, taste ± farinaceous. Gills crowded, short-decurrent, narrow, ± chestnut brown. Stipe 2-6 cm x 1-3 mm,

base white-mycelioid and mycelium extending over substrate; surface more or less concolorous with pileus beneath the fibrils. Pleurocystidia none. Cheilocystidia often developing a protuberance up to ± 50 μm long.

Scattered or in small clusters on debris in hardwoods, Great Lakes area, apparently fairly rare.

36b Chrysocystidia present in the hymenium **37**

37a Spores 11-13 × 6-8 μm; stipe 4-13 cm x 2.5-4 mm; scattered to gregarious on wet soil .... *N. ericaeum* (Fr.) **Singer**

Pileus 1.5-3 (6) cm, campanulate to ± plane, margin appressed against stipe at first, soon glabrous, subviscid to viscid, olive to olive-brown becoming tawny and fading to yellowish; context pale yellow, odor and taste slightly raphanoid. Gills adnate, then adnexed, ± subdistant, broad, grayish, finally violaceous fuscous. Stipe equal, yellowish above, dingy brown below, often with a faint veil-line.

Apparently southern in distribution in North America.

37b Spores (8) 9-11 x 5-6 μm; stipe 3-10 cm x 1.5-3 mm; northern in distribution .... *N. squalidellum* (Pk.) **Smith**

Pileus 1-3 (4) cm, conic to campanulate, glabrous, moist, reddish cinnamon to rusty brown fading and then yellower to greenish yellow. Gills close, narrow, adnate, whitish to olivaceous gray or finally greenish yellow. Stipe flexuous, brittle, rusty brown to blackish brown near base in age, olive-yellow above.

Scattered, gregarious or caespitose on piles of organic debris such as left along a stream by the overflow, but on wet soil generally, often abundant when rains follow a hot dry summer. It was very abundant at Lake Timagami, Ontario in the late summer of 1936.

CORTINARIACEAE Roze

Pileus and stipe confluent (if a stipe is present); spore deposit yellow (ochraceous), yellow-brown, orange-rusty to orange-brown, rarely ± vinaceous brown to cocoa-brown; spores with colored wall (mount in KOH) except in *Tubaria*, and usually ornamented; the ornamentation various: of wrinkles, warts, nodules, fine spines, etc., but *not blue* in Melzer's, lacking an apical pore. *Pholiota* may sometimes key out here. It has smooth spores which usually have a germ pore.

The family is a large one showing great diversity in the details of the pileus cuticle, the types and morphology of the cystidia as well as their location, and in the development of veils. It is the largest family of mushrooms with *Cortinarius* alone having nearly 800 taxa (species, varieties, and forms) in North America. Some species are deadly poisonous, some "mildly" poisonous, and some are edible and choice.

KEY TO GENERA

1a Stipe absent, lateral or ± eccentric and then reduced in size to ± rudimentary .... (p. 286) *Crepidotus*

1b Stipe typically central (if eccentric, not reduced in size) 2

2a Veils absent; stipe with a long pseudorhiza; cap margin long remaining inrolled .... (p. 300) *Phaeocollybia*

2b Not as above 3

3a Spore deposit orange-rusty to orange-brown or bright rusty brown; lignicolous .... (p. 289) *Gymnopilus*

3b Not as above 4

4a Spores smooth to angular or nodulose .... (p. 295) *Inocybe*

4b Spores warty-rugulose to punctate often appearing ± smooth 5

5a Stipe 1-2 cm thick; partial veil leaving a distinct annulus on stipe; terrestrial .... (p. 303) *Rozites*

5b Not as above 6

6a Stipe typically cartilaginous (and narrow); spores typically with a plage .... (p. 288) *Galerina*

6b Stipe typically fleshy (and mostly thicker than in *Galerina*), seldom with spore showing a plage 7

7a Fruiting body always with a cortina when young; young gills usually distinctly colored; cheilocystidia lacking in most species; spore-wall rigid and spore not readily collapsing .... (p. 264) *Cortinarius*

7b Not as above 8

8a Spores with relatively thin almost colorless walls and often one observes many collapsed spores in a mount of revived material; spore deposit ochraceous to pale tan .... (p. 303) *Tubaria*

8b Not as above 9

9a Young gill edges typically white and crenulate .... (p. 291) *Hebeloma*

9b Young gills not as above; white, very soft and easily separated from the pileus .... (p. 136) *Ripartites*

Cortinarius Fries

Pileus and stipe confluent; spore deposit rusty brown to ochraceous tawny; spores at least weakly ornamented but not amyloid; stipe typically fleshy even when thin; partial veil a cortina; outer veil fibrillose and rarely leaving an annulus on the stipe; pileus typically with a cutis or an ixocutis to an ixolattice; species typically terrestrial and forming mycorrhiza with woody plants. Over 600 species are estimated to occur in North America; some are poisonous, some edible, and most are untested.

KEY TO SUBGENERA

1a Pileus and stipe both viscid to slimy or (if dry) ± shining as if varnished .... (p. 264) *Myxacium*

1b Stipe dry; pileus viscid, moist or dry 2

2a Pileus viscid to slimy (shiny when dry) 3

2b Pileus dry to moist and if the latter ± hygrophanous 4

3a Stipe with a marginate bulb at first or with an abrupt oblique basal flange .... (p. 269) *Bulbopodium*

3b Stipe clavate to equal when young .... (p. 273) *Phlegmacium*

4a Pileus dry and fibrillose to scaly .... (p. 276) *Cortinarius*

4b Pileus moist and hygrophanous (or subhygrophanous in some, but then glabrous and not fibrillose) .... (p. 282) *Telamonia*

SUBGENUS MYXACIUM

Key to Sections

1a Stipe equal or narrowed downward when young .... (p. 264) *Elastici*

1b Stipe clavate to bulbous at first, nearly equal in age in many species .... (p. 266) *Delibuti*

Section Elastici

1a Stipe 3-6.5 cm thick; pileus 11-35 cm broad; lamellae staining russet if injured .... *C. ponderosus* Smith

Pileus slimy, russet on disc, color at margin mustard-yellow; context pallid, taste disagreeable. Lamellae narrow, crowded, on edges tinged purplish vinaceous at first, soon yellow ochre, russet in age. Stipe surface brownish becoming russet, slime-veil yellow. Spores 8.5-11 x 5-6 μm.

Scattered to gregarious under ponderosa pine, southern Oregon and northern California, late fall.

1b Not as above 2

2a Lower portion of stipe surface typically breaking up into zones or rings of veil and cuticle tissue (often obscure) .... *C. collinitus* (Fr.) sensu lato

Pileus 4-10 cm, obtuse to convex then plane or plano-umbonate, dull yellow to ochraceous tawny or tawny, slimy; odor and taste slight. Lamellae pallid to grayish (violaceous in one variant), close, broad, ± adnate. Stipe 6-15 cm x 7-15 mm, slimy and with a fibrillose veil interior to the slime, generally discoloring in age. Spores 10-13 x 6-7.5 μm.

Very common under aspen, late summer and fall in northern United States and in Canada.

2b Not as above 3

3a Violaceous, purplish, vinaceous or blue colors present somewhere on the fruiting body when it is young (often disappearing) 4

3b Lacking the above colors in the immature fruiting bodies 6

4a Lamellae pale tan when young; stipe with a violaceous slime sheath. Fig. 372 .... *C. vanduzerensis* Smith & Trappe

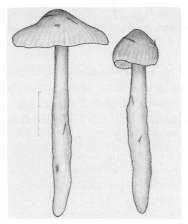

Figure 372

Figure 372 *Cortinarius vanduzerensis*

Pileus 4-8 cm, covered with a thick layer of slime, dark chestnut becoming ± cinnamon brown; context pallid then pinkish buff; odor and taste not distinctive, with $FeSO_4$ olivaceous. Gills pale tan (pinkish buff), at maturity dull cinnamon, close, adnate, broad. Stipe 10-18 cm x 1-2 cm, narrowed downward, pallid then brownish within, surface coated by a thick violet slime-veil. Spores 11-14 (15) x 7-9 μm.

Solitary to gregarious under spruce and hemlock, Oregon Coast, not common, late fall.

4b Lamellae pale violaceous when young 5

5a Gill edges white and ± fimbriate from numerous cheilocystidia; spores 13-17 × 5.5-7.5 μm; growing under beech and other hardwoods .... *C. cylindripes* Kauffman

Pileus 3-7 cm, violaceous-umber, soon ± vinaceous brown then tawny or paler, often radially wrinkled; context violaceous becoming pallid; odor and taste mild. Lamellae broad, close, adnate, violaceous when young. Stipe 8-10 cm x 8-17 mm, with a violaceous slime-veil, white within. Spores 12-15 x 6.5-8 μm.

Gregarious in low, wet, oak and beech woods, Great Lakes area, summer and early fall, common during some years. It may be significant that *Vaccinium* bushes are nearly always present near by.

5b Lacking white-floccose gill edges; growing under conifers, often under spruce in bogs; spores 14-18 × 7-9 μm. Fig. 373 .... ***C. splendidus*** **Peck**

Figure 374

Figure 374 *Cortinarius mucosus*

Pileus 4-9 cm, slimy, subferruginous to tawny, in age ± ochraceous; context whitish, odor and taste mild. Lamellae broad, crowded, ± adnexed, pallid becoming tawny. Stipe 4-7 cm x 12-20 mm, subequal, slimy, whitish, a superior white fibrillose zone left by the broken cortina. Spores 11-15 x 5-6.5 μm.

Scattered under conifers, especially 2-needle pines, Pacific Northwest, fall; some seasons it is frequently encountered.

6b Lamellae ochraceous becoming cinnamon; spores 14-17 × 7-8.5 μm .... ***C. mucigineus*** **Peck**

Pileus 3-6 cm, margin finally uplifted, viscid, tawny-orange, margin striate when moist; context merely tinged with yellow. Gills broad, yellowish then cinnamon, close, ± veined on faces. Stipe 7-10 cm x 6-8 mm, viscid, white or whitish. Spores coarsely roughened.

Scattered under balsam, New York, September.

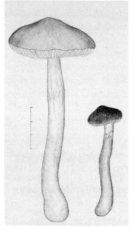

Figure 373

Figure 373 *Cortinarius splendidus*

Pileus 3-5 cm, obtuse then campanulate to plano-umbonate, slimy, somewhat striate on margin, dark rusty brown (liver-brown), slowly paler to tawny or pinkish cinnamon finally; context lacking a distinct odor or taste. Gills whitish to violet, then clay-color to cinnamon brown, edges even. Stipe 6-9 cm x 6-10 mm, with a violaceous slime sheath. Spores 14-18 x 7-9 μm.

Scattered to gregarious in the fall, northeastern and Great Lakes areas, late summer and fall.

6a Gills white to grayish then tawny; spores 11-18 × 7-9 μm. Fig. 374 .... ***C. mucosus*** **(Fr.) Fr.**

Section Delibuti

1a Fruiting body violet to lilac or purple in some part 2

1b Fruiting body lacking above colors 6

2a Fruiting body at first violaceous over all 3

2b Not as above 4

3a Taste of slime on pileus surface bitter. Fig. 375 .... *C. iodioides* Kauffman

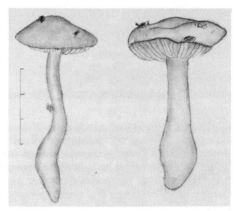

Figure 375

Figure 375 *Cortinarius iodioides*

Pileus 2-5 cm, convex to broadly umbonate, slimy-viscid, fading to yellowish; context pale violaceous then white, odor none. Lamellae narrow, close, violaceous at first then whitish and finally yellowish cinnamon. Stipe 2-6.5 cm x 4-6 mm, slime veil violaceous and surface whitish beneath it, nearly equal in age. Spores 7-9 x 4-5 μm.

Scattered to gregarious under hardwoods, late summer and fall, east of the Great Plains, abundant at times. Not edible.

3b Taste of pileus mild .... *C. iodes* Berk. & Curt.

Pileus 2-7 cm, convex to campanulate, becoming yellowish on disc; context violaceous becoming pallid; taste mild. Gills close, adnate, $\pm$ broad. Stipe 5-7 cm x 4-8 mm, slimy, slime violaceous. Spores 8-10 x 5-6.5 μm.

Gregarious on low ground under hardwoods, summer and fall east of the Great Plains, often abundant after heavy rains in August.

4a Pileus bright yellow; lamellae at first violet; spores 6-7.5 $\times$ 5-6.5 μm .... *C. sphaerosporus* Peck

Pileus 3-7 cm, convex to plane, straw yellow, slimy if wet; context violaceous then pallid, yellowish under the cuticle, odor and taste $\pm$ mild. Gills close, broad, $\pm$ adnate, violet at first. Stipe 5-10 cm x 5-8 mm, with an outer yellow slime-veil, at first pale violaceous near apex. Spores minutely roughened.

Gregarious in low hardwoods on wet soil, summer and fall, east of the Great Plains, occasional.

4b Pileus some other color when young; spores $\pm$ elliptic in face view 5

5a Pileus ferruginous to chestnut brown over disc; gills violaceous at first. Fig. 376 .... *C. castaneicolor* Smith

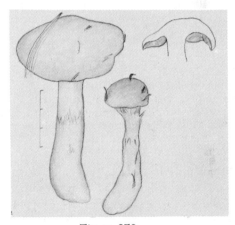

Figure 376

Figure 376 *Cortinarius castaneicolor*

Pileus 4-9 cm, broadly convex, slimy when fresh, disc soon showing minute patch-like scales, ferruginous on disc, margin pale tan; context caesious but soon buff colored; taste mild. Gills narrow, close, adnate. Stipe 8-11 cm x 10-15 (20) mm, whitish, lower portion showing remains of a pale tawny outer veil, only moderately viscid when young and fresh. Spores 8-10 x 4-5.5 μm.

Gregarious under conifers, Pacific Northwest, fall, not common.

5b Pileus violaceous drab becoming olive-ochraceous; gills pale vinaceous gray or more violaceous. Fig. 377 .... ***C. griseoluridus* Kauffman**

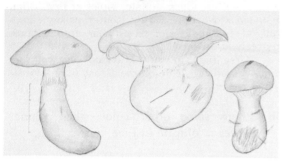

Figure 377

Figure 377   *Cortinarius griseoluridus*

Pileus 5-10 cm, convex to broadly umbonate, slimy; context tinged violaceous but soon pallid or tinged olive-yellow; odor and taste mild. Gills adnate-subdecurrent, close, finally rusty brown. Stipe 4-10 cm x 1-2.5 (3) cm near apex, clavate-bulbous to ± equal, violaceous-tinged over upper part, soon pallid, with a slime-veil. Spores 8-10 x 6.5-8 μm.

Scattered to gregarious under spruce and fir, Rocky Mountains, common after summer rains.

6a Pileus cuticle very bitter, color tawny to pale tan; pileus 1.5-5 cm broad. Fig. 378 .... ***C. vibratilis* (Fr.) Fries**

Figure 378

Figure 378   *Cortinarius vibratilis*

Pileus obtusely campanulate, slimy, hygrophanous, ochraceous to tawny later and finally pale tan; context pallid, thin, odor slight. Gills adnate to subdecurrent, thin, close, pallid becoming ochraceous and then ± ochraceous tawny. Stipe 3-7 cm x 4-10 mm, clavate and 10-15 mm below, white, slimy. Spores 6-7.5 x 4-5 μm.

Under both conifers and hardwoods, scattered, summer and fall, widely distributed in North America but infrequently collected.

6b Taste not bitter **7**

7a Odor sharply fragrant; context bright yellow; stipe staining brown where handled .... ***C. citrinifolius* Smith**

Pileus 3-5.5 cm, convex to broadly umbonate, slimy, yellowish orange; context citron yellow; taste slight. Gills close, broad, pale yellow, cinnamon brown in age. Stipe 7-9 cm x 9-12 mm, ± clavate, slimy, pale yellow above, dingy yellow below at first. Spores 8-10 x 5.5-7 μm.

Under fir, hemlock and spruce, Pacific Northwest, fall, not common.

7b Odor not distinctive; context white; not staining brown where handled. Fig 379 .... ***C. pallidifolius* Smith**

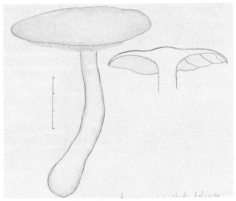
Figure 379

Figure 379 *Cortinarius pallidifolius*

Pileus 5-9 cm, convex to ± plane or umbonate, slimy if wet, tawny; context white; odor and taste mild. Gills whitish, slowly changing to grayish brown, close to crowded, broad. Stipe 10-15 cm x 10-15 mm near apex, up to 30 mm at base, pallid within, surface sheathed by a yellowish slime-veil which breaks up into zones or patches, a white fibrillose cortina beneath the slime-veil. Spores 9-13 x 5-6.5 μm.

Gregarious to solitary under spruce and fir, in the mountains of western North America, abundant at times.

SUBGENUS BULBOPODIUM

1a Gills at first violaceous to lilac 2

1b Gills at first some color other than above
.... 10

2a Pileus violet or lilac overall at first 3

2b Pileus some other color 6

3a Pileus with a patch or patches of a submembranous outer veil usually remain-
ing over the disc ....
.... *C. calyptrodermus* Smith

Pileus 5-10 (15) cm, convex to plane at maturity, dull lilac to violet over all beneath the remains of the veil; context pale lilac finally going to whitish, odor and taste not distinctive. Lamellae violet when young, close, ± broad, adnexed, not spotting. Stipe 5-9 x 1-2.5 cm above a broad (3-4 cm) marginate-depressed bulb; violaceous overall; cortina violaceous. Spores 10-13 x 6.5-8 μm. Cheilocystidia 24-36 x 4-7 μm, narrowly clavate.

Gregarious under second-growth hardwoods, Great Lakes area, late summer, sporadic.

3b Lacking patches of a submembranous
outer veil on pileus 4

4a Fruiting body a pale lilac; under conifers
in the Pacific Northwest. Fig. 380 ....
.... *C. olympianus* Smith

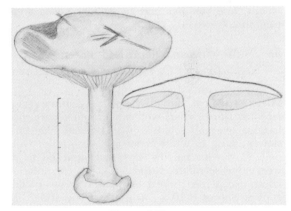
Figure 380

Figure 380 *Cortinarius olympianus*

Pileus 3-7 (10), convex to nearly plane, margin long remaining inrolled, glabrous, slimy at first, pale lilac over all, finally lilac white, at times yellowish on disc; KOH on pellicle pink to red; context pallid, odor and taste mild. Gills a pale pinkish lilac, narrow, crowded, ± adnexed, not spotting if bruised. Stipe 4-6 x 0.8-1 cm, equal above a broad depressed-marginate bulb 2 cm or more broad; pale to medium lilac. Spores 8-10 x 5-6 μm. Cheilocystidia basidium-like.

Scattered to gregarious under spruce fir and hemlock, Pacific Northwest, fall rainy season, not common.

4b   Fruiting body ± dull violaceous; on low ground under hardwoods; east of the Great Plains **5**

5a   Bulb small and oblique ....
.... *C. aggregatus* **Kauffman**

Pileus 5-12 cm, convex to plane, often irregular from crowding, dull violaceous over all, viscid, white-pruinose when young; context violaceous becoming dingy, odor and taste mild, not changing color where bruised. Gills violet-purple becoming grayish violaceous, broad, close, rounded next to stipe. Stipe 4-7 x 1-2 cm above a small oblique bulb which disappears in aging; cortina deep violet. Spores 7-9 x 5-5.5 μm. Cheilocystidia none (basidium-like).

Caespitose in arcs under oak and other hardwoods, late summer and fall, Great Lakes area, common.

5b   Bulb wide and depressed marginate ....
.... *C. michiganensis* **Kauffman**

Pileus 8-15 cm, broadly convex, glabrous, violaceous, slimy when wet, when young pale violaceous over all; context thick, tinged lilac and slowly going to white, odor and taste mild. Gills pale violaceous narrow, crowded, adnexed to ± free, edge serrulate. Stipe 3-6 x 1-3 cm, interior white except near apex; cortina violaceous-pallid, copius. Spores 8-10 x 5-6 μm. Cheilocystidia basidium-like.

Gregarious to clustered under hardwoods, late summer and fall, Great Lakes area, infrequent.

6a   Pileus radiately corrugated to wrinkled; under beech; gills violaceous when very young. Fig. 381 .... *C. corrugatus* **Peck**

Figure 381

Figure 381   *Cortinarius corrugatus*

Pileus 5-10 cm, obtuse to ± campanulate, surface viscid, coarsely radiately corrugated to reticulate, tawny to rusty ochraceous to ochraceous; context white to buff, odor pleasant, taste mild. Gills adnate broad, close, at first obscurely purplish violaceous, soon rusty cinnamon, edges becoming eroded, not spotting where injured. Stipe 7-12 x 0.6-2 cm, bulb rounded-oval and its margin oblique and often disappearing, tawny; cortina very thin. Spores 12-15 x 7-9 μm. Cheilocystidia basidium-like.

Scattered to gregarious under beech, summer and early fall, east of the Great Plains, common.

6b   Pileus not corrugated or conspicuously wrinkled **7**

7a   Pileus bright yellow at first **8**

7b   Pileus not yellow, or if yellow is present, the color pattern mixed **9**

8a   Growing under conifers; spores 9-12.5 $\times$ 5-6.5 μm .... *C. metarius* **Kauffman**

Pileus 4-10 cm hemispheric then broadly expanded, slimy, glabrous, bright yellow; context pinkish-violaceous soon becoming pallid and finally yellowish. Gills crowded, narrow, ± adnexed, pinkish violaceous (lilac) slowly more violaceous (duller), finally ± clay-color. Stipe 4-6 x 1-2 cm above a broad marginate-depressed bulb, at first ± violet throughout; bulb ± covered by yellow outer veil remnants; cortina pallid. Spores 9-12 x 5-6.5 μm.

Scattered to gregarious under spruce and fir, Rocky Mountains and the Pacific Northwest, sporadic, summer and fall.

8b   Growing under hardwoods; spores 8-10 × 4.5-5 μm; bulb small but depressed-marginate at first. Fig. 382 ....
.... *C. calochrous* Fries

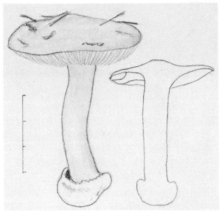

Figure 382

Figure 382   *Cortinarius calochrous*

Pileus 3-6 cm, convex to plane, slimy to viscid, glabrous; context whitish, odor and taste mild. Gills purplish-violaceous at first, narrow, crowded, adnexed, edges serrulate. Stipe 3-5 x 0.5-1 cm; bulb at first coated with yellow fibrils from an outer veil; near apex violaceous becoming pallid and finally yellowish overall. Cheilocystidia basidium-like.

Gregarious under hardwoods on low ground, summer and early fall, infrequent, widely distributed east of the Great Plains.

9a   Lamellae distinctly violaceous; spores (6) 7-9 (10) × 4.5-5.5 μm ....
.... *C. glaucopus* (Fr.) Fries

Pileus 5-12 cm, convex to plane or irregular from crowding, viscid, at first with a few scattered fibrils, soon glabrous, color ± yellowish-olive on margin, ochraceous to cinnamon-ochraceous on aging (color variable), surface often virgate; context violaceous but soon ochraceous, odor and taste mild. Gills narrow but finally broad, close, adnate, not spotting. Stipe 6-8 x 1.5-3 cm above an oblique ± evanescent bulb; near apex violaceous but soon dingy ochraceous, copious mycelium often present (some at times left on the cap as stipe elongated).

Gregarious-caespitose often in arcs under spruce and fir, summer and fall, common in the conifer forests of the West, less common east of the Great Plains. It is one of our most variable species. We have reports of people eating it, but cannot recommend it because of its variability and the fact that some *Cortinarii* are, apparently, deadly poisonous.

9b   Gills in face view at first violaceous but as seen across the edges olivaceous; spores 9-12 (13) × 5-6.5 μm. Fig. 383 ......
.... *C. montanus* Kauffman

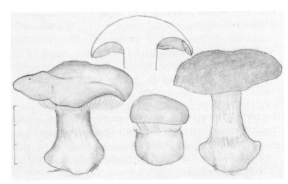

Figure 383

Figure 383   *Cortinarius montanus*

Pileus 5-10 cm, convex to broadly expanded, slimy to viscid, dingy rusty brown to clay-color streaked with olive or olive-brown (color pattern very confusing); context pallid becoming tinged the color of the pileus; odor and taste mild. Gills dingy brown over all in age. Stipe 4-7 x 1-2.5 cm; bulb depressed at very first but soon oblique; surface above bulb pale blue to apex, at first with remains of greenish yellow outer veil, finally dingy brown over all. Cheilocystidia basidium-like.

Growing mostly solitary to scattered under conifers in our western mountains, especially in the Cascade range; fall. It can be found almost every season in the Cascades.

10a Stipe soon becoming pale lavender within; gills honey yellow at first, slowly becoming lavender to purplish; spores 11-14 $\times$ 6.5-8 μm; under conifers. Fig. 384 .... *C. cedretorum* **Maire**

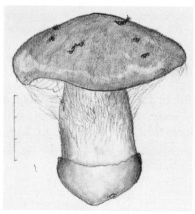

Figure 384

Figure 384   *Cortinarius cedretorum*

Pileus 8-15 cm, convex to broadly convex, slimy, bright yellow but soon tinged brick red and purplish brown by late maturity; context with mild odor and taste. Gills close, broad, adnate, greenish yellow but soon changing, edges crenulate. Stipe 8-12 x 1.5-3 cm, usually pale lavender throughout; bulb 4.5-7 cm broad, marginate-depressed, yellow from veil remnants, apex livid purple in age. Basidia containing purplish red granules in KOH.

Gregarious under conifers, Pacific Northwest, fall, uncommon. It is one of our most striking species. East of the Great Plains under hardwoods *C. atkinsonianus* Kauffman occurs. Its gills change in color as in Maire's species, but the cap

is dark reddish brown at first. It is one of the best edible fungi known but cannot be recommended because of what has been discovered relative to poisonous species in the genus during the last ten years, and the number of "variants" known around both of these species.

10b Not as above **11**

11a Gills olive to olive-yellow at first; spores 10-13 $\times$ 6-7.5 μm; basidia with olive granules as revived in KOH. Fig. 385 .... *C. prasinus* (**Pers.**) **Fries**

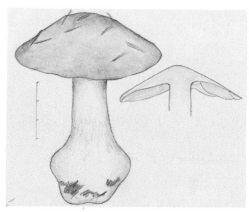

Figure 385

Figure 385   *Cortinarius prasinus*

Pileus 4-10 cm, convex to broadly convex, glabrous, viscid, evenly olive-color over all; context yellowish pallid, odor and taste not distinctive. Gills adnexed, close, moderately broad. Stipe 4-8 x 1-1.5 cm above the bulb which is depressed-marginate, and the surface olive to olive-yellow toward the apex from remains of the cortina. Cheilocystidia basidium-like.

Scattered to gregarious under conifers, Pacific Northwest, fall, most abundant during warm wet seasons.

11b Gills whitish becoming pale tan; spores 8-10 $\times$ 5-5.5 μm, pileus canescent at first .... *C. multiformis* (**Fr.**) **Fries**

Pileus 5-10 cm, convex to broadly expanded or with a low broad umbo, canescent at first, viscid, ochraceous buff to tawny; context pallid, ± lutescent, odor and taste mild. Gills whitish then pallid, finally ± rusty cinnamon. Stipe 4-9 x 1-2 cm above bulb; bulb oblique or merely a flange and gradually ± obliterated; surface above bulb whitish at first becoming ± alutaceous; cortina white and scanty.

Common under conifers and widely distributed, summer (Rocky Mountains), or fall (northern USA and southern Canada).

SUBGENUS PHLEGMACIUM

1a Odor and/or taste of pellicle or context distinctive 2

1b Not with a distinctive odor or taste **6**

2a Taste of pellicle bitter **3**

2b Not as above **4**

3a Pileus whitish to pale tan; young gills pallid .... *C. crystallinus* Fries

Pileus 3-5 cm, obtuse becoming expanded-umbonate, glabrous, slimy viscid, whitish to pale buff or pale tan; context pallid to buff; odor none. Gills becoming pale tawny finally, narrow, close, adnate, not staining where bruised. Stipe 4-8 x 0.9-1.5 cm, 15-20 mm at base, pale tan in age, whitish at first, thinly fibrillose. Spores 5.5-7 (8) x 3.5-4 μm.

Solitary to gregarious under spruce and fir, Pacific Northwest, fall, not uncommon. Not edible.

3b Pileus sooty olive to olive-brown, finally clay-color; gills dark olive to tinged violaceous at first. Fig. 386 ....
.... *C. infractus* (Fr.) Fr.

Figure 386

Figure 386 *Cortinarius infractus*

Pileus 4-10 cm, convex to obtuse becoming broadly convex to ± plano-umbonate, glabrous; context thick, pallid or tinged violaceous, odor slight. Gills close, ± broad, adnate. Stipe 4-9 x 0.8-1.5 cm, solid, clavate, dull violaceous above at first, dingy olive-brown downward. Spores 7-8 x 5-6 μm, ellipsoid to subglobose. Basidia (some of them) olive green in KOH.

Gregarious and often abundant, late summer and fall, either under hardwood or conifers, common and widely distributed. Obviously not edible. There are a number of color variants of this species.

4a Odor fragrant-subfoetid; fruiting body ± bright lilac-violaceous overall; spores 7.5-10 × 5-5.5 μm ...... *C. subfoetidus* Smith

Pileus (3) 4-10 cm broad, obtusely umbonate to plane, surface slimy, soon dry, appressed-fibrillose beneath the slime; context about concolorous with surface at first; taste mild. Gills close, adnexed, broad. Stipe 5-8 x 1-2 cm, ± equal, ± concolorous with pileus, sheathed over lower third with a lavender sheath.

Under conifers (especially hemlock), fall, Pacific Northwest, not abundant but frequently encountered. Edibility not known.

4b Not as above **5**

5a Pileus and stipe staining vinaceous brown where bruised; odor strong of fresh green corn. Fig. 387 .... *C. superbus* Smith

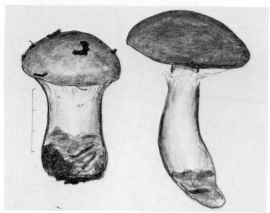

Figure 387

Figure 387 *Cortinarius superbus*

Pileus (4) 6-15 cm, convex then ± plane, slimy, pale yellow with olive tones, gradually becoming vinaceous brown or redder context pale yellow, soon dingy brown where cut, taste mild. Gills yellow staining brown, broad, close, adnexed. Stipe 6-12 x 1-2.5 cm or up to 4.5 cm at base, finally ± equal; cortina yellow and copious. Spores 11-13 x 6-7.5 μm. Basidia (at least some) with purple content as mounted in KOH, the pigment in granules.

Scattered under conifers, Pacific Northwest, fall, after heavy rains, apparently rare.

5b **Odor aromatic and very pleasant; injured parts of fruiting body not staining brown** .... *C. percomis* Fries

Pileus 5-8 cm, obtuse to convex, dull greenish yellow becoming honey yellow, viscid, glabrous; context yellow, with a slightly disagreeable taste. Lamellae crowded, narrow, narrowly adnate, pale yellow becoming sulphur yellow before masked by spores. Stipe 4-8 x 1-1.5 cm, clavate, yellowish white, fibrillose from the sulphur yellow veil. Spores 10-13 x 5-6.5 μm. Some basidia with a vinaceous red content in KOH.

Under conifers, western United States, fall.

6a **Fruiting body violaceous over all except the mature gills** 7

6b **Fruiting body lacking above colors or these only on young gills** 9

7a **Stipe with a large clavate bulb, its cut surface slowly staining dark vinaceous red to vinaceous brown. Fig. 388** .... *C. cyanites* Fries

Figure 388

Figure 388 *Cortinarius cyanites*

Pileus 7-15 cm, convex to broadly convex, surface appressed-fibrillose, moderately viscid to tacky, when fresh dull blue to bluish gray overall, finally becoming deep vinaceous brown; context thick, dull blue. Gills dark dull blue at first, close, broad, Stipe 10-15 x 2-3.5 cm at apex, 4-8 cm near base, fibrillose. Spores 8-10 x 5-6 μm. Cheilocystidia 18-36 x 4-9 μm, filamentous to clavate.

Usually solitary under conifers, Pacific Northwest, fall and early winter, not common.

7b **Not as above** 8

8a Stipe short and thick (5-12 × 1-4 cm), ± equal; growing under oak, *Vaccinium* present also; Great Lakes area .... *C. balteatus* (Fr.) Fries

Pileus 5-15 (25) cm, convex to plane, ± viscid, at first dull lavender over all, soon tawny olive with a violaceous margin; context thick, compact, soon whitish, odor and taste slight. Gills violaceous gray at first, broad, crowded, adnate, to adnexed. Stipe equal to tapered below when mature, dull brown in age, at times staining yellow when injured. Spores 9-11 x 5-6 μm.

Gregarious under hardwoods in the Great Lakes area; generally reported as from under conifers. In the Great Lakes area it is often abundant where shrubby *Vaccinium* plants occur under oak, and such are also often present in conifer forests. Thus *Vaccinium* may possibly be a "bridging genus." When we learn whether the American variant is poisonous, the species would be worth testing for edibility—it is very firm and "meaty."

8b Stipe 1-1.5 cm thick; cut context becoming bright lilac; spores 7-9 × 4.5-5.3 μm. Fig. 389 .... *C. mutabilis* Smith

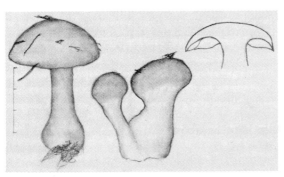

Figure 389

Figure 389 *Cortinarius mutabilis*

Pileus 4-8 cm, convex to plane, viscid, glabrous; context violaceous becoming brighter when cut, odor and taste mild. Gills persistently dull violet until masked by spores, adnexed, close, broad. Stipe 6-8 cm long, clavate.

Gregarious under conifers on very rotten wood and duff, fall, Pacific Northwest, often common late in the fall. Edibility ? (A number of other species closely resemble it).

9a Gills pale grayish blue at first; stipe with yellowish zones of veil material over lower part .... *C. claricolor* Fries

Pileus 5-9 cm, umbonate to convex or ± plane, glabrous, tawny over disc, ochraceous over margin. Context pallid to yellowish; odor very faintly pleasant at first (hardly distinctive). Gills close, broad, adnate. Stipe 8-12 x 1-1.5 cm, 2.5-4 cm near base, pallid to yellowish, staining brown around worm holes. Spores 10-13 x 6-7.5 μm.

Gregarious on humus under hardwoods, late summer and fall; abundant during warm wet seasons; Great Lakes area eastward. Not recommended. The European material cited by Moser as edible has spores 8-9 μm long.

9b Gills whitish at first 10

10a Veil well-developed and leaving patches on pileus margin and ± of an annular zone on stipe where it breaks .... *C. turmalis* Fries

Pileus 8-15 cm, obtuse to convex to plano-umbonate, viscid, slimy if wet, yellowish tawny to reddish tawny and in age ± chestnut brown on disc. Context thick, white, firm. Gills white, slowly dark tawny, close, broad, becoming adnexed. Stipe 8-12 x 1-3 cm, near base 3-5 cm at first, solid, whitish to pallid, copiously fibrillose. Spores 8-10 x 5-6 μm.

Solitary to gregarious under conifers in the mountains of the Pacific Northwest and in the Great Lakes area, fall, not uncommon. Edibility: not recommended—there is a cluster of variants around this species which makes critical testing or chemical analysis difficult.

10b Veil not copious; spores 9-12 × 5.5-6.5 μm. Fig. 390 .... *C. crassus* Fries

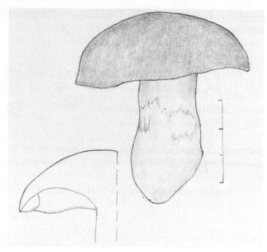

Figure 390

Figure 390 *Cortinarius crassus*

Pileus 8-15 (20) cm, convex to broadly convex, viscid, soon dry, ± clay-color at first, russet in age; context thick, firm, white. Gills white becoming buff, finally ± fulvous. Stipe 8-13 x 1-3 cm, ± equal or narrowed near the base, whitish becoming dingy brown and then brownish within also.

    Gregarious to scattered under conifers, frequently collected in our western mountains but also known from the northern conifer forests generally. The North American variant described here is slightly different from species as currently understood in Europe.

SUBGENUS CORTINARIUS

1a Gills and/or pileus blue to violet when young 2

1b Not as above 8

2a Pileus soon becoming squamulose 3

2b Pileus appressed fibrillose, at times the fibrils arranged in appressed fascicles 5

3a Pileus covered with dark brown squamules; stipe with scales or patches of brown fibrils below veil-line. Fig. 391 .... *C. pholideus* (Fr.) Fries

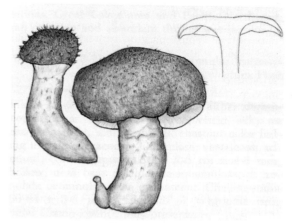

Figure 391

Figure 391 *Cortinarius pholideus*

Pileus 4-8 cm, obtuse to campanulate or convex to plano-umbonate, surface dry, ± cinnamon brown; context slightly violaceous then whitish to brownish, odor and taste mild. Gills narrowly adnexed, ± close and broad, violaceous then clay-color or browner. Stipe 4-10 cm x 5-12 mm, apical region violaceous; spores 7-8 x 5-5.5 µm.

    Solitary to gregarious on or near rotting logs of birch (*Betula*), common in the Great Lakes area and eastward, rare in the Pacific Northwest, fall. Edibility: not recommended.

3b Not as above 4

4a Pileus brown strongly tinged with purple, becoming chocolate brown; stipe with a thick ± clavate bulb 4-6 cm diameter; fruit bodies growing under hardwoods. Fig. 392 .... *C. squamulosus* Peck

Figure 392

Figure 392 *Cortinarius squamulosus*

Pileus 4-10 cm, convex to broadly umbonate, surface dry, appressed-fibrillose and the layer breaking into squamules, brown strongly tinged purple, becoming chocolate brown; context thick in the disc, pinkish white to grayish pallid, odor ± spicy (stronger in age), taste mild. Gills close, broad, deep purple-umber becoming chocolate brown, edges flocculose. Stipe 8-15 x 1-2 cm (at apex); with a ± median bandlike ring; dull purple becoming chocolate color; cortina pallid. Spores 6-8 x 5-7 μm, ellipsoid to subglobose. Cheilocystidia present.

New England to Wisconsin, late summer and fall, not common. Edibility: not recommended.

4b   **Pileus dark violet over all; stipe ± equal; under conifers. Fig. 393** ....
.... **C. *violaceus* (Fr.) Fries**

Figure 393

Figure 393 *Cortinarius violaceus*

Pileus 5-15 cm, obtuse to convex then broadly convex to broadly umbonate, dry, scaly; context thick, dark violet, unchanging when bruised, odor and taste not distinctive. Gills broad, subdistant, adnexed. Stipe 7-12 (16) x 1-2.5 cm, dark violet within. Spores 13-17 x 8-10 μm. Pleurocystidia (54) 66-90 x 9-16 (20) μm, often with violaceous content which becomes wine-red in KOH. Cheilocystidia resembling the pleurocystidia.

Solitary to scattered in old-growth conifer forests of the United States and southern Canada, fall. Edible: BUT NOT RECOMMENDED. The North American variant apparently lacks "taste appeal" and there are several variants of the species. It occurs under hardwoods in Europe.

5a   **Pileus and stipe ± lilac, interior of stipe pale to rusty cinnamon; odor slightly pungent-fragrant. Fig. 394** ....
.... **C. *traganus* Fries**

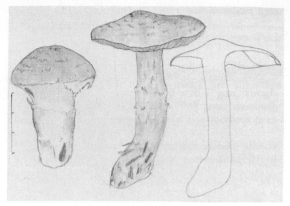

Figure 394

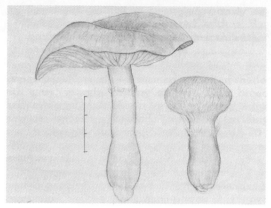

Figure 395

Figure 394 *Cortinarius traganus*

Pileus 5-12 cm, obtuse becoming broadly expanded, dry, fibrillose, evenly lilaceous or showing pallid sectors extending to pileus margin. Gills broad, subdistant, adnexed, pale cinnamon fulvous. Stipe 5-12 x 1.5-3 cm near apex, 3-5 cm near base, solid, surface fibrillose with remains of lilac-pallid veil. Spores 7-9 x 4.5-5.5 μm

Scattered to gregarious in old-growth conifer forests of the Pacific Northwest, fall, not infrequent. Edibility: not recommended.

5b Not as above **6**

6a Pileus grayish buff becoming ± ochraceous; gills dull purple, broad, thickish and ± distant. Fig. 395 ....
.... ***C. subpulchrifolius* Kauffman**

Figure 395 *Cortinarius subpulchrifolius*

Pileus 4-10 cm, convex to broadly convex, surface dry and innately appressed fibrillose, grayish soon tinged buff, in age more ochraceous and with rusty stains; margin adorned with pallid veil remnants; context thickish, pale caesious becoming pallid, odor and taste mild. Gills dull purple at first, finally dark cinnamon, broad, adnexed. Stipe 5-10 x 1-1.5 cm, ± equal, solid, sheathed with a pallid veil terminating in an evanescent fibrillose annulus; cortina white and copious. Spores 8-10 x 5-6 μm.

Solitary to scattered under hardwoods, especially oak, Great Lakes area, summer and fall, common at times. Edibility: not recommended.

6b Not as above **7**

7a Pileus grayish violaceous, becoming reddish brown; gills thin and close; lower part of stipe decorated with pale buff zones or patches of veil tissue. Fig. 396 ....
.... ***C. caninus* (Fr.) Fr.**

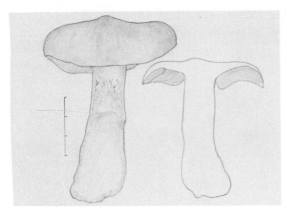

Figure 396

Figure 396   *Cortinarius caninus*

Pileus 4-12 (15) cm, obtuse to convex, often broadly umbonate, dry, grayish violaceous but very soon cinnamon-tinged; context firm, pallid then brownish, odor and taste mild. Gills violaceous when young, gradually becoming dark cinnamon, close, broad, adnexed. Stipe 6-14 x 1-2 cm, clavate, soon equal, violaceous above, pallid below. Spores 7-8.5 x 5-6.5 μm.

Scattered to gregarious in conifer and hardwood forests, late summer and fall, northern and widely distributed. Edibility: not recommended.

7b   Not as above ...... *C. subargentatus* Orton

Pileus 5-10 cm, obtuse becoming convex or broadly expanded to nearly plano-convex or umbonate, surface silky, silvery violaceous-white, with brighter violet-blue tints at first. Contex violaceous but soon pallid, odor and taste not distinctive. Gills adnate, narrow, close, violaceous to pale violet, finally ± cinnamon. Stipe 5-10 x 1-2 cm above an abrupt bulb 3-5 cm broad, silvery violaceous over all or deep violet near apex; cortina violaceous-white. Spores 7-9 (10) x 5-6 μm. Cheilocystidia scattered, 40-70 x 4-6 μm, filamentous.

Solitary to gregarious under hardwoods on low ground, especially near woodland pools and swamp edges; summer and early fall, common in the Great Lakes area. Edibility: not recommended.

8a   Pileus decorated by red fibrillose squamules or streaks on a pallid ground color .... *C. bolaris* (Fr.) Fries

Pileus 3-8 cm, convex-expanded, often umbonate, surface dry; context white to yellowish, odor and taste mild. Gills close, broad, adnate, pallid when young, soon pale cinnamon. Stipe 5-10 x 0.5-1.2 cm, equal coated to veil-line with fibrils colored as on pileus, where bruised the surface staining saffron yellow to red; cortina white. Spores 7-8 x 5-5.5 μm.

Scattered under hardwoods on wet soil often under oak and *Vaccinium* stands near edge of woodland pools and bogs, summer and fall, Great Lakes area, rare during most seasons. Edibility: not recommended.

8b   Not as above 9

9a   Pileus white at first, fibrillose; gills pallid to pale brown when young. Fig. 397 .... *C. pinetorum* (Fr.) Kauff.

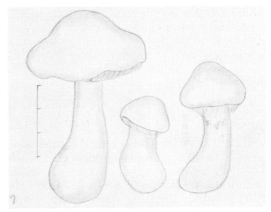

Figure 397

Figure 397   *Cortinarius pinetorum*

Pileus 3-10 cm, obtuse, becoming convex to campanulate, dry, innately silky-fibrillose (± tacky when wet), silvery gray and shining, becoming pale drab; context watery-mottled when fresh; odor penetrating (earthy), taste ± disagreeable. Gills adnate, becoming emarginate, ± broad and becoming ventricose, close becoming subdistant, pallid then avellaneous, finally clay-color. Stipe 4-9 x 0.8-1.2 cm, clavate, pallid, sheathed below middle by white outer veil remnants, glabrescent and in age silky-shining. Spores 7-8.5 x 5-6 μm.

Scattered to gregarious, Rocky Mountains of Colorado, under pine and spruce, late summer. Edibility: not recommended (apparently not tested).

9b   Pileus distinctly colored **10**

10a Pileus cream-buff to tawny yellowish; lamellae pale yellow; under hardwood. Fig. 398 .... *C. flavifolius* **Peck**

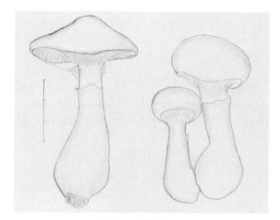

Figure 398

Figure 398   *Cortinarius flavifolius*

Pileus 4-10 (15) cm, convex to ± plane, dry, appressed fibrillose, becoming somewhat squamulose, in age dingy ochraceous to clay-color; context whitish, odor and taste mild. Gills subdistant, broad, finally rusty cinamon. Stipe 6-18 x 0.6-1.2 cm (4 cm ± at base), solid, sheathed below with outer veil remnants; cortina copious. Spores 7-9 x 5-6 μm.

Gregarious under hardwoods, especially beech (*Fagus*), summer and early fall, Great Lakes area east and southward, common during wet seasons. Edibility: not recommended.

10b Stipe equal to clavate but pileus some other color than in above choice or a brighter yellow **11**

11a Pileus, gills, and stipe blood red; taste ± radish-like. Fig. 399 ....
.... *C. sanguineus* (Fr.) **Fries**

Figure 399

Figure 399   *Cortinarius sanguineus*

Pileus 2-4 cm, obtuse, becoming campanulate to convex or ± plane, dry, silky, evenly colored; context blood red, odor slight to ± fragrant. Gills adnate to adnexed, close to subdistant, narrow then ± broad. Stipe 4-8 (10) cm x 3-7 mm, equal, darker where injured, cortina tinged red. Spores 6.5-7.5 (8) or 7-8.5 μm long, 4-5 μm wide. Basidia revived in KOH with purple to vinaceous red content in at least some of them.

Scattered in mossy moist conifer forests in the United States and Canada, late summer and fall, not common. Edibility: not recommended.

11b Pileus stipe and gills not concolorous **12**

12a Pileus and stipe ochraceous; gills deep red. Fig. 400 .... *C. semisanguineus* (Fr.) **Gill.**

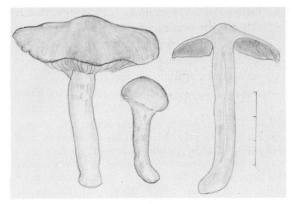

Figure 400

Figure 401

Figure 400 *Cortinarius semisanguineus*

Pileus 3-9 cm, obtuse then campanulate to convex or finally plano-umbonate, surface dry and silky, ochre yellow to a cinnamon-yellow, rarely ± squamulose; context pallid, odor and taste mild; with KOH on cuticle quickly inky-black. Gills narrow, crowded, adnate to subdecurrent. Stipe 3-8 cm x 3-6 mm, equal, yellow becoming duller in age, fibrillose from yellow to tawny fibrils. Spores 7-8.5 x 4.5-5 μm. Basidia as revived in KOH with vinaceous red content in some.

Scattered on moss under conifers and around decayed conifer stumps, northern United States and Canada; summer and fall, not uncommon but seldom in abundance. Edibility: not recommended.

12b Not as above **13**

13a Pileus garnet red, gills deep vinaceous red; stipe ochraceous. Fig. 401 ....
.... ***C. phoeniccus* var. *occidentalis* Smith**

Figure 401 *Cortinarius phoeniceus* var. *occidentalis*

Pileus 3-8 cm, convex to plane or broadly umbonate, surface dry, appressed-silky, often rimose in age; context reddish near cuticle, olive-brown near stipe, odor and taste mild. Gills with a changeable sheen, broad, subdistant, adnate. Stipe 4-10 cm x 6-12 mm, ± equal, coated with yellowish fibrils, interior "old gold"; basal mycelium ochre yellow becoming vinaceous red in age. Spores 7-8 x 5-5.5 μm. Basidia hyaline to pink in KOH.

Gregarious under conifers, fall; Pacific Northwest, rather common in the fall. Edibility: not recommended.

13b Pileus gills and stipe yellow; stipe clavate; spores 7-8.5 × 6-7.5 μm. Fig. 402 ....
.... ***C. callisteus* (Fr.) Fries**

Figure 402

Figure 402 *Cortinarius callisteus*

Pileus 4-8 cm, campanulate to convex, glabrous, surface soon broken into numerous minute squamules, evenly bright apricot yellow, slowly going to ochraceous-orange, or orange-rufous in age; context yellow, odor and taste slight. Gills adnexed, distant, broad and finally ± ventricose, bright yellow-ochre, finally rusty brown from the spores. Stipe 5-9 cm x 6-10 mm (at base 20-30 mm), yellowish within, surface yellow to pallid, at times streaked with fulvous fibrils. Spores 7-8.5 x 6-7.5 μm.

    Scattered to gregarious under conifers, northern United States and the conifer areas of Canada (?); not common, fall. Edibility: not recommended.

SUBGENUS TELAMONIA

1a   Stipe 1-4 mm thick near apex 2

1b   Stipe 5-20 mm or more thick near apex 6

2a   Fruiting body violaceous over all when young; Spores 9-11 (12) x 5-6 μm .... *C. pulchellus* Lange

Pileus (5) 10-30 mm, conic then campanulate, finally plano-umbonate, glabrous, moist, vinaceous brown when faded; context violaceous at first, odor and taste slight. Gills broad, adnexed, subdistant, finally dull rusty brown. Stipe 1-4 (5) cm long, grayish at first from a thin coating of fibrils terminating in a faint annular evanescent zone.

    Solitary to gregarious under alder (*Alnus*), Great Lakes area and Pacific Northwest, usually fruiting during early fall in relatively dry seasons.

2b   Young fruiting body not entirely violaceous 3

3a   Odor of geraniums (*Pelarogonium*); stipe with copious zones and patches of white veil material; base of stipe at times with violaceous mycelium; often on sphagnum under spruce .... *C. paleaceus* Fries

Pileus 2-5 cm, conic to campanulate to plano-convex or umbonate, blackish brown when young and moist, fading to dingy brown, surface decorated with remains of a copious white outer veil especially at the edge; context brown, taste slight. Gills close, pallid, then dark cinnamon, broad, adnate. Stipe (3) 8-10 cm x 2-4 mm, undulating or strict, brownish and darker near base, surface ± glabrous at times in age. Spores 8-10 x 5-6 μm.

    Gregarious on wet moss, often in bogs; Great Lakes area and northern United States and Canada generally, sporadic.

3b   Not as above 4

4a   Gills and apex of stipe violaceous at first; pileus rusty brown soon fading to ochraceous; annulus superior and submembranaceous; veil whitish .... *C. subflexipes* Peck

Pileus 1-3 cm, conic, then campanulate and finally ± plane with a conic umbo, glabrous, moist, hygrophanous, near cinnamon brown, soon tawny to ochraceous tawny (paler), the margin often whitish from remains of the veil; context brownish. Gills thin, close, rather broad, soon clay-colored. Stipe 3-6 cm x 2-4 mm, equal, flexuous, lower portion ± honey-color, subannulate from veil remnants. Spores 6-7 x 4-4.5 μm.

    Scattered to gregarious under conifers, northern United States and Canada in conifer forests, late summer and fall.

4b   Not as above 5

5a   Gills violaceous at first; pileus squamulose with yellow veil remnants; stipe with yellow veil fibrils. Fig. 403 .... *C. lacorum* Smith

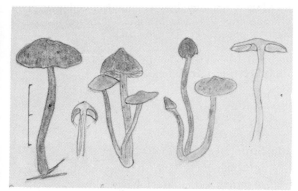

Figure 403

Figure 403 *Cortinarius lacorum*

Pileus 5-25 mm, conic to conic-campanulate, margin finally spreading to uplifted, ground color yellow-brown becoming rusty brown, context dull violaceous at first, soon yellowish, taste mild. Gills distant, adnate, moderately broad, dark cinnamon at maturity. Stipe 2-6 cm x 2-3 mm, concolorous with pileus below or in age over all. Spores 8-10 x 5-6 μm.

Scattered to gregarious under alder, late summer, during relatively dry seasons, Great Lakes area, seldom collected.

5b   Gills brown to ochre yellow at first; pileus glabrous. Fig. 404 ....
.... ***C. gentilis*** **(Fr.) Fries**

Figure 404

Figure 404 *Cortinarius gentilis*

Pileus 2-5 cm, conic becoming campanulate to ± expanded-umbonate, glabrous, moist, hygrophanous, rich yellow-brown to ± ochre yellow or amber yellow, paler and duller if faded; context thin, yellow, odor and taste ± mild. Gills broad, subdistant, thickish, adnate. Stipe 3-8 cm x 3-5 (7) mm, ± equal, about concolorous with pileus and usually with a yellow zone of veil fibrils near midportion (faint and ± evanescent in North American collections). Spores 7-9 x 6-7 μm.

Gregarious in large numbers in the fall in the Pacific Northwest, less common in the Great Lakes area and eastward. Edibility: thought to be DANGEROUSLY POISONOUS, the symptoms being very delayed.

6a   Gills violet; stipe with zones and patches of vinaceous red fibrils; under conifers in western mountains ....
.... ***C. boulderensis*** **Smith**

Pileus 2-5 cm, obtusely conic to campanulate to plano-umbonate, moist, hygrophanous, deep violaceous brown to dark vinaceous buff finally, at times chocolate brown, margin striatulate when moist and fading usually to dull cinnamon; context thin, violaceous brown fading to vinaceous buff, odor and taste ± mild. Gills violaceous becoming dull cinnamon, close, broad, adnate and with a decurrent tooth, edges ± uneven. Stipe 5-8 cm x 4-7 mm, clavate, base 10-15 mm, pale violaceous above, brownish below. Spores 7.5-10 x 5-6 μm.

Gregarious under conifers, fall, abundant some years in the Olympic National Park. Edibility: not recommended.

6b   Not as above **7**

7a   Stipe ± fire-red to orange over the basal area and the basal mycelium also orange-red; growing under hardwoods ....
.... ***C. rubripes*** **Kauffman**

Pileus 5-12 cm, obtuse to convex, expanding to broadly convex or plano-umbonate, watery cinnamon or at first violaceus tinged near the edge, becoming ± tawny (a reddish tone); context reddish to violaceous-tinged at very first, soon paler, odor and taste ± mild. Gills subdistant to distant, broad, adnate-seceding, pale bluish purple soon becoming tawny to reddish cinnamon. Stipe 5-9 x 0.5 x 0.5-1.5 cm, at base 2-2.5 cm, brownish pallid above. Spores 7-9 x 5-5.5 μm.

Gregarious under hardwoods, east of the Great Plains, late summer and fall, abundant in the Great Lakes area after heavy late August rains. Edibility: not recommended.

7b Base of stipe not fire-red **8**

8a Fruiting body ± violaceous to grayish violet overall or in part before maturing **9**

8b Fruiting body when young lacking violet tints **11**

9a Stipe clavate bulbous and annulate; gills broad, distant, deep purple at first. Fig. 405 .... **C. torvus** (Fr.) Fries

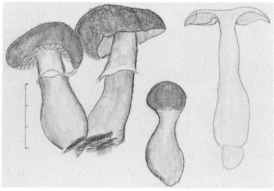

Figure 405

Figure 405 *Cortinarius torvus*

Pileus 3-6 cm, obtuse to convex becoming broadly convex or with a low umbo, surface at first ± glaucous and variegated, color dark dull purple

to deep vinaceous brown, grayish veil material often along the margin. Gills adnexed at maturity. Spores 9-11.5 x 5-6 μm.

Scattered to gregarious under beech-maple and under hemlock, summer and fall, not common. Edibility: not recommended.

9b Not as above **10**

10a Stipe 10-20 cm × 10-20 mm ± equal; violaceous overall; with zones and patches of outer veil material over lower part .... **C. evernius** Fries

Pileus 3-10 cm, campanulate to expanded-umbonate, deep violaceous fading to vinaceous brown, margin at first silky from the veil; context thin, violaceous, odor ± radish-like, taste slight. Gills distant, thick, broad, adnate, at first deep violet with whitish edges. Stipe deep violaceous, marked by veil remnants. Spores 8-11 x 5-6 μm.

Solitary to scattered in mossy conifer forests, frequently in *Sphagnum* moss, northern United States and Canada, late summer and fall; not common. Edibility: not recommended.

10b Stipe 8-12 mm thick, only the apex violaceous. Fig. 406 .... **C. brunneus** Fries

Figure 406

Figure 406 *Cortinarius brunneus*

Pileus 3-6 cm, obtuse becoming expanded-umbonate, hoary at first but soon glabrous and deep reddish brown, reddish tawny in fading; context deep brown (but lilaceous above the stipe), odor and taste ± mild. Gills deep brownish violaceous but soon ± walnut brown, close, adnexed, narrow to moderately broad. Stipe 8-10 cm long, clavate becoming equal, brown over lower 2/3 at first with a whitish sheath terminating in a zone of fibrils (this breaking up in age). Spores 7.5-9 x 4.5-5.5 μm.

Scattered under conifers in the Pacific Northwest, less common elsewhere in conifer forests, fall, not infrequent. Edibility: not recommended.

11a Stipe with dull red zones from the outer veil; spores 10-13 × 6-7.5 μm; growing under or near birch. Fig. 407 ....
.... *C. armillatus* (Fr.) Fries

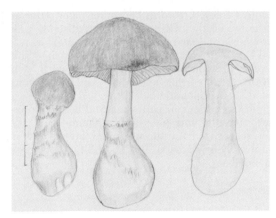

Figure 407

Figure 407 *Cortinarius armillatus*

Pileus 5-12 cm, obtuse then broadly campanulate to expanded umbonate, surface moist, glabrous, subhygrophanous, dull tawny-reddish to dull vinaceous brown, rarely becoming slightly squamulose; context brownish-pallid, odor and taste not distinctive. Gills broad, ± distant, adnate becoming adnexed, pale cinnamon but finally more rusty brown. Stipe 7-14 x 1-2.5 cm, clavate and 3-4 cm at base, brownish within; cortina copious and white. Cheilocystidia 3-4 μm wide and ± filamentous, scattered.

Solitary to gregarious under birch especially, late summer and fall, common in the Great Lakes

area and eastern North America, but rare in the Pacific Northwest. Edibility: edible but not recommended.

11b Not with both large spores and reddish zones on the stipe 12

12a Pileus, gills, and stipe red to dull orange-red or reddish orange ....
.... *C. californicus* Smith

Pileus 3-9 cm, obtuse becoming expanded-umbonate, glabrous, hygrophanous, margin straight at first; context watery, orange-red, odor and taste mild. Gills rusty orange, adnate to adnexed, subdistant, narrow to moderately broad, edges slightly serrate. Stipe 8-15 (2) x 0.5-1.5 cm, ± equal, sparsely orange-fibrillose from the cortina. Mycelium around base orange-red. Spores 8-10 x 5-6 μm. Cheilocystidia mostly 30-42 x 10-14 μm, content pinkish when mounted in KOH.

Scattered under conifers, fall and early winter, Pacific Northwest, not common. Edibility: not recommended.

12b Neither pileus nor gills red to orange 13

13a Stipe equal, pileus deep reddish bay-brown; gills pale tan when young ....
.. *C. dilutus* Fries

Pileus 3-9 cm, convex to nearly plane, glabrous, moist, finally fading to dull tan; context thin, fragile, odor and taste mild. Gills adnate to adnexed, broad, close. Stipe 4-7 cm x 5-20 mm, cortina white and copious but stipe not annulate, ground color paler than pileus. Spores 6-7 x 5-6.5 μm.

Scattered to gregarious, northern United States and in Canada (?), fairly abundant in the Pacific Northwest, fall. Edibility: not recommended.

13b Stipe clavate at first; pileus not as above 14

14a Gills distant; growing under hardwoods
.... *C. distans* Peck

Pileus 3-8 (10) cm, obtuse becoming campanulate to broadly umbonate, glabrous to scurfy, rather hygrophanous, cinnamon brown fading to dull tan; context thin and brittle, concolorous with surface, odor and taste mild. Gills adnexed, broad, thickish, rigid, yellowish tan becoming ± cinnamon. Stipe 4-9 x 0.5-1.2 cm, with a pallid median annular zone, above it brownish (paler than pileus). Spores 7-9 x 5-6 μm.

Scattered to gregarious under hardwoods, eastern North America, summer and fall, not abundant but frequently collected. Edibility: not recommended.

14b Gills close to subdistant **15**

15a Spores 8-10 × 5-6 μm; pileus and stipe reddish cinnamon; growing under conifers. Fig. 408 .... *C. laniger* Fries

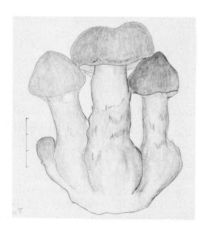

Figure 408

Figure 408 *Cortinarius laniger*

Pileus 4-11 cm, convex to broadly convex, surface canescent, subhygrophanous, fading to tan, margin white and silky from the veil; context pallid to cinnamon, odor and taste mild. Gills rusty brown at first, adnexed at maturity. Stipe 8-10 x 1-3.5 cm (at base 3.5-4 cm), with a white fibrillose outer veil leaving a zone or zones and patches over lower portion.

Gregarious under conifers, fall northern United States and in Canada but particularly in the Pacific Northwest. Edibility: not recommended.

15b Spores 7-9 × 4-5 μm; stipe pallid brownish to dull brown .... *C. bulbosus* Fries

Pileus 5-12 cm, convex to broadly convex, with a thin white silkiness, dull brown beneath this; context thick, brownish becoming paler, odor and taste ± earthy. Gills close to subdistant, pallid brownish at first becoming ± rusty brown. Stipe 5-11 x 1-2 cm (near base 2.5-3.5 cm), solid, pallid brownish within, decorated with white fibrils from cortina and outer veil, the annular zone soon obliterated.

Gregarious in hardwood and conifer forests, late summer and fall, fairly common but often not recognized, northern United States and undoubtedly in Canada also. Edibility: not recommended.

Crepidotus (Fr.) Staude

Spore deposit dull brown, earth-brown, fulvous or rarely reddish (salmon pink); spores lacking an apical germ pore, surface smooth to roughened-punctate; pileus sessile or only short-stipitate and a stipe (if present) eccentric to lateral; pileus typically small (1-4 cm but extremes vary from 5 mm to 130 mm). Cheilocystidia typically present; pleurocystidia typically rare. (mentioned here only if present); habitat mostly on wood but also on soil or various types of organic detritus.

The genus contains approximately 125

species for North America, and none of them appear to have been adequately tested as to edibility.

KEY TO SPECIES

1a Pileus 5-15 mm, scarlet to cinnabar red; gills scarlet on the edges .... *C. cinnabarinus* **Peck**

Pileus conchate to fan-shaped, surface dry and fibrillose. Gills broad and subdistant. Stipe rudimentary, lateral or lacking, if present reddish tomentose. Spores 7-10 x 5-6 μm. Cheilocystidia 36-63 x 5-11 μm, clavate, cylindric, or fusoid-ventricose and with a ± acute apex. Clamp connections absent.

On basswood, poplar and beech, Great Lakes area eastward and southward, rather rare, late summer and fall.

1b Colors not as above **2**

2a Spore deposit ± salmon pink; pileus ± fibrillose, bright orange-tawny; spores 5.5-7.5 × 5-7 μm, brown in KOH; gills subdistant and salmon-color to dull orange ....
.... *C. subnidulans* **(Overh.) Hes. & Sm.**

Pileus 5-20 mm, sessile, fan-shaped, taste ± mild. Stipe absent. Spores smooth. Pleurocystidia 43-53 x 3-6 μm, cylindric to ± clavate, rare. Cheilocystidia 38-50 x 8-13 μm, clavate to fusoid-ventricose. Clamp connections present.

On rotting wood, Missouri. Apparently southern, at least it has not been found in northern areas.

2b Pileus and gills not colored as in above choice **3**

3a Pileus 4-13 cm, ± fan-shaped, viscid; gills staining to purple-brown where bruised ....
.... *C. maximus* **Hes. & Sm.**

Pileus white to pallid, coarsely rimulose-reticulated. Gills white then snuff-brown, close, ± narrow. Stipe none. Spores (6) 7-9 x 4-5 μm, smooth.

Cheilocystidia 48-96 x 5-10 μm, clavate to subcylindric or subcapitate. Clamp connections present.

Southern, fall, on hickory, Tennessee. Very likely it will be found eventually on a number of species of hardwoods.

3b Pileus smaller than in above choice and not staining purple-brown **4**

4a Pileus at first fibrillose to squamulose with fulvous hairs and/or squamules; spores ellipsoid; clamp connections absent. Fig. 409 ....
.... *C. mollis* **(Fr.) Staude**

Figure 409

Figure 409 *Crepidotus mollis*

Pileus 1-5 (8) cm, ± fan-shaped, rarely glabrous when young. Gills pallid at first, broad, close to crowded, edge becoming gelatinized. Spores 7-10 x 4.5-6 μm, smooth. Cheilocystidia 30-60 x 6-8 μm, ventricose near base, and others 70-105 x 4-6 μm and filamentose, gelatinizing.

On hardwood debris and remains (logs, stumps, branches, etc.), common, late spring, summer, and fall, widely distributed in North America. It is often the first *Crepidotus* a collector finds. The common variant is that described by Peck as *C. fulvotomentosus*.

4b Pileus glabrous, milk-white, with small black spots generally by maturity or old age ....
.... *C. maculans* **Hes. & Sm.**

Pileus 2-6 cm, fan-shaped, glabrous, when moist margin translucent-striate. Gills broad, close to subdistant, white at first. Spores 5-7 μm, globose, punctate. Pleurocystidia 27-40 x 6-8 μm, ± fusoid-ventricose, ± imbedded in hymenium. Cheilocystidia 26-42 x 5-10 μm, clavate, fusoid-ventricose or irregular in outline (variable in shape). Clamp connections present.

Very common on hardwood slash in the Lake Superior area of Michigan, summer.

Galerina Earle

Spores ochraceous to rusty brown in deposits, in most species having a distinct ± smooth area (a plage) just above the apiculus on the face view of the spore, mostly lacking an apical pore; stipe slender and brittle, continuous with the pileus; pileus very thin and usually striate on margin when moist; on moss beds, organic debris of various types, on humus or typically lignicolous, spring, summer or fall, or during the winter in the south.

Galerina is a large genus of over 200 species including a small group of deadly poisonous species, some of which are Tropical and some North Temperate in distribution.

KEY TO SPECIES

1a On *Sphagnum;* with a conspicuous white veil leaving a white superior annulus and/or patches and zones lower down; late spring to fall. Fig. 410 ...... *G. paludosa* (Fr.) Kuh.

Figure 410

Figure 410 *Galerina paludosa*

Pileus 10-30 mm, conic to convex, becoming nearly plane or plano-umbonate, pale tawny when moist; taste ± mild. Gills broad, close, tawny. Stipe 7-16 cm x 1-3 (4) mm, equal, ochraceous. Spores (8) 9-11 x (5) 6-7 (8) μm, very slightly punctate. Cheilocystidia 25-44 x 6-12 μm, (3-5 μm at subcapitate apex).

It is the most abundant species in bogs in North America during most seasons. The copious veil readily distinguishes it from other bog-inhabiting species.

1b Not as above (typically lignicolous) 2

2a Stipe with a thin appressed superior membranous annulus; spores 8-11 × 5-6.5 μm; pleuro- and cheilocystidia similar, 40-65 × 9-12 μm, fusoid-ventricose, apex ± acute. Fig. 411 ...... *G. autumnalis* (Pk.) Sm. & Sing.

Figure 411

Figure 411 *Galerina autumnalis*

Pileus 2.5-6.5 cm, yellow-brown to dark tawny, glabrous, viscid, margin ± translucent-striate.

Gills adnate to ± decurrent, close, broad, ± tawny. Stipe 3-8 cm x 3-8 mm, with a thin coating of appressed fibrils below the annulus, darkening appreciably in ageing at least over basal area; annulus sometimes absent in old specimens.

Scattered to clustered on hardwood and conifer logs, stumps, etc.; spring, summer, and fall; common and widely distributed. POISONOUS. *G. platyphylla* (Kauff.) Sm. & Sing., *G. marginata* (Fr.) Küh., *G. megalocystis* Sm. & Sing., and *G. venenata* Smith are easily mistaken in the field for Peck's species, and we suspect all of them of being poisonous. We know this to be true for *G. venenata*.

2b Annulus absent or merely a fibrillose zone; spores 6.3-8.7 × 4-5 μm; pleurocystidia absent, cheilocystidia narrowly ninepin-shaped (apex capitate), 23-28 × 3.5-8 μm. Fig. 412 .... *G. stylifera* (Atk.) Sm. & Sing.

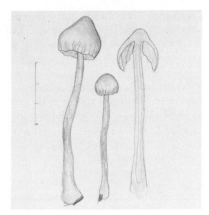

Figure 412

Figure 412   *Galerina stylifera*

Pileus 1.5-5 cm, glabrous, ± plane or slightly umbonate, viscid, ± striatulate when moist, cinnamon brown to tawny. Gills close, broad, adnate, colored like pileus. Stipe 4-6 cm x 2-6 mm, appressed fibrillose over lower half.

Gregarious on sticks, debris, logs, etc., mostly on conifer wood, northern United States and in Canada. In the field this species is easily confused with exannulate specimens of *G. autumnalis*.

Gymnopilus Karsten

Spore deposit orange to rusty orange to bright rusty brown; spores typically finely ornamented (roughened); stipe and pileus confluent; stipe usually central and fleshy, rarely eccentric or thin and cartilaginous; habitat typically on wood and in North America frequently on wood of conifers. Hesler recognized 73 species for North America.

KEY TO SPECIES

1a Veil fibrillose to submembranous and in breaking leaving a ring or zone ± persistent on the stipe 2

1b Veil absent to rudimentary 4

2a Taste of raw context bitter (usually strongly so) 3

2b Taste of raw context mild to ± disagreeable but not intensely bitter; on wood of hardwoods .... *G. validipes* (Pk.) Hesler

Pileus 7.5-15 (20) cm, ochraceous, floccose-squamulose; context pallid. Gills pallid yellow becoming ochraceous before colored by spores, narrow becoming broad, close. Stipe 2-5 cm thick, length variable, pale ochraceous; ± annulate from a zone of fibrils. Spores 7.5-10 x 4.5-5.5 μm. Pleurocystidia 23-28 x 5-7 μm, imbedded. Cheilocystidia 23-30 x 3-7 μm, fusoid-ventricose, apex enlarged. Clamp connections present.

Caespitose on hardwood stumps, Great Lakes area eastward, late summer and fall. POISONOUS: Psilocybin is present in this species.

3a **On wood of hardwoods; annulus submembranous to fibrillose; spores 8-10 × 4.5-6 μm, Fig. 413** .... *G. spectabilis* **(Fr.) Smith**

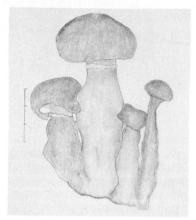

Figure 413

Figure 413 *Gymnopilus spectabilis*

Pileus 5-15 (18) cm, broadly convex to ± plane, ± bright orange-yellow, odor pungent. Gills yellow becoming rusty, broadly adnate, broad, close. Stipe 8-30 mm thick, orange-ochraceous, ± fibrillose below veil-line; veil pale ochraceous; FeSO₄ olive on stipe and pileus; KOH on context dark red-brown. Clamp connections present.

Not uncommon in the Great Lakes area and eastward and southward; late summer and fall, usually clustered. It is suspected that this species intergrades with *G. validipes*. Some collections contain psilocybin and some, apparently, do not.

3b **On wood of conifers, western North America** .... *G. ventricosus* **(Earle) Hesler**

Pileus 6-18 cm broad, orange-ochraceous to reddish brown, ± fibrillose becoming squamulose; context yellow. Gills broad, crowded, dark cinnamon in age, ochraceous when young. Stipe 2-4 (7) cm thick, ventricose, ± radicating; annulus ± apical, thick and persistent, at times not forming and veil remnants left on margin of pileus. Spores 4-5.5 (6.5) x 3.5-4 (5) μm. Pleuro- and

cheilocystidia similar, capitate, 20-40 x 3-5 μm. Clamp connections present.

Common and conspicuous in the Pacific Northwest, fall. Numerous tests have failed to show that psilocybin is present in this species.

4a **Pileus lilac-vinaceous to dull green at first, more variable at maturity and green, blue and yellow in a variable pattern, at times with a bluish bloom. Fig. 414** .... *G. punctifolius* **(Pk.) Sing.**

Figure 414

Figure 414 *Gymnopilus punctifolius*

Pileus 2.5-10 cm, convex, margin inrolled, glabrous or faintly squamulose around the disc; taste very bitter. Gills ± sinuate, broad, becoming about subdistant, olive-yellow young, with rusty red stains in age. Stipe 5-15 cm x 5-15 mm, staining brownish yellow to olive-ochre; veil absent. Spores 4-5.5 (6.5) x 3.5-4 (5) μm. Pleuro- and cheilocystidia similar, capitate, 20-40 x 3-5 μm. Clamp connections present.

On wood of conifers and on debris, usually only a few in one locality, fall, Pacific Northwest, not uncommon.

4b **Colors not as above** **5**

5a **Pileus 1-2.5 cm, veil none; spores 3.5-5.5 × 2.5-3.5 μm. Fig. 415** .... *G. bellulus* **(Pk.) Murr.**

Figure 415

Figure 415 *Gymnopilus bellulus*

Pileus dark rusty red to orange-brown, glabrous to scurfy, taste bitter. Gills bright then dull yellow, finally ferruginous, close, narrow. Stipe 1.5-3 cm x 1.5-3 mm, rusty to bay brown, finally staining darker, apex pruinose to scurfy. Pleuro- and cheilocystidia similar, 14-26 x 3-6 μm, fusoid-

ventricose, apex capitate to subcapitate. Clamp connections present.

On conifer stumps and logs, northern United States, June to late fall; often collected but not found in quantity.

5b Pileus 3-9 cm; veil rudimentary and evanescent; spores 7-10 $\times$ 4-5.5 μm .... *G. sapineus* (Fr.) R. Maire

Pileus soon plano-convex, $\pm$ golden ochraceous or duller, thinly fibrillose to minutely squamulose; odor pungent, taste often bitter. Gills yellow becoming rusty ochraceous, close, broad. Stipe 3-7 (9) cm x 4-8 (12) mm, ochraceous, $\pm$ fibrillose; veil fibrillose, yellowish. Cheilocystidia 22-40 x 5-7 μm, ventricose, capitate to merely obtuse. Clamp connections present.

On conifer slash and other debris, common, late summer and fall, widely distributed. Clusters of over-sized fruiting bodies may occur on sawdust piles.

Hebeloma Kummer

Pileus and stipe confluent; spore deposit dingy brown to (rarely) pinkish brown; spores not truncate at apex but at times with a beak; edge of gills often whitish from copious development of cheilocystidia; pileus cuticle typically an ixocutis; gill trama regular; habitat mostly terrestrial in conifer and hardwood forests, forming mycorrhiza with woody plants (presumably); veil absent in many species, and fibrillose in others but not forming a true annulus.

The genus is closely related to *Cortinarius*, especially through those species with a fibrillose veil. About 200 species occur in North America.

KEY TO SPECIES

1a Gills becoming pinkish tan; spores in a deposit a medium cocoa-brown .... *H. sarcophyllum* (Pk.) Sacc.

Pileus 3-7 cm, convex to plane, pure white becoming reddish gray, glabrous, subviscid; taste $\pm$ bitter. Gills close, adnate, broad, ventricose, white at first. Stipe 4-6 cm x 3-6 mm, white, surface coated with soft fibrils. Spores 8-10 x 4.5-5 μm (in some collections 9-13 x 6-7 μm). Cheilocystidia fusoid-ventricose to cylindric or contorted, 35-50 x 4-6 μm. Clamp connections present.

Solitary to widely scattered under hardwoods, Great Lakes area eastward, summer and fall, not common.

1b Gills not pinkish when young; spore deposit $\pm$ yellow-brown 2

2a Veil remnants evident on mature fruiting bodies 3

2b Veil absent (check buttons) 7

3a On *Sphagnum*; pleurocystidia present .... *H. paludicola* Murrill

Pileus 1-2 cm, convex to plane, viscid, glabrous, "grayish rosy isabelline" (Murrill), bay on disc. Gills ventricose, subdistant, pallid to clay-colored. Stipe 5-6 cm x 3-4 mm, whitish-fibrillose from veil. Spores 11-13.5 x 6-7 μm, faintly marbled, clay-color in KOH. Pleurocystidia 30-44 x 8-11 μm, fusoid-ventricose, apex obtuse to enlarged. Cheilocystidia resembling pleurocystidia, rarely with a secondary septum. Clamp connections present.

On marshy ground and in bogs, Adirondack Mountains of New York, October, rare.

3b   Habitat various; pleurocystidia absent 4

4a   Stipe with a cottony annular zone or a heavy fibrillose sheath up to a distinct persistent annualar zone 5

4b   Veil relatively thin, seen as patches on cap margin and/or a thin coating on the stipe below the midportion 6

5a   Spores 7.5-9 × 4-5.5 μm; veil a heavy sheath ending in a fibrillose annulus or zone. Fig. 416 .... _H. strophosum_ (Fr.) Sacc.

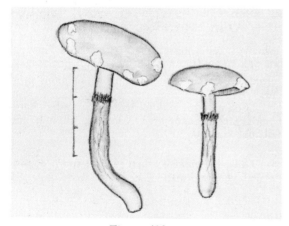

Figure 416

Figure 416   *Hebeloma strophosum*

Pileus 3-7 cm, broadly umbonate, viscid, margin with 1-2 rows or patches of veil material, dingy brown to (when faded) dull yellowish; taste ± bitter. Gills pallid, becoming dull cinnamon, mod-

erately broad, close. Stipe 5-8 cm x 5-9 (18) mm, darkening slowly from the base progressively upward. Cheilocystidia 28-66 x 3-10 μm, fusoid-ventricose to cylindric, in some the apex subcapitate. Clamp connections present but rare.

On soil under conifers, especially in plantations, Great Lakes area and Pacific Northwest, fall common and abundant during wet seasons.

5b   Spores 8-11 × 5-7 μm; annulus cottony-fibrillose and persistent .... _H. velatum_ Peck

Pileus 1.5-6 cm, convex to plane or either slightly depressed or umbonate on disc, viscid, silky on margin at first, soon glabrous, chestnut color fading to pale ochraceous. Gills close, ventricose, adnexed, whitish young. Stipe 2-6 cm x 4-6 mm, hollow, near base ± floccose-squamulose, ± annulate or annular zone evanescent. Cheilocystidia 30-64 x 5-8 μm, cylindric, or ventricose near base. Clamp connections present.

On soil under conifers, New York and southward, fall, not often reported.

6a   Stipe darkening slowly from base upward; pileus merely dingy pinkish brown. Fig. 417 .... _H. mesophaeum_ (Fr.) Quél.

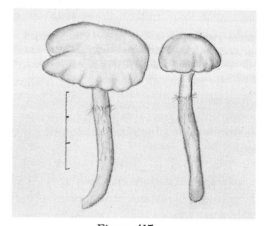

Figure 417

Figure 417   *Hebeloma mesophaeum*

Pileus 2-6 cm, convex to broadly convex, some with an obtuse umbo, dull brown to dark pinkish brown slowly fading to clay-color, margin decorated with patches of veil material; odor and taste raphanoid. Gills pallid, finally dull brown, broad, close, edges white-floccose. Stipe 3-7 (9) cm x 3-8 (11) mm, ± fibrillose striate; veil thin and cortinate. Spores 8-11 x 5-7 μm, roughened. Cheilocystidia 24 x 54 (70) x 5-9 (12) μm, ventricose near base or subcylindric. Clamp connections present.

Gregarious under conifers, spring and fall, often abundant, regarded as a "cold weather" species, appearing as early as April in the Great Lakes area, widely distributed in northern United States and Canada. NOT recommended for table use.

6b Stipe not darkening; pileus dull yellow ....
.... *H. gregarium* **Peck**

Pileus 2-4 cm, ± plane, clay-color, viscid, at first fibrillose along margin, odor raphanoid, taste similar but becoming bitter. Gills pallid then dingy cinnamon brown, close, broad. Stipe 3-6 cm x (2) 3-6 (8) mm, whitish, apex mealy, fibrillose toward base; veil copious, forming an evanescent fibrillose zone. Spores 8-11 x 5-7 μm. Cheilocystidia 28-54 x 5-9 μm, fusoid-ventricose to subcylindric, some ± capitate. Clamp connections present.

Scattered under pine and on heaths, fall and winter, New York south to Tennessee, not common.

7a Pileus white to white over a broad marginal area and with disc pale honey-color when young **8**

7b Pileus more distinctly colored when young **10**

8a Odor and taste distinctly radish-like; gill edges beaded with drops at first. Fig. 418 ....
.... *H. crustuliniforme* **(St. Amans) Quél.**

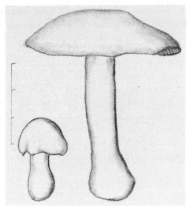

Figure 418

Figure 418 *Hebeloma crustuliniforme*

Pileus 3-10 cm, broadly convex, margin inrolled, margin pallid, disc pale buff, disc darker in age, surface viscid, glabrous. Gills crowded, narrow, pallid going to clay-color. Stipe 4-9 cm x 6-12 mm, solid, equal to an abruptly enlarged base, white, apex pruinose; veil none. Spores 10-13 x 6-7 μm. Cheilocystidia 50-85 x 7-9 μm, narrowly clavate but not capitate. Clamp connections present.

Gregarious in arcs or rings under conifers, late summer and fall widely distributed, common and abundant. POISONOUS.

8b Odor and taste not distinctive **9**

9a Stipe 1-2 cm thick, apex beaded as well as being squamulose to furfuraceous; gills gray-brown at maturity ...... *H. sporadicum* **Smith**

Pileus 5-13 cm, convex to broadly convex, some with watery spots and zones, glabrous, disc ± pale honey-color but in age yellow-brown. Gills broad, close, adnexed, white at first. Stipe 4-10 cm long, white, dingy near base where handled, solid. Spores 9-12 x 4-7 μm. Cheilocystidia 50-70 x 7-10 μm, elongate-clavate to nearly cylindric. Clamp connections present.

Clustered in rings or in large arcs under spruce, Michigan, apparently often overlooked or mistaken for *H. crustuliniforme*. Not recommended for table use.

9b Stipe 4-6 mm thick, apex not beaded; gills "brownish ferruginous" (Peck) .... *H. albidulum* **Peck**

Pileus 2.5-6 cm, convex to ± plane. Gills close, narrow, whitish when young. Stipe 3-6 cm long, glabrous, white. Spores 11-13 x 6-7 μm, roughened. Cheilocystidia 40-50 x 7-9 μm, narrowly clavate to ± filamentose. Clamp connections present.

Among fallen leaves in hardwood stands, October, New York; not often recognized if collected.

10a Pileus pinkish gray to pecan brown; gills at first ± pinkish gray; spores 7-10 × 5-6.5 μm .... *H. avellaneum* **Kauffman**

Pileus 3-10 cm, ovate-campanulate becoming expanded-umbonate, viscid, glabrous; taste ± bitter. Gills narrow, crowded, ± adnate, edges white-floccose. Stipe 5-10 (12) cm x 6-15 mm, at times ovate-bulbous at base, ± pruinose-mealy, glabrescent, basal mycelium white. Spores 8-10 x 5-6 μm. Cheilocystidia 30-80 x 5-8 μm, narrowly clavate to filamentose, agglutinated. Clamp connections present.

Caespitose to gregarious under conifers, Great Lakes area and the Pacific Northwest along the coast, not rare.

10b Not as above **11**

11a Spores 10-15 × 6-8.5 μm; taste mild; stipe 2-6 mm thick; found on sandy areas .... *H. colvini* **(Pk.) Sacc.**

Pileus 5-7 cm, broadly umbonate, convex or nearly plane, glabrous, viscid, grayish to yellowish gray. Gills crowded, broad, adnexed, whitish at first. Stipe 2.5-8 cm long, flexuous, silky fibrillose, whitish. Cheilocystidia of 2 types: 30-45 x 8-10 μm, cylindric to clavate, and the other 36-44 x 10-18 μm and broadly clavate to utriform. Clamp connections apparently absent.

Scattered, on dunes and sandy beaches, etc., late summer and fall during wet seasons, New York and Great Lakes area, rarely collected.

11b Spores smaller than in above choice and stipe thicker **12**

12a Spores 10-12.5 × 6-7 μm; stipe scaly and 1-3 (5) cm thick .... *H. sinapizans* **sensu American authors**

Pileus 4-12 (18) cm, convex to ± plane, viscid, deep pinkish brown to cinnamon tan, often shaded with gray, margin cottony at first. Gills broad, close, adnexed, pale clay-color when young, edges serrulate and often beaded. Stipe 6-12 cm long, base ± abruptly bulbous. Cheilocystidia 48-70 x 8-12 μm, clavate to subcapitate. Clamp connections present.

Common, gregarious to caespitose in fairy rings or arcs on grassy ground under oaks (as in cemetaries) and in thin upland woods during wet seasons, widely distributed, late summer and fall. POISONOUS.

12b Spores 7.5-9 × 4.5-6 μm; stipe 3-6 mm thick; growing in bogs. Fig. 419 .... *H. lubriciceps* **(Kauff. & Sm.) Hesler**

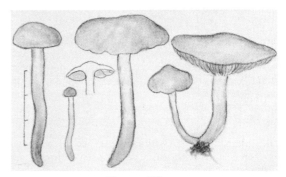

Figure 419

Figure 419 *Hebeloma lubriciceps*

Pileus 1-5 cm, campanulate to convex or plane, with or without a low umbo, hoary when young, lubricous, pale clay-color to pale reddish cinnamon, darker brown in age, at times blotched with dingy yellow-brown areas. Gills whitish when young, close, moderately broad. Stipe 4-9 cm long, innately silky, darkening slowly from base upward, apex naked. Cheilocystidia 28-36 x 5-7 μm, subcylindric to narrowly fusoid-ventricose. Clamp connections present.

Gregarious in bogs after heavy fall rains, Great Lakes area, fairly common during some seasons.

Inocybe (Fr.) Fries

Pileus and stipe confluent; spore deposit brown (earth-brown to dull yellow brown); spores smooth or angular to nodulose or angular-nodulose, lacking a germ pore at apex; pleurocystidia present or absent and if present thick- or thin-walled, apex often incrusted; veil present or absent but partial veil not membranous; pileus typically fibrillose to squamulose or lacerate-scaly; gill trama ± regular; clamp connections usually present; cheilocystidia present. Edibility: for the genus, not recommended.

KEY TO SPECIES

1a Fruiting body with olive to bluish green stains or discolorations **2**

1b Fruiting body not with above stains or discolorations **4**

2a Spores nodulose; pileus rimose at maturity .... *I. insignis* **Smith**

Pileus ± 5 cm, acutely conic then broadly campanulate, dry, fibrillose to scaly, becoming rimose, medium to dark date brown; taste bitter, odor heavy-aromatic. Gills close, narrow, adnate, dingy cinnamon brown. Stipe ± 6 cm x 4 mm, ± equal to a bulbous base, greenish gray where handled, otherwise about concolorous with pileus; pruinose to pubescent overall. Spores (8) 9-12 x (6) 7-10 μm (ornamentation included), shape irregular and surface bearing 9-13 prominent nodules. Pleurocystidia 40-65 x 12-23 μm, thick-walled.

Solitary under beech, hemlock and oak, Great Smoky Mountains National Park, rare (?), summer.

2b Spores smooth; pileus not rimose **3**

3a Base of stipe with bluish green to dull blue stains; spores 10-12 × 5-6 μm. Fig. 420 .... *I. calamistrata* (Fr.) **Gill.**

Figure 420

Figure 420 *Inocybe calamistrata*

Pileus 2-6 cm, convex-campanulate to nearly plane, dark coffee-brown, fibrillose-scaly, cut context tinged reddish. Gills adnate, seceding, broad, close, dull cinnamon when mature. Stipe (2) 3-6 mm thick, 4-10 cm long, colored about as pileus except for base. Pleurocystidia none.

Solitary to scattered, on the ground and humus, conifer and mixed forests alike, widely distributed but seldom abundant, summer and fall.

3b Base of stipe not bluish or green; umbo of pileus soon ± olivaceous; spores 8-10 × 5-6 μm .... *I. corydalina* **Quélet**

Pileus 3-5 cm, obtuse, becoming campanulate, finally expanded-umbonate, appressed fibrillose over marginal area, appressed-squamulose around disc, margin cottony at first, fibrils and squamules dark date brown; odor strong and pungent. Gills adnate, narrow, crowded, pallid then cinnamon brown. Stipe 4-8 cm x 8-15 mm, ± equal, whitish, darkening from base upward. Pleurocystidia 40-55 x 10-18 μm, thick-walled.

In conifer and hardwood forests and under brush along roads, widely distributed in North America but apparently rarely collected.

4a Gills and/or apex of stipe violaceous to lilac **5**

4b Not as above **6**

5a Pileus and apex of stipe violaceous to lilac; spores 7-9 × 4-4.5 μm .... *I. lilacina* (**Boud.**) **Kauf.**

Pileus 2-4 cm, conic to conic-campanulate, finally expanded-umbonate, dry, innately silky and ± smooth, not fading completely; taste ± nauseous. Gills adnate, close, broad at maturity, pallid to pale lilac, finally clay-color. Stipe 4-6 cm x 4-7 mm, more or less equal innately fibrillose, cortinate. Pleurocystidia 40-60 x 10-15 μm, thick-walled.

Under either hardwoods or conifers, common, summer and fall, widely distributed.

5b **Pileus with red to reddish-tawny fibrils** .... *I. pyrotricha* **Stuntz**

Pileus 1.5-3 cm, conic, then umbonate-expanded, umbo broadly rounded, appressed-fibrillose then diffracted scaly, color various shades of rusty red, tawny in drying; context pale lavender but soon pallid. Gills rounded at stipe, broad, close, pale bluish lavender at first, slowly becoming light gray. Stipe 2.5-5 cm x 2.5-5 mm, base ± clavate, yellow at base, lavender above, fibrillose with rusty red fibrils. Spores 7-10 x 4.5-6 μm, smooth. Pleurocystidia 66-80 x 12-17 μm, thick-walled.

Gregarious under conifers, Pacific Northwest, fall, apparently rare.

6a Spores smooth 7

6b Spores angular to nodulose 16

7a **Pileus with a blackish, glabrous, subviscid disc; spores 7-10 × 4.5-6 μm** .... *I. fuscodisca* (**Peck**) **Massee**

Pileus 1-2.5 cm, obtusely conic then campanulate and finally expanded-umbonate, marginal area dull-brown and ± virgate with agglutinated fibrils; odor ± disagreeable. Gills adnate, close, broad, white becoming dingy clay-color. Stipe 4-7 cm x 2-3.5 mm, equal, appressed fibrillose, apex pruinose, grayish in age. Pleurocystidia 40-60 x 10-20 μm.

Under conifers, scattered to gregarious, summer and fall, southeastern and Pacific Coast regions, not rare.

7b **Pileus glabrous, subviscid, disc not blackish** 8

8a **Odor soon persistently fragrant or fruity; context slowly reddish where cut. Fig. 421** .... *I. pyriodora* (**Fr.**) **Quél.**

Figure 421

Figure 421 *Inocybe pyriodora*

Pileus 3-7 cm, conic-campanulate to plano-umbonate, dry, pallid at first, soon dingy ochraceous to grayish brown, becoming lacerate-scaly. Gills adnexed, broad, close, pallid becoming dingy cinnamon, in age ± reddish tawny. Stipe 4-9 cm x 4-10 mm, equal, cortinate at first, surface thinly fibrillose, pallid at first, finally dingy brown. Spores 7.5-10 x 5-6 μm. Pleurocystidia 40-55 (60) x 10-15 (20) μm, thick-walled.

Solitary to scattered in low hardwood stands and in brushy places east of the Great Plains, late summer and fall, fairly abundant at times after heavy rains in August.

8b **Odor various: of green corn, nauseous, disagreeable, or none present** 9

9a **Fruiting body white at first but gradually developing extensive orange, reddish or rusty red stains** .... *I. pudica* **Kühner**

Pileus 2-6 (8) cm, conic to conic-campanulate or ± expanded and conic-umbonate, white and appressed-fibrillose at first; odor nauseous. Gills close, adnexed, ± broad, white becoming dark clay-color. Stipe 6-8 cm x 5-10 (12) mm, equal, appressed-fibrillose, solid, apex pruinose. Spores

8-10 x 5-6 μm. Pleurocystidia abundant, 40-60 x 10-18 μm, thick-walled.

Very common under conifers, Pacific Northwest, less common elsewhere in North America but by no means rare, late summer and fall, POISONOUS.

9b Fruiting body colored or white, and not developing orange to red stains or flushes 10

10a Pileus brown with margin brass-yellow; stipe apex ± salmon-color .... *I. laetior* Stuntz

Pileus 2-3.5 cm, campanulate becoming expanded-umbonate, finally plane, margin incurved, splitting radially, smooth, appressed silky, marginal area finally rimose, disc tawny brown to rusty red; odor ± radish-like. Gills adnate, broad, ± subdistant to close, pallid then finally olivaceous brown. Stipe 2.5-7 cm x 2.5-5.5 mm, terete, slightly bulbous, base white-mycelioid. Spores 9-11 (13.5) x 5.5-6.5 μm. Pleurocystidia (53) 60-80 x 20-30 μm, thick-walled.

Gregarious under conifers, Pacific Northwest, fall, not common.

10b Not as above 11

11a Pileus white and silky-fibrillose, conic at first; spores 8-10 x 5-6 μm. Fig. 422 .... *I. geophylla* (Fr.) Kummer

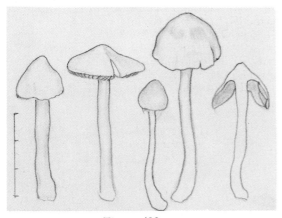

Figure 422

Figure 422 *Inocybe geophylla*

Pileus 1.5-4 cm, conic, finally conic-campanulate, dry; odor nauseous. Gills adnate to adnexed, close, narrow becoming broad and ventricose, whitish becoming ± clay-color. Stipe 3-6 cm x 2-4 mm, equal, firm, white, silky fibrillose to the pruinose apex. Spores ± inequilateral in profile. Pleurocystidia abundant, 43-58 (65) x 10-18 μm, thick-walled.

Scattered to gregarious under brush and in hardwood as well as conifer forests, summer and fall, widely distributed in North America. POISONOUS.

11b Not as above 12

12a Pileus soon conspicuously rimose 13

12b Pileus not rimose or very slightly so 14

13a Pileus cream color to dull yellow; spores 9-13 (17) × 5-6 (8) μm. Fig. 423 .... *I. sororia* Kauffman

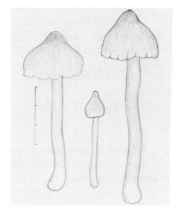

Figure 423

Figure 423 *Inocybe sororia*

Pileus 2-7 (10) cm, conic to campanulate, dry, cream color to dull yellow, disc often pale brown; odor pungent. Gills narrow, close, adnate. Stipe 3-10 cm x 2-5 (7) mm, pallid to dingy brownish, innately fibrillose. Pleurocystidia none.

On ground under hardwoods, Great Lakes south and eastward, also in the Pacific Northwest, late summer and fall; frequently collected. Very likely poisonous.

13b Pileus ± date-brown to dingy clay-color; spores 7-9 (10) × 5.5 μm ....
.... I. fastigiella Atkinson

Pileus 2-5 (6) cm, date-brown to dingy clay-color, campanulate to expanded umbonate, dry, at times ± scaly. Gills nearly free, narrow, crowded. Stipe 4-8 cm x 4-7 mm, equal to slightly enlarged base, ± fibrillose but becoming glabrous, pallid but brown by maturity. Pleurocystidia none.

Scattered to gregarious on the ground in hardwood stands, not uncommon, summer and fall, east of the Great Plains.

14a Stipe becoming fuscous brown from the base upward .... I. atripes Atkinson

Pileus 1-3.5 (5) cm, campanulate, then expanded-umbonate, dry, fibrillose, dull yellow-brown to darker; odor pungent-disagreeable. Gills adnate, close, moderately broad, white then dingy clay-color or darker. Stipe 3-6 (7) cm long, 3-6 mm thick, solid, pruinose above, fibrillose downward. Spores 7-10 x 5-6 μm. Pleurocystidia 38-56 x 9-14 (20) μm, thick-walled.

Under pine, hardwoods, or brush and along roadsides, Great Lakes area eastward and southward, summer and fall, not rare.

14b Stipe not darkening as in above choice 15

15a Spores 7-9 × 4-5 μm; pleurocystidia 60-90 × 10-16 μm; pileus dull cinnamon to dingy yellow-brown. Fig. 424 ....
.... I. olympiana Smith

Figure 424

Figure 424 *Inocybe olympiana*

Pileus (2) 3-7 cm, obtuse to campanulate or convex, at times finally nearly plane, innately fibrillose becoming ± squamulose; taste ± farinaceous. Gills close, broad, adnate, whitish becoming dingy dull clay-color. Stipe 6-12 x 0.8-1.2 cm, equal above a submarginate bulb, solid, pallid but soon dingy brown or finally ± concolorous with pileus sparsely fibrillose. Pleurocystidia 60-90 x 10-16 μm, thick-walled.

Gregarious under conifers, Pacific Northwest, common, late summer and fall. Probably poisonous.

15b Spores 10-14 × 4-5.5 μm; pleurocystidia 40-60 × 12-18 μm; pileus dark brown to dark grayish brown. Fig. 425 ....
.... I. lacera (Fr.) Kummer

Figure 425

Figure 425 *Inocybe lacera*

Pileus (1) 2-4 (5) cm, obtuse to convex, finally ± expanded-umbonate, surface dry and loosely appressed-fibrillose, margin fibrillose. Gills broad, close, adnate, pallid becoming brown. Stipe 3-5 cm x 2-4 mm, floccose fibrillose at first, ± concolorous with pileus. Spores elongate and smooth to obscurely angular Pleurocystidia thick-walled.

Very common in spring and fall in sandy soil especially under aspen, throughout northern United States and in Canada. POISONOUS.

16a Spores 10-14 × 4-5.5 μm, mostly angular see .... *I. lacera*

16b Spores all distinctly angular to nodulose **17**

17a Odor at first nauseous then sweely fragrant .... *I. suaveolens* **Stuntz**

Pileus 2-4.5 cm, campanulate then expanded-umbonate, dry, silky smooth and ± shining, margin becoming rimose, dull yellow. Gills broad, ventricose, close, variously attached, finally brownish-olivaceous. Stipe 3-9 cm x 2.5-7 mm, with a marginate bulb, discoloring in age. Spores 7-10 x 5.5-6.5 (7) μm. Pleurocystidia 43-60 x 10-17 μm, very thick-walled.

On humus and moss under conifers; Pacific Northwest; fall.

17b Not as above **18**

18a Pileus glabrous, ± hygrophanous, dark pinkish brown when fresh, furfuraceous and hoary when faded .... *I. tubarioides* **Atkinson**

Pileus 1-3 cm, convex and remaining so, margin faintly striate when moist. Context watery brown. Gills close, broad, adnate to decurrent, vinaceous buff young, dingy brown in age. Stipe 3-4 cm x 2-3 mm, equal, solid, colored like pileus or toned more pinkish brown, with a thin coating of whitish fibrils, whitish at base. Spores 7-8 x 4-5 μm, elliptic-nodulose in optical section. Pleurocystidia 45-50 x 10-15 μm, obtuse, thin-walled.

Solitary to scattered, often on very rotten wood, Great Lakes area eastward and southward, late summer, rarely collected.

18b Pileus fibrillose to scaly and dry **19**

19a Spores with prominent blunt spines as ornamentation; pileus soon lacerate-scaly. Fig. 426 .... *I. calospora* **Quélet**

Figure 426

Figure 426 *Inocybe calospora*

Pileus 1-3 cm, conic to conic-campanulate, finally expanded-umbonate, dry, fibrillose, near cinnamon brown to chestnut brown, paler if faded. Gills close, ± broad, narrowly adnate, grayish becoming dull cinnamon. Stipe 3-5 cm x 1.5-2 mm, equal or at times with a small bulb, solid, concolorous with pileus, pruinose then ± naked. Spores 9-12 x 8-10 μm including spines, spines ± 2.5 μm long.

Scattered on soil, widely distributed, summer and fall east of the Great Plains.

19b Spores not spiny (as in above choice) **20**

20a Spores with ± crown-shaped warts over the spores .... *I. multicoronata* **Smith**

Pileus 1-2.5 cm, sharply conic then campanulate, dry, fibrillose, cinnamon brown, becoming rimose and ± scaly, buff-color in age when surface fibrils are gone. Gills close, narrow, adnate, becoming cinnamon brown. Stipe 6-8 cm x 1.5-2 mm, equal, fairly tough, pallid brownish, fibrillose over lower portion, pruinose above. Spores 8-11 μm diameter with 6-9 warts each with some secondary ornamentation along the rim of the wart.

Scattered on soil under hardwoods, known from Nova Scotia in Canada, rare.

20b Spores not as above **21**

21a Pileus with a whitish disc that is glabrous; spores 6-8 × 5-6 μm. Fig. 427 ....
.... *I. albodisca* **Peck**

Figure 427

Figure 427 *Inocybe albodisca*

Pileus 2-5 cm, obtusely conic to campanulate, finally ± expanded-umbonate, surface moist, color violaceous gray except for the disc, in age ± rimulose on marginal area. Gills close, ± adnate, narrow, pallid then grayish brown. Stipe 3-7 cm x 3-6 mm, equal down to a marginate bulb, paler

than pileus. Spores ± nodulose. Pleurocystidia 45-60 x 10-15 (18) μm, thick-walled.

On the ground in mixed woods, northern United States, solitary to gregarious, late summer and fall; common at times in old logging roads.

21b Not as above **22**

22a Pileus thinly coated with pale brown fibrils; spores 11-13 (16) × 5.5-9 μm ....
.... *I. rainierensis* **Stuntz**

Pileus 1.5-4.5 cm, obtusely campanulate, then umbonate-expanded, dry, dull brown in age. Gills broad, close, adnate, finally olivaceous brown. Stipe 2-4.5 cm x 3.5-8 mm, equal to an abrupt bulb 7-11 mm wide and bearing tufts of fibrils. Spores with 4-5 coarse nodules. Pleurocystidia 58-78 x 12-25 μm, thick-walled.

Scattered under conifers in subalpine habitats, Pacific Northwest, apparently rare.

22b Pileus and stipe distinctly fibrillose with dark brown fibrils; spores 9-12 × 7-9 μm ....
.... *I. lanuginosa* **(Fr.) Kummer**

Pileus 2-4 cm, ± hemispheric to campanulate, finally expanded-umbonate to plane, surface dry and densely fibrillose-squamulose, evenly dark reddish brown or duller in age. Gills adnate, rounded near stipe, pallid brown then dull rusty cinnamon. Stipe 2-5 cm x 2-4 mm, equal, fibrillose-squamulose to lacerate-fibrillose, ± concolorous with pileus. Spores 9-12 x 7-9 μm (incl. ornamentation), covered with blunt nodules. Pleurocystidia 50-60 x 12-18 μm, thin-walled.

Mostly a few fruiting bodies at a time on very rotten wood but fruiting almost every year, summer and fall, widely distributed.

Phaeocollybia Heim

Pileus and stipe confluent; stipe distinctly cartilaginous and tapered down into a long pseudorhiza arising from deep in the substratum; veils absent; spore deposit rusty brown; spores ornamented (warty-wrinkled as viewed with a microscope using an oil-immersion objective), apex of spore in some species ex-

tended apically to a snout-like extension (but apex not truncate from an apical pore as in *Agrocybe*); margin of pileus inrolled at first or at least strongly incurved; species probably forming mycorrhiza with woody plants.

The genus is a small one, with less than 25 species in North America, most of which are known only from the Pacific Northwest. Very little is known in regard to their edibility, and experimenting with them is not recommended since numerous poisonous species occur in closely related genera.

KEY TO SPECIES

1a Pileus olive becoming green; young gills violet .... *P. fallax* **Smith**

Pileus 1-5 cm, glabrous, conic, finally conic-umbonate, slimy when wet; context olive to greenish, odor raphanoid. Gills close, free or hardly attached, narrow, edges serrate. Stipe 8-12 cm x 4-8 mm, grayish-caesious at apex, reddish brown below, tubular. Spores 7-8.5 x 4-5 μm, $\pm$ inequilateral in profile. Cheilocystidia 35-42 x 7-9 μm, clavate. Clamp connections none.
    Gregarious under Douglas fir, Pacific Northwest, not common, fall.

1b Color combination of pileus and gills not as above 2

2a Pileus olive to green 3

2b Pileus various shades of brown 4

3a Spores 7-9 $\times$ 4-5.5 μm; stipe usually less than 10 mm thick near apex. Fig. 428 .... *P. festiva* (Fr.) **Heim**

Figure 428

Figure 428   *Phaeocollybia festiva*

Pileus 2.5-6 cm, $\pm$ convex; odor raphanoid. Gills free, pallid at first, finally rusty brown to rusty red, in age strongly ventricose. Stipe (3) 5-8 (10) mm thick, 3-9 cm long, some with appressed dark fibrils or squamules, toward apex red to grayish green (rarely with a violaceous tinge). Spores inequilateral in profile view, ovate in face view, apex not snout-like. Cheilocystidia clavate, 23-35 x 6-10 μm.
    Scattered under redwood in northern California, late fall and winter, not common. Clamp connections absent.

3b Spores 8-11 $\times$ 5-6 μm; 1-2.5 cm thick at apex .... *P. olivacea* **Smith**

Pileus 4-11 cm, convex to expanded-umbonate, glabrous, slimy, dark olive fading to olive buff; odor of raw cucumbers but soon fading. Gills pallid then rusty brown from spores; broad (up to 2 cm), deeply adnexed to $\pm$ free. Stipe 12-22 cm long, often 3.5 cm thick at ground line, watery olivaceous above. Spores broadly inequilateral in profile view, $\pm$ elliptic in face view, apex snout-like. Cheilocystidia 25-35 x 4-10 μm, filamentose to clavate, gelatinizing. Clamp connections absent.
    Gregarious and common some seasons, Oregon and northern California in oak-pine stands, late fall.

4a Stipe 10-30 mm thick **5**

4b Stipe 2.5-8 (10) mm thick **7**

5a Gills lilac at first. Fig. 429 ....
.... *P. lilacifolia* **Smith**

Figure 429

Figure 429 *Phaeocollybia lilacifolia*

Pileus 3-10 cm, conic to obtuse, then expanded-umbonate, slimy, dark pinkish brown fading to a pale pinkish tawny; taste unpleasant. Gills finally dark rusty brown, narrow, somewhat crowded, nearly free. Stipe lilac above at first. Spores 7-8.5 x 5-5.5 µm, apical snout small. Cheilocystidia 30-35 x 4-9 µm, filamentose-subcapitate to clavate. Clamp connections absent.

Gregarious under conifers, fall and winter, Pacific Northwest, along the coast in particular, not rare but usually only a few found at a time.

5b Gills not violet at first **6**

6a Pileus broadly umbonate to nearly plane, 8-25 cm broad; stipe 1.5-4 cm thick ....
.... *P. kauffmanii* **(Smith) Singer**

Pileus glabrous, slimy, cinnamon to reddish cinnamon, finally liver-brown. Odor and taste ± farinaceous. Gills crowded, nearly free, broad (± 2 cm or more), pallid when young, ± cinnamon brown in age. Stipe 20-40 cm long, glabrous. Spores 8-10 (11) x 4.5-6 (7) µm, in profile view

inequilateral, with a slight apical snout. Cheilocystidia 30-40 x 5-9 µm, ± clavate (basidiole-like). Clamp connections absent.

Scattered to gregarious along the coast of the Pacific Northwest late in the season, frequently collected but we have no reports on its edibility.

6b Pileus 4-12 cm; conic then expanded and with an abrupt umbo; stipe 1-2 cm thick ....
.... *P. spadicea* **Smith**

Pileus slimy, umber brown to dark dingy pinkish brown; odor of cut flesh pungent-farinaceous, taste slightly bitter. Gills nearly free, pallid then avellaneous (pinkish gray), finally cinnamon brown. Stipe 15-20 cm long, glabrous, near apex pinkish brown, toward base dingy reddish brown. Spores 7-9.5 x 4.5-5.5 µm, apical snout well developed. Cheilocystidia 23-32 x 3-8 µm (ventricose part) 1.5-2 µm (neck), 2.5-3 µm (diameter at apex); apex acute to capitate. Clamp connections absent to rare.

Under Sitka spruce, Pacific Northwest, late summer and fall, fairly rare. *P. lugubris* (Fr.) Heim is very closely related but has pleurocystidia and spores lacking an apical snout.

7a Spores 5-6 × 3-3.5 µm; cheilocystidia 18-30 × 2.5-4 µm, apex acute to capitate; taste mild .... *P. radicata* **(Murr.) Sing.**

Pileus 2-3 cm, convex or with a conic umbo, subviscid, a rusty red-brown on disc, pale tawny on margin. Gills broad, narrowly attached, crowded, reddish cinnamon. Stipe 6-18 cm x 3-5 mm, very fragile, dark reddish brown below in age, paler above. Clamp connections present.

Scattered to gregarious under redwood, late fall and winter, northern California.

7b Spores 7-9.5 × 4.5-5 µm; cheilocystidia resembling basidioles; taste becoming very disagreeable .... *P. attenuata* **(Smith) Sing.**

Pileus 1.5-5 cm, soon broadly umbonate, glabrous, subviscid, amber brown fading to yellowish; odor strongly radish-like. Stipe 10-12 cm x 3-5 mm, glabrous, polished, very cartilaginous, dark rusty brown to blackish in age. Clamp connections absent.

Densely gregarious to scattered, Pacific Northwest, along the coast especially, very abundant at times.

Rozites Karsten

Pileus and stipe confluent; spore deposit ± rusty brown; spores clay-color in KOH under the microscope, ornamented by warts and wrinkles; an annulus present on the stipe (in our species); outer veil present but poorly developed. For a "thumb-nail" characterization, this genus may be described as a *Cortinarius* with a membranous partial veil. In the annulate *Cortinarii* the annulus is of outer veil tissue. We include only one species. Fig. 430 .... ***R. caperata* (Fr.) Karsten**

Figure 430

Figure 430 *Rozites caperata*

Pileus 5-12 (15) cm, campanulate to expanded-umbonate, markedly wrinkled or grooved, usually hoary at first around the disc, ± ochraceous brown otherwise. Gills pallid then dingy tawny, close, adnate, broad. Stipe 6-12 × 1-2 cm, ± equal, pallid to ochraceous, with a median annulus. Spores 12-14 × 7-9 μm, elliptic in face view, inequilateral in profile, warty-wrinkled.

Scattered to gregarious in woods of conifers and hardwoods alike but when found under hardwoods, species of *Vaccinium* (blueberry bushes) have been present, indicating that they may be the mycorrhizal host. The fungus is common during late summer and fall in northern regions. Edible and Choice.

Tubaria (W. G. Smith) Gillet

Pileus 5-12 (15) cm, campanulate to expanded-delicate; spores pale yellow to pale cinnamon in deposits, wall thin and some spores remaining collapsed when mounted in KOH, nonamyloid; gills broadly attached to distinctly decurrent; with or without a veil; stipe typically slender.

The genus is represented in North America by 20-25 species, but no reasonably accurate account of them has been published. Only species based on type collections (which have been studied) are included here.

KEY TO SPECIES

1a Pileus glabrous; gills distant; spores 7-9 × 3.5-4 μm .... *T. tenuis* **Peck**

Pileus 1-1.5 cm, convex to hemispheric, subumbilicate, reddish cinnamon moist, ochraceous faded, margin becoming sulcate. Gills ventricose, ± decurrent, ochraceous tawny, broad. Stipe 2.5-5 cm x ± 2 mm, flexuous, pruinose above, downy at base. Spores narrowly inequilateral in profile, very pale ochraceous in KOH. Basidia 4-spored, clavate. Cheilocystidia 28-36 x 7-10 µm, fusoid-ventricose, apex subacute to acute, rarely capitate.

Among mosses on gravely soil, southern California, apparently rare.

1b Pileus with fibrils on surface or floccose; gills subdistant or crowded; spores 8-10 (11) × 5-6.5 µm **2**

2a Gills long-decurrent, subdistant; cheilocystidia none .... *T. alabamensis* **Murrill**

Pileus ± 1 cm, subcampanulate; clothed with white silky hairs, becoming glabrous; brown fading to clay-color. Gills pale cinnamon. Stipe ±

2 cm x 1 mm, white-silky fibrillose then glabrous. Spores yellowish hyaline in KOH, ovate in face view.

Solitary to scattered on fragments of decaying wood, February, Alabama, rare.

2b Gills crowded, decurrent; cheilocystidia 20-26 × 9-12 µm, clavate, yellow in KOH, walls of pedicels ochraceous .... *T. earlei* **Murrill**

Pileus 1-2 cm, deeply umbilicate, surface ochraceous, floccose, not striate; context fleshy. Gills narrow, ochraceous. Stipe ± 2.5 cm x 2-3 mm, densely floccose, ochraceous. Spores thin-walled, yellowish in KOH. Clamp connections present.

Clustered on soil in thickets, Lousiana, September, rare (?).

RHODOPHYLLACEAE Singer

Pileus and stipe confluent; gill attachment to stipe various or the gills free; spore deposit pink to vinaceous or reddish cinnamon; spores angular to longitudinally striate or grooved; veil typically absent.

The family is a large one in North America, there being over 100 species in *Rhodophyllus* alone, but as yet we have no critical account of them. The family contains a number of edible species, a few which are highly rated, a number of poisonous ones, and the majority of little interest to the mycophagist. The name *Rhodophyllus* Quélet is not a valid name, but is exceptionally appropriate, and is still used by Singer in his system. It should be conserved. The generic names applied to its species in the Friesian system are, among

others, *Entoloma, Leptonia, Nolanea,* and *Eccilia*. These genera were never clearly distinguished from each other. In the following treatment where our authorities for species are incomplete, it means we did not find a valid combination of the specific epithet with the generic name.

KEY TO GENERA

1a Spores angular to angular-nodulose .... (p. 305) *Rhodophyllus*

1b Spores longitudinally striate or grooved .... (p. 304) *Clitopilus*

Clitopilus (Fr.) Kummer

Pileus and stipe confluent; context soft and delicate; lamellae decurrent at maturity; stipe central to eccentric; spore deposit pinkish

(flesh-color); spores longitudinally striate or grooved.

This is a small genus with less than half

a dozen species in our region, one of which *C. prunulus*, is highly rated for the table.

Pileus 3-10 cm, convex becoming ± plane to centrally shallowly depressed, tacky to the touch when moist, white to grayish; context soft, both odor and taste strongly farinaceous. Gills close to subdistant, white then pink from spores, decurrent, narrow. Stipe 3-8 cm x 4-15 mm, ± equal, solid. Spores 9-12 x 5-6.5 μm, subfusoid, longitudinally striate. Fig. 431.........
.... **C. prunulus (Fr.) Kummer**

Figure 431 *Clitopilus prunulus*

Scattered to gregarious in conifer and hardwood forests. In Michigan it often occurs on sandy soil under scrub oak, and the pileus is consistently white. In other habitats in other localities, however all shades from white to drab pilei have been found. Kühner & Romagnesi give it a 3-star rating as one of the best of edible fungi. *C. orcella* is here considered a synonym of *C. prunulus*.

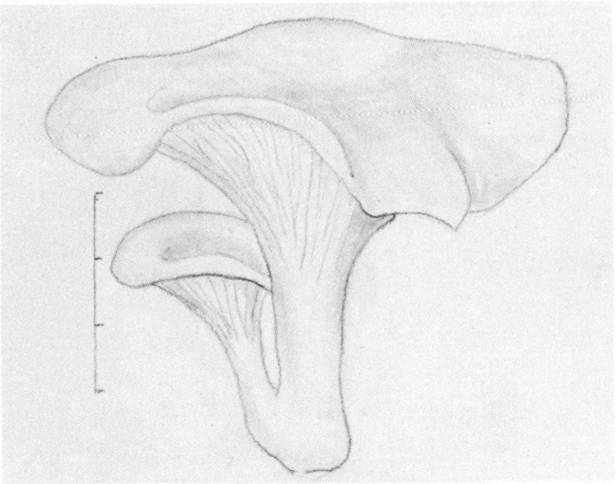

Figure 431

Rhodophyllus Quélet

For a characterization see family description and key to genera.

KEY TO SPECIES

1a Stipe 6-30 mm thick 2

1b Stipe 1-3 (5) mm thick 6

2a Pileus and stipe dull violet to grayish blue; gills pallid at first. Fig. 432 ....
.... *R. madidus* (Fr.) **Quél.**

Figure 432

Figure 432 *Rhodophyllus madidus*

Pileus 6-15 cm, glabrous, tacky to touch if fresh; context violaceous-umber near cuticle; taste farinaceous. Gills close, sinuate, broad, becoming bluish gray before colored by spores. Stipe 4-10 x 1-2.5 cm, ± equal or at apex flared, solid, white within and over surface of base. Spores ± globose, 7-9 μm or 7-9 x 6-8 μm. Pleurocystidia and cheilocystidia not differentiated.

Solitary to scattered under conifers in the Pacific Northwest, especially along the coast, fairly abundant during warm wet fall weather. Edible according to European authors.

2b Fruiting body lacking violaceous tones 3

3a Pileus pale gray and innately appressed-fibrillose; gills grayish at first; fleshy masses of whitish soft tissue occurring near the normal mushrooms. Fig. 433 ....
.... R. abortivus (Berk. & Curt.) Sing.

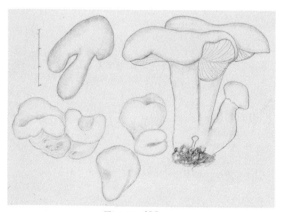

Figure 433

Figure 433 *Rhodophyllus abortivus*

Pileus 4-10 cm, convex and margin inrolled, at times minutely squamulose, sometimes watery-spotted or subzonate near margin; context thick, white, taste farinaceous. Gills close, adnexed to decurrent, edges becoming eroded. Stipe central to eccentric, 4-10 cm x 8-20 mm, ± clavate and at times ± scurfy, base with a coating of white mycelium. Spores 8-10 x 4.5-6 μm, angular-elliptic. Pleurocystidia and cheilocystidia none.

Scattered on and around decaying wood or on humus near it, late summer and fall, common and widely distributed in North America. Edible. The fleshy masses of tissue are now thought to be young mushrooms which have been parasitized by mycelium of *Armillariella mellea*. They are also edible, but be sure decay has not set in. They decay through yeast and bacterial action much faster than the normal fruit bodies.

3b Not as above 4

4a When young the gills yellowish; stipe 1-2.5 cm thick. Fig. 434 ....
.... R. lividus (Fr.) Quél.

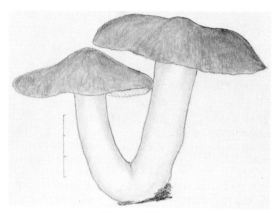

Figure 434

Figure 434 *Rhodophyllus lividus*

Pileus 6-15 cm, obtuse becoming expanded-umbonate, pallid to grayish, glabrous, slightly tacky when wet, not hygrophanous, becoming dingy tan in age over disc; context firm, white, odor and taste farinaceous. Gills close, broad, sinuate. Stipe 8-15 x 1-2.5 cm, equal, solid, white, apex pruinose, dull and silky toward base, not discolored from handling. Spores ± globose 7-10 μm diameter. Pleuro- and cheilocystidia absent.

Scattered to gregarious under oak in woods, early fall after heavy rains, abundant at times, Great Lakes area eastward and southward; *POISONOUS*.

4b Gills not yellowish when young and stipe typically less than 12 mm thick 5

5a Pileus 3-9 cm, obtuse to convex becoming ± plane, dark to pale gray or brownish gray; taste strongly farinaceous. Fig. 435 .... *R. griseus* (Peck)

Figure 435

Figure 435 *Rhodophyllus griseus*

Pileus in age often shallowly depressed over disc, glabrous, margin striatulate when wet and then surface slightly tacky; context watery gray when moist. Gills broad, adnate, close. Stipe 4-9 cm x 6-12 mm, fibrous striate at maturity, dingy grayish pallid to a whitish base, solod. Spores 7-9 x 6.5-8 μm, angular-globose. Pleurocystidia and cheilocystidia absent.

Scattered to gregarious, and abundant during wet weather in late August and September in the Great Lakes area east and southward, it fruits in rather dry upland hardwood stands. It is a species also occurring under conifers. We include it here because it is an example of a ubiquitous mushroom easily confused with half a dozen other species in the genus some of which are poisonous. Not recommended.

5b Pileus conic becoming conic-campanulate, watery cinnamon-colored to grayish cinnamon; taste mild .... *R. strictior* (Pk.) Singer

Pileus 2.5-7 cm wide at base, often equally high, glabrous, hygrophanous, margin often translucent-striate; context thin and fragile. Gills close to subdistant, broad, ascending-adnate, pallid when young. Stipe 7-15 cm x 3-8 (10) mm, fragile, longitudinally- to twisted-striate, pallid or

tinged with color of pileus, whitish at base. Spores 9-12 x 6-8 μm, angular-elliptic. Pleuro- and cheilocystidia none.

Solitary to scattered, seldom in quantity, spring, summer and fall in the Great Lakes area eastward. It is a beautiful species, but not recommended for the table. We find it in boggy and swampy situations generally.

6a Pileus distinctly conic at first **7**

6b Pileus convex-depressed to merely convex **9**

7a Fruiting body ± salmon-color when fresh. Fig. 436 .... *R. salmoneus* (Pk.) Sing.

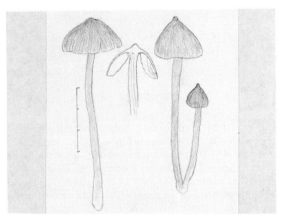

Figure 436

Figure 436 *Rhodophyllus salmoneus*

Pileus 1.5-4 cm, sharply conic, finally conic-campanulate, glabrous, moist, margin at first translucent-striate; taste and odor mild. Gills close, broad, ascending-adnate. Stipe 4-10 cm x 1.5-4 mm, equal, fragile, about concolorous with pileus, base with appressed white mycelium. Spores 9-12.5 μm angular-quadrate (± square in optical section). Pleurocystidia and cheilocystidia absent.

Scattered in bogs or on boggy ground in low wet woods, very abundant at times but usually one finds only scattered fruiting bodies, Great Lakes area eastward, late summer and early fall. It seems to favor logs rotted to the extent that their outlines are hardly visible.

7b Colors not as above **8**

8a Fruiting body bright yellow; pileus cuspi-
tate; spores 9-11 × 8-10 μm. Fig. 437 ....
.... *R. murraii* **(Berk. & Curt.) Sing.**

Figure 437

Figure 437 *Rhodophyllus murraii*

Pileus 10-25 mm broad, faintly striate; context
yellow. Gills close, ascending-adnate. Stipe 5-10
cm x 2-4 (5) mm, equal, strict, longitudinally
striate. Spores quadrate. Pleurocystidia and cheilocystidia absent.

    Scattered to gregarious in mixed conifer-
hardwood forests on rich humus, summer and
early fall, Great Lakes area eastward and southward, not common but abundant during some
seasons.

8b Pileus ± umber brown to dark reddish
brown; pileus ± conic; fruiting early in the
spring. Fig. 438 ....
.... *R. vernus* **(Lundell) Romag.**

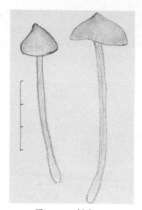

Figure 438

Figure 438 *Rhodophyllus vernus*

Pileus 2.5-5 cm, pale brown when faded, glabrous. Gills subdistant, broad, at first grayish
brown, ascending. Stipe 3-8 cm x 2-4 (7) mm,
± equal, often compressed, innately fibrillose but
no veil evident. Spores 9-11 x 7-8 μm, angular-
elliptic. Pleurocystidia and cheilocystidia none.

    On soil along roads, under brush, and in
waste areas, abundant at times. It is one of our
earliest fruiting mushrooms in the Great Lakes
area, probably widely distributed especially in
Canda.

9a Pileus greenish to greenish yellow; odor of
mouse dung (acetamide). Fig. 439 ....
.... *R. incanus* **(Fr.) Quél.**

Figure 439

Figure 439 *Rhodophyllus incanus*

Pileus 1-3.5 cm, moist, glabrous to minutely squamulose over disc; context bluish green where bruised, taste mild. Gills subdistant, about concolor with pileus, adnate, broad. Stipe 1.5-4 cm x 1-3 mm, concolorous with pileus, glabrous, staining greenish blue where injured. Spores 9-11 x 7-8 μm, angular-elliptic. Pleurocystidia and cheilocystidia absent.

Gregarious on moss and in grassy areas, woods borders, waste land, etc., summer and early fall, east of the Great Plains, rare (?).

9b Not as above 10

10a Gill edges dark violet. Fig. 440 ....
.... *R. serrulatus* (Fr.) Quél.

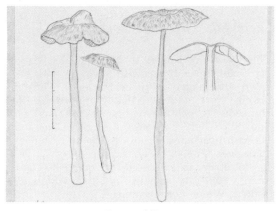

Figure 440

Figure 440 *Rhodophyllus serrulatus*

Pileus 15-30 mm, dark violaceous, squamulose over disc, fading to violaceous gray; context thin, taste and odor not distinctive. Gills bluish gray at first, adnate to short-decurrent, ± subdistant. Stipe 3-7 cm x 2-3 (4) mm, violaceous, naked or furfuraceous to scabrous toward the apex, base thinly coated with whitish mycelium.

Solitary to gregarious on rich humus, in bogs, etc., widely distributed in North America, summer and fall, common but not in large numbers.

10b Gills, including edges, white at first ....
.... *R. albinellus* (Pk.)

Pileus 1-4.5 cm, convex with a ± depressed to merely flattened disc, plano-depressed in age, white overall until flushed pinkish as the spores mature, innately fibrillose or squamulose around disc, odor fragrant. Gills white then pink, close, narrow, adnate. Stipe 3-5 cm x 3-5 mm, white, fragile apex pruinose, base white-cottony. Spores 9-12 x 6-8 μm, angular-elliptic. Pleurocystidia and cheilocystidia none.

Solitary to scattered on *Sphagnum* under larch and poison sumac and under ferns along swamp and bog edges. It was found abundantly during the dry years of the 1930s but has been rare since then according to Smith's experience. It is to be expected from the Great Lakes area eastward.

PAXILLACEAE R. Maire in Maire, Dumée and Lutz

Pileus and stipe confluent (when a stipe is present); spore deposit pale to dark yellow-brown to cocoa-brown; spores lacking a germ pore; hymenophore typically readily separable from pileus, formed of gills and the latter often intervenose; gill trama ± bilateral; growing on soil, humus and dead wood.

The family, including *Phylloporus,* has under two dozen species here in North America. Some are frequently collected for table use; NEVER should they be eaten raw. In our treatment here we have included *Phylloporus rhodoxanthus* in this family in spite of its having boletus-like spores. Singer places the genus in the Boletaceae even though it has well-developed gills.

KEY TO SPECIES

1a Stipe present and central to eccentric 2

1b Stipe absent to lateral and poorly developed (note: none of these species are included here.)

2a Gills broad, subdistant, thickish and bright yellow. Fig. 441 .... *Phylloporus rhodoxanthus* (Schw.) Bresadola

Figure 441

Figure 441 *Phylloporus rhodoxanthus*

Pileus 3-12 cm, broadly convex, dry, velvety to subtomentose, dull to bright red to reddish brown; context pallid to yellowish, taste mild. Stipe 4-10 x 0.5-1.5 cm, equal to ventricose, red to rusty yellow in a variable pattern. Spores 9-12 x 3.5-5 μm, in profile view $\pm$ inequilateral. Pleurocystidia and cheilocystidia numerous, 60-70 x 9-15 μm, content yellow in KOH.

Solitary, scattered or gregarious on humus in either hardwood or conifer forests, summer and fall, rather frequent and widely distributed. Edible.

2b Gills close to crowded, thin, narrow 3

3a Stipe 1-3 cm thick, soon dark brown over basal area and soon covered with a dark brown pubescence; spores 5-6 $\times$ 3.5-4 μm, strongly dextrinoid. Fig. 442 .... *Paxillus atrotomentosus* Fries

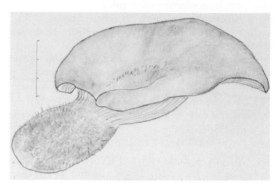

Figure 442

Figure 442 *Paxillus atrotomentosus*

Pileus 6-15 cm, convex to $\pm$ plane, dry, $\pm$ velvety or unpolished, yellowish tawny to dark rusty brown (or in age at times blackish). Gills decurrent, close, narrow (finally $\pm$ broad), dull ochraceous to ochraceous tan, often forked near stipe. Stipe 3-12 cm long, often eccentric, solid, yellowish near apex. Pleurocystidia and cheilocystidia none.

Solitary to clustered on or near conifer stumps, etc., late summer and fall, widely distributed. We do not recommend it.

3b Not as above 4

4a Spore deposit cocoa-brown; stipe 2-4 cm thick near apex. Fig. 443 .... *Paxillus vernalis* Watling

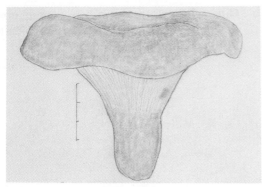

Figure 443

Figure 443 *Paxillus vernalis*

Pileus 5-20 cm broad, broadly convex to plane, whitish to pale pinkish buff when young, darkening to about snuff brown. Gills close, decurrent, staining brown on bruising. Stipe 3-10 cm long, glabrous to appressed-fibrillose, soon dark brown from handling. Spores 7-9 x 5-5.5 μm. Pleurocystidia abundant, 40-50 x 8-11 μm.

On sandy soil in balsam-birch-aspen stands, Great Lakes area, late spring to early fall, common during wet seasons. Edibility not tested.

4b   Spore deposit deep yellow-brown; stipe 4-20 mm thick; pileus pale ochraceous brown when young. Fig. 444 .... *Paxillus involutus* **(Fr.) Fr.**

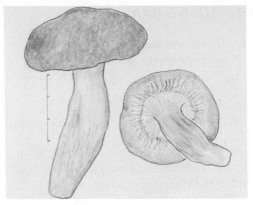

Figure 444

Figure 444 *Paxillus involutus*

Pileus 4-15 cm broad, plane or broadly depressed, the margin inrolled and ribbed, dry, matted fibrillose; context yellowish pallid soon brownish where bruised. Gills decurrent, crowded, anastomosing, pale olivaceous-ochraceous, brown where injured. Stipe solid, glabrous, central or eccentric, dingy ochraceous brown. Spores 7-9 (10) x 5-6 μm. Pleurocystidia 50-70 x 9-12 μm.

Solitary to gregarious on ground in woods, especially in bogs or along their edges, common but sporadic, widely distributed, summer and fall. Often abundant during dry seasons. It is listed by many authors as edible, but we do not recommend it. NEVER should it be eaten raw.

GOMPHIDIACEAE R. MAIRE

Gills decurrent, thick, distant to subdistant or close; spore deposit smoky gray to blackish; spores long and narrow, in profile often ± inequilateral, smooth, pale tawny in Melzer's; pleurocystidia projecting well beyond the basidia, content often lilac to reddish as seen in KOH mounts; clamp connections not present on hyphae of fruit body but often present on vegetative mycelium which may surround the base of the stipe; stipe and pileus confluent; veils present or absent.

Solitary to gregarious or at times caespitose under conifers, especially pine and larch, apparently all species are mycorrhiza-formers with conifers. Fruiting occurs from late June through November or December or later in California. More species occur in the Pacific Northwest than anywhere else, but the total world flora is probably less than 25 species. All species known to date are edible or at least not poisonous.

KEY TO GENERA

1a Gills, pileus, and stipe bright to dull ochraceous to ochraceous tan .... (p. 312) *Chroogomphus*

1b Gills white or pallid when young; context of pileus white at first; stipe typically lemon-yellow over basal area .... (p. 314) *Gomphidius*

Chroogomphus (Singer) O. K. Miller

Context of stipe ochraceous throughout when young; at least some hyphae of the fruit body violet in Melzer's; surface of pileus dry and fibrillose, seldom slimy, usually merely viscid when moist. The genus has around a dozen species.

KEY TO SPECIES

1a Surface of pileus dry and appressed fibrillose or subviscid (tacky) in wet weather, appearing dull when dry 2

1b Surface of pileus viscid to slimy, appearing shiny when dry 3

2a Pileus evenly colored pale to bright ochraceous; pleurocystidia thick-walled. Fig. 445 .... *C. tomentosus* (**Murr.**) **Miller**

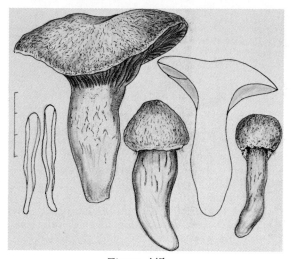

Figure 445

Figure 445 *Chroogomphus tomentosus*

Pileus 2-8 cm broad, obtuse to broadly conic to expanded-umbonate. Gills distant, thick, ochraceous at first. Stipe 4-17 cm x 2-20 mm, colored like the pileus; at first with an ochraceous fibrillose veil. Spores 15-25 x 6-8 μm. Pleurocystidia 118-225 x 20-21 μm.

On moss under conifers, often with Douglas fir and hemlock, from sea level to ± 4500 feet. Fruiting from late August to late October, common in the Pacific Northwest.

2b Pileus typically gray or at least usually gray over the margin; pleurocystidia thin-walled. Fig. 446 .... *C. leptocystis* (**Sing.**) **Miller**

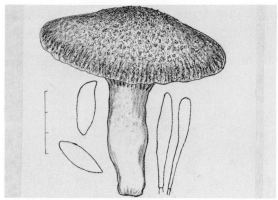

Figure 446

Figure 447

Figure 446 *Chroogomphus leptocystis*

Pileus 2.5-9 cm, at times merely tinged ochraceous or salmon-color variously, usually more glabrous than in above species; context pale orange, becoming slightly purplish red variously. Gills broad, subdistant, ± clay-color. Stipe 6-14 cm x (2) 4-12 mm, yellowish; fibrillose veil pale ochraceous and leaving a slight superior zone, fibrils on stipe often stained reddish. Spores 12-18 x 6-7 μm. Pleurocystidia 103-187 x 15-18 μm.

Under conifers from sea level to ± 4000 feet, fruiting generally from September through October, not common, Pacific Northwest.

3a   Pileus pinkish to vinaceous when young, 1-4 cm broad; spores 18-29 $\times$ 6-8.5 μm .... *C. flavipes* (Pk.) Miller

Pileus surface moist but not viscid, striate to radially rimose; context pallid vinaceous, odor and taste mild. Gills broad, distant, pale salmon-color at first. Stipe 3.5-6 cm x 4-6 mm, pallid above, lemon-yellow below; veil slight, surface dry. Pleurocystidia 119-249 x 9-26 μm, thin-walled.

Scattered under conifers in or at edge of bogs, late summer and fall, Great Lakes area eastward; rare.

3b   Pileus color not as above 4

4a   Pleurocystidia thin-walled. Fig. 447 .... *C. rutilus* (Fr.) Miller

Figure 447 *Chroogomphus rutilus*

Pileus 2.5-12 cm, convex to umbonate, viscid, ochraceous to vinaceous or finally blackish brown; context ochraceous to tinged salmon; taste mild. Gills distant to close, broad, thickish to thin in age, ochraceous but finally clouded olive-brown from spores. Stipe 4-18 cm x 10-20 mm, a thin fibrillose veil present; surface ochraceous but stained or flushed vinaceous in age. Pleurocystidia 82-178 x 13-22 μm, narrowly clavate to cylindric. Spores 14-22 x 5-7.5 μm.

Solitary to scattered, rarely gregarious under pine, common during wet years in the northern United States and Canada. Edible, used more than others in the genus.

4b   Pleurocystidia thick-walled 5

5a   Stipe 5-15 mm thick. Fig. 448 .... *C. vinicolor* (Pk.) Miller

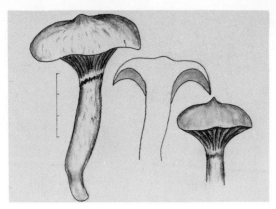

Figure 448

Figure 448   *Chroogomphus vinicolor*

Pileus 1-8 cm, obtuse to convex finally turbinate to umbonate, viscid but soon dry, squamulose in age pale brownish ochraceous to smoky ochraceous, toned vinaceous in age or with reddish orange stains; context orange at first; taste mild. Gills broad, distant, decurrent, dingy ochraceous, smoky ochraceous in age. Stipe 5-10 cm long, orange-buff, tapered downward, pale ochraceous to orange-buff to vinaceous red; veil slight, fibrillose. Spores 17-23 x 4.5-7.5 μm. Pleurocystidia 112-164 x 13-20 μm, narrowly clavate to narrowly fusoid.

Solitary to gregarious or caespitose on the ground under pine in particular, late summer and fall, rather common during wet years in the north-ern United States and Canada and the Pacific Northwest.

5b   Stipe 2-5 cm thick near apex. Fig. 449 ....
.... *C. pseudovinicolor* **Miller**

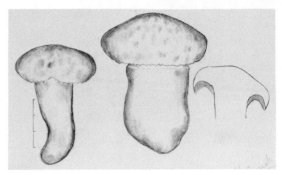

Figure 449

Figure 449   *Chroogomphus pseudovinicolor*

Pileus 6-12 cm, dry, somewhat mottled, ochraceous becoming orange to dull red, margin fringed at first. Gills forking and frequently anastomosing, thickish, subdistant. Stipe 6-12 cm long, solid, colored about like the pileus, dry; veil rudimentary. Spores 15-20 x 5-7.5 μm. Pleurocystidia 88-200 x 16-20 μm, fusiform to cylindric.

Solitary to caespitose on ground under conifers, Pacific Northwest, September and October.

Gomphidius Fries

Pileus viscid to slimy when wet, shiny when dry; flesh of pileus pallid to white in immature fruiting bodies; veil if present a slime veil or an outer slime veil and an inner white, fibrillose veil; stipe often blackening and at base typically bright lemon yellow.

The genus is a small one with under a dozen species, none of which is popular here in North America for the table because of the slime.

KEY TO SPECIES

1a   Pileus purple drab to brownish drab, soon stained black; caulocystidia absent to scattered. Fig. 450 .... *G. glutinosus* (**Fr.**) **Fr.**

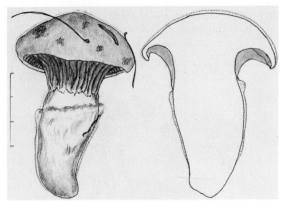

Figure 450

Figure 451

Figure 450 *Gomphidius glutinosus*

Figure 451 *Gomphidius oregonensis*

Pileus 3-10 cm, broadly convex, glabrous, slimy when fresh. Gills close to subdistant, broad, decurrent, white becoming smoky fuscous. Stipe 4-10 cm x 10-20 mm, white above, yellow over basal area; with a white, fibrillose veil beneath the slime veil. Spores 15-21 x 4.5-6 μm. Pleurocystidia 74-146 x 11-14 μm. Hyphae of gill trama 4-6.5 μm wide ± gelatinizing.

Solitary to scattered, occasionally caespitose, under conifers, especially spruce. It is circumboreal in distribution and fruits during late summer and fall. It is probably the most frequently collected species in the genus. *G. largus* Miller is quite similar to it but the gill tramal hyphae are 20-40 μm wide. Its pileus is up to 20 cm broad and it fruits in the summer and fall in the Rocky Mountains and the Pacific Northwest.

1b Pileus pink to rose-colored or pallid when young; caulocystidia in clusters near the apex of the stipe 2

2a Spores 10.5-14.5 × 4-6 μm. Fig. 451 ....
.... *G. oregonensis* **Peck**

Pileus 2-15 cm, broadly convex, ochraceous-salmon to salmon buff when young, becoming dark sordid brown and blackening in age; context pallid at first. Gills ± close, narrow to moderately broad, decurrent, whitish at first. Stipe 6-15 cm x 1-5 cm, often deeply rooting, white above the annular zone, yellow near base, slime readily blackening; a fibrillose veil present beneath the slime veil. Pleurocystidia 80-120 x 8-13 μm; hyaline to yellow in Melzer's sol.

Typically under Douglas fir late in the fall or during the winter along the Pacific Coast, rather common. It is often caespitose and generally very unattractive.

2b Spores larger than in above choice and fruiting bodies seldom caespitose 3

3a Stipe lacking a slime veil; soon blackening on handling or in age; associated with larch. Fig. 452 .... *G. maculatus* (**Fr.**) **Fr.**

Figure 452

Figure 452 *Gomphidius maculatus*

Pileus 3-11 cm broad, light cinnamon to reddish brown, slimy at first, glabrous; context pallid; taste pleasant. Gills ± decurrent, becoming distant, many of them forked, white to pallid at first. Stipe 6-8 cm x 4-12 (20) mm, equal, whitish to the yellow base when young, lower two-thirds covered with dark purplish to black fibrils (or finally dark over all from the staining reaction). Spores 14-22 x 6-8 μm. Pleurocystidia 95-170 x 15-30 μm, thin-walled, hyaline in Melzer's.

Solitary to scattered or gregarious throughout the range of *Larix* (larch) in North America, but most abundant in the Priest Lake region of northern Idaho, late summer and fall. In the Great Lakes area a slender form with stipe 3-5 mm thick is usually encountered.

3b Stipe viscid to slimy from the slime veil; pileus dull rose red. Fig. 453 ....
.... *G. subroseus* **Kauffman**

Figure 453

Figure 453 *Gomphidius subroseus*

Pileus 4-7 cm, obtuse to expanded umbonate, glabrous, slimy; context pallid at first, taste mild. Gills pallid becoming smoky gray, close to subdistant, decurrent. Stipe 3.5-10 x 0.6-1.5 cm, nearly equal, whitish above, yellow near base, discoloring in age, inner fibrillose veil very poorly developed. Spores 15-20 x 4.5-7 μm. Pleurocystidia 85-129 x 13-17 μm, cylindric to subfusiform.

Solitary to scattered under conifers, up to 6000 feet elevation, June to October in the Rocky Mountains, September to December on the Pacific Coast. Rare in eastern North America.

Appendix: Identifying Mushroom Genera by Macroscopic Characters

The way most people learn to identify mushrooms in the field is to go out with someone who already knows the mushrooms and can name them for the learner. In this method one learns to recognize the mushrooms (as in sight reading) simply by their aspect without being conscious of the individual characters (letters). However when one is dependent solely on her/his own resources to learn mushrooms, the first step is to notice particular characters, i.e., size, color, shape, and how they vary. Soon certain genera become easy to recognize, i.e., *Lactarius* with milky juice, *Russula* with its squatty appearance. The following key is designed to help the user learn to recognize the genera (and in a few instances families) in the field by macroscopic characters alone. It is not to be considered a substitute for the main key which will lead to more accurate identification because anatomical and chemical characters are also considered.

It cannot be too strongly emphasized that this key is applicable only to the mushrooms included in this book, and that even with the included species one will often have trouble running them down to genus. One reason for this difficulty is that several genera may be quite similar in appearance but are found to be quite different when anatomical consider-

ations are taken into account. Many genera have intergrading characters and in the case of borderline species it is difficult for the specialist to assign them to the correct genus even when all the anatomical and chemical characters are known. It can be readily seen that it is impossible for the layman using only the relatively small number of macroscopic characters to make accurate generic identifications in many instances. The following suggestions may make the macroscopic study of mushrooms somewhat less frustrating.

One of the most important characters for field identification is the color of the spores as represented by the spore deposit. Gill color is not a reliable indication of spore color as the two may differ markedly. The best method of making spore prints as described in the introduction is not always possible in the field. However, one can often find a spore deposit on the upper surface of a pileus that is underneath a taller fruiting body. Also there may be a spore deposit represented by radiating lines on the upper surface of an annulus, or a fine dusting of powder over the upper surface of the stipe or on the upper surface of a basal bulb. If a natural spore deposit cannot be found a spore print can be started in the field by cutting the stipe from a pileus and placing the pileus gill side down on a piece of paper, wrapping them in waxed paper and placing in the basket gill side down. To test for the effect of iodine on spores (if Melzer's reagent is not available, ordinary tincture of iodine will work) simply put some of the spores from a deposit on a glass slide, white china, plastic wrap or similar surface and touch with a small amount of iodine solution. One can usually readily decide whether the spore powder turns blue or not (be sure to use plenty of spore dust). A less precise way is to macerate a few gills and place a drop of iodine on them. NEVER test for iodine with the spores on paper—the paper itself will probably give a strong amyloid reaction.

Determining viscidity in the field in dry weather poses a problem. The surface of a viscid cap will feel dry to the touch but will usually have a somewhat glazed or shiny appearance; sometimes one can tell if the surface is viscid by putting a little water on the cap and see if the surface becomes viscid—this is not a foolproof method. In dry weather it may be hard to get latex from the usual type of cut across the gills of species of *Lactarius*. Try making a small cut on the stipe near the pileus or a tangential cut on the margin of the pileus.

Careful field observations are very important in determining the presence or absence of a veil or veils. *Always* dig out the base of the stipe and examine it for a volva, rolls, patches, or fragments of tissue that may be present; if none are found check in the debris around the base to see if fragments of veil were left in the substrate. Also look at the pileus, particularly on young specimens, to see whether or not patches of veil material were left there. Veil material occurring on the pileus and at the base of the stipe indicate the presence of an universal veil. To determine whether a partial veil is present examine the gill cavity in a young button. If the gill cavity is covered with cobwebby material, fibrils, slime, or a membrane of some sort extending from the margin of the pileus to the stipe, a partial veil is present.

In spite of the utmost care in observation it is sometimes difficult or impossible to make a good choice between the two choices in a couplet. In this event run the specimen down both ways. It may be impossible to arrive at a satisfactory identification. If an identification cannot be made with this key nor with the main key it is quite possible that the species is not incuded in the book. The more than 800 species of mushrooms included here represent only a fraction (probably less than 1/4) of the gilled mushrooms of the United States and Canada so the majority of species are not included.

KEY TO SPECIAL KEYS

1a Parasitic on, and growing on, other mushrooms .... Key 1

1b Not obviously parasitic on other mushrooms 2

2a Stipe absent, lateral, or eccentric, i.e., habit "pleurotoid" .... Key 2

2b Stipe present and central or nearly so 3

3a A universal and/or partial veil present (look for a covering of some kind over the gill region in buttons, a volva or patches of material at the base of the stipe or on the pileus, a definite annulus or fibrillose zone or other evidence of a partial veil) .... Key 3

3b No veils present (the gill cavity exposed to the atmosphere throughout the entire development of the fruiting body) 4

4a Spore deposit white to whitish, very pale cream, pale buff or very pale lilac gray .... **Key 4**

4b Spore deposit distinctly colored (not yellow or buff or whitish to white) .... **Key 5**

Key 1: Mushrooms Parasitic on Other Mushrooms

1a Parasitic on fruiting bodies of *Clitocybe* species (especially *C. nebularis*); gills pink at maturity; stipe with a membranous volva .... *Volvariella surrecta*

1b Not parasitic on *Clitocybe;* gills not pink at maturity; volva absent 2

2a Fruiting bodies of parasite having ± chocolate brown gills at maturity .... *Psathyrella epimyces*

2b Gills almost lacking (rudimentary) or if present not chocolate brown .... *Asterophora*

Key 2: Pleurotoid Mushrooms

1a Pileus sessile; gills bright orange; spore deposit pink .... *Phyllotopsis nidulans*

1b Not as above 2

2a Pileus ± reticulate and watermelon pink when fresh and young; stipe typically eccentric .... *Rhodotus palmatus*

2b Not as above 3

3a Spore deposit cinnamon to brown; gills pale yellow to brown at maturity 4

3b Spore deposit white, yellowish, or lilac-gray; gills typically white or nearly so at maturity 5

4a Stipe typically present, eccentric; gills ± readily separable from pileus (test by pushing fingernail from stipe toward margin of pileus); terrestrial or near stumps .... *Paxillus*

4b Stipe typically absent; gills not readily separable from pileus; predominantly lignicolous .... *Crepidotus*

5a Gills with serrate edges; taste of raw flesh in some acrid to bitter; spore deposit blue to violet when treated with iodine .... *Lentinellus*

5b Not as above 6

6a Taste of raw flesh mild; pileus fibrillose to glabrous but neither tough nor rubbery; spore deposit not blue to violet when treated with iodine .... *Pleurotus*

6b Not as above 7

7a Fruiting bodies fleshy to firm or rubbery; spore deposit blue to violet when treated with iodine .... *Panellus*

7b Fruiting bodies tough to rubbery; spore deposit not blue to violet when treated with iodine 8

8a Stipe absent; fruiting bodies with a rubbery feel .... *Hohenbuehelia*

8b Stipe present or absent; fruiting body tough, reviving when moistened, typically pliant but not rubbery .... *Panus*

Key 3: Universal and/or Partial Veil Present

1a Universal veil present (look for patches of material on the pileus and a volva or patches or rolls of material at the base of the stipe) **2**

1b Universal veil lacking or remains as fibrils (often inconspicuous) (see *Rozites* also) **4**

2a Gills free from stipe or nearly so, white at first and remaining so or sometimes staining in age; spore deposit white or nearly so; partial veil sometimes present also ...... *Amanita*

2b Not as above **3**

3a Gills distinctly brownish at maturity; spore deposit pale tawny; annulus present .... *Rozites caperata*

3b Gills distinctly pinkish or pink at maturity; spore deposit also pink; partial veil absent .... *Volvariella*

4a Fruiting bodies disintegrating into a black inky fluid at maturity .... *Coprinus*

4b Fruiting bodies not as above **5**

5a Gills at maturity and spore deposit dull green; pileus white with pale brown scales .... *Chlorophyllum molybdites*

5b Not as above **6**

6a Spore deposit white or whitish **7**

6b Spore deposit strongly colored **16**

7a Fruiting bodies obviously attached to wood (sometimes the wood buried but the connection apparent with some excavation) **8**

7b Not as above **10**

8a Gill edges serrate; fruiting bodies tough .... *Lentinus*

8b Not as above **9**

9a Annulus cottony; mycelium producing black rhizomorphs; fruiting bodies often clustered .... *Armillariella*

9b Not as above .... see *Armillaria* and *Tricholomopsis*

10a Gills free from the stipe or practically so **11**

10b Gills attached to stipe at first (sometimes becoming free in age) **13**

11a Some evidence of a universal veil present as patches of tissue on surface of pileus, small warts over a swollen stipe base, or small loose patches of tissue which stay in the soil when the fruiting bodies are collected .... *Amanita*

11b No evidence as above that a universal veil is present **12**

12a Pileus subviscid to slimy when young and fresh .... *Limacella*

12b Pileus dry (rarely somewhat viscid in wet weather) .... *Lepiota*

13a Stipe massive, usually 3 cm or more wide at apex and narrowing toward the base; annulus well formed, double .... *Catathelasma*

13b Not as above 14

14a Pileus dry, appearing granular to powdery or somewhat suede-like; stipe usually narrow, more or less equal; annulus sometimes well-formed .... *Cystoderma*

14b Not as above 15

15a Fruiting bodies usually stout (stipe 8-30 mm thick); pileus viscid, glabrous, or innately fibrillose to fibrillose-scaly; gills notched; partial veil scant and not forming a membranous annulus .... *Tricholoma*

15b Not as above; gills resembling candle wax in texture or appearance, not notched .... Hygrophoraceae

16a Pileus small, surface powdery, dull grayish brown; young gills bright brick red .... *Melanophyllum echinatum*

16b Not as above 17

17a Young gills white to pinkish or pinkish gray, becoming cocoa-brown to chocolate-brown at maturity; spore deposit purple-brown to blackish brown; annulus frequently well developed; gills free or soon becoming so .... *Agaricus*

17b Not as above 18

18a Gills decurrent, relatively thick, typically subdistant to distant; spore deposit smoky gray to blackish 19

18b Not as above 20

19a Gills, pileus, and stipe bright to dull ochraceous to ochraceous-tan ...... *Chroogomphus*

19b Gills white or pallid when young; stipe typically lemon yellow over the basal area .... *Gomphidius*

20a Pileus dull tan with a silvery overlay; gills resembling crepe paper; annulus usually distinct, membranous; fruiting on the ground, fall .... *Rozites caperata*

20b Not as above 21

21a Fruiting bodies terrestrial, not arising from decaying wood 22

21b Fruiting bodies associated with living or decaying wood (wood sometimes buried, i.e., roots) 30

22a Partial veil cobweb-like (cortinate); spore deposit yellowish brown to orange-brown to deep rusty brown or earth brown 23

22b Not as above 27

23a Pileus dry and fibrillose to scaly; stipe ± fleshy; gills not brightly colored when young; pileus never viscid .... *Inocybe*

23b Not with the above combination of characters 24

24a Pileus viscid to subviscid at first; young gills white to brownish or grayish; gill edges typically white and crenulate .... *Hebeloma*

24b Not as above 25

25a Cobweb-like veil present when young; pileus viscid or not but gill edges not white-crenulate; young gills *usually* distinctly colored (red, blue, olive, yellow, orange, but in some reddish brown to brown); stipe if narrow more fleshy than cartilaginous .... *Cortinarius*

25b Not as above 26

26a Stipe fragile (cartilaginous) and narrow; pileus typically conic at first (may be convex finally); spore deposit ± pale tawny to tawny .... *Galerina*

26b Stipe ± pliant; pileus convex becoming convex-depressed to flat; spore deposit yellow to pale tan .... *Tubaria*

27a Fruiting bodies typically fragile and usually ± cinnamon brown when moist; spores and mature gills typically chocolate-brown (if gills blackish and mottled see *Panaeolus*) .... *Psathyrella*

27b Fruiting bodies not especially fragile; spores and mature gills not as above typically 28

28a Spore deposit bright to dull rusty brown or dull brown 29

28b Spore deposit dull brown to purple-brown or blackish brown .... Strophariaceae

29a Stipe mostly over 4 mm thick at apex; spore deposit dull brown .... *Agrocybe*

29b Stipe mostly under 4 mm thick at apex; spore deposit bright rusty brown .... *Conocybe*

30a Spore deposit deep bluish fuscous, black, deep olive-brown, purple-brown, or cocoa- or chocolate-brown 31

30b Spore deposit ochraceous, yellowish tan, tawny, orange-brown, dark rusty brown or earth brown 32

31a Fruiting bodies typically fragile and ± cinnamon brown when moist, occasionally grayish .... *Psathyrella*

31b Fruiting bodies typically not fragile and typically more brightly colored than in previous choice .... Strophariaceae

32a Fruiting bodies medium to large (cap 5 cm or more), often somewhat stout 33

32b Fruiting bodies small to medium; stipe typically narrow ...... see *Galerina* and *Conocybe*

33a Pileus viscid, the viscidity sometimes obscured by fibrils and scales in young specimens; spore print cinnamon brown to tawny or earth brown .... *Pholiota*

33b Pileus cuticle of appresssed fibrils, squamulose or glabrous but not viscid or slimy; spore deposit orange, rusty orange or bright rusty brown .... *Gymnopilus*

Key 4: Spore Deposit White or Lightly Colored; Veils Absent Even in Young Specimens

1a Stipe usually 1-3 cm thick, interior punky to hollow, white or colored like the cap; gills often broad and thickish but frequently brittle; spore deposit blue to violet when treated with iodine 2

1b Not as above 3

2a Exuding a colored, white, or clear juice (latex) when young gills or apex of stipe are cut with a sharp instrument .... *Lactarius*

2b Lacking a distinct latex .... *Russula*

3a Fruiting bodies fleshy, ± pliant and firm, medium to large, ± pumpkin orange over all or sometimes with brown or olive tones on pileus 4

3b Not as above 6

4a Gills foldlike or at least the edges obtuse when gills are young, gills often distant, forked (see "How to Know the Non-Gilled Fleshy Fungi" for this genus) .... *Cantharellus*

4b Gills with sharp, knife-like edges, thin, close to crowded 5

5a Gills dicotomously forked; fruiting bodies typically terrestrial, not clustered .... *Hygrophoropsis*

5b Gills not prominently forked; fruiting bodies typically clustered and arising from rotting wood .... *Omphalotus*

6a Stipe tough and fibrous; gills thick, violet, lilac, vinaceous-red or purplish (see Hygrophoraceae also) .... *Laccaria*

6b Not as above 7

7a Fruiting bodies thin and pliant, reviving when moistened after having been dried out 8

7b Fruiting bodies fleshier than in the above choice, or if thin then more fragile, generally not reviving when dried then remoistened 11

8a Spore deposit becoming blue to violet when treated with iodine .... *Xeromphalina*

8b Spore deposit not becoming blue to violet when treated with iodine 9

9a Pileus radially fibrillose-scaly to appressed fibrillose with brown fibrils and white flesh .... *Crinipellis*

10a Fruiting bodies bright lemon yellow; fruiting on wood of deciduous trees .... *Cyptotrama*

10b Fruiting bodies of various colors; mostly terrestrial .... *Marasmius*

11a Gills appearing clean and ridgid (waxy) or with the feel of wax when crushed .... Hygrophoraceae

11b Not as above 12

12a Growing on old cones of conifer trees, magnolia cones and cone debris; stipe slender (± 1-1.5 mm) and pliant .... *Strobilurus*

12b Habitat not as above 13

13a Injured areas of gills and stipe staining gray to black, sometimes slowly .... *Lyophyllum*

13b Not staining as above 14

14a Gill edges serrate at maturity; flesh of fruiting body rather tough; spores in mass not becoming blue to violet when treated with iodine .... *Lentinus*

14b Not as above 15

15a Fruiting bodies clustered to densely gregarious, with black shoestring-like strands extending from the stipe base into the substrate; cap yellowish to reddish brown, often squamulose .... *Armillariella*

15b Not as above 16

16a Fruiting bodies attached or wood or having a pseudorhiza which is attached to wood 17

16b Fruiting bodies terrestrial 22

17a Stipe with a well-developed pseudorhiza (see *Collybia* and *Mycena* also, especially if specimens small) .... *Oudemansiella*

17b Not with a prominent pseudorhiza 18

18a Stipe dark brown and velvety over lower half at maturity; fruiting on dead hardwoods (elm and aspen especially) .... *Flammulina*

18b Not as above 19

19a Densely clustered on old conifer logs; cap grayish brown; spore print blue to violet when treated with iodine .... *Clitocybula*

19b Not as above 20

20a Stipe less than 4 mm thick, brittle to cartilaginous 21

20b Stipe thicker and typically fleshier (see *Collybia* also) .... *Tricholomopsis*

21a Pileus conic at first and usually remaining so .... *Mycena*

21b Pileus plane or with a depressed disc at first, often funnel-shaped by maturity (see *Xeromphalina* also) .... *Omphalina*

22a Cap typically conic at first and long remaining so, fleshy thin, stipe narrow and brittle to cartilaginous .... *Mycena*

22b Not as above 23

23a Gills decurrent 24

23b Gills differently attached 26

24a Pileus gray; gills and stipe white; staining reddish in age; flesh soft, fruiting bodies of medium stature .... *Cantharellula*

24b Not as above 25

25a Pileus small, thin-fleshed and translucent striate near the margin typically .... *Omphalina*

25b Pileus small to large but margin not translucent striate (see *Leucopaxillus* also) .... *Clitocybe*

26a Pileus glabrous and moist; gills crowded; stipe strict .... *Melanoleuca*

26b Not as above 27

27a Copious white mycelium present at base of stipe .... *Leucopaxillus*

27b Not as above 28

28a Gills broadly adnate to somewhat decurrent .... *Clitocybe*

28b Gills sinuate to adnexed (notched) 29

29a Stipe fleshy .... *Tricholoma*

29b Stipe cartilaginous to tough or fibrous .... *Collybia*

Key 5: Spore Deposit Distinctly Colored; Veil Absent Even in Young Specimens

1a Spore deposit (or color of mature gills) pink, reddish cinnamon, or vinaceous 2

1b Spore deposit color not as above 3

2a Gills free from stipe; flesh of cap very soft .... *Pluteus*

2b Gills attached to stipe at first and tissue of pileus ± pliant .... Rhodophyllaceae

3a Gills typically readily separable from the underside of the pileus (push from the stipe toward the pileus margin with a fingernail and the gills should separate from the pileus readily) 4

3b Gills not readily separable from the pileus 5

4a Gills ± distant, broad, and thick .... Phylloporus

4b Gills close to crowded, thin, and typically narrow .... Paxillus

5a Gills turning into an inklike black liquid as the spores are matured and discharged; spore dust black .... Coprinus

5b Not as above 6

6a Fruiting bodies soon collapsing (but not dissolving into a liquid) in about a half day to a day; pileus viscid; spore deposit pale rusty brown .... Bolbitius

6b Not as above 7

7a Spore deposit purplish brown, black, chocolate- or cocoa-colored 8

7b Spore deposit yellow, orange-brown, rusty brown, umber brown, or earth brown 11

8a Pileus membranous, plicate striate to disc when mature .... Pseudocoprinus

8b Not as above 9

9a Gills mottled with light and dark areas; spore deposit black (see Psathyrella also) .... Panaeolus

9b Not as above 10

10a Fruiting body fragile .... Psathyrella

10b Fruiting body ± pliant, often viscid .... Strophariaceae

11a Stipe with a well-developed pseudorhiza and a very cartilaginous cortex; spore deposit rusty brown .... Phaeocollybia

11b Not as above 12

12a Pileus viscid at first; gill edges often white-crenulate; spore deposit clay-color to dull or reddish brown (check mature gills) .... Hebeloma

12b Not as above 13

13a Spore deposit and mature gills earth brown .... Agrocybe

13b Spore deposit and mature gills tawny to orange 14

14a Spore deposit orange-brown to tawny 15

14b Spore deposit cinnamon brown to pale dull tan or dull ochraceous 16

15a Spore deposit orange-tawny (bright); stipe thickish or if thin pliant .... Gymnopilus

15b Spore deposit duller than in previous choice; stipe slender and fragile .... Conocybe

16a Pileus pale to broadly convex or disc depressed .... Tubaria

16b Pileus conic to convex or convex-umbonate .... Galerina

Index and Glossary

CRENATE: scalloped, often used to describe the pileus margin.
CRENULATE: having small scallops (diminutive of crenate).
CRISPED: finely wrinkled as in crepe paper.
CROWDED: a type of gill spacing in which the gills are very close together, fig. 7
CUSP: a sharp point.
CUSPIDATE: of pileus, with a cusp, or pointed umbo, fig. 4
CUTICLE: the outermost covering layer of the pileus or stipe in a mushroom. It may be subdivided into 1-3 layers, fig. 20
CUTIS: a cuticle composed of dry, interwoven, narrow, more or less cylindric hyphae, fig. 20
CYLINDRIC: resembling a cylinder in shape (with parallel sides), fig. 2
CYSTIDIUM: (pl. cystidia), a sterile hyphal end-cell, at times distinctive in form or content or both, fig. 18

D

DECURRENT: a type of gill attachment in which the gills extend down the stipe, fig. 6
DECURVED: used to describe a condition where the margin of the pileus slopes abruptly downward a short distance back from the edge.
DELIQUESCENT: undergoing a process of self- (auto-) digestion to form a liquid from the tissue of the fruiting body. It is best shown by species of Coprinus.
DEPRESSED: used to describe a pileus which has a shallow depression over the disc, fig. 2
DEXTRINOID: a wine-red to red-brown reaction of a spore wall or content when treated with iodine.
DISC: the center of a pileus; usually the region above the stipe.
DISTANT: a type of gill spacing in which the gills are relatively far apart, fig. 7
DIVERGENT: a type of gill trama in which hyphae extend downward from the pileus and diverge outward to form the hymenium of each of the gill faces; also called bilateral, fig. 19
DRAB: a dull medium gray or brownish gray.

E

ECCENTRIC: of stipe, off-center (not central) to the pileus, fig. 9
ECHINATE: with small pointed spines.
ELLIPSOID: a 3-dimensional solid with the outline of an ellipse, fig. 16
ENTIRE: of gill margin, even, not toothed, fig. 8

EPICUTIS: the outermost differentiated region of a multizoned (complex) cuticle.
EQUAL: of stipe; the same diameter throughout, fig. 10
ERODED: of gill edges; broken, jagged, irregular, fig. 8
EVANESCENT: vanishing, as do the fibrils of a superficial outer veil.
EXPANDED: of a pileus; one which has reached its maximum size.

F

FACE: the broad side of a gill.
fairy ring mushroom, 81, 113
FARINACEOUS: a taste or odor often likened to that of freshly ground meal, also used to describe a surface with a granular appearance (appearing as if covered by meal).
FASCICLES: of hyphae; small bundles or strands, also groups (bundles) of hyphal ends.
FERRUGINEOUS: the color of rusted iron or rusty red.
$FeSO_4$: an abbreviated formula for a solution of about 10% iron sulfate in water; the solution is applied to surface layers and context of fruit bodies and the color changes noted.
FIBRILLOSE: furnished with fibrils.
FIBRIL: an aggregation of hyphae to form a thread-like strand.
FIMBRIATE: fringed with hairs of fibrils (often used to describe the edge of a gill or margin of the pileus, fig. 8)
FLACCID: limp or flabby.
FLEXUOUS: of a stipe; one which undulates somewhat, not strict.
FLOCCOSE: cottony.
FOETID: (fetid), an offensive odor, like that of decaying proteinaceous material.
FREE: of gills; gills which do not reach the stipe, fig. 6
FRIABLE: readily breaking up, usually into small pieces, especially the outer veil of some mushrooms (see Amanita).
FRUITING BODY: the spore-producing phase of the mushroom plant, fig. 1
FUGACIOUS: lasting only a short time, fleeting.
FULVOUS: the color of a red fox (presumably the back).
FURFURACEOUS: scurfy, covered with bran-like particles.

FUSCOUS: dull dark gray, i.e. the color of a dark storm cloud.
FUSOID: (fusiform), tapered at both ends, spindle-shaped, figs. 16, 18
FUSOID-VENTRICOSE: tapered toward both ends and distinctly enlarged at more or less the midportion; the term often applied to the most frequently encountered type of cystidium in mushrooms, fig. 18

G

GELATINOUS: resembling gelatin in consistency.
GERM PORE: a differentiated area on a spore, often apical, through which the germ tube (the first hypha of the new mycelium) extends during the process of germination. It is not just a hole in the wall as the term seems to indicate, fig. 15
GILL: one of the plates of tissue attached to the under side of the pileus and on which the hymenium develops and produces spores, fig. 1
GILL TRAMA: the internal tissue of the gill, the region between the two faces, fig. 19
GLABRESCENT: becoming glabrous (bald).
GLABROUS: lacking hair or fibrils (bald).
GLAUCOUS: covered with a whitish, waxy bloom like a fresh prune plum.
GLOBOSE: resembling a sphere in shape, used mainly to describe spores and pilei, fig. 16
GLOEOCYSTIDIUM: a cystidium with a specialized content.
GLUTEN: (slime), the viscous material which makes some fungi slimy.
GRANULOSE: resembling grains of sand or finely ground meal.
GREGARIOUS: a pattern of

HEMISPHERIC: resembling half a sphere, usually used to describe a pileus, fig. 2

HETEROMEROUS: having two or more cell types in a tissue, especially found in the Russulaceae where more or less globose cells in groups as well as narrow elongate hyphae together constitute the tissue, such as the context of the stipe.

HIRSUTE: bearing fairly coarse hairs.

HISPID: bearing coarse hairs or bristles and coarse to the touch.

HOARY: a surface with a sheen, as if covered with frost.

HORNS: projections on the cystidia usually at the apex, fig. 18

HYALINE: clear and colorless.

HYGROPHANOUS: changing color as moisture is lost.

HYMENIFORM: resembling a hymenium, but the cells not producing spores, usually used to describe the cuticle of pileus or stipe, fig. 20

HYMENIUM: the palisade layer of spore bearing cells and associated structures, fig. 1.

HYMENOPHORE: the region or tissue of a fruiting body which bears the hymenium. The gills in a mushroom.

HYPHA: the basic, thread-like structure making up the vegetative phase of the fungous plant. The mushroom is the fruiting phase and is also made up of hyphae many of which become highly modified, fig. 1

HYPODERMIUM: a differentiated region just below the pileus cuticle in some mushrooms.

I

IMBRICATE: resembling overlapping shingles, one partly covering another.

INCURVED: a type of marginal curvature, see fig. 5

INEQUILATERAL: of spores; in a profile view of a spore, in optical section, the spores are more or less fusoid in outline but the widest point on the ventral side of the spore is not directly opposite the widest point on the dorsal line, fig. 16

INFERIOR: of an annulus; located below the middle of the stipe.

INROLLED: of the edge of the pileus, fig. 5

INTERVENOSE: numerous veins connecting one gill to another.

INTERWOVEN: a type of gill trama in which the hyphae are tangled and not in a distinct pattern such as parallel or divergent; also known as irregular, fig. 19

ISABELLA COLOR: a dingy dull greenish yellow-brown.

IXOCUTIS: a cutis with a slime-matrix, or one which the hyphae gelatinize, fig. 20

IXOLATTICE: a cuticle composed of branching, ascending, tangled hyphae in a slime-matrix, fig. 20

IXOTRICHODERMIUM: (or ixotrichoderm), a trichoderm in a slime-matrix or one in which the trichodermial elements gelatinize, fig. 20

K

KOH: potassium hydroxide; the usual solution for reviving mushroom tissue is a 2.5% aqueous solution. A 25-30% solution is also used for spot testing for color changes.

L

LACERATE: torn or ragged, often used to describe the stipe surface.

subserifluus, 41
subvellereus var. subdistans, 31, 32
  var. subvellereus, 31
subvernalis, 31
theiogalus, 47
thyinos, 30
torminosus, 39, 40
  var. nordmanensis, 40
trivialis, 41, 42
uvidus var. montanus, 37
  var. uvidus, 37
vellereus, 32
vietus, 42
vinaceorufescens, 43, 45
volemus var. flavus, 35
  var. volemus, 34, 35
LACTIFER: a duct which contains latex.
LACTIFEROUS SYSTEM: the sum total of all lactifers in a fruiting body.
LAMELLAE: (lamella sing.), the technical term for gills.
LAMPROCYSTIDIUM: a thick-walled cystidium with more or less colorless walls (often found in the hymenium), fig. 18
LATERAL: of a stipe; one which is attached at one side of the pileus, fig. 9
LATERITIOUS: brick red (dull red).
LATEX: a liquid, often viscous, produced by some mushrooms, especially Lactarius.
LECYTHIFORM: shaped like a small ninepin; used to describe a type of cystidium, fig. 18
Lentinellus, 71, 104, 319
  cochleatus, 104
  montanus, 105
  ursinus, 105
  vulpinus, 105
Lentinus, 73, 106, 320, 323
  elodes, 106
  kauffmanii, 106
  lepidus, 107
  ponderosus, 106, 107
  sulcatus, 106
  tigrinus, 106
Lentodium squamosum, 106
Lepiota, 173, 320
  acutaesquamosa, 182, 183
  americana, 174, 175
  atrodisca, 179
  barsii, 176
  bucknallii, 181
  caerulescens, 177
  castanea, 180
  cepaestipes, 177
  clypeolaria, 183, 184
  clypeolarioides, 184
  cortinarius, 183
  cristata, 179, 180
  cystidiosa, 181, 182
  eriophora, 182
  flammeotincta, 177, 178
  flavescens, 180
  lutea, 176
  luteophylla, 183
  naucina, 173, 174
  petasiformis, 182
  procera, 8, 175
  pulcherrima, 179
  rachodes, 174

roseilivida, 178
roseotincta, 177
rubrotincta, 173, 178, 179
scabrivelata, 182
seminuda, 181
tinctoria, 175
Lepiotaceae, 26, 172
LEPTOCYSTIDIUM: any thin-walled cystidium.
Leptonia, 304
Leucoagaricus, 173
Leucocoprinus, 173
  birnbaumi, 176
Leucopaxillus, 74, 107, 324
  albissimus var. paradoxus f.
    var. piceinus, 109, 110
    albiformis, 110
  gentianus, 108, 109
  laterarius, 109
  paradoxus, 108
  subzonalis, 108
  tricolor, 108
LIGNICOLOUS: with fruiting bodies attached to wood or arising from buried wood, presumably the mycelium is living in the wood.
LILACEOUS: lilac colored.
Limacella, 171, 320
  glioderma, 171
  glishera, 172
  illinita, 172
    var. argillaceae, 172
    var. rubescens, 172
  lenticularis, 171
    var. fischeri, 171
LIMB: the free portion of the volva as in some species of Amanita, fig. 12
LUBRICOUS: greasy to the touch.
LUTESCENT: becoming yellow.
Lyophyllum, 9, 73, 74, 110, 135, 323
  decastes, 111
  loricatum, 111
  montanum, 112
  multiforme, 112
  semitale, 111, 112

M

MACROCYSTIDIUM: a large gloeocystidium wih oily content and relatively constant form, found especially in the Russulaceae, fig. 18
Macrolepiota, 173
MARASMIOID: resembling a Marasmius, i.e., a small thin fruiting body which can dry out and then rehydrate and continue producing spores.
Marasmius, 73, 95, 112, 113, 137, 323
  capillaris, 116
  cohaerans, 115
  cystidiosus, 115
  delectans, 114
  iocephalus, 113
  magnisporus, 114
  oreades, 113
  pallidocephalus, 116
  plicatulus, 114, 116
  rotula, 116, 117
  scorodonius, 115
  siccus, 117

sullivantii, 117
umbilicatus, 114
urens, 113, 114
MARGIN: of gills or pileus; the edge (or, for the pileus the area near the edge—as contrasted to the disc).
MARGINATE: of gills; having the edges differently colored from the faces; of bulbs, one with a raised edge or rim, fig. 11
Matsutake, 75
Meadow mushroom, 198
MEALY: resembling coarse meal such as corn meal; of taste, like that of freshly ground meal.
MEDIAN: middle.
Melanoleuca, 74, 117, 324
  alboflavida, 119
  angelesiana, 118
  brevipes, 119
  cognata, 118
  eccentrica, 117
  humilis, 118
  lewisii, 117
  melaleuca, 119
  reai, 118
Melanophyllum, 27, 194, 206, 321
  echinatum, 206, 207, 321
MELZER'S REAGENT: a solution (water 22 gm. chloral hydrate 20 gm, iodine 0.5 gm, potassium iodide 1.5 gm) used to determine the amyloidity of a tissue or structure (a blue reaction indicates a starch-like compound—it is then said to be amyloid).
MEMBRANOUS: resembling a membrane or a thin skin.
Mica cap, 211
MICACEOUS: appearing covered by small glistening (mica-like) particles.
Monadelphus subilludens, 130
Montagnites, 209
MUCRONATE: having a short abrupt point, fig. 18
MYCELIUM: (pl. mycelia), the mass of hyphae which is the fungous plant, fig. 1
MYCELIOID: resembling a mycelium.
Mycena, 72, 73, 110, 120, 127, 323, 324
  alcalina, 126
  amabilissima, 120
  amicta, 123
  cooliana, 125
  elegantula, 122
  epipterygia, 123, 124
    var. lignicola, 124
  euspeirea, 121
  haematopus, 120
  leaiana, 121
  lilacifolia, 123
  maculata, 127
  megaspora, 125
  murina, 125
  niveipes, 126
  osmundicola, 125
  overholtsii, 127
  pelianthine, 121
  pura, 122
  purpureafusca, 121, 122

rosella, 120
rutilantiformis, 121
strobilinoides, 121
stylobates, 124
subcaerula, 123
tenerrima, 124, 125
texensis, 121
viscosa, 123
MYCOPHAGY: the eating of fungi.
MYCORRHIZA: an association of a fungus (mycelium) and the rootlet of a green plant which is a balanced relationship and of advantage to both partners.
MYCOTOXIN: a toxin produced by a fungus.

N

Naematoloma, 237, 249
  capnoides, 255
  dispersum, 259, 260
  ericaceum, 262
  fasciculare, 255, 256, 259, 260
  squalidellum, 262
  sublateritium, 254, 255
  subviride, 256
  udum, 261
NAPIFORM: resembling a turnip in shape, often applied to a bulb, fig. 11
NECK: the narrow portion of a capitate cystidium, fig. 18
NINEPIN-SHAPED: shaped like a bowling pin, fig. 18
NITROUS: a sharp odor, as of certain nitrogen-containing compounds.
NODULOSE: having bumps or nodules, fig. 16
Nolanea, 304
NON-AMYLOID: not amyloid.

O

OBOVATE: inversely ovate.
OBLONG: longer in one direction than in another, the sides parallel or nearly so.
OBTUSE: blunt or rounded at the apex, fig. 4.
OCHRACEOUS: dingy yellow to dull brownish yellow.
OLEIFEROUS HYPHAE: those hyphae which presumably contain waste material; they are usually more irregular and more opaque than regular hyphae.
OLIVACEOUS: with olive tones (those of a green olive).
Omphalina, 73, 75, 127, 324
  ericetorum, 128, 129
  luteicolor, 128
  postii, 128
  wynniae, 128
Omphalotus, 21, 74, 129, 323
  illudens, 130
  olearius, 130
  olivascens, 129
ORNAMENTATION: of a spore wall, the material and the pattern of its disposition

V

VEIL: a thin layer of tissue, figs. 7, 8. The partial veil extends from the stipe to the margin of the pileus, figs. 12, 13. The universal veil envelops the young button, fig. 12

VENTRICOSE: broad in the middle, tapered to each end, fig. 10

VERRUCOSE: bearing small rounded warts.

VESICULOSE: resembling a vesicle, a bladder-like sack, fig. 18

VERSIFORM: having a variety of shapes.

VILLOUS: bearing long soft hairs.

VINACEOUS: as used here a color term for a dull pinkish brown to dull grayish purple.

VIRGATE: streaked.

VISCID: sticky to slimy.

VOLVA: the remains of a universal veil around the base of the stipe, figs. 12, 13

Volvariella, 157, 185, 191, 320
  bombycina, 185, 191
  var. *flaviceps*, 192
  gliocephala, 185
  hypopithys, 193, 194
  pusilla, 192, 193
  smithii, 193
  speciosa, 185, 192
  surrecta, 191, 319
  taylori, 193
  villosavolva, 192
  volvacea, 185, 192, 193

W

White matusake, 75
Winter mushroom, 101

X

Xeromphalina, 72, 152, 323, 324
  campanella, 153, 154
  cauticinalis, 154, 155
  fraxinophila, 153
  fulvipes, 154
  kauffmanii, 153
  orickiana, 152
  picta, 152
  tenuipes, 153
Xerulina chrysopepla, 96

NOTES

NOTES

NOTES

NOTES